THE STATURE OF
THOMAS MANN

THE STATURE OF

Thomas Mann

Edited by Charles Neider

Essay Index Reprint Series

BOOKS FOR LIBRARIES PRESS, INC.
FREEPORT, NEW YORK

THE STATURE OF
THOMAS MANN

To my parents
Olya and Kolya
with gratitude

TABLE OF CONTENTS

Part III. Comparative

Part IV. Thematic

Part V. General

TABLE OF CONTENTS

PREFACE

Of the several possible forms of a critical anthology I have chosen the present one because it seemed best to mirror and illumine the activities and significance of the subject. Approaches such as methodology and chronology seemed too restrictive. Mann is one of those rare gifted men whose significance looms beyond the confines of their art. His recent serious illness touched many people, some of them not personally familiar with his work, but for whom he has come to stand as a great and necessary symbol. Mann has the distinction of simultaneously appealing to the person of esoteric leanings as well as to the general reader. He has been influential in novelistic and stylistic techniques, in theme and thought and in political affairs. He has continued to grow with age and exile, and his influence, both social and artistic, happily has grown accordingly. The breadth and quality of his creative endeavors are such as to make comparison fruitful between him and the greatest figures in the arts. For these and other reasons the ecumenical approach seemed appropriate.

Its disadvantages are readily apparent, not least of which is a flavor of idolatry, with which much of the literature on Mann is tinged. In this connection it is well to state that, on the other hand, not all voices are lifted in praise of him, that not all spirits find him congenial. There are those who feel that he has lived too little and too safely; and some object to the almost exclusively bourgeois nature of his writings.

I have necessarily had to exclude many good essays—for a variety of reasons: length, copyright, et cetera. In general I have favored the newer criticism because it possesses a longer perspective on Mann's work. Mann literature goes back to the beginning of the century, yet with few exceptions I have drawn only upon the last twenty years. Also I have favored work of merit which has not been widely disseminated.

It is fitting that this book should be prepared in America— as a belated cultural welcome supplementing all the social and political ones which have preceded it. To our art Mann brings solidity and tradition, a great sense of form, intellectual substance, artistic longevity and perfectionism; to our thought, the German metaphysical tradition of the nineteenth century tempered by the rationalism of the eighteenth and by twentieth-century scientific humanism. The affinity we have for each other is best expressed by the words democracy, humanism and unification. In turn we offer him the practical benefits of liberalistic eighteenth-century thought; also the regenerating power of youth and freshness and geographical vastness.

We honor Mann the symbol as well as the man. While to his fellow newcomers he is a sort of father-image offering consolation and protection in the face of the immensity and tempo of the new land, to us he stands as a symbol of the most talented and pathetic wave of immigration that has struck these shores. Mann, the devotee of myth and music, has become, ironically, a symphony of myths. Myth is tradition, he has said; to live in tradition is to live in myth. He himself carries within him some of the great myths of our time—the world citizen, the prophetic, scornful exile, the skeptical humanist, the poet as scientist. We honor all these in honoring him.

For all the size and variety of this volume, one feels, almost a little sadly, that somehow the main thing, the elusive essence, has mockingly danced away. It is always the case between criticism and art, as it is between the mind and the senses, that one without the other may have the color but not the flavor of life. Perhaps the best and most important things about any great artist must remain unsaid because they cannot adequately be set down in words—in critical words, at any rate. The nature of criticism— intellection—does not seem to permit the expression of the *quality* of the artistic experience; on the other hand dithyrambic homage tends to overstate, to make garish and thereby to cheapen it. Perhaps the only fitting expression is the work of art itself; at least it comes closest to it; such a work, paying homage to the Goethe-experience, is *The Beloved Returns*. But even the work of art, even poetry, in the end fails to give adequate justice. Is it possible that only life itself, new forms and degrees of living, can do justice to the experience of great art? What is the Mann-experience? An education, certainly: a mental, moral and sensuous education. But how the words fall flat: they do not even approximate the idea of *heightened and guided living* which is the essence of it. The hot sensuousness of *Death in Venice*, the luxurious warmth of the *Joseph*, the brilliant iciness of *The Magic Mountain*—these are no substitutes for life, of course, but neither are they pale shadows of it. They have an exclusive existence of their own, valid and palpable; and it is as difficult to describe them as it is difficult to catch in words the quality of an apple or a color. And yet, criticism is not without value, for just as art serves to prune life and thereby enriches the life-experience, so criticism performs a pruning service for art itself, guiding one through the mazes of its bewildering richness.

NEW YORK   CHARLES NEIDER

ACKNOWLEDGMENTS

Permission to reprint copyright matter has been courteously granted by the following:

Conrad Aiken, for his essay on Thomas Mann (*Dial*, 1928).

Alfred A. Knopf, Inc., for the chapter from *Modern German Literature* (1933), by Arthur Eloesser, the introduction to *Death in Venice* (1930), by Ludwig Lewisohn and the excerpt from *Theme and Variations* (1946), by Bruno Walter.

Manfred and Hannah Altmann, for the essay by Stefan Zweig from *Zeit und Welt* (1943). Translation, Copyright, 1947, by Manfred and Hannah Altmann, joint executors of the Estate of Stefan Zweig, Deceased, 109 Regency Lodge, London, N.W. 3, England.

The American Scholar (Winter 1945-46), for the essay by Albert Guérard.

D. Appleton-Century, for the chapter from *The Twentieth Century Novel* (1932), by Joseph Warren Beach and the chapter from *Thomas Mann's Novel Der Zauberberg* (1933), by Hermann J. Weigand.

The Atlantic Monthly (February 1943), for the essay by Thomas Mann. Copyright, 1943, by *The Atlantic Monthly*.

Aufbau, New York (June 8, 1945), for the essays by Rudolf Kayser and Erika Mann.

Lydia Baer and the University of Pennsylvania, for excerpts from her *Concept and Function of Death in the Works of Thomas Mann*, 1932.

The Helen Black Office, New York, for the excerpt from the essay by Georg Lukacs (*International Literature*, Moscow, June 7, 1945) and for the essay by B. Suchkov (*The Literary Gazette*, Moscow, June 30, 1945).

Creative Age Press, for excerpts from the chapter on Thomas Mann from *No Voice Is Wholly Lost* (1945), by Harry Slochower.

Deutsche Blätter (Santiago, Chile), for the essays by Julius Bab (September-October 1945), Berthold Biermann, Hanns Fischer and Gabriela Mistral (May-June 1945).

De Fakkel (May 1941) and the Netherlands Information Office, New York, for the essay by Menno ter Braak.

Fantasy (Number 27—1943), *New Mexico Quarterly Review* (Autumn 1944) and *Rocky Mountain Review* (Summer 1945), for parts of the editor's essay. The revised essay as it appears in this edition, Copyright, 1947, by Charles Neider.

Mrs. Bruno Frank, for the essay by Bruno Frank, which appeared originally in the *Wuerttemberger Zeitung* and later in *Die Neue Rundschau,* both in 1913.

The Germanic Review, for the essays by André von Gronicka (April 1945) and Friedrich Carl Sell (December 1940).

Harcourt, Brace and Co., Inc., for the chapter from *Counter-Statement*, Copyright, 1931, by Kenneth Burke; and an excerpt from *The Condition of Man*, Copyright, 1944, by Lewis Mumford.

Houghton, Mifflin Co., for the chapter from *Escape to Life* (1939), by Erika and Klaus Mann.

The Kenyon Review (Summer 1945), for the essay by Philip Blair Rice.

F. J. H. Letters, for the section from his book, *An Introduction to Thomas Mann* (1945).

Robert Morss Lovett, for the chapter on *Buddenbrooks* from *Preface to Fiction* (1931).

Lavinia Mazzucchetti and *L'Unitá Europea* (Milan, Italy; July 21, 1945), for the essay by Lavinia Mazzucchetti.

Michigan Alumnus Quarterly Review (Autumn 1945), for the essay by James H. Meisel.

Helen Muchnic and Smith College for the essay by Helen Muchnic.

The Nation (November 28, 1942), for the essay by Reinhold Niebuhr.

Die Neue Rundschau (Stockholm, June 6, 1945), for the poem by W. H. Auden, the essays by Tor Bonnier, G. A. Borgese, Lion Feuchtwanger, Hedwig Fischer, Martin Gumpert, Charles Jackson, Erich Kahler, H. T. Lowe-Porter, Heinrich Mann, Klaus Mann, Agnes E. Meyer, Alfred Neumann, Bruno Walter, Joseph Wittlin.

The New Republic (July 10, 1944), for part of the essay by Harry Levin.

The New York Herald Tribune (April 14, 1937), for the essay by Dorothy Thompson, Copyright, 1937, New York Tribune, Inc.

Oxford University Press, for the chapter from *Directions in Contemporary Literature* (1942), by Philo M. Buck, Jr.

J. B. Priestley and *The Friends of Europe Publications,* London, for the essay by J. B. Priestley.

The Saturday Review of Literature for the translation of the essay by Joseph Wittlin.

University of Toronto Quarterly (October 1938), for the essay by A. F. B. Clark.

The Virginia Quarterly Review (Winter 1938), for the essay by Vernon Venable.

Whittlesey House, for the chapter from *A Panorama of German Literature* (1935), by Félix Bertaux.

A number of the essays in this book have not been published previously—those by Bergel, Hatfield, Kaufmann, Kesten and Monika Mann. A few have been revised extensively: the Baer, Gronicka, Lukacs and Slochower essays appear in more or less abbreviated form; the Levin essay has been expanded by the author; the Jackson essay corrected by the author and expanded slightly. A few contain minor alterations: the Beach essay has a new beginning, written by the author; and the Mistral and Niebuhr essays have undergone minor changes.

Many of the essays appear in translation. To the translators I wish to express my thanks: *E. B. Ashton,* from the German (Frank, Kesten, Wittlin); *Lienhard Bergel,* from the German (Kahler, Lukacs, Zweig), from the Italian (Mazzucchetti); *Berthold Biermann,* from the German (Biermann); *Doris Dana,* from the Spanish (Mistral); *George Davis,* from the French (Gide); *James Galston,* from the German (Walter); *Fima Haimson,* from the Russian (Suchkov); *Konrad Katzenellenbogen,* from the German (Thomas Mann); *Jo Mayo,* from the Dutch (ter Braak); *S. C. Meyer,* from the German (Bab, Hanns Fischer); *Fred Morton,* from the German (Bonnier, Feuchtwanger, Neumann, and with the editor, from the German (Hedwig Fischer, Gumpert); *Marie Rapp,* from the German (Kayser, Erika Mann); *John J. Trounstine,* from the French (Bertaux); and *Marianne Zerner,* from the German (Heinrich Mann).

I am especially indebted to G. B. Fischer, editor of *Die Neue*

Rundschau and head of the Bermann-Fischer Verlag, Stockholm, for having graciously given me access to the issue of *Die Neue Rundschau* dedicated to Thomas Mann on his seventieth birthday.

I wish, finally, to record my deepest thanks to all those who so generously helped to make this volume possible, chief among whom, of course, were the contributors themselves. I wish also to thank Lienhard Bergel, B. W. Huebsch, Hermann Kesten, James Laughlin, Klaus Mann, Fred Morton, and F. C. Weiskopf. Particularly do I wish to thank Mark Neider, Doris Dana and Dr. and Mrs. Thomas Mann. But above all and inevitably am I grateful to Vivien Breslove Neider for her fruitful suggestions and gracious aid.

C. N.

A TOAST

W. H. Auden

To Her, the Empress of the Double Kingdom, who in her sleep and by her sleep alone knows and alone defends those answers our enigmas must obey, the compensation of so many victims, a list which includes, I may say, some very important names.

To Them who so wisely took with them none but the finest equipment, the latest medicines, the most reliable maps, who so carefully asked only sensible political questions, and in consequence, either by Her fire or Her water, perished the moment they opened their mouths, to Them, naturally, our sincerest and oldest regrets.

To Him, the young fool who cannot shudder, but with his hands in his pockets and a straw in his mouth wakes Her for a lark, so that in sheer astonishment She blurts out her most precious secrets which only make him laugh, to Him, the dear boy, our gayest homage.

This, you know, happens over and over again. There remains, though, still to be mentioned that which makes each encounter a unique triumph, that which, unknown to Him or Her or ourselves personally, stands behind Him and, no doubt because it wishes him ill, arranges the whole business suggesting what only innocence can do and only ignorance can ask. To whatever it is, then, that produces from mere child's play such a serious and necessary result, to the anonymous and sexless shadow that gives to our eternal artist a name, a place, a time, a birthday in fact like this, to It, ladies and gentlemen, the silence, surely, of our devotion.

Written in honor of Thomas Mann's seventieth birthday.

PART I

Personal

WORKS AND DEEDS

Hermann Kesten

Strange fate!

Thomas Mann, born June 6, 1875, is a merchant's son from Lübeck, with a Creole grandmother. At fifteen he lost both his father and interest in his studies—he never got beyond Senior High, but he "wrote." At twenty he thought of suicide, read Schopenhauer and Nietzsche and got a job in Munich, as a writing insurance clerk. His first printed story was entitled "Fallen." He heard lectures at the university to fit himself for a journalistic career; a fellow-student and friend later became leader of the German Democrats and died in exile. Thomas Mann followed his brother Heinrich to Rome, where they lived as petty *rentiers.* In Palestrina he started a novel about his forebears. A humorous weekly in Munich hired him as editorial assistant; a publisher in Berlin printed some of his stories. He spent three months in the army, most of it in the hospital. In 1900 the youth published the work of his age, the *Buddenbrooks* which earned him a Nobel Prize a generation later. In his further life Thomas Mann seemed to grow constantly younger and gayer in spirit. *Tonio Kröger,* the popular novella, appeared a few years after the first novel. Thomas Mann lived in Schwabing, was a passionate bicyclist, and called the poet Martens, well-known at the time, by his first name. The Hungarian Holitscher, a writer of travel stories who became a Communist, thought after a few sentimental hours that he was a friend of the author from Lübeck—in fact, he only modeled for a character in "Tristan," a short story. In Florence Thomas Mann came close to marrying Molly, a traveling English girl. At thirty he married Katia Pringsheim, the daughter of a wealthy Munich mathematician. Of their six children—who delighted their father by appearing in pairs—the oldest son, Klaus Mann, became one of the most courageous and talented writers of the next generation and the oldest daughter, Erika, an actress and war correspondent.

Thomas Mann's two sisters committed suicide. One of his two brothers, Heinrich Mann, himself a great writer, plays many parts in Thomas Mann's life and work; once, in the volume of political memoirs, he even appears as the imagined antagonist, the representative of the "literati of civilization."

In 1909 the second novel, *Royal Highness,* appeared, followed after some years by the second popular novella, *Death in Venice.* Shortly before the First World War, Thomas Mann visited his wife in a tuberculosis sanitarium in Arosa and conceived his third novel, *The Magic Mountain,* which did not appear until 1924.

The war interrupted work on the unsurpassed *Confessions of Felix Krull, Confidence Man.* In the war Thomas Mann sided with embattled Germany in *Wartime Thoughts,* in the essay, *Frederick the Great and the Grand Coalition,* and in the *Reflections of a Non-Political Man.* He "bore the arms of thought for more than two years" and "returned a disabled veteran." One of his children was born while the Red revolution was being suppressed in Munich.

In 1923, in honor of Gerhart Hauptmann's sixtieth birthday, he delivered his *Oration for the German Republic* in Beethoven Hall in Berlin. *The Magic Mountain* was followed by the novella, *Disorder and Early Sorrow,* and the essay, *Goethe and Tolstoy.* He traveled in Spain and Poland and Paris (of which he rendered his *Parisian Account*); he visited Egypt. He was elected to the Poet's Section of the Prussian Academy and awarded the Nobel Prize, and in October 1931 he delivered in Berlin his *German Address—An Appeal to Reason* for the Social-Democratic Party.

When Hitler started to rule, Thomas Mann was on a lecture tour in Switzerland. From Munich, Erika and Klaus Mann told their father over the telephone that "the weather was too disagreeable for the parents to come back home." From 1922 to 1933 Thomas Mann had spoken out with increasing vigor against National Socialism—and likewise, by the way, against Fascism and Bolshevism. More and more he had become one of the representative figures of the democratic, peace-loving Weimar Republic. Until 1935 the first two volumes of his fourth great novel, the Joseph myth, and a collection of essays, *Sufferings and Greatness of the Masters,* still appeared in Berlin. He received an honorary degree from Harvard in 1935, and lost his honorary degree from Bonn in 1936. The third volume of *Joseph* had by then been published in Stockholm. Thomas Mann was deprived of his German citizenship. In Switzerland he published *An Exchange of Letters,* the rebuff to the dean of Bonn which has become famous, and the *Third Reich*—after four years of claiming the "right to be silent" in exile, in the belief that his link with the German public was more useful than his public judgment on the German tyrants. He lived in Switzerland, became a citizen of Czechoslovakia, and in Zurich published the conservative anti-Fascist magazine, *Mass und Wert.* In 1938 he moved to Princeton, N. J., to lecture at its university and soon all over the United States. New publications were his novel, *The Beloved Returns,* his selections from Schopenhauer with an essay about the philosopher, his Indian legend, *The Transposed Heads,* his Moses novella, *The Tables of the Law,* and in 1943 the final volume of the Joseph tetralogy.

Directly after his arrival in America he had published a pamphlet, *This Peace,* against the betrayal of Czechoslovakia at Munich. In the following years he spoke and wrote pamphlets against the enemies of humanity and delivered addresses to the friends of democracy. Thomas Mann became an American citizen and adviser on German literature to the Library of Congress in Washington, D. C. He moved to California. His three sons fought against Germany in the American Army. His daughter Erika was an American war correspondent (and a British subject) who on occasion interrogated German war prisoners. Thomas Mann has mastered "the art of being a grandfather," and in his seventieth year is working on a *Doctor Faustus*—a new novel about a German composer's life.

He started as a writer of decadence, an aesthete, a cultural pessimist. His philosophical mentors were the anti-progressive, Schopenhauer, and the "dithyrambic-conservative" revolutionary, Nietzsche. Like Nietzsche, he followed the tradition and the style of Heine, the apostate romanticist who ridiculed his own feelings.

Thomas Mann, the bourgeois scion, regarded the poet, too, as an apostate with a guilty conscience. The spirit also was an apostate romanticist rebelling against life. From such antitheses, Thomas Mann created the dramatic conflicts in his work. Besides, he liked to call himself a moralist. Irony was a moral attitude and "self-abnegation, the self-betrayal of the spirit in favor of life." He was against politics. He was for "music."

This antipolitical attitude was argued in 1918 in his *Reflections of a Non-Political Man.* They constitute an eminently political pamphlet, the memoirs of a pamphleteer. He called the book "almost a work of poetry," and "romanticism, nationalism, a bourgeois nature, music, pessimism, humor . . . in the main the impersonal elements" of his existence. He loved "order." He praised the "positive German character" of his work. He appeared as the "last conservative," as a fiery nationalist.

He was always very proud of his ability to change and develop. It is a very humane ability, and a highly novelistic talent.

In every spiritual character into which he grows, and in which
he represents himself, the novelist strives for perfection as though
he were one of his own characters.

In the Empire a nationalist and friend of culture, in the
Weimar Republic a democrat and friend of the people, he turned
into one of the most representative German enemies of the Third
Reich; he became a friend of mankind and spiritual leader of
banished Germans, exiled Europeans and global oppositionists.

"Born rather to represent," as he called himself in the letter
to Bonn, he was always driven to rebel (and remained representative even in exile and opposition). A North-German *grand bourgeois* in looks and bearing, a *pater familias* blessed with many
children, a home owner, a dignitary, sedentary by nature, regular
in his habits, a man bound to his desk, he was driven into exile
and forced to live as a nomad by a terroristic mass movement.
Thus he exchanged one public for another, exchanged nationalities and places of residence; he who seemed completely at home
in Germany moved restlessly through the world. In vain, again
and again, he settled as if for good in villas in Tölz on the Isar,
in Munich, in Nidden on the Baltic, on Lake Zurich, in Princeton,
New Jersey, and near Hollywood in California. In vain he sought
permanence. He did not want to leave his German publisher, S.
Fischer, so the publisher was driven from Berlin to Vienna and
Zurich and Stockholm and New York. The bourgeois poet satirized both bourgeois and poet in his work, showing the disintegration of the one and the treason of the other. In the
ancient German squabble between "culture" and "civilization" he
sided with culture, and came to lead Western civilization. The
romanticist mocked romanticism. When the aesthete went to
the people, the masses drove him out of the country and into the
loneliness of exile, into a world partnership. The champion of
Germany became a preacher to Germany, an advocate of Europe,
an American citizen of the world. The writer of myths became
an anti-Fascist. The conservative arch-German, the son of a
Lübeck senator, took the part of Czechoslovak patriots and
Spanish republicans, of the new Russia, the coming German revolution, President Roosevelt and the ostracized of all countries, of
Jews, Negroes and fugitive German poets. He proclaims a new
social humanism. He is the prophet of "the return of the genius
of peace, work, and the dignity of man."

Strange figure!

He is so utterly German in his external appearance, so German also in his internal one, in the language and style that weigh

as heavily as do his mental processes. He is so German in his ambiguous universal candor. At first glance he once seemed to resemble a North-German provincial, a younger brother of Novalis and Fontane, of Reuter, Raabe and Storm. Germanic he also seemed in certain dangerous romantic leanings toward decadence, disease and death, in his brooding and in his pedantries, in the taste which led him to choose his first artistic cousins, like Platen and Richard Wagner. His sense of humor was as German as were his sort of irony, his entire romanticism, his Lutheran faith.

So he might perhaps have remained the "scion of the bourgeois German narrative art of the nineteenth century" (as he termed himself in the *Reflections of a Non-Political Man*) and the creator of a new German baroque literature and a baroque style—if he, like other great Germans, had not crossed the German frontiers, in spirit first and then in action.

Besides the German frontiers he also crossed those of the nineteenth century whose heir he appeared to be, and the frontiers of naturalism which he had refined. He turned to historical universality and Indian and Egyptian mythology. Like so many Christians he dined at the Jews' table and drew his themes from the Bible. He also changed models: instead of Maupassant and Gautier, or Hermann Bang and Dostoyevsky, he studied with Goethe, Tolstoy and Sigmund Freud, compounding mythology with psychoanalysis, religion with poesy, the West with the East, ethics with irony. A tremendous mixture was appropriated in his work. He is extraordinarily open and subject to suggestions. This makes him so entertaining. This, at times, lends an encyclopaedic character to his work. Curiosity, an eminently epic trait, lifts his work above the best bourgeois entertainment, beyond his bourgeois limits. From the beginning, he had a historic feeling about his person and work. He was a man "who set store by himself," as he wrote in his *Reflections*. Thus he became a continuous writer of memoirs. Thus he was called upon to adopt the profession of an educator. Thus he was moved to turn his own problems into examples. His irony, his skepticism, his knowledge, his world sympathies, his world-educating, all but prophetic features, are due to this exaggerated self-regard and restless curiosity.

Curiosity, in epic play, becomes delight in associations. Thomas Mann repeatedly confesses being in love with associations, and on the detour over associations his little plans often grew into heavy tomes.

And his great talent for happiness made him obliging, even entertaining, and topical. Thomas Mann, for all his coquettish flirtations with nocturnal darkness and chaos, has always proved his great gift of living happily. He always knew how to arrange things for himself, and for the best. Like all spiritual leaders he often was led astray, but his very aberrations proved so interesting as to seem like merits. For all his deliberation and reserve, his mind was always open to the world; for all his Germanism he was always cosmopolitan, for all his stiffness always ready to help. In his work, chaos itself seems reasonable and humane. His constantly unfolding personality changed much dangerous oscillation into fascinating perfection. A certain pedantic streak confirmed the moralist. Certain egotistical tendencies caused him to seek and find his own best interest in the interest of the world. The aesthete repulsed the journalist. His German sturdiness protected him from the smooth assimilation of certain exiles. In the end both his fate and figure became parts of his creation, as artful and consistent as his literary work.

Strange work!

Is it the melancholy play and mythical dream of a born humorist? He certainly is a natural story-teller. But is the telling of stories his basic literary trait? Or is it the entertaining *esprit* manifested in his language? Or the insatiable curiosity mentioned before, the educational urge appearing in the analytical essay? Or the element of autobiography and pamphleteering?

Is he an artful heir, the beautiful late flower of the nineteenth century? Or is he one of the fathers of the disagreeable twentieth century? "In the days of my youth," he wrote, "I owed everything to models." In October 1944, writing in the *Atlantic Monthly*, he made mention of his late political maturity and stated that as an artist he had been precocious—"for at twenty-three years of age I wrote a book which still lives and may perhaps survive all that I have written since."

Thomas Mann reports that his critical essayistic writings mostly were by-products of his novels, and that each of his principal novellas was written and published in conjunction with one of these larger works. All his essays, novels and novellas of fifty years, the broad work of an author who moved from the right to the left—all of them bear strikingly related features. There is the eternal dualism, the noisy spectacle of conflicts eternally reviewed!

Bourgeois and artist, society and genius, art and fraud, family and outsider, death and transfiguration, order and disorder, music and politics, nationalism and internationalism, culture and civilization, tribe and state, disease and spiritualizaion, life and death, and so forth—applied to the social, political, moral, aesthetic, physical and spiritual fields, but always with the same leitmotif of struggle!

Buddenbrooks, the tragic family novel; *Royal Highness,* the "attempt at comedy in the form of a novel"; the *Confessions of Felix Krull, Confidence Man,* the parody of an educational novel in the form of memoirs; *The Magic Mountain,* the "novel as thought architecture," including illness as the education for death; the biographical novel of art, *The Beloved Returns;* and the last and gayest of his novels (although a constantly increasing gaiety is noticeable throughout his work), the Joseph legend—what rich and colorful cultural pictures and collective portraits! How many broad symbols, returning like leitmotifs but turned from the musical into the epic-moral! The portraits of Germany in the eighteenth and nineteenth centuries, the portrait of pre-war Europe, the myth of Egypt, land of the dead, and of the birth of the twelve tribes of Israel—what a huge epic expenditure for the colossal self-portrait, for the great self-realization of a born story-teller!

It is but a step from young Hanno to the sun-worshipping Pharaoh, but a step into profundity. The German bourgeois novelist executes merely a half-turn and appears as the sculptor of Oriental myths. A half-turn—and the national poet reveals the universal man of letters. Only fifty years' difference, and in the tired aesthete's place the patriarch appears voicing the wrath of the prophet.

Did we not early see the clownish trait in him? It remained the same trait, but now it belongs to the philosopher. The dangerous, abysmal elements are now apparent as wealth. The suspect, the disreputable, the sensually loose ones have acquired a deeper meaning.

All the charms of Thomas Mann's narrative art have remained: the German coziness and the artful contortions, the precious entertainment and the all but Catholic intoxications of the rational Lutheran, the civilized accessibility of the ironical humanist, the humor and the deeper meaning. . . .

There has remained the basically epic impression of the grand stream of life. The flow of time and the movement of events are the good old elements of all epical magic. This seemingly endless stream of life permeates and carries Thomas Mann's classically great phrases, his thousand characters and his constant conflicts, the music and song of his prose, the imitated little humanity with the living charm of transience and the artistic gleam of permanence.

Strange language!

It is inimitable, even though often imitated, and in fact inviting parody. It is a well-to-do, indeed a gluttonously entwining prose, with the grace of the Biedermeier style. It is extraordinarily rich in words, in every sense. It is a cultured language, in the best sense. It borrows its components from the pulpit and from the chancellery, from dialects and from mystics, from Goethe and the Bible. Most of the time it conceals itself, as in a thicket. Or it draws meanderingly through mazes. It has the sharpness of the pamphleteer, the vanities of the autobiographer, the precision of the pedant, the luxuries of the blushing voluptuary. Like a wise serpent it crawls through many technical terminologies. Ponderously, like a champagne-drunken Falstaff, it executes a leaping, bobbing snake dance over whole pages, with its constructions that may encompass more than a hundred distinct sensual perceptions and as many lines. It is a wisely weighed mixture of odd, erudite insights and precise, living trivia. This language is rich in subjectives and adjectives, and therefore epically slow, descriptive rather than narrative.

It oscillates and appears cryptic, even equivocal, because of a deeply moral effort to achieve a full, carefully shaded precision.

This language might seem like an utter mannerism, were it not for the ease with which in one graceful turn or poetic leopard's leap it is apt to leave the mannerism behind like a hedge, and suddenly, in the grammatically sheltered maze of civilization, to open undreamed of vistas of naked nature, of the hidden god.

It is a completely personal language, distilled for home use, so to speak, in the home pharmacy. But it fully suffices for speaking deceptively like a German Philistine, and almost like Goethe. It naturally flows from the lips of Egyptian gods, of frauds of all sorts, and of well-bred boys. With equal perfection it describes snow and love, the sentiments of gods and of triviality, of a man with a transposed head and of a ghoul like Hitler. It is always quite unmistakably the language of Thomas Mann, and one of the loveliest adventures of the German language, the good harlot of us all.

Strange man!

Thomas Mann's well-known witticism, "that the writer is a man who finds writing more difficult than other people," presumably does not apply to him. This methodical writer writes his quota every day; he carries on a voluminous correspondence; he undertakes lecture tours; he represents; for decades he has

been aiding other writers, younger ones in particular, and reading
and judging manuscripts and new books; he helps many people
who turn to him; in exile he performs the functions of a German
shepherd or an emigrated German Pope.

How much intelligence, how rigorously economical a mode
of living, and how much active kindness are required to combine
all this with a rich and intensive work—although this is the place
to quote Thomas Mann's word about his wife and recall "the
wise, courageous, delicate but energetic assistance of my incomparable companion and friend."

By works and by deeds he attempts to fulfill the "duty to
mankind" which he mentioned in his essay *This Peace*. I have
had frequent occasion to observe his readiness to help, his practical kindness. How much time and strength and money I have
seen him expend in the service of others! If he always saw himself as great, he also always felt that greatness imposes obligations. How many letters I have read from him, or at his request
from his energetic, witty, kindhearted wife—all of them full of
what might perhaps be done for this or that person in danger,
how money or visas might be obtained for him, and to how many
more persons or agencies Thomas Mann might yet appeal! And
how much he has done—how many, in these last murderous
years, have literally come to owe their lives to his action and
care! Tirelessly, privately and publicly, he has stood up for all
the persecuted, for all the righteous, for friends and for unknown
individuals, for the good causes and for the good people.

Good men, thank God, are to be found in all countries. With
luck, one may even find a great man here and there.

A good man, to be sure, is usually too busy to become a
great man, even if he has the gift. The needy await him at
every corner; widows and orphans clutch his coat tails. He feels
in debt to everyone. And so he belongs to the community and
obeys the commandment of God.

When would a great man have time to become a good man,
even if he had the heart? In his failures he detects a failure of
the world. Like God, he is not pleased by sacrifices offered to
others. What a human pleasure it is, then, to know a great man
who is a good man too.

[1945]

THE POSITION OF THE PUBLISHER

Tor Bonnier

Everybody who has read Thomas Mann's Joseph novels knows that the author has access to the "higher spheres and rank" where it is decided which place each one of us will occupy in the scheme of repetition and renewal that represents the history of the human race. Perhaps Thomas Mann has also inquired up there just what is the position of a publisher. The publisher is the modern version of the papyrus scribe, the copyist, the book transcriber and the book vendor. As little as his predecessors does he wish to be forgotten in the great scheme of things. Perhaps Thomas Mann could award him a place in connection with one of the four freedoms, to use a modern expression, of whose past history the author of the Joseph novels knows so much. Perhaps he would leave to the publisher the modest but not unimportant task of acting as doorkeeper at the proud edifice of intellectual freedom.

In large countries the publisher may choose his speciality. He may publish medical or military works. He may introduce dictionaries or popular science books to the public. He may publish native literature or devote himself to translations. Again, he may confine himself to the publication of books meant solely for entertainment. In a small country, however, a publisher's work becomes perforce motley and versatile. The small nation lacks the specialized audience which supports the specialized publisher of the large countries, and he therefore has to look for readers in all of the various fields. Still, that must not keep him from performing his duties as a doorkeeper.

But since he has no access to the higher ranks among which Thomas Mann is moving, he often fulfills his task only in a blind and groping manner. Sometimes he admits too many, sometimes too few through the portals of the edifice of journalistic and intellectual freedom, too many or too few of those who intend to use the printing presses and the dissemination devices which are available there.

If the publisher is an ambitious person—and nearly all publishers are ambitious—he can, however, add to his catalogue those classics which he as well as all men know are great and famous masterpieces. If he is very alert and sensitive of reception and if he, like my father, belongs to a new generation with a new intellectual program, then it may be granted to him to publish the works of renewers of native literature like Strindberg, Fröding and Selma Lagerlöf. Should he possess good connections abroad, he can, like my grandfather, publish a book that attracted considerable attention in Germany and Russia and which bore the title *The Cossacks,* and thus become, gradually, to his own astonishment, the Swedish publisher of Leo Tolstoy.

When I, in my youth, read the exciting and entertaining novel *Buddenbrooks,* it was by no means clear to me that in doing so I was destined to be the Swedish publisher of works like *Tonio Kröger* and *Death in Venice,* like *The Magic Mountain, The Transposed Heads* and the Joseph novels; that, in a word, I was to receive a task rare and elevating for a publisher, to be Sweden's publisher of a unique phenomenon: a contemporary, living, genius.

[1945]

WANDERLIED

G. A. Borgese

There are Orphic poets—such as Virgil, Dante, or, among the prose epicists of our own era, Dostoyevsky—and there are Homeric poets, in prose or verse, such as, of course, Homer himself. The former are "makers,' or prophets. They move the mountains, or would like to. The latter are "historians," and witnesses rather than judges; their main interest being in reporting on the world as it is and painting a credible likeness of it.

Thomas Mann belongs to the second species; and this is, I suppose, what one recent interpreter had in mind when singling out above his qualities the "genius of comedy." As a poet realizes that reality is untamable, a tough datum, and that no one's fingers are strong enough to mould it otherwise, a complacent despair becomes his leading state of mind. It ripples frequently in smile, it roars occasionally in laughter. Virtually or actually, a Homeric narrator is an ironist.

No doubt Thomas Mann is a witness of the age of decadence, perhaps the outstanding one—also in the literal sense that he "stood out" of it. Unlike, say, Proust or Joyce, or Picasso, who, even in spite of Guernica, dived deep into those waters, he did not drink of them, he swam over them, chin up, inspecting them with a captivated but uncaptured eye: neither a disgusted moralist nor an accomplice. This attitude was unique.

Hitler unexpectedly acted as a catalytic on that superior constancy. Through him Thomas Mann was tossed into exile and fight; for, while willing to take much of very many things, he was unable to take anything of Nazism. Hence pathos, not irony, is the necessity that forced this umpire to become a partisan, and burdened him in dead earnest with a role (Settembrini's in *The Magic Mountain*) he had contemplated not without some slight— and slighting—humor. The exponent turned an opponent, an "anti." The historian or memorialist drew closer and consciously to the "maker's" missionary will.

Yet it did not perturb the flow, as limpid and vast as ever, of his aesthetic invention. Veronese-like in the late maturity of *Joseph* no less, nay more, than he had been in the spring of the

Buddenbrooks or in the summer of *The Magic Mountain,* he
painted on, never hurrying, never stopping his oversize murals:
filled with tapestries, jewels, goblets, jesters, cripples, parrots, and
full-length portraits of heroes and lovers. The feelings and motives
of humans are open sesames to him. Their twists and oddities are
his delight. If you step back to the proper distance and grasp
the whole in its finality, you see life's labyrinth summed up in
an arabesque, fate and freedom knit together in a Leonardesque
knot.

I know the man better than the work, for he happens to be
the young father-in-law of this old son-in-law.

Remiss as most writers past apprenticeship are in learning
from their contemporaries, I think I did not come in direct touch
with any of Mann's works before late in the 20's. Life, occasionally, builds out of mere chance concomitances that dissemble
the symmetries of art. It so happened that the first of Mann's
works I came across while still in Milan was the long short story,
Disorder and Early Sorrow, whose protagonist, the author's
youngest daughter, I call Elisabeth. In her home she was Medi,
meaning simply Mädchen, the Girl. The father, in the thin alias
of an absent-minded professor circling above all disorder in the
pure orbit of his meditation and ken, descends from those heights
when the hour strikes; bends over that small bed, almost a crib,
rocked by precocious passion; spends, a merciful Olympian, on
those sobs the comfort of an illusional yet wholly satisfactory
fulfillment.

No one else of the family—or as I call it, "the clan"—holds
so visible a place in his work; perhaps not even Katia, his wife,
the mother of six, the selfless, the tireless, the bright, the brave,
(they call her Mielein), who takes on herself the winds and waves
of the days that his wall of silence and security may stay un-
breached. She, Medi, fills *Disorder and Early Sorrow.* She
walks, a live Palladium of candor clad only in light and air, on
the Italian beach of *Mario and the Magician.* Hers entirely had
been long since, by birthright, the *Gesang vom Kindchen, ein
Idyll,* in hexameters, the least of his writings, and his one accomplishment of some length in metric language ("Am I a poet? was
I one at times? I do not know"), a story of birth and baptism
attuned to cheerful-pious strains of eighteenth-century German
poetry, soft-pedaled, however, by German defeat and misery. For
she was a war baby, of 1918, a late comer, even though, it seems,
not quite too late for me.

I had never met any of the family in Europe. With Thomas
and Katia Mann my first contact was in Chicago, not long before

Munich. Soon after Munich, in the fall of 1938, I knocked on
his door, in Princeton, with the hope of winning his support for
a green idea of mine: the *City of Man,* a free association of philosophers and poets, self-appointed leaders of democracy toward
victory and global peace. I won his support and that of several
others. Our words, none the less, were to fall on deaf ears, for
practically everybody believed at that time—as a few still believe
today—that colonels and diplomats know better.

Thus we did not build the "great society." But we did build
a measurable one. Medi, in a kind of glow radiating from herself
no less than from the lights, had "sat in" during the discussion,
and what she said at the end was as terse and unspoiled as if
Nausicaa were speaking at the court of Alcinous. We were married a year later in the University Chapel at Princeton. A British
friend presented us with a joint picture of Duce and Führer, set
jocularly in gaudy tinsel, for they, the worst, were our "best
men," who brought us together, a Rome-Berlin Axis in our own
right. But the father, not long thereafter, sent a tenderer offering: a copy of the *Gesang vom Kindchen,* which, a rarity in itself, had become a unicum with the author's inscription in his
wiry, far-flung, rather elusive hand:

> Niemals verleugn' ich das Lied und seien auch holprig
>   die Verse.
> Lässig wird wohl die Kunst, wenn wir das Leben beschenkt.
> Nimm es denn hin, mein Sohn, am besten weisst Du's zu
>   lesen!
> Dem ich das Kindchen vertraut, hege sein Loblied denn auch.

> (I shall never disown this poem, no matter how limping the
> verses. Art is apt to grow neglectful when we have made a
> gift to Life. So take it, my son; you know best how to read it.
> He to whom I entrusted the little child will care for the song
> in her praise too).

Our own little children, English-speaking, have been chris-
tened in the Unitarian All Souls' Church of Santa Monica, California. There, or more exactly on the slow slopes of Pacific
Palisades above the bay, rises moderately the American home of
the Manns. Their guests more than once in protracted vacations,
I came as close to him as his halo of self-defense consents.

Often, in the orange-blossoming mornings, the window of my
room framed him stepping quick and erect along the groves, a
confident hunter of images and cadences, with his black poodle,
an un-Mephistophelean companion (or, though, Mephistophelean
somehow?) I watched his rhythm of work and rest, as reliable as

Kant's, whose daily walks, as is well known, regulated the clocks of the citizenry. The conversation at meals was mostly political, yet never rising to pitches of debate, for he dislikes pugnacity. Evenings he would tap, from radio or victrola, music whose overtones might glide into the paragraphs to be written next morning. Occasionally I too was in the circle of relatives and friends listening to him, a perfect reader of perfect pages from the work in progress.

The senior offspring may refer to him as *der Zauberer*, the Magician, in reminiscence of the role he impersonated once upon a time in a costume ball. The younger call him Herr Papale, meaning Mister Daddy.

What stands out in my experience as a reader and a neighbor is the accord in him of passion and detachment. It results in supreme dignity.

You may envision him as a Platonic charioteer driving the conflicting team of vice and virtue—or, as we should call them, of decadence and reconstruction. He cracks no whip (except when thinking of Hitler). His hand trembles because it is a very sensitive one, a knowing one; yet it does not lose its grip. He is firm and relaxed.

To this inner behaviour he owes whatever luck has embellished his destiny: the prosperous work, reaching far, but rooted in the ground of the days, unravished by wild winds of prophecy, hence appealing to many, not to the chosen few alone; the resonance of his name; the loyalty of his kin; and permanence in change. A magic carpet—speaking of a Magician—has carried behind him through the lands of exile his most precious goods; the yarns, the language, a few books and keepsakes, the dearest persons, and a household which, it seems, is fairly the same always and everywhere, a recurrent embodiment of his spirit as interpreted by the demiurgic hand of his busy Frau. It used to be in Munich, or in Memelland. It was, during the first phase of expatriation, in Küssnacht. It landed transitionally in Princeton, it settled for good in California. Here or there, on hill or shore, it has size and leisure, space and time, and large windows on heartening vistas.

The Greek word, Praos—so wrote an unfamiliar neighbor of Thomas Mann, Gerald Heard—is inaccurately rendered in the English Gospel sentence, The meek shall inherit the earth. "The trained do inherit the earth," he proposes; and anyhow he prefers the French translation "debonair." "This training is neither impossible nor a leap in the dark. It does develop inevitably and step by step out of that ordinary and spontaneous considerate-

ness, that generous dealing, that fine behavior of the debonair
which every human being likes, in the moments when he is aware
of others, to imagine that he possesses and that they recognize
in him." Such a picture resembles Thomas Mann. His imagination is investigation with wonderment and no bewilderment, his
style is drapery softly thrown on a continuous contour, his de-
meanor is courtesy—that gyroscopic evenness above the billows,
that fragrance of high civilization, a charity, as elegant as unassuming, which understands everything and rejects nothing
(except brutality, which he calls Nazism).

Relentless athletes like Luther and Lessing are not his genius. The parallel with Goethe is too obvious, and not deep enough,
to be significant. One is rather reminded of total humanists like
Erasmus or Leibnitz; or, more closely, of the great composers,
rightly called so, who composed the intricacies and discrepancies,
even the frenzies of he German mind in ultimate, hard-won
harmonies.

When Germany becomes European and human again, she
will recognize herself in this son.

[1945]

ON FIRST MEETING THOMAS MANN

Hedwig Fischer

When I first met Thomas Mann he was still quite a young man and I quite a young woman. It was around 1900 and I had just been introduced to the literary world by my husband, S. Fischer, the publisher. Thomas Mann came up from Munich together with Jacob Wassermann, both having been invited to recite from their works at the "Literarischen Gesellschaft" in Berlin. The response was so great that these two young men had to recite the same things fourteen times at short intervals. They groaned not a little but there is no help for it; and after all, this trial of their patience was a sign of the strong interest they had awakened at such an early stage of their careers. Thomas Mann read his novella *Tonio Kröger*. I still remember the delight it evoked, especially the figure of the "sweet blond Inge."

On that visit I showed the two young writers some of the sights of Berlin, with which they were not acquainted. They were, each in his own way, unusually pleasant and interesting although basically different in nature and appearance. Greater opposites could not easily be imagined. Thomas Mann a little aloof, somewhat uncommunicative, with the elegant certainty of pose which betrayed the good breeding of his Hanseatic patrician background—and beside him Wassermann, the gypsy descended from a small Jewish family in Fürth, with hot blood and flashing black eyes. Only much later, when I myself had become a bit more mature and experienced, did I realize how much temperament there was in Thomas Mann too; I realized only then that he knew how to tame his inner passion and I understood how much shrewdness—which in later years became wisdom—how much knowledge of people and of life lurked behind his apparent coolness.

I was filled with the deepest admiration for his first major work, *Buddenbrooks,* in which the young author recounted the tale of his family and at the same time portrayed the German bourgeoisie of those years. My husband and I had devoured the voluminous manuscript, whcih was written in longhand and teemed with corrections, as soon as it came into our hands. We had laughed over all the droll and the comical which came to life in his narration, over Tony Buddenbrook, who became Frau Grünlich and then Frau Permaneder but who always remained "child Tony." We were moved deeply by the figure of Thomas and his tragic death and also by that of his precocious son Hanno and by the sad end of the family. We had felt immediately that this was a truly epoch-making work which would be a great success both for the author and the publishing house. But the proportions of the success, especially in the subsequent cheaper edition—whose appearance coincided with the award of the Nobel Prize to the author—we could of course not foresee.

But what I expected in Thomas Mann and estimated greatly was not only his talent but his character as well, his faithfulness to himself and to others. One could count on him in every situation in life as friend and as man. This is a great rarity. There were very good reasons for his being given the honorary title of "Praeceptor Germaniae." When the Hitler-spook drove him out of Germany, his strong character enabled him to be true to his title to an even stronger and exemplary degree. It will never be forgotten how he associated himself with the few towering men who with heavy hearts left their homeland and went abroad. But he did not limit himself to that. Abroad, in Küssnacht, Switzerland, near the Zurich Sea, where he lived for a fairly long period, and then in America, which gave him protection and citizenship, he never let his voice be stilled. Rallying all his creative powers, he brought to completion his greatest and most powerful work: the Joseph tale. This tale, originally planned as a small novella, astonished and moved his friends as it grew into the gigantic work which scintillated with an incomparable wealth of color. I am fond of all four volumes of the Joseph, but my heart goes out to the fourth, the final volume published last year. How strange it all is: we have known the story since childhood, yet we are enthralled by suspense until the moment when the long-awaited scene emerges, in which Joseph makes himself known to his brothers and the "I am he" is heard from his lips. For me that is always overpowering. Often I open the book at this very spot and each time I am moved as if I were reading it for the first time; I feel then the deepest emotion and a cleansing, relieving surprise. At these times I always see before me the scene from Gustave Doré's Bible illustrations in which Joseph, standing on a pedestal and clothed gorgeously as an Egyptian overlord, receives his brothers, embraces them and lifts them up out of their misery. It was really strange: at other times while reading the Joseph story I had to think of these Doré woodcuts, which I had become acquainted with in my grandparents' house. That was especially true of the meeting of Jacob and Rachel at the well. Once I spoke to Thomas Mann about it; it was strange to hear him, astonished, confess that before him too these illustrations had hovered while he worked, illustrations which he too had known since early childhood.

Nor could I ever forget the portrayal of Rachel's death on the way, a piece of poetry with its sweet, sad melody. Rachel's figure, her surrender, her feminine willingness, belong to the fairest inventions of Thomas Mann. And beside her, her counterpart: the bewitching portrait of Madame Chauchat of *The Magic Mountain,* with her piquant, slanted eyes. The details of the portrait have impressed themselves upon every reader with indelible poignancy—how she slams the door or how she slinks, catlike, into a room. Oh, how well we understand that all men must fall in love with her, not only young Hans Castorp of the North German commercial town but also the resplendent Mynheer Peeperkorn, one of Mann's most enjoyable creations. Because of such jewels alone one loves and honors Thomas Mann.

It was a great delight to see how Thomas Mann, used to themes of universal significance, could transform a simple, small experience into a narration of such sweetness as *Disorder and Early Sorrow.* With deft, careful hands he weaves a delicate flower-wreath: the children of the beautiful house in the Herzog Park of Munich, the mother, the "blue Anna," the enchanting depiction of the atmosphere of scarcity following the First World War, the wonderfully droll jargon with which these lovely people communicate with each other, the somewhat aloof personality of "Herr Papale," as Bibi Mann addresses him in a charming poem by Erika on the occasion of his fiftieth birthday—up to the delightful episode of Medi's first love.

Thomas Mann's strong relationship to music was always clear to me, in his work as well as in his person. Although he himself is not a practicing musician he has an extraordinary knowledge of music, extending to minute details. His eclectic record collection is eloquent testimony of his kinship with the world of music. The after-dinner concerts in his home in California are among my unforgettable memories. In the old days I could do him a musical favor now and then. There were many musicians among those who visited our house in Grünewald and evenings of chamber music were easily arranged; I remember especially Schubert's B-Major Trio; three young musicians played it, musicians who were later destined to become very successful:

the pianist Franz Osborn, the cellist Gregor Piatigorsky and the violinist Joseph Wolfsthal, who died in his youth. At the celebration of Thomas Mann's fiftieth birthday in the Munich city hall I arranged to have the orchestra play his favorite melodies, those melodies with which Hans Castorp tries to console himself after the departure of Madame Chauchat.

I have the strong conviction that Mann's creative work, above all *Buddenbrooks, The Magic Mountain* and *Joseph and His Brothers,* will retain their importance and their value for a long, long time. They will help to educate to the good and genuine those people who are capable of noble thoughts and experiences. This is my firm belief. And as it is with me, so it is with innumerable others: until the end of my life I shall honor and praise him as a great artist and psychologist, one who was conferred upon us as a gift; and may he remain for us as youthful as he is now, when he celebrates his seventieth birthday.

[1945]

FOR THOMAS MANN

Martin Gumpert

Whenever I had visions of homeland in these years, it was always in the proximity of Thomas Mann. At any place, at any hour he might draw the pages out of his folder, pages covered densely with his steep, spare and somewhat obstinate German script, which only Frau Katia could decipher well; and, adjusting his spectacles and sitting up quite straight, he would proceed to read what, only a short while ago, had been unspoken, unwritten and unthought. His proud and manly face, lost in revery, his austere, absorbed voice were for us, following the movements of his eyes and lips, a center of appraisal and strength. There were always a glass of wine at hand, a few friends, a few of his children and the good genius of his labors, Frau Katia. Exile was easy to bear so long as one could, from time to time, participate in these festivities: one was at home.

In the difficult, strange and painful course of immigration Thomas Mann was for us a saving moral power. We orphans learned to stand, to walk and to speak on foreign soil. We experienced all the ills of solitude, forlornness and shame. Today we are richer, not poorer. We have been strengthened, not destroyed. The madness which drove us out was a favor and a show of mercy on the part of fate. We have a new land but we have also the old homeland common to all of us. Our homeland never deserted us and we never relinquished it, although it is now nothing but a mutilated shadow. Had we remained in Germany we would have died of nostalgia. Here, in freedom, under the great, good and gay American sky, we have not been deserted. The misery of exile was never felt here in the asylum of humanity. Our language was preserved for us, our dignity restored us and friendship, knowledge and warmth streamed upon us.

It was Thomas Mann who protected our first years in America. If the word "German" still harbors a hope today, it is him we have to thank for it. For he who saw him, read him and to whom he spoke knew that this too is Germany and it is good. The respect which was rightfully his was also conferred upon us.

For many years his voice drowned out the diabolic music of the
Nazis. At a time of life when others are old and finished, he became younger and more valorous, wiser and more fertile. At a
time when he was deprived of the resonance of his language he
began his new flight up to the power and profundity of expression. Goethe's Germany was reborn in the small university town
of Princeton; the almost disconcerting mythology of the Joseph
legend thrived in the California sun; and a portrayal of the tragic
twilight of German artistry has almost been completed. But in
all these years of tireless and undeviating labor even the pauses
were brimming with work. Since his historic letter to the
Faculty of Bonn, which ended a span of discomfiting silence,
Thomas Mann has never ceased to exhort, to warn and to accuse
Hitler's Germany. And the great experience of American democracy, of which we knew and divined nothing until it stood palpable and overpowering before our eyes, was for him the point
of departure for a new world hope, a hope worth living and dying
for.

All of us have in our own and more feeble efforts found
confirmation of Thomas Mann's experience. Many of us speak,
write and feel in two languages today. It has done us no harm.
It has strengthened our responsibility toward the word and deepened our sense of the secret and the mystical power of language.
This bridge of the spirit on which we moved uneasily at first and
then with ever-increasing certainty has vouchsafed us a new and
sublime panorama. Innumerable doors are opening which before
were closed to us and only now are we really learning to feel
at home on this greater and more beautiful soil, a soil which
knows no boundaries.

Thomas Mann was not only a leader but also a reliable and
intimate friend on this happy path towards a new and unaccus-
tomed freedom. No one went away empty-handed who sought
his help. His cheerful and dignified attitude gave consolation in
the darkest hours of sorrow. Whenever I saw him—before the
Christmas tree in Princeton, on the Pacific beach, in a small room
at the Hotel Bedford in New York—he seemed to be growing
ever more healthy, more alert and youthful. It is hard to believe
that Thomas Mann will be seventy soon. He shows not the slightest trace of decay or senility. His is an existence on the ascent,
without decline: the portrait of a man full of plans and beauty,
for whom the later years promise to constitute a colorful and
active time of fulfillment.

When the eyes of a Germany awakened from the night shall
turn upon America it will happen with trust and gratefulness,

for here in America the Germany of Thomas Mann has found
refuge and nurture. This German voice from America may become the signal for a new day, when the unhappy, distorted land
begins to rise from debris, ignominy and death.

[1945]

STRICTLY PERSONAL

Charles Jackson

This appreciation of Thomas Mann is by no means an intellectual one. I have never felt up to Dr. Mann's intellectual level, and would not presume to write a serious essay on his work. Rather, this is a kind of "personal" appreciation—and I use the word "personal" not because I have recently had the honor to meet and know Dr. Mann but because, for nearly twenty years, I have been possessed by a passionate admiration for his work, amounting, I confess, to hero-worship. Because of this very attitude of mine, I am probably, out of the many thousands of his admirers, the one least likely to write something interesting about his work and its meaning. And as if my lack of intellectual equipment were not handicap enough, another stumbling-block lies in the essay itself. This is the first time I have ever attempted such a thing; I only do it because my enthusiasm for the man outweighs my commonsense. Let these paragraphs, then, be regarded as a kind of conversation piece, merely, on the subject of those works which have brought me greater pleasure than the work of any other living contemporary. Indeed, my devotion to his books is equalled only by my devotion to the novels of Tolstoy. He has contributed more not only to my pleasure but to my education than any other single name I can mention. Last year, when I published my first novel, it was only natural—it was inevitable, in fact—that I should mention his name or allude to certain passages in his writing at least half a dozen times during the course of the book. In doing this, I was not trying to "borrow" from his work or lean on the great reputation of Thomas Mann; I was merely trying, in some small way, to acknowledge my indebtedness to him.

My first experience of any kind with the name of Thomas Mann was when, in 1925, while working in a Chicago bookstore, a new book came in called *Death in Venice*. I thumbed it through and decided it was highbrow, probably because there was so little dialogue; probably, too, because it was a translation. I was twenty-one at the time. Anyhow, we always recommended it to those readers who sought, whether they read them or not (and we suspected they didn't), "deep" books; and, during the year, we sold maybe a dozen copies.

Three years later I lay for many months in a New York hospital, waiting for admission to a sanitorium for tuberculosis in New Mexico. Somebody told me I ought to read *The Magic Mountain* because it was all about TB. The title didn't appeal to me much; it sounded like a fantasy, romantic, "mythical"; but since I was interested in knowing something about the disease, I ordered the book.

With abject apologies to Mrs. Lowe-Porter, who has since developed into an extraordinarily brilliant translator of Dr. Mann's work, I thought the translation abominable. It was like the time when I first read Dostoyevsky and Tolstoy and was nearly stopped by the "English" of Constance Garnett. I didn't know Russia or Russians, but I did know that characters never spoke as Mrs. Garnett made them speak, anywhere in the world, in any age or time. But the great truth and drive and thrill of Dostoyevsky and Tolstoy—their content, in short—soon overcame and shone through the awkward English version. So it was with Thomas Mann; to us who cannot read him in German, so it will always be, I feel sure, with any translator who gives us his work at all.

It is true I learned a good deal about tuberculosis from *The Magic Mountain,* but I learned a great deal more about art, about politics, about science, about psychology, about Europe, and about myself. I had been scheduled to go to a sanitorium in Santa Fe in the summer of 1929; but after reading *The Magic Mountain* I went to Davos instead. I well remember how my new German doctor, Hans Staub, asked why I had come all the way to Switzerland for the cure; didn't we have health resorts in the United States? We had a dozen such, I replied, but I chose Davos because I had read *The Magic Mountain.* I was careful, of course, to call it *Der Zauberberg* so that he would understand. But I am afraid he didn't understand at all. "What," shouted the loyal and outraged member of the community which had been given such wide "notoriety," "you read *Der Zauberberg* and *then* came to Davos?" He threw up his hands and looked at me aghast, and his bewilderment plainly said, "Crazy American!"

Of course I did not expect to meet, in person, Hans Castorp or Frau Chauchat or Mynheer Peeperkorn, but I did see the place with my own eyes and did live, for over two years, in the scenes I had loved reading about. Apropos of the characters in the novel, there was a Russian by the name of Licochine who I was sure was the original of Settembrini (and not entirely be-

cause he lived in a little *pension* near the Dorf Station) and whom
I did get to know very well, so well that we used often to go down
the bob-run together as a team. I also knew the wealthy young
German who was alluded to in the book as "a twelve-year old lad
who bore the name of a champagne known the world over." It
is both sad and ironical to recount now, incidentally, that this
youth later became one of the leaders of Hitler's Storm Troopers.

I remember the first time I went to call on a Swedish friend
in the Wald Sanitorium. He suggested we go down to the smoking room in the basement. From the first moment I walked into
that room I had the feeling, almost the certainty, that I had been
there before. I felt distinctly uncomfortable about it but I
couldn't say why. During the smoking of several cigarettes I
puzzled about this strange feeling. Only later, when I learned
that the Wald Sanitorium was the "Berghof" of *The Magic Mountain,* did I realize that I had been sitting in the very room where
Hans Castorp and his friends had evoked the dead Joachim at
one of their midnight séances.

It was during my first winter in Davos that Thomas Mann
was awarded the Nobel Prize. In February, I believe, I read in
the paper that he was stopping at the Suvretta Hotel in St.
Moritz. If I could travel all the way from New York to Davos
because of Thomas Mann, I could certainly travel a few more
miles, doctor or no doctor, to St. Moritz. I stopped at the Palace
Hotel, and for a whole week tried to get up courage enough to
go out to the Suvretta and call on him, to speak with him on the
telephone, or merely write him a note. After a week of this tor-
turous indecision, I went back to Davos where I belonged—and
back to his books.

Since I have no critical pretentions whatever, it would be
silly of me to attempt a valuation of the works of Thomas Mann.
But I wish I knew how many times I have read, with increasing
astonishment each time at the mastery with which the artist
handled his material, *Death in Venice* (it is certainly more than
twenty times); I think this story is the only single work of fiction
I have ever read that can be called, on all counts, an absolute
work of art. Nor can I begin to say how much a part the works
of Thomas Mann have played in my education, such as it is. *Tonio
Kröger, Tristan, Buddenbrooks, Disorder and Early Sorrow,
Mario and the Magician, Lotte in Weimar,* the Joseph books, and
the essays, have long been and always will be a vital part of my
life, as important and necessary to me (dare I say?) as my own
family. Even *A Man and His Dog* and *The Transposed Heads* I
admire and cherish more than I can easily state—and I say "even"

because, I am told, Dr. Mann wrote the former as a kind of recreational piece and the latter as a kind of joke. (But I love *A Man and His Dog*, from its beautiful opening paragraph to the last glimpse we get of Bashan; and *The Transposed Heads* seems to me one of the wittiest books I have ever read, one of the most pleasantly erotic and one of the most beautifully written.) To show that my worship is not entirely blind, I have never been able to read *Royal Highness*, which, though I have tried it half a dozen times, simply does not hold my interest.

To go back to *Death in Venice* for a moment. When my second novel, *The Fall of Valor*, was published, almost every reviewer compared or contrasted it with *Death in Venice*, saying that my book was like it or not like it, better or not so good, told the same story or missed the story as Thomas Mann had told it, and so on. This constant allusion to *Death in Venice* in the reviews of my novel embarrassed me considerably, for, of course, not only are the two stories totally unlike and on a different plane entirely, but to me there seems no resemblance whatever—and certainly I never intended one, consciously or unconsciously. *Death in Venice* is a thrilling intellectual experience, esthetically conceived and esthetically satisfying in the deepest and purest sense, while my slight story was merely an emotional tale.

I think the greatest experience I ever had in reading was when I first read the first volume of the Joseph books. I know of no love story in all literature more beautifully or movingly handled than Thomas Mann's telling of the Jacob-and-Rachel story. It is an exalting experience, for example, to read the chapter describing their wedding-night. The story of Dinah is so beautifully told and realized that I cannot read it without shivers of excitement—and the excitement is always caused as much by the mastery of its telling as by the moving events themselves. I remember lying on the grass with my wife one summer afternoon and reading aloud to her the chapter about Dinah. I myself knew the passage almost by heart, but suddenly she interrupted my reading to say, "Look at your arms—the hair is standing up!" Speaking of the Joseph books as a whole, it is almost presumptuous of me to say that I think the story represents, in its entirety, the greatest feat of the human imagination ever brought off by an artist.

At this point in my "essay," I had occasion to speak to my wife about some family matter or other, and she inquired what I was doing at the moment. "I'm trying to write something about Thomas Mann," I replied, "but what can one say?" By which comment she understood, of course, my difficulty in trying to write about his work with objectivity. I repeat, what is one to say? Perhaps this last detail will suffice—and again, it is strictly personal:

During the summer of 1944 I was invited to dinner one evening at the home of Edwin Knopf, a Hollywood producer and the brother of Alfred Knopf, who is Thomas Mann's American publisher. When I arrived, there were several "celebrities" from the world of books, music and the movies already present. Across the room I saw a quiet distinguished-looking man with a cigar, whom I immediately recognized as Thomas Mann. Suddenly I suffered an attack of what I can only call "stage-fright." I simply did not know what to say or what to do with myself. My being there at all was a terrible mistake; I wanted to get out of that room as fast as I could. I had feelings of panic; I felt I could not be held accountable for my actions—which would be largely those of a man suddenly struck dumb. I managed to speak to my host in private and asked him if I couldn't help with the drinks—anything rather than meet or talk with the man I had revered so highly for so many years. To my shame, I even avoided being introduced to Dr. Mann. My relief was enormous when, on going in to dinner, I discovered he had been placed far down the table from me. Mrs. Mann however (who turned out to be the most delightful dinner partner and one of the liveliest and most fascinating of women) was on my left, and during the course of the dinner I told her about having been in Davos. This gave us, for the time being, a topic of conversation, and gradually I spoke of my admiration for her husband. She said, "Then you must talk with him yourself, after dinner"—and later she arranged it so that we were left alone together for more than an hour. Afterward I visited often at Dr. Mann's house in Santa Monica. But what I want to speak about at this point is something that his wife and I discussed during dinner.

Mrs. Mann said to me, "You read him in German, of course?" I said no, more was the pity, I had to read him in translation. Whereupon she exclaimed, "Oh, but to get anything out of Thomas Mann, you've got to read him in German!" I told her that in the past, when I was younger and more ambitious, my passion for his work had been such that I seriously considered devoting several years of my life to studying the German language thoroughly, but only in order that I might be able to read Thomas Mann in the original. Again she exclaimed. "Oh, but it would have done you no good," she said vehemently; "you would have to know German all your life, be educated and brought up in German, know the great German poets, in order to be able to appreciate the nuance, the subtlety, the various styles, and often the parodies inherent in Thomas Mann's writing." So it was a hopeless situation whichever way you looked at it. But I did have a rejoinder. I told Mrs. Mann of my astonishment and chagrin, so exactly like hers, when my Brazilian friend, the painter Candido Portinari, told me that he loved Shakespeare as I did but read the plays in Portuguese. I was aghast, and pitied him from the depths of my heart, "But Portinari," I cried, "Shakespeare is the greatest poet in our language. You can't *possibly* read him in anything but English!"

Portinari put his hand on my arm and tried to calm me— and he did calm me by his reply: "Listen, my friend, Shakespeare in translation is like a millionaire who has lost his money: he is still a rich man."

Well, as we Americans say, for my money Thomas Mann is still a rich man; and with the extraordinarily beautiful translations of the Joseph books, Mrs. Lowe-Porter has again restored him to his millionaire status.

[1946]

AN ADDRESS

At the end of Plato's *Symposium,* the protagonist Socrates
is shown at dawn, after a night of feasting, sober and wide awake;
and while the mug of wine still goes the rounds among him and
two friends, he is absorbed in discussing whether or not there
should be a personal union between two types of playwright,
the tragedian and the comedian.

How can the poet put asunder what is one in life—the elements of the tragic and the comic? They are not separated in
your work, Thomas Mann, inspired as it is by a deep and lasting
sympathy with figures tragic or laughable or both at once; and
it is to the latter ones that you, like your Tonio Kröger, were
particularly drawn.

When your unassuming hero, Hans Castorp, envisions the
truth of our life from a vantage point above the struggle of
human opinions, he sees men acting together in a serene and
composed performance, but against a background of carnage and
barbarism. In their own formful and disciplined way they be-
have like Wilhelm Busch's little bird which, aware that the tom-
cat will shortly devour it, has good humor enough to sing and
warble once more to its heart's desire.

Janus-faced as it is, the whole is always sensed though never
grasped completely. But while even Joseph, the expert in God's
psychology, fails to decipher the mysteries of the divine whole, he
may still play his role so as to bring a smile to the face of Him
who does not deign to answer all our questions.

Like Dürer's Knight between Death and Devil—dangers
lurking both outside and within the German mind—you know
the valley of the dark. Like Nietzsche, you had to fight in your
own soul the struggle against the metaphysical pessimism of
Schopenhauer and Wagner. You know the eternal "Die and
Rise." You have suffered as much as anyone from the Christian
dualism of body and spirit, from the disintegration of modern
life, from the artist's homelessness in bourgeois society; and as

Delivered at a dinner in honor of Thomas Mann's seventieth birthday, Chicago,
June 29, 1945.

an analyst you could not help exposing and thus accelerating
this process of decadence.

Still, the Romantic tradition lives on in you—cherished, cultivated, transformed, passionately loved even if conscientiously
rejected: nothing that contributed to your growth has ever become meaningless to you—you never forget. Thus today—after
three score and ten years whose strength was labor and sorrow—
you are the true representative of the German tradition which
was betrayed by those who tried to monopolize it. Your very criticism of the German people is an outgrowth of love and com-
miseration; and all of your work carries the blessing which their
false prophets had turned into a curse.

As a poet you use not only the bow that wounds but also
the lyre that comforts—just as both symbols are united on the
cover of your books. You embrace, at once, the past, the present
and the future of life in a spirit of charity, of faith and of a somewhat skeptical, somewhat bitter hope. You see and show us in
the agony of the Old World the labor pains of a new age.

In what first seemed a limited attempt to account for your
own being you dug more and more deeply into its origins, only
to be led in ever widening circles from self to family, to nation,
to the very foundations of the human being as such, like Saul
who went out to find his father's she asses and found a kingdom.
Thanks to that unity of masculine creativeness and feminine
receptivity which makes the artist an androgyne, you made your
work world-literature by gathering into it the manifold voice of
the people. In a unique productive effort you came to assimilate
the sacred literature of the East with the refinement of intellect
and sense of dynamics of the West. The dialectical process of
your thought has led beyond the dialogues and antinomies of *The
Magic Mountain.* Naphta and Settembrini have ceased to be
mortal enemies; they have found their common center in man—
he who keeps beyond the opposites in what may be called an
existential irony: he does not commit himself to the parts and the
parties, because he is concerned above all with the Whole and the
Holy One. This worship of the One and the Whole has always
been the religious spring of your works.

There is no other means of realizing one's individual being
than that of Leibnitz's monad—the increasingly clear and distinct
representation of the universe. You have always stood for totality against the totalitarian claims of the particular. Once you
pleaded most fervently for the organic growth of national life
which you felt endangered by the emancipation of the intellect,
by the programs and technique of rational organization. Again

in recent years you fought the claims of the spirit against its
surrender to the forces of unfettered bestiality. The positions
have changed—the ultimate end has remained the same.

This is—to use a philosophical term—the Wholism of your
thought, being advanced in different ways at the different steps
of your career as a writer. You were at first tempted to drown
the individual in the ocean of India's, Schopenhauer's, Wagner's
Nirvana. Hans Castorp's adventures in the flesh and the spirit,
his assimilation of every possible experience, is a later expression
of this process of universalization. And the same holds true of the
ethical as well as mythical doctrine of imitation in your Joseph
legend—another conquest of the *principium individuationis* of
time, another illustration of how man transcends the limits of his
finiteness—*come l'uom s'eterna*—by identifying himself with
great ancestors and reenacting the roles and motives which they
created and developed. Through them you gave the individual
his part in the drama of human life as a whole:

Welchem der Bilder Du auch im Innern geeint bist
(sei es selbst ein Moment aus dem Leben der Pein),
fuehl, dass der ganze, der ruehmliche Teppich gemeint ist.

With whatever pattern you find yourself inwardly blended
(even a moment out of the life of pain),
feel that the whole, the glorious carpet's intended.

In your work man is defined by the sense of the Highest, the
principle of the Whole. The principle lives in man and works
through him. His self-knowledge is, at the same time, knowledge
of God. Only to man is God explicitly present, only in this presence is he properly realized and truly revealed. In recognizing
and sanctifying his God, man verifies and sanctifies himself.

The idea of the artist is inseparable from the devotion to the
whole of Being. But you have served and extolled this whole
not only through your work but also through your life and have
thus grown beyond the limits to which you would modestly confine the artist—beyond the stage of a *joculator Dei,* God's jester,
and have become one of the foremost champions for God's cause
in our world.

Such a representation of the whole is no mere shadow of
true reality. Such art is not for art's sake, but art for God's
sake. Such story becomes a phase of history; an action in which
man accounts for himself before the face of the Highest and the

court of mankind. What Plato says at the end of his *Republic*
about the myth of Er applies also to your story (thus I may conclude with Plato as I began with him): "This story," the story
of man in crisis, the eternal history of the soul, "is never out and
dead; it goes on, is saved and will save those of us who believe in
its message."

[1945]

LETTER TO MY FATHER

Erika Mann

Dear Magician:

So you are seventy! And only yesterday you taught me to
tell the green book from the red book on Franz Joseph Street
in Munich. You were younger then than I am today. But your
face has not changed for me: the light attentive eyes under the
dark, jagged brows, one of which you like to raise, pensive or
astonished; the straight and prominent nose, heritage of all your
sons and lifesaver for your cartoonists; the long upper lip with the
correctly styled mustache and the long oval chin. Young and soft
and sensitive as it may be, this face of yours in my earliest memory, it is the same as that severer and more narrow one of which
I think with tenderness as I am writing now. And then the voice!
It has changed so little that its spell ever takes me back into the
most distant past. You only need to read aloud—sitting under
the lamp near the desk in the darkened study while we make
ourselves comfortable around you (as usual, chairs and sofas
have had to be cleared of books, papers and assorted printed
matter before we could find room), you only need to read to
us like that, dearest, and time and place fade into dreamery.
That which is of today is no longer binding. Only that which
always was is valid.

There is the smell, a mixture of leather, printer's ink, cigar
smoke and tart *eau de cologne* of which we said as children that
it was "just like the magician." There is your head, small and
dark, with the soft, closely cropped hair. As you are reading we
can see it more clearly than at any other occasion. More clearly,
for instance, than during our short meals or when we are having
music—"abundance of sweet sound"—after dinner and you are
taking care of the records. There are your hands—not very
small, strong, but with slender fingers—and the manuscript
which they hold. It looks as always, your manuscript—many
white pages with your neat writing on them, German words in
Gothic script, each letter showing a tendency to fall below the
line while the whole remains firmly horizontal. You haven't
been reading for a long time yet. The cigarette is still alight.
When it goes out, which will happen soon enough, you will crush

it without interrupting yourself. The brass cup into which it will disappear is of Turkish origin, neither good nor bad but very much where it belongs, just like the Empire lamp on your desk and the black lacquered cigarette case, the Russian one, with the painted troika, which you find so useful and yet never fill.

Who is with us? One or the other of the "children," as fate wills it, and perhaps—but not necessarily—a guest. First and always there is "Mielein," by whose side and with whose help and under whose protection you have become seventy. Today and whenever there is something to be celebrated she must share honors with you. The way she listens! And yet it is possible that she has heard it all before, that you have read the same passages in her presence more than once to various people. But you wouldn't guess that, watching her attentive and vividly interested face, listening to her hearty laugh whenever you are funny—and sometimes, you know, you are excruciatingly funny. She is your most faithful and by no means least critical audience.

What are you reading? Is it Adrian, the musician, the German, who is talking? But he speaks with Joseph's voice, with Hans Castorp's, with Aschenbach's or with that of Tonio Kröger. Not as if he, this amazing hero of your new and most amazing book, were like them! It is rather as if he were their brother without being similar to them, just as Jacob, the legend-laden one, is with all his uniqueness, across thousands of years, a brother of Abel Cornelius, professor of history, and Tony Buddenbrook-Grünlich-Permaneder is a sister of *Hofrätin* Kestner, born Buff. That which links them all together becomes plastically clear in the tone of your voice. The themes are the same as those we heard when we were children. Only what then appeared as if lightly and impressionistically breathed out by each single, nostalgic instrument has returned today in full orchestration—deepened, broadened, elevated from the level of the melancholic-particular to that of the representative and all-human, magnificently transformed and yet astoundingly true to itself.

After reading for a while you stop. "Well," you say without lowering your voice, "that's enough." As we contradict, you leaf through several pages and jump to the end of the chapter to a temporary finale.

Where are we? In the study! But in which one? In *Tölzhaus* with the shadowy pine woods behind it, and the beautiful view upon the snowy peaks of the *Karwendel* mountains from the open terrace? The only thing is that this vacation paradise of our childhood was lost long ago, having been put into war bonds

during the First World War when things began to go badly in
Germany. In Munich then, on the banks of the Isar? But that
house, in which we all grew up and in which you thought you
would grow old, is no more. It had passed out of our lives long
before the day when the news came, the horrible news, which
we could receive with but a melancholy smile. "Our house," it
said, "repeatedly bombed structure fairly intact, interior previously changed, now completely destroyed." It was bitterly
ironic, this communication in its neat precision. "Our house!"
It hadn't been ours for quite some time, this house. It had been
an instituton—one of many—for what they called "Hitler-
brides" over there, a place where illegitimate children were born,
children dedicated to the "Führer." "Previously changed!" Why,
of course. Those Nazi ladies would not have felt comfortable in
your study!

We like it where we are. But where are we? In the *Niddenhaus* perhaps, on the Courland promontory? The thought would
seem natural (for obviously we are at home, and these are sum-
mery breezes from the ocean streaming through the open windows!) if it were not for a certain German prisoner of war and
his report. Our little *Niddenhaus*, too, has been changed and
made unrecognizable. It is much more magnificent now, elabor-
ately furnished, surrounded by stables and servants' quarters
and paved walks. Nevertheless, it is usually empty. The owner,
a gay hunter chasing our elks, is otherwise occupied. He has
time on his hands now, though not for long. His name? Hermann
Göring.

No, it is clear, we are where we shall stay: at home, at Pacific Palisades. The road was long. When we started upon it, Europe's skies were darkened by the black thunderclouds which
had already burst down upon Germany. Had the great storm
come earlier, it might not have developed into the deluge which
it was destined to become. The worst part was to know all that
—and everybody knew it who came from "over there" and was
no fool—and to be unable to make this knowledge effective. We,
and you my dear above all, have tried our best. We have often
been separated in these years. But since we travelled in the
same direction we have been able to travel together for long
stretches of the way, much to my joy. How many lives have we
known together since the old one ended? There was the one in
Sanary, another in *Küssnacht*; there was the life in lecture halls,
hotels and Pullman cars in the United States; there was one in
Princeton, and finally there is the one just started, in the new
house. The air which became harder and harder to breathe with

every hour that passed before the outbreak of the war is much cleaner today. And though its purity still leaves a lot to be desired, this is precisely my birthday wish for you: a world in which it will be worth while to live to eighty. Farewell and let me embrace you.

Very much your own,

Erika

[1945]

PORTRAIT OF OUR FATHER

Erika and Klaus Mann

When did our father's image first take on living form for us?
Let us return for a moment to the land of our childhood, to the
meadows and hills of the Bavarian uplands where we used to
pass the summer months. Father, who looms very large in our
childish eyes (he is actually of medium height and lightly built),
is coming up the path that leads from the garden gate to the
house. Our Tölz house—so called because it was in Bad Tölz,
a health resort—stood in full sunshine against a gigantic black
forest and looked out on the Karwendel Mountains, covered with
eternal snow. We are busy weeding the tennis court; it is very
hot, and the sound of our parents' footsteps on the gravel path
is good to hear, for it means dinner. They are wheeling their
bicycles; they have been in the village shopping. The way there
is pleasant, it runs downhill, and we watched them as they went,
gliding idly downward on their glittering machines. Now they
are returning slowly on foot.

We seldom saw our father. In spite of or because of that, we
felt him as a great power in our lives, as the final authority
against which there was no appeal. He worked every morning
from nine till a quarter past twelve. In the afternoon he rested.
Later, after tea, he wrote letters. During all these hours we had
to be quiet, and there were terrible moments when he would
come to the door of his study, demanding, 'Qui-et, there!' in a
voice in which vexation struggled with the incapacity to believe
that we had forgotten again. Sometimes, toward evening, when
we were sitting in the nursery on the chairs we had long since
grown out of, and feeling very bored with our box of bricks, he
would call us. We would tumble downstairs as fast as we could;
to be called in the evening meant being read to, and being read
to by Father was the height of our dreams. We were allowed
into his study only for that purpose—a moderate-sized room
full of books, with a red plush carpet, a scrupulously tidy writing-
table, a round oak table covered with books, a chaise-longue
covered with books—every chair stacked with books. The room
was never quite free of cigar smoke, and the smell of it, mingled

with a faint redolence of glue and dust from the books, was always associated in our minds with our father.

Father would shut the door behind us—there was a book in his hand: a volume of the *Arabian Nights,* or *Grimm's Fairy Tales,* or Tolstoy's *Popular Tales.* He read beautifully; the figures came out of the stories and filled the room; the funny ones made us all laugh till we cried. We were moved, thrilled, saddened or shocked according to the story. We knew that Father wrote stories himself, though we were 'too young for them yet,' but we knew, too, that he could have gone on the stage if he had wanted to.

He was passionately fond of the theatre, and would often talk about what it would be like the first time he took us there. We were to see *Lohengrin* together as soon as we were a bit bigger. We used to think he could have been a musician; he played the violin and whistled beautifully. When we sang carols on Christmas Eve, he would whistle the alto tunefully. But the fact of the matter was that he ought to have been an artist. Sometimes he would make little sketches for us—a gentleman with a goatee who, he declared, Heaven knows why, was the Brazilian Ambassador, or another in tails who was 'The Pride of the Ballroom.' One thing is certain: if for any unimaginable reason his career as a writer had not come about, he could have easily found another medium of expression for his talent. Most likely he would have become an orchestra conductor—that is what he used to tell us when we asked him what he would have liked to be if he had not become a writer. Sometimes, when we had been very good, or at least said we had been, we were allowed to look at a picture-book which our father and Uncle Heinrich had made as young men in Italy for their sister Carla, who was an actress and died young. Heinrich, who would have liked to be an artist, painted the 'finer,' more serious pictures, while our father's contributions tended to the fantastic and bizarre side. They were full of weird dwarfs, of apparitions and comic monsters. There were rhymes and stories to all the pictures. It was really a lovely book, and we had our private doubts as to whether the books he wrote from nine till a quarter past twelve could be nearly so lovely.

Sometimes the children at school would ask us, 'Does your father ever trouble his head about you?' It was our mother who took charge of our school reports, and when we had any 'row' at home to tell about, it was generally she who had intervened to settle things. It was obviously she who managed our education, and so we used to tell our friends, 'No—I mean yes—you can't really describe it.'

It is a fact that he did not *seem* to trouble his head about us.
He thought it was better to give us 'a living example' than to
make any attempt to bring us up in the way we should go.
The atmosphere of our home, the feeling of spiritual responsibility, the discipline of work, the regularity of life, the cheerful-
ness, the calm, the gravity always tinged with irony, and, as it
were, 'between inverted commas,' which is peculiar to him, and
which he brought to bear on our childish affairs with just the
same kindliness as on the 'grown-up' matters which touched him
personally, his talks with our mother, or with the friends who
came to lunch—all these things, he thought, were of a nature
to help in the formation of our characters; besides, he relied on
what he believed was our innate good sense.

Had secret pedagogical intentions possibly prompted him to
speak to us of his own youth, his development, his life? It happened only rarely; maybe that is why we were so deeply impressed by what he told us. Incidentally the anecdotes from his
childhood were by no means 'moralizing.' Nevertheless, in some
way, they had the power to enlighten us and to stimulate our
ambition.

Our father confessed: as a boy he had been very lazy—not
thoroughly lazy, of course, for he had been an avid reader, had
played the violin and written poetry; he had, however, been a
lazy pupil, received poor marks, and besides he had been re-
fractory toward his teachers. He told us many tales about the
teachers in his native town, Lübeck—to us one story seemed
more humorous than the other. And he also told us about the
fine old patrician home in which he grew up—to this day it is
shown to visitors as the Buddenbrook House, although the man
who was born there has been living in exile for some time, as a
traitor to his country; he told us about the room which he shared
with his brother Heinrich for many years, of his grave, very
correct father, of his beautiful mother, who hailed from Brazil.
'And then?' we inquired. 'After you left Lübeck and were no
longer a school-boy, what happened?' It might occur that on such
occasions he wasn't inclined to talk and answered only briefly,
'Well—then I had grown up, of course.' Sometimes, however, he
was more talkative. He sat in his armchair—a particularly nice
old armchair, which he uses to this day—his legs crossed, a cigar
in his mouth, and said: 'Yes, then the years in Munich followed
—we left Lübeck soon after the death of my father, your grandfather. At that time I had already begun to write—or, to be more
exact, I had never stopped. . . . But the family was of the opinion
that I should have a "regular profession." For a while I worked

for an insurance company—but only for a short time; I knew
that wasn't the right thing for me; I had other plans. . . .' Then
he would smile mysteriously, almost gaily, as though the thought
of those 'other plans,' then already shyly enshrined in his heart,
amused him. 'Military service was definitely not the right thing
for me,' he continued 'my feet could not get used to the German
gait. I became quite ill, was taken to the hospital and had to be
released from military service after a few weeks. I was more
fortunate in another position, which I accepted about that time: I
was made editor of *Simplicissimus*—you know, that magazine
with the funny pictures, a copy of which you will always find on
my desk. The first money I ever earned was paid by this magazine. They had accepted one of my short stories and the publisher remunerated me with three shining gold pieces: to this day
I can feel them as they lay in my hand then. The man who presented these first gold pieces to me was Jakob Wassermann!' 'The
real, dear old Jakob Wassermann?' we asked. 'Have you known
him that long?' 'Yes,' he said, 'I have known him that long. And
we were always good friends.'

Beautiful evening hours under the lamp, the air filled with
heavy blue cigar smoke—that was almost better than being read
to. Our father spoke to us of Italy, where he had spent several
years, together with our Uncle Heinrich. 'It was there I began
my work on *Buddenbrooks*. At first I wasn't at all serious about
it. I thought to myself: why not tell a little about Lübeck? I have
so many memories . . . that will amuse my friends in Munich. . . .
And then the book increased in volume—I was terrified at such
a growth . . . but I soon realized that was the only way; not one
bit of it must be eliminated. That is the reason why I was so
very much upset by the cruel suggestion of my publisher in Berlin, dear old S. Fischer—then quite a young man—to curtail the
material to half its size, so that it could be published in one volume. I was quite unwilling to do this. While it was really meant
only as a sort of joke for my friends, yet it was to be a very
exhausting joke. I wrote Fischer: "I cannot permit deletions! I
would rather abandon the publication!" I was taking a great risk;
but I was fortunate—and Fischer listened to reason. . . . The
novel appeared in two volumes, and gave pleasure not only to
my Munich friends. Success came gradually—not with exaggerated speed, but steadily. And now the Buddenbrooks have
become so famous. . . .' It sounded almost melancholy, just as
though fame meant a kind of degradation. ('Fame is the sum
total of all misunderstandings circulated about a person,' Rainer
Maria Rilke says in one of his works.)

'And then? And then?'—We wanted to hear still more; it was so fine and exciting to learn a great deal of our father's life; to determine that he, too—our father—had been young once, had played silly pranks, that he, too, had had to struggle for his first success. 'And then?'—Now, however, he adopted the manner of the teller of tales. He took our mother's hand and caressed it a little, while slowly he said: 'And then one day I was invited to a beautiful home in Munich. I went there often—as often as possible—and there were special reasons why I did. For the daughter of the house was so pretty and so clever and quite unusual in every respect—like a little princess.'—Possibly he would have told us more, and we would have given anything just to be permitted to go on listening; but our mother suddenly said, 'Now it's high time to go to bed, children!'

Our mother was often troubled because we were so naughty; we were, for instance, great liars, would tell stories of which not one word was true, and lie ourselves out of it if things went wrong. Erika especially was an accomplished liar. Once, when she had gone rather too far, it came to the point that our father had to speak to her about it. He was to make her realize that things could not go on in that way. His clear eyes rested on the sulky, obstinate face of the defiant little girl. They were thoughtful, but, it seemed to her, not quite, not utterly, not deadly serious. 'It's very silly and no use at all,' he said, 'for you to go on telling fibs like this. But I think you'll give it up of yourself soon, because I believe you are sensible. It is perfectly nonsensical to lie. Just imagine what would happen if we all told each other lies. It would be awful. As soon as you are big enough to realize that, you'll see that it's beneath your dignity to tell untruths, and now, looking at you as you stand there, I see that you're big and old enough to feel that already.' Then he gave a little laugh and turned back to the book he was busy with when our mother had pushed Erika into his study. The fibber was dismissed. Of course, she did not forthwith give up hoodwinking her parents for good and all. No child ever believes the grownups who say she will change, that she will know better one day than she does at the moment, for she always regards her present state as final, and herself as unchangeably what she is. But Erika did not forget the little exhortation on silliness and dignity, and it was not long before she found, to her own surprise, that she was not *enjoying* telling lies any more, and gave it up, not because it was 'naughty' or 'forbidden,' but because she felt she had grown out of it.

Although 'times' were so bad, and we knew that our parents

had many troubles, both personal and general, we had our family celebrations, great and small, which were carried out with loving attention to every detail. Our father loved festivals; he used to look forward to Christmas almost as eagerly as we did. He would himself set up an old Christmas manger, arrange the pretty wax figures under the Christmas tree, give the dog, whom he had adorned with a bow of ribbon, his Christmas dinner and wait with us in the dark study while the tree was being lit. Its candles shone on and transfigured the presents lying beneath it, which our father admired with us. He could be as thrilled by some little present somebody had given him—a refill pencil, a reading-lamp—as we over our box of bricks or Punch and Judy.

In summer, 1918, our Tölz house was exchanged for a slice of war loan, and life went on, winter and summer, at our house in Munich. A thousand little scenes in which our father played a leading part flash before our mind's eye. What kind of picture do they make up?

It is very hot; we four children, ranging from five to twelve, are lying in our bathing costumes in front of the house on the lawn. Father appears with the garden hose. His technique with the hose is particularly expert. It is not only that he can aim better than anyone else; he can also command the greatest possible variations in the play of the cooling jet of water. 'It's the flick of the wrist that does it,' he cries. 'It's an art!'

Indoors, the pleasantest room was the hall. That is where we held all our celebrations, and where we used to sit in the evening to listen to the music. The hall was panelled in brown wood. The bookcases reached to the ceiling. It narrowed down to a bay with three big windows looking onto the garden, and there its whole width was taken up by the big black oak table, stacked with portfolios of pictures and magazines. The globe stood there, too. From the other end of the hall a folding door led into our father's study, which in its turn led to the terrace and the garden. On each side of the glass door leading to the terrace there stood the beautiful, gilded, five-branched candelabras which our father was so much attached to because they came from his grandparents' home in Lübeck, like the slender, aristocratic Empire cupboards in the 'upper hall.' There were some good pictures in the house—a very charming study of a child's head by Lembach, showing our mother as a little girl, two or three Dürer engravings, a very attractive picture by Ludwig von Hoffmann of slim and shapely youths bathing in a spring, a few prints, reproductions of Breughel and van Gogh. Our father took a great pride in these prints. He thought they showed what astonishing progress the world had made; they gave hardly less pleasure than the originals.

The big gramophone was in the hall. Our father loved organizing concerts; one evening there would be German songs, another Tschaikovsky, or Wagner—very often it was Wagner. If a record squeaked or a woman's voice cracked on the top note, Father was as upset as a pianist who has come to grief over his show-piece.

When we were seven or eight years old—that is, since the beginning of the war—politics began to play a part in the talk at table. We listened with all our ears even at a time when we could not understand what it was all about. We were much better pleased when the conversation took other turns. Politics was an alien and hostile domain.

As soon as we were old enough, we were allowed to be present when our father read his own work aloud in the evening. It was in this way that we came to know *The Magic Mountain, Felix Krull* and the *Joseph* novels as they came into being. At first the audience on these occasions numbered three—Mother, Erika and Klaus. Then the little ones, Golo and Monika, were allowed in, and finally the littlest ones came too. By this time we formed quite a good-sized audience.

For his part, our father enjoys listening to others. 'Parlour tricks,' especially when they are amusing, give him the liveliest pleasure. He is in the highest degree 'amusable' ('It wouldn't be difficult to amuse people—if they were only amusable,' exclaimed Goethe), and this quality of being 'amusable' is a beautiful nuance in our father's portrait, like his childlike pleasure in pretty things, in 'feasts,' in attractively got-up meals and all the little delights of life. His friends would read their work aloud to him, and us; even the children had something to produce, and they found the most kindly and sensitive critic in our father.

Politics, that calamity of the grownups, among whom we were now numbered, put an end to our peace. It was not long before our father realized and hated the monstrous thing he saw coming. His hope that it would suffice to give his fellow-countrymen a living example (as he had given his children a living example rather than to 'bring them up') proved illusory. He felt that it was his duty to grapple with the evil directly, risking his whole physical and moral self in doing so. Were the Germans, in actual fact, 'sensible'? Would they realize of themselves a bit later that what they were doing was 'awful'? On the contrary, they sedulously cast all 'good sense' overboard and plunged into a vortex of mass madness, to which reason was a horror and

which was a horror to reason. After the September elections of
1930, in which the Nazis won their first alarming victory, our
father went from Munich to Berlin, where in a great, urgent
speech, he besought his audience to be on its guard. Nazi youths,
scattered all over the hall, began to riot. They were hissed down
by those who had come to listen to the voice of reason. Our
father, small and still, stood above the noise; he went on speaking—said what he had to say into the row and in spite of it. He
is no orator, we thought, sitting somewhat anxiously down in
the centre of the hall; he is not meant to howl down yelling
rowdies. Why didn't we prevent him? Why didn't we implore
him to stay at home, at his writing-table, where he belongs? Yet
we were proud of him all the same. And it is certain that Germany could have been saved from the worst even then, in autumn, 1930, or still later, in the autumn and winter of 1933, if the
men of mind, the prominent artists and intellectuals, had brought
their influence to bear on the situation, and had made a stand to
defend reason and morality against barbarism. They made no
stand, and the enemy won practically without a fight.

On March 11, 1933, we put through a trunk call from Munich
to Arosa, for our parents were having a few weeks' holiday there
after a lecture tour. We told them that the weather at home
was unpleasant, and that we would not advise them to come
home the next day as they had planned. We could hardly make
our father understand. 'It's rough weather up here too,' he said,
to which we replied: 'We're having the house spring-cleaned.
You'd better stay where you are.' It was a long, distressing conversation. In the end our parents consented; they would wait
and see how the weather and the spring cleaning turned out, and,
for the moment, not return to the Isar.

When we ourselves arrived at Arosa the next day, we found
our father calm and resolute. He had done what lay in his power
to prevent what had now happened. In Germany, his voice
would be lost in the rattle of weapons and the clamour of those
who had raised up the new leaders—a clamour which drowned
every other sound, both the sweet voice of reason and the cries
of suffering which issued from the concentration camps and
prisons—his place was no longer there, but outside, where his
voice could be heard, and whence it might gradually penetrate
into the misguided country.

That spring was an ordeal. From Arosa we went to Lugano,
where milder breezes blew. In Germany they were beginning to
resent the absence of the 'Aryan' Nobel prize-winner, whose
former delinquencies they would certainly have been ready to

overlook. His passport had expired; at the consulates he was given to understand that it would be renewed without difficulty if the holder would take the trouble to have it done at Munich, the issuing office. But that is just what he would not do. Then came reprisals. First our car was taken from the garage; then our house and money were confiscated. But the news coming from Germany was so ugly that all personal hardship faded into the background. The weeks immediately following the 'seizure of power' were the worst because the unimaginable had to be grasped and the incredible gradually believed. We had become homeless; we belonged nowhere. It was a matter of complete indifference whether our hotel rooms were in Lugano or the south of France.

Of course—now we were poor. And our mother must often have been more disturbed than she permitted us to see, because she didn't know how things could continue this way. Everything our father had achieved and earned—yes, even the honour bestowed upon him by the Swedish Academy, the Nobel Prize— had been taken from us. There must be a new beginning—in foreign countries and languages.

We went down to the Côte d'Azur, spent a few weeks in Lavandou, a few more in Sanary sur Mer, near Toulon. Father had stopped working; for the first time in our lives we found him, between nine and a quarter past twelve, out walking, or talking to our mother, with friends or alone, brooding over the disaster that had come. The world—our world—was out of joint.

The house above the sea in which we came temporarily to rest, was small. But there was a study, there was a room in which we could sit together in the evening, there were a few books, and instead of the familiar rushing of the Isar in Munich we could hear the waves breaking on the rocky shore. We spent the summer in Sanary. Some of the big chapters of *Joseph in Egypt* were written there, and when, in autumn, we returned to Switzerland, to settle provisionally by the Lake of Zurich, we were already experienced exiles, who knew that life goes on whatever happens, and are at home wherever their writing-table happens to be.

It is one of the good things about exile that it intensifies a man's contact with the world; indeed, that it creates a contact with the world which those who come from home, go for a tour abroad and return home hardly know. We had travelled about a good deal 'before Hitler'; we imagined we knew our way about in Europe, and even in the United States. In reality, we had always been 'on a visit'; we had never participated in the life of the countries we had stayed in. That has all changed now. And the friendship which unites our father today, say with Switzerland, or with Czechoslovakia—he is a citizen of the Czechoslovakian Republic—or with America, is deeper and means more than any connection he could have established from home. In Germany he has been 'deprived of his nationality'— not that that has caused him any trouble whatsoever. He is a German writer, whether Hitler and his henchmen will admit it or not. He knows that where he is, Germany is—more of Germany than there is in the vicinity of those who today set themselves up as the arbiters of what is German and what is not. But at the same time he is at home in the free world—everywhere where there is sympathy for things of the mind, and where a man can work in peace and with self-respect. During these years he has been a frequent visitor to America. In the winter of 1937-38 he made his first lecture tour 'from coast to coast,' and it was that tour which confirmed what he had till then only suspected—that here was the country in which life was fullest, most promising, finest. The most important democracy in the world received the exiles kindly. She opened her gates with special cordiality to those who had paid for their loyalty to democratic ideals with the loss of their homes. On the great tour which took our father into every corner of the continent, he met with so much understanding, so much interest and receptivity, so much enthusiasm for art and the spiritual things that are above nationality that, moved and grateful, he felt, 'I should like to stay here.' He has immigrated to America and accepted an invitation to settle at Princeton, where he delivered several lectures at the university and has worked on his Goethe novel and the fourth part of *Joseph*. The German University of Bonn has withdrawn the honorary doctorship it once conferred upon him. But it was unnecessary for him to relinquish the title of Doctor, since Harvard University has conferred the degree on him, likewise Columbia and Yale. At Yale he had the pleasure of being present at a ceremony which took place at the opening of the Thomas Mann Archive. The fine and well-stocked collection of first editions, manuscripts, photographs and appreciations of his work which has been brought together there is a testimony of great and active love. While his books are being removed from the German libraries, while the school-children there are not allowed to learn his name, here in a foreign land, which has long ceased to be 'foreign' to him, a home has been made ready for him.

Does this image of our father correspond to the one which

rises from the depths of our childhood into the clouded present? Do we recognize the face that bent over us tiny children as we played in the garden of the Tölz house—which we saw sombre when politics had found its way to us, and which rose so calmly above the noise of the Nazi rowdies in Berlin? We recognize in it the clear eyes under the dark brows, which rise high in surprise or indignation, the urbane kindliness and the gravity tinged with irony of our early days. The face has remained narrow, with the prominent nose we have all inherited and the little, close-clipped moustache whose neatness and patrician conventionality is belied by the reflective and shimmering depth of the eyes. Can we merge the figure of our father as it is today with that we first saw? At any rate, the voice, which, as we sit together of an evening in Princeton in America, tells us the story of Lotte in Weimar, is the same that issued from the corner of the Munich 'study,' in the persons of Hans Castorp and Madame Chauchat talking in French. We recognize the voice at once, we recognize the figure from which it issues as the one we once knew, though time has transformed it. For between and behind the slim silhouettes, his work rises, uniting, clarifying and linking them.

It is difficult, perhaps almost impossible, to see and judge as a public figure one to whom we are closely attached by human ties. It seems hardly possible to separate the man from his work, particularly in a case like Thomas Mann, whose work is so intimately bound up with his personality. All his books, and even the great literary essays, are autobiographical in character, a trait clearly recognizable in *Buddenbrooks* and in *Tonio Kröger*, which can be discerned as it were under a mask in *Royal Highness*, *Death in Venice* and *The Confessions of Felix Krull*, and which, for the keen-sighted, is even to be divined in *The Magic Mountain*. Not until *Joseph and His Brothers* does the autobiographical and confessional element seem quite to fade into the background. Yet what a thrill of surprise it gives us to discover and recognize it even here. For those characters from a far-distant time and an alien scene take on strangely familiar traits. Young Joseph is not unlike Tonio Kröger; at the same time he has a vague resemblance to Tadzio, the lovely Polish boy, whose charm laid so mortal a spell, in Venice, on Gustave Aschenbach, the aging man weary of his own dignity. The torments of hopeless love which Joseph causes Potiphar's wife, the priestess and *femme du monde*, who is, in her way, as dignified as Gustave Aschenbach in his, and who, like him, suffers degradation in that

mortal enchantment, not only recall the bitter-sweet end of the
German writer in Venice, but also the dubious delights into which
a certain Hans Castorp sank with a guilty conscience when he
suffered his heart to be overwhelmed with love for Madame
Chauchat. That love for a sick woman, that forbidden adventure
on the magic mountain, was 'hopeless,' like Aschenbach's passion,
like Madame Chauchat's desire, like that rather contemptuous
yet very powerful attraction which Tonio Kröger, the brooder,
felt for the 'fair and commonplace,' the frivolous and harmless.
And yet again, the motive of a love which burns the more un-
quenchably just because it is hopeless returns, like some great,
sorrowful musical theme recurring throughout a composer's
work, in the novel now in the process of writing, centred round
the aged Goethe, *Lotte in Weimar*. For Goethe too loved hopelessly, and wanted to love hopelessly, when he loved Lotte, the
betrothed of his friend. All these torments and ecstasies are interwoven, all these figures bear faces which are akin, and in all
these faces we recognize, with reverence and love, the poet who
created them. It is the face of Jacob, the thoughtful face of the
father watching his son, young Joseph, with anxious yearning.
Then a mysterious and comical change passes over it, and it melts
into the features of Felix Krull, that genius at 'making faces,' and
when it settles again, it takes on the lineaments of upper middle-
class dignity, the likeness of Thomas Buddenbrook, the last patrician, who indulged in Schopenhauer like a drug fiend, then
simply fell dead in the street because a dentist had hurt him—
or because he would not put up with life any longer. But then
again there is a change; the face turns more solemn on the one
hand, smoother and more callow on the other. It is the face of
Prince Klaus Heinrich, the beloved and secretly melancholy
Royal Highness, who had to keep at a severe ceremonial distance
from 'ordinary people' and in the end found happiness all the
same, an 'austere' happiness, when the sweet and capricious betrothed, the strange girl Imma came. And we recognize even this
Imma! Familiar features we have loved since earliest childhood
—for the fairy-tale betrothed, the capricious guardian angel of
the Prince, has turned into the wife and mother—our mother.

   Given such a wealth of memories and associations, of touching relationships, it is not easy to remain 'detached.' On the
other hand, we should not wish to turn our personal intimacy
with the author's life into a fatal handicap by regarding his work
merely as a complex of family allusions, and hence losing the
power to appreciate it as one of the fullest manifestations of
the German, of the human spirit which our time has seen.

The range of problems and human affairs which has entered into this creation, and formed its artistic and spiritual themes, has grown gradually but steadily wider until it has attained the magnitude we know today. It is characteristic that the great essays, that is, the writings of a more general and social nature, have played a preponderating part in Thomas Mann's work only since the World War. The complex of problems which pre-occupied and exercised his mind for years, almost exclusively and with painful insistence, could find concrete artistic form in the ironic sadness of the confessional novels. The problem that dominated Thomas Mann's work solely and uniquely, up to the war, was the problem of the creative spirit. The problem of decadence, which gave the great chronicle of the decline and fall of an upper middle-class family, the Buddenbrooks, its spiritual content, was only a part, a section of the problem of the creative mind. For the artistic temperament already afflicts the last of the Buddenbrooks, not only the oversensitive, over-affectionate boy Hanno, but his father too, who was, to all appearances, still sound. They are estranged from the solid business life of their family; they have been touched by the dangerous breath of the spirit.

The last, and actually the first great bourgeois epic of Germany, *Buddenbrooks*, is the story of bourgeois decay. In its decadence, the race of great merchants gives birth to the artist. It is true that he still harbours a yearning for the 'ecstasies of the common-place,' the soothing solidity of bourgeois life. This longing is also the fate of Tonio Kröger, who weaves his nostalgic monologues between two worlds—the bourgeois and the bohemian. In a way that gives one pause, the notions 'bourgeoisie' and 'strong, simple life' are here identified. Tonio Kröger is estranged from life because he is estranged from the bourgeoisie.

'The creative spirit' after that appears in many guises and under many masks, for he is, after all, an actor too and likes to wear all kinds of strange costumes; but we can always recognize him as the man standing aloof from life, and isolated, the man who does not really 'belong.' Once we find him under the mask of the Prince, who merely represents instead of living; once in the disguise of the swindler who, for his own dubious purposes, apes the respectability which is the genuine lot of other 'bourgeois' human beings. And between the two spheres, between 'mind' and 'life,' Eros hovers, a graceful, cunning go-between.

Eros can appear in many forms. Sometimes he even assumes the form of hate, and instead of vows of tenderness, we hear curses. It is curses, not vows of love, which Savonarola the

ascetic hurls at the luxurious sensuality of the Florence of the
Medicis. But all the same, Eros is at work here too; the hatred
of the ascetic is only the extreme, despairing expression of his
longing, and the priest with the burning eyes, the man of the
'spirit,' confesses it in so many words to his adversary, the 'goddess of the flesh' in a highly dramatic scene (*Fiorenza*, Act III).
'I have always loved you,' Savonarola declares in the end to the
great courtesan. 'Can you understand me? I have always loved
you with a hopeless love.' And the courtesan smiles an unfathomable and rather contemptuous smile. Eros does not always appear wreathed with roses; the perfumes he exhales are at times
highly suspicious; they are the exhalations of the stagnant lagoons
of Venice, shot through with other, acrid odours given off by the
disinfectants used against the cholera.

'Whoever has looked upon beauty is dedicated to death,' said
a German poet whose knowledge of all things concerning death,
beauty and love was profound. That poet was August von Platen,
to whom Thomas Mann has paid homage in a great study: *Platen,
Tristan and Don Quixote*. For Eros can also appear in the likeness of the angel of death. His seduction is at times the seduction of annihilation—that very fascination which so ensnared
poor Thomas Buddenbrooks as he sat reading Schopenhauer in
the summerhouse and to which Hans Castorp, in *The Magic
Mountain*, owed so many strange experiences, physical and spiritual. The most cunning and equivocal of all gods—thus Plato describes Eros—is revealed in that feeling of which Platen sang, and
which Thomas Mann has described as 'the bias towards death.'

This formula, 'the bias towards death,' is one of the intellectual *leit-motifs* which run through a long critical and philosophical study, *Reflections of a Non-Political Man*, on which Thomas
Mann worked during the four war years, 1914-1918. This book
marks a turning-point in his inner life and in his work. For the
first time the problem of the creative spirit recedes. The antithesis 'mind' and 'life,' which had predominated in all Thomas
Mann's creative work from *Tonio Kröger* to *Death in Venice*, is
replaced by other antitheses, other spiritual polarities.

Rather paradoxically, the author's interest in social and political matters is earliest manifested in the *Reflections of a Non-
Political Man*. It is true that this interest at first takes the form
of a long and bitterly angry attack on that type of intellectual
who concentrates his efforts and interests primarily on social and
political matters—that is, the western, democratic type most
clearly represented in Germany by Heinrich Mann. This 'literary prophet of civilization,' with his optimism and his belief in

progress, is thrown into contrast with the conservative, non-political German Romantic; French rhetoric is contrasted with German musicality, the western idea of civilization with the German ideal of Kultur (ostentatiously spelt with a capital K instead of a small c). The *Reflections* are a pamphlet in the grand style, written with passion and grief against the spirit of the Entente Cordiale, the spirit of the democracies with which the Germany of Luther and Bismarck was at war. The author of this strange and at times movingly beautiful book has long since outgrown all the *opinions* expressed in it. All the same, within the whole compass of his work, it is of decisive importance. It is in a way beside the point that his interest in political and social matters should first appear in the guise of patriotic fervour. The profound and painful preoccupation with the 'problem of Germany,' with the difficult task of *being a German,* was only the first expression and symptom of a great inward process. The creative spirit had quitted his tragic, ironic isolation to enter a community. Suddenly the man who till then had held aloof from life, half quizzically, half sadly, participated directly in life with his whole heart, struggling and suffering. It is true that he showed at first no great aptitude for life in the new community, as might be expected of a creative spirit and a Don Quixote. For instance, he entered on a long, intricate and wearing dispute with the 'literary prophet of civilization,' only to realize soon after how groundless and senseless the quarrel was. It may well have been a tragic moment for him when he became aware that he had fought with windmills in the *Reflections* and had given warning through five hundred pages of dangers which, for Germany, were never really dangers. For there is no serious reason to fear that Germany will ever fall victim to a 'facile belief' in progress, to a civilization functioning too smoothly and too perfectly. The reasons there are to fear *for* Germany, which are also the reasons to fear Germany, are of a very different order.

For that matter, the *Reflections* themselves, in their deepest sense, are fraught with the premonition that this somewhat hectic battle is being fought for a cause already lost. The patriotism of this strange war book is by no means the hearty, flag-flapping kind; it is a melancholy patriotism, a kind of suspicious enthusiasm, familiar not only with all the greatness of Germany, but also with all her evil potentialities. It is a pessimistic enthusiasm which lends the book its almost musical charm and its vibrant but dubious verve. It is not mere chance that one of the *leitmotifs* of the book should be the recurring phrase 'the bias towards death.'

It is that very bias which had to be overcome. As Nietzsche overcame in suffering his love for Schopenhauer, Wagner and romanticism, thereby winning a brighter, austerer happiness, the author of the *Reflections* overcame the melancholy conservatism, the secretly rather sceptical enthusiasm for what is already doomed and marked by death. *The Magic Mountain* is the epic record of a process which leads from the interest in sickness, death and decay to the interest in life and finally to an all-embracing sympathy with life and the living. But through this new and brighter melody other notes run, the old notes rising from the depths. The experiences that were gathered 'down there,' in the depths, are not to be forgotten up in the light. It is the man who knows darkness who loves the light most. 'Is he an earth-dweller?' Rilke asks of Orpheus, who made all earthly things bow themselves when he played. 'No, his wide being sprang from both domains.'

This new humanism, which is treated dialectically in *The Magic Mountain*, and is the great finale of its intellectual symphony, could not but have political consequences. Its political implications make their first appearance in the *Speech on the German Republic* which Thomas Mann held on a Goethe Memorial Day in Frankfort-on-Main and in which he made his first explicit avowal of democratic principles. The nationalist circles in Germany, who had, with extreme shortsightedness and lack of penetration, imagined that the author of the *Reflections* would now be one of them for all time, were beside themselves with anger and disappointment. They howled 'treachery,' and did not stop howling when Thomas Mann showed that he was going to remain faithful to the convictions at which he had arrived after a long and conscientious process.

His moral and political development by no means came to an end with the *Speech on the German Republic*. It went on, and the pace at which it progressed was hastened by the fatal turn things took in Germany. The struggle against the barbarism which first menaced, then overwhelmed Germany, was in very truth no 'fight against windmills.' The 'literary prophet of civilization' and the German writer, who was a disciple not of Zola and Flaubert but of Goethe and Nietzsche, found themselves side by side in the struggle and joined forces in brotherly fashion. The creative antithesis, which had at one time borne the name of 'Mind and Life,' had long since ceased to be called 'Kultur and Civilization,' 'Optimistic Faith in Progress and Romantic Pessimism.' It now bore the simpler, clearer name of 'Culture (or *Kultur*) against Barbarism.' Barbarism—the degradation of

human beings by the 'totalitarian state,' the atavistic relapse
into the pre-civilized stage of life, subject to the 'law of might,'
where the notions of justice, freedom and compassion provoke
either scorn or helpless stupefaction. But the new humanism, the
new, age-old goal of a culture no longer based on social injustice
—that is the idea under whose aegis Thomas and Heinrich Mann
came together, and for the sake of which they both became irreconcilable enemies of Fascism.

For this notion of culture is comprehensive. It contains the
idea of civilization without being absorbed or fulfilled by it. It
is broader and deeper. It is faithful to the great values, the
inalienable heritage of the past; hence it is also conservative. But
it points boldly to the future, it has social hopes; hence it is
revolutionary. It is in its nature synthetic rather than antithetic,
since it reconciles opposites by uniting them within itself, instead
of playing them off against each other. It has both dignity and fire.
It has room for all that is human, and is the sworn, inexorable
enemy of the dogmatic inhumanity represented by Fascisim.

The example which Thomas Mann follows with reverence in
his new vision of man is above all the great figure of Goethe. The
being of Goethe, the greatness of Germans, seems to him to show
the most wonderful fusion of nature and culture, of national
and supernational qualities. And yet in that huge mind of
Goethe, who could endure 'injustice rather than disorder,' there
is an element of rigidity, of aristocratic exclusiveness, of *fear* of
changes that might occasion disorder—traits and tendencies that
might well narrow the concept of a coming humanism and check
its development. Thomas Mann knows that; he has never observed the great objects of his admiration—Nietzsche or Wagner,
Frederick the Great or Tolstoy—with a curiosity untinged by
criticism and scepticism. No one will venture to doubt that
Goethe would have turned his back on the Third Reich with a
still deeper disgust than on the patriotic clamour of the Wars of
Liberation in 1813. Yet we have also reason to doubt whether
he would have achieved more than the gesture of cold disdain,
whether he would really have made up his mind to enter the
struggle. It is a well-known fact that the great man of Weimar
never quite fell out with those in power.

But as soon as the Nazi danger became acute, that is what
Thomas Mann resolved to do—namely to enter the struggle, and
to enter it publicly. He could no longer be satisfied with serving
the new form of humanity with his creative power alone, by conjuring up, in *Joseph and His Brothers,* primeval human figures,
by bringing them close to us and 'humanizing' early myths of

humanity. His love of the future made him indignant with the
horror of the present. As long as there was time he warned his
fellow-countrymen, in a host of articles and speeches, and when
it was too late, when the disaster he had seen coming made it
impossible for him to live in his native country, he first fell into
a silence of grief, then found words again—eloquent words,
glowing, angry, sorrowful and yet not comfortless words, words
that were confident for all their indignation and pain. They were
not only heard by the world. They found an echo within the
Reich itself—we know it. The famous letter *To the Rector of
Bonn University,* that great answer to a petty action of with-
drawing from the author of *Buddenbrooks* the honorary degree
of Doctor once conferred upon him, that letter, which aroused
attention in five continents, was greedily read in Germany. Read
with danger as may well be imagined. But thousands in the
Third Reich really wanted to hear Thomas Mann's voice and ideas
again, instead of the everlasting 'voice of their master,' which
has long since become nauseous to them. And they risked prison
and the concentration camp for the sake of that joy, that refreshment.

It cannot be assumed that those who dared to do so were
moved merely by literary curiosity. In their indescribable degradation they realized that they were not utterly degraded as
long as that voice still spoke. The solace which that calm yet
fiery pronouncement brought them came on the one hand from
the memory of a better past; on the other, the message was a
message of hope. The future of Germany, of Europe, of the world
cannot be so gloomy as long as a few proud and greatly gifted
minds continue their active endeavors. That those few do not fail,
but courageously carry on their difficult work, the work that so
often creates new enemies for them—that is a guarantee.

A guarantee of what? Of the nearness of the golden age, of
that lasting peace which would be a boon to all mankind? By no
means. But a guarantee that the struggle is not quite hopeless,
and that it has aims which make it worth while.

[1939]

PAPA

Monika Mann

When I compare Papa to other papas, essential differences do not strike me. Every papa has his peculiarities; but his, since he is a great papa, may be held under a special light and seized upon in a special manner. This may be the reason for that certain shyness and reserve he shows toward us. But I am convinced that he feels much the happier when in intimate hours these are forgotten.

He is filled with honest and naive pride when his children prove to be efficient in one way or another; and he is sincerely pleased if we are alert to his little wants. He has a great taste for traditional family gatherings. A birthday or wedding or Christmas celebration is for him a deeply serene event which he looks forward to and plans for a long time ahead; and when it arrives at last, he indulges in it with childlike joy. Papa is a little excited when he expects guests. Even if they are close friends their visits are ever new and rousing and he is much contented if the evening proves pleasant. Every diversion, everything which lies outside his creative hours, is a sort of festivity: he is always a little the schoolboy on his holidays, as it were. Yes, Papa, you put on your best tie for the movies; you'll be there overpunctually and enjoy your ice cream afterward. At a silly comedy you will laugh tears, and a little journey is a big adventure. (Well, he who must daily chastise and shape his imagination as you do fully deserves to taste the little joys of life.) At times Papa has something of a grandfather about him—not that he looks old —because his relation to us children seems to skip one rung of kinsmanship, smiling more affably and tolerantly. This grandfather quality is further strengthened by the readings aloud in the huge arm chair in the cozy lamplight.

Papa has for everything a great respect, which takes the form of love, fear or personal irritation. Nothing is insignificant—man, beast, object or occurrence. When a child cries, when the dog gets a bone in his throat, he breaks into full action to settle the incident. With the barber or the workman he is eloquent and accepts him as he would a famous man. A thing—the trickiness of the object—has for him an importance, a soul and understanding; and he takes it as a personal affront if, let us say, he doesn't succeed in opening a box or if the thing just doesn't obey. Toward nature he has a peculiar awe—even fear. I remember well many a family walk in Germany at the shore of the sea, which he so loves and which causes him such deep and manifold thoughts and emotions—when he was suddenly seized by panic in face of the silent, monotonous, immense, inconceivable whiteness of the dunes. A nameless terror seemed to take hold of him so that his countenance resembled the paleness of the sand, and with agonized, haunted eyes and as if under protest he toilsomely hastened toward solid ground and human traces.

Papa is perhaps a little superstitious—that is, in a permissible way: he is very figurative, he sees things symbolically and in their entire coherence. A universal spirit may well have an occult vein . . . as if we were not spun all round by phenomena and miracles, and as if anything weren't just as possible. . . .

Papa is not at all vain. His fame and ovations he takes as a necessary consequence, as a logical result of his troubles. He does not directly refer the praise to himself but feels it rather to be the unavoidable thanks for his creation—a justification for it rather than a reward. Conceit, pride, jealousy are unthinkable because he transfers the superpersonal character of his art to its consequences. We may, without running the risk of being sentimental, call him a pious artist. (Have I not often observed how he submits to the festive racket with an expression that suggests, clearly enough: Ladies and gentlemen, whom do you celebrate? You don't mean *me*?)

With other artists he is modest, almost intimidated. Toward them he feels something brotherly and admiring as well. Everything in the realm of art interests and fascinates him so much that when he talks to a fellow creator he seems to forget that he is one himself. What other artists are prone to do—to brag, to try conclusions with this and that genius—is unknown to him; not so much because he feels sure of his fame and position but because he is more concerned with the subject than with himself.

For everything he reads, for every magazine article, he has enthusiasm; his receptive spirit is as indefatigable as his productive one. When he reads Goethe or Dostoyevsky or Joseph Conrad, he will speak at dinnertime about his reading with naive ardor as if he had just come out of an author's world where he

has been received as an honored guest. On the other hand, an
arch collegiality is evident in his words and countenance as he
addresses the author and "brother" as *du*, saying in effect: You
do express yourself handsomely and you have a great soul; I too,
I know a little about how it feels to give expression to oneself
and to things. Isn't it rather devilish and grandiose fun and
worth the trouble? For the rest, many thanks. Thou couldst not
have said it better.

As a husband, Papa is very gentle. It is generally agreed
upon that everything ticks, to be sure, but apart from the traditional arrangements of the daily routine he is quite complaisant
and mild with Mama. Theoretically he is the head, practically he
is the child. He feels lost without her. Outside of his artistic work
he relies on her in small and great matters and intrusts her with
everything. If he happens to answer a telephone call or go by
himself to a party or even on a little journey, he is, I believe, very
proud indeed. Papa is in no way pretentious. He takes great care
of his wardrobe and is contented with a hearty, homely fare. But
if the soup is scorched or the butter not quite fresh he is awfully
hurt—it comes near to a downright catastrophe. Papa and Mama
are a real little couple. For instance, when you watch them pro-
menade arm in arm—they match excellently in stature—or when
the two of them of an evening sit together on the sofa listening to
music, they are the picture of a most intimate, classical couple.
Papa loves it when Mama wears her beautiful red silken gown
and when her white hair neatly and handsomely frames her face.
But he is not ambitious to see her particularly stylish and elegant. He himself has a dark steel-blue house jacket, rather long
and sashed, which he wears with a shawl of the same color close
to the neck. It is exceedingly becoming to him. However, he wears
it only until the hour of noon; the rest of the day he is always
in complete street attire. That jacket gives him a slight suggestion
of the bohemian—just enough to soften, to improve his appearance. In the morning, after he has spent a considerable time in
refreshing rites, he comes down to the breakfast table brisk, comfortably prepared, ready for action. Other men might yawn, be
ill-humored, take it easy. Not he. Papa in his damask jacket, before his cup of tea and his morning paper, looks more aristocratic
and harmonious than at other hours of the day. And we need
not fear that his work will fail. . . .

Papa's rhythm of life is striking. The day follows its course
like a well-rehearsed performance. Both energy and caution become noticeable in his very movements in the way he opens and

shuts a door (I know it's he, even if I am far away) and in the
way he walks along the hall and down the stairs. Everywhere
is the energetic, cautious rhythm: the way he uses his cane when
he walks, the way he eats his soup. . . .

Papa can't easily bear to see suffering—not because of
cowardly egoism, but because he puts himself so intensely into
the sufferer's condition that he is seized by the torture with all
its might. (That he can and must put himself into other men's
lives is of course an essential part of his artistic existence.)

Music is the only weakness Papa has. He regards it with a
mixture of adoration, envy and disdain. "They" have a better life
than I, he may think—although this might be but another rendering of his artistic longing, an incitement for the unattainable, for
the sublime. Music is known to be the most beautiful Muse—
and you musicians are happier than I. And yet I might have had
the power to be one, and not a bad one either, God forbid. But
I didn't *want* to. *Ecco!* I had my reasons. And it is just as well.
But it gnaws at me all the same. . . . And nearly always when
Papa is listening to music he arouses in me the idea that he is
more musical than most musicians taken together but that, had
he chosen it or been chosen by it, he would have fallen into an
abyss. Its inarticulateness would have corrupted him and delivered him to the devil. He is too fully and wholly the man of
the word—of the prosaic, the intrinsic, the ascetic—so that music
for him is necessarily somehow linked with sin. For all that, it
may be a divine sin, and no small stimulus to his own art.
Shouldn't the divers arts long for each other? (What could be
more ideal and fruitful than a poet possessed by music?)

Papa has much taste for virtuosity, for brilliance and graceful precision. It may be a skillful cabaret singer to whom he
offers his praises so proudly that you might get the impression
that he himself has performed the song or at least rehearsed it
with the singer. Schubert's chamber music delights and moves
him most. The B Flat Major trio is his pet. Once he exclaimed
with a deeply grateful, almost baffled smile: "Delightful. *Delightful.*" And then, grieved, questioning reproachfully: "Why don't
they compose like that today? It is a pity, a pity indeed."

When Papa had his new home built in California and on the
first night entered the living room, which still smelled of new
paint and looked sparsely furnished—bookcases, pictures and
chairs standing about higgledy-piggledy—he found himself a
little place on the sofa opposite the radio, and Mama seated herself by his side. Somewhere sat the dog, and someplace I was

seated. Only one lamp was burning, rather dimly. The room lay almost in darkness and seemed enormous, chaotic and strange; everything in it seemed to be without contact. Oh, everything would be very comfortable and nice and would have the wonted atmosphere in good time. It would even be his most beautiful house—with the terrace abundant with flowers, and the vast bright view of the California land and ocean. The deep blue sky contrasting with the light smooth walls, a strong, slightly gilded sun and the odd trees remind you, Papa, a little of Egypt. . . .And his private domain—studio, a little hall with books, from which a small staircase leads up to his bedroom—would be cozy and inspiring. He inclined his head on Mama's shoulder and listened to the music. The sounds may have mingled with reveries. The smell of paint, the damp, exciting promise of a new building may have awakened in him familiar things—thirty-five years ago in Munich. . . . Almost unthinkable what lies in between then and now, how long a time and how many changes. . . . And of one's own constancy one is almost a little tired. One might almost feel a bit ashamed to take root again and again in spite of all—and to defy everything. . . . But to be your own master, your own god, to pitch your tent somewhere in this world, to be free, to have a home again, is not bad. It is even very good. And eventually you deserve it. The music was interrupted, the dog rattled his collar, and Papa and Mama talked softly to each other. It reached me as from far; I didn't understand it. Perhaps Mama asked him, "Well, and are you then really happy with your new house?" And he may have answered, "Oh, surely!" and his glance quickly turned inward, while he thought with a smile (possibly Dvorák's *New World* was being played): It is touching—and by the way worthy of appreciation, and fine—how one has the courage. You need your property and your liberty. You must be able to hide and to represent yourself. You have to juggle and say you are at home, until you believe it, and nobody can touch you really! How else could you spend yourself in such a way and present the world with beauty and wisdom? *Punktum.* Here shall you yet bring about something unheard of. Something—something—just wait.

And we wait indeed. Never before has Papa seemed so absorbed and possessed by his work. It is as if he carries about with him a great burden. He is tense, exalted, very sad frequently. Deep chaos, despair, ecstasy, destruction are to be shaped. With unequaled intensity he conspires with phantoms, infernal specters of the universe. Surely it is to be an incomparable and agitating tale. A sort of trial, a doomsday. After a particularly violent working-day his eyeglasses sparkle in an uncanny way (Papa's spectacles are like a being, brought to life by the power of his glance, and in their turn take on a glittering or dull aspect) and his eyes behind them are menacing and evasive. How thankful and relieved he is when someone at the family table has some cheering story to tell. He laughs more heartily than is his wont— although he doesn't feel like it. But without laughter in between, without serenity, his book might go up in flames under his very hands. And where would he himsef remain? The devil has an insatiable appetite these days. But we shall yet master him. We'll handle the business, all right!

[1947]

MY BROTHER

Heinrich Mann

After my brother had moved to the United States he declared simply: "Wherever I am is German culture." Only here do we fully grasp the words: "What you have inherited from your fathers, earn it so that you may possess it!" That is our heritage of concepts and convictions, of images and visions. They do not change essentially in a lifetime, although they grow and deepen. They are furthermore not bound up with any nationality.

Our culture—like every other—has the nation of our birth as its point of departure and its pretext, so that we may become completely European. There is no world citizenship without a birthplace; no penetration into other languages and literatures unless simultaneously we have lived our native idiom, from despair to bliss, whether it be printed or spoken. In his early twenties my brother was devoted to the Russian masters; half my being consisted of French phrases. Both of us learned to write German—I believe for that very reason.

I see him at my side, youths both of us, on trips mostly, together but alone: without bonds, one might have said. Can one fathom what relentless obligation a youth marked for a creative existence bears with him everywhere? It was more difficult than I can recall today. Later the agony of expectation would have been unbearable. We needed all the resilience of our youth.

I would not like to penetrate too deeply; I left the probing of my own pains for better days for fear of baring them forever; but the good days never come. Learning to live with one's pains, which vary in their rich diversity, is the lesson of life. My brother learned this sooner than I.

We walked down to the highway from our little Roman mountain town—the scene of my *The Little Town* ten years later —after a hot summer day. Before us, around us, we had a sky of massive gold. I said: "Byzantine pictures are gold-grounded. That is not a metaphor, as we can see, but an optical fact. Just add the slender head of the Virgin and her much-too-heavy crown which look down indifferently from their plastic zenith!" My brother disliked the aestheticism in my remark. "That's its external aspect," he said.

He never left his little dog at home. "Should we really go without him?" he asked if Titino was not around. We had found him on a haystack. His little ways, the manifestations of his little instincts, like ours—only more natural—they taught and comforted him. Titino, the realist, was a jolly corrective when the young soul of his master grew melancholy.

The best antidote was called *Buddenbrooks, the Decay of a Family.* In our cool stone-walled hall, halfway up a street of stairs, the novice, still a stranger to himself, began his work; soon many would know it; decades later it belonged to the world. In the first draft it was simply our story, the life of our parents and grandparents, down to the generations we had heard about —directly or indirectly.

The old people had counted their days more thoughtfully than we do, they kept accounts. Births in the family house, a first schoolday, sicknesses, and what was called the "establishment" of their children, joining the firm, marriages—all was recorded, in particular detail recipes, with their surprisingly low food prices, great-grandmother nevertheless complaining about the rise in prices. These things, as we recalled them, were gone a hundred years, our own memories not older than ten.

If I may claim the honor, I have had my share in the famous book: simply as a son of the family who had something to contribute to the given subject matter. But if a departed gentleman with powdered hair and embroidered coat had looked over our shoulder, he would have had more to say than I. The young author listened to him: the details of every character's life were indispensable. Each demanded to be *mise en scène.* The essence of the book, namely its harmony, the direction in which the array of characters moved—the idea itself belonged to the author alone.

Only he understood the decay at that time; his own fruitful ascent taught him how it is that one declines, how a numerous family becomes a small one and can never survive the loss of its last able man. The delicate boy who remains succumbs, and all is said for eternity. In reality, as became clear later on, much had to be added, if not for eternity, at least for the few decades which were given to us. What was called the "rotten" family by a hasty clergyman was still to become conspicuously productive.

This was a beginner's robust manner of freeing himself from the tribulations of insecurity. After his novel and its success had arrived I have never again seen him despair of life. Or perhaps he was now strong enough to settle it with himself. The last able man of the family was by no means gone. My brother vindicated thoroughly the perseverance of our father, as well as the ambition which was his virtue. Egotism is ennobled by ambition, or rather, ambition may divert one from it.

After sixty years I again hear my father, his answer to a remark of an acquaintance that he is, of course, again nominated as a member of a committee. "Yes, I am always on hand where nothing is to be gained." A businessman, he valued unremunerative work which served the common good. The taxpayers of his city-state cost him more trouble and time than a member of the ruling senate was compensated for. I do not believe the capital of the firm increased during the twenty-five years that he was at its head.

His business was to buy grain, to store and ship it. When I was a boy he took me with him to the villages. He still hoped at that time I would be his successor. He let me christen a ship, introduced me to his employees. All this subsided when I read too much and could no longer recite the houses of our street. We traveled in rented carriages; no one, hardly a millionaire, had his own carriage then, while nowadays the have-nots own them. At the clatter of the horses the farmer stepped out of his house and the deal was made sight unseen; they trusted one another. My father traveled just to keep up the friendship.

His popularity, which was great and sincere—sincerely acquired and offered—seems to me a prefiguration of the extraordinary recognition for which my brother was destined. He began, so to say, before he was present in person. His fame transcends all ranks, like that of a patrician who carries his tradition with him. We forgive the descendant the prejudices inherent in tradition, prejudices often combined with skepticism. The uncontrollable aversion of the *nouveaux-riches* toward innovations which spell danger for these prejudices in a social sense is spiritually stimulating for the insecure.

Our father worked for his family and for public welfare with the same conscientiousness. Neither the one nor the other would he have left to chance. He who preserves and who carries on has to fear nothing so much as he does chance. But in order to create something lasting one must be accurate and on time. There is no genius after business hours. The most solemn personages of the past have laughed and prattled with their friends. One should keep one's hours. We have after all no power over genius, but only over perfection, provided we are strong and dependable.

If I am not mistaken, more than for his talent my brother is respected for finishing what he began. To achieve perfection completely exceeds human capacity. To approach it untiringly is already the highest permissible achievement. Disinterested ambition is selfless because it wills the work and, if it be spurned, alienates while it compels men as well as nations. For when both are involved they are more likely to be negligent and easygoing as long as possible.

This would explain to a certain extent why a new audience of many Americans have agreed to call Thomas Mann the foremost writer of the world. We may recall that most Germans held the same opinion but were prevented from uttering it. If an individual achieves this unquestionable recognition he must represent more than himself: a country and its tradition; but more than that, a whole culture, man's supernational consciousness. The one as well as the other bore to this day the name of Europe. It *was* Europe.

Americans are probably justified in their conviction that they are destined to help form the future culture of the world. Some doubt whether this can be done so easily arises from their unreserved recognition of the man who writes German, is German. He could not deny his origin and lifelong training, even if he would. He uses English daily now, even in public, but I have heard him call German his "hieratic" language.

Erasmus of Rotterdam, whose picture, as an intimation of the future, hung over the desk of my brother years ago, wrote in Latin. German is dead—but for how long? We must be translated to be read. Leibnitz, although fluent in the languages of the scholar, preferred to express himself in French for the layman. Who was prompted by the higher ambition, Leibnitz or Erasmus? It is amazing how many newly arrived authors after a short pause utter their thoughts now in English—an approximate English and approximate thoughts. The most respected of all writers remains German and becomes hieratic.

This may be permissible in old age, after many trials, toward the end of a significant representative existence. His destiny, he says, has been to represent, not to condemn. He formerly stood by Germany as it was, against the wrath of the world and against his own scruples. His conscience traveled a stony road until it decided against his country. His decision is only valued the more, with love here, with hate there. He is a witness outside the ranks. And he is not half-hearted.

The Princess of Orange, Mme. d'Orange as she was called by her century, confessed through me: "I pass through events unchanged: that is a great shortcoming. We ought to be laden with afflictions so that we can heal them through understanding and will power. I had nothing to renounce, neither arrogance nor ambition nor selfishness." In conclusion the Princess repeated: "And all this cost me nothing. I did not fight. I was guided by a serene obstinacy which is erroneously called virtuous."

The Christian lady obviously seeks justification in self-chastisement when she says "Never to err—this our Father in heaven calls half-heartedness."

She fails, however, to realize how she is idealizing her fallibility. She has never been as she would have herself be. This degree of immunity to the common passions is foreign to us. But there are gradations of sensitivity and half-heartedness. Today my brother is the more deeply affected. His Germany must have disappointed him more than it did most others. What Germany has since made of itself—or as it has permitted itself to appear—the enemy of reason, of thought, of man: an anathema, that struck him personally, or all its lateness in striking him. He felt himself betrayed.

At a time when he had still published little, he once referred to himself in another author's words, which I no longer remember exactly. "A people is breathing down my back," was their meaning. Already then, alone before his manuscript, he wished that a nation might look over his shoulder and agree with him. His need was to be new and profound, but to be so for a community of the congenial. How would it be when a nation really offered him to the world as a master! If a nation does not do it, the world will hear from us late or never.

As matters stand, however, only a number of foreign countries may know him; no longer all, and his own last. Yet his words were always intended for his own country: the others were reached through his excellence among the utterances of other Germans. It is true that the peaks of European literature approach one another above the nations. Their roots and beginnings have disappeared from sight. Surely it no longer concerns just a single country when in the hands of an author the Joseph legend becomes an allegory for mankind unchangeable in its essence. This lives for us all, lives in us all.

But the *Joseph* is, as *The Magic Mountain* was before, a pedagogical novel: since *Wilhelm Meister* the truly German form of the novel. *The Magic Mountain* too teaches only how to live. To teach how to live is the purpose of literature, theology and medicine. From each of his books to the next, he who is gifted with imagination must study all three and add several disciplines so that he can invent. "I have really invented nothing," said this author, so convinced was he by his stories.

A man educates himself in writing, embraces life with every book, from expanding knowledge he gradually reaches wisdom, the wisdom which is his goal. What does Germany matter here? It adds nothing to the work, and can take nothing from it. Yet there it stands, though its houses are rubble. The old house from which he came stands unscathed in his memory; so, too, the country as it was, as he wanted it to be. The agony over its moral collapse is fiercer than that over wrecked cities. He had thought Germany morally secure; hence his unrelenting wrath.

One's relationship to one's country changes sometimes. A man may clash with it early, not knowing why. Perhaps on account of his youthful adjustment to other zones or to causes which are prior to his birth. I had soon begun to question the Germany of my time to the justified annoyance of my brother. But how can one help one's impressions?

In 1906, in a café on Unter den Linden I watched the pushing bourgeois crowd. I thought them loud and without dignity; their ostentatious manners betrayed their secret cowardliness. They pressed against the large windowpanes as the Emperor rode by outside. He had the bearing of an indolent conqueror. When he was greeted he smiled—not sternly, but with frivolous disdain.

A worker was ejected from the café. He had had the absurd notion that he could drink a cup of coffee here for the same price as those who were dressed differently. Under a ceiling from which hung life-size stucco figures! Between badly painted military parades along both walls! Although the man did not offer resistance, the manager and the waiters could not calm down for some time before the annoying incident was forgotten.

I needed six years more of intense experiences before I had matured for *The Patrioteer,* my novel of the bourgeoisie in the era of Wilhelm II. The novel of the proletariat, *The Poor,* was written during the war year of 1916. I ventured to deal with the leading figures of the Empire in the summer of 1918, a few months before its collapse, of which the definite moment was uncertain until the end. In my first draft I still thought it advisable to place the action in a fictitious country with fictitious names.

I had not risen up early; my inspiration had nothing of a prophecy. To be sure, I began as the facts dawned. They can hardly be said to have risen as suns. Did I suffer from a knowledge which could have been anyone's at the time? Was I a fighter? I do not believe so. I expressed what I saw and tried to make my knowledge convincing and at best applicable.

It has not applied. After the Empire I sized up the Republic and appraised it for about as much as it was worth. The conditions which followed it, this gruesome outcome of earlier conditions, this Hitler Germany had to nauseate me as it did every other person of taste, self-respect and compassion. Thanks to Hitler, his rule, his war, I suffered anxieties, agonies and the deepest humiliation of my existence.

Not really wrath. Wrath takes us by surprise. We must believe those who enrage us incapable of their infamy. Only the mild are infuriated by them. It would not do for us to have recorded too accurately the early symptoms, the preliminary stages of their infamy, if some evil day we are to learn anger. My brother has learned it now.

That is to say, he was kind. He needed to believe in Germany—certainly for the sake of his work; it had need of the moral, the German soil which had brought forth much work that was honest. But from his kindness he also trusted the Germans. How could he otherwise have helped them, how could he have spread abroad their good name, not only his? Such a knower of souls as he is does not base his knowledge on a troublesome multitude. The individual German—Goethe differentiates him from the nation—was often good.

He who was taken by surprise must be on his guard that in his wrath he does not condemn the whole nation with a few scoundrels or with a generation of the malicious. When we now talk—we talk little and rarely—about what our epoch has accomplished, the whole beautiful mess, it is I rather than my brother who does not see a unique monster in the unfortunate country of our birth.

To be sure, I too know what that country has been guilty of, or at least instigated. I have had sufficient examples of its wretched depravity perpetrated upon me and others.

I claim only that this is not the first attempt at world conquest and will not be the last. The realist Stalin said: "There will always be wars." But what do wars mean in a world whose spaces are easily controlled? They can mean only the subjugation of mankind by one or two world powers. That must repeat itself—if one Napoleon, who should have been enough, was not. This time the lot of history fell upon Germany. The next war is perhaps not too far away. "The feet of those who will carry you onward are at the door."

Oh, conquerors do not resemble one another in convictions and conception of life! The France of the Emperor brought the peoples of the world the best—human rights, liberty—made secure by imperial fortresses. Hearts swelled thereat, for years one

breathed admiration, and the friend of nations streamed forth
genuine superiority.

How different has been the fate of the hated Germans. The role
they chose did not wait for the last act to become monstrous; it
was designed so from the beginning. They had nothing to take
along on their blitz through the world, nothing at all for themselves or others that could swell the heart. Their breath was lies
and destruction their nurse. Frightful, is it not? But aside from
the fact that they thirsted for revenge and bred a depraved pride,
they might have become noble men provided they had been
received as the longed-for unifiers and protectors of the continent.

This was hardly conceivable and they knew it. It was for this
reason that they were horrible and became more and more horrible. The next conqueror will again be full of the best intentions.
We may be sure of that! The motives change; after those of the
Germans, the opposite are in the offing. Unfortunately they cannot change the consequences. Twenty millions, thirty if it should
last longer, may be counted as direct victims of the present war—
the indirect appear later. The next war would sacrifice the
greater half of mankind to the ruthless advance of the sciences.

I am not sure of a word of all this. I have only seen in the
course of my life that everything runs its course to the very end
as long as it is wicked. Nothing is proved; my skepticism is
wrong. The irrationalism which turned me out of my country and
far beyond it has been drunk to the dregs. Next, perhaps, reason
might be—not almighty but admitted as an attempt which promises the germ of novelty and a few other things besides.

My brother would not express these doubts about the absolute,
almost detached guilt of the Germans and the lasting lesson
taught the whole planet. I, too, should perhaps keep my doubts
for myself. It is only to confess to my half-heartedness. I have
done what is commonly called fighting—only I was not conscious
of a fight. I did not hate blindly enough for that, and I was not
surprised by anger.

I loved fervently, that is true. But my love? Where has it gone,
where is a trace of it? Still, it will survive me in one I loved.

Already in the first years of our literary activity my brother
and I shared the same secret thought. We wanted to write a book
together. I spoke first but he was prepared. We have never come
back to it. Perhaps it would have been the strangest of all books.
One is not given one's earliest companion for nothing. My father
would have recognized his house in our partnership. I almost
forget that it is more than fifty years since he was called away.

[1945]

SOLEMNLY MOVED

Klaus Mann

With the American Army in Italy, Christmas, 1944.

Joseph the Provider is the only German book in the luggage of an American soldier. I am the American soldier. The book has been a very consoling, strengthening, indeed paternal, friend to me at a time when I have often been in need of strengthening and consolation. Yes, precisely under the harsh, unpleasant conditions of my present warrior life has my spirit proved itself especially grateful and susceptible to the encouragement of this solemn wit, this ingenious piety.

Those were strange circumstances in which I experienced the beautiful tale, the artistry of the God-invention. Usually I read at night by the light of a candle stump, in an icy tent through whose canvas roof the Italian winter rain slowly seeped. The book accompanied me on my journeys through the mangled land. I had it with me when I was quartered in the granary of a shelled and deserted Italian farm. While I enjoyed Joseph's profound pranks the strangest and most disquieting events occurred around me. Heavy artillery—ours as well as the enemy's—made a truly infernal noise. Sometimes I had to stop reading in order to take cover against shells. And so I would descend from my granary into the cellar—the book under my arm.

I would not let my fun and my devotion be disturbed by the din. Whenever I caught myself slightly nervous I would think of Mai-Sachme, the calm prison official who—rather to his sorrow—simply could not take fright, however much he tried. After that it was easy to overcome my own fear almost completely, no matter how fearfully the enemy raged.

The enemy is Germany. Yet the book in which I was so deeply engrossed that it actually made me forget the fear of the enemy—this book is written in German by a German. All this is decidedly strange.

During the day I often dealt with German prisoners of war. What jargon did these lads speak? Was that German? It did not sound like the language which my father taught me to speak

and to love. Would these paratroopers and SS men understand
the archaic-ironical finesse of the *Joseph* style? What faces
would they make if it should occur to me to recite a few passages
from the Biblical novel to them?

Meanwhile one of my buddies seemed very intent upon reading *Joseph* in the German original. The young man who wished
to borrow my volume was German by birth but had lived in
America for a number of years and had become completely ac-
climatized there. He was extremely popular and respected in
his unit: a capable soldier and a good egg to boot, helpful and
gay, gifted with a natural charm and an unpretentious grace.

One morning, at breakfast, I said to him: "Say, by the way,
I finished the thick book, you can have it."

He said: "That's swell. I'll pick it up tonight."

With that we parted. Five minutes later he crossed the
village street just when the enemy resumed firing. He was hit
in the back. He could not have suffered long.

I want to mention the name of my young friend here. It
was Johnny Löwenthal. He was one of Joseph's old, sorrow-
experienced family.

It is well said that men prove the reliability and strength
of their characters in critical situations. That also applies to
books. A book which manifests its validity and power of attraction during gunfire, in the midst of death and destruction,
must be a book made of genuine, powerful stuff. It has ac-
quitted itself well in the trial by fire.

When I recall the grim days in the shelled Italian village it
is primarily Joseph the Provider who comes to my mind. The
wild visions of war pale, become untrue and shadowlike, while
the figures of the beautiful God-invention gain in plastic reality.
See, there they are again—carefully equipped with their unique
and yet human qualities! There are the old friends: Joseph, who
develops from an inspired lamb to the King's Shadow-Dispenser
and Lord of the Bread in the most natural and delightful manner;
Jacob, the solemn, who waxes considerably more story-rich and
reminiscence-heavy as the narrative progresses, and Joseph's
brethen, who also do not grow younger while the tale runs grain
by grain through the hour-glass waist. And there are new faces:
Mai-Sachme, the nonchalant administrative official, Chief Physician and man of letters; the King's Baker and His Eminence
the Lord of the Wine-Press—two unforgettable court officers
created specifically for the purpose of testing Joseph's sooth-
saying power for the first time on them; Amenhotep, the tender

and spoiled God-seeker who holds the great God-conversation
with Joseph in the Cretan loggia; Tamar, that fascinating person
who knows how to get her way with such amazing determination,
and Serah, the childish musician whose shrewd and lovely song-
improvisation drowns out the thunder of heavy artillery pieces
in my memory. I always hear her touching voice:

> God He can scourge and can heal;
> How marvellous all His ways can be
> For human children's weal!

Oh, how marvellous are his ways. . . . I, too, am in a marvel-
ling mood. I am deeply and solemnly moved. Everything seems
somewhat dreamlike to me, the surroundings in which I pen
these lines and the occasion for which I am writing.

Is my father really seventy years old? That sounds extremely dreamlike to me! Then twenty years must have passed
since we celebrated his fiftieth birthday with portly official solemnity in Munich's city hall. . . .

What twenty years! If all that is but a "divine jest"—as
Serah maintains of Joseph's pit-falls and resurrections—then
God's jests are indeed incomprehensibly grim. He has truly
proved that he is capable of scourging us thoroughly. A little
healing is more than due.

Or are there in this chastisement elements of a coming universal elevation and world-atonement? The patiently creative
septuagenarian whom the literary public will fete the world over
on June 6, 1945, seems to carry such divinations in his story-rich,
reminiscence-heavy heart. He is well versed in divinations, allusions and anticipations. The seemingly absurd dispositions of
divine waywardness become less incomprehensible and easier to
bear when he contemplates them smilingly and interprets them
creatively.

                                                    [1945]

AN INTIMATE GLIMPSE

James H. Meisel

As a person, Thomas Mann does not radiate that magic strength and inspiration we expect of our great ones. His flame burns inward. At first sight he suggests a retired ship's officer rather than a poet. Reporters looking for human interest stories are in for a disappointment. His autobiography is wholly in his fiction. He also wrote the best commentaries to his own works.

If there is anyone who knows about the ways of the genius, who is very conscious of his gift, and still endowed with enough naiveté to do creative work, it is Thomas Mann. One may say of him that he has daily intercourse with inspiration—from nine to twelve o'clock sharp, writing from forty to fifty lines, not more. He conquers by patient toil. Like his Jacob, Thomas Mann is daily wrestling with the angel of benediction. His long experience tells him that there is no use in waiting for the kiss of the Muse—you have to provoke it. And so he slowly warms himself up to that gracious enthusiasm of his, temperate even in high spiritual ecstasies. He confesses to a hearty dislike for the great gesture, for all excited declamation. His model is Goethe, of whose style he says, in his Weimar novel, *The Beloved Returns*:

> One might almost call it dry or even punctilious, but no—for what he says always goes to extremes. . . . Everything is uttered in the middle register and volume . . . entirely matter-of-fact. And yet it is full of shrewd, innocent magic, presented with restraint and boldness at once.

Bold restraint, shrewd innocence—the whole Thomas Mann is in these attempts at reconciling what is as irreconcilable as the spirit of ironic reasoning for which he stands and the rebellion of his time that made bold to abolish all restraints, hailing irrationality as the New Innocence.

It is interesting to watch him lecturing to a crowd—clinging to the desk at first, scholarly, bespectacled, bent upon his manuscript with his inquisitive, bold nose; then, by degrees overcoming the handicap of expressing himself in a foreign language, tossing up his head, stirring in his soles, until finally a rhythmic, almost dancelike wagging of the tiptoes accentuates the progress of thought; leading at last, with an unobtrusive crescendo, to the conclusion of his sentence—sentences that have the long, sober breath of patience. His attention is unflinching, although he sometimes makes feints, pretends to forget about the main point, but, to quote a figure in his Goethe novel once more: "I seem to be talking at random—but do not be alarmed, I forget nothing and hold all the threads in my hand."

"Speaking at random" is Thomas Mann's trick to divert the grim watchdog of his overconsciousness. He has to tease himself into attacking his stupendous, epic tasks. For, by nature, Thomas Mann is a short-story teller, a craftsman of the filigree. Not without reason his children, ever since they were little, called him to his face: "Magician." Indeed, there is something uncanny about the way he built such an elaborate and roomy literary house out of such delicate and, at times, brittle material. To conjure the powers of the great form, he called up the spirit of music, and it is Richard Wagner, the Führer's favorite composer, to whom the love of the greatest living anti-Nazi belongs —as a private person he likes to indulge in the very emotionalism he has so severely curbed as an author.

It is an experience to see him listening to phonograph records of *Tristan* or *The Twilight of the Gods*. A strange abandon slowly invades his disciplined face. It is that of a man who has taken off his spectacles: limp, mellow, suffering, and enthusiastic. You feel that as a youth Paul Thomas Mann must have thought of himself as a musician, as his Goethe meant to be a painter. And when, through Wagner's roar and thunder, you hear the composer of the Joseph tetralogy chanting to himself, see his arms beat time, you feel like an intruder and look the other way.

The work from which he thus relaxes is a record of great fortitude—and great fatigue. A sacrifice of strength that would have worn out many a stronger man. It is the triumph of will power over a frail and sensitive disposition. Dr. Mann likes his coffee very light because he is not in need of any artificial stimulants; he once confessed: "I am sufficiently excitable without it!" His creative restlessness, his utter inability to loiter, to relax, come from the same source of ever-wakeful doubt that rejects even the best chapters of a newly written book once the joy of creation is gone.

He is, of course, very conscious of his stature, and his relationship to fame is one of—affectionate reluctance. An admiring lady once carried him off to his study to read to him something she had written about Thomas Mann. When they reemerged, a certain pallor on his face caused the jubilant authoress to exclaim: "I'm afraid I've abused your kindness, Dr. Mann!" "Oh no," he said, with a vicious frown, "not at all! Everything that deals with my important personality is of the greatest interest to me!"

They say of another shy genius, T. E. Lawrence of Arabian fame, that he always happened to retreat into the limelight. Thomas Mann is too obliging to retreat. He does not see himself as an Olympian, but he knows we need an oracle to put into its mouth the answers to our questions. He has accepted his role as a repository of the Free Spirit with gallant resignation. He will protect his privacy behind an appearance sometimes stiff, sometimes deliberately jolly. He may enter the room with a smart "Hello, hello," stepping forward in a sprightly gait, his face cocked sidewards, eyebrows raised in the same amazement which he attributes to old Goethe: "The naïve, wide-open gaze —it seemed to be saying: Who are all these people? . . . His features wore a rather disingenuous look of innocent surprise at sight of the after-all expected guests. . . ."

Thomas Mann's home life has not changed through all these decades, regardless of whether his address changed from Munich, Germany, to Küssnacht, Switzerland, and from there to Princeton, New Jersey, and finally to Pacific Palisades, California. His workshop is an island of planned economy surrounded by much domestic laissez faire. His family used to be large—now the children have gone to war, and the uproar of grand pianos and busy typewriters has quieted down. But even while it was still going on, Thomas Mann must have been, during these last years, a lonely man. He had lived to see the twilight of his gods. He had been taking leave of them ever since he had begun to write— to write with that peculiar irony of his which he once defined as a "parting with love." Sheltered as he was, he must nevertheless have suffered intensely under the impact of the Hitler age. Thomas Mann said somewhere that the Führer had to conquer Vienna in order to get hold, get rid, of his bad conscience, Sigmund Freud. We may wonder whether the American citizen Thomas Mann, in turn, did not see in this war something like a personal contest between the false Messiah of the Germans and himself.

Is he happy now? Relieved, no doubt. But he is far too wise not to know that the battle with the destructive forces is continuing in our own midst. *The Coming Victory of Democracy* which Thomas Mann foretold at a time when many freedom-loving people began to despair of it will be a process of slow growth. Nobody knows that better than the wary genius whose lifework slowly grew into perfection.

[1945]

THOMAS MANN RECITES

Alfred Neumann

A kind destiny led me, almost two decades ago, into the
neighborhood of the venerated man; it was this proximity
which brought it about that during this long span of time I heard
the work of Thomas Mann come into being, heard it through the
medium of his own voice.

I therefore do not allude to his public recitations, which
belong to a different category. These remove him somewhat,
not only spatially, by means of the lecturer's desk, but also personally, by a perceptible desire for distance peculiar to him on
such occasions—an attitude that probably eases his being faced
with so many people.

I wish to express rather the nearness which he has bestowed
upon me, the nearness in Munich's *Herzogpark,* in the hillhouses
at Küssnacht and at Pacific Palisades, his workshop nearness and
that which was perhaps the nearness of his heart. If there were
a word more cautious than "perhaps" I would have used it. For
it is not only the nobility of his heart which puts one under obligation but also its austerity—and two decades are of no mean
importance in such a matter.

The first half of his cigar is in full swing when he puts on
his spectacles and goes to his desk to select the manuscript
sheets. The visitor knows and values the brand not only because
his own smoking is in full swing but also because it is a vener-
able if not an already anecdotal brand that changes only by force
of radical shifts of residence; which means that whole worlds
may lie between Hans Castorp's mildly leafed Maria Mancini
and the rounded slimness of America's Santa Fe, but very few
cigar brands. But the visitor also knows that the reciter's cigar
will soon puff its last. Encumbering the first words a bit, it
will go out in the course of the first page and be put away with
a quick side glance of regret.

He recites not at the desk but in the arm chair next to
the standing lamp; he prefers to have only this lamp lit, leaving
the rest of the room in a mild gloaming. He leans back, crosses
his legs but never fails to keep his back straight; in this stance

of poised relaxation, comfortable, yet dignified and extremely seigniorial, he remains throughout his reading. And he says "Tja. . ." before he makes the few, very pointed introductory remarks which precede his recitation. And the dog lies at his feet. Since Bashan the Great, whom I know only from his immortalization in print, the metamorphosis of the dog has proceeded quicker than that of the cigar; indeed I remember a hysterical canine at Küssnacht, a gloomy Alsatian who was definitely not to be trusted. But here, in the New World, an angel of a dog has been conferred upon the master; he is a black poodle called Nikko, who has Othello's eyes and Jonathan's soul, a creature of passionate kindness whose literary manners are so perfect, and whose surrender to the reader's voice is so complete that, though enticed by an itch he may lift his hindpaw to his belly, he nevertheless will not scratch himself but will drop the paw again slowly—with just a tiny little sigh.

The extraordinary quality of Thomas Mann's reading manner—a peculiarity closely related to the nickname Magician which his children gave him—is the magic of his correctness. His oral tone is sonorous, Hanseatically colored, yet without the faintest admixture of dialect, his delivery steady, distinct enough for scansion. Someone listening to him for the first time (and listening to him as he starts to read) may think of the "Magister Germaniae" and will be mistaken. And he will quickly realize his mistake. For this is a peculiar intonation whose magic soon comes into play; both, the black and the white magics, spread their spell. The timbre undulates constantly, moves and is being moved, modulates and models, forms word, sentence and meaning and captivates the listener. Yes, this magisterial voice snares men into its captivity, and since it does so in portrayal as well as in effect, captures both the person of the book as well as the listener, it is a magic if not a demonic phenomenon. But it achieves its end not by dint of dark conjurings but on the contrary by a kind of overillumination, by a lucidity of portrayal and effect that spares the listener every difficulty of absorption. Thomas Mann's style fugue, the syntactical composite which taxes the reader and frightens some, transfigures itself to self-evidence while one listens to his interpretation; and Jacob's well-deep time image of God assumes personal dimensions.

Yet this is but part of the magic of his recitation; and a more obstinate auditor may call it pedagogic sorcery, even though he sees how a guarded and deeply concealed unmagisterial temper moves the reciter or at least moves his free hand. But another part is even more pregnant, and I believe it to be a

product of maturity, for even magic can develop. I mean the
sorcery of irony. There is a senile irony which turns acid, even
wicked—Goethe did not escape it. Begotten in Thomas Mann,
however, of a living wisdom and a moderation of feeling, it
has become the diametrical opposite, namely tolerance, a kind,
conciliatory smile—and I speak here of the voice which com-
municates his work. It is that rare irony which represents not
only humor but also kindness, love, suffering and death, and
which inspires not only the Joseph volumes and their divine
caprice and joviality (with the unforgettable, amusingly moving
recitation of Serah's sweet doggerel), but also the gloomy Faust
book about the sick German, which is now being born under
California's Western sun and an old master's benign propitiation.

The visitor hears the grass of new creation grow and fares
well with so much magic landscape yet to come. For, after all,
what are seventy years to a magician?

[1945]

TO THOMAS MANN

Dorothy Thompson

We are glad you are here, Thomas Mann. No nation can exile you. Yours is a larger citizenship, in no mean country. Wherever men love reason, hate obscurantism, shun darkness, turn toward light, know gratitude, praise virtue, despise meanness, kindle to sheer beauty; wherever minds are sensitive, hearts generous and spirits free—there is your home. In welcoming you, a country but honors itself.

If you should never see again the German landscape you have loved so well—that landscape, natural, springlike, almost dewy, yet so formal, so humane, it will live behind your eyeballs, and because of you, exist for us. Exiled from that landscape, none can exile you from the culture which molded its fields, its shaped woodlands, its lively, gracious cities, its dreamy towns. For you are of that culture, inalienably, and carry it with you wherever you go, moving in a German air, limpid with light, vibrant with music, an air which all of Europe once could breathe.

The very ghosts who walk with you are more robust than the living. They are secure in time: Wagner and Nietzsche and the colossal Goethe—all Germans, but all Europeans, men of the West, carriers of the

"Torch that flames from Marathon to Concord, its dangerous
     beauty binding three ages
Into one time; the waves of civilization and of barbarism has
     eclipsed but never quenched it."

All sharers, like yourself, in the great Western passion: the love of freedom.

Let them cast you out of Germany! No one saw earlier or more clearly than you the coming blight. When Germany was strongest, most powerful, before the war when Europe trembled, you spotted the canker, scented decay, wrote *Buddenbrooks,* seeing the decline of the bourgeois world. In 1927, at the height of the feverish after-war prosperity, you laid the conflicts in the

---

Written on the occasion of Thomas Mann's arrival in the United States.

European mind in a mountain-top sanatorium, and showed us
all the illness of Europe, in *The Magic Mountain.* Out of what
have you been cast, Thomas Mann? Out of the German language? All its words are in your mouth, under your hands,
emerging in forms and colors and sounds to make us love a
tongue defiled by others. They cannot cast you out of literature.
Let them burn Tadzio in Berlin. A wraith of smoke floats out
across the borders, across the seas, drifts down in shapely form
amongst the skyscrapers of New York, and there he stands again,
his honey-colored hair bright about his temples, his smile win-
some and shy, as alive as when he stepped from the Lido's waves
in Venice.

Despite the world's dark hocus-pocus Mario still defies the
Magician, despite gas masks for babies, some hearts still weep
for childhood's early sorrow. And if we look at Germany with
pain instead of rage, it is because we still see Hans Castorp,
"Life's problem child," stumbling through No-Man's-Land, with
a rifle in his hand.

Inextricable is the relationship between you and Germany
and Europe, and through Europe with all men and women still
loyal to the spirit of the Western World. The worshippers of
Blood and Soil cannot obliterate German earth and German
landscape from your pages. When they admit again *Geist*—
mind and spirit—to make a trilogy, they will again admit you.

Many share your exile, Thomas Mann, whose feet are still
on home ground, whose houses are safe, whose language is spoken
in the streets where they live. But they, like you, live between
two worlds—between a present which they believe to be in dissolution and a future which they hardly hope to live to see. If
they have faith in the grandeur and dignity of that future, if they
look ahead bravely and serenely, they feel themselves kin of
yours, though they speak English or French or the racy, ironic
idiom of the Americans.

And of your future in history we have no doubt. Generations from now men may speculate about your persecutors, however the circle turns. But of you they will say: His virtue was
equal to his gifts. He served with humbleness a most exacting
art and with nobility the loftiest human aims.

[1937]

RECOLLECTIONS OF THOMAS MANN

Bruno Walter

Near our house in the Mauerkircherstrasse, a short street branched off. At its end, close to the bank of the Isar, and shielded by an extensive front garden, stood the stately and dignified villa of Thomas Mann. Around a corner, one came upon a white garden gate. Visitors were frightened at first by Bauschan's barking, but quickly reassured by the overwhelming affection displayed by the dog whom the poet had immortalized. Soon the wide terrace of Mann's house was reached. We spent many an unforgettable hour on that terrace during the warm season and in the comfortable sitting room adjoining the author's fine library and study during the winter.

I do not recall where I first met Thomas Mann. It may have been at the home of Dr. Hallgarten, the art-lover, or at that of his father-in-law, the well-known mathematician Professor Alfred Pringsheim, a collector of exquisite Italian ceramics. He was quite a character and had formerly been associated with Hermann Levi. A musical enthusiast, he had gone so far in his passionate Wagnerism as to make piano arrangements of some fragments of Wagner's operas. His wife, Hedwig Pringsheim, née Dohm, retained her beauty until far into old age. Her father was the publisher of the Berlin *Kladderadatsch*, her mother the well-known feminist Hedwig Dohm. On gala evenings all Munich met at the hospitable house in the Arcisstrasse, but we naturally preferred quiet meetings in a more intimate circle.

Having read Thomas Mann's *Buddenbrooks* and *Royal Highness* and the novelettes *Tonio Kröger* and *Tristan* before making his acquaintance, I was naturally looking forward eargerly to meeting the author. Katia Mann was not in Munich in 1913. Not until the early summer of 1914 did she return from Arosa, where ill health had compelled her to go, but a young girl's enchanting portrait by Kaulbach in the Pringsheim home had shown me her features. That, and the figure of Imma in *Royal Highness*,

Reprinted from *Theme and Variations* by Bruno Walter, by permission of Alfred A. Knopf, Inc. Copyright 1946 by Alfred A. Knopf, Inc.

a poetic paraphrase of her being, had to some extent prepared me for the acquaintance with the theme of the two variations.

A friendly intercourse soon developed, encouraged by the proximity of our houses and enlivened by our daughters' comradeship with Klaus and Erika Mann. The children's wild pranks and their mutual instigation to imaginative mischief kept furnishing us with material for excited telephone calls and personal consultations. But the misdeeds of the children were not the only cause of discussion among the grownups. More amiable pursuits of the young generation frequently served to entertain us and to provide a topic of general conversation. I particularly recall a juvenile performance of Lessing's *Minna von Barnhelm*, in which our daughters played the parts of Minna and Francisca, Erika the part of Sergeant-Major Werner, Klaus that of Just, a young Hallgarten that of Tellheim, and—an irresistibly funny episode—Mann's youngest son, the eight-year-old Golo, that of the Lady in Mourning. He was quite little and spoke with a lisp. His earnest endeavors to portray a ladylike sadness contrasted most strikingly with the rakish hint at the cleft of a woman's bosom by means of a self-devised charcoal line on his extremely *décolleté* childish breast. The young actors attended to their tasks with a fiery zeal. Not only did they have the benefit of two grown-up stage directors, but—a strange artistic whim!—they had even asked for criticisms, for which Thomas Mann and I had volunteered. I suppose that on the occasion of a subsequent performance of Wilde's *Bunbury* I sinned against the supreme moral of criticism, that of strict impartiality, by unjustly giving the evening's chief honors to seven-year-old Monika Mann, whose cherubic sweetness had quite overwhelmed me.

Our amicable relations, so charmingly stimulated by incidents connected with family life, were still further benefited by a proximity more beautiful and inward than that of our homes. I felt instinctively captivated by the singularity of Mann's creative work—I had been profoundly moved by his *Tristan*, while his essentially musical nature seemed in turn to be attracted by my musicianship. Soon it came about that I played for Thomas and Katia Mann from the works I happened to be rehearsing and with which I was therefore overflowing, works like Weber's *Euryanthe* and Mozart's *Don Giovanni*, symphonies by Beethoven or Mozart, Schubert or Mahler. I also made them acquainted with Pfitzner's *Palestrina*. Mann's essay on the subject sounded the very depths of this work. I also recall my playing for him the second act of *Tristan* and my amazement at his unbelievably thorough knowledge of the work when he subsequently pointed out that I had omitted the soft E-flat of the trumpet at the words "*Das bietet dir Tristan.*"

I cannot undertake to speak of the poet Thomas Mann within the framework of this book. I can merely try to say a few words about my relation to his work. It seemed to me the young poet's gravest problem—a problem to which he gave the most thoughtfully clear expression in *Tonio Kröger*—that his nature was so wholly governed by art; that, in other words, he felt so irresistibly driven to formulate artistically his every experience. There was the danger that this urge to contemplate life and to mirror it poetically would cause him to become lost to life itself. The mystery of his instrument, language, might indeed have tempted him to see in man and fate nothing but the material for brilliant writing. He had to beware of the artist's "ivory tower," of egoistic self-enjoyment. He was saved from its allurement by the warmth, the moral strength, and the humanity of his deeper self. The gentle irony and toleration characteristic of the tone and mood of his earlier works never induced me to conclude that he was cool, stood aloof from life, or looked down upon man with condescension. They were to me rather symptoms of his artistic style, bashfully cloaking a wealth of heartfelt sympathy, all-understanding, and pity. Had there still been any doubters, works like *A Man and His Dog*, *Lied vom Kindchen*, and *Disorder and Early Sorrow* would have utterly convinced them of the poet's love of the creature and of nature, and of his devoutly tender involvment in elemental human relations. Larger works like *The Magic Mountain* tend to put the author himself in the shade. The way leading from *Buddenbrooks* to the *Joseph* story seemed to me symptomatic of the development from the "growing" to the "being" Thomas Mann, to his "idea"; the way from the poetical representation of temporal happenings to that of eternal man and his fate; and I am tempted to say from the word to music. Anyway, Thomas Mann and music! Does it not dominate him more than he himself suspects? How enlightening that at the climactic moment of the Joseph story the poet bids music to lead the son, believed to be dead, into his father's arms, that the supreme pathos of an incomparable human event is dissolved in the lovely song of the child Serach!

And does not the poet's path of life run parallel with his creative work—if such an apposition be at all permissible? The man who belonged to the bourgeoisie grew out of it as soon as political events sharpened his gaze and took hold of his heart. He turned toward the people. The man who by his language, his culture, and his soul was a German became a European, and the European became a citizen of the world.

It was my good fortune to make Thomas Mann's acquaintance at an early stage of his interesting and admirable wandering through life, before the revolutions that steeled his forces and raised him to the twofold apostolate as a poet and a citizen of the world. Many a thoughtful Munich conversation during the War and the years immediately following it revealed to me his endeavor to grasp the sense of world events, his emotional affection, but also his effort to preserve the poet's inward quiet as a thing apart from the onrush of wildly agitated reality. It was this tendency that, in 1926, made him hasten into the world of his Joseph, into whose distant domain he returned again and again, throughout seventeen years, from his campaigns against the dragon world of the present.

Although I had left the Munich Opera at the end of 1922, there were occasional later meetings with Mann and his family. His indignation at rising Nazism had in the meantime been expressed with increasing vehemence. I vividly recall his Berlin lecture at Beethoven Hall in 1930, which the Nazis, scattered among the audience, disturbed so threateningly through outcries and interruptions. Mann was forced to bring his drowned-out remarks to an *accelerando* close and to leave the hall, much to the relief of the wife of his publisher, S. Fischer, who had sat in the front row and had kept whispering to him tremblingly: "Stop as soon as possible!" The demonstrations were directed by the "poet" Arnolt Bronnen, rendered partly unrecognizable by monstrous black spectacles. No sooner had Mann left the platform than my wife and I hastened to his side to save him from coming into contact with the rabble. Using a number of familiar connecting corridors, we led him and his family from the artists' room to neighboring Philharmonic Hall, groping our way through the darkness to the Köthenerstrasse exit. A gloomy foreboding had made me park my car there. It finally carried us to safety.

The tender vulnerability of the poet's existence, endangered in spite of his philosophical armor, had been entrusted by a kind fate to his wife Katia's thoughtful protection, without which Thomas Mann's creative power would hardly have been able to remain undisturbed by world events. Back of charming mockery and pliable agility of mind of his model for Imma stood the reliable straightforwardness of a vigorous and brave nature, dedicated as much to the sixfold obligations of a mother as to the thousandfold ones of a wife, a helpmate, a guardian, a fighter, a congenial companion, and an efficient intercessor with the world. My gratitude for the enrichment of my life goes out to the poet and friend as well as to Katia Mann. Although I have not at my command the verses in which her rare combination of mental strength and worldly efficiency ought to be sung, I hope that her tenderly attuned ear will discern with satisfaction the latent enthusiasm in the prose of my paean of praise.

[1945]

PART II

Operatic

BUDDENBROOKS

Robert Morss Lovett

Genealogical novels, represented by Thomas Mann's *Buddenbrooks*, must be distinguished from the simpler family novels such as *Clarissa Harlowe* or *The Newcomes*. In these, the destiny of the individual hero or heroine is visibly influenced by his membership in a family group which thus assumes a role more active than mere background. In the genealogical novel, however, the family itself serves as hero, and its fortunes are followed through several generations. Such a plan is usually dictated by an interest extending beyond personal histories and problems; by a more scientific concern with the principles of environment and heredity, which can be discerned only by observations carried through a cycle of individual lives.

Because of its unusually large canvas, this type of novel requires a particular sort of ability. And because so much of its interest is based on biological and sociological concepts, it is of fairly recent development. One of the best examples is found in the *Small Souls* series by the Dutch author, Louis Couperus, whose novels indicate the current preoccupation with abnormal psychology and the revelations it offers concerning the normal. In Russian literature the book which immediately comes to mind is Gorky's *Decadence*. Several contemporary English novels are of the genealogical type, and several others come very close to it. The outstanding English contribution to this category is Galsworthy's *Forsyte Saga*. This was not originally planned as a genealogical novel, but grew into one long before the author or his public were ready to call a halt. It began as a study of the property sense in an upper-middle-class family; but the last three volumes have been novels of manners, a shift of emphasis which reveals the principle of evolution at work upon John Galsworthy and modern society, as well as on the Forsyte family. *The Matriarch* and *A Deputy Was King*, by G. B. Stern, unite to furnish another example of the English genealogical novel at its best. *The Way of All Flesh* has some claim to be counted one of this *genre* since it deals with four generations of Pontifexes, but its focus is so exclusively upon Ernest that it falls rather under the biographical heading.

As a matter of fact, *Buddenbrooks* itself covers little more than fifty years, but it brings into prominence four generations of the family whose name supplies the title. It focuses particular attention on the third of these four generations: Tom, Tony, and Christian, of whom Tom is the most important since in him the story of the Buddenbrooks is recapitulated. But Tom is a mere episode in that larger narrative which concerns the gradual dissolution of the family and the dissipation of the wealth acquired by its progenitors.

To describe a novel as a story of decay is to suggest an emphasis on the morbid and unpleasant which is quite apart from the actual tone of Mann's book. The tragedy of dissolution is foreshadowed even in the heyday of Buddenbrook prosperity, but the process is effected in a manner which brings out the beauty inherent in decay, and reminds one that the term decadence implies an increase in refinement and sensibility as well as a decrease in vitality. The very style, even in translation, carries that suggestion of beauty in death which is called elegiac. It is a suggestion always, for in this, his first novel, Thomas Mann established himself as a craftsman who accomplished his effects by means so subtle as to seem only a happy accident. He also established himself as perhaps the foremost contemporary writer of German prose, a position recognized by the award of the Nobel Prize in 1929.

A novel covering so many years and dealing with so many characters demands an unusually convincing background. This Mann has supplied in terms of the physical, the social, and the historical. Most of the action takes place in the little Hanseatic city of Lübeck, and before the book is finished the reader is comfortably familiar with its geography. One becomes acquainted with its climate as with its topography—its rain, its snow, its mist, the occasional burst of sun and heat, are an integrated part of the lives and deaths of the people who move through its pages. These include not only Buddenbrooks, but also the numerous families who compose the social stratification of Lübeck: the aristocratic Krögers, with whom the Buddenbrooks are intermarried, the upstart Hagenströms and Köppens who are *nouveaux riches* and so inferior to the Langhals and Möllendorpfs. All this human background is unobtrusive, but it supplies that social third dimension which adds solidity to *Vanity Fair,* and even more strikingly to Proust's *A La Recherche du Temps Perdu.* The same unobtrusive presence of detail achieves the same sense of solidity with regard to the routine of daily life. One knows how the family mansion is furnished, what the characters wear, what they eat. This matter of menus is apt to be prominent in genealogical novels, since the dinner table is a natural gathering place of the family. The *Forsyte Saga* includes a surprising number of meals; and a comparison of the two novels would bear out the statement that perhaps no other typical scene is so helpful in suggesting the atmosphere and mores of a group.

The historical events which occur during the course of *Buddenbrooks* creep in as casually but as correctly as the gradual changes in fashion and manners. The Napoleonic epoch is still a lively memory to old Consul Buddenbrook and his contemporaries. The Revolution of '48 furnishes to his son an opportunity for displaying his solid bourgeois courage. To Tony it vouchsafes the slogans of liberalism which she employs long after the event is as remote as the lover who preached them is to her. The Austro-Prussian War brings to Lübeck the benefits of having sided with the winner, but strikes at the Buddenbrooks through their financial interests in Frankfort. The Danish and Franco-German conflicts, however, reach the town chiefly as an echo of distant marching and a painless flare of patriotism. War is thus a significant element in the background of the century.

Against this firm, though lightly indicated background, the more immediate drama of the Buddenbrooks is enacted. The structure of the novel depends on a series of family scenes, beginning with the joyous housewarming at the mansion on Mengstrasse—" 'Such plenty, such elegance! I must say you know how to do things!' " Thus the ill-bred wine merchant, Köppen, proud to be admitted to the gathering, sounds the keynote of the occasion. Years later, the celebration of the family centenary furnishes a companion piece to this introductory group picture. Again the atmosphere is one of prosperity. The family has reached the pinnacle of its worldly position. But Tom, now acting patriarch, already feels within him the symptoms of decay; and during the festivities he is called out to receive a telegram announcing his disastrous failure in a wheat speculation. One feels that his ancestors, who had amassed the fortune which he inherited, would not have speculated; but if they had, they would have won. So the family scenes progress, each marking a step in the rise and fall of the collective hero's career; until at the final gathering, after the death of the last male Buddenbrook, his mother announces her decision to return to her girlhood home in Holland. She is the first member by marriage to resist the assimilative power of the clan; and its members are left, convicted and convinced of ruin, to seek in some mystical assurance the compensation for worldly decline.

Birth and death of necessity bulk large in the chronicles of a family. But it is significant that the death scenes are far more elaborated than the births; and that the one birth which is dwelt upon—that of little Hanno, last of the line—is in itself the threat of a death temporarily averted. Because he comes into the world ill equipped to cope with the life his lusty ancestors had relished, his birth is really a signal to prepare for the funeral.

Death was one of the great literary values in the nineteenth, as in the seventeenth century. Of late its role in fiction has dwindled. But Thomas Mann himself has experienced ill health and has been in contact with suffering and death in hospitals and sanatoria, so that it is natural the shadow of death should brood over much of his work. It plays a large part in his short stories, such as *Death in Venice,* and dominates *The Magic Mountain,* which has for its scene a Swiss sanatorium. In this book illness, both physical and mental, plays a far greater part than in *Buddenbrooks,* which for all its study of decadence is essentially normal.

The death scenes throughout *Buddenbrooks* bear witness to Mann's consummate blending of realism and symbolism, and this is true whether they are taken singly or considered as a progression. For the earlier ones are easily passed over, while with the growing decadence of the family the demise of its members assumes an ever more tragic aspect. It is as if the author placed himself on the very line where the two types of writing merge, so that this book in itself demonstrates how realism may develop into symbolism, how the choice of significant naturalistic details inevitably suggests a meaning beyond its concrete limits. He has not spared unpleasant physical trivia —the minute odors and sensations which can be made to endow a scene with reality. But neither has he overlooked symbolical values. Part of the horror of Tom's death rises fom the fact that he who had been so immaculate in life was borne home to his deathbed coated with mud and slush, his white kid gloves streaked with filth. And when his son Hanno comes to die, we are made to feel that he has succumbed, not to the power of death, but to the weakness of his own grasp on life.

This blend of realism and symbolism makes itself felt in the constant use of physical detail, and of objects that serve almost as stage properties: the Buddenbrook hand, "too short but finely modeled," modified to an almost unearthly delicacy and whiteness in Tom, but still recognizable in Hanno; the leather-bound volume wherein are inscribed the family births, marriages, deaths and important events as they occur. A reverent perusal of this record impresses upon Tony Buddenbrook the duty to family which must come before her individual happiness; and her submission is registered by inscribing in her own hand, wet with the tears she is weeping, her betrothal to the despised Grünlich. Little Hanno also peruses the book years later, and is moved to rule in, after his own name, the double line which signifies in book-keeping that an account is closed. When rebuked by his father, he stammers: "I thought—I thought —there was nothing else coming." Contrary to Mann's custom, the symbolism here is patent. And it is doubly significant, indicating the end of the family, and also, the commercial element which is inseparable from Buddenbrook history.

This pecuniary motif, developed with such meticulous detail, is a comparatively recent element in fiction. Before Balzac, novelists tended to belittle the fact of money, which in the form of dowries, sudden inheritance, buried treasure, they showered on their principals with the fine generosity of children dispensing make-believe coin. Balzac was one of the first to undertake careful calculations, to mete out exactly what he thought his characters should have, and to cause the action of a story— as in *Père Goriot*—to turn on money or the lack of it. *The Way of All Flesh* brought a respect for money into English fiction, condemning Ernest's inability to handle it as one of his chief weaknesses. *Buddenbrooks* is still more explicit about the size of the family fortune, the various losses it suffers through marriage settlements and bad speculations. Because this is a commercial family, the state of its fortune serves as an index to its general state. When its possessions decline, its morale and its very hold on existence likewise deteriorate. Even the crimes which affect its standing are commercial crimes, the bankruptcy of Tony's husband, the embezzlement of her son-in-law.

In portraying his characters Mann has, for the most part, been content with classical methods. There is no attempt to limit the point of view, which shifts easily from one to another, though it is always given to some member of the family. Nor is there much stress on that exploring the unconscious which recent psychological developments have brought so strongly to the fore, and which plays so large a part in *The Magic Mountain*.

The restraint which makes Mann's literary devices almost imperceptible is admirably illustrated in the case of Tom Buddenbrook, who is revealed as much through behavioristic as through analytical detail. His "Buddenbrook hand," and his death have been mentioned as examples of realism and symbolism. The modification of the hand may be taken to indicate the suppressed artistic impulses hinted at in his choice of a wife and openly expressed in his son. The strange deterioration which takes place within him so that he feels himself eaten away by a species of spiritual dry rot, is revealed through his growing obsession with details of wardrobe and toilet. As the inner man melts away he strengthens his armor of spotless elegance, till in the end he is but the exquisite shell of a man. Here Mann achieves a realistic and far more effective treatment of the theme which Henry James played upon more crudely and more fantastically in *The Private Life*.

The character of Tom is effective, just as the general technique of *Buddenbrooks* is effective, because it hovers on the border-line between two types, and benefits by both. Apparently normal, he yet suffers from conflicts and suppressions which play a large part in abnormal psychology. One feels that he is straining against the bars which hold him to stolid decorum, and this sense of stress increases the poignancy of his characterization. The distance he has traveled between self-confident young manhood and his final state, is well brought out by two scenes which also illustrate Mann's masterful economy: the first, Tom's interview with his mistress, the little florist's assistant, when moved, but very much master of himself, he bids her a final good-bye; the second, his suffering as he sits alone in his office listening to his wife and the handsome lieutenant making music in a room above—a prey to suspicions of a spiritual betraying far more torturing than those based on physical infidelity.

Tom's evolution from assured and almost callous conservatism to anguished sensitivity is counter-balanced by that of Tony, who changes from an impetuous young girl into the spirit of conventionality and the personification of the family point of view. Her very conversation grows to be a compote of clichés in which the jargon of the Forty-eighters, sole vestige of her youthful revolt, clashes oddly with the bromides of the seventies and eighties, by which she shapes her life.

The family deterioration, recapitulated in Tom's character, takes final form in Hanno's physical weakness and artistic temperament. His tooth troubles, described with extreme realism, also serve as a symbol of general debility; and that his weakness stems directly from his father is emphasized by the fact that it is a decayed tooth which precipitates Tom's death. In addition, the teeth offer opportunity for implied comment on the role of dentistry in modern life, and the essential impotence of dentists, doctors, and all the agents of science to exercise that helpful control which is supposed to be their function. As for the aesthetic leanings suppressed in Tom and evident in Hanno, they too become symbols of decadence since they are wholly at odds with the sturdy commercialism which is the essence of the Buddenbrooks. The genius of the family has been the sort that could be reflected through rooms shining with comfort and cleanliness, opulent fur coats, and superabundance of good things to eat. When it descends to such a vessel as a frail, tearful boy with bad teeth, a weak digestion, and a burning love for music, it has declined indeed!

Because the point of view is limited to the family which is the group hero, the real touch of caricature is reserved for outsiders, such as Tony's second husband, Herr Permaneder from Munich, who is sketched with something of the good natured satire turned upon those beyond the pale. The Buddenbrooks are always sympathetically portrayed. Yet irony is never far from the surface, though so suavely insinuated that the reader feels it his own, developed from a strictly realistic representation of the material. Herein lies Mann's triumph. *Buddenbrooks* seems to take seriously the family and the family ideals; it almost does so. Nevertheless, by methods more veiled than innuendo, it does imply a satirical comment on pride of family, on provincial, and even national pride. One suspects, even though it is not hinted, that Tom's later preoccupation with clothes is a sly dig at the last Kaiser.

The irony strikes deeper, however, down to the very roots of human aspiration, both worldly and other-worldly. Its full force is for an instant released during Tom's one moment of vision, which gives the most eloquent passage in the book, and which by implication adds to the painfulness of his death when at last it comes. Dipping into a stray treatise on philosophy he seems to find an inkling of the strength he needs, and an assurance of some deeper portent in life itself. The assurance grows as he thinks it over during the night:

> "I shall live!" said Thomas Buddenbrook almost aloud, and felt his breast shake with inward sobs. "This is the revelation; that I shall live." . . . He wept, he pressed his face into the pillows and wept, shaken through and through, lifted up in transports by a joy without compare. . . . He never succeeded in looking again into the precious volume—to say nothing of buying its other parts. His days were consumed by

nervous pedantry harassed by a thousand details, all of them unimportant, he was too weak-willed to arrive at a reasonable and fruitful arrangement of his time. Nearly two weeks after that memorable afternoon he gave it up—and ordered the maid-servant to fetch the book from the drawer in the garden table and replace it in the bookcase.

This might be, as it purports to be, merely an account of what happens. Yet it carries overtones of comment on Tom and his species as well as on the value of mystical assurances concerning the life everlasting. A similar chord is struck in the very last scene. The Buddenbrook women on the eve of the family's final disintegration, meet in a pathetic conclave that recalls by contrast the buoyant group with which the novel began. There are quiet tears but there is also courage; and Tony in a moment of exaltation asks whether there can be an after life in which may occur a joyous reunion of Buddenbrooks. Her kinswomen are silent—this is not their field. But Sesemi Weichbrodt, Tony's old teacher and the family's staunch friend, undertakes to answer:

"It is so!" she said, with her whole strength; and looked at them all with a challenge in her eyes.

She stood there, a victor in the good fight which all her life she had waged against the assaults of Reason: hump-backed, tiny, quivering with the strength of her convictions, a little prophetess, admonishing and inspired.

Does Thomas Mann see Sesemi as sublime or ridiculous, or a little of both? The essence of his art lies in leaving the question open.

[1931]

DEATH IN VENICE

Bruno Frank

Among the arts in our new German Empire the art of poetry is Cinderella. Not mere indifference but actual hostility exists between spirit and empire. Every prologue before any official ceremony, every festive play supposed to glorify national achievements must be utterly trivial and far removed from art, and this strikes all of us as natural; hardly anyone knows any longer that it is just a matter of custom, not of necessity. It must not be so, for it is not so everywhere. When *Cyrano de Bergerac* was first performed in Paris, the President of the Republic went backstage and presented M. Rostand, the author, with the cross of the Legion of Honor. *Cyrano de Bergerac,* of course, is a consummately French play; but then in France the poets generally need not be ashamed to write national plays, so this cannot have been the only reason. One may perhaps assume that the President in his box, as every spectator in the orchestra, throughout the performance had been saying to himself: "What language—oh, what language! My God, what beautiful verses!"

If the France of today had a writer like Thomas Mann, so deeply in love with the language and so beloved by it—a writer armed besides with such form-giving strength and such a wealth of understanding—it would have a spiritual throne prepared for him. There, the literary art is not regarded as a rather superfluous ornament on the edifice of national consciousness. As strong cement it is admixed to the mortar which holds the structure together. I think of the intellectual tremors evident there during the publication days of a new work by Anatole France, for instance—who is not half so new, so significant and forward-looking as, for us, the German Thomas Mann whose story, *Death in Venice,* his most profound work and, so far, his work of highest artistry, is in these days brought to light, not without evoking murmurs of approval from the experts.

But there should be shouts—not murmurs. There should be shouts: hats off, bow deeply, deeply to the ground—for here, and this time in his most princely garb, comes Europe's ranking epic poet of the day, the writer of what linguistically is the most powerful prose written by a German since Schopenhauer closed his eyes.

No injustice! The German public has certainly not been shabby in its treatment of the great figure of Thomas Mann. Tens of thousands have bought his books. Hundreds of thousands have read them. And yet, in the consciousness of the German intellectuals of today, he seems like just one more excellent author and not many know that in spiritual history it was a great year which gave him to us.

No man before Thomas Mann (let this be stated aloud, for once) has written so fully animated a German—a German, to be sure, which refrains from all the word-forming excesses that are now commonplace, but a German full of awareness and breathing force, down to the very last particles. It is not highly selective taste alone which so expresses itself; the real source of such peculiarity can be only quite an egregious earnestness, quite an egregious sincerity of thought and feeling. And as water returns to the cloud from which it descended, one psychic state will here, *via* art, turn back somewhere into the same psychic state. Although slowly and hardly noticeably at first, it cannot but affect the character of certain strata of a nation when such qualities as the clarity and incorruptibility of knowledge and form, with which a great man here entertains them, start through the medium of linguistic habit to exert their influence upon the soul.

Serving art, in the higher sense, is a service for heroes, and this, for the first time quite extensively and candidly, is the subject of the new story by Thomas Mann. It is not as if here he were speaking of himself for the first time; fundamentally, like every poet, he never did anything else. But the disguises in which he used to appear were too convincingly genuine and too sumptuous for people to look underneath. Today one cannot think without amusement of the time when the novel, *Royal Highness,* appeared and one member of certain court circles lifted his voice in defense of the modernity of his class, against that picture of courtly, disciplined serfdom and representative asceticism—while the writer really was just speaking fraternally and parabolically of the lonely dignity of him who also "represents": himself, and thereby the world in the forms of beauty.

The struggle which such an artist wages against himself, against the chaos erupting within him, his heroic struggle and his heroic defeat are related in the novella, *Death in Venice.*

It describes the passing of a senescent individual enjoying great and well-deserved fame—his end on a southern journey taken for his health, an all but fugitive interruption of the artistic slavery at home, with which he felt no longer able to cope. Formlessness, dissolution, nothingness overtake him in the disguise of a late, strange, sensual adventure, a love story experienced fully and exclusively within, tingling his every nerve although he does not even dare address a single word to the object of his tender feelings. It is as though he were no longer able to speak to her. It is as though there were no longer the figure of a living, truly desired woman but a congealed fever-vision, . a dream-product. But in the main—some eerily two-faced spectres notwithstanding—the dreams which the sinking one dreams and weaves into the light, clear, sunny oceanic landscape of the South are rather unlike the frightening spooks to which we have been accustomed by Germans and Scandinavians: they are bright, light, Greek dreams; and walking therein, softly calling to each other, are Plato's beautiful and knowing figures. Until the black cavern yawns and the shadowy abyss devours the world. The world—that is to say, here, this one man alone. For while Thomas Mann again has us walking in radiantly clear surroundings, while a ride in a gondola or a mass in San Marco or a summer morning on the sand of the Lido were surely never shown with such convincing veracity, while this epic master's absorption of all the virtues and capabilities of the naturalist way of presentation is not denied at any point here, either—yet it is, and ought to be, as though all characters of the novella except the hero himself were soaring, a hand's-breadth above the ground. They are phantoms, even though radiant phantoms. They are dream creatures, and Aschenbach, the poet, has brought them along with him. Moreover, he has brought the very cholera that he will die of along with him to Venice. Not in the real, medical sense, of course. We are told quite plainly how Syrian traders bring the cholera from overseas, how it simultaneously shows up in several Mediterranean ports, while Europe still trembles with fear lest it might come overland, from East Asia, by way of the Russian plains . . . This is what happened in fact, two years ago, and so we find it admitted. And yet, somehow the disease seems linked to the great failing spirit who came down in flight from the North. He really is finished already; he really has been submerged in darkness and dissolution at the moment when a nauseous inability to work seized him at home and put him to flight. In a sense, his Venetian experiences are phases after death.

In point of style, of the technique of language, this new work also is unmistakeably the child of its masterful creator. It resembles its elder brothers and sisters and yet is plainly distinguishable from them, in accordance with its destined end. After all, to the experts the fascination of Thomas Mann's epical writing has always lain in his employment of style to characterize divers events and persons, while remaining wholly true to his own. This time, a significant change occurs even within one and the same work — from the Nordically severe, dogmatic manner of the early chapters (in which the formalistic, the somewhat "officiously didactic" traits attributed to Aschenbach the artist are apparent) to the sensuous wealth of the later ones, when the soft, well-rounded sentences flow as if waves were rolling on a blue Southern sea. Or as if ringing beneath the beautiful words were the gentle melody of a Greek pastoral flute.

Aschenbach the artist perishes. Not, of course, like the typical representative of the literate *literati*, who at some point has failed to make the grade and now quits and decamps, or is redeemed from his sterility. On the contrary: as one who has given his greatest, Aschenbach pays for a fertile life based on the spirit alone with an eruption of the repressed and proudly denied sensual forces—an eruption with which he can cope no longer.

The problem of artistry in our time which has become so conscious is here fearlessly handled. Whoever is great today— so states a man who is in a position to know—owes his greatness less than ever before to an inspired, quickly grasping naiveté; the sap of his artistry has passed through a filter of the most painful knowledge, and a tenacious will has formed the vessel. But today, as ever, all creative powers rise in the end from the well of spurned sensuality.

Aschenbach perishes; but Thomas Mann lives and gives his scarcely veiled pledges for his own future. We learn that the coming years may expect a great work from him, a work in which he will recreate the figure of Frederick of Prussia—out of a feeling, proudly and modestly indicated, of fraternal familiarity with this great genius of discipline and duty. And we learn more: a bright vista opens to those who love our language and our poetic art.

But why does Aschenbach perish, since his creator and brother lives and promises so much? Because more than a mere human, an entire moral condition is to die in him. For Thomas Mann, despite all his intelligence and insight, is like all poets something of a Utopian. Of those who come after us he longingly expects what the living generation still lacks: the conciliation of the ancient struggle of senses and spirit, the completely easy conscience. If today the best have still so hard a time of it, if to be able to accomplish their work they cannot relax their grip upon themselves for even a poor instant, if today their "reborn ingenuousness" (their "superficiality from depth," to speak with Thomas Mann's ethical forebear) still resembles a heavily assaulted fortress—the grandsons will dwell in it as in a flowering garden, under Greek skies, no longer knowing that it could be otherwise. The great artists who then are on earth will be able to live more easily than Aschenbach, the hero who succumbs.

Will they? Will human greatness, will artistic greatness ever grow on any soil other than struggle and suffering? No matter—there is no poetry without faith: Pan's flute, whose sound we hear, faithfully leads our march into the future.

[1913]

DEATH IN VENICE

Ludwig Lewisohn

Death in Venice, a sovereign masterpiece of modern prose, stands both chronologically and spiritually at the centre of its author's life. It was published in 1911; it was the successor of *Royal Highness;* its author, who had already written *Buddenbrooks, Tonio Kröger, Tristan,* and *Fiorenza,* was not to publish another major imaginative work until *The Magic Mountain,* thirteen years later. In order to grasp the high significance of these bare facts it will be necessary to define both the sources of Thomas Mann's work and the character of the unity of tone and intention which renders that work so homogeneous.

In 1921 the University of Bonn conferred an honorary doctorate upon Thomas Mann. In his letter of acknowledgment to the Dean of the Philosophical Faculty, Mann emphasized the liberal spirit of the university in selecting him for this honour. "For," he wrote, "I am neither learned nor a teacher, rather a dreamer and a doubter who is hard put to it to save and justify his own life." In using these words Mann defined not only his own character but the character, as it seems to him, of the literary, the creative process itself. "Only where the 'I' is a problem is there any sense in writing." But this impulse to save and justify the creative "I" is, in the deepest of all senses, an other-regarding, even a "pedagogical" impulse. For man is a social being; he desires to justify himself first to himself as a responsible and metaphysical creature, next to his kind, to his contemporaries and even to posterity. And in this justification of the creative self there is inevitably inherent and implicit the justification both of other individuals and of the species they represent. An austere but vital feeling for human brotherhood is at the core of this conception of the creative process. "One loves the human creature because he has a hard time—and because one is human oneself." The artist, the articulate one, saves and justifies not only himself but others; both his suffering and his work, though so intimately his own, are vicarious. Thus all true art is at the same time

autobiographical and, however subtly and implicitly, propagandist—propagandist, if only through form, through beauty,
because autobiographical, *because* all men are brothers and
none can save or justify himself without saving and justifying
his fellows and his race. In these facts and not in this or that
conduct of fable or choice of .principles or intentions or maxims
reside the moral quality and power of art as such—as such,
in its own inevitable nature.   Under this aspect the æsthetic
and moral categories are one. . . . This bare and brief outline
of Thomas Mann's theory of art and of the life of the artist
cannot pretend to touch upon its thousand fruitful implications
and applications. He has unfolded and elucidated these in a
number of essays; he will be seen, in the long run, to be
not only a great novelist but perhaps the profoundest critic
of his time.

In what special sense was the "I" of Thomas Mann a
problem and a conflict? Why did he have to save and justify
himself? One must assume, of course, the ultimate organization—the innate blending of sensitiveness and responsibility—
which makes the artist. This being assumed, it may be said
that Thomas Mann's problem and need for justification arose
from the exact balance within him of sensitiveness and responsibility. The overwhelming impulse towards art, with its
necessary accompaniments of superficial sloth, of dreamy in-
activity, of worldly unpracticalness, gave him a bad conscience,
produced in him what the psychoanalysts call a feeling of
guilt. Sprung of a line of patrician merchants, he did not, as
perhaps the very greatest artists do not, rebel against the normal
life of man in its freer and nobler forms, but conceived it to
be his duty, no less than another's, to guard, to conserve, or
creatively to change and enlarge the fundamental values of man
and of society. He has been magnificently able in the long
run to achieve his ideal of artist and citizen. But this achievement lay far in the future in those early days when he retired
to a little room in Rome to write *Buddenbrooks*. It was his
task and his ideal then to save and justify his existence by a
scrupulous account of its sources, its special character, and to
lend this account its moral weight by the perfection, fullness,
grandeur of its form. Thus he might be able to return to
the conscientious North and, from within at least, feel that
an equivalence had been established between himself and those
comrades of his youth, the beloved of life and reality, who
trod blithely and earnestly the honourable ways of their fathers
and their kind. The lovely story of *Tonio Kröger* is the record,

fresh, musical, youthful, more lyrical than his other works, of those days. Tonio is Mann, is the young author of *Budden-brooks,* is the artist soul born into a settled and honourable society and seeking to justify itself and its being. . . .

With the publication of *Buddenbrooks,* probably the most massive and permanent prose work ever written by a man of twenty-five, that justification was outwardly achieved. But outwardly only! Mann himself continued to struggle with the demon—the demon of beauty which is sloth, withdrawal from life, vagabondage, romanticism, and therefore love of death and of war and so anti-civilizatory in drift and character. In this enchainment of ideas we see already of course the germ of *The Magic Mountain.* But what Thomas Mann wrote in those early years was both more fragmentary and more one-sided. He wrote the short story *Gladius Dei,* which stated the theme and foreshadowed his dialoguized novel *Fiorenza,* the least perfect of his works, in which he settles his account with the Renaissance, with Lorenzo the Magnificent and his friends and city, with the menace of beauty that is mere beauty and therefore corrupts and cloys and creates the other extreme and its antithesis: Savonarola. But now—it was towards 1905—Thomas Mann was ready to begin the structure of a human life that was still further to save and justify the life of art. In a house, patrician by both culture and inheritance, he found that admirable "companion," as he is fond of calling his wife, who has sustained and fortified him for a quarter of a century and who is the mother of his six children. It was a happy young husband who wrote the symbolic comedy *Royal Highness,* that story of one who, like the artist, stands outside of the normal necessities and duties of life and who is saved by a woman's energy and freshness and love. But neither wife nor child nor house nor gear can wholly save the artist. The menace of beauty remains. From some ambush the fatal arrow may fly. Neither fame nor years nor stringent labour nor civic virtue and its rewards can guard his feet from the edge of the abyss. For he treads the edge of an abyss—to do so is his nature and the nature of his task. He may grow dizzy when he seems most sure of himself. That dizziness is the theme of *Death in Venice.*

To project his idea Thomas Mann thought at first of re-telling the story of the septuagenarian Goethe and that last tragic love of the aged poet for Ulrike von Levetzow. But that story was found to be too well documented to admit of the play of the creative imagination. A sojourn in Venice

furnished Thomas Mann with incidents and visions that con-
densed about the remembered face and head of Gustav Mahler,
and from these observations and visions arose the character
of Gustave von Aschenbach and the story of his dizziness on
the edge of the abyss of art. With all this there may have
blended, though our author has barely admitted it, memories
of the story and Venetian fate of the poet Platen, whose verses
might well serve as a motto to *Death in Venice*.

> *Wer die Schönheit angeschaut mit Augen,*
> *Ist dem Tode schon anheimgegeben,*
> *Wird für keinen Dienst der Erde taugen.* . . . .

In the light of these observations *Death in Venice* may
yield to the reader some of its brimming significance and beauty.
In Aschenbach Thomas Mann projected, of course, a personal
vision of his own later years. Aschenbach's methods and motives
of work are his own—the strong sense of the artist's responsibility, the moral power that comes from the mastering of mighty
tasks, and striving after "that noble purity, simplicity, and
harmony of form" which, we are told, characterized Aschenbach's later works. And this personage grows dizzy on the
edge of the abyss. Spirit succumbs to pure beauty without
having first spiritualized it and must therefore suffer death.
Were the Greeks able to look upon beauty bare and not perish?
That question is woven into the story; it is suggested in the
music of the very rhythms which here and there are unobtrusive echoes of the first hemistich of hexameters. Perhaps
they were; perhaps the memories of them helped to lure Aschenbach to his undoing. We, at least, cannot. In us—to use the
later phraseology of Thomas Mann—*Natur* and *Geist* are divided
and we must, upon some plan, bring nature under the subjection
of spirit before we can begin to live at all. Let it not be thought
for a moment that Thomas Mann has anything in common with
the conventional Christian denial of nature or the Christian
identification of nature with sin. His ideas dwell on a wholly
different plane, and Christianity, in this aspect, is to him part
of that romantic love of death which fills him with dread.
Nature and spirit must make peace upon other terms than
the historic ones, and from that new blending a new humanism
may arise.

Of the form of *Death in Venice* it is difficult to speak.
What is said in the story of sensuous beauty applies here, that
words can praise, but neither communicate nor reproduce it.
Nor, by the same token, can even the ablest translation render
either the savour of words nor the musicality of their com-

bination nor, above all, the contributions of both structure and rhythm to the projection of the creative idea. I have read *Death in Venice* in the original text many times and it is but sober fact that each time I seem to grasp more fully its astonishing richness and perfection as a piece of prose—the complete embodiment of its intention in its form, the consummate union of precision with musicality, of philosophical scrupulousness with the flesh and blood of art. The miracle of art—the perfect union of *Natur* and *Geist*—is here achieved. The miracle of art, which life must imitate if our civilization is to be saved.

[1930]

DEATH IN VENICE

Vernon Venable

I

In a literary epoch that has produced such figures as Gertrude Stein, James Joyce, Paul Valéry, and T. S. Eliot, it is not surprising that little should have been said about Thomas Mann as an innovator. Orderly interest in contemporary spiritual and social problems and respect for the orthodoxies of syntax are virtues that have not been at an artistic premium. Any new ways Mann has of saying things occasion so little cognitive discomfort that they have been generally assumed to be old, familiar ways, and the things he says are so clearly to the contemporary point that his chief fame has been as a kind of mentor, like André Gide and D. H. Lawrence.

To be esteemed as a mentor, however, is doubtless quite as embarrassing to Mann as to have his artistry taken for granted. Although he makes frequent use of ethical subject-matter, the inspiration of his fiction differs fundamentally from the messianic muse of Lawrence and Gide and acts neither from prophetic ardor nor towards doctrinal conclusions. (I speak only of his fiction, of course, not of his essays or of his recent public letters and addresses.) And while he misbehaves with his medium no more than they do with theirs, he manages, nevertheless, to make it serve a new technique.

The clue to this new technique lies in the dualism or polarity which always characterizes Mann's subject-matter. Such large antitheses as life and death, time and individuality, fertility and decay, flesh and spirit, invariably constitute the themes of his novels. Mann never allows this dualism to become vitiated, for it is the formal and operative principle of his æsthetic. He never prefers one term of his antithesis to the other, for his interest is not in arguing theses but in developing themes. Hence we misunderstand his fiction if we isolate individual symbols from their dualistic context in order to lend the weight of Mann's authority to questions of conduct.

The life-death theme, which has been more often the focus of his attention than any other, is a good case in point. Not once in any of his novels, so far as I have been able to discover, does this theme assert the simple, unequivocal proposition that all men are mortal. People sometimes die, to be sure; death often negates life in a kind of dialectical way, but quite as often we find life spoken of in such terms as "inorganic matter become sick," or "the existence of the actually-impossible-to-exist." In Mann's scheme death and life, life and death both unremittingly affirm and unremittingly negate each other in a paradox worthy of Zeno. Actually, Mann's interest in paradox is even more final than was Zeno's, for Zeno saw in his paradoxes only a convenient means of refuting those philosophers who held that the world was plural; while Mann sees, in his, the very core and heart of his world:

> Beautiful is resolution. But the really fruitful, the productive, and hence the artistic principle is that which we call reserve. In the sphere of music we love it as the prolonged note, the teasing melancholy of the not-yet, the inward hesitation of the soul, which bears within itself fulfilment, resolution, and harmony, but denies it for a space, withholds and delays, scruples exquisitely yet a little longer to make the final surrender. In the intellectual sphere we love it as irony: that irony which glances at both sides, which plays slyly and irresponsibly—yet not without benevolence—among opposites, and is in no great haste to take sides and come to decisions; guided as it is by the surmise that in great matters, in matters of humanity, every decision may prove premature. that the real goal to reach is not decision, but harmony accord. And harmony, in a matter of eternal contraries, may lie at infinity; yet that playful reserve called irony carries it within itself as the sustained note carries the resolution.

Mann, then, is first and foremost an ironist, but this is scarcely a novelty for a writer. Secondly, he is a symbolist, and in one respect his symbolism is not even modern. His cemeteries mean death, his jungles stand for life, his Peeperkorns mean spontaneous vitality, and his Naphtas mean overrefined intellectuality in the conventional way in which Dante's *selva oscura* stands for spiritual darkness, or the flag for the country—not in the *symboliste* manner in which "patience amiable, amiably" signifies Gertrude Stein's idea of Bernard Fay, or "the hyacinth girl" a very personal aspect of Eliot's *Weltschmerz*.

Now Mann could doubtless have accomplished many of his ironic purposes within the bounds of conventional symbolism. Every typical death symbol, for example, could have been given its counterpart in a typical life symbol, every jungle could have

its adjacent cemetery, every Peeperkorn his Naphta. But so
deepseated, so radical is Mann's irony that it will not allow him
an unambiguous feeling even about an individual symbol: in the
jungle, which represents life at its most lush, he sees the breeding place of the plague; the "little O" which Peeperkorn is
forever shaping "with forefinger and thumb . . . the other
fingers standing stiffly erect beside it," is clearly a phallus, but
to Mann it is just as clearly a cipher; the "lying-down position"
of the body is the posture of repose, healing, and love-making,
but it is also the posture of sickness, dying, and the grave; the
bark of the quinine tree is medicinal but poisonous, that of the
deadly upas tree both aphrodisiacal and lethal; the ancient
burial urn is covered with fertility symbols.

It is to this insatiable ironic temper, I believe, that we may
ascribe chief responsibility for the newness of Mann's symbolism.
In the process of trying to achieve the symbolic identifications
which his irony demands, he has created a new technique for
the exploitation of poetic meaning, a technique in which no
symbol is allowed univocal connotation or independent status,
but refers to all the others and is bound rigorously to them
by means of a highly intricate system of subtly developed
associations. Such a system constitutes the structure of each
of his major novels. Its function is always synthetic: one by one
the various antithetical symbols are identified with each other
and finally fused into the single, nuclear, paradoxical meaning
which Mann wishes to emphasize.   There is no escape from
this meaning; at every point the reader's characteristic tendency
to stray off into realms of private association is checked by
the rigid poetic logic of the story, and he is led ineluctably
to the specific response which Mann intends that he shall experience.   This represents, I believe, a singularly successful
solution to what Stevenson thought the most difficult of all
poetic problems: not that of getting the reader to feel, but
of making him feel in precisely the way in which the poet
thinks he ought to feel. Poets who work within the bounds
of rigidly controlled symbolic references sometimes achieve results more like mathematical demonstrations or bank statements
than poems.   Mann, however, consistently manages to produce
effects that are genuinely poetic.   I should like to examine the
short novel, *Death in Venice,* which is perhaps the finest expression of his genius in this respect, in order to discover how
his system of structural symbolic associations operates.

II

Death in Venice is a powerful, strangely haunting, and

tragic story about a middle-aged artist who takes a holiday from his work, and finds himself held in Venice by the charms of a twelve-year-old boy until he goes to seed in a most shocking way, and at last succumbs to the plague which he might otherwise have fled. There is no more of a plot than that. There are other people, however, who wander in and out of the story apparently at random, but who leave their mark both on the artist, Aschenbach, and on the reader: a red-haired, snub-nosed traveler, whose vitality and air of distant climes first suggest to Aschenbach that he himself go off on a trip; a painted and primped old scapegrace from Pola who gets on Aschenbach's Venice-bound steamer with a coterie of young men; a gondolier, of sinister aspect, who rows Aschenbach from Venice to the Lido and vanishes without collecting his money; a mendicant singer who, shortly before Aschenbach's death, goes through his comic turns on the porch of the hotel, smelling all the while of the carbolic acid which has become associated with the plague.

These people seem to serve only as atmosphere, to be quite unrelated both to one another and to the development of the story, but in truth they constitute the very structure of its elaboration. One is reminded of the musical form known as the passacaglia, where a ground bass, repeating the same theme over and over again for progressive variations in the upper register, occasionally emerges into the treble itself, with the effect of affirming emphatically the singleness of the thematic material in both registers.

In *Death in Venice*, the treble is the simple narrative sequence of Aschenbach's voyage, his life on the Lido, his love for the boy Tadzio, and his death. The ground bass is the "life and death" theme repeated as a sort of undertone to the story by those characters who seem to have no very obvious connection with the proper narrative content.

Before attempting to understand how the symbols of the bass are related to those of the treble, it should be remarked that despite the almost mathematical precision with which the intricate associations are accomplished, they are not meant to be understood. To be free from artificiality, from the appearance of tour de force, such a highly complicated formal pattern must gain its effectiveness immediately; that is, not through rational processes. This is a comparatively easy accomplishment for the musician, whose medium does not involve meaning, but it demands rare subtlety from a writer. Mann's deftness is, of course, prodigious, and he contrives to keep his formalized meanings from the explicit attention of the reader largely by the simple technical expedient of hiding them from Aschenbach himself.

For example, Aschenbach never notices—and hence the reader seldom does—that the vital stranger who aroused in him the desire to stop working and to try merely living for a while, is the same man as the sinister gondolier who later ferries him to the Lido and his eventual death, and that the clowning beggar of the hotel porch is none other than the gondolier still further down at the heel. Nor is he ever aware that this ubiquitous person bears a shocking resemblance to the loathsome old fop from Pola. Least of all does it occur to him that all of these questionable people, as morbid caricatures of the heroes of his own novels, are really merely images of himself and his loved-one Tadzio, though it is this final identification which constitutes the meaning and effect of the entire story.

If, as readers, we are not supposed to be consciously aware of these relationships, we may, as critics, proceed to seek them out. The life and death theme is announced at the very beginning of the story: Aschenbach is waiting by the North Cemetery when he sees a wandering stranger. His reveries proper to the funereal setting, sober, necroscopic, are changed by this man's striking vitality into extravagant fancies of the jungle, lush with phallic imagery. Death and life, entering the scene thus hand-in-hand, induce their characteristic emotions, and Aschenbach's heart knocks "with fear and with puzzling desires."

At this point, a retrospect of Aschenbach's life as man and artist breaks the narrative, and we are introduced to the second important symbol. This time, it is not a person of the story, but a *type* of person found in Aschenbach's own stories—a kind of character that proclaims much the same virtues as does the figure of Saint Sebastian in painting, and that represents to Aschenbach's readers a new ideal for spiritual and moral heroism. This figure is really Aschenbach's artistic projection of his own personality. an apotheosis of his own "distinguishing moral trait," and though it is not yet at this place associated with the first symbol, the stranger of the cemetery, it already begins, obviously, to reflect its symbolism on Aschenbach. Equally important, it reintroduces the life-death theme of the ground bass, for this paradoxical "hero-type" combines "a crude and vicious sensuality capable of fanning its rising passions into pure flame" with "a delicate self-mastery by which any inner deterioration, any biological decay was kept concealed from the eyes of the world."

These are the grounds for a gruesome association which

soon follows; the shameless old fraud from Pola—Aschenbach's fellow-traveler to the southland where he has been drawn by his "puzzling desires"—this revolting old man, weazened and rouged, decayed and feeble, but more waggish and gay than any of his young companions, is none other than a loathsome travesty of the Sebastian-like hero-type: in him, the hero's "crude and vicious sensuality" burns no "pure flame" but reeks of perversion; the "delicate self-mastery" which distinguishes Aschenbach's characters and is the controlling principle of his own art, appears here as ugly artifice, and "biological decay" shows doubly horrible through the old man's paint.

But Aschenbach fails to see the image of himself; indeed, even when, towards the end of the story, he himself resorts to cosmetics in his wooing of Tadzio, the kinship does not occur to him. And though he is now "fascinated with loathing" at the old man on the boat, he does not remember his "fear and desire" of the cemetery, or even the vital stranger, whose insolence and habit of grimacing were not unlike the old dandy's. Neither does the reader make this association consciously, but the ground is nonetheless well prepared for the reappearance of the stranger when the ship docks at Venice.

This time the stranger is not framed in the portico of a funeral hall, to be sure, but he *is* riding a gondola: "strange craft . . . with that peculiar blackness which is found elsewhere only in coffins—it suggests silent, criminal adventures in the rippling night, it suggests even more strongly death itself, the bier and the mournful funeral, and the last silent journey." And as Aschenbach transfers from the ship to be rowed by this modern Charon on his own last journey, he observes guilelessly "that the seat of such a barque, this arm-chair of coffin-black veneer and dull black upholstery, is the softest, most luxurious, most lulling seat in the world." This time the "desire" has taken the form of a "poisonous but delectable inertia." But "fear" is there also, deriving from the illicit aspect of the gondolier, whose present dilapidation hides his identity both from us and from Aschenbach and renders his vitality and pugnacious insolence distinctly menacing. The red hair, however, the snub nose, the long, white savage teeth and the frail build are those of the vital stranger; there are even certain frayed remnants of his former costume if we were but to observe them, and his second disappearance is quite as uncanny as his first.

The life-death theme, firmly established by these devices, is now taken up for development by the story proper, the

details of which I need not enter into here. Rumors of the
plague run an increasingly sinister counterpoint to Aschenbach's growing love for Tadzio, his young fellow-guest at a
hotel on the Lido. An ominous odor of death thus conditions
but intensifies the seductiveness of this new life-symbol until
the climax of the story when the stranger, entering for the
third and last time, performs his antics for the hotel audience.

He is a beggar now, and smells of disinfectant. Even his
arrogance has become tainted with obsequiousness. In the re-
pulsively suggestive movements of his mouth, in "his gestures,
the movements of his body, his way of blinking significantly
and letting his tongue play across his lips," our symbol of
organic life reveals himself to be as rotten at the core as the
sleazy old cheat of Pola. The latter, we may remember,
"showed a deplorable insolence . . . winked and tittered, lifted
his wrinkled, ornamented index finger in a stupid attempt at
bantering, while he licked the corners of his mouth with his
tongue in the most abominably suggestive manner." And the
vital stranger's smell is the smell that has become associated
with the constant rumors of death. Aschenbach goes, the next
day, to the tourist office to inquire about these rumors. He
learns that they are true: there is death in Venice, death that
was hatched as pestilence in jungle swamps. And the jungle
had meant *life* to Aschenbach, had lured him away from the
stern and desiccating discipline of his existence to seek "an
element of freshness" for his blood, to live!

That night he has a dream in which he joins a fertility dance
in the heart of the jungle—an orgiastic nightmare, compounded
of fear and desire, which completes the annihilation of his
"substance . . . the culture of his lifetime." "His repugnance"
at the awful carousal, "his fear, were keen—he was honorably
set on defending himself to the very last against the barbarian,
the foe to intellectual poise and dignity. But . . . his heart
fluttered, his head was spinning, he was caught in a frenzy,
in a blinding, deafening lewdness—and he yearned to join the
ranks of the god." When the obscene symbol was raised at
last, he could resist no longer; he abandoned himself to the
hideous debauchery and "his soul tasted the unchastity and
fury of decay."

A short coda-like section completes the development of
the symbol of imposture; then, in a concluding synthesis, the
hero-type symbol is resolved. The symbol of fraud is no longer
the old fop, but Aschenbach himself. Harassed by chronic
apprehensiveness, ravaged by his illicit passion, undone by

the anguish of his dream, Aschenbach begins to show the marks of death. But "like any lover, he wanted to please. . . ."

And when, after a scandalous pursuit of his loved one through the infected alleys of Venice, he sits by the cistern in the deserted square with his mouth hanging open, panting for breath, sticky with sweat, trembling, lugubrious and old, but with blossoming youth painted on his lips and cheeks, dyed into his hair, sketched about his eyes—as he sprawls thus in ghastly caricature of his own spiritual and moral ideal, we not only do not loathe him, but we temper with a new access of sympathy the loathing we originally felt for the old cheat of Pola. For when the magnificent stranger showed his frailty, we felt how it must be with everyone.

The synthesis which brings the story to an end reveals the full meaning of the hero-type symbol, and effects at the same time a final merger of all the other meanings. At the sacrifice of his art, of his ideals, of his very life itself, Aschenbach found Tadzio; now Tadzio, the object of his sacrifice, the goal of his desire, the instrument of his death, reveals that he *is* Aschenbach's art, his own ideal creation, and thus is Aschenbach himself no less than are the stranger and the cheat.

The scene which accomplishes this dénouement was prepared for in Aschenbach's first meeting with Tadzio. After days of worshiping the god-like beauty of the boy at a distance, but of giving no outward sign of his feelings, indeed scarcely admitting them even to himself, Aschenbach chanced to come face-to-face with him so suddenly one evening that "he had no time to entrench himself behind an expression of repose and dignity," but smiled at him in infatuated and undisguised admiration. And the exquisite smile which Tadzio gave back to his smitten admirer was *"the smile of Narcissus* (the italics throughout are mine) bent over the reflecting water, that deep, fascinated, magnetic smile with which he stretches out his arms *to the image of his own beauty* . . . coquettish, inquisitive and slightly tortured . . . infatuated and infatuating." Quite broken up by the episode, Aschenbach sought solitude in the darkness of the park, and as he whispered fervently the "fixed formula of desire . . . 'I love you!' " his voice was for none but his own ears. That the *"night-smell of vegetation"* pointed up the frenzy of his passion in his scene, is typical of the faithfulness and subtlety with which Mann introduces fragments of his bass theme into the details of the treble.

Unknowing, Aschenbach was confronted with the image of his own beauty. What was this image but the Sebastian-like hero-type, his own apotheosis, his spiritual essence—parodied in the old cheat, revealed in its uncompromising duplicity in the stranger, and displayed in its pathos in the painted Aschenbach?

Now, in the final scene, that ideal is at last glorified again by the frail, the exquisite Tadzio. Tadzio is out on a sand-bar in the ocean. His playmates of the beach have brutalized and humiliated him, but he stands haughty and graceful, "separated from the mainland by the expanse of water, separated from his companions by a proud moodiness . . . a strongly isolated and unrelated figure . . . placed out there in the sea, the wind, against the vague mists." Here he is the true Sebastian, the living hero-type—that figure which by a power of "more than simple endurance," by "an act of aggression, a positive triumph . . . (is) poised against fatality . . . (meets) adverse conditions gracefully . . . stands motionless, haughty, ashamed, with jaw set, while swords and spear-points beset the body." He is Aschenbach's ideal incarnated.

And he is outlined against the sea. Once before he was outlined thus—long ago, when for the first time Aschenbach learned the full poignancy of his beauty. Aschenbach then, too, was seated in his beach chair, but he had been watching the sea, pondering its power over him, feeling himself drawn to it "because of that yearning for rest, when the hard-pressed artist hungers to shut out the exacting multiplicities of experience and hide himself on the breast of the simple, the vast; and because of a forbidden hankering—seductive, by virtue of its being directly opposed to his obligations—after the incommunicable, the incommensurate, the eternal, the non-existent. To be at rest in the face of perfection is the hunger of everyone who is aiming at excellence; and what is the non-existent but a form of perfection?" And then, suddenly, "just as his dreams were so far out in vacancy . . . the horizontal fringe of the sea was broken by a human figure; and as he brought his eyes back from the unbounded, and focused them, it was the lovely boy who was there. . . ."

Now, at the last, Tadzio is standing out there again, beyond the shore this time, out in the vast expanse itself. Slowly he turns from the hips, looks over his shoulder with twilight-grey eyes toward the artist seated on the shore, and seems to beckon to Aschenbach to come. Once more arousing himself to the call of his own spiritual form—out from the incommensurate, the incommunicable, the non-existent—the stricken artist stands up to follow, then collapses in his chair.

III

This is an outline, by no means exhaustive, of the symbol structure of *Death in Venice*. The clearest view of Mann's synthetic technique, and of the nature of the change that occurs in an individual symbol during the process of synthesis, is furnished by the episodes which involve the vital stranger, first in the cemetery, second in the gondola, and third on the hotel porch.

To connote the life-death antithesis in the episode of the cemetery, three pairs of symbols are used: the stranger versus the funeral hall, Aschenbach's jungle fancies versus his necroscopic reveries, his desire versus his fear. These fall roughly into the three realms of physical things, of ideas, and of emotions.

In the gondola episode, the same three realms are preserved, each with two symbols: in the world of things the gondola opposes the stranger; ideally, Aschenbach's attention is divided between the gondola's luxurious comfort and the illicit aspect of the stranger; and feelings of fear still mingle with his desire.

Some interesting things follow from this rather dull arithmetic. In the first episode, the symbols were for the most part unambiguous: the stranger meant life and life only; the cemetery, death and death only. Further, they were mutually exclusive in their functions: the stranger supplanted the cemetery as a focus of attention, the jungle images disposed entirely of thoughts of the grave. Finally, the causal progression between Aschenbach's physical impressions and his emotional reactions seemed also to be without ambiguity: the stranger was solely responsible for his jungle fancies and these fancies alone aroused his desire, just as the funeral hall alone inspired his morbid reveries and these, presumably, his fear. But let it be noted that even in this first episode, fear and desire held the emotional stage together! Ambiguity had already begun.

In the gondola episode the situation is very different. Synthetic activity is well under way, and the ambiguity which marked the emotional realm in the first instance extends here to the other two realms. The stranger still seems to be the physical symbol of life and the gondola of death, but in the realm of Aschenbach's ideas the whole thing is confused; the vital stranger looks "illicit" and "perverse" to him, capable, indeed, of those very "criminal adventures in the rippling night" which were originally brought to mind by the death-symbol, the gondola. And the gondola, "coffin-like barque" though it be, is by this time, in Aschenbach's dream fancy, naught but the "most luxurious seat in the world." Thus his desire—that "poisonous but delectable inertia"—issues from the death-symbol, "from the seat of the gondola itself," while his fear is of the vital stranger!

The merging of the life and death symbols, initiated in the emotional realm during the scene in the cemetery, now absorbs the symbols in the realm of Aschenbach's ideas, and, because one is never sure which of his ideas is caused by the gondola and which by its conductor, even the symbols of the physical realm begin to be drawn in.

It remains for the third episode to complete the synthesis. Here the same three realms are preserved: the stranger goes through his physical antics on the hotel porch; Aschenbach indulges in some new reflections about the jungle, and his dream is an orgy of emotion. But in each realm there is now only one symbol, no longer two: the fuzzy boundaries distinguishing life from death have disappeared entirely and these antitheses have become functions of single symbols: decay is seen in the vital stranger himself; the lush jungle is known as the source of the plague; the fertility-dance is felt as a carousal of death. Even the causal chain which, in the other episodes, connected the three realms, is missing here; indeed, the three realms are quite separate in time. The stranger, with no necroscopical setting now but smelling of death itself, makes his final, awful bow, and departs from the story. *The next day,* in no connection with the stranger, Aschenbach learns from someone at the tourist office that the plague was hatched in the jungle and thinks his morbid thoughts. The anguish of fear and desire, which he experiences in his dream many hours later, constitutes still a separate event.

What has happened to the symbols in these transmutations? In the episode of the cemetery, and even in that of the gondola, each symbol in each realm contributed its own small part to the construction of the total life-death meaning. In the last episode, however, the entire connotation is contained in each symbol, and the others are not needed to complete it. The symbols have lost their discursive character and taken on, each for itself, a sort of synoptic one; so their function in the climax is not, as in the other instances, to build up to the meaning in three separate times. The intensifying effect of such synoptic repetition needs no comment.

The same general principles govern the resolution of the fraud and the hero-type symbols, though these, of course, are more inclusive in their synthetic function, embracing Aschen-

bach and Tadzio as well as the stranger. A single, total meaning
is slowly built up out of separate elements—the vital stranger,
Aschenbach, the hero-type, the old cheat, and Tadzio, each contributing his small share. This meaning is summarized first in
the climax by the stranger alone; then it is given again in its
entirety by Aschenbach in the episode of the cosmetics; finally
it is repeated a third time, in still a different way, by Tadzio on
the sand bar.

The most interesting product of the complicated structural
relations which this analysis has brought to light is, to me at
least, the poetic simplicity of mood which distinguishes one's
response to *Death in Venice*. The type of control which makes
it possible has been rejected by most contemporary poets, probably under the influence of the tradition of *symbolisme*. Two
points are usually raised against it: first, that the rational or
logical element in it tends to falsify poetry's true object—indeterminate, fluctuating, concrete reality as presented to immediate experience; and, secondly, that it leaves no room for
that exquisite quality of response which, under the name *sens
du mystère*, is often identified with what Poe referred to as
the "vague and therefore spiritual effect" of "suggestive indefi-
niteness." How Mann provides for what Poe was talking about
we have already remarked. His control operates entirely below
the reader's conscious attention; meanings are never forced,
they are intimated and suggested rather than stated, and the
reader is allowed the illusion, at least, of a good deal of imaginative freedom.

But the feeling of mystery which characterizes authentic
poetic response is not, I believe, merely this feeling of freedom
of reference. The problem is less simple; it is probably not a
technical one at all. Poor poets fail to conjure up mystery even
with methodical mystification, yet it often flourishes in classical
poetry in the full light of logical reference from symbol to
meaning. I suspect that *mystère* is to be sought rather in the
aspect of experience comprehended in a poem than in the form
of its elaboration. At this level there is essential, not artificial,
mystery, deriving, perhaps, from the nature of experience itself. Both the nuance of private feeling, the "immediate experience" of the *symbolistes*, and Mann's "infinity" where, "in
a matter of eternal contraries," harmony lies—both of these are,
in the last analysis, quite un-understandable, and hence, un-
susceptible of totally adequate communication. At the level
of *mystère*, the mediated experience is no less valid a poetic
object than the immediate one.

These, however, are properly questions for æsthetics rather than for literary criticism. Here I have been concerned less with the latent content of poetry, with its mystery, than with that other quality which is often forgotten today but which Mann has so richly remembered—the quality of lucidness, of intelligibility, by whose virtue the incommunicable *seems*, at least, to be communicated.

[1938]

THE MAGIC MOUNTAIN

Joseph Warren Beach

The use of the novel as a vehicle for ideas is a dubious undertaking and beset with difficulties. But there are instances to show that, where these difficulties are overcome, the novel may take its place alongside tragedy as a literary form of deepest human significance. One thinks of *War and Peace*, of *The Brothers Karamazov*, and of several of Zola's *Rougon-Macquart* series. In our own time, I am inclined to name *The Magic Mountain* as the most indubitable instance of what genius can do in assimilating philosophy to the purposes of fiction. To this book I came with every favorable prepossesion. Works like *Buddenbrooks, Death in Venice, Tristan* had made me think that he was perhaps that one of living novelists who most perfectly suited my personal taste in quality and method. Above all, *Buddenbrooks*, with its epic sweep in the representation of life through several generations, its authoritative treatment of family life among the wealthy "bourgeoisie," so parallel to the work of Mr. Galsworthy, but having to my seeming so much more depth and mass resonance.

It was of Thomas Mann I thought when I wished to represent to myself what it was that seemed to me lacking in contemporary American fiction, and for which I can find no word but that one of strictly European connotations, "soul" (*âme, Seele*). I do not refer to that entity which it is the function of religion to save immortally, and I am far from meaning sentimentality. Thomas Mann is not a writer who specializes in sentimental characters, and still less does he interpret them in a sentimental way. What I have in mind may perhaps be denominated simply quality in personal experience, the sense on the part of the author of value in personality itself. It is this which gives what I have called resonance, which gives depth and a kind of bloom to the work of Continental writers such as do not often characterize present-day novelists in England, and still less in America.

This quality I find in almost any French writer of distinction, whatever his rank, in the scale of "greatness." I find it in Colette, in Mauriac, in André Gide. I find it in Russian writers of the Soviet age, in Gladkov, author of *Cement*. In Italy I find it in highest degree in Pirandello (for example in *Il fu Mattia Pascal* and *Si Gira*). Almost invariably I find it in Scandinavian writers, in Hamsun, in Lagerlöf, in Sigrid Undset.

I do not find it in Aldous Huxley or in Sinclair Lewis. And in writers like Maurice Baring, Charles Morgan, and Hugh Walpole what I find is a sentimental substitute for it. The American writers who interest me most are sometimes those who have the least suggestion of it. They are clever and smart and inventive no end, sophisticated as the devil, but they do not seem to invest the human personality with that sense of value in and for itself which comes so natural to any European writer. Of course there are exceptions. There is Sherwood Anderson in *Winesburg, Ohio* and *Poor White*.

I do not know how to account for this lack in our contemporary fiction of a quality which was formerly there in plenty (witness Hawthorne, Melville, Howells, James), unless that somehow, for the moment, we are younger and cruder than we were; or else that we have been strongly infected with English utilitarianism. However that may be, Thomas Mann is the author who most stands in my mind for the possession of this quality. Tragic and cruel as his picture of life may be, there is always in his treatment of character a sensitiveness, a *feeling* quality, as of one who realizes that he has to do with living creatures. And what could be a better equipment for the art of making characters *live*?

In *Buddenbrooks* that is all he undertakes to do. There is no philosophy to be found there, at least on the surface. The book may imply some theory of cyclical rise and fall in the social organism. At any rate, there is no overt philosophical speculation. But *The Magic Mountain* is as full of philosophy as it can hold. There is page on page of exposition of scientific matters—physiology, embryology. There are hundreds of pages of overt discussion of matters political, religious, social. And there is, not quite so much on the surface, a subtle and elusive theme involving a philosophy of personal conduct.

The central theme of the book, if I rightly understand it, is that sickly disposition to turn one's back on reality and retreat into some ivory tower of speculation, or, otherwise phrased, that will to death, which the author must have found to be a dominant feature of pre-war mentality.

The leading character is a certain Hans Castorp, a young

engineer from Hamburg. Before starting out on his professional career, he will make a three weeks' visit with a cousin who is taking a temporary cure at a famous hospital for consumptives at Davos Platz. So great is the power of suggestion, that Hans Castorp has not even stayed out his three weeks before he comes down with a bad cold, and before long he has been found to have certain rough spots (*feuchte Stellen*) in his lungs. He is condemned to a several months' stay at the sanatorium.

The thing drags along, and the months extend themselves to years. He gets the habit of this invalid life; he loses touch with the world below; he gets absorbed in the endless business of "balancing his accounts" intellectually and spiritually; and it comes to pass that he loses track entirely of that time by which ordinary mortals measure their experiences. As a matter of fact, he has been there seven years at the outbreak of the World War. This event it is that wakens him from his long sleep. He is one of the seven sleepers in the Magic Mountain roused at last by the thunder-stroke.

And what was he doing all those years in the Magic Mountain? He was taking the rest-cure on his airy balcony, comfortably installed in a reclining-chair and wrapped up in excellent blankets which he had learned to wind about himself with expert skill. He was eating five hearty meals a day at the well-provided table, and recording his temperature seven times a day. He was nursing his love for a married lady with Asiatic eyes and cheek bones, with ill-kept finger nails and a beautiful skin, who had the habit of slamming the glass door every time she came into the dining-room.

But above all, he was "balancing his accounts." In this he was helped by several interesting men—three men of striking personalities and decided opinions, who alternately swayed his mind.

The first of these is Lodovico Settembrini, an Italian suffering from tuberculosis, a Freemason, a humanist, the descendant of patriots and rebels, a believer in the Reason of the eighteenth-century Enlightenment, member of an "International League for Organizing Progress." Another is Herr Naphta He is by origin a Jew, a Catholic and Jesuit by conversion and education. He believes in the dictatorship of the proletariat as the best means in our time for bringing about the salvation of men's souls. He has a great theoretical contempt for the body, and is inclined to defend the methods of torture of the Inquisition as a means of purifying the spirit. He too is suffering from tuberculosis.

Herr Naphta is a subtle and persuasive reasoner, and, like Herr Settembrini, is fond of arguing and making converts. And they often engage in passionate and interminable debates. Thomas Mann refrains conscientiously from intervening in these combats, and the reader is left to infer for himself how far he agrees with this or that one of the disputants. But in one matter he seems to weight the balance in favor of the Italian humanist. Herr Settembrini is very much opposed to what he considers Naphta's cult of suffering and death. He is for life and action; and if he were consulted, Castorp would long ago have given up his idle, self-indulgent ways. He seems to think Castorp's illness is self-induced, and that he would do much better to return to the lower world.

Neither Settembrini nor Naphta, however, quite has the secret of the riddle. In both of them there is lacking something essential to a true philosophy of life. And this, I take it, is what the author undertook to supply in the person of Mynheer Peeperkorn. He is a Dutchman from Java, who has come to Davos badly attainted with tuberculosis and alcoholism. He is an elderly man of great stature, with face deeply and nobly lined and a beard to match. Everyone instinctively feels him to be a great, a royal personality. And that in spite of his want of practical prudence, and the almost complete incoherence of his speech. In the end he commits suicide, in order to make way for Castorp with the woman he loves. Thus he puts an end to that Life of which he has been the prophet and devotee, and gives a demonstration, perhaps of cowardice and morbidity, perhaps of the Love which he is evidently meant to symbolize.

The above outline will serve to show what an enormous freight of abstract thought is carried by this novel. But the beautiful thing is the high degree to which the thought is objectified in the story. Not story in the sense of incident and intrigue, for there is very little of these, infinitely less than in Dostoyevsky, less even than in Zola's *Lourdes* or *Vérité*. The principal action of the story is simply the battle over the soul of Hans Castorp. But this is sufficient, and the reason why it is sufficient is that Thomas Mann has such a prodigious, such an exhaustless faculty for giving life to the creatures of his imagination. He is simply incapable of inventing a character who shall be the mere mouthpiece of an idea—as we may say of Marie de Guersaint and the Abbé Pierre. There is not a single one of the major or minor characters of *The Magic Mountain* who has not his own unmistakable and unforgettable personality.

To begin with, he has imagined them to the least detail in their looks and dress, their several habitats, as we may say, their idiosyncrasies of speech. There is the crisp and alarming manner of Fräulein von Mylendonk, the ugly head nurse, with the enormous sty, who is called in to see Hans Castorp because he has "caught cold." Catching cold is something not in favor at this sanatorium. Nothing short of a rough spot in the lungs is worth the attention either of patient or doctor, and they all look with the same air of mingled suspicion, indignation, and superiority on any one who announces he has a cold—that air of suggesting that he must be out of his mind if he thinks there can be such a thing as a mere cold in a tuberculosis sanatorium. So when Fräulein von Mylendonk comes to see Hans Castorp, and he says he has a cold, she soon puts him in his place by her way of asking, "What sort of a cold is that?" In ten minutes this medical dragoness has reduced the young man to a proper state of submissiveness and alarmed concern, has inoculated him with the notion of fever and noxious infection, has sold him an expensive thermometer and convinced him of the importance of taking his temperature at frequent and regular intervals.

The clinical side of sanatorium life is handled, my professional friends assure me, with competence and thoroughness. What a layman can answer for is the visibility, as I may call it, the complete realizing for the imagination of the details of the history. There are certain features of person and object which are notable instances of the writer's power of giving human significance to physical detail. Much has been made by critics of Charles Bovary's hat so meticulously described by Flaubert as rendering objectively the character of the schoolboy. Quite in a class with this are the descriptions of Frau Chauchat as seen by Hans Castorp during Dr. Krokowski's Freudian lecture. As it chanced, he sat directly behind her. She "sat slouching and hunched up; her back was round, she let her shoulders slump forward; and more than that, her head was shoved forward, so that her vertebrae stuck out above the neck of her white blouse." As the lecture goes on Castorp is greatly distracted by the close-up view of her hand and arm as she fusses with her back hair. These members he finds himself studying as if under a magnifying glass. He reflects with alarm on the well-nigh miraculous arrangements of nature for making women seductive—"for the sake of posterity, for the perpetuation of the species"—and of the wrongness of such displays where a woman is inwardly diseased. The earnest young man! "What was the sense of her wearing gauze sleeves and attracting male attention to her physical parts if these were actually unsound? Obviously that made *no* sense; it ought to be considered indecent, and forbidden as such."

The most minute material documentation is consistent in Mann with our confident assurance that we are never stopping on the surface of things. In this respect I find him superior to Zola— not to speak of Zola's American counterpart, Mr. Dreiser —and that without yielding to any one in my admiration for performances like *L'Assommoir*. I am speaking now of that art by which infallibly the objective detail is made to render the individual quality of scene or character, and translates itself directly into what we may call spiritual values. It is in this art that Thomas Mann is such an unusual figure.

He is a writer, for one thing, who takes his time. The passage I have just cited is an example of his use of the "close-up." The classic French naturalist would consider that too much was made of Frau Chauchat's hand and arm, that they should have been left to speak for themselves in their own hard, sharp, objective manner. But, then, it would scarcely occur to a French naturalist to handle a subject so simple, shy, and elusive as the mind of Hans Castorp. The hand and arm of Frau Chauchat—typical of everything at variance with his German and Occidental notions of a civilized and orderly life, and yet so strangely fascinating to him—these physical details are part and parcel of Castorp's moral problem and the "balancing of accounts" in which he is occupied at Davos Platz. And the tempo in their description is made to correspond to that of his spiritual process.

Mann is one of those rare writers who can afford to take his time and to make much of apparently small details. That is because he is so substantial, and in two directions—in that of objective detail and in that of subjective discrimination. He is so much of a scientist, and he is so much of a philosopher. He is a profound and humane writer because he reveals beneath every external appearance that animating essence which makes of each human being something so much more than a differentiated mass of protoplasm. It is almost as if he did this in spite of himself. His characters are representative types—they all stand for something in his philosophical scheme. But he cannot leave them there. Once he sets them on their feet as persons, they begin to act like persons, and he could not stop them if he would.

All this means creative imagination in a high degree. And it means something more, and something perhaps even rarer.

What it comes down to in the last analysis is the extraordinary humaneness of the man. This writer has wisdom and ripeness of understanding far beyond those of the average successful novelist. And that brings me to his personal style, which is the intimate language of his wisdom.

Perhaps the outstanding feature of his style is its simplicity. He has none of the smartness that characterizes so much of the most interesting contemporary fiction in the English language. He seems to have more faith in his subject, more confidence in his power to get his effect without facetiousness or straining at cleverness. He takes his characters seriously. It is true that he sees all round them. But he also sees deeply enough into them to know they are more than Babbitts, more than musical motifs in a philosophical counterpoint.

He has that supersophistication which brings the wisest men back to the conception of value. Thomas Mann is perhaps in our day the novelist most conscious of those spiritual essences which our mathematicians and physicists are laboring to bring back to a mechanical and materialistic world. He knows as well as any one what frail wisps and motes we are on the shoreless tides of destiny. But he thinks no less of us for that. He is "humanist" enough to realize that values are ideal entities, and that the human mind is all there is to furnish a gauge of human values.

Hans Castorp he means for a type of the ordinary serious, bewildered intellectual dilettante of the pre-war period. A German of course. The German author is fully conscious of the Teutonic mentality of his hero, and goes to some lengths to bring his German quality into relief. None but a German could have been so grave and thorough in his researches, so easily impressed with learning, and so inveterately metaphysical. There is nothing extraordinary about him except his seriousness and tenacity. He means infinitely well and goes far astray. He loses touch with reality and with humanity. But his heart is sound, and the author brings him back in the end to those contacts through which he may be fulfilled. He is a most amusing character, and more likable than he is amusing. It is with a mild, enveloping, insinuating, and ever discreet humor that the author unfolds his somewhat pathetic story.

If there is one thing more beautifully "done" than another in the book, it is those earlier chapters in which he shows him falling into the trap of invalidism and the sanatorium mentality; growing hourly more nervous under the polite insinuations of the doctors and nurses; alarmed by the nosebleed that comes upon him in his mountain walk; taking the rest-cure on his balcony and falling under the spell of reclining-chairs and peaceful hours, wrapped up in woolen blankets. The first serious intimation that all was not going well with him was the loss of his power of enjoying tobacco.

Nothing could be more delicious than Hans Castorp's eloquent connoisseurship on the subject of cigars and his bewildered reflections over the fact that he can no longer take a real pleasure in his favorite Maria Mancini. It is one of those material details that in the hands of a master serve to render the very idiosyncrasy of a man. And it brings us back to the moral of our discussion, which is this: what an enormous amount of discursive philosophy can be conveyed in the form of fiction if the writer has the genius of Thomas Mann for "dramatizing" it, for rendering it in the proper terms of story.

[1932]

THE MAGIC MOUNTAIN

Lewis Mumford

The actual force of barbarism can easily be over-rated: any positive minority of equal energy, even one as weak as Christianity in the second century A. D., would possibly have enough élan to take over Western society. For we are living through a time of decay. The oldest and most obvious form of decay is that of Christianity, with its millions who go numbly through the motions of a faith that every waking hour of their day contradicts. Even the Sabbath is no longer a day of spiritual change: no longer a day dedicated to inner communion and contemplation.

With all the talk of reunion between the Churches and sects, which has occupied the leaders of Christianity during the last half century, there are few real signs of the deeper spiritual effort required for Christianity's renewal—its admission of the local and relative nature of its original mission and its willingness to merge, for the sake of the universal values all men should share, with the faiths of other races and peoples which Western man too long spurned. An unchristian pride, disguising itself as a unique revelation of a truth not granted to other peoples, still blocks that essential sacrifice. A Hindu sage, like Ramakrishna, could understand Christianity by espousing it, disciplining himself to it, thinking and willing himself into its very marrow: but the Christian Churches sought to conquer the rest of the world on easier terms, with the aid of Andrew Undershaft's devices, money and gunpowder. The fruits of Christianity's decay have ripened to rottenness in our own generation: the Quaker pacifism that would not resist fascism, the Buchmanism that flattered fascism, the Roman Catholicism whose hierarchy, with a few noble and memorable exceptions, openly co-operated with fascism.

The decay of secular ideals has been equally conspicuous; but until the present generation they were not so visible, not so distressing: those who were aware of them, like Thoreau and Melville and Tolstoy and Ruskin in the nineteenth century, like Albert Schweitzer or Reinhold Niebuhr in our own time, were looked upon as spoil sports and eccentrics—though in fact it was society itself that was eccentric.

Moreover, as long as the machine itself was still in a formative state, its limitations were less significant than its emancipations; and man's pride in his new discoveries in physics and chemistry, in biology and physiology, was a wholly legitimate one: positive knowledge replaced mere opinion, as rational opinion had once replaced authority. In a whole and integrated community, none of these advances would have been inimical to the personality: on the contrary, they would have nourished man, as under the favorable conditions that prevailed from 1830 to 1860 in New England, they nourished the mind and personality of Ralph Waldo Emerson: his journals are proof of that.

In our time, the forces that counter cultural decay have been weakened: weakened by death and desertion, by psychological depression and economic depression. What positive values does a disintegrated society possess for those who have lost their inner go, who are no longer a dynamic part of a visible or imaginable whole? Outside the values of raw barbarism, the only values that remain are those derived from decay itself: the black opalescent film on putrid flesh which obsesses the imagination of a Hemingway. Here again art is prophetic: some of our best modern works of art are those in which the dissolution of our world is pictured with masterly fidelity: Proust's *Remembrance of Things Past*, Joyce's *Ulysses*, Eliot's *Wasteland*. Were these not the most eloquent witnesses of the generation whose disillusion and dissolution touched bottom at the end of the First World War, and sank deeper into the mud for the next two decades? Each of these works stands high as literature: each is proof that some of the best energies of this society were the energies of decomposition.

After 1918 those with a gift for action became gangsters, fascist hoodlums, organizing terrorism and corruption on an ever-widening scale: now drawing tribute (in America) from chicken-hearted citizens, themselves willing to break the laws themselves had made, or again seizing possession of whole states, as in Italy, Germany, Spain, Hungary, Poland, in order to work out larger schemes of blackmail and plunder. Those who had no taste for action could only carry the processes of decay further by a passive acquiescence and an inner corruption, seeking nourishment from the spiritual products of decomposition. The incoherent language of Dada and the irrational forms of surrealism made their entry at the same moment: further symptoms of an emptiness and a debasement that was not uncoupled with technical ingenuity, even esthetic mastership. These artists had a twofold audience: the connoisseurs of illness and the connoisseurs of violence; and a positive antipathy to beauty, wholeness, or health was a qualication for discipleship.

Under the circumstances, it would seem futile to look for evidences of integration; but out of the surviving energies of this society more than one such work of art appeared. Perhaps the most satisfactory esthetic symbol of this period was Thomas Mann's *The Magic Mountain.*

The Magic Mountain portrays an ailing world: symbolized in a tuberculosis sanatorium, the Berghof, situated on a high mountain in Switzerland. Everyone who inhabits this world is ill or deeply involved in illness, from Hofrat Behrens, the chief physician, to life's delicate child, Hans Castorp, who is the hero of this romance of hypochondria, this Odyssey of disease. Yet the illness of the inmates is an essential part of their life: the source of their drama and the plot of their days. A plentiful supply of food, continuous medical attention, the luxuries of perfect service and studious care, endless sports, diversions, amusements, not a care in the world except the disease itself make this house of disease that very paradise of the heart toward which the New World had concentrated its energies. Is it not to universalize the "happiness" or at least the euphoria of the Berghof that the modern world has come into existence—that self-consuming happiness which has, as the only corrective to the pleasure principle, the perfect routine of science, the lofty zeal of medicine and surgery, with the X-ray, the radiograph, the surgical resection of the ribs, the deflation of the diseased lung, a thousand little ingenuities for arresting or diverting the forces of disintegration?

As in Melville's *Moby-Dick* all the races of the world compose the crew that has gathered to pursue the White Whale, so in *The Magic Mountain,* all the nationalities of Europe, even Mynheer Peeperkorn from the East Indies, and all classes of society, the penniless intellectual, the vulgar bourgeois widow, the business man, the soldier, have a place in this sick institution. No matter how healthy they may seem when they arrive, they belong there, and despite their efforts do not easily escape the Rhadamanthus who presides over its destinies. Only the members of the working class seem to escape the luxury of the disease, though they are present as waitresses and porters.

Mann's characters are ill, and they form part of an ailing world, a world he had depicted in his numerous stories of a decadent Germany, from *Buddenbrooks* to *Tristan* and *Death in*

Venice. It is not the vulgar strength of modern man, but his tendency toward perversity, self-defeat, and suicide that Mann shows best in these imaginative works. All these elements come together in *The Magic Mountain.* Perhaps consciously, perhaps by a more hidden process, Mann causes every personality to caricature and betray his function in society: not one of these people is genuinely what he professes to be. Hofrat Behrens, the purveyor of health, is himself a hypochondriac, perhaps tubercular: worse than that, his very sanatorium, famous for its pure mountain air, is surrounded for a good part of the year by clouds and fogs that are never acknowledged to be such: atmospheric conditions which the people of the flatlands fancy they have escaped. Even worse, one suspects that some of the patients, beginning with the hero, acquire the disease in the very act of taking precautions against it: in them is a will-to-illness, first stage of the will-to-dissolution. Hans Castorp, the engineer, dreamy and reflective, is fit for anything but engineering: his cousin Joachim Ziemssen, the soldier, dies before he establishes himself in his profession: Peeperkorn, the incarnation of inarticulate vitality, commits suicide: Naphta, the jesuitical advocate of violence, cannot even fire a gun to kill his enemy, Settembrini: instead he shoots himself.

All this elaborate care of the diseased has produced a counterfeit life; but out of the situations Castorp encounters he discovers truths he would never have had time to reflect upon had he remained healthy enough to take his place among "normal" people in the shipyards of Hamburg. Two men wrestle for Castorp's soul, the Italian humanist, Settembrini, a liberal but a windbag, the disciple of reason, convinced that even madmen can be brought to their senses by merely commanding them to become rational, and the Jewish convert to Catholicism, Naphta, who speaks for all the dark forces, for superstition, terrorism, violence, and death—who in fact rejects the too bland heaven of republican humanism for the "annointed Terror of which the time has need," thus linking a totalitarian state to an authoritarian church.

The true climax of the book occurs in the chapter called "Snow." Lost in a snowstorm, after he has wandered far out of bounds on skis, prey to hallucination and dream, utterly alone, close to death, Castorp rejects the teaching of both men: he has a vision of both a dark underground cruelty close to life's roots and a redeeming light that transfigures the mind and the world. But Castorp is still ill: his new vision of life quickly fades from him and his actions are unaffected: at the end of seven

years he is drawn away from the sanatorium, not by any inner
growth of character, not by any will of his own, but by the call
to war. He has grown, he has veritably matured: yet he remains
unconnected with life, except through war and death. The disease that afflicts this ailing world has realized itself at the expense
of life, which has become, not reality, but the form of illusion.

The moral of this novel does not have to be underscored: it
is present on every page and is amplified by the scene that greets
the eye when one looks away from the pages of the book. Disease
has counterfeited life: disease has reorganized science, technics,
art, love for its own purposes; and death has now become the
main goal of our living, lovingly circumvented, profitably elaborated, but no less inexorably perverting every hour of life.
War alone can bring awakening: can renew the sense of self-
direction and responsibility that a healthy personality always
carries with it.

Here, then, is the modern world, with its over-charges of
empty stimuli, its perpetual miscarriage of technique, its materialistic repletion, its costly ritual of conspicuous waste, its highly organized purposelessness: here is a veritable clinical picture
of the cultural disease from which that world suffers. The X-ray
photograph, the bacteriological analysis of the sputum, the aus-
cultation, the temperature chart, all add up to a prognosis of the
final result, death. The patient is in the midst of a mortal illness,
and his feverish efforts to remain alive are themselves a disguised mechanism of the death wish. Syphilis, tuberculosis, can-
cer, hypertension—they come to the same end. The power of
choice has gone: paralysis seizes every limb. When the President
of the most powerful industrial nation on the earth boasts that
no act of choice, such as Woodrow Wilson had been brave enough
to make, brought his people into the war against fascism, few
challenge that avowal or question its morality. Invalids do not
choose.

Now we see the perfection of Thomas Mann's central symbol: the sanatorium. In terms of current ideals, what life could
be more perfect than that of the sanatorium? What life more
secure, more carefree, more capable of realizing to the full all
the modern world can offer, not least by way of medical and
psychological knowledge—even psychoanalysis, that last refinement in medical care? If life is a matter of multiplying pleasures
and skillfully fending off death, what better use can be made of
it than these sick people make? The essential sickness of the
modern world, with its defective understanding of the personality
and its needs, is that its ideal existence is really an invalid's

existence, even as the repetitive motions that it inflicts upon its busy, hard-driven workers transform into a collective ritual the elements of a compulsion neurosis: the mechanical repetition of a limited set of motions. With illness and hypochondria and neurosis as the *norms* of civilization, is it any wonder that life itself reappeared in savage, pre-civilized guise as the will to violate, the will to kill, the will to destroy?

Once the death wish has become so prevalent one conclusion is inevitable: the present condition of man admits no easy relief. No minor remedies, no small, timid measures of reform, will bring life and health back to such a society: only the most dire catastrophe can now summon up the energies necessary for the reassertion of life and the values of life. Anesthetics may temporarily blot out the terrors of this state: chloral and whiskey, sexual dilation and speed, may ease the tensions; but in the end they add to the enfeeblement. Barbarism and war: these were the re-awakeners. And the catastrophe came. For that reason, perhaps, we may sardonically hail Hitler as the friend and redeemer of modern man.

[1944]

THE MAGIC MOUNTAIN

Hermann J. Weigand

The Magic Mountain presents itself as a pedagogical novel. It is repeatedly styled so in its own pages. We may as well be warned from the outset, however, that there is the same flavor of ironic modesty about this designation as there is about Thomas Mann's frequent reference to his hero as a simple young man, a youth without guile. The literary *genre* of the pedagogical novel, as known to histories of literature, is always concerned with a very specific sort of education,— an education that sets out to mould the plastic personality of a child along lines determined by its educators; and the process of education is pronounced complete when the youthful personality has come to conform dependably to the moral pattern that represents the educator's ideal. In *The Magic Mountain*, true enough, we have two educators, educating at cross purposes to each other, each coveting the mastery over Hans Castorp, like God and the Devil in the medieval mysteries fighting for the possession of the human soul; the pedagogical point of the novel, however, consists in the fact that the hero steers his course between the two, without committing himself to the orthodoxy of either. While deriving enormous stimulation from their exhortations, warnings, and disputes, he dodges all direct attempts to force him into the role of a disciple. Hans Castorp develops, not according to the lines of a pattern imposed from without, but according to an inner law of his own personality that becomes manifest by degrees. We are in reality dealing, then, with a novel of self-development rather than with a pedagogical novel, except in the wider sense in which Hans Castorp himself formulates the principle of his "pedagogy," when he says to Clavdia in one of those rare moments of ultra-clear consciousness:

> You, of course, do not know that there is such a thing as alchemistic-hermetic pedagogy, transsubtantiation, from lower to higher, ascending degrees, if you understand what I mean. But of course matter that is capable of taking those ascending stages by dint of outward pressure must have a little something in itself to start with."

Hans Castorp has it *in sich*—to an extraordinary degree, in fact. And this established, *The Magic Mountain* reveals its affiliation with that aristocratic and exclusive group among the novels of self-development which constitutes Germany's most distinctive contribution to the world's fiction. I am referring, of course, to the *Bildungsroman*. Goethe's *Wilhelm Meister*, Keller's *Grüner Heinrich*, Stifter's *Nachsommer*, Thomas Mann's *The Magic Mountain*—these most outstanding representatives of the type all focus upon a quest of *Bildung* that transcends any specific practical aims. *Bildung*—a term quite inadequately renderable by "culture"—we might define as the approach to a totality of integrated human experience, provided we stress the integration. This result is always but a by-product of the hero's conscious activities. He may see as his goal a brilliant career on the stage like Wilhelm Meister, only to discover, years later, that he lacked the fundamental qualifications for success; he may be buffeted about like Keller's artist-apprentice Heinrich, and return home, after years of struggle and hardship, a complete failure, as measured by all specific worldly standards; or again, like another Heinrich, the hero of Stifter's I-novel, he may be spared all violent shock and noisy commotion in the tranquil if eager scientific exploration of his physical environment in all its aspects; he may finally, like Hans Castorp, sacrifice all prospects of a practical career to the pursuit of a quixotic passion. In each case the by-product of these strivings, struggles, pursuits, and passions is something infinitely richer than the specific result coveted, altogether regardless of success or failure, and each author could dismiss his hero with the valedictory that stands at the end of *Wilhelm Meister's Apprenticeship*: "You appear to me like Saul, the son of Kish, who went out to seek his father's she-asses, and found a kingdom." The keynote of the true *Bildungsroman* is, thus, an affirmative attitude toward life as a whole.

If the by-product of Wilhelm Meister's adventurings can be formulated as *Lebenskunst*, if the upshot of the disappointments of Keller's hero is spiritual freedom, if the studious pursuits of Stifter's Heinrich blend into polyphonic harmony,—what is the incidental yield of Hans Castorp's hermetic existence? It is the development of genius! Genius, present in the germ as an element of his native endowment, is awakened and nurtured by a series of highly abnormal factors. Thomas Mann's irony scores its most surprising point, perhaps, in the transformation of this simple young man into a genius in the realm of experience. Perhaps it takes a long time for it to dawn upon the reader that this is what has been happening—it certainly takes Hans Castorp long enough to find out, but no false modesty keeps him from acknowledging the fact, once discovered. We remember his telling Clavdia about the alchemistic-hermetic pedagogy, as involving transsubstantiation, *Steigerung*, and his emphasizing that for this pedagogy to take effect, the subject exposed to its workings "must have a little something in itself to start with." And he continues:

> And what I had in me, as I quite clearly know, was that from long ago. even as a lad, I was familiar with illness and death . . . for death, you know, is the principle of genius. . . . There are two paths to life: one is the regular one, direct, honest. The other is bad, it leads through death—that is the way of genius.

There is no ambiguity about this self-appraisal, nor can there be any doubt but that it coincides with Thomas Mann's own version, as we shall see when we come to analyze the factors involved in the awakening of Hans Castorp's genius.

It accords with the character of *The Magic Mountain* as a *Bildungsroman* that the hero is repeatedly styled "ein Bildungsreisender" (a cultural traveller). In a spirit of irony, of course; —this designation being patterned to suggest the familiar commercial traveller—and this irony is in line with the traditions of the German *Bildungsroman* and derives its sanction from the prototype of the class, from *Wilhelm Meister* itself. The host of Goethe's contemporaries who bent their efforts to producing variations of the Wilhelm Meister theme were equally keen in exploiting its comic possibilities. Thus Tieck, himself the author of a variation of the Meister theme, introduces, in the prologue of his *Kaiser Oktavianus*, a *Bildungsreisender* whose plodful musings on what is in store for him include the following pedestrian lines:

> Good fortune will smile on me now and then,
> Occasionally I may come in for a drubbing
> For the most part Tomorrow follows Today.
> Every day has something or other in store,
> And you get nothing for nothing on earth.
> For that reason I'll make light of hardships
> If only I acquire a little 'Bildung.'

And one thinks, of course, of the frank travesty of the ideal of *Bildung* in Heine's *Bader von Lucca,* where we make the acquaintance of the self-styled Marchese Christophoro di Gumpelino and his valet Hirsch Hyazinth, the little shrimp of a lottery

agent who accompanies his master on his ludicrous tour of
Italian galleries and cathedrals solely "der Bildung wegen."
Thomas Mann's irony, it goes without saying, is of a different
sort.

Viewed from another angle, *The Magic Mountain* belongs in
the class of novels of unilinear development, as opposed to the
novel of multiple strands of action. Most of Wassermann's novels,
for example, represent the latter type. Thus his *Gänsemännchen*,
and his *Christian Wahnschaffe* even more so, trace the lives of a
veritable host of characters that have their own experiences and
their own fates. It is only at salient points of the action that they
become linked with the development of the central hero; and
after they have effected their contribution to his experience, it
is just as likely as not that they again become detached from the
line of the hero's life and continue to move in orbits of their own,
where the reader glimpses them from time to time before they
lose themselves on the periphery. This type of novel, if the loose-
ness of its unity is to be something other than a bewildering
jumble, has very definite problems of organization to cope with,
and Wassermann's way of handling these problems makes one of
the most fascinating elements of his technique. The closest conceivable unity, on the other hand, is represented by the type of
the I-novel, where the content of the narrative is filtered through
the medium of the narrator's personality in its entirety. *The
Magic Mountain* steers a middle course between these two types.
Although we are introduced to approximately one hundred men
and women in its pages, Hans Castorp dominates the action from
start to finish; his personality makes itself felt in every scene.
We never for a moment lose sight of the fact that it is Hans Castorp's experience which the author is transmitting to us; not a
single incident is developed which does not affect him directly,
and not one is included but for the reason of its effect upon him.
The principle of unity is, then, the unity of the hero's experiences. But there is a second angle to the case. While the author
identifies himself with his hero in the most far-reaching way, he
is at the same time distinctly present in the novel over and above
the hero. The author is Hans Castorp plus ever-present resources
of insight and conscious interpretation that transcend the normal
level of Hans Castorp's experience. Only in those rare moments
of *Steigerung* when it is given to Hans Castorp to turn an X-ray
beam of intuition upon himself, is the merging of the two personalities absolutely complete.

This dual author's role involves recognition of the fact that
The Magic Mountain is a psychological novel. The author fre-

quently comments on his hero's behavior and subjects it to searching analysis. And the behavior of this apparently simple young man is a most intricate business, for it harbors ever so many elements that have to put on the shrewdest of disguises in order to slip by the alert "censor" that guards the threshold of consciousness. We encounter in Hans Castorp all that complex functioning of the subconscious forces of the self on which the genius of Freud has trained the searchlight of psychological study. We sense the omnipresence of the libido as the psychic fluidum, impregnating Hans Castorp's behavior, coloring his every gesture, act, and utterance. But it would be an unfair distortion of the antecedents of Thomas Mann's psychology to stop at the name of Freud. His ready assimilation of Freud's discoveries is largely due to the fact that Nietzsche's pioneer work in tracing the genealogy of morals had been one of the great formative influences of his youth. Nor can we afford to forget how largely Ibsen and Hebbel and Kleist intuitively anticipated the principles of modern psychoanalysis.

All the foregoing attempts to classify *The Magic Mountain* have turned on the hero-author relationship. But this relationship, enormously important though it is, is far from exhausting the significance of *The Magic Mountain*. The reader who has allowed himself to be engrossed by Hans Castorp's story to the exclusion of everything else is certain to feel that he has missed a great deal. He may even confess to being puzzled as to what it is all about. It is well to emphasize, therefore, that, in addition to several other things, *The Magic Mountain* is a symbolic novel. The hero, the secondary characters grouped about him, the *milieu* of Haus Berghof—they are all charged with a meaning over and above what is visible on the surface, and it is this aspect of things that may make the reader who found pure delight in following the saga of the Buddenbrook family, leave *The Magic Mountain* in bewilderment,—the more so as, to the superficial view, both novels are couched in the same naturalistic manner and excel in the same meticulously accurate portrayal of the characters and their environment. No doubt, this difference between *Buddenbrooks* and *The Magic Mountain* is fundamental, and while it is partly to be accounted for by a revolutionary change in temper of the literary age, it is equally indicative of the course of Thomas Mann's own development. It will be one of our most interesting tasks to pursue the implications of the symbolic principle in detail. At this point I can only outline the symbolic relation that obtains between the concrete elements of *The Magic Mountain* and the more general phenomena they aim to encompass. But lest I be accused of manufacturing a symbolic perspective which the author did not even remotely dream of, it is well to make clear once for all that such an approach has the author's authoritative sanction. In one of those passages of *The Magic Mountain* where the author speaks in his own person we find a definition of the concept of the symbol, phrased evidently with an eye to its application to the novel in which it occurs. Leading up to his interpretation of the song nearest to Hans Castorp's heart, "Der Lindenbaum," in Schubert's setting, he says:

> A conception which is of the spirit, and therefore significant, is so because it reaches beyond itself to become the expression and exponent of a larger conception, a whole world of feeling and sentiment, which, whether more or less completely, is mirrored in the first, and in this wise, accordingly, the degree of its significance is measured.

Goethe might have written this sentence without changing a word, so thoroughly does it accord with his philosophy of art. It is perfectly possible, of course, that a theme may lend itself to symbolic interpretation without any internal evidence of the author's having had any specific symbolism in mind. Heine's well-known poem about the northern fir-tree that dreams in its wintry slumber of the sun-scorched palm of the Orient, is a good example in that it may, but by no means need be taken as an expression of Zionistic longing. The case is very different, however, when it is an integral feature of the author's conscious design to make us sense, over and above the concrete action unfolding before us, and without sacrificing any of its vitality, the presence of an elusive shadow play of larger import, running parallel to it, on a higher plane. Thomas Mann does this in *Royal Highness*, where it is his immediate concern to develop the problems confronting a grave little prince who has to take life very seriously, whereas the accompanying shadow play reveals corresponding problems, dangers, temptations, and compensations as typical features of the literary artist's life pattern. There are moments when the characters, together with the stage on which their lives are unfolding, become transparent, as it were, allowing us to glimpse the archetypes of which they are but variations.

The same is the case with *The Magic Mountain*. Hans Castorp, Joachim, Settembrini, Naphta, Peeperkorn, the social *milieu* of the Sanatorium generally, are intensely real in their individuality, but they stand, besides, for something larger and more

inclusive. Thus the *clientèle* of Haus Berghof—this motley international group drawn from the middle and upper strata of society, all of them stamped with the mark of disease—is readily felt
as a symbol representing pre-war Europe. The analysis of the
prevailing mental attitude, flighty, frivolous, thrill-hungry, and
insincere, becomes a searching indictment of Western civilization, and *The Magic Mountain* thereby reveals itself as a *Zeit-
roman*, in that it strives to express the psychic temper of a whole
age. As for the principal characters, they frankly function as
representatives. "You are not, to me, just any man, with a name,
like another," Hans Castorp says to Settembrini on the night of
the carnival. "You are a representative, Herr Settembrini, an
ambassador to this place and to me." And it is with a smile that
we recall how, at their very first meeting, the simple young man
from Hamburg had been grandiloquently hailed by Settembrini
as "the representative of the whole world of labor and practical
genius"—a role not exactly expressvie of his natural bent, as
we have occasion to find out later. Settembrini henceforth functions in Hans Castorp's thinking as a concrete symbol: "a representative—of things and forces worth hearing about, it was
true, but not the only forces there were." But this new mental
slant of Hans Castorp's is not limited in its application to Settembrini; in the same context from which I have just quoted he
becomes conscious of Joachim also as the impersonator of a
type—the military type of existence as opposed to his own, the
civilian type. And we are doubtless aware of a similar representative character applying to Clavdia Chauchat and to Naphta.

To anticipate further discussion, Settembrini stands forth
as the exponent of the philosophy of Western enlightenment, the
philosophy of the bourgeois-capitalist world, a blend of generous
idealism and shallow utilitarianism. Precise and self-assured,
master of the rhetorical phrase and the withering jibe, ardent
apostle of humanity and inveterate cynic in one, Settembrini is
kin to a succession of illustrious figures ranging from Voltaire
to Woodrow Wilson, as every reader recognizes. Little as one
might at first suspect it, the German phase of the enlightenment,
too, has contributed delicious traits to his character. From time
to time we catch unmistakable echoes of Goethe's Mephisto, of
Schiller, of the young Nietzsche, and of the early Thomas Mann
himself in Settembrini's gestures and phrases. But he comes
nearest, we have good reason to believe, to being a portrait
likeness of his countryman, the flamboyant Italian agitator, Gui-
seppe Mazzini. As for his name—like the names of all Mann's
characters an integral part of his portrait, and not a mere label

—it carries a suggestion of bloody radicalism (the September massacres of the French Revolution, in 1792, after which the verb "septembriser" came to be coined as a slogan for radical action) that Settembrini would be painfully embarrassed to avow in all but his most ardently patriotic moments; it thus contributes an indelibly humorous, if somewhat alarming accent to his humanitarian pipings.

If Settembrini is the eloquent representative of the enlightenment, there is a magnetism about Clavdia Chauchat's mute presence that serves as a focus gathering into itself all those elements of Hans Castorp's personality that assert their instinctive opposition to this way of life. In this way Clavdia becomes a symbol of the East, as opposed to the West. In Naphta, again, the spirit of protest against the bourgeois ideology and all its implications finds an articulate spokesman who is altogether a match for Settembrini. He is a much more complex type than the Italian. His personality, rooted in no steadying tradition, is a discordant blend of motley elements that have coalesced solely because of their mutual bond of hate against the bourgeois world. Naphta, a much more trenchant thinker than Settembrini, and always on the alert to expose the logical flaws concealed under the magnificent drapery of his eloquence, represents all those modern currents of thought that focus their attack upon the existing order, and he borrows his weapons alike from the Kabbala, from medieval mysticism, from the later Nietzsche, and from Karl Marx. His only positive principle is that of negation, and it is altogether in keeping with his part that he should end by blowing out his brains.

In sharpest contrast to these two intellectuals is the inarticulate Peeperkorn. It is his function to make Hans Castorp experience the phenomenon of "personality on a grand scale." Its effect, while eluding rational analysis, is overwhelming. In the great Peeperkorn's presence the two debaters shrink to diminutive stature. As for his character, it is not easy to find a just formula for this weird synthesis of the reeling Dionysus and Jesus in Gethsemane. At first blush it may seem absurd to group him with characters like Senator Thomas Buddenbrook, Lorenzo de'Medici and Fra Girolamo of *Fiorenza,* and Gustave Aschenbach of *Death in Venice,* all of whom live a life of unrelaxed tension and self-discipline; nevertheless he is related to them. He is another, albeit a grotesque member of Thomas Mann's gallery of "heroes." An idealist, like any devotee of the ascetic life, a modern Don Quixote, he consumes himself in the service of an idea.

His cult of life is a form of worship, a continuous act of self-immolation. Goaded on by a constant dread of failure, he exacts a phenomenal degree of performance from his frail physique. There are rumors afloat as to the identity of the real "model" that stands back of Peeperkorn; but the pursuit of such clues, besides forgetting the fundamental distinction between life and art, invariably leads away from the work of art instead of closer to its core. Regardless of any flesh and blood individual who may have contributed certain traits to Peeperkorn's portrait, Peeperkorn is—to reduce the matter to simplest terms—a life-size portrait of Goethe's *König in Thule*.

And what of Hans Castorp himself? Gravitating as he does between Settembrini and Clavdia; steering his cautious course between the two rival educators after Clavdia's departure, he stands as a symbol of Germany, *das Land der Mitte*, politically and philosophically. Between the lines we see Thomas Mann intent on defining the role that Germany is called upon to play in the family of nations, holding a middle ground between the voices of the East and the West, and if we rise to a more abstract realm we read his formulation of what is the essence of the German spirit, as he conceives it. This is a feature of *The Magic Mountain* which it will certainly be worth our while to probe rather thoroughly.

So *The Magic Mountain* is, in addition to its other aspects, a philosophical novel. It is this in more than one sense of the word, in fact, for its deepest concern is not man's relation to the universe as a whole. The almost complete omission of the economic realm from the range of its discussion is significant. Thomas Mann even delves into the realm of metaphysics and contributes views of a profoundly startling nature on the relation of appearance and reality. It is one of the many angles of the problem of Time which lures him into this boldest and most questionable of all his ventures.

[1933]

CHILDREN AND FOOLS

Conrad Aiken

The process by which one comes to know an author, or that part of him which appears in his books, is exactly the process by which one comes to know a person in the flesh. One moves from one impression to another; he is this to-day, and that to-morrow; at first he seems predominantly sad. later one finds that this sadness conceals an undercurrent of irony or secret glee; his face is immobile, but one discovers that his talk is full of emotional or affective overtones; or one moves forward from a first impression of copiousness to a second one of essential thinness. And by slow evolution, all these separate impressions fuse in one image. The glee is added to the sadness, the thinness to the copiousness, the mysterious hint to the impassivity. One acquires a single image, in which, if the first magic of mystery is lost, one finds a kind of definite consolation in the fact that it now quite clearly seems to belong to a category.

The writer's acquaintance with Thomas Mann, or his books, has been of that sort. It has been kaleidoscopic, confused, directionless, delicious. *Buddenbrooks* created the first image—solid, distinct, forthright, almost of the Arnold Bennett order. A four-square three-decker, but with a German, or Gothic, distortion. *Death in Venice* broke this image, precisely as a dropped pebble breaks an image in a surface of water. This was something new— here was an affective overtone not experienced before. What, exactly, was this added something? As before, the story was simple and direct and naturalistic. The secondary characteristics were all, apparently, of the realistic school, if one may be permitted so loose a term. But decidedly there was something else. On the surface, everything was clear and simple and distinct. The story—what there was of it—moved with no subterfuges to its tragic and quiet climax. And nevertheless, there was this queer something else, this nameless undertone, deep and melancholy, which gave the story a different quality, and gave the author, in one's memory, a new reputation. Perhaps the easiest epithet for this added quality is "poetic." If one had felt this in the earlier

work, here and there, one had forgotten it in the prevailing sense
of the real, or (as Henry James preferred to call it) the actual.
But in *Death in Venice,* this became the dominant tone; the poetic or allegorical quality was precisely what one most remembered
afterward. One remembered a tone, a haze, a vague disquieting tapestry effect, as of the smoke from autumnal burnings of
leaves; an atmosphere heavy and *charged;* a feeling of that kind
of poetic counterpoint which was habitual with Poe and Hawthorne. The tale was deep, melancholy, almost (in a sense)
horrible. Beauty and horror were met, here, in a kind of balance.

The *Magic Mountain* moved one's general impression back
again toward *Buddenbrooks,* but not all the way. Is one perhaps
right in calling this enormous novel a kind of "secondary" masterpiece? It resembles *Buddenbrooks* in its leisure, its copiousness, its massive employment of circumstance. It differs from it
in a slight dislocation toward what one might call the spiritual.
This again is a three-decker: one of the finest examples of the
really "exhaustive" novel which the present generation has
given us. But it moves away from *Buddenbrooks* in at least one
particular: one feels in it just a trace of an *arrière-pensée,* a
mystic or pseudo-mystic current, barely revealed, a preoccupation with ultimates and eternals. Its superlative leisure, like
that of Proust's great novel, annihilates time: it is indeed, in a
sense, as the prologue makes clear, preoccupied with the sense of
time, or of timelessness; and it is also curiously, and perhaps
naturally (given this circumstance) preoccupied with death, and
with the scale of values peculiar to the man who stands on the
brink of death. Here we have a sanatorium full of tuberculosis
victims, all of them obsessed with death, all of them charged
with that queer recklessness and detachment which supervenes
in such cases, where the approach of death is gradual, and all
of them subnormal, as regards energy; the characterization is
acute, detailed, profound; the hero, and Mynheer Peeperkorn,
and Madame Chauchat, are magnificent; and the amount of time,
for a patient and cynical review of the world, is unlimited.
Except for the slight and intermittent love-story, which comes
to no climax, there is no plot: the novel has its excuse first in
its richness as a microscosm (which everywhere refers to a mac-
roscosm) and second in is exquisiteness of tone. It is a three-
decker with a deep undercurrent of poetry: a kind of *William
Clissold* written by a poet who happens, also, to have a streak
of morbidity.

This streak of morbidity comes out most clearly, apparently, if one may safely judge by what has thus far been translated from the German, in the latest of Thomas Mann's books, *Children and Fools*. These are short stories, of which the most recent and best is dated 1926, and the others from twenty to thirty years earlier. In all of them is this queer Gothic something-or-other which one has obscurely felt from the beginning in Mann's work —most definitely in *Death in Venice*, perhaps, but also, as just noted, in *The Magic Mountain*. Knowing little of contemporary German literature, one hesitates to say that this is a mere Germanness: and nevertheless one is constantly feeling how curiously these tales resemble—if one may speak wholly of *affects*— the German fairy-stories which one read when one was a child. Here again is that blending of beauty and horror: of the mystic with the terrible: of life and the most morbid aspects of death. One feels that Mann is a victim of certain obsessions which he cannot escape. He must torture, and be tortured: he must die, and see death; he must be weak, and submit to the brutal; he must manage the scalpel which dissects an anguish, and manage it with a surgeon's scientific detachment. *Disorder and Early Sorrow* is one of the most beautiful stories the writer has ever read: the story of a child's first love, and of the father's jealousy; but even in this is the note of Gothic morbidity. And in the earlier and shorter stories, which are more purely analytical, and less circumstanced—almost, indeed, clinical statements—one detects a nearly unintermittent note of morbidity. They all deal with psychological disaster. The difference between these and the later stories is simply that the later ones are more poetic, more sublimated. *The Path to the Cemetery*, in the present volume—a story dated 1901—is a bare pathological or psychiatrical outline for what might, in 1926, have been another *Death in Venice*.

Eventually, therefore, we begin to see Thomas Mann as a very special and slightly warped figure. But he is a poet, and that is all we need.

[1928]

MARIO AND THE MAGICIAN

Henry C. Hatfield

Since 1936, when Thomas Mann remarked that *Mario and the Magician* was a "tale with moral and political implications," critics have belatedly realized its essentially anti-fascist intention. It is amazing how many writers had managed to miss the point up to that time. The present day reading of *Mario* goes to the other extreme: the tendency is to take the novella as an allegory of Italian fascism; no more, no less. Some interpretations try to force every character and every detail of the action into a rigid and elaborate allegorical pattern. Mann, of course, does not write in so mechanical a fashion. Simply as a story, *Mario* has importance of its own, on the literal level; it is thus symbolic rather than allegorical. And the symbolism is not limited to the political realm; there is the philosophic as well: the struggle of free will against the forces of the occult and the subconscious.

Yet it is easy, I think, to show that the political meaning of *Mario* is central in its importance. From any other point of view the tale seems to lack unity, falling into two disparate parts: the apparently trivial events in the Grand Hotel and on the beach—an English critic calls them "pleasant anecdotes"; and the terrifying account of the performance given by Cipolla, the magician. Once the political implications are grasped, as soon as one sees fascism in the crowds at the resort and the fascist leader in Cipolla, the structure becomes clear; the seemingly formless takes shape. Indeed, the first part, serving as a prelude, gives an added dimension to the second. And, of course, the converse is true also: one can best understand the patriotic children, the Italian in the bowler hat, and so on, retrospectively, after getting to know the magician and his victims. The incidents of the plot, which seem but loosely strung together, are actually combined into a unity of the most careful design. Nor should one be deceived by the casual, anecdotal style; it is art to conceal art.

Within the two main divisions of the story, the structure is developed symmetrically. In the first part, events rise in significance from the slight and seemingly irrelevant annoyances of the

Grand Hotel to the incident of the naked child on the beach. This is a semicomic crisis, but still a crisis; the first head-on clash with the fascist mind. Like the children of the narrator, we are disturbed by the self-consciously patriotic Italians, with their "solemn phrases that spoilt the fun"; but we do not at first take them too seriously. After a sort of philosophical intermezzo, the scene changes to Cipolla's performance. The same process of intensification, of rising tension, is repeated, though this time on a more serious—and more obviously political—level. The focus has shifted from a group more or less tainted with fascism to a leader who gradually bends the crowd to his will. The magician's feats advance from the comic and apparently harmless through the grotesque to the horrible. Thus there is a parallel rising action, a *Steigerung* as Mann would call it, in each division of the story. Gradually a situation is built up which can be resolved only tragically. When the magician is assassinated (no other word is adequate, for he has completely become the symbol of the tyrant) one feels liberation from terror, a genuine catharsis. Mann's subtitle, "a tragic travel experience," is amply justified.

In his opening scenes, Mann works with the greatest care to put the reader in the desired frame of mind about Italian fascism. Very early in the story, he equates the nationalism of the crowds at Torre di Venere with lower middle-class vulgarity and contrasts it devastatingly with the international and somehow aristocratic atmosphere of the Pensione Eleonora. (Indeed, fascism is seen throughout from the point of view of the highly cultivated patrician, rather than that of the militant democrat.) Without denying the attractive qualities of the Italians, Mann implies—of course for the benefit of his German audience— that Italy is a politically backward nation which could never serve as a model for the more enlightened Reich. When his children are puzzled and hurt by the boorishness of the patriots on the beach, they are told: "These people . . . [are] passing through a certain stage, something like an illness perhaps; not very pleasant, but probably unavoidable."

It can't happen at home! Later in the tale, fascism is taken far more seriously but at this point Mann appeals to his reader's conviction of German superiority. To turn for a moment to the background of the story: *Mario* was published in 1929, at the time when the Nazis began to appear as a real menace in Germany, rather than as grotesque charlatans; in Munich, where Mann had been living for many years, they were more in evi-

dence than elsewhere. Their power grew as the economic crisis
deepened. In 1930 Mann was to deliver his first major attack on
Nazism: *Appeal to Reason.* The point of view of this speech has
much in common with that of *Mario.* In both there is the combination of patrician scorn for fascism with the almost incredu-
lous realization that it must be taken seriously.

It is in the appearance and character of Cipolla that the
political implications of the novella are most clearly brought
out. Again and again he has recourse to two great sources of
power in carrying out his magic: the claw-handled whip and the
stimulus of cognac. Force and fraud, as it were; and Mann draws
our attention to these symbols with almost Wagnerian insistence.
Cipolla is a mixture of apparently contradictory traits; he looks
like a "charlatan and mountebank," a veritable Cagliostro; yet
like the *petite bourgeoisie* on the beach he is completely devoid
of humor. He is grotesque and ridiculous, but one does not feel
like laughing at him. There is something almost fantastically
old-fashioned about his dress. (In the essays and speeches in
which Mann warned the Germans of the implications of fascism,
it was precisely its reactionary, "old-fashioned" character which
he stressed.) Like the fascist leaders, he deliberately appears late
before his audience, and he displays the striped sash of a highly
dubious nobility.

The magician speaks with such brilliant eloquence that he
gains the grudging respect of the uneasy listeners. There is in
him a curious combination of boastfulness and self-pity; he
claims that it is he, not his victims, who suffers during his feats
of hypnotism. He paints himself, in other words, as the all-wise,
all-enduring hero, the leader of the people. Arrogance predom-
inates in his character, but it is an obvious compensation for
ugliness and deformity; his sensitiveness about "national honor"
repeats that of the bowler-hatted man on the beach. Indeed,
Cipolla's chauvinism is such that he does not shrink from the
most obviously absurd lies: "In Italy, everybody can write." Just
before he is killed, he shows a strong homosexual tendency, a
tendency for which the German fascists were already notorious.
Above all: one must not underrate the magician's powers; he
gradually reveals himself as "the most powerful hypnotist I have
ever seen in my life." (One remembers that he had billed himself as a mere prestidigitator.)

At least one critic conceives of the magician as another of
those "marked men" whom Mann delights to describe. In this
view, he would be but another of the symbols of the artist, a

relative, as it were, of Tonio Kröger, Gustave Aschenbach, Felix Krull and all the others. This interpretation seems to rest on the unflattering assumption that there is only a single theme in all Mann's work, that of the lonely and maladjusted artist. Seen in this way, *Mario* loses its individuality and becomes a sort of *"Death in Venere."* But Cipolla, for all of his occult powers, is no artist. He lacks the all-important trait which, in Mann's view, distinguishes the creator: a frustrated and at times scornful love for ordinary humanity, for the "blond and blue-eyed."

In his handling of the audience, Cipolla is a master of demagogic tactics. Divide and rule is his method, and he uses it with supreme skill. Before his performance starts, he is challenged by a brash youth; by hypnotic powers the magician makes him insult the rest of the audience. He reduces another youth, significantly enough, to a state of "military somnabulism." At first Cipolla leaves the better-dressed spectators alone, concentrating on those whom ignorance or lack of self-assurance render vulnerable. To break down the barrier between the leader and the masses he leaves the platform and circulates among the audience. Finally the aristocrats, including an army officer, a lady of cultural pretensions, and even a "long-toothed Anglo-Saxoness" fall under his spell. By flattery, tricks, intimidation, and above all by hypnotic powers of whose genuineness the author leaves no doubt, Cipolla subdues practically the entire audience.

At one point he assumes a seemingly passive role, performing prodigies of mind-reading in obedience to the will of the spectators. The leader must be able to sense what his people desires. But Cipolla makes it clear that his will is still dominant after all. His remarks about the unity of commanding and obeying and the oneness of the leader and the people sound like direct quotations from some work of fascist dogma.

The audience, it is worth stressing, has never liked the magician. Its attitude towards him is shifting and ambivalent, and generally it shows sympathy for his victims. Yet no one leaves the performance; Cipolla exudes a fascination as a person, "independently of the program." A new theme is established: this is a story of the will, as well as of fascism; or rather, the two elements, moral and political tyranny, are closely interrelated and finally fused into one.

Cipolla suggests to his first victim that "it would be a pleasant change for you, to divide up the willing and the doing." This, obviously, is what happens throughout the evening, and the spectators, more and more reduced to puppets, find that will-lessness is an enjoyable condition. Even the Roman gentleman succumbs, after a stubborn and courageous attempt to assert his will, and finds that he is happier after yielding. The flight from freedom becomes universal; people of all backgrounds and all classes are overcome.

Why does the Roman aristocrat submit? He is sympathetically presented, obviously a person of unusual character and intellect. Mann is quite explicit about it: the Roman has no positive goal, and a purely negative will cannot resist suggestion. This "fighter for freedom," as Mann calls him with a certain irony, is doomed; his position is purely defensive. Freedom, as Mann's master, Nietzsche, observed, must be freedom to some end; merely to be free *from* something is not of particular significance. The Roman is, like Settembrini in *The Magic Mountain*, an admirable person who does not understand the powers of the irrational: his philosophy is superficial and he is made to appear, again like Settembrini, a bit ridiculous.

For Mann, like the magician, believes that there are "forces stronger than reason or virtue." Again we are reminded of Mann's intellectual heritage: the Romantic emphasis on the "dark" side of life: Schopenhauer, Wagner, Nietzsche and Freud. Many in the audience—most of them, perhaps—have a strong subconscious wish to be dominated; they meet the magician at least halfway. When Cipola leads Signora Angiolieri away from her husband in a sort of trance, Mann notes that the poor fellow is bald, middle-aged and physically unimpressive.

Cipolla's powers, at least in part, are "really" occult; for example, the trance into which Mario falls is no ordinary hypnosis. Although Mann feels that subliminal manifestations are unworthy of human dignity and somehow unclean, he believes in them nonetheless. One thinks of his essay *An Experience in the Occult*, and of the chapter in *The Magic Mountain* in which the ghost of Joachim Ziemssen is quite literally conjured up.

How then can the magician be overthrown? Mario, who finally strikes him down, is a person of no particular distinction; quite the contrary. Despite the heroic and republican associations of his name he can hardly be taken as the champion of militant democracy, antifascism or free will. He is a real person, not a figure in an allegory; but his action has symbolic significance. Mario is notable only because he is unusually likable and decent. Though he is destined to kill, he is without a trace of brutality. He has been trained to obey; he has no desire for a clash with Cipolla and tries to escape from him before the crisis occurs.

Mario strikes only when the magician, in his *hubris*, humiliates him beyond endurance; he acts from some instinctive sense of personal dignity. This dignity, Mann seems to imply, is in itself a force stronger than free will or the conscious mind; it brings down the tyrant after they have failed. Cipolla lies on the platform, "a huddled heap of clothing"; and one cannot help thinking of the corpse of Mussolini lying in the square at Milan. There is an end of terror; the tragedy is finished. One is left with the sense of liberation, a liberation both political and human.

[1946]

AN EXCHANGE OF LETTERS

J. B. Priestley

In these pages there will be found two Germanies, address-
ing one another across a dreadful gulf. The first Germany is that
which can strike at one of the most distinquished living men of
letters through an ignoble communication, dated—with horrible
irony—from the Philosophical Faculty of the ancient University of Bonn. That the signature to this letter should be illegible
is not surprising, for the signature to all communications from
this strange new Germany of violence, intolerance and superstition, is illegible. Bewildered, saddened, we stare at its mysterious
scrawl, and wonder what evil enchantment now possesses our
world.

The reply, a noble if melancholy document, comes from another and older Germany, that land of great poets, musicians,
philosophers and scientists, and to comment on its quality would
be almost an impertinence. But something must be said of its
author, Thomas Mann. He is generally acknowledged to be the
best novelist-writer in the German language, and I do not know
that any other language can show us a better living novelist.
The awards of the Nobel Prize Committee sometimes astonish
us, but nobody who knew anything about contemporary literature was surprised when, some years ago, Thomas Mann received
the award. In short, he is one of the recognized Masters of creative literature. He is not a Jew, for he comes from an old North
German family of merchants in Lübeck; and he is not a political
revolutionary. He merely has the misfortune to be a great Liberal
man of letters. And that, it seems, is enough.

He has been deprived of his German citizenship. This is a
bitter loss to a sensitive man deeply attached to all that is most
nobly characteristic of the German people; but he has the consolation of knowing that now he is proudly accepted as a citizen
of the whole wide world of liberalism and culture.

Ironically enough, his work is essentially German, and could

J. B. Priestley's essay appeared as a preface to the English edition of Thomas
Mann's An Exchange of Letters.

not have been created by a writer who belonged to any other people. It is German in its massive intellectuality, its mystical brooding quality, and, at times, its faintly morbid melancholy. His first and most popular novel, produced when he was still in his twenties, is *Buddenbrooks,* an epic of the decay of a prosperous middle-class German family. It may be compared with Galsworthy's *Forsyte Saga,* but it is actually a far finer piece of creative literature, being both richer and stronger. Mann is not so severely conditioned by his own social status as Galsworthy was, has more creative energy, and a far more massive mind. Omitting some slighter things, his next important work was the enormous novel known in its English translation (which is excellent) as *The Magic Mountain.* This is one of the major achievements of modern fiction. It is a work of terrible power, haunting the reader's imagination. Its setting is a sanatorium in Switzerland; its characters are mostly the patients, diseased and doomed; it contains scenes in which the German passion for the grotesque runs riot, and at times the narrative breaks down and we are given elaborate discussions of ideas and seem to take leave of fiction altogether. Many readers, by no means unintelligent, find themselves repelled or bewildered by it. Yet it is undoubtedly a great work. It has a strange symbolic quality, as if it contained level after level of meaning; and it is one of those works that, if you accept them at all, you must return to, perhaps over and over again. On an even vaster scale is Mann's most recent fiction, in which he goes to the antique pastoral world of Jacob and Joseph for his people and his fables; but it is too early yet to pass judgment on the work. But together with these big novels he has brought out some little things that are almost perfect in their kind: that sombre little study of decay, *Death in Venice;* the vivid glimpse of family life and childhood, *Disorder and Early Sorrow* and—a little masterpiece—*Mario and the Magician,* a very fine example of a story with an equal appeal on many different levels. It is not difficult to see in the sinister figure of the magician a symbol of Fascism. When Fascism can reply with a similar little masterpiece of symbolic fiction, its cultural claims may be taken rather more seriously.

Nothing has been said of Thomas Mann's critical essays. It is enough to add that they have the force and penetration of the letter printed here, a letter that should have a place in all final editions of his work. That such a man should find himself compelled to write such a letter is a terrible comment on the world we have made. Germany is a great country, and Thomas Mann, no matter how distinguished he may be, is merely one of its many authors. Yet, although enforced exile is an unhappy fate for a serious man whose roots strike deep in the life and culture of his own country, it is true to say that Germany stands in even more bitter need of Thomas Mann than he does of Germany. He has lost a great deal, but Germany is losing even more. And behind the noble melancholy of this remonstrance of Mann's, we may discover what, unhappily, so few people seem to understand, namely, real patriotism, the patriotism that brings us the duty—in our author's own fine phrase—of keeping pure the image of one's own people in the sight of humanity.

[1937]

EUROPE BEWARE!

André Gide

I deem it a great honor to preface this little book. The men of our time whom we can admire without reserve are rare: Thomas Mann is one. There are no falterings in his work, and there are none in his life. His ripost to a silly snub of Hitlerism is worthy of the author of *Buddenbrooks, The Magic Mountain* and the Joseph trilogy. The importance of the work gives to the gesture its importance and its powerful meaning.

Henceforth Thomas Mann is Czechoslovakian. I saw him recently in Küssnacht, near Zurich, where he lives in self-imposed exile. Once again I was moved by the gentle manners and the exquisite consideration with which he conceals a great firmness of character, an inflexible will. Qualities which I admire in his wife as well, and which are to be found in his children along with, on occasion, a charming turbulence.

Because Thomas Mann has never been officially exiled the Germans within Germany insist on this point.

"Nothing," they say, "forced him to leave our country. There was no particular proscription to drive him out. All he had to do was to remain, just as we have done, and to join us in acknowledging that an adjustment can very well be made to a regime that asks nothing of us, after all, but acquiescence. Instead, he chose to be difficult. So much the worse for him. All the rest came as a result: the seizure of his properties in Bavaria; the loss of his rights; and the revoking finally of his German citizenship and his degree from the University of Bonn."

Thomas Mann had never mixed in public affairs. "I was born to bear witness not in martyrdom but in serenity, to bring the world a message of peace rather than to nourish conflict and hate," he tells us. Doubtless; but he was "born to bear witness"; such is his role; it is that of a man of letters; and when a despotic government tries to bend the souls of men to its will, one mixes in politics by refusing to submit. To him may be applied

André Gide's essay appeared as a preface to the French edition of Mann's *Achtung Europa!*

what Sainte-Beuve said of the "politics" of André Chenier: "It is never a concerted and consistent action; it is an individual protest, logical in form, lyrical in source and jet, *the protest of an honest man* who at one and the same time defies those whom he refutes, and fearlessly exposes himself to the sword." Happily, there is no question here of the guillotine; but Thomas Mann has a perfect right to declare: "If I had remained in Germany, or if I had returned there, I would probably be no longer alive." Thomas Mann is compelled, by his own integrity, to assume a political role in a country where "gentlemen" who still insist on thinking are regarded as nuisances and troublemakers. As for us, we have enough love for Germany to recognize her voice rather in the protest of a Thomas Mann than in the letter of the dean of the University of Bonn. In this protest, his indignation is still moderate in expression; Thomas Mann lets himself go far more when he is concerned with the fate of Spain in the third of the papers collected here. And I admire his anger for manifesting itself where there is the least self-interest. It is in this, too, that we recognize the utter sincerity of these pages; not only do they all come from the same man, but from the same ink, the same inspiration; an unflinching belief gives them their life. No, it is not self-interest that is behind them; Mann remains authentically on the side of the spirit: a humanist, in the fullest sense of the word.

"Humanism," he explains in an address given in Budapest, during the course of a forum organized recently by the Institute of Intellectual Cooperation, "humanism . . . is in no way an academic matter and has no direct concern with erudition. Humanism is, rather, a state of mind, an intellectual leaning, a condition of the human soul that involves justice, liberty, knowledge and tolerance, grace and serenity; doubt, too, not of what concerns the end, but in how we may reach truth, in what is the most whole-hearted effort we can make to rid truth of the presumptions of those who would hide it under a bushel." He began by saying: "Would it not be simplest and best to consider humanism as the opposite of fanaticism?"

Humanism, as Thomas Mann presents it here, might seem, in a peaceful period of history, to merge with a kind of smiling Renanism; but let us not be deceived: comes the time when force tries to break the spirit, to bend it to some arbitrary and brutal statute, and at once the true humanist is made aware of his role; refusing to yield, he opposes to material force another

force: the irreducible one of the spirit—of which, for better or
for worse, all tyranny should realize the token value.

If I have made a point of quoting the statements above, it
is because the speech from which they are taken is not part of
this volume. But all the pages which may be read farther on
give out the same true and solid sound. Certain truths which
are therein expressed should invite young people to reflection;
in particular, this: "The young (of today) are ignorant of culture in its loftiest and profoundest sense. They refuse all self-
discipline. They no longer know anything of the individual's
responsibility and find all their conveniences in the collective
life. The collective life, compared to the life of the individual,
is the sphere of facility. Facility which permits the worst self-
indulgence. The present generation wants only to bid a lasting
farewell to its own identity. What it craves, what it loves, is
drunkenness. In a new war, it will achieve its final aim and
there our civilization will perish."

The flood of barbarity that Thomas Mann anxiously watches
break over our world has not yet reached France; and that is
perhaps the only reason why I, a Frenchman, feel rather less
gloomy than he does. But the thoughts which are developed
in his *Warning to Europe*—how can we fail to recognize their
truth? "The highest values are no longer sheltered from destruction," he says, "nor perhaps the fate of our entire civilization."
He refuses to hold the war of 1914 responsible for our present
degradation. His *Buddenbrooks*, in portraying for us through
three generations the "story of the decline of a family," testifies
to the torment which was already his in 1901. "I repeat," he
writes today, "that the decay of European culture has not been
the doing of the war, which only accelerated it and made it more
apparent." And very subtly, but very sagaciously too, he attempts to show that, arrived at a certain stage, culture begins
to attack itself. "In all humanism, there is an element of weakness," he remarks, "that comes from its contempt for all fanaticism, from its tolerance and from its bent toward an indulgent
skepticism; in a word: from its natural bounty. And that can,
under circumstances, be fatal to it."

Doubtless the present Hitler regime puts culture in great
peril; but the worst danger Thomas Mann sees is this: that,
in our time, reason is usually flouted, and the man who seems
to be more intelligent than the reasonable man is the one who,
in the name of Life, disowns reason.

"The world is perhaps already lost," he concludes. "It is

surely so unless it manages to tear free from this hypnosis and regain awareness of itself." It is toward this goal that the following pages strive. And, thanks to them, I dare think: No, Thomas Mann; no; our world is not yet lost; it cannot be as long as there is a voice like yours to raise itself in warning. As long as consciences like yours remain awake and faithful, we shall not despair.

[1938]

THE BELOVED RETURNS

Menno ter Braak

The Goethe who is the "magnetic" hero of the novel *The Beloved Returns* is sixty-seven years old; thus, in September 1816, shortly after the death of his "bed sweetheart" Christiane Vulpius and shortly before the marriage of his son August to Ottilie von Pogwisch, he was only a little older than Thomas Mann, who has chosen this episode from Goethe's life as the "inset" of his book. I say: inset, not subject; the word subject would awaken wrong associations which do not correspond at all with *The Beloved Returns*. For nothing was probably farther from Mann's intention than to write a historical novel of the type of those half-invented, half-documented narratives that attracts so many readers; with this sort of book this writer has scarcely the form in common. The inset here is the enigma Goethe, in other words, the mysterious "great," "objective" Goethe of Weimar, who became a figure of international renown in 1816 and who had come far from the young "subjective" Goethe to whose complicated love for Charlotte Buff, later spouse of Johann Christian Kestner, the world owes in part the existence of *The Sorrows of Young Werther*. This later Goethe is a result of a vital process: he is an official personality, surrounded by admirers, commentators and other creatures who try to maintain themselves in his domain; his life has been characterized by unparalleled productivity; and it is just this productivity which has formed him into something which can no longer be undone; the great Goethe is a tyrant with a court, before whom intellectual Europe bows as temporal Europe bowed not so long ago, before that other tyrant Napoleon.

But Napoleon was transported to St. Helena, and Goethe, the isolated German, lives in Weimar: fruitful analogies could be drawn between St. Helena and Weimar, which go precisely as far as the analogies between temporal and intellectual tyranny go. This Goethe of 1816 felt the German wars of liberation with all their loud-spoken idealism and patriotic rhetoric least of all as liberation; he treated them with aversion, sometimes with pronounced hostility because he saw something loom up behind the pathos of which the enthusiastic contemporaries had no notion: German barbarism; but he identified himself just as little with Napoleon, because he knew the latter's interests were not his. After the Napoleonic period Goethe becomes a despot in his own sphere; he entrenches himself behind his symbols, he "resides in culture" and the scene of the provincial. Weimar suits him, the Privy Councillor, just insofar as he is a finished product who no longer undergoes the process in the form of subjective revolution. The official Goethe of 1816 has the traits of the reactionary and royal servant, but with all his presentation at Court he is beginning to grow lonely; his great objectivity, his Olympian attitude conceal the enigma that he himself suppresses with his productivity and his symbolism. The enigma Goethe is the inset of *The Beloved Returns*.

It is not the first time that Thomas Mann measures himself against Goethe because he feels related to the teacher of his youth, without wanting to surrender to him minus criticism. In the volume of essays *The Sufferings and Greatness of the Masters* (1935) we come across an essay on Goethe, some parts of which form, so to say, the nucleus of *The Beloved Returns;* what was written there about Goethe's ambiguity and irony found application in this novel, which is really just as little and just as much a novel as *The Magic Mountain:* "There are in Goethe, if one looks more closely, as soon as the innocence of youth is over, traits of a deep sorrow and despondency, of a dull displeasure which without doubt are profoundly or uncannily connected with his ideal incredulity, his natural indifference toward what he calls his amateurishness, his moral dilettantism. There is a strange frigidity, malice, backbiting, a Bocksberg mood and unpredictability about which one cannot muse enough and which one must love too if one loves him." These sentences one could call the key sentences of *The Beloved Returns*. In the same essay Mann quotes a contemporary's utterance about Goethe: "Out of one of his eyes looks an angel, out of the other a devil, and his speech is deep irony concerning all human things"; and a remark by Charlotte von Schiller: "So he spoke in sentences which also had a contradiction in them, so that one could think anything one wanted to; but the master, one feels with a kind of pain, thinks of the world: I have built my house on sand." On nothing—Goethe as the representative of nihilism! Is he therefore a nihilist? No, for he was Privy Councillor, even with productive ambition;

but in his role of enemy of the democratic and nationalistic ideas of his day he was above all an enemy of the abstractions which threaten to put a pattern of man in the place of his un- predictable multiplicity, his intuitivity and loftiness; for his schematizing environment he was thus a nihilist, as soon as he ap- plied his irony maliciously. As citizen, Goethe stands between the people and the aristocracy; his social position is accurately defined by this contradiction; also his cultural position (at least, if one can speak of something like that); the notion that he is like a reaction- ary from one distinct aspect and a nihilist from another aspect can be made plausible only if one starts out from the inimitability, the uniqueness of the personality of Goethe, who displays these two accents without falling apart or splitting. No second Goethe could live; he would be an ape of the real Goethe. Every effort to thrust Goethean veneers on our culture is ridiculous because the phenomenon Goethe, the "demoniac," enigmatic creature contra- dictory within himself and yet to the world an Olympic repre- sentative, who is a result and a finished product, can never serve as precept for those who have come after him.

The literary Werther of the famous novel committed sui- cide: a choice. But his creator, Goethe, lived on at Werther's expense: another choice. Herein already lies the whole prob- lem, the whole secret, the whole demonism of this figure. All inspiration in Goethe comes from his personality; that is, his inimitability, the concatenation of choices that made Goethe irrevocably what he was, including the devilish irony toward his own choices: all opposition that we feel toward Goethe arises from his tyranny toward himself and his environment, the humorous side of which is also all too clear. It is also this tyranny, official and symbolic, that has made him old-fashioned as a writer, so that today, strangely enough, we esteem Goethe's productive personality more highly than his individual works.

Is *The Beloved Returns* a novel, an erotic novel? Let us guard against the word *novel* that in our epoch has become almost synonymous with vulgarity. In the sense of vulgarity *The Beloved Returns* is no novel and no erotic novel; the action is limited to the arrival and the sojourn of Charlotte Kestner, née Buff, in Weimar. She has come ostensibly to visit her family but she is really driven by the desire to see after forty years whether the possible is still to be found in the reality of the official Goethe. It is the need of verification of an old woman who had too much common sense four decades earlier to allow herself to be dissuaded by genius from her life's destination (marriage to Kestner). For the lover of novels with action and plot that is now about all; he will have to admit that this novel, seen from the standpoint of the realistic or romantic theory of literature, has bitterly disillusioned him because conversations are interminably carried on and because this does not fit into our tensely and dynamically living age.

To repeat: this novel has no subject but an inset, it deals neither with Goethe's youthful love nor with Goethe himself, but tries to penetrate into the problems of subjectivity and objectivity, of becoming and become, of possibility and reality, of genius and the commonplace, of officious and official personality. Altogether, this is the problem of time, its irrevocability and irreparability, of remaining, passing into or passing away, of metamorphosis. Lotte became famous as a figure of romance, but in her ordinary life remained a sensible woman and mother. Goethe became the official genius and Privy Councillor who at the same time presented and concealed his secret; what interchange is possible between these two finished beings after so many years? It is an excellent stroke of Thomas Mann to have Lotte received at her hotel by a comic figure. The literarily interested waiter Mager is a kind of Goethe clown who represents the entire Goethe reputation on the level of the speechmaking community of Weimar. "To help Werther's Lotte out of Goethe's carriage, is an experience—what shall I call it? It is worthy of a book." This Mager is grotesque with literary solemnity; he proves, as it were, how close the ceremonious style of Thomas Mann is to the grotesque—how close all ceremonial is to the grotesque if it is carried by nothing but a fashionable convention. This educated fellow opens and concludes the book which therefore lies enveloped in cultural grotesqueness—a delightful ironic effect. Just as in *The Magic Mountain,* all the personages in this book are "educated," even the relatively "uneducated"; this too is characteristic of Thomas Mann's style in general, of the dialectic character of *The Beloved Returns* in particular. One recollects the modest Hans Castorp of *The Magic Mountain* who, like Charlotte Buff, is introduced as quite an ordinary representative of the human race, but has so much dialectic fluency that he certainly does not seem a duffer.

Since in this new book even the waiter is an "educated person" who can add his say about Goethe, one can expect much more of the average intelligences of the master's environment: Dr. Riemer, Goethe's zealous subject; Adele Schopenhauer, the intellectual woman; and August von Goethe, the son, who on account of his famous father's presence is unable to be anything but a crude imitator of the latter's philosophy of life. These personages come to Charlotte to pay their respects, and all three show they are not only dialectically skillful but even dignified. Here one immediately sees how far we are removed from the ordinary historical novel: by confronting these figures with Charlotte, Mann tries to bring the elderly official Goethe of 1816 through the eyes of third parties nearer to the picture she remembers; before she meets Goethe she passes through a kind of inauguration, so that she can picture the finished product before she meets it.

These dialogues at Charlotte's arrival fill the first 284 pages of the book; nothing, oh novel devourer, has as yet happened. And after that, again nothing happens. Mann creeps into Goethe's skin and presents the latter's "wild sayings" in the form of a *monologue intérieur*. That this adventure has been entirely successful proves firstly the degree of intimacy of his relationship with Goethe and secondly his masterliness as writer: for one does not feel this monologue is forced, the leap of thoughts blasphemy; I believe one could not indicate with subtler means of what precisely Goethe's famous demonism consists, how productivity and irony alternate, conflict and complement each other in this personality, how Goethe's legendary development is everywhere full of genesis, but a genesis which at the same time curbs and directs.

After these two kinds of preparations, the two meetings between Charlotte and Goethe, the official at the dinner and the officious in the carriage, are such excellent solutions of the created tensions that one must be blind to overlook the masterliness of the treatment, although it has not much in common with the customary tools of the novel. The first-class writer of *The Magic Mountain* is here operating at full force; cumbrousness and involution, into which Mann's style must immediately develop if he loses his masterliness, and of which he indeed makes conscious and ironic use for Mager, the waiter, does not occur here, even as a threat.

The whole atmosphere of the dinner at Goethe's with that delightful Eckermann touch, with which the official privy councillor characteristics of the genius are underlined with rare refinement, is sublimely drawn; no less sublime Charlotte's drive in the empty carriage which Goethe has placed at her disposal (still official politeness), her lonely watching of the rhetorical drama of Karl Theodor Körner in the theatre, her meeting with the officious Goethe (surprising and yet for so long prepared) in the same carriage, and their conversation which rounds off the dialogues—the final truth of this novel, prelude to death, that will again relate the irreparability of the finished man . . . metamorphosis, "play of the metamorphoses." . . .

One understands why Mann has chosen the novel form for this meeting with Goethe (Charlotte's meeting, but also his), or rather, why the dialectic novel form was the indicated choice for him here. "Despite everything it seems to suffice to be an artist, a creator, as Goethe was, to love life and remain faithful to it," he wrote in his above-quoted essay. The artist does not wish in the last instance to judge, to convince; he wants rather to portray life with all its contradictions, because of its contradictions; and Mann is such an artist to his fingertips. Most treatises concerning Goethe remain academic theory because they wish to persuade that Goethe is this or that; in Mann the subjective and the objective Goethe cannot be separated any more than the historical Goethe could be chopped in two; in the metamorphosis of the imagination these two themes are the more intimately linked the more clearly they are weighed one against the other. This result is musical; *The Beloved Returns* is Goethe music, the only solution of which is Goethe.

If one speaks of relationship between Goethe and Thomas Mann (both, in different moments and with different antecedents, representatives of bourgeois culture) one must first of all postulate that this relationship can only exist in the contradiction. A Thomas Mann who is supposed to be a reiterated Goethe would have to be more like Gerhart Hauptmann and he would certainly not have been the great German and European that he now is for us. Also Mann came to be isolated from his country by his thoroughly German unpatriotism; but while Goethe could still live in Weimar as privy councillor and official (hated but nevertheless respected), an enigmatic figure, Mann was compelled, after the republic of another Weimar had had to give up its hopeless existence, against many of his instincts, to emigration and to democratic leadership outside the German frontier, even in America; here already is an important difference that shows how much a Goethe of 1816 is inimitable, how much Goethean outwardness had to belie a real Goethean personality to be able to convey something of Goethe's demonism. Mann is least of all a copy of Goethe; he is a kindred spirit in irony, in contradiction, in inimitability, and *The Beloved Returns* testifies to it in the most striking manner, just because the book is a Goethe novel. Every platitude about the official Goethe, every concession to his reputation would have been obvious in the case of a lesser god; one can only admire in Thomas Mann the fact that he has not allowed himself to be tempted by any of the concessions with which the historical novel usually tempts the writer.

His relationship with Goethe manifests itself in a ceremonial which in his own way (not Goethean) is inimitable. This ceremonial coincides with his style, which is no subtle arabesque art as one might assume for a moment at the beginning of the novel; in his slowness, his cumbrousness, his rejection of vulgar directness, his elegance and his irony Mann may remind one of Goethe's example by his attitude to analagous friends and foes; he has found the distance that excludes every by-thought of epigonism. The picture of the sixty-seven-year-old, as Mann with delicate details lets it gradually take shape before the reader, is determined as much by his admiration and love as by his criticism; in other words, criticism is admitted in admiration and love; admiration and love here no longer need indiscrimination.

[1941]

THE BELOVED RETURNS

Stefan Zweig

In these days of gloom we must be doubly grateful for any pleasure. We have received intellectual pleasure of the highest and purest sort from Thomas Mann's new novel, *The Beloved Returns*. This book is perhaps his most perfect masterpiece, despite *Buddenbrooks, The Magic Mountain* and the *Joseph* epic. It is perfect in structure and language; the latter here reaches its fullest maturity. But it is not only in these respects that *The Beloved Returns* seems to me to surpass all his preceding works; we find here also an inner rejuvenation and a brilliance of technique which easily hurdle the most difficult problems and which combine ironical wisdom with a noble pathos in a manner surprising even in Thomas Mann. The substance and weight of this book written in exile easily outweigh everything written during these last seven years inside Germany under Hitler's literary despotism.

At first glance it might appear as if the material of this novel could hardly yield more than a masterfully told anecdote or a graceful story. One is at first inclined to take it as an apercu of literary history: Lotte Kestner, the former Charlotte Buff, whom Goethe loved in his youth and who will always be remembered as the Lotte of *The Sorrows of Young Werther*— this lady cannot resist the temptation of meeting again, after fifty years, Goethe, the Theseus of her youth. She is now a grandmother; time has worked deleteriously upon her but has also given her wisdom. And still she commits the sweet folly of dressing again in the white Werther dress with the pink sash, in order to remind the richly decorated dignitary, Goethe, of the sweet folly of his youth. And he sees her, a little disturbed, a little embarrassed. And she sees him and is a little disappointed and yet secretly touched by this somewhat ghostly encounter after half a century. That is all. A plot not larger than a dew drop; but, like one, a miracle of color and brilliance under the light from above.

Lotte Kestner has hardly entered her name in the register

when the people of the small town, curious and gossipy, begin to throng around her. One after the other of Goethe's circle comes to see her, and all of them, whichever turn the conversation takes, feel impelled to speak of Him, who keeps them all under his spell despite their inner resistance and their injured vanity. Thus gradually a picture of Goethe is shaped out of these manifold images he has impressed on the minds of others. Each image reflects a different side of his nature, and finally he himself enters the gallery of mirrors. He is represented with such a compelling concreteness that one believes one can feel his breath. The portrait is so real and so convincing that in my experience no other novel can offer anything to approach it. The petty traits inherent in any human being are observed and preserved, but they gradually disappear before the full light emanating from the majestic personality. With an incomparable plasticity which does not shun boldness and daring this personality is artistically presented from the center outward. Every minute detail of gesture, voice and behavior is brought alive to such an extent that, in spite of all philological knowledge one may possess, one is at a loss to distinguish the historical facts from the poetic addition and elaboration. Fictionalized biography is esthetically unbearable if it romanticizes, idealizes and falsifies; here for the first time it has become a perfect work of art. I am convinced that the way the coming generations will view Goethe will be determined by this sublime representation.

No word of enthusiasm seems to me too great for this work in which artistic insight is raised to the level of human wisdom and in which an almost uncanny versatility of expression masters the greatest and most difficult subject. The future will see an absurd curiosity of literary history in the fact that this thoroughly German book, which is superior to anything which has been written in German in decades, at the time of its publication was forbidden to eighty million Germans. It is almost a cause for malicious joy to think that only to the Germans in exile fell the privilege—though indeed they had to pay so dearly for it in other respects—of being able to read this book in the original, for only in the original can it offer perfect enjoyment. I fear that in a translation much of its charm will be destroyed, many of its most delicate qualities of subtle allusion and concealed reference will be lost. We should consider this book not only as a work of art but also as a comforting demonstration of the fact that, for an artist, exile need not mean only bitterness and intellectual impoverishment, but may mean also an increase in power and intellectual enrichment. Let us be thankful that we are permitted to receive this book today, while those others who inside Germany remain in spirit faithful to Goethe and therefore are the real exiles, will receive it only after this war, as a reward for their sufferings.

[1939]

ORDER OF THE DAY

Reinhold Niebuhr

With the publication of Thomas Mann's political essays, one is naturally prompted to ask some more or less fundamental questions about the relation of Thomas Mann to German culture and the relation of German culture to Nazism, despite the fact that it might be sufficient to accept the essays with grateful admiration for the noble proportions of Mann's thought, for the elevated and slightly tragic mood of his style, and for the depth of his understanding of the issues involved in the world crisis.

Yet it may be well to begin more simply with the essays and to express the satisfaction which any sensitive reader must feel in reading Mann's moving defense of democratic civilization. Though some of the essays have been published before, the most important ones—particularly those written in Germany before Hitler came to power—are new to us. The first essay in the book, *The German Republic*, was delivered as a lecture in Berlin in 1923 and represents Mann's first explicit defense of democracy. He was obviously speaking to a hostile youthful audience, already deeply infected with the virus which would bring disaster to them, to Germany, and to the world. He responds to their jibes with the dignity of a patrician and a great humanist, and in the process of countering their hostility he expresses forebodings which have since been tragically justified. The whole chapter, and many subsequent ones contain the vitality of living history and are more than the mere words of a wise man.

In all of his various appeals Mann is defending something more than democracy as a form of government against the rising tide of obscurantism, militarism, and mystic nationalism. He speaks as a protagonist of the common element in the classical and Christian tradition which has informed the culture of Europe for ages; and he seeks vainly to stem the tide of synthetic barbarism which the youth of Germany so pathetically regarded as the resurgence of German vitality.

It is not possible to do full justice to all the facets of Mann's thought in his polemic against Nazism. One may say, however,

that no one has been able to express disgust for something
loathsome with so nice and calculated a contempt. His essay
on Hitler entitled *A Brother,* in which he measures the man as
a perverted artist and perverse genius, is a perfect piece of
irony.

Thus while one may hail Thomas Mann as the most authentic voice of the "true" Germany, as the most persuasive
exponent of a culture to which Germany made as many significant contributions as any other Western nation, one may be
pardoned if one detects in Mann's spiritual history some clues
to the pathos of Germany's genius. He protests eloquently
against the degradation of Nazism. He sees it as a perversion
of the romantic tradition in German culture. Yet he is himself
deeply indebted to the romantic tradition. He is quite right
of course in not holding Schopenhauer or Nietzsche responsible
for Nazism; and equally right in detecting a closer affinity between Wagner and Hitler, despite his own honest admiration
for Wagner. Yet one wonders whether the Nazi dregs could
be what they are if the best wine of German culture had not
been what it was and had not been a little too heady. Much
has been made of the tension which Mann felt and expressed
between his tradition as a *Bürger* and his vocation as an artist,
between the solidity, respectability, and conservatism of a scion
of a patrician family and the freedom and creative irresponsi-
bility of art. Yet it may be that the difficulty of German culture
lay in an insufficient tension between characteristic bourgeois
virtues and artistic feeling in the German middle class.

In other parts of the Western world the rise of the bourgeoisie was concomitant with the destruction of feudal traditions
and loyalties and the establishment of political justice based upon
careful rational discrimination. But for Mann and for Germany
bürgerlich had other connotations. The point of Mann's original
disavowal of politics in his *Reflections of a Non-Political Man*
was that Germany was a land of music and not of politics. His
preference for music as the highest art was prompted by his
conviction that it expressed depth of feeling without the conscious intellectual discrimination other art forms demand. In
his debate with the youth of Germany, after he had renounced
his former indifference to politics and had come to the significant conclusion that an intelligent interest in politics was synonymous with concern for democratic politics, he states the
position of those who oppose him thus: "Literature and art, I
am told, romantic literature at least, German art, are they not

dream, simplicity, feeling, or better yet temperament? Whatever have they to do with intellect, which like the republic is more the concern of sharp-witted Jews and to be disapproved of on patriotic grounds?" He refutes this position, which was once his own, and his whole volume of essays does handsome penance for his previously avowed indifference to politics. But they can scarcely hide the original mistake. It would be ungenerous to call attention to the mistake had it been unique rather than typical. It was not the mistake so much of a German artist who was in conflict with his middle-class traditions as the mistake of the German middle classes. They were informed by romantic traditions which might be universalist or nationalistic, individualistic or *Völksch,* but which scorned the plodding, discriminating social and political disciplines which bore the fruit of political justice.

What would have become of democracy in the non-German world if only Rousseau and not John Locke had informed our tradition? It is significant that even after Mann espouses democracy he makes much of the similarity between the thought of the German romantic, Novalis, and our own romantic, Walt Whitman. Rousseau, Novalis, and Whitman may persuade us to love the people en masse, but more is required to save the people from themselves and each other.

In short, the tragedy of a non-democratic Germany slipping into the morass of tyranny and obscurantism which the democratic Thomas Mann tried so nobly and so futilely to avert may be partly explained, or is at least illumined, by the thought of the non-democratic and non-political Thomas Mann. The futility of his later efforts is, at any rate, partly determined by the typical, rather than unique, character of his early position.

It is necessary to make this indictment of German culture for the sake of refuting such indictments as those of Lord Vansittart, which attribute a congential defect to German character. Nazism is not merely an accidental aberration in German life. But neither are its cruelties typical of German character. Nazi tyranny is the bitter fruit of a congenital political ineptness in German culture; and that ineptness is at least partly derived from the romantic tradition.

All this does not derogate from the stature of Thomas Mann. Only a very great man could rise to the height of his noble disavowal of Nazism and his humble and ironic recognition of Hitler as a "brother." Hitler is of course a brother to all of us, in so far as his movement explicitly avows certain evils which are implicit in the life of every nation. Yet it is not unfair to regard him as, in a special sense, the evil fruit of the German romantic movement. The greatness of that movement is not refuted by the fact that Nazism is really its fruit; but neither can the relation of the fruit to the tree be denied. The most tragic aspect of German culture is that it frequently illumined the ultimate issues of human existence more profoundly than any other culture. But meanwhile it scorned all the proximate issues. In a sense all Thomas Mann's arguments since his conversion to the importance of politics are a plea to the artist and the philosopher to deal with proximate as well as with ultimate issues of existence, lest failure at this point wipe out the ground upon which men stand when they concern themselves with the ultimate.

[1942]

JOSEPH AND HIS BROTHERS

Julius Bab

Bearing the title *Joseph the Provider*, there has now appeared the final volume of Thomas Mann's prodigious Joseph novel. It was more than ten years ago that the first volume, the *Joseph and his Brothers*, appeared, soon to be followed by the second, *Young Joseph*, and two years thereafter by the third, *Joseph in Egypt*. The completion of this undertaking invites a consideration of the whole, longer and more exhaustive than is usually accorded in these pages to new arrivals on the book market. Such study is due not only to the eminence of the author and the magnitude of the work, but is especially excited by the fact that here for the first time, as far as I know, there appears among the so numerous publications by German emigrés a great imaginative work that eschews any direct reference to the events of our time, and seems to be formed wholly out of a subject matter that is timeless. Now if the history of literature has established any rule (one merely confirmed by its few famous exceptions), it is this, that any direct trafficking with actuality prevents the writer from approaching the sphere of permanent values. And this holds true not "even when" but particularly when that actuality is so disastrously uprooting, so loud with catastrophe, as the one we are facing. A creative work of lasting power, one in which the deepest problems of the time are genuinely "resolved," becomes possible only when the work does not take its way through the stridency of the day's battles. Hence we may hope to come upon matters of significance in following the course of Thomas Mann, and for this reason we must proceed slowly and circumspectly.

What prompted Thomas Mann again to go over the world-famous Biblical tale of Joseph, Jacob's son, who was sold by his jealous brothers into Egypt, where he rose to high honors as an interpreter of dreams and where, with much cunning, he afterward induced his father and brothers to follow him—how Thomas Mann came to give a whole decade of his life to the re-creation of that legend—is not difficult to understand. From the

first this great author has been preoccupied with a single theme
which presents itself to him in an ever-changing variety of
forms: beginning with the Buddenbrooks, that vigorous family
of merchants whose vitality is undermined by the growth among
them of spiritual awareness, until at last it bleeds to death in the
person of a boy possessed only by music; past the purely repre-
sentational existence of *Royal Highness,* and down to the modest
but intellectually sensitive Hans Castorp, serving his apprenticeship on the Magic Mountain, the theme is always the same: the
conflict between mind and life. (Such as the mindlessness of
those who are efficient at the business of life, and the ineffec-
tuality of the thinkers, a dangerously German theme!) Thomas
Mann has labored endlessly over this problem: it is represented
in the writer who succumbs to Death in Venice, and it is alive
even in the dog that yelps contemptuously after his master because he has seen another master with a gun, shooting down
real ducks and hares that a proper dog can run to fetch! The
obscure problem is illumined by a hundred tragic and comic
refractions in the mirror of Thomas Mann's work. The human
spirit is in league with death, is dissolvent to life—in his most
recent work Thomas Mann pursues this apperception into the
depths of gnostic mysticism. But is not the story of Joseph a
primal instance of the one Thomas Mann must tell again and
again? Here is Joseph, with his beauty and his cajoling ways,
his father's darling, attired in the robe of splendor, a dreamer
and interpreter of dreams; and bitter enmity arises between
him and his sound, substantial brothers who are destined to be
the forefathers of a great people. The artistic, intellectual man
arouses instinctive hatred in those best fitted for the business
of life. The poet, in whom esthetic and intellectual gifts are in-
termingled, presents a threatening challenge to those who simply live and multiply. For Joseph, whom we find at the outset
of the story engaged in "fine language" with his father on a
moonlit night—Joseph is a poet! For what is "fine language?"
" 'Fine language'—in other words, conversation which no longer
served the purpose of a practical exchange of ideas or of intellectual discussion but consisted in the mere relation and utterance
of matters well known to both speakers: in recollection, confirmation, and edification, a kind of spoken antiphony. . . ." All
of this vast prose-epic by Thomas Mann is in fact nothing but
such a restatement of something that is quite well known.

Let us proceed with that outwardly dry, scientific manner
which Thomas Mann loves to assume when he wishes to dis-

simulate a profound sympathy: The four volumes of the work
under discussion have a total of two thousand, one hundred and
thirty-four pages; the Joseph story as it appears in my good old
Bible, including the stories of Jacob, covers not more than
twenty-one pages of print. The very first question is: What
accounts for this ratio of a hundred to one? What did Thomas
Mann do to swell to such an enormous span his treatment of
basically the same events?

To begin with, his material is derived not only from the Bible
itself. He found a number of fine points in the Koran and other
oriental sources, all of which reveal a familiarity with the story
of Joseph and relate it in their own fashion. But primarily, the
imagination of the Jews never ceased to busy itself with the
Joseph legends; in the story-telling part of Jewish scripture, the
Midrash, a good many variations of the Joseph story are given,
and Thomas Mann has drawn upon these also. But even if we
considered that these various sources contribute as much as the
Bible does (although they certainly do not contribute so large
a part) there would still remain, comparing the length of the
entire work with its sources, the amazing ratio of fifty to one.

Did he, then, invent so much of his story? Did he add a
great many original characters, tales, adventures? No, certainly
not. To be sure he did insert a few figures for whom no prototypes exist, as far as I know, in the source material. There are
the two dwarfs in the princely household of Potiphar: Dudu,
"the plain man," tremendously proud of the fact that he has a
wife and children despite his "somewhat diminished stature,"
who, in his dwarfish respectability, hates the wondrous beauty
of Joseph from the first; while his rival, little "Beauty" (translation of an intricate Egyptian name) just as unconditionally
loves Joseph and watches over his interest. Nor did Thomas
Mann have a source, that I know of, for the character of Potiphar's overseer, the modest, serious, and loyal ·Mont-kaw, or
Mai-Sachme—who appears in the final volume first as Joseph's prison-warden, and later as his steward—that placid
man who loves the medical arts and ponders the novel he is
writing. I believe that he needed these two men (as, for example, he needed Eliezer, the "eternal servant of Israel's house"
in the earlier volumes) to provide a calm, unaccented background for the gleaming, glittering portrait of Joseph. They
remain, even though touched by the breath of spirit, men of
solid substance.

The "exalted parents" of Potiphar, those ghostly whispering

ancients, from whose dispute we learn to what dark superstition the manhood of their child, the great dignitary Potiphar, was sacrificed, are also, it appears, characters created by the author. These are the principal "inventions" of Thomas Mann but even if I have overlooked any others of importance, only an insignificant fraction of the entire so-called "original invention" did not exist in some earlier version of the Joseph story.

Actually this great work contains almost as little that is "new" as the *King Lear* which Shakespeare created out of a worthless old play, or the most delightful of all Shakespearian comedies, *As You Like It,* which is indebted to a mediocre novelette even for some of its lines. Actually there is nothing so difficult as to convince the average reader that so-called original invention is a quite subordinate and sometimes a wholly superfluous feat in a great work of art, where the decisive role is played by the stylistic emphasis and the formal organization of the subject matter. These are the essential gifts of the artist that made a masterpiece of dramatic poetry out of the coarse, clumsy "truthful chronicle of King Leir and his Three Daughters." They are also what transformed, with not much less effect, the beautiful story of twenty Bible pages into the two thousand pages of Thomas Mann's novel. A change of verbal expression and of formal arrangement are what turn poesy from an "alluring, seductive thing" into the language of the spirit, the spirit which strives in true concern for God, that is to say, for all the most serious meaning of our existence.

A great part of the work is taken up with introducing us to the age of the patriarchs, i.e., a period of about 1200 years before the beginning of our chronology, or more than 3000 years before our time. For Mann does not merely set us down amidst the costumes of that distant civilization and the machinery of its functioning; he tries to give us a genuine feeling for the culture of the time, for the way in which these people think, feel, believe. It is just this that makes Thomas Mann's historical portraiture, which in point of accuracy and perfection is comparable only to Flaubert's *Salammbô* perhaps, something more than an esthetic means of making the period come to life for us— and a bit of learned sport besides. It is both of these as well, no doubt; but above all this "descent into hell," into the abyss of a very ancient world, serves to provide a foundation for the religious experience which is Thomas Mann's first and last concern.

It is almost ten years since Thomas Mann wrote in a letter to me: "The mythologists among our Bible scholars consider the scriptural characters as legendary, and their stories as expressions of mythical concepts and mythical motives. It was my idea to see the characters as real, but as living their myth and feeling themselves as its actual embodiment."

If Thomas Mann, therefore, believes with all of a poet's naive passion in the real existence of Jacob and Joseph, he does not because they ever existed historically but because they live for him today. Similarly alive for the people of that time were the great figures of their tradition, who grew to be their own reality as they re-enacted those legendary lives. This fundamentally poetic form of consciousness is undoubtedly more widespread in the East even today than it is with us. In Biblical times it was, as Thomas Mann points out, of universal prevalence. The language of the day was informed not by the clear sun of reason but by "moonlight grammar." Related phenomena found their identities mixed; time and number played a quite subordinate role. Ishmael *is* Cain, and Esau is Ishmael and Cain. Joseph, likewise, is Abel, is Isaac and Jacob. The conflict between brothers recurs and is always the same.

But it is not in the patriarchal tradition alone that the children of Israel live. We must remember that this three-thousand-year-old moment of man's history is still very far from representing the beginning of all human affairs, or even of just the cultural tradition alone. Abraham himself, the first forefather, came from the land of Ur, the land of the Euphrates and the Tigris, with its infinitely ancient traditions and myths. They are all alive for Joseph and in him. He even comes close to thinking of himself as a reincarnation of Gilgamesh, whom an Assyrian myth describes as a "glad-sorry" man, and whose fateful refusal to love the Goddess Ishtar bears an amazing likeness indeed to a familiar episode in the course of Joseph's chiaroscuro destiny.

But then Joseph comes to Egypt, and we stand entirely on the solid ground of an ancient tradition. We find ourselves in the year 1400 B. C. under the 18th Dynasty at the height of what is termed the "new" kingdom! The oldest documented accounts of Egypt's fortunes date back 3000 years, making them much more remote from the events of Mann's novel than we are from the age of Augustus. All life and thought of this period are molded to a most rigid ceremonial style. With infinitely painstaking industry and art (and, to be sure, with a good deal of learned playfulness as well) Thomas Mann has reconstructed this ancient culture for us—a culture of such a strangely materialistic spirituality. Its greatest concern is the continuity of

life, the life after death. Their graves, from the gigantic pyramids to the rocky caves, are what they build first, and more
carefully than any habitation of the living. Joseph says to
them: "Your dead are gods and your gods are dead, and you do
not know what is *the living God.*"

And we have penetrated, past all concealment, to the core
of the entire work. For at its roots lies the fact that Jacob has
inherited Abraham's legacy, the news of the living God. And
the question arises: Who shall bear the message and the blessing after him? Can it be Joseph? From the first one feels vague
doubts (Thomas Mann's perennial problem emerges here once
more) that this wondrously handsome, dreamy, gifted youth
with his playfully cajoling ways is likely to become the bearer
of the blessing. His playful nature leans toward compromise
and his considerable vanity would gladly see him in the role
of a pagan god. Even before his Fall he roams with his little
brother Benjamin through the sacred grove of Adonis, whose
death and resurrection is the faith of the women in Syria and all
the East; here Joseph winds the flower sacred to this god, the
myrtle, through his hair, half dreamily and half well-knowing
what he does. When, later, he has been thrown into the pit by
his brothers and has seen the light again in Egypt he is more
than ever given to such toying with godhead and takes to calling himself "Osarsiph," which means nothing other than "Joseph
as Osiris." Osiris is the Egyptian Adonis, the mangled king and
god, ruler of death's kingdom, whence he is always resurrected.

While Joseph, who clings earnestly and anxiously to the
faith in one God taught by Jacob, is nevertheless given to flirt-
ing with the religions of other peoples, we see how, on the
other hand, the highest exponent of the Egyptian God-idea
moves from the polytheism of his ancestors toward the one
living God. Readily accessible, yet nonetheless inspired—a true
"glimpse of the open secrets"—is Thomas Mann's identification
of Joseph's Pharaoh as Amenhotep IV, the religious revolutionary who called himself Ikhnaton in token of his efforts to
replace the cults of Ammon and all other Egyptian divinities by
the worship of the sun, called Aton. This notion is not without
historical foundation, if the Joseph cycle is to be regarded as
historically valid, for we have an inscription dating from the
time of this Pharaoh, which tells of shepherd tribes that came
out of Syria into Egypt crying for bread.

What is far more important in any case, however, is the

spiritual dialectic by which the religious revolutionist upon the throne becomes the counterpart of the Hebrew youth.

It is quite undiscerning not to appreciate the fact that Thomas Mann takes Ikhnaton very seriously indeed. One may well wonder how, after forty years of Bernard Shaw's dramatic teaching, so many people still fail to grasp the point that men do not cease to be worthy of serious consideration, and significant, because we are tempted to laugh at some of their peculiarities. This Pharaoh is, at the time of his ascension to the throne —the meagre documentation of the period indicates the probable truth of this—a youth in delicate health; his visionary spirit makes him prone to fits akin to epilepsy; that he speaks of his divine majesty in the ceremonial style which has been traditional for thousands of years is a matter of course. Yet he is passionately in earnest about his religious reform; his full devotion to this idea is just what makes him inept in matters of practical politics. His sun-worship, however, is so profound that he is enabled to tread upon the bridge built for him by the wise Joseph and to surmise that it is not the sun, but the "Lord of the Sun" whom he adores. The conversation between Pharaoh and Joseph at their first meeting, of which the Bible knows nothing but the interpretation of Pharaoh's dreams, becomes one of the important subdivisions of the entire work. It is also a leading instance of the way in which the modern author culls a hundred pages of text from a single page of the Bible. It is the meeting of the two minds, that of the God-seeking King and the God-wise son of Israel, which is the real content of this impressive exchange. More than his interpretation of dreams, more than the clever measures Joseph recommends to prevent the feared famine while contributing to the aggrandizement of Pharaoh's glory, more than all of this, it is Joseph's encouragement of Pharaoh in his striving toward God that moves Pharaoh to draw the stranger from his prison so warmly to himself and to raise him to the highest post in the land. Then Thomas Mann, who takes such pleasure in donning the mask of the dry-as-dust scholar at the very moment of creative triumph, declares in his drollest serious tone: "It is well that this conversation between Pharaoh and Joseph—this famous and yet almost unknown conversation—has now been re-established from beginning to end in all its turnings, windings, and conversational episodes. Well that it has been set down with exactitude once and for all . . . "

In the course of their conversation Ikhnaton is moved to one of his ecstatic outbursts (ending in epileptic rigidity) and begins his great hymn in praise of the sun. This is based on the historical record of Pharaoh's hymn to the sun. However, Thomas Mann gives us much more than a new translation, for his version is most skillfully adapted to the dramatic moment and the character of the speaker while still retaining its great lyrical rhythms. Clearly it is Thomas Mann's intention to contrast the religious passion of this somewhat decadent late-comer to an over-aged culture with the young faith of high destiny, which is ripening among the children of Israel; nevertheless the purity and strength of feeling Ikhnaton brings to his cult of the sun here comes to fervent lyrical expression.

The poet Thomas Mann!—his existence is no new discovery to me, to be sure. (Who, if not a great lyric poet, could have written the sunrise passage of *Death in Venice* or the deeply stirring two pages that conclude *The Magic Mountain?*)

But the great Joseph epic contains many remarkable testimonials to his existence. For a poet is not a man who, as they used to say, writes short lines which rhyme behind. Even if the lines are long and do not rhyme at all, as a more recent fashion dictates, the requirements of the lyric art are not, therefore, exhausted. Lyric poetry exists wherever a poet's deepest emotion impels him to give it rhythmic verbal expression. Nor can any great dramatist or novelist achieve his most successful effects entirely without moments of lyrical revelation. Now in the storyteller Thomas Mann, that keen ironist who masters his emotion by using the tonalities of scientific reports, there is also a hidden poet who stands fully revealed more than once in the course of this Joseph novel. A case in point are those subdued, fine passages in which Potiphar's steward, the modest Mont-kaw, is nearing his end—he is dying of a kidney ailment the symptoms of which Thomas Mann has just described with grimly scientific thoroughness. But now Joseph is comforting the dying man; the charming, varied sayings with which he regularly bade Mont-kaw good-night, to the delight of the old house-steward, culminate in a veritable litany for the dying by Joseph as poet: "The dungeon of your sore trouble opens its door, you can come out and stroll strong and hale down the path of consolation."

But in one of the final chapters we actually come upon rhymed verse! It is the moment of the "annunciation"; the brothers face the task of imparting to Father Jacob the news that his son Joseph, whose bloodstained ketonet they brought him twenty years ago, is in fact alive and Governor of Egypt.

This revelation, which might throw the old man dangerously off balance, is finally brought home to him by means of song. Here too Thomas Mann is using elements of traditional plot, this time out of the Midrash. Jewish story-tellers of that later day employed the pretty conceit that Serah, the daughter of Asher, is the one who brings the dangerous message of good fortune. "She was a comely and wise little maid, skillful at playing the lute." She seats herself beside the patriarch, singing: "Joseph, my uncle, is still alive, not dead is he, but Governor over all Egypt." This much from the Midrash. And Thomas Mann's version?

First of all, the maid does not begin by sitting down at Jacob's feet but comes singing over the wide meadows; shepherds prick up their ears and follow her, until at last a great retinue enters Jacob's tent behind her, already preceded by disturbing rumors. What she sings is in verse form, long stanzas not without some awkwardness and stumbling measures, as befits the improvisations of a child, but surging up at last into a marvellously familiar music. What manner of music is this? No one who has grown up with the German language can be in any doubt about it. It stems from the school of Goethe!

> "Ah, he was no longer present
> Desolate the barren earth
> Till we heard: He is arisen—
> Dear old Father, pray have faith!"

So sings Serah. But for us there echoes inwardly, inescapably, Goethe's "Magic Song" sung by the boy in the *Novella*:

> "From the graves in this ravine
> I can hear the prophet singing."

When Serah's song rises to its full climax, we hear:

> "Read it in his laughing features
> All was but a godlike jest
> And in late-believing raptures
> Take him to thy father-breast."

Could this not be a particularly fine stanza from Goethe's *West-Eastern Divan*? And could the author have chosen a better model than the old poet who fled "Eastward and there to breathe pure, patriarchal air." And could anyone but a born poet follow so worthily in the footsteps of such a master?

But this novel contains other lyrical outpourings wherein

Thomas Mann follows no example but his own. There is the famous story of Potiphar's wife, whose intricate Egyptian name Thomas Mann usually abbreviates to "Eni." We must mention this story in any case, since it is a further example of the way in which the artist's labor gives us a hundred for one. The Bible has only this to say: " . . . his master's wife cast her eyes upon Joseph and said: 'Lie with me.' " Thomas Mann finds the unsympathetic curtness of this shocking, and considers it his duty as an artist to relate the real story of this woman and her passion. Now we begin to know the ceremonious Egyptian noblewoman who is married to the grand dignitary Potifera. We mentioned previously that he was stripped of his manhood at birth, through religious superstition. Indeed he is in every respect a purely titular personage, bearing the title of War-Lord-to-Pharaoh without ever having anything to do with real war. It is just such remoteness from the sphere of practical vitality, however, that nourishes in him certain esthetic and ethical instincts, making him sensitive to Joseph's beauty and wisdom. In the noble castrate's wife, on the other hand, the extraordinary beauty of the youth engenders a passion flaming up by degrees before our eyes, until at last it has become a conflagration devouring all of the lady's poise and reason. Thomas Mann was able to borrow many a telling point for the development of his love story from the Koran and the later Eastern poets, who never ceased singing of Jussuf and Suleika. But when Eni's infatuation is at its height (though before it has degenerated to murderous madness), her words attain to a curiously musical quality; they are quite openly transformed into lyrical song such as this: "O paradise of feeling! Thou hast made rich my life—it flowers!"

Thomas Mann long ago confessed to me that these are verses of his own youth, never before published, which now after many years have found their place here as an organic part of the whole, to save the honor of a much-maligned woman. It seems to me that such a knightly defense as this does the artist honor.

Joseph comes through this trial by the wife of Potiphar, as Thomas Mann puts it, far from brilliantly; he barely skims through. He lets himself go far enough with the alluring lady, at any rate, so that the setting for her recklessly false accusation becomes possible; he loses his coat once again and is thrown into the dungeon pit. But that which enables him at the last moment to resist the woman's seduction, the root of his overly-cited "chastity," is "the vision of his father." It is the memory of Jacob, who had nursed and taught only the most relentless

contempt for the debauchery of Egypt. And it is at the same
time his mindfulness of God-the-Father, whose insistence upon
the dignity and purity of man Israel had so deeply implanted
in his children. In the end Joseph goes to prison innocent, to be
resurrected from the pit a second time and to rise much higher
than before.

And yet Thomas Mann's profound doubt of the poet, of
beauty, of intellect, is consistent with the fact that it is not
Joseph who in the end receives the blessing. We know from
the scriptures that not one of the twelve tribes is named for him,
although two are named for his sons Ephraim and Manasseh.
The interpretation and clarification of this tradition is the real
aim of Thomas Mann's great work.

It is now time to recall the fact that the novel is entitled not
Joseph but *Joseph and his Brothers*. Thomas Mann, who is certainly no blind partisan of the man with the greatest esthetic
charm, did his utmost to develop vivid portraits of the eleven
brothers from their meagre outlines in the Bible: beginning
with the towering Reuben, who is "like a rushing torrent," impetuous and seething with inhibited passion, and yet "a thoroughly good fellow"; to the savage, rude "twins" Simeon and
Levi"; Dan, "the serpent," full of legalistic subtleties; the bony
Issachar and the smooth Sebulon, the forthright Gad, the "fleet-
footed" Naphthali, Asher with his sweet tooth, and finally Benjamin, the youngest, at whose birth Rachel died, so that his
father watches over him with anxiety but without real love. And
Thomas Mann takes great care to make us realize that the brutal action of the brothers in tearing Joseph's coat, beating him,
and throwing him into the well (selling him to the Midianites is
an afterthought) is not to be condoned, certainly, but is to some
extent understandable. For the lovely and clever Joseph is,
putting it mildly, an insufferable fellow, who almost of necessity drives his elder brothers into a rage by the superiority of
his wit, the preferential treatment he enjoys as his father's darling, his arrogant dreams, all connoting his privileged position.
"Tactlessness" is a very soft word for his behavior and the immaturity of his sixteen years is his only excuse. No wonder that
nine of these substantial and simple brothers finally assault him.
Only nine, for little Benjamin is not present and Reuben, unlike
the others, tries to save Joseph.

Undeniably present, however, is the most important of all
the brothers, the one who has not yet been mentioned, namely
Judah, Judah the lion with the eyes of a deer, the beloved legend-

ary, hero, whose name will come to signify the chosen people
as a whole. Now Judah is by no means a "simple" man. He is
eternally plagued by feelings of guilt—the episode of Joseph
adds its share to these—but always and everywhere tormenting
himself because of his abject enslavement to Astarte; he succumbs to lust without having any joy of it. But conscience,
Thomas Mann points out, is the attribute of one who is highly
conscious, spiritually gifted, superior—the really commonplace
never suffer in their conscience. Judah is accordingly the chosen
one, not despite his guilty conscience but because of it.

Thomas Mann probably arrived at this unique characterization of the most noteworthy brother only because the story of
Tamar enters abruptly into the midst of the Joseph story. Tamar
is the remarkable woman who marries two sons of Judah, one
after the other, only to be left a childless widow each time. She
then demands Judah's third son in marriage. When Judah
refuses she tricks him into lying with her and eventually gives
birth to twin boys whom Judah must acknowledge as his sons
when she shows him certain pledges he had left with his unknown companion of that one night.

This fable has attracted writers often enough—one version
is Walter Harlan's thoughtful comedy, *In Canaan*. Thomas Mann
brings it into the course of his Joseph novel but it is far from
being an unrelated episode. He establishes its basic continuity
with his God-romance by a single brilliant stroke: his Tamar,
the Canaanite, is introduced to us sitting admiringly at old Jacob's feet, learning and believing. She becomes inflamed with
longing for the salvation which is God's gift to his own people,
the children of Israel, and her desire to play a role in its coming
accounts for the boundless determination with which she acts.
For Reuben, the eldest, who forgot himself with one of Jacob's
concubines, and the two rude inseparables, Simeon and Levi,
whom Jacob cursed for their bloody doings at Shechem, have
forfeited their right of inheritance to their father's blessing. It
must fall to Judah, the fourth son, from whose progeny Tamar
will have to receive the seed; but if not from one of them, then
it must be from Judah himself. It is a fact that the legend names
her son Perez, fathered by Judah, as an ancestor of David; several references are also made by Thomas Mann to the Messianic salvation that is to come from the seed of David. The story of the
magnificent, somber woman Tamar and her Astarte-like determination is itself a masterpiece within the wider framework of
Thomas Mann's novel. Her significance within the conceptual

unity of the whole, however, derives from the way she helps to characterize Judah as he yields to the temptress, which serves to emphasize the relationship between his guilt-ridden conscience and his eventual emergence as the bearer of the blessing.

As the novel nears its end Judah comes impressively to the fore as leader and spokesman for his brothers. When the Governor of Egypt, still unrecognized by the brothers, demands that Benjamin be surrendered to him, Judah comes forward with a stirring plea for the youngest, offering to give himself up instead, to atone for his old sin against his brother Joseph, which he now confesses. At this point Thomas Mann heightens the traditional account by many skillful touches that lend stature and dignity to the figure of Judah. At the end, the lion with the ailing conscience stands amazed, saying to himself: "Who would have thought it? For the oil is trickling down on my head, God have mercy on me, for I am the one."

But what of Joseph's blessing? Unquestionably his father had often toyed with the idea that he, who was beautiful, witty, and charming, the son of Rachel, the grievously beloved, might be raised above the heads of the sons of Leah and the sons of the maid servants, to be Israel's heir. For Jacob, we are told at the very beginning of this long story, had two passions: God and Rachel. Thomas Mann was fully aware of the impressive fact that the story of Jacob, who wrestled for God, and won the name of Israel, is also the oldest account we have of a personal love. Whatever is great and new in the world is brought into it not by the undifferentiated mass which clings necessarily to traditional forms but by the *individual* with the vitality and the instinct to *choose* for himself. In this case, the individual decided against the multitude of nature deities bound to their special localities, and for the one, universal God; and decided also against the personally indifferent marriage which is concerned only with perpetuating the tribe, insisting instead on a love-match with the one woman of his choice. Jacob's two passions are accordingly of identical origin; they are not equal in rank, however. This is the painful insight to which the patriarch has attained and which Joseph must accept.

Probably the most profound turn Thomas Mann has given to the traditional version is his identification of the distinguishing coat of many colors—which Joseph obtains from his father by his coaxing—with the multicolored veil worn by Leah on that fateful night when she entered Jacob's tent in Rachel's stead. "Leah was only arrayed in it but Rachel was the owner of the robe . . . I and my mother are one . . . and Jacob means Rachel when he looks at me." So speaks Joseph, and so it is. The bestowal of the veil is indeed the strongest sign of Jacob's deep-rooted predilection for the beautiful son of Rachel; it very nearly proves that he has been designated as the heir of Israel, sufficiently to infuriate the brothers so that they tear it to shreds and throw the boy into the well.

Twice does Joseph go down into the pit, and twice he rises again. But at his second resurrection he has learned enough to restrain his naive self-complacency and his supercilious playfulness; despite his worldly splendor he is not too surprised to find that he is not to be the bearer of the blessing. His life was "play and playing . . . approaching salvation yet not quite seriously a calling or a gift." Such is Thomas Mann's final verdict of ineradicable mistrust against the function of the artist, the poet.

Jacob has also learned much in twenty years of sorrow and endless mourning for his beloved lost son. He has realized that he had yielded too completely to his second great passion, his love for Rachel, and that God's blessing was not meant for the lovely one. This quiet tragedy of Jacob's makes the chapter entitled "Of Withholding Love," to my mind, the most moving of the entire novel. It tells of the meeting between Jacob and the son he had believed to be dead. When the old man whispers into the ear of his dearest son: "My heart loved you and will always love you, whether you are alive or dead. . . . But God tore your garment . . ." Jacob goes on, saying: "He has raised you in a worldly way, not in the sense of salvation and the inheritance of the blessing. . . . Through you salvation is not to reach the peoples, and the leadership is denied to you . . . you are the set-apart . . . you are not like the fathers, for you are no spiritual prince, but a worldly one."

At this point it would seem that there is a gap between Thomas Mann's idea and the legendary plot he has chosen to be its vehicle. That the artist-thinker, the poet and dreamer becomes possessed of too much worldly power and glory, which estranges him from the path of true salvation, does not exactly correspond with our historical and our everyday experience. However, a poetic metaphor is no mathematical equation, dealing only with exact counterparts. Every attempt to express the purely abstract through sensuous forms can and must leave such dangling residues as this. It remains for us to note that Joseph, the friend of Pharaoh and Governor of Egypt, has absorbed enough of Abraham's blessing to become in the end, if not the bringer of salvation, at least a true and unassuming human being. What is, after all, Abraham's vital discovery which must be passed on to future generations? This emigrant from the land of Ur is resolved to serve none but the Highest. " 'One should serve the Highest alone!' Remarkable indeed. For the answer revealed a self-assertiveness which might be called excessive and arrogant. The man might have said to himself: 'What am I and of what avail is the human being in me? What mattereth it which little god or idol or minor deity I serve?' He would have had an easier time. But instead he said: 'I, Abram, and humanity within me, must serve the Highest and nought else.' And that was the beginning of it all."

That, indeed, is the beginning of everything. It is the beginning of individual life: liberation from dependency on anything less than the ultimate power. In a drama by Moritz Heiman it is said: "God is the pride in our breast." The discovery of this God leads to holding in low esteem all that is not the Whole. It reduces to their modest place all the idolized powers of nature and even the sun of earlier cults. And it teaches us also how insignificant all worldly honor and power become before that final pride in God, which can alone justify us. Joseph, in his dreamy self-love, had played so long at being the buried and resurrected god; yet when he makes himself known to his brothers, and Benjamin, released from the "indescribable" torment of knowing-while-not-knowing, cries aloud, hailing his brother as the risen one, "the inner prince who has overturned the great abode of the shadow of death," then Pharaoh's Vice-Regent replies: "Little one, do not talk, it is none of it so great nor so remote, and I have no such glory and the great thing of all is that we are twelve once more." —And so the pseudo-god has become a thoroughly honest man.

And when, at the very last, after Jacob's death and burial, the brothers fear that Joseph will seek revenge after all, he only smiles: "For a man who uses power only because he has it, against right and reason, is absurd. If he is not today, he will be. And it is the future we are interested in . . ." —In this way Thomas Mann allows us to see, at the end, how deeply his timeless story is bound up with our actuality. Deeply precisely because it is timeless, because it looks down on the struggle and the spasms of our time from the vantage point of eternal truth, not of temporal confusion. Primeval divine wisdom that leads to love, though the furious hatreds of our day try to destroy it;

primeval wisdom discloses itself in this Joseph tale, shedding
its light into the darkness in which we live.

Thomas Mann has called his great work "a game with
words." He does so by the same right by which Goethe, speaking of his *Faust II* in his last great letter to Wilhelm von Hum-
boldt, called it: "These very serious jests." Every poem, to be
sure, is such a "game with words"; provided that "the playful
spirit does not forget itself in play, and remains concern for
God." And it does remain so in the great work now completed by
the German novelist Thomas Mann, who was driven out of his
homeland.

[1945]

JOSEPH THE PROVIDER

Harry Levin

"Except a grain of wheat fall into the earth and die, it abideth by itself alone." To this text Mann's earlier works provide a comment, with their dying fall, their concern for the pathological, and their consciousness of isolation. The title of his first story was *Fallen*; the subject of his first novel, written at twenty-five, was the decadence of the German burgher; in a remarkable sequence of sketches he went on to expound the riddle of the artist, whose gifts were a blessing to mankind and a curse to himself. In 1918 Mann contributed to the German war effort his *Reflections of a Non-Political Man*, an earnest and unhappy defense of *Kultur* against such exponents of *Zivilisation* as his pacifist brother Heinrich. His own arguments for the old order were later ascribed to the authoritarian Naphta, and answered by the humanist Settembrini: "Everything is politics." Thus *The Magic Mountain*, written at fifty from the alpine summits of postwar internationalism, broadened the dialectic between art and society. The large-hearted Peeperkorn set an example of brotherhood and sacrifice; the convalescent Hans Castorp, singing a *lied* of Schubert, marched down again into the battles of the flatland. The Naphta-Settembrini debate could only be settled by force; taking a leaf from Turgenev's *Fathers and Sons*, Mann staged a duel between them; his liberal fired in the air and his fascist committed suicide. Germany would have to choose, his Russian heroine warned his ambivalent hero. Germany chose soon afterward—and Mann, after what must have been an agony of hesitation, chose the other side. Already *Mario and the Magician*, as early as 1929, had dramatized the fall of Italian fascism with the portentous detonation of a pistol-shot.

"But if it die," and in 1933, when the first volume of *Joseph and his Brothers* was published, Europe was nearing the crisis, "it beareth much fruit." With the publication of *Joseph the Provider*, the last volume of his tetralogy, Thomas Mann, looking toward his seventieth year and the completion of the Second World War—might be said to have reaped his harvest. His lit-

erary self-consciousness, the conviction of his high calling, accentuates the parallel between himself and his latest hero, and
allows him to look—with Joseph's detached attitude of irony
and complacency—upon the vicissitudes that have turned his
exile into a triumph. The story-teller's wandering star, which
he so poignantly invoked at the outset of his story and of his
wanderings, has brought him a long way. It has ended by bringing him the kind of public reception that Joseph received at
the foreign court of Egypt: even the ceremony of "gliding" is
not without its analogies in the sphere of publishng and review-
ing. Just as Joseph considers the Egyptians a "quaint and
comic" people, so Mann, in the environs of Hollywood, must know
what it feels like to live in a "monkey-land." He must also know
the significance of the gesture he made when he came to America a few years ago: the isolated artist taking out his citizenship
papers. And American fiction, with its symbolist traditions, offers
an appropriate haven for his writing. We cannot read of the declining Buddenbrook family or of Hans Castorp lost in the snow
without recalling the ponderous fancy that plays around Judge
Pyncheon in *The House of the Seven Gables* or the allegorical
zeal that glosses the whiteness of the whale in *Moby-Dick*.

We are less likely to remember that Mann is still working in
the Goethean tradition of the pedagogical novel. That genre, to
our way of thinking, is scarcely a novel at all; but the forms of
fiction, always protean, are changing faster than ever today. Once
more we seem to be accustoming ourselves to didacticism in the
arts; indeed hagiography has become a best-seller. Hence it is
not impertinent to suggest, of a writer who has just completed
a prose narrative of more than two thousand pages, that he is
scarcely a novelist. (Neither was Sterne, and Mann has recently
testified to the stimulation his work derived from *Tristram
Shandy*.) Mann is more interested in projecting ideas than in
telling stories. Both *Buddenbrooks* and *The Magic Mountain*
were conceived as short stories, and then amplified with Teutonic thoroughness to their encyclopedic scale. As for the Joseph
story, it would be hard to improve upon the succinct narration of
Genesis xxv-1, and Mann has not tried. He is rather a commen-
tator than a narrator; he comments so fully on the circumstances
and implications of his theme that little is left for the critic except to admire. Repeating—or perhaps we should say anticipating
—Schiller's distinction between naive and sentimental poetry,
Mann is acutely aware of the distance that separates primitive
myth from modern knowledge. He bridges it by playing the scho-

liast, enveloping his text in word-play and numerology, notes and queries, exegetics and homiletics. A full page of Talmudic explication follows the three words, "I am he." Often the very simplest assumption requires the most complicated explanation. Sometimes the reader nods, and sometimes the author, as when he calls photography to his aid. Such imagery helps us to visualize not Joseph, but a German tourist in pith helmet and sun-glasses.

To hold your audience, while discarding the habitual devices and advantage of the *raconteur,* is a technical feat which few writers could accomplish. Mann does this by sustaining a rich texture, by embroidering what he has called—referring to the imaginary masterpiece of Gustave von Aschenbach—a "tapestry-novel." With a virtuosity which we may recognize, if not appreciate, he echoes the sonorities of Luther's German; we may well be grateful for Mrs. Lowe-Porter's skill in handling the comparable English of King James. If the book is not a novel, it is a fruitful collaboration of poetry and scholarship, a brilliant exercise of the historical imagination, a striking exhibit in the museum of latter-day culture. Mann's development out of naturalism toward symbolism—"from the bourgeois and individual to the typical and mythical," in his own significant phrase—is thoroughly consistent; for he is continually seeking the symbolic in the temporal, continually finding "the eternal present." Writing of the twentieth century A. D., he indicates the typical in a welter of particulars. Writing of the fourteenth century B. C., he particularizes his archetypes, as Joseph candidly admits. Into the deep well of the past Mann has taken his naturalistic equipment; he has conveyed life out of the tombs that the Egyptologists have excavated; he has created some memorable vistas of the ancient world, not quite so vivid as Flaubert's perhaps, but impressively solid. As if it were yesterday, or indeed today, he has re-created the New Kingdom at the end of the Eighteenth Dynasty. He even permits us an archeologically accurate glimpse of the perennially fascinating Nefertiti. He plausibly identifies the Biblical Pharaoh with the youthful mystic Ikhnaton, whose cult of the sun-god does not seem far removed from prehistoric Jewish monotheism. Mann thereby strengthens the identification between his mythical theme and our contemporary diaspora.

Our reviving preoccupation with myth, he has elsewhere stated, represents "an early and primitive stage in the life of humanity, but a late and mature one in the life of the individual." Taking as long a retrospect as the mind can reach, the saga of Joseph is a work of old age. Stately and studied, visionary and discursive, it has the minor key and the complex orchestration, the grand manner and the flagging intensity, that we expect from the later works of the masters. In its cyclic structure it closely parallels the contemporaneous productions of Joyce and Eliot: "In my end is my beginning." The tale has been told—and Mann's repetitions and anticipations stress the point—not once nor twice but many times. Everything has happened before and will happen again. "After all it was a sacred play," the moribund Jacob declares by way of epilogue. Characters enact their parts with the sense of fulfilling a pattern, breaking out into songs and rhymes at the happy ending. Ikhnaton is half-embarrassed in his role of *deus ex machina*, Joseph supremely confident as he reincarnates the mystery of Adonis. Since he is not merely the dying god but also the hermetic trickster, "not only a prophet but a rogue as well," his career is picaresque as well as prophetic. Something of a prig, something of a show-off, he has flaunted his marvelous dreams and his coat of many colors. His sin has been artistic self-absorption; the favorite son has held aloof from his brethren. He must learn to place his gifts at the disposal of society, to interpret the dreams of others. Literally he has gone down into the foul pit; figuratively he has gone down into the nether world of Egypt; still a third time he must go down into the house of bondage before he can emerge triumphant, bringing fruitfulness to the land. The downward movement of the first three volumes ripens into the success story of *Joseph the Provider*.

For provision is foresight; in telling, as Mann points out, there is an element of foretellnig; and his eyes, as he approaches the climax of the epos, turn toward the future. The artist, never a mere custodian of tradition, is forever *rerum novarum cupidus*. Having been ushered in by a Dantesque introduction, a vertiginous "Descent into Hell," the cycle is now rounded out by a "Prelude in the Upper Circles," spoken by a Miltonic angel with a cosmic sense of humor. To suggest still further continuities, the disturbing episode of Tamar is interpolated, with its promise for the Messianic line of David and the subsequent cycle of Jesus. Mann's self-confessed "mania for treatment *ab ovo*" has taken him back to the cradles of civilization in Ur of the Chaldees and the valley of the Nile. His far-ranging prospect, not less timely than timeless, extends to the current outposts of UNRRA. To a world which is undergoing the widest realization of Pharaoh's nightmares, Mann offers the newest application of Joseph's prophecies. Reading between the hieroglyphics, they all add up to a planned economy: the stars, the sheaves, the dying grain, the bread and wine of communion, the lean and fat kine of scarcity and abundance. Joseph himself, no longer a scribe and a slave, must now be a minister of agriculture with a global conscience. It is hardly coincidental that, in Mann's lecture on *The Theme of the Joseph Novels*, he expressed such warm admiration for Henry Wallace. Joseph's agrarian reforms, his ever-normal granary, his rationing and taxation, his exploitation of the rich barons and generosity toward the little men, his tact with the priests of Amon, his regulation of business, his socialization of property, his Nile Valley Authority, his Office of Price Administration—his platform, in short, should win the liberal vote. Osiris comes forth by day and lo, a New Deal! "And ye shall eat the fat of the land," we read in the Bible and John Steinbeck.

It is strange how so familiar a tale can maintain its suspense. Each successive book involves the protagonist in a more entangled set of human relationships: ancestry in the first, brotherhood in the second, sex in the third. In the fourth book all of these conflicts attain their resolution. No recognition-scene is more strongly charged with conflicting emotions than the meeting between Joseph and his father, and Mann is at his masterly best in treating "the painfully beautiful motif of reunion." The paternal quest of so many modern writers ends here in the patriarch's arms. The *Brüderkriegs* of recurrent folklore resolves in forgiveness and reconciliation. For resisting temptation Joseph has already paid the penalty; now he reaps the reward. As he fulfils his mission and emerges from Mann's commentary, he is no longer a portrait of the artist, nor the culture hero of a persecuted race; he is civilization itself. And Mann, by the unanswerable dialectic of events, has become our most enlightening *Zivilisationsliterat*—not less enlightening because he has brought along, to the heights of his final accomplishment, his darker vision of the depths. His final symbol is the Thummim, the synthesis of light and shade, blessing and curse. "What constitutes civilized life is that the binding and traditional depth shall fulfil itself in the freedom of God which belongs to the I," he has learned. The ego, in discovering the idea of God, has emancipated itself from collective unconsciousness. Having veered toward the opposite extreme of artistic individualism, it has gradually found its ultimate equilibrium in the recognition of social responsibilities. It has lived up to the original covenant. "And," to let the author supply the most important footnote, "the contrast between esthetic and civic tendencies, between isolation and community, between individual and collective is fabulously neutralized."

Between the thesis of the *Bürger* and the antithesis of the *Künstler,* the dialectical interchange is now complete. Mann has vastly changed, and so has the old Hanseatic town of Lübeck, since the days when he described himself to his fellow citizens as "a bourgeois story-teller." As a citizen of the world, a *Weltbürger,* in the years that have hurriedly followed the Weimar Republic, he has painfully adumbrated his own conception of the city of men. Humanistic as well as humanitarian, this would unite the best features of Athens and Moscow; it would realize the contrasting ideals of Hölderlin and Marx. And if it is somewhat rhetorically proclaimed in Mann's articles and speeches, it is imaginatively approximated in his later fiction—particularly in *Joseph the Provider.* Consequently, the outcome of Mann's tetralogy is life and fertility, where the burden of Wagner's was death and destruction. Always the exponent of German culture, Mann, beginning to write in its decadent period, premised his writing on Nietzsche's definition of a human being: "the sick animal." Inevitably, as Mann's position became more central, his biography has become what he once termed an *imitatio Goethe,* and his emphasis has shifted from sickness to health—in Goethe's terms, from romanticism to classicism. In an early sketch, *A Weary Hour,* Mann associated the artist's vocation with the sickly genius of Schiller. In *The Beloved Returns,* gravitating toward his healthier and more cosmopolitan model, Mann has latterly reenacted Goethe's quarrel with his short-sighted countrymen: "They think they are Germany—but I am."

It is good to be reminded of that other Germany, whose voice now rises with some of its former authority above the Tohu-Bohu of muddled motives and opportunistic attitudes, whose recuperating wisdom will be profoundly needed in the epoch of privation and plenty that lies ahead. The immediate situation confronting Europe, which is rather a famine than a feast, hardly accords with the festival spirit of Mann's concluding volume. But his love-feast is the necessary sequel to the "feast of death" that was predicated by his military conclusion to *The Magic Mountain.* The naturalism of *Buddenbrooks* reached its last decaying stage in Mann's detailed prognosis of a typhoid case. The symbolism of *The Magic Mountain,* taking the sanatorium as its point of departure, was basically therapeutic. But the upward direction of Hans Castorp's pilgrimage terminated in a sudden descent, while Joseph's underground explorations—happily end-

ing after many ups and downs—ascend toward an *O altitudo!*
On that rarefied level it is not Joseph but his descendant, it is
Moses who appears in a postscript as Mann's avatar. The Germans, by an ironic reversal of circumstance, are now identified
with the children of Israel; while the expatriate writer, no longer
a displaced person, is virtually recognized as the father of his
people. In *The Tables of the Law* he does not lead them out of
the wilderness; he righteously administers a shattering rebuke
for the profanation of their heritage. Mann's recent decision to
make this country his Pisgah will not make milk and honey flow
in Germany. His continued presence, however, should enlarge
our own perspective. It is his contribution as much as anyone's,
if we can look back to the war and say, as Karl Jaspers said at
the rededication of the Heidelberg Medical School: "We have won
insights into the reality of the world and man and of ourselves."

[1946]

THE JOSEPH NOVELS

Thomas Mann

I

It is, perhaps, not a matter of indifference to those who listen to an address to know the inner circumstances and the feelings of the speaker standing before his audience. Let me begin, therefore, with the statement that this is a precious and great, a festive and stirring hour for me. To speak here, not as a stranger or outsider, but, to a degree, in an official capacity, as a member of the staff of the Library of Congress—that is a great honor, a great joy for me.

It is a fortunate coincidence that the topic on which I am to speak is in itself a festive topic, not only because all art as such has, or should have, a festive character, but because a literary work is to be discussed whose very object is the idea and nature of the festival.

You have been told, of course, that I am to speak about *Joseph and His Brothers,* a tetralogy of novels, or epic in prose, of which the final volume, *Joseph the Provider,* is just about to be completed. Let me say first that I was quite startled and disconcerted when Archibald MacLeish suggested this book to me as my topic for tonight—I was much more inclined to refuse than to accept. Would it not seem terribly presumptuous, vain, and egocentric if I talked today, and here, about my own affairs, my own work—in other words, about highly personal and private matters instead of general and important ones, of the great cares and hopes of our time, of the war and its objectives?

This is a time when it makes almost no difference what we talk about—we always talk about one and the same thing. Categories crumble, the borderlines between the different spheres of human thought become unessential.

Once it was possible to distinguish between a "purely aesthetic," "purely philosophic," "purely religious" sphere and the sphere of politics, of human society, of national and international community life, and to declare that we were interested in the

Originally delivered as an address at the Library of Congress.

one but not in the other. This is no longer possible. We are interested in the whole or we are interested in nothing. "Totalitarian" is an oppressive word in its strictly political meaning; we
do not like to hear it because it signifies the voracious absorption
of all things human by the state. But then, we are indeed living
in a totalitarian world, a world of totality, of spiritual unity and
collective responsibility, before which all sovereignties have to
abdicate. Unity is the word of the historic hour. The world wants
to become *one*, all the way, in practical reality, down to economic
matters. It is a world of infinitely mutual *implications;* and to
talk about belletristic literature, about a novel, is not necessarily
insipid infidelity toward the great and burning concerns of our
time, and toward the plight, the struggle, the longing of humanity. Of course, it depends a little on the novel.

I have often been asked what induced me to transform the
Biblical legend of the Egyptian Joseph into a broad cycle of
novels requiring many years of work. In answering this question
there is little importance in the circumstances which prompted
me, almost a decade and a half ago when I was still in Munich,
to reread the story in my old ancestral Bible. Suffice it to say that
I was delighted and that immediately a preliminary probing and
productive searching began in my mind as to what it would be
like to renew and to reproduce this charming story in fresh narrative and with modern means—with *all* modern means, with the
spiritual ones and the technical ones.

II

Almost immediately these inner experiments significantly associated themselves with the thought of a tradition: the thought
of Goethe in fact, who relates in his memoirs, *Dichtung und
Wahrheit*, how he as a boy had dictated the Joseph story to a
friend and in doing so had woven it into a broad narrative. However, it soon met the fate of destruction because, in the author's
own judgment, it still lacked too much in "substance." As an explanation of this youthful and premature venture the sixty-
year-old Goethe observes: "This natural story is highly amiable;
only it seems too short, and one is tempted to carry it out in all
its details."

How strange! Immediately, these words from *Dichtung und
Wahrheit* came to my mind, in the midst of my reveries. They
were in my memory, I did not have to reread them, and indeed
they seem most fitting as the motto for what I then undertook.
They furnish the simplest and most plausible explanation for

my venture. The temptation which the young Goethe had naively followed—namely, to carry out the short legendary report of Genesis in "all its details"—repeated itself in my case at a stage of my life when the poetic execution could obtain definite human and spiritual substance as well. But what does that mean? It is exactness, realization; it is to draw into proximity something very remote and vague, so that you believe you see it with your eyes and grasp it with your hands, and you think that finally you have learned the definite truth about it.

I still remember how amused I was, and how much of a compliment I considered it, when my copyist in Munich, brought me the typewritten copy of the first volume, *The Stories of Jacob*, and said: "Now we know at last how all this actually happened." That was touching—for, after all, it did not happen. The exactness, the realism are fictional—they are play and artful illusion, they are realization and visualization forcibly brought about by all the means of language, psychology, presentation, and in addition critical comment; and humor, despite all human seriousness, is their soul. What above all is inspired by humor in the book is the analysis and scientific research, which are, just like the narrative and the descriptions, a means of establishing reality; and the command to the artist to create forms and not to talk is invalid in this case.

The reasoning also is playful; it is not really the language of the author but of the work itself; it has been incorporated in its linguistic sphere; it is indirect, a stylized and bantering language, a contribution to the pseudo-exactness, very close to persiflage and at any rate to irony; for scientific treatment of wholly unscientific and legendary matters is pure irony.

It is quite possible that such secret charms played their part at the time of the earliest conception of the work. But this does not answer the question as to how I came to select this archaic subject matter from the dawn of mankind. Different circumstances, some of a personal and others of a general temporal character, contributed to it. The readiness is all. As a man and as an artist, I must somehow have been in *readiness* to be productively attracted by such subject matter, and my Bible reading was not mere chance. The various stages of life have different inclinations, claims, tendencies of taste—as well as abilities and advantages. It is probably a rule that in certain years the taste for all purely individual and particular phenomena, for the individual case, for the "bourgeois" aspect in the widest sense of the word, fades out gradually. Instead the typical, the eternally

human, eternally recurring, timeless—in short, the mythical—
steps into the foreground of interest.

The attainment of the mythical viewpoint is of decisive
importance in the life of the narrator; it signifies a peculiar enhancement of his artistic mood, a new serenity in recognizing
and shaping which, as I suggested before, is ordinarily reserved
for the later years of life: for the mythical, it is true, represents
an early and primitive stage in the life of humanity, but a late
and mature one in the life of the individual.

There, the word "humanity" has been pronounced—in connection with the ideas of the timelessly typical and the mythical
it automatically made its appearance. I had been in readiness to
feel productively attracted by a subject matter like the Joseph
legend because of the turning of my taste away from the bourgeois toward the mythical aspect. But at the same time I was
in readiness for it because of my disposition for generally human
feeling and thinking,—I mean a feeling and thinking in human
terms,—a disposition which was not only the product of my individual time and stage of life but that of the time at large, and
in general of *our* time, of the historic convulsions, adventures,
and tribulations by which the question of man, the very problem
of humanity, was presented to us as an indivisible whole and
imposed upon our conscience as hardly ever to a generation before us.

I believe that the sufferings and stirring adventures through
which humanity has been going now for decades will bring forth
a new, deepened feeling of humanity, indeed a new *Humanism*,
remote from all shallow optimism but full of sympathy, which
will be only too necessary for the work of reconstruction that
will confront us after the tremendous moral and material de-
vastations, after the collapse of the accustomed world. In order
to build up, or at least lay the foundations for, the new, better,
happier, and more social world, freed from unnecessary suffering, which we want our children and grandchildren to have—the
City of Man, as I should like to call it—we shall need a binding
and all-determining basic pathos, guiding us all the way to detailed and practical matters; we shall need sympathy for it, and
love. And with all this the mythical novel has something to do
which was conceived in 1925 and of which I am speaking to you:
it is by no means an out-of-the-way, evasive, extra-timely product, but inspired by an interest in humanity transcending the
individual: a humorous, ironically softened—I am tempted to say
a "bashful" poem of man.

Rather, it turned out that way unintentionally; for the author was far from attributing it this quality in the beginning. Once again it came to pass that a work developed a much greater aspiration than was inherent in the rather skeptical and by no means ambitious nature of the one on whom it imposed itself, and from whom it exacted efforts far beyond all plans and expectations.

III

To begin is always terribly difficult. Until one feels oneself master of a subject, until one learns the language it speaks, and can reproduce it, much courting and laboring, a long inner familiarization, are required. But what I planned was so new and unusual that never did I beat about the bush longer than this time. There was the need of establishing contact with a strange world, the primitive and mythical world; and to "make contact" in the poetic sense of the word signifies something very complicated, intimate—a penetration, carried to identification and self-substitution, so that something can be created which is called "style" and which is always a unique and complete amalgamation of the artist with the subject.

How much of an adventure I considered this mythical enterprise of mine is indicated by the introduction to *The Stories of Jacob,* the first volume of *Joseph and His Brothers,* which forms the anthropological prelude to the whole work. Entitled "Descent into Hell," it is a fantastical essay which seems like the cumbersome preparation for a risky expedition—a journey down into the depths of the past, a trip to the "mothers." The overture was sixty-four pages long: that might have made me suspicious in regard to the proportions of the whole, and did so to a degree—especially as I had decided that the personal story of Joseph alone would not do, but that the primeval and original story, the history of the world, demanded to be included at least in perspective. The stories of Jacob filled a heavy volume. In mingled order, anticipating and reverting, I recited them, strangely entertained by the novelty of dealing with human beings who did not quite know who they were or who knew it in a more pious, deeply exact way than the modern individual—beings whose identity was open in back and included the past with which they identified themselves, in whose steps they trod, and which again became present through them.

Novarum rerum cupidus—this characteristic fits the artist better than anyone else. Nobody is more bored than he by the old and worn out, and more impatient for the new, although nobody on the other hand is more bound to tradition than he is. Audacity in confinement, fulfillment of tradition with exciting news—that is really his calling and his business, and the conviction that "such a thing has not been done before" is the indispensable motor of all his industry. I have always needed this spurring conviction in order to accompish anything; and it seemed to me that I had never experienced it more strongly than this time.

The Stories of Jacob and its successor, The Young Joseph, were completed while I was still in Germany. During my work on the third volume, Joseph in Egypt, the break in my outward existence occurred: the trip from which I could not return, the sudden loss of my life's basis—the larger part of Joseph in Egypt is work born in exile. My oldest daughter, who dared to return to our already confiscated house in Munich after the revolution, recovered the manuscript and brought it to me in Southern France; and slowly, after the first shock of my new, uprooted situation, I resumed the work which was continued and completed in the Swiss refuge which we enjoyed for five years.

Now, then, the narrative enters into the highly developed and sophisticated cultural sphere of the Nile Empire, which through sympathy and reading had been familiar to me since the time of my boyhood, so that I knew more about it than even the teacher who during Religion Class had questioned us twelve-year-old boys as to the name of the holy steer of the ancient Egyptians. I showed that I was eager to answer, and was called upon. "Chapi," I said. That was wrong in the opinion of the teacher. He reproached me for having raised my hand when I knew only nonsense. "Apis" was the right name, he corrected me angrily. But "Apis" is only the Latinization or Hellenization of the authentic Egyptian name which I had given. The people of Keme said "Chapi." I knew better than the good man, but discipline did not allow me to enlighten him about it. I kept silent—and all my life I have not forgiven myself for this silence before false authority. An American boy would certainly have spoken up.

Occasionally I thought of this early incident while I was writing Joseph in Egypt. A work must have long roots in my life, secret connections must lead from it to earliest childhood dreams, if I am to consider myself entitled to it, if I am to believe in the legitimacy of what I am doing. The arbitrary reaching for a subject to which one does not have traditional claims of sympathy and knowledge seems senseless and amateurish.

Because of its erotic content, this third volume is the most novel-like part of this work which, as a whole, had to make of the novel something different from what is generally understood by this term. The variability of this literary genre has always been considerable. Today, however, it almost looks as though nothing counts any more in the domain of the novel except what is no longer a novel. Perhaps it was always that way. As far as *Joseph in Egypt* is concerned, you will find that its novel-like erotic content too has been turned into the mythical by stylization, despite all psychology. That holds true particularly for the sexual satire which is centered in the figures of the two dwarfs: the asexual one in his kindly nothingness, and Dudu, the malicious and procreative midget. In a humorous spirit a connection is shown here between the sexual and arch-evil, a connection which must help to reconcile us to Joseph's "chastity," his resistance to the desires of his unfortunate mistress, as given by the Biblical model.

IV

This third of the Joseph novels grew under the constellation of my parting from Germany. The fourth grew under that of my parting from Europe. *Joseph the Provider,* the final part of the work, which brings its length to over 2000 pages, came into being entirely under America's sky—in fact, largely under the serene, Egyptian-like sky of California.

Now Potiphar's demoted favorite slaves as a prisoner in a Nile fortress commanded by a good man—so good a man that Joseph later makes him his major-domo, accepting him into the divine story as a helpful friend. In the fortress Joseph is commissioned to act as a valet to the distinguished servants of the royal court who arrive one day as prisoners under investigation: the baker and the cupbearer. Now the dreamer interprets dreams, and the day comes when he is taken from the prison in haste and stands before Pharaoh. He is thirty years old then and Pharaoh is seventeen. This hypersensitive and tender youth, a searcher after God like Joseph's forefathers, and enamored of a dreamy religion of love, has ascended to the throne during the time of Joseph's imprisonment. He is an anticipating, a premature Christian—the mythical prototype of those who are on the right way but are not the right ones for that way. It is a widely ramified sequence of chapters in which Joseph gains the unlimited confidence of the young ruler, and at whose end he receives the ring of power.

Now he is viceroy, takes the well-known measures of Providence for the coming famine, and enters into a matrimony of state with Asnath, daughter of the sun priest of On-Heliopolis. But here the story returns from the Egyptian soil to the theatre of the first and second volumes, to Canaan, and a complete long short-story is interpolated which gives to this volume its outstanding female character, as the first volume had it in the person of the lovely Rachel, the third volume in the fruitlessly desiring Mut-em-enet. It is Tamar, the daughter-in-law of Judah, a figure of grand style, the female paradigm of determination whose spiritual ambition scorns no means that might help her, the pagan child of Baal, to get on the path of Promise and to become a forebear of the Messiah.

Now the famine assumes reality, and dramatically the well-known action takes its course, which is nothing but a precious childhood memory, and for which the curiosity of the reader can be captivated only by the most detailed presentation and visualization of every how and why. The arrival of the brothers, the meeting with the prescient Benjamin, the play with the silver cup, the great scene of recognition, the scene in which a musical child sings to the aged Jacob that his son Joseph is alive and lord over the land of Egypt—in minute detail we learn (and some day my Munich copyist, too, will probably learn) how it all really happened. The novel extends to the solemn passing away of Jacob, the father, in the land of Goshen. And with the tremendous procession which brings home the body of the patriarch, so that he may rest in the twofold cave with his fathers, ends the whole work which through one and a half decades of outer stress was my steady companion.

Some people were inclined to regard *Joseph and His Brothers* as a Jewish novel, even as merely a novel for Jews. Well, the selection of the Old Testament subject was certainly not mere accident; most certainly there were hidden, defiantly polemic connections between it and certain tendencies of our time which I always found repulsive from the bottom of my soul: the growing vulgar anti-Semitism which is an essential part of the Fascist mob-myth, and which commits the brutish denial of the fact that Judaism and Hellenism are the two principal pillars upon which our Occidental civilization rests. To write a novel of the Jewish spirit was timely just because it seemed untimely. And, it is true, my story always follows the dates of Genesis with semi-jocular faithfulness, and often reads like an exegesis and amplification of the Torah, like a rabbinical Midrash. And yet all that is Jewish throughout the work is merely foreground, just as the

Hebrew cadence of its diction is only foreground, only one style element among others, only *one* stratum of its language which strangely fuses the archaic and the modern, the epical and analytical.

In the last book is a poem, the song of annunciation which the musical child sings for the aged Jacob, and which is an odd composition of psalter recollections and little verses of the German romantic type. That is an example of the character of the whole work, which seeks to blend a great many things, and because it conceives and imagines everything human as a unity it borrows its motives, memories, allusions, as well as linguistic sounds from many spheres. Just as all the Jewish legends are based on other, timeless mythologies, and made transparent by them, so Joseph, the hero, is also a transparent figure, changing with the illumination in vexatory fashion: he is, with a great deal of consciousness, an Adonis and a Tammuz figure; but then he perceptibly slides into a Hermes part, the part of the mundane and skillful businessman and the intelligent profit producer among the gods; and in his great conversation with Pharaoh the mythologies of all the world, the Hebraic, Babylonian, Egyptian, and Greek, are mingled so thoroughly that one will hardly be aware of holding a Biblical Jewish storybook in one's hands.

V

There is a symptom for the innate character of a work, for the category toward which it strives, the opinion it secretly has of itself. That is the reading matter which the author prefers and which he considers helpful while working on it. I am not thinking in this connection about factual sources and material research, but about great works of literature which in a broad sense seem related to his own effort, models whose contemplation keeps him in the right mood, and which he seeks to emulate. All that can be of no help, does not fit, has no reference to the subject, is hygienically excluded—it is not conducive at the moment and therefore disallowed. Well then, such strengthening reading during the last Joseph years was provided by two books: Laurence Sterne's *Tristram Shandy* and Goethe's *Faust* —a perplexing combination, but each of the two heterogeneous works had its particular function as a stimulant; and in this connection it was a pleasure for me to know that Goethe had called Sterne one of the finest intellects that had ever lived.

Naturally, it was the humorous side of the *Joseph* which profited by this reading. Sterne's wealth of humorous expressions and inventions, his genuine comical technique, attracted me, for to refresh my work I needed something like this. And then, Goethe's *Faust*—this life's work and linguistic monument developed from a tender, lyrical germ cell, this enormous mixture of magic opera and mankind's tragedy, of puppet show and cosmic poem. Time and again I returned to this inexhaustible source— especially to the second part, to the Helena scenes, the classical Walpurgis Night—and this fixation, this insatiable admiration, indicated the secret immodesty of my own endeavors, they revealed the direction in which the ambition of the Joseph story pointed—its own, for the author as usual had at the outset been quite innocent of such ambition.

Faust is a symbol of humanity, and to become something like that in my hands was the clandestine tendency of the Joseph story. I told about beginnings, where everything came into being for the first time. That was the attractive novelty, the uncommon amusement of this kind of fable telling—that everything was there for the first time, that one foundation took place after the other, the foundation of love, of envy, of hatred, of murder, and of much else. But this dominant originality is at the same time repetition, reflection, image, the result of rotation of the spheres which brings the upper, the starlike, into the lower regions; carries in turn, the worldly into the realm of the divine so that gods become men, men in turn become gods. The worldly finds itself pre-created in the realm of the stars, and the individual character seeks its dignity by tracing itself back to the timeless mythical pattern giving it presence.

I dwelled on the birth of the ego out of the mythical collective, the Abrahamitic ego which is pretentious enough to assume that man should serve only the Highest, from which assumption the discovery of God followed. The claim of the human ego to central importance is the premise for the discovery of God, and from the very first the pathos for the dignity of the ego is connected with that for the dignity of humanity.

At the same time, these humans remain confined in the mythical, the collective, to a large extent of their being. What they call spirit and culture is just the conviction that their lives are the embodiment of the myth; and their ego detaches itself from the collective in the same way that certain figures of Rodin wrest themselves out of the stone and awaken from it. Jacob, weighty with stories, is also such a half-detached figure: his solemness is still mythical and already individual; the cult which he devotes to his feelings, and for which he is punished by the

jealousy of the Highest, is the bland but proud assertion of an
ego which loftily feels itself the subject and hero of its stories.
It is still a patriarchial and respectable form of human individual-
ization and emancipation.

It grows far more bold and daring in the complicated case
of his son Joseph. There is one who has not only discovered
God, but knows how to "treat" Him; one who is not only the
hero of his stories, but also their director, indeed the one who
poetically "adorns" them; one who it is true still participates in
the collective and mythical, but in a banteringly spiritualized
and playful, purposefully conscious manner. In short, we see
how the ego in the process of its emancipation soon becomes an
artistic ego, attractive, delicate, and—endangered; a tender concern for the respectable father, but with inborn possibilities of
development and maturing that have not existed before. In its
youth the artistic ego is of inexcusable egocentricity: it lives
under the dangerous assumption that everybody must love it
more than himself. But because of a sympathy and friendliness
which nonetheless it never renounces, it finds its way into the
social, while it matures, and becomes the provider and benefactor of a foreign people and of its own. In Joseph the ego flows
back from arrogant absoluteness into the collective, the common;
and the contrast between artistic and civic tendencies, between
isolation and community, between individual and collective, is
fabulously neutralized—as, according to our hopes and our will,
it must be dissolved in the democracy of the future, the coöpera-
tion of free and divergent nations under the equalizing sceptor of
justice.

VI

A symbol of humanity—in a certain way my work was entitled to this secret opinion of itself. After all, from the original
and simple, the typical and canonical, it led to the complicated,
involved, late. The way from Canaan to the Egypt of the New
Kingdom is the way from the piously primitive, the God-crea-
ting God-contemplative idyl of the arch-fathers, to a highly developed and sophisticated culture with its luxuries and absurd
snobberies in a land of the grandchildren, a land whose atmosphere is so much to Joseph's taste because he is himself a grand-
child and a late soul.

The feeling for the way, the advancement, the change, the
development, is very strong in the book; its whole theology is
connected with it and derived from it: namely, from its concep-

tion of the Old Testament "bond" between God and man—from the conviction that God and man are mutually dependent upon each other in common aspiration for enhancement. For God too is subject to development; He too changes and advances, from the desert-like and demoniacal to the spiritual and holy; and He can do so without the help of the human spirit as little as the human spirit can without Him.

Were I to determine what I, personally, mean by religiousness, I should say it is *attentiveness* and *obedience*—attentiveness to the inner changes of the world, the mutation in the aspects of truth and right; obedience which loses no time in adjusting life and reality to these changes, this mutation, and thus in doing justice to the spirit. To live in sin is to live against the spirit, to cling to the antiquated, obsolete, and to continue to live in it because of inattentiveness and disobedience. And whenever the book speaks about the "concern with God" it speaks about the just fear of this sin and folly. "Concern with God" is not alone the creating of God in one's thoughts, and determining and recognizing Him, but principally the concern with IIis will with which ours must coincide; with the demands of the present, the postulate of the aeon, of the world hour. It is the intelligent listening to what the world spirit wants, to the new truth and necessity, and a special, religious concept of *stupidity* follows from that—the stupidity before God which does not know this concern, or complies with it as clumsily as Laban who still believes that he must slaughter his little son and bury him in the foundation of his house, a custom which once was quite beneficial but is so no longer.

Must I add that we owe the tribulations which we now have to endure, the catastrophe in which we are living, to the fact that we lacked intelligence toward God to a degree which had long become criminal? Europe, the world, was full of stale and outworn things, of evident obsolete and even sacrilegious anachronisms which had been clearly outdistanced by the world will and which we permitted to continue, in dull mind and in disobedience to this will. It is understood that the spirit is always ahead of reality, that reality follows it clumsily. But never, perhaps, had there existed before such pathological, such unmistakably dangerous tension—in the social, political, and economic life of the peoples—between truth and reality, between things long reached and accompished by the spirit and between things which still took the liberty of calling themselves reality; and foolish disobedience to the spirit or, religiously speaking to God's will, is undoubtedly the true cause for the world explosion which stuns us. But explosion is equalization, and I think that here in this hall is quite the right place to express the hope that after this war we—or our children—shall live in a world of happier equalization between spirit and reality, that we shall "win the peace." The word "peace" always has a religious ring, and what it signifies is a gift of intelligence before God.

You understand I am eager to prove that it is not wholly vain and idle to speak about my private work at a moment like this instead of general and important matters. I may tell myself that there are connections between my work and general and important matters—indeed underneath all badinage that is its secret motor. In a discreet and unpathetic manner, the case of mankind is tried in it; and therefore the manner in which this book treats the myth is so different from a certain contemporary manner of employing it—a malevolent and anti-human manner whose political name we all know.

After all, the word "myth" has a bad reputation nowadays —we only have to think of the title of the book which the "philosopher" of German Fascism, Rosenberg, the preceptor of Hitler, has given to his vicious textbook, *The Myth of the Twentieth Century*. So often in the last decades had the myth been abused as a means of obscurantic counter-revolution that a mythical novel like the *Joseph*, upon its first appearance, in evitably aroused the suspicion that its author was floating with the murky stream. This suspicion had to be discarded, for at a second glance a process could be observed similar to what happens in a battle when a captured gun is turned around and directed against the enemy. In this book the myth has been taken out of Fascist hands and humanized down to the last recess of its language. If posterity finds anything remarkable about it, it will be this.

In the idea of humanity, the human idea, the sense for the past and that for the future, tradition and revolution form a strange and, to my mind, infinitely attractive mixture. The slogan of the "conservative revolution" has played a pernicious part; Fascism has seized it as it seized the myth, and has pretended to be the conservative revolution. Its nature is fraud. But what better formula than just this "conservative revolution" could be found for the spirit and meaning of that famous speech which an American opponent of Fascism, Henry A. Wallace, Vice President of the United States of America, held before the members and guests of the Free World Association on May 8 of this year? This

speech, "The Price of Free World Victory," is, I think, a beautiful example of the unification of tradition and revolution in the
sphere of the Humane, the stirring proof that today the con-
serving and the revolutionary will are one and the same, are
simply the *good* will.

May I say that my composition is of a somewhat similar
nature? It bases its concept of piety upon the idea of time, of
change, of development, of advancement toward perfection—an
advancement for which God and man ally themselves; but at
the same time the idea of tradition plays in it a thematic part of
the first order. I related to you how a Goethe memory, a word
of his about the Joseph tale, entered into my first reveries when
I tried my hand at this subject; I also told you of the secret reference to Goethe's *Faust* which my work dared to take while it
grew. That was playful boldness which sprang from the sense of
tradition and succession and corrseponded to the inner nature of
my task, a mythical task. For what else is myth but succession
and recollection, the forming and coining of the present with the
past, the childlike identification with an admired idol—in short,
tradition? Myth is tradition, and to live in tradition means to
live in the myth.

VII

An artist's life is a life of *experience*, in manifold ways;
when it strives to follow the great, it also becomes a means of
experiencing greatness—not like the scientist, nor like the historian; not objectively and from without, but in a subjective,
practical, productive way. Three times, at different stages of my
life, have I lived under the prolonged tension of tasks which
have a certain affinity to greatness: at the age of twenty-five,
when I tried my hand at the novel of the German bourgeoisie,
Buddenbrooks; at the age of fifty, when in *The Magic Mountain*
I made a friendly *alter ego* pass through the adventures of European intellectual controversies; and between sixty and seventy,
when I told mankind's fairy tale of Joseph and his brothers. To
participate playfully in the consciousness of great creativeness
and to acquire thereby the right to a more familiar celebration of
greatness than the wholly inexperienced and unitiated possess—
that is something, that is worth a life. "That a man entertains
himself and does not spend his life like dull cattle," I have my
Joseph answer a critic of his mythical temerity, "is after all what
matters most; and what heights of entertainment he is able to
reach—that is what counts."

And now let me finally return to the fact which seems to me to have a certain symbolic value, after all—namely, that the mythical play of Joseph and his brothers, begun in Germany, continued in Switzerland, transplanted to America, was completed here, in contact with the American myth. For there is such a thing; you, too, live in a tradition here, walk in footsteps, in paternal footsteps, which you call your "Way of Life." The pioneer-like optimism and hearty faith in man, the mental youthfulness, the benevolent and confident ideas and principles upon which the Union was founded by the fathers, amount to the American myth, which is alive today.

In his biography, Goethe speaks about an "alleviation for humanity" effected by the American war of liberation; and the European emigration to America (which finds its way into the final parts of *Wilhelm Meister*) sprang from the constant desire to participate in this alleviation—it was the pilgrimage to a pure fountain of health. But the measure and the significance which this flight and migration has assumed at present are something new. The diaspora of European culture which we are witnessing, the arrival of so many of its bearers, representatives of all categories of science and art, to these shores; their more or less involuntary decision, transformed however into an *amor fati,* to complete their work in the American air of life—that is something very strange and unprecedented; it opens unexampled possibilities of exchange and equalization and may be supremely helpful in creating the new feeling of humanism of which I spoke. Our emigration thus assumes an entirely different significance from that of any former emigration: the significance of the coalescence of the hemispheres, of the unification of the earth. "Europe wants to become one"—that is long obsolete; the *earth* wants to become one. "Unification" is the word and command of the world hour, and the future belongs to the union of knowledge *and* hope; of profundity *and* courage; of faith *and* labor in the face of all doubt, and despite all doubt.

[1942]

PART III
Comparative

THOMAS MANN AND BENEDETTO CROCE

Lienhard Bergel

In 1932, Benedetto Croce dedicated his *History of Europe in the Nineteenth Century* to Thomas Mann with these words of Virgil to Dante:

> *This moment came thy thoughts*
> *Presented before mine, with similar act*
> *And countenance similar, so that from both*
> *I one design have framed.*

This fervent expression of a spiritual affinity, at the beginning of one of his major books, is the more significant since Croce has never dealt explicitly with Thomas Mann's writings, though he has frequently referred to them as confirming his own views. It is the purpose of this essay to establish the agreement between the world of Thomas Mann and that of Croce in their essential points.

Both writers begin their careers by studying the region of their origin: Thomas Mann finds his early subjects in Lübeck; Croce explores the political and cultural history of the old Kingdom of Naples. For Thomas Mann, the psychology of the artist and his position in society soon becomes a dominant theme; Croce's first philosophical concern is the nature of art and its place in the totality of human existence. Croce's *Esthetics* gradually grows into the comprehensive *Philosophy of the Spirit,* in which the theory of the contemplative activities of intuition and rational thinking is complemented by that of practical activity in the economico-political sphere. Similarly the world of *Tonio Kröger* enlarges into that of *The Magic Mountain* and the political essays.

This parallelism in the development of Croce and Thomas Mann is of organic necessity; it is an unfolding of problems which were potentially present from the outset. Croce's *Esthetics* contains the germ for the whole *Philosophy of the Spirit;* only because all other forms of the spirit were philosophically determined from the beginning was it possible for Croce to delimit the specific nature of art with such precision, and the fact that Croce's esthetics is part of an original and complete philosophical system, and not the product of a "specialist," accounts for its lasting and fruitful influence.

The distinguishing feature of Croce's esthetics is the new place it assigns to the intuitional faculty. Croce divests art and the artist of the mystic glory with which romanticism had surrounded them; here art is conceived no longer as "the final ballet which follows the opera and the drama and at which the audience might just as well choose not to be present," but as an "elementary fundamental indispensable form of the life of the spirit." The aristocratic and esoteric concept of art, which was that of the romanticists, is replaced by a democratic one, which recognizes in the artistic faculty a basic human activity, shared by all. The difference between the artist and the non-artist is no longer qualitative but merely quantitative. The artist ceases to be an exceptional individual subject to divine illumination.

For Thomas Mann also the artist loses most of his remote splendor. If the artist feels himself to be "exceptional," he finds in this a cause for suffering; he no longer basks in the romantic glory of the superman or the inspired priest or prophet, but humbly tries to find a place for himself. While Gerhart Hauptmann and Arthur Schnitzler are mainly concerned with the conduct of the artist as a private person, Thomas Mann searches consistently for an ethical justification of the existence of the artist in society. The romantic conception of the artist is carried to its extreme by Stefan George; Thomas Mann has repeatedly emphasized the difference between him and the prophet of the "new Reich." The only one among Thomas Mann's German contemporaries who came close to his views was the young Hofmannsthal, and Hofmannsthal's opposition to George rested to a large extent on convictions similar to those of Croce.

The romantic views on art and the artist have far-reaching historical implications. The cleavage between the artist and the non-artist is easily broadened until the artist is no longer bound by the common laws of ethics; the separation of art from other human activities leads to pseudo-mystical concepts of art as a way into a transcendental world. These are essential elements in nineteenth-century decadence, with its *paradis artificiels*, its *l'art pour l'art* and the haughty contempt of the artist for reality, particularly social reality. Croce's philosophy, particularly in its application to history, concerns itself to a large extent with the problem of decadence; the criticism and theoretical dissolution of modern decadence in all its aspects is one of its most beneficial services. An important instrument in this task is the *History of Europe in the Nineteenth Century*. Here the separation of the theoretical from the practical is recognized as the main feature of decadence. The consequences of this process are demonstrated as destroying man in his humanity; Croce scorns the "half men," the artists and thinkers who consider participation in the common affairs of man below their dignity. The course of the evil is traced from its beginnings, in what Croce calls "morbid" or "practical, sentimental and moral romanticism," to its most recent manifestations in the philosophy of brute force as exemplified by Bismarck and his contemporary disciples. This historical analysis finds its systematic complementation in Croce's writings on ethics and politics. Here the dialectical relationship between the theoretical and the practical is demonstrated, and ethico-political ectivity is defined as a synthesis between ideal and reality.

If we turn to Thomas Mann we find an exact parallel. Also for him the most urgent task becomes the bridging of the gap between the theoretical and artistic and the practical and political. Thomas Mann's criticism of romanticism has much in common with Croce's analysis of morbid tendencies in the nineteenth and twentieth centuries. But there is a difference in the way in which Croce and Thomas Mann deal with the same phenomenon. For Thomas Mann the probing into the problem of decadence is a form of self-medication; he is a patient whose healthy energies overcome an illness. The remarkable thing about Croce is that he has never been touched by the disease. Croce is of an intellectual robustness which is the envy of those who are less immune to infection; his treatment of the disease has the cold impersonal precision of the surgeon; it sometimes does not lack harshness and is more inclined to remove too much of the endangered tissue rather than too little. Thomas Mann, on the other hand, has a warmer understanding of the patient.

The question of decadence is intimately related with that of the relationship between Germany and Europe. Neither Croce nor Thomas Mann approaches the problem in the crude form in which it was frequently treated, particularly by French writers on romanticism to whom the role of Germany in the nineteenth century appears simply as a barbaric invasion. It is a fact, however, that Germany had developed many aspects of romanticism more fully than any other country, and, for good or bad, she had been the *magistra mundi* in these matters. Croce, in his *History of*

Europe, has shown how the morbid elements of romanticism, an irrational adoration of the past and a mystical glorification of brute force, had a better opportunity to flourish in Germany than in any other country because of her political backwardness. For Thomas Mann the world of German romanticism was a heritage, at first unquestioned, of the moral and intellectual atmosphere into which he was born; for Croce it was an artistic and philosophical complex of foreign origin, which had to be integrated into his own and different tradition. Croce was brought up among people who were accustomed to respect and revere *il libro tedesco;* Germany was the country foremost in his mind when he was a young man. The task for Thomas Mann was to reconcile his national heritage with the traditions of Western Europe from which Germany had broken away. Croce, as an Italian, was from the beginning in possession of those European criteria which Thomas Mann was to acquire gradually in the course of an often painful self-education; Croce was anxious to graft those elements of German romanticism upon the trunk of common European traditions as promised to thrive there. Their respective situations may be expressed in the simile which Croce uses in order to determine the relationship between linguistics and esthetics: "Both find themselves like workmen piercing a tunnel: at a certain point they must hear the voices of their companions who have been at work on the other side."

The two ends of the tunnel met. Thomas Mann's culminating formulation of his views on the German problem, his essay *Germany and the Germans,* has its counterpart in Croce's little book *Germany and Europe, A Spiritual Dissension,* which appeared a year earlier. Neither Croce nor Thomas Mann is an adherent of that popular school of thought concerning Germany, the "manhole theory": the Germans are basically good and healthy; their present situation may be compared to that of a man who inadvertently walked into a manhole and hurt his leg; all he needs to get well again is to be pulled out, treated sympathetically and well fed. Both Croce and Thomas Mann agree that the dissension between Germany and Europe has its deep roots in the past, that the evil is to be overcome only if it is recognized in its origin and in its historical manifestations. To them Germany is not the victim of an accident but a sufferer from a chronic disease; a mere treatment of symptoms will not lead to recovery.

In his historical analysis Croce is more radical than Thomas Mann. He goes further back in time, observing the tendency

toward national boasting and the effort at dominating Europe by
mere force, without the justification which may be found in ethical and intellectual superiority, in the Germanic tribes of the
migration, in the struggle of the medieval German emperors toward continental supremacy and in the first *Drang nach Osten*
of the Teutonic knights. Thomas Mann begins his historical survey with the Reformation. Their agreement in the evaluation of
Martin Luther and his time is remarkable. Here both observe the
beginning of the fundamental evil of German life: the separation of inner liberty from political liberty; here the breeding of
"half men" has its beginnings. In their reflections on Martin Luther both Croce and Thomas Mann observe another characteristic
of Germany: good and evil are intricately, almost inextricably
bound together; that which is good in them often becomes the
cause of their evil. It is the subject of most of Croce's writings
dealing with German matters to define more precisely this relationship between the good and the evil, to distinguish the
"dead" from the "living." It appears as though the products of
the German mind have a similarity to certain drugs: they are
poisonous in their state of rawness and become beneficial only
after they have been decomposed and chemically rebuilt and
filtered. Croce is the greatest living master in this art of analysis
and synthesis. If he has often occasion to say harsh words about
them, the Germans should never forget that Croce's work is one
of the few channels through which things German can join the
large stream which represents Europe.

In German philosophy Croce finds abstruseness and empty
professorial speculation, a contempt for reality, interspersed with
most fruitful conceptions. He demonstrates how the same philosophy which outside Germany contributed so significantly to the
development of the new political philosophy of liberalism, became inside Germany an instrument of political reaction; how
German historiography, the child of the new philosophy, for a
while the model of Europe, the special pride of the Germans
instead of stimulating healthy political activity became a play-
thing or an opiate in the hands of its most illustrious representatives, Rancke and Burckhardt, and, was turned into a tool of
German aggression. Thomas Mann carries Croce's criticism of
German philosophical and historical research even further: in
Faust he sees the representative symbol of Germany: "an irrationally inspired professor, clumsy in worldly things and at the
same time filled with the arrogant feeling that he is superior to
the world because of his 'profundity.'" "Where arrogance of the

intellect is joined with an archaic and illiberal attitude of the mind, there is the devil." The most apt and ample commentary on this criticism in its application to modern Germany are Croce's reviews of German books in the *Critica*. If ever a comprehensive history of the intellectual development of Germany in the twentieth century were to be written, these reviews could serve as a foundation and as a guide.

There are other significant agreements between Croce and Thomas Mann in their critical appraisal of Germany. Both stress the spurious basis of the German claim for national unity. They see in it, in contrast to similar European efforts, a purely nationalistic drive for more concentrated power, without any justification in a liberal political philosophy. When Thomas Mann condemns the "coarse and sinister misunderstanding of the concept of political activity" of Bismarck and his admirers and disciples, and the inability of the Germans to "harmonize ideal and reality, the desirable and the necessary, conscience and action, ethics and power," he uses arguments which find their full justification in Croce's philosophy, and when he blames the German "inner-worldliness" for this failure, he corroborates Croce, who criticized the metaphysical topheaviness of the Germans and the shortcomings of their idealistic philosophy, which did not fully succeed in reconciling the finite wth the infinite.

It is the tragedy not of Thomas Mann but of Germany that there was none among his own countrymen, but rather an Italian, who diagnosed the German problem with equal clarity. The only German counterpart to Thomas Mann's criticism of modern Germany are the *Letters of the Returned* of the young Hofmannsthal. He recognized just as clearly as Thomas Mann where the root of the German evil was to be found: "Their left hand does not know what the right hand is doing, their thinking does not agree with their feeling, their professional opinons not with their theories . . . their public life not with their private life." Hofmannsthal reminded the Germans of Addison's dictum: "The whole man must move at once," and the possibility of a synthesis between spirit and reality became his increasing concern in the latter part of his life. But the German "inner-worldliness" which had always stood in the way of accomplishing this synthesis claimed in Hofmannsthal another victim. In his last plays the main characters either renounce political action or fail in it because of their "inner-worldliness." Hofmannsthal would have sided with Luther and the princes against the peasants. He lacked that sense for the "demands of the day" which both Thomas

Mann and Croce possess to such a high degree. At bottom Hofmannsthal did not go beyond the stage of Professor Cornelius in
Disorder and Early Sorrow; he remained a sensitive and tasteful
lover of the past. Hofmannsthal, like Croce and Thomas Mann,
was ready to measure German values against those of Europe,
but he overlooked the fact that an essential part of the European
tradition is the shaping of social reality in the service of ethico-
political ideals; that, in order to be a "good European" it does not
suffice to be at home in several literatures. In this, Benedetto
Croce and Thomas Mann are *d'un sol consiglio.*

[1946]

THOMAS MANN AND GOETHE

Berthold Biermann

In the past hundred years an individual version of the literary theme "and Goethe" has been applied to every German writer. However, the relationship of Thomas Mann and Goethe has an unusual, indeed unique aspect in that it becomes more and more intimate as time passes. Never, as elsewhere in the history of literature, is this relationship confined to the influence of the work of one great man on the writings of a later author. The phenomenon Goethe assumes a direct, consciously expanded bearing on the very life pattern of Thomas Mann. This process in the true sense of the word is "Bildung" (formation of the mind) and paraphrased by Mann himself in his lecture on Freud, with an apparent allusion to Goethe's influence on him, as "the shaping of the human being through the powerful influence of admiration and love, the childlike identification with a father-image elected out of profound affinity."

It took Mann a long time to achieve this harmony with Goethe. The father-image of his youth was not Goethe but Schopenhauer. He has recreated his experience of Schopenhauer in that scene of *Buddenbrooks* where Thomas Buddenbrook, having shortly before his death accidentally come upon the philosopher's chief work, embraces with joy and trembling the words of the great pessimist as a deliverance from the confusion of his life. In *The World as Will and Idea,* Thomas Mann found, at twenty-three, sanctioned by the authority of a superior mind, the feeling which determined his Weltanschauung—sympathy with death.

"Ah, youth, with its sacred pangs, its urgency, its disorders!" exclaims Thomas Mann when three decades later he pictures this period of his youth in the *Sketch of My Life*. He confesses how close he was to the thought of suicide at the time he wrote *Buddenbrooks*. The longing for death overshadowed his will to live. What made him a disciple of Schopenhauer was the atmosphere of worldly renunciation which had already fascinated Nietzsche. We do not know the particular reasons for this crisis.

It may well be that there were no particular reasons at all, just
the disgust of an oversensitive artist for the brutality of life. The
problematic gift of such oversensitivity, through which life is
wedded to suffering, seems to be a heritage of the Mann family.
Two sisters of Mann died by their own hand. Was it creative
ability which helped him and his brother Heinrich overcome all
dangers? Possibly it was—at least in so far as artistic creation is
the expression of another faculty: tenacity.

Sensibility and tenacity—Mann considers this blend the particular vitality of the genius. This "tenacity" has a purely spiritual
origin without any connection with physical vigor and toughness.
It is the disposition for order and form, the selective and organizing faculty, enabling the artist to master the impressions of
life which affect him more directly and more dangerously than
others.

Thomas Mann has lived and created for decades in the ambivalent state of a man who sees through the pretense of life
and worships it with a sad love at the same time. To soften the
opposition between the mournful doctrine of Schopenhauer and
a sentimental attachment to the little things in life, he has made
ample use of irony. Irony is detachment, and from afar even the
pessimist may show some kindness for life. In the *Reflections of
a Non-Political Man,* which sums up his experiences at the end
of his first period, Mann defines this irony more closely. "It is
directed against the intellect as much as it is against life," he
says, "and that makes it restrained, tints it with melancholy and
modesty." The sarcasm of Thomas Mann has indeed something
of melancholic resignation; with good reason, as it is only an
expedient for a conflict in the artist's soul which seems to be
irreconcilable. This role of a detached spectator is best for a *ver-
irrter Bürger* like Tonio Kröger in the autobiographical story.
Irony is an essential element of all the creations of Mann, yet a
close observation would reveal that as years pass the sarcasm
somewhat changes its tone. There is a shift of accent in *The Magic
Mountain* which is still more distinct in the Joseph novels as
compared with the early works. The marks of a painful compromise begin to heal. It is no longer the remoteness of a by-
stander but rather that of someone who views things from above.

I

Polemic Prologue

The Goethe-experience was not a dramatic event as that of
Schopenhauer was. A classic to be studied in school as a subject

for essays can hardly have the effect of a revelation. There is no possibility of discovering Goethe, but there is one of finding him again, by becoming more mature. Mann reports how the words "deserving life," which Goethe used in a poem to denounce the aburdity of Schiller's death, impressed him at first reading; this concept gave him a strange sensation of being pardoxical and imposingly bold at the same time. With sarcasm turned against his own past, he says: "Here, life was considered the highest achievement, and to deserve it such a great distinction that it should be a protection against annihilation; that was something to confuse my youthful conception of superiority, which rather included a refined unfitness and unsuitability for this earthly life." The impression of the pardoxical seems in every respect to prevail in Mann's first contact with Goethe's sphere. That was due not only to the optimistic accent of Goethe's writings (repugnant to the disciple of Schopenhauer); what irritated him even more was the cliché "Dichterfürsten," one who, like Jupiter, lives far removed from the earthly disorder. This attitude of Goethe seemed somehow inhuman to Mann and did not suit his idea of a poet. He could feel familiar only with men who struggled with themselves and suffered. *A Weary Hour,* a story about Schiller, one of Mann's earliest works, reflects this antagonism to Goethe.

Having this personal attitude, one cannot be surprised that the first consciously accepted influence of Goethe on Mann's writing is expressed as parody. About the origin of *Felix Krull* the author confesses: "There was a fantastic intellectual charm in the burlesque idea of taking a much loved tradition—self-portraiture in the Goethe manner, the introspective confessions of the born aristocrat—and transferring it to the criminal sphere." It is a favorite topic of Mann to point to the obscure relationship between artist and criminal. Tonio Kröger is apparently pleased with the story of the fraudulent banker who wrote stories, something that would never have come to the mind of an honest business man. The young Thomas Mann is very suspicious about the respectability of artists. Even his own success cannot assure him completely.

The story of Felix Krull's youth illustrates how a boy, lost in imaginary visions, may become a swindler for trifling reasons. This sensitive and daydreaming child really has the disposition of an artist, but an unfavorable milieu forces his talents in the wrong direction; instead of applying his abilities to artistic production he tries to satisfy his fancies by fraud and ends up as an imposter. The fact that Mann has shaped the confessions of the swindler after the pattern of Goethe's autobiography may be interpreted as a polemic against the too-refined Goethe. He simply does not believe in Goethe's dignity, which has become a model for the whole fraternity of poets, because he has his own convictions about the irresponsible tendencies in the make-up of the artist. Goethe himself is only once mentioned in the confessions and this in a connection which is not quite flattering. Godfather Maggotson (who enjoys telling the story of Phidias' theft of gold) comforts the otherwise well-shaped and satisfied Felix about his being short-legged with this remark: "The princely genius at Weimar was short-legged too and yet he could acknowledge great personal successes in his life-time." But somehow the analogy of artist and swindler seems to be defective; or did the parodic manner prove insufficient to treat this obscure relationship? The confessions of an impostor were not finished, though the character of the charming, narcissistic adolescent continued to preoccupy Mann's mind for a long time. Unexpectedly he was resurrected decades later in the legend of the Biblical prince Joseph. The narration of a "mission," intelligently supported by the hero, though now treated as a typical experience in the evolution of mankind, implies a certain resemblance to the projected great swindler novel.

To recuperate from the strain of the memoirs of Krull, which the author himself calls a most difficult feat of equilibrium, Thomas Mann wrote *Death in Venice*. The difficulties of the artist's character, a subject which had been treated in *Tonio Kröger* in a sentimental manner and in the confessions of the impostor parodically, is transferred this time to the tragic scene adorned with a faint light of irony. The fate of the writer, Gustave von Aschenbach, who achieved masterliness by a complete devotion to his work and then was ruined so utterly by a perverted love, certainly can be called tragic. Nevertheless, by emphasizing indifference in his narration the author indicates that he disapproves of his hero's pattern of life. By his sensitivity the artist is subjected to a sensual existence; he should not try to suppress his nature and become a statue. Aschenbach is lured to chaos and death because he wants to deny the problems of the artist and supersede them with discipline. The way in which this story is told recalls Goethe's technique. Aschenbach, too, is one of the variations of the artist type, yet the author never shows a personal attachment and keeps the distance of the true narrator. Something else reminds one of Goethe in this work—the diction. The skillful selection of words, always aiming at the highest precision, consciously imitates the style of the old Goethe.

II

The New Humanism

Thomas Mann was already a man halfway between forty and fifty when he felt for the first time impelled to examine more closely the phenomenon Goethe. Up to that time he knew the work of the poet but was not familiar with Goethe as a personality. Indeed, he was inclined, as his occasional allusions prove, to accept without question the traditional cliché of the godlike genius who passes his life undisturbed by human afflictions. It may well be that it was this impression which instigated the comparative study, *Goethe and Tolstoy,* which he delivered as a lecture at Lübeck on the occasion of Nordic Week, 1921. The first draft of that literary parallel was evidently influenced by the *Reflections of a Non-Politcial Man,* the book which he composed during the First World War and in which he bitterly opposed politically-minded writers. The point of departure of his lecture was to confront the natural poetical forces as embodied in Goethe and Tolstoy with the artifices of the partisan scribblers. But as Mann scrutinized the problem, he discovered that it was far more significant than he thought at first glance; besides which he was now in a better position to see the question of principle behind the political controversy, as the excitement of war and revolution no longer interfered with his judgment. The counter-types of the naive geniuses Goethe and Tolstoy, the children of nature, were elevated now to intellectual geniuses, the children of spirit, and represented by such eminent figures as Schiller and Dostoyevsky. However, it seems that the antithesis of the world of nature and the world of spirit could not be dissolved, and although Mann treated the question of rank cautiously, he did not conceal his sympathy with the children of nature. Seen from that angle, Goethe appears as a representative of the Teutonic race and looks almost like the ancient pagan god Wotan.

Thomas Mann himself shortly realized the deficiency of such a Goethe portrait. He revised and perfected the original manuscript of the lecture, elaborated it into a significant essay—significant, too, for his own intellectual development. Only now did the work receive his personal imprint. It mirrored his searching intellect, which can never be satisfied completely, and his individual style, full of reservations and hesitations. He recognized the antithesis of the worlds of nature and spirit as so highly complicated that he refrained from taking sides. Mann must have studied the Goethe literature assiduously in the year between the lecture at Lübeck and the conclusion of the essay. We are now introduced to a different Goethe, one who has by no means the simplicity of an elemental force of nature but is a human being with a character full of problems, trying hard to attain harmony. Certainly Goethe had the childlike naiveté and the instinctive self-confidence of the children of nature, yet the obscure and chaotic tendencies of his disposition are part of the authentic portrait too. The graceful lucidity of his work was not a gift of nature but the fruit of a consistent effort. Mann says: "What Goethe is, in stature and lineaments, in his outline and bulk, in the eyes of the nations today, is the work of renunciation." The true intention of the biographical study about Goethe and Tolstoy is revealed by the sub-title, which Mann added later: *Fragmentary Thoughts about the Problem of Humanity*. The descendant of Lübeck patricians had been deeply disturbed by the repercussions of war and revolution. The collapse of Imperial Germany meant for him the destruction of his pattern of life. Still his faith in the future was so strong that he could not be satisfied for long by the role of a deceived spectator lamenting the past and deriding the present. He was in quest of the new humanism which was to embrace and harmonize all the confusion stirred up by the sudden change. Unexpectedly Goethe became the patron of this bold enterprise which sometimes meant denial of formerly cherished convictions. The essay explored only part of the perplexing question, that is, the professional dilemma of a contemporary writer. The process of liquidation and revaluation was expanded in full detail in the novel, *The Magic Mountain,* which, begun before the war, and interrupted by it, was brought to a conclusion two years after the Goethe essay.

Mann now followed Goethe's method of approaching personal problems, and instead of studying philosophical principles he peopled the issues with human beings. *The Magic Mountain,* like *Wilhelm Meister,* is an epic of the formation of a mind, in which the hero is led through a complicated educational process until he attains that final knowledge which the author acquired by his life experience. However, while the attitude of Goethe to Wilhelm Meister reflects the detachment of a mature mind, in the case of Thomas Mann he himself learned a good many things through the calamities of his fictional hero.

When he began the story of Hans Castorp before the First World War, Mann did not yet know what he wish to teach Hans in the end. It may be questioned if he intended originally to practice much pedagogy. There is good reason to believe that the vacation adventures of Hans Castorp were supposed to serve only as a pretext for a melancholy and somewhat sarcastic description of the milieu of a tuberculosis sanatorium. Thomas Mann, who in the pre-war period had shown such delight in ambiguous characters like the youthful swindler, Felix Krull, could hardly be suspected of special interest in education. It was the collapse of the bourgeois world which made him conscious of certain vexing problems of his own character and preoccupied him with pedagogy, a tendency predominant in the second period of his career.

What is the beneficial effect of Hans Castorp's seven years of "hermetic pedagogy?" This question cannot be answered simply. *The Magic Mountain* is a work of many strata reflecting the uncertainties and endeavors of a decade of intellectual crisis. Mann defended his novel against the charge of advocating the advantages of illness. In an open letter to the editor of the "Medizinische Wochenschrift" he called the book "an ideological challenge to many cherished things, a withdrawal from dangerous sympathies, enchantments and temptations—a farewell address and an attempt at self-discipline." It is this atmosphere of transformation which envelops the work with a sort of twilight, delightful but sometimes confusing. We cannot rely on Hans Castorp's utterances—he is embarrassed by too much education—for information on Mann's own beliefs but must watch closely his mentor, the humanist, Ludovico Settembrini. In the beginning of the novel this fanatic of reason and progress (his oratory reminds Hans Castorp of an official speaker) appears to be a caricature. The rampant republican, who wants to save Hans Castorp from the exciting adventures of illness, could easily be interpreted as a travesty of the political pamphleteer. As time goes on the personality of Settembrini expands; the extravagances of the pedagogue are softened; he becomes more human and convincing. The humanist likes to refer to Goethe, and in one of the discussions with his adversary, Naphta, he even makes a little speech about "deserving life," the very words which once seemed to Thomas Mann full of parody and imposing boldness.

Viewed against the uproar of disease and death and repeated by the tubercular Settembrini, the eulogy of life manifests only boldness. And Hans Castorp in the end does what the pedagogue exhorted him to do every time they met for seven years. He escapes from the entanglement of illness, deserts the dangerous license of the moribund and returns to the banal and healthy people of the plains. Mann, however, having finished the manuscript of *The Magic Mountain,* delivered his speech *Von Deutscher Republik,* which centered around the idea of humanity.

In the address, which expressed Mann's adherence to the young German Republic, he said: "There is no metamorphosis more familiar to me than that which begins with sympathy with death and ends with the decision to be a partisan of life." Service for life, duty to life, have now become preferred formulations for Thomas Mann. There is no higher virtue for that "delicate child of life," the artist, than to be well-disposed toward life. When the city of Munich honored the poet on his fiftieth birthday he stated: "I hope it will be said of my work that it was well-disposed toward life while being acquainted with death."

III

Parallels in the Infinite

Thomas Mann was now completely at ease in the world of Goethe's ideas. There was no more temptation to show disapproval by parody and irony. He had adopted Goethe's well-meaning conception of life, his courageous belief in the evolution of man. Under these circumstances, having achieved an agreement on fundamental questions, the relationship of Mann to Goethe revealed a new and very particular aspect. The connection assumed the form of a spiritual brotherhood, a kind of intimacy with a colleague as if Mann were Goethe's contemporary and not separated from him by a century.

At first this personal relationship was still expressed with some restraint, for even a successful writer might well shrink from pretending to equality with such an eminent predecessor. "I am no Goethe," assured Thomas Mann in his address on the German Republic, when he referred to Goethe's pacifism. "I am no Goethe, yet a little, afar off, somehow or other, as Adalbert Stifter put it, I belong to his family—" It took some time before Mann overcame the natural shyness revealed by such reservations. The great success of his work and the honors bestowed on him were certainly of help in strengthening his self-confidence. But even without the applause of the public, the completion of *The Magic Mountain* would have established his status as a great artist. By this accomplishment he proved to himself that he was more than merely a good narrator like the romancers of the nineteenth century.

With the address on the German Republic, Mann started his political and representative career. It was the necessary supplement to his new outlook, attained with great effort. The responsibility of an educator compelled him to overcome the inherent repugnance of the non-political man to public life. While he had once considered the artist almost as a social outcast, now he himself became one of the principle speakers for intellectual Germany.

When Thomas Mann now spoke of Goethe—as in the two lectures on the occasion of the hundredth anniversary of the poet's death—he was depicting through experienced familiarity a revival "out of his own substance and his own being." The consciousness of this deep affinity gave him the assurance necessary to draw a Goethe-portrait which was so different from that of the literary historians. In his arrangement there was no more room for the legend of the natural genius, the innate harmony of a superior being. The assumed Jupiter is in truth a bitter skeptic, very close to the abyss of nihilism. How difficult it is for him to make up his mind about anything; the rigidity of his behavior is nothing but a disguise to protect him against the impertinence of visitors. It is strange how little things can irritate him, how easily he is tired out. He needs decades to mature his poetic visions and he would probably never have completed a major work if the pedantic father had not inoculated the youth with the categorical imperative to finish everything. Is this Goethe—full of problems—now the genuine, the authentic? Or did perhaps the wish to find similarities with the poet-colleague induce Mann to bring so much shadow into his portrayal of Goethe?

As last and conclusive proof of the authenticity of *his* Goethe, Mann chose the novel form. The fragmentary parts of a life can be restored to an organic unity only with the help of imagination. *The Beloved Returns* is a chapter of Goethe-research written by a poet. Science and poetry combine in this creation to form a delightful blend. A remarkable knowledge of the biographical material and the Weimar milieu are the secure foundation for the magical experiment of resurrecting Goethe. However, the decisive factor in the novel's success is that the biographical traits are boldly filled in with autobiographic details.

The autobiographical aspect of the work becomes manifest in a two-fold manner, paralleling the dualistic nature of Thomas Mann. His critical vigilance is represented by Goethe's secretary, the savant Riemer. Riemer's attitude towards the poetic genius, a curious combination of enthusiasm and terror, corresponds to the apprehensions of the essayist Thomas Mann in regard to Goethe—and to his own genius. Quite logically, the savant, Rie-

mer, when he endeavors to understand the enigmatical phenomenon of genius, refers to Mann's essays; indeed, sometimes he
repeats these formulations almost literally. Riemer's speech has
the same ambiguity when he approaches the secret of his master—
namely the distressing skepticism behind Goethe's virility, which
can find relief only in the ardent devotion to art. "That terrifying approach to the godlike-diabolic which we call genius," loves
himself exclusively and all his benevolence is not natural but the
result of a moral decision. Goethe himself has only vaguely
alluded to this problem of his character. The fact that Thomas
Mann discerns this trait so easily suggests that he has something
similar in his own nature.

The long and painful process of self-examination qualified
Mann at last to identify himself with Goethe. They became truly
one—the aged Goethe, lonely in all his splendor because his
superiority places him apart, and the exiled Thomas Mann, who
had severed his bonds with a nation which had succumbed to
barbarism. This portrayal of Goethe by means of Mann's own
experience achieved an authenticity superior to any biography.
As never before an insight was achieved into the genius of
Goethe, that particular combination of the daemonic and the
bourgeois. In a great monologue Mann revealed the play of
Goethe's spirit and indicated how the important and the commonplace were intimately related in his mind.

This Goethe of Thomas Mann has a surprising way of trifling
with his poetic calling, which he himself considers a limitation of
his nature. Once he exclaims: "As though a man wrote *Werther*
at four-and-twenty and then lived and grew another four-
and-forty without outgrowing poetry!" And to the wiseacres who
criticize his dilettantism in the natural sciences, he addresses this
remark: "How do they know it isn't the poetry that's the dab-
bling and the serious work which lies somewhere else, namely
in the whole of life?" Thomas Mann, too, could profit from this
defense. His work is loaded with medical and philosophical,
with sociological and political reflections, which from a merely
aesthetic point of view may seem an encumbrance. Nevertheless,
the contemplation of the universe, the outlook on the whole of
life, bears results for the artistic work too. It is a preparation for
the habit of regarding life as mythical and typical; a conception
which gives to Goethe's and Thomas Mann's later works a mysterious profundity. "What is gained," explains Mann in his lecture on Freud, "is an insight into the higher truth depicted in
the actual; a smiling knowledge of the eternal, the ever-being

and authentic; a knowledge of the schema in which and according to which the supposed individual lives, unaware, in his naive belief in himself as unique in space and time, of the extent to which his life is but formula and repetition and his path marked out for him by those who trod it before him."

It is this outlook on mankind which enables Thomas Mann to give the final interpretation to his relationship with Goethe. He can now point with frankness to the correspondence between *Buddenbrooks* and *Werther,* between *The Magic Mountain* and *Wilhelm Meister,* between the *Joseph* and *Faust.* This *imitatio Goethe* is by no means mere imitation; it is rather legitimate succession, necessary and inevitable, because the great man, too, despite his refined individuality, represents a type; and the path of his life and work is marked out for him by those who trod it before.

[1945]

THOMAS MANN AND ANDRÉ GIDE

Kenneth Burke

When Gustave von Aschenbach, the hero of Thomas Mann's *Death in Venice*, was about thirty-five years of age, he was taken ill in Vienna. During the course of a conversation, one keen observer said of him: "You see, Aschenbach has always lived like this," and the speaker contracted the fingers of his left hand into a fist; "never like this," and he let his hand droop comfortably from the arm of a chair. It is with such opening and closing of the hand that this essay is to deal.

In the early writings of both Mann and Gide the characters are exceptional, though always in keeping with our metaphor. Mann's concern is with serious and lonely fellows, deviations from type, who are overburdened with a feeling of divergency from their neighbors. In stories like *The Dilettante* the deformations are more mental, but generally the subject is simplified by his imagining characters who are physically extravagant. There is Tobias Mindernickel, whose ill-dressed, gaunt, ungainly figure excites the persecution of all healthy children. He buys a little puppy and names it Esau. They become inseparable, but one day as Esau leaps for food, it is accidentally wounded by a knife which Tobias is holding, whereupon Tobias nurses his puppy with great tenderness. After some days it is cured, it no longer lies gazing at him with bewildered, suffering eyes, it leaps down from its sick-bed, goes racing about with full delight in its puppyhood, with no thought that it is showing how it no longer needs Tobias's morbid tenderness. It is a cheerful little mutt—and maddened at his loss, Tobias plunges his knife into it again, then forlornly gathers its dying body into his arms. Similarly there is little Herr Friedemann, who humble as he is, can by the course of his story be still further humiliated and, in the very act of taking his life, grovels. Mann also writes of an abnormally fat man, who worships his adulterous wife abjectly, and falls dead of apoplexy at a particularly comical moment, topples like a collapsing building, when he feels the full weight of the indignities which have been heaped upon him. And Piepsam, Praisegod Piepsam, a decayed alcoholic, a victim of life if there ever was one, is insulted as he goes to visit the grave of his wife. On the path to the cemetery he is passed by a boy on a bicycle, the merest child, who is too happy to be anything but well-meaning, yet Piepsam resents him and works himself into a fatal rage— the story being told fancifully, even cheerfully. After Piepsam has been bundled off in an ambulance, one feels how brightly the sun is shining.

These outsiders (Mann later took over the word "outsider" from the English) appear under many guises. They watch, they compare themselves with others to their own detriment, they are earnest to the point of self-disgust, and they are weighted with vague responsibilities. In *Tonio Kröger* the concept has matured. Tonio's divergencies are subtler. As a writer, he observes the unliterary with nostalgia. Vacillating by temperament, one might almost say vacillating by profession, he seeks simple people, who form for him a kind of retrogressive ideal. He does not fraternize with them, he spies upon them. A bohemian, he distrusts bohemianism. He watches these others, awed by the healthiness, or the ease, of their satisfactions. It is a kind of inverted praising, since he envies them for qualities which he himself has out- grown. And it is melancholy.

Against this earnestness, this non-conforming mind's constant preoccupation with conformity, we find in the early writings of Gide much the same rotten elegance as characterizes Wilde's *The Portrait of Dorian Gray*. Religious thinking is perverted to produce an atmosphere of decay and sinfulness. There is the Baudelairean tendency to invoke Satan as redeemer. Even in a work as late as *Les Nourritures Terrestres*, we find a crooked evangelism, calling us to vague and unnatural revelations. These artificial prophecies, with a rhetorical, homiletic accent which Gide has since abandoned, suggest a kind of morbid Whitmanism. In place of expansion across an unpeopled continent, we have a pilgrimage through old, decaying cities, erotic excitations at the thought of anonymity and freedom among the ruins of other cul- tures. The hero who cries out to Nathaniel is seeking, not the vigour of health, but the intensity of corruption. The mood, if I understand it correctly, has by now lost much of its immediacy, but in his later works Gide has shown it capable of great readap- tation; what we find earlier, in an archaistic terminology, is sub- sequently transformed into something wholly contemporary.

The most thorough contrast between these writers probably arises from the juxtaposition of Mann's *Death in Venice* and Gide's *The Immoralist*. Gustave von Aschenbach is nationally respected as a master of his calling. Parts of his works are even among the prescribed reading of school children. His austerity, his "morality of production," is emphasized. Aschenbach has clearly erected a structure of external dignity in keeping with the sobriety, the earnestness, which he has brought to the business of writing. But he is now undergoing a period of enervation. He finds that he cannot tackle his page with the necessary zest. As a purely therapeutic measure, he permits himself a trip to Venice, and here becomes fascinated by a young Polish boy, Tadzio, who is living in the same hotel. In his shy and troubled contemplation of this boy he finds an absorption which is painful, but imperious. Von Aschenbach remains outwardly the man of dignity honoured by his nation—he does not, as I recall, ever exchange a word with this Tadzio, whose freshness, liquidity, immaturity are the sinister counterpart to the desiccation of Aschenbach's declining years. But inwardly he is *notwendig liederlich und Abenteurer des Gefühls*. Necessarily dissolute—an adventurer of the emotions—the words are Mann's, when discussing this book in his *Reflections of a Non-Political Man* years afterwards. We thus find again the notion that the artist faces *by profession* alternatives which are contrary to society. The theme of Aschenbach's gloomy infatuation coexists with the theme of the plague—and we observe the elderly man's erotic fevers metamorphose gradually into the fevers of incipient cholera. A poignant and inventive passage describing his cosmetic treatment at the hands of a barber is followed by Aschenbach's delirious remembrance of lines from the *Phaedrus,* wherein Socrates is speaking words of courtship and metaphysics indiscriminately, a merging which Aschenbach makes more pronounced by his own diseased reworking of the Platonic dialogue. A few pages later "a respectfully shocked world" receives the news of his death.

The same themes, sickness and sexual vagary, underlie Gide's *The Immoralist.* Michel, after being at the verge of death and being nursed by his bride into vigorous health, subtly drives her to her own grave. Throughout the novel he is profuse in his tenderness, he is almost hysterically attentive to her, but at the same time he is steadily destroying her—and during the final march of her illness he takes her on that savage pilgrimage from city to city which inevitably results in her death. There has been a young Arab on the fringes of this plot, an insolent fellow who first charmed Michel by stealing from his wife. The reader places him unmistakably as a motive in this unpunishable murder. Despite the parallelism between *Death in Venice* and *The Immoralist*, the emphasis is very different. Whereas in Mann we feel most the sense of resistance, of resignation to the point of distress, and Aschenbach's dissolution is matched by a constant straining after self-discipline, in Gide we hear a narrator who relates with more than pride, with something akin to positive advocacy, the unclean details of his life. "Je vais vous parler longuement de mon corps," he opens one chapter in a tone which I sometimes regret he has seen fit to drop from his later work; there is no mistaking its connotations; it is the accent of evangelism, of pleading.

Buddenbrooks and *Lafcadio's Adventure* do not fall in corresponding stages of their authors' developments. *Buddenbrooks,* a remarkably comprehensive realistic novel of life in North Germany, comes much earlier. But the same contrast in attitude is apparent. We might interpret *Buddenbrooks* as having the theme of *Tonio Kröger* greatly subtilized and ramified. This "fall of a family" through four generations is also the "growth of an artist" through four generations. What is lost in health and moral certitude is gained in questioning and conscientiousness, in social and aesthetic sensitiveness, until we arrive at little Hanno the musician, who, like Aschenbach, finally mingles inspiration with disease, as we watch his improvisations become the first symptoms of the typhoid fever that is to result in his death. In *Lafcadio's Adventure*, however, we meet with a brilliant type of villainy, an "aesthetic criminal" who commits crimes for pure love of the art. The character of Lafcadio is perhaps Gide's most remarkable discovery. It suggests a merging of Stendhal's Julien Sorel with those criminals of Dostoyevsky whose transgressions are inexplicable from the standpoint of utilitarian purpose.

In *Lafcadio's Adventure* Gide makes a notable change in nomenclature, recasting his "corruption" in more characteristically contemporary moulds of thought. The transgressions have become "secular," advancing from sin to crime. If theology remains, it is relegated to a more superficial function; it becomes background, the story being built about a swindle whereby certain picturesque crooks fleece Catholic pietists. Lafcadio, who remembers five uncles but no father, has placed villainy on a distinguished and difficult plane. The author endows him with accomplishments somewhat lavishly, perhaps even a bit credulously; he seems eager that our sympathies be with this experimenter in crime, who can look upon kindly and vicious acts as almost interchangeable:

The old woman with the little white cloud above her head,

who pointed to it and said: "It won't rain today!", that
poor shrivelled old woman whose sack I carried on my
shoulders (he had followed his fancy of travelling on foot
for four days across the Apennines, between Bologna and
Florence, and had slept a night at Covigliajo) and whom
I kissed when we got to the top of the hill . . . one of what
the curé of Covigliajo would have called my "good actions." I could just as easily have throttled her—my hand
would have been as steady—when I felt her dirty wrinkled
skin beneath my fingers. . . . Ah! how caressingly she
stroked and dusted my coat collar and said *"figlio mio!
carino!"* . . . I wonder what made my joy so intense when
afterwards—I was still in a sweat—I lay down on the moss
—not smoking though—in the shade of that big chestnut-
tree. I felt as though I could have clasped the whole of
mankind to my heart in my single embrace—or strangled
it, for that matter.

We shall not reconstruct here that gratuitous murder which
recommends the hero particularly to our attention when poor
Fleurissoire, attracted by this pleasant-seeming lad, chooses to
seat himself in the same compartment with him and unknow-
ingly excites Lafcadio to homicidal criticism. Gide exacts a very
complex reception on the part of his reader. He asks us to observe
a moral outrage committed by a charming scoundrel to whose
well-being we are considerably pledged. Fleurissoire is the butt
of much injustice in this book, but it is Lafcadio, insolent, despotic, with his mercurial slogan "what would happen if . . . " who
earns our suffrage.

The war ends, the mythical post-war period begins, and
Thomas Mann issues *The Magic Mountain,* Gide *The Counterfeiters.* Our contrast is by no means imperiled. Mann shows how for
seven years, during his illness in the mountains, Hans Castorp
has lain exposed to moral questionings. While each day observing his temperature and eating five enormous meals to combat the
wastage of his phthisis, he is privileged to hear the grave problems of our culture aired by sparring critics, themselves diseased,
who speak with much rhetorical and dialectic finish. In particular,
a humanist and a Jesuit altercate for his benefit, until Mynheer
Peeperkorn enters (a much grander version of Herr Klöterjahn
in the story *Tristan*) and routs them both by his inarticulate
vitality. He is life, himself ailing, to be sure, but magnificent
and overwhelming while he lasts—and Castorp's melancholy
respect for him is, in a matured and complex form, Tonio
Kröger's respect for the burghers whom he watched with aloof
humility. Castorp has the attitude of a student. Under ordinary

circumstances he would probably have been unthinking, but he
is made sensitive by his illness and his seven years' elevation
above the century. He amasses greater understanding chapter by
chapter, or at least learns to play one statement against another—
until once more we come to that bewildered fever which marks
the close of both *Buddenbrooks* and *Death in Venice*. At the last,
as we see him on the battlefield, advancing to the aimless business of slaughter, simplified, regimented, unquestioning, we comprehend his evasion. For years he has been uncertain—he now
embraces the arbitrary certainty of war. "Moralism, pessimism,
humour"—these three qualities, whose interrelation Mann himself has stressed, are the dominant traits of this momentous novel,
a summarizing book, a comprehensive and symbolic work to be
included in the world's literature of last wills and testaments.

To turn from *The Magic Mountain* to *The Counterfeiters* is
to turn from brooding to shrewdness. Cruelty, malice, sensuality,
intrigue—such elements are assiduously welded into an entertaining volume, of much subtle literary satisfaction. The reader
of *The Magic Mountain* may have to deal with the fruits of complexity on the part of the author, but he receives them simply.
The reader of *The Counterfeiters* finds complexity unresolved—
he is not even at liberty to differentiate between the absurd and
the beautiful. He is left fluctuant, in great tenuousness of moral
values. The book continues Gide's development from sin to
crime, and reaffirms his sympathy with deviations from the average ethical stock.

Returning to Aschenbach, ill at the age of thirty-five in
Vienna, we find ourselves with correspondences for the closed
and opened hand. It seems that Mann, who himself has situated
the mainspring of his work in conscientiousness, is like his protagonist Aschenbach, with the hand contracted. And Gide, whose
works could readily be taken by the immature or the trivial as
invitations to the most unscrupulous kinds of living, who masters
an air of suave corruption beyond any possible corrupt act, Gide
can be the hand relaxed. *Gewissenhaftigkeit, Einsamkeit*—loneliness, the sense of responsibility—are Mann's words; but as the
most distinctive device for Gide, I would quote from his *Journal*
the triptych: "nouveauté, vice, art."

Our primary purpose, however, in establishing this distinction between the conscientious and the corrupt is to destroy it.
One need not read far in the writings of Gide to discover the
strong ethical trait which dominates his thinking. Perhaps no
other modern writer has quoted the New Testament so frequently

or shown such readiness to settle secular issues by formulas drawn from religion. His critical work on Dostoyevsky, with its theological distinction between the psychology of humility and the psychology of humiliation, is throughout an exercise in moral sensitiveness. And his Lafcadio is a mass of categorical imperatives. We learn from entries in his diary, how, with the athleticism of an anchorite, he plunges a knife into his side for penance, one thrust "for having beaten Protos at chess," another thrust "for having anwered before Protos," four thrusts "for having cried at hearing of Faby's death." Faby was one of his "uncles." Protos was his master in adventure, his accomplished rival, and Lafcadio punished himself, it seems, for not having been disdainful enough to let Protos win. Lafcadio's lamentable conduct might even be derived from an excess of scruples, though these scruples are peculiar to himself.

"I began to feel," Gide has written on this subject in his autobiography, *Si le Grain ne Meurt*, "that perhaps all men's obligations were not the same, and that God himself might well abhor the uniformity against which nature protests but towards which the Christian ideal seems to lead us in aiming to bring nature under control. I could concede none but an individual morality, its imperatives sometimes in conflict with those of other moralities. I was persuaded that each person, or at least each one of the elect, had to play a role on earth, which was wholly his own and did not resemble any other. And every attempt to submit to a general rule became treason in my eyes, yes, treason which I likened to that great unpardonable sin against the Holy Ghost, since the individual lost his precise, irreplaceable significance, his 'savour.' "

We should also consider Gide's *Strait Is the Gate*, which constructs a sympathetic idyll out of the perverse rigours of chastity. As Alissa is courted by Jerome, the two progress into a difficult relationship, obscuring their sensual attraction beneath complex forms of tenderness, and living in a state of pietistic exaltation. Jerome seeks her patiently and unerringly—and with the vocabulary of nobility she beckons to him while continually delaying the time of their union. At first she can offer logical pretexts for this delay, but as they are one by one removed she retreats behind the subterfuges of her faith, and with the assistance of Biblical quotations, morbidly chosen, she remains to the end difficult, pure, intact, a treasure, while loving Jerome with hysterical effusiveness. From the standpoint of its genesis the book is doubtless a companion piece to *The Immoralist*. Both are per-

verse studies in the frustration of heterosexual union, the one
with the connotations of corruption, the other with connotations
of great conscientiousness. When bringing the two together, we
see that Alissa's moral sensitiveness was no greater than that of
Michel. Similarly we should recall in *The Counterfeiters* the brutal letter which the bastard Bernard Profitendieu writes to his
nominal father, a dutifully vicious letter, and the first step, we
might say, in the growth of Bernard's affection.

Has not Mann, on the other hand, spoken with fervour of a
"sympathy with the abyss," an admitting of the morally chaotic,
which he considers not merely the prerogative, but the duty, of
the artist? Aschenbach is committed to conflict: whatever policy
he decides upon for his conduct, he must continue to entertain
disintegrating factors in contemplation. That practical "virtuous"
procedure which silences the contrary is not allowed him. He
must contain dissolution. In "the repellent, the diseased, the degenerate" Mann situates the ethical. Distinguishing between the
moral and the virtuous, he finds that the moralist is "exposed to
danger" and "resists no evil." As essential components of art he
names "the forbidden, the adventurous, scrutiny, and self-aban-
donment." Defining sin as doubt, he pleads for sinfulness. His
work might be called an epistemology of dignity, for he never
relinquishes the love of dignity and never ceases to make the
possession of it difficult.

Mann has defined the problematical as the proper sphere of
art ("art is the problematical sphere of the human"). In any
event, the problematical is the sphere of his own art. Implicit in
his work there is a cult of conflict, a deliberate entertaining of
moral vacillation, which could not permit a rigid standard of
judgments. He has said that the artist must contain his critic,
must recognize the validity of contraries. This attitude would
make such simple certainty as moral indignation impossible. It
would imply exposure to mutually exclusive codes of conduct,
diverse modes of behaviour. Aesthetically, as he himself has said,
he finds the unification of this attitude in irony, which merges the
sympathetic and antipathetic aspects of any subject. Unlike the
satirist, the standpoint of the ironist is shifting—he cannot maintain a steady attack—by the standards of military morale he is
treacherous; he belittles the things he lives for, and with melancholy praises what he abandons. He is equally tentative towards
Leben, life, nature, and Geist, spirit, the intellectual order erected above life. The vigour of the pamphleteer is denied him. To
the Rooseveltian mind he is corrosive—wherefore that "sympathy

with the abyss" which any one of rigid criteria, of sure distinctions between the admirable and the reprehensible, must feel as corrupting and which Mann himself, approaching from the attitude of alien criticism, chose to designate as "dissolute." The ironist is essentially *impure*, even in the chemical sense of purity, since he is divided. He must deprecate his own enthusiasms, and distrust his own resentments. He will unite waveringly, as the components of his attitude, "dignity, repugnance, the problematical, and art."

To the slogan-minded, the ralliers about a flag, the marchers who convert a simple idea into a simple action, he is an "outsider." Yet he must observe them with nostalgia, he must feel a kind of awe for their fertile assurance, even while remaining on the alert to stifle it with irony each time he discovers it growing in unsuspected quarters within himself. It will continue to rise anew, for man has a tremendous fund of certainty—and one will find only too little of Mann's best ironic manner in his essays written during the war, or will find it without its counterpart of melancholy. Yet I grant that the slogans of his opponents were enough to infuriate any subtle man in his position; the temporary disorientation which turned him away from the ironist and towards the pamphleteer is readily understandable. In *The Magic Mountain*, however, the author has recovered from his citizenship to become again the artist. Castorp descends, not to a specific European war, but to regimentation, to the relief, even the suicidal relief, of the slogan-minded. He, the hero, represents the ultimate betrayal of his author's own most serious message. After years of vacillation he seeks the evasion of a monastery, though in these secular days, when the power of theology has dwindled, the dogmatic certainties for which people are burned will more often be those of patriotism, and the equivalent of churchly penance becomes the advance in numbers under arms.

What Mann does with irony, Gide parallels with experimentalism, with curiosity. He views any set code of values with distrust, because it implies the exclusion of other codes. He speculates as to "what would happen if . . . " He is on guard lest the possible be obscured by the real. In his autobiography we find him, characteristically, considering a whole civilization gratuitously different from our own:

> I thought of writing the imaginary history of a people, a nation, with wars, revolutions, changes of administration, typical happenings. . . . I wanted to invent heroes, sovereigns, statesmen, artists, an artistic tradition, an apocryphal literature, explaining and critizing movements, recounting the

> evolution of forms, quoting fragments of masterpieces. . . .
> And all to what purpose? To prove that the history of man
> could have been different—our habits, morals, customs, tastes,
> judgments, standards of beauty could have all been different—
> and yet the humanity of mankind would remain the same.

By recalling *Gulliver's Travels,* we see again how far removed we are from satire. Perhaps, in a much simpler and more lyrical form, Gide did write this book. I refer to *La Symphonie Pastorale,* where he speculates upon a world foreign to him, an arbitrary world so far as this author is concerned, the world of blindness. He even contrives to forget his own knowledge, as when his blind heroine, trying to meditate her way into the world of sight, surmises that sunlight must be like the humming of a kettle.

Perhaps one may interpret Gide's "corruption" too literally. I do not believe that his work can be evaluated properly unless we go beyond the subject-matter to the underlying principles. His choice of material even implies a certain obscurantism, assuming a sophistication on the part of the reader whereby the reader would not attempt too slavishly to become the acting disciple of his author's speculations. Surely Gide would be the first to admit that we could not build a very convenient society out of Lafcadios, however admirable they are. I should take the specific events in Gide as hardly more than symbols: their parallel in life would not be the enacting of similar events, but the exercising of the complex state of mind which arises from the contemplation of such events with sympathy. To live a life like the life in Gide's books would be to commit under another form the very kind of exclusion which he abhors—Lafcadio is for the pious, he is not for poisoners and forgers. Nor must one, in placing this author's malice, forget his *Travels in the Congo,* with its protests against the systematic injustice meted out to the Negroes at the hands of the concessionaires.

Irony, novelty, experimentalism, vacillation, the cult of conflict—are not these men trying to make us at home in indecision, are they not trying to humanize the state of doubt? A philosopher has recently written of this new wilderness we now face, a wilderness not of nature, but of social forces. Perhaps there is an evasion, a shirking of responsibility, in becoming certain too quickly, particularly when our certainties involve reversions to an ideology which has the deceptive allurement of tradition. To seek the backing of the past may be as cowardly as to seek the backing of the many, and as flattering to our more trivial needs of conformity. Need people be in haste to rebel against the state of doubt, when doubt has not yet permeated the organs of our body, the processes of our metabolism, the desire for food and companionship, the gratification with sun and water? There is a large reserve of physical unquestioning, and until we find this reserve itself endangered by the humiliation of tentative living and unauthoritative thinking, are we compelled to reach out impetuously for set criteria? Since the body is dogmatic, a generator of belief, society might well be benefited by the corrective of a disintegrating art, which converts each simplicity into a complexity, which ruins the possibility of ready hierarchies, which concerns itself with the problematical, the experimental, and thus by implication works corrosively upon those expansionistic certainties preparing the way for our social cataclysms. An art may be of value purely through preventing a society from becoming too assertively, too hopelessly, itself.

Could action be destroyed by such an art, this art would be disastrous. But art can at best serve to make action more laboured. To be sure, so long as we feel the need of certitude, the state of doubt is discomforting, and by its very prolongation can make for our hysterical retreat into belief, as Hans Castorp descended from his mountain to the battlefield. But why could one not come to accept his social wilderness without anguish, utilizing for his self-respect either the irony and melancholy of Mann, or the curiosity of Gide? In the unformed there are opportunities which can be invigorating to contemplate. One need not suffer under insecurity any more than an animal suffers from being constantly on the alert for danger. This state of technical apprehension can be a norm, and certainly an athletic norm.

No, our fellows want the seasoned stocks and bonds of set beliefs, and they hope to enrich themselves in these securities as rapidly as possible. Meanwhile, there is an art, a questioning art, still cluttered with the merest conveniences of thinking, a highly fluctuant thing often turning against itself and its own best discoveries. How far it will go, how well it can maintain its character, I should not venture to calculate. But working in the traditions of such art are the two conscientious, or corrupt, writters, Thomas Mann and André Gide. When art is asked to set itself up as "praeceptor patriae, haranguing youth in the classical style of virtue, without shame," they remain men who, with considerable literary endowments, maintain "the Bohemian, the ironic and melancholy, the unattached, the grimly humorous, the innocent, the childish." They do so, it is true, under a deceptive guise. They are not Villons, or Baudelaires. Nor will they relinquish the Villon, the Baudelaire.

[1931]

THOMAS MANN AND THOMAS HARDY

Helen Muchnic

The above title calls for apology, presenting as it does a combination even more "arbitrary and unseemly" than that which
Thomas Mann himself in his *Goethe and Tolstoy* found it necessary to explain at some length. What right, he asked, with a critical glance at the proposed juxtaposition, had one to bring the two
together? There was, to be sure, the frail chronological link in
the person of Stötzer, the schoolmaster, who in the course of his
life had been vouchsafed a glimpse of both great men and so
could serve to make the *and* between their names "more palatable." But he was not enough; a better excuse was the antithetic
implication of the troublesome combining word itself, the conjunction *and,* which, Mann explained, marked differences as well
as similarities in the elements it joined, as was true, for instance,
in the familiar combination "Goethe and Schiller," to which
Nietzsche had objected, and even more clearly, in Schiller's own
Naive und Sentimentalische Dichtung. So also in the case of
Goethe and Tolstoy, for whom there was a place of meeting at
the point of their greatness. That indeed, in spite of differences,
was the obvious excuse, if not the primary reason, for confronting the "wild and primeval" paganism of the Russian and the
"human divineness" of the German. The epithet "Olympian,"
so right for Goethe, was hardly applicable to Tolstoy, in whom
there was too little of the Greek; but since there was something
of kinship in all forms of divinity, these two godlike creatures
might, without impropriety, shake hands as equals across the
humble head of Stötzer. As the essay proceeds we discover that
perhaps, after all, there was not so much difference between the
humanistic German and the "Russian god under the golden lime-
tree"; but that comes later, and the fact of their godhead is
enough to begin with. "The question of rank," says Thomas
Mann, "the aristocratic problem, is no problem at all" in the
grouping he has chosen.

But with "Hardy and Mann" the aristocratic question does arise and cannot be passed unchallenged. There is nothing for it; Hardy is simply not so great an author as Mann, who belongs in the company of epic writers, of Goethe, or Milton, or Tolstoy, so that in the matter of rank, one must use the *and* between them wholly as antithesis and only for want of a better term to express contrast rather than comparison. Why bring their names together at all? To which the answer—were there not a more interesting problem involved—might be: to explore, on the analogy of Mann's examination of godhead through Goethe and Tolstoy, certain distinctions between the earthly and the divine. The more interesting problem, however—so one dares consider it —has to do not so much with apportioning laurels as with looking into some of those concepts and artistic procedures by which the work of these authors is characterized, a problem of analysis rather than one of judgment, wherein the antithetical-uniting conjunction happily appears as better serving in its double capacity. For these two authors, the earlier and lesser, and the later, greater one are more close in their beliefs and methods than in the range and depth of their poetic vision. The contrast presented by the more purely intellectual problem, in other words, is not so immeasureable as that of the aristocratic one. Still, in behalf of the latter it might be said that the ways in which Hardy's work suggests Thomas Mann's, prefiguring it, as it were, tempt one to see the simple chronological factor as very, perhaps as chiefly, important in making for the differences between them. Mann, with knowledge at his disposal not available at an earlier age, seems to answer the questions that Hardy asked; and because the very fact of his answering, the assuredness of his statement, is a measure of his superiority, in fairness one is driven to the query: could Hardy possibly, however great his genius, have given answers to his own questions? He might have asked them better—that is conceivable; but what of answers in an era wherein tentativeness was the very essence of its intellectual ventures, as assertiveness is that of ours?

The difference appears, for example, in their professed attitudes to their role as artists,—Hardy annoyed with all attempts to force his "mood-dictated" writings into some ordered pattern of philosophy, Mann humbly—the term is advisedly and justly used—accepting his position as spokesman and prophet of his day. He had "repeatedly stated," said Hardy, "in prefaces and elsewhere" that the views which his works expressed were "*seemings,* provisional impressions only, used for artistic purposes" because they were plausible enough until "somebody produced better theories of the universe." One must, he said, be satisfied with "tentativeness from day to day." This waiver of the artist's responsibility, this retreat from the perplexity of formulating convictions proceeds, of course, from the common and indisputable observation that Art and Life are not the same, and from its not so unquestionable corollary that the artist as man is not the artist as artist, that the aesthetic validity of his work has little to do with his personal conclusions as an individual among other individuals in a shared universe. As an artist he is a spectator, divided from his fellows—such is Hardy's implication; and the public is at liberty to take or leave the record of his impressions. The problem of the difference between Art and Life Thomas Mann has also emphasized. Time and again he has presented the artist's dilemma, the situation wherein a man's divinely prescribed function among the living makes him a stranger in life. But whereas Hardy underscored the difference as unbridgeable, Mann has evolved a remarkable integration, seeing all those characteristics that apparently set the artist apart as an unhappy and useless creature, combined in eminently social functioning. For although the artist's dreaming—this seems to be the final argument—distinguishes him from others, his dreams are no mere impressions of the reality before him, nor are they so private as to be inexplicable to others: their substance is a vision of human destiny; and he comes close to his fellows through his understanding of their needs, is one of them and loved by them as their prophet.

This is not to say that Hardy's work lacks coherence, nor that his characters are coldly presented. On the contrary, despite his renouncement of philosophies, his "impressions," threaded on a belief in brute destructiveness as the fundamental, tragic, and only unquestionable rule of life, are extraordinarily unified. In their very unity, however, they exhibit a stark and unresolved dualism: on the one hand, the irrational, the powerful, the unknown; on the other, the sentient, the victimized, the ignorant— so much so that man's nature and his experience appear to have little to do with each other; and all that an individual can know about himself and about his destiny is that he is helpless and unbefriended by the gods. It is as if humanity were a small child, lost without the security of parental care, but accepting his unhappy loneliness as something prescribed and wholly in the nature of things. That is why Hardy's poor, victimized heroes and heroines are not coldly presented; why their author weeps for them, and we weep with him, shedding the tears for Tess and Jude and Marty South which they do not shed for themselves.

Mann's view is not so pitying. There is—to take the point for symbolic comparison—all the difference in the world between Michael Henchard's defeated "I must suffer, I perceive and Hans Castorp's "challenge" to the elements. In the remarkable chapter of *The Magic Mountain,* entitled "Snow," in which Castorp throws down his challenge, there is a sentence that might have been Hardy's:

> . . . the storm burst, the storm that had threatened so long. Or may one say "threatened" of the action of blind, non-sentient forces, which have no purpose to destroy us—that would be comforting by comparison—but are merely horribly indifferent to our fate should we become involved with them?

Is this not very like that early little poem, called *Hap,* in which Hardy laments the absence of a vengeful deity on whom he might blame life's fortunes and declares it a greater bitterness to know one's existence ruled by Crass Casuality, irrationally and uncaringly dispensing good and evil, than to suffer whatever sorrow it might decree? The difference between Hardy and Mann on this score is that whereas the theme of "horrible indifference to our fate," which is the subject of *Hap,* remains the leitmotif of all Hardy's work down to *The Dynasts* and *Jude the Obscure,* with Mann it is passed over lightly, as held for granted, taken by a man in his stride, casually, without so much as a shrug of the shoulders. Eustacia Vye's rebellious acquiescence, Tess d'Urberville's passionate but unquestioning passivity, Michael Henchard's hard-headed struggle and equally stubborn surrender, the unassuming dignity with which Jude Fawley meets the destruction of his hopes—all these infinitely pathetic attitudes are not the ways of Thomas Mann's humanity. The sense of division between man and his destiny, between his limited consciousness and the limitless mystery in which it plays so pitiful a part, this view of a tragic concatenation of events to the meaning of which the very men who suffer from it are blind—this dark and melancholy conviction which is the root of Hardy's pathos and of his irony is foreign to Mann, for whom irony resides not in ignorance but in knowledge, not so much in the way events happen to shape themselves as in man's own occasionally mistaken perception of himself or his role. His heroes are by no means all-knowing or free from mistakes. A man's illusion may be so complete as to rouse, in a false situation, love or grief as ardent as if there had been no mistake. But with Hardy, although illusion plays a most sinister and important part, it is of a different order. The error is nearly always another's; when a being suffers because of error, the mistake is seldom his own but another's about him: in his relation to his fellows, as in his relation to the universe, an individual is helpless in the grip of an ignorant outside force. Hardy's villains, it is notable, are not more consciously vicious than his heroes are consciously good; they *happen* to be crude and destructive just as Nature happens to be crude and destructive. The verb "to happen" is indeed as essential in Hardy's idiom as it is inappropriate to Mann's. Mann speaks more readily of what a man does in his life, or with his life, as of what happens to him. To such a degree, in fact, is he predisposed to see a unity between the *outside* and the *in,* that the monstrous and incalculable Chance of Hardy's thinking is reduced for him to almost infinitesimal proportions; even the blindness that strikes a man, it is possible for him to conjecture, although not with complete seriousness, might be the result of the man's privately not *wanting* to see.

They differ, that is, these two ironists, in their estimates of human capacities, and in the measure of this difference, in what they hold to be unquestionably real. So complete is Hardy's mistrust of the wavering impressions which he sees as constituting the sum total of man's understanding, that he turns from them, in his search for the real, to the greater security of that which is least changeful and least sentient. For Thomas Mann, on the other hand, immobility and changelessness are not prime requisites of reality. Trusting man's changing, growing, even mistaken and groping intelligence, he accepts it as no less real than the empirical data open to its intuitions. Under Hardy's command, reason gives knowledge over to the enemy in unconditional surrender and waves a rather sickly flag in truce with the unthinking and unknowing. The problem as to what is real remains unanswered; there can be only tentativeness and a guess as to the existence of a mysterious reality. No doubt at all, however, as to the unreal: all that a man perceives, all that he lives through, all that he thinks. The "insight into the higher truth depicted by the actual" which, according to Mann, grants a "smiling knowledge of the eternal" is for Hardy the dimmest of hopes. His man may question the eternal but never can he reach a "smiling knowledge" of it. He may believe darkly in a truth behind the "veil of things," but as for tearing away the veil—

the possibility of doing that is one of his most sad delusions. His
life, if he could but see it, is will-less entirely; he is led on strings
in the hands of unknown and uncaring Immortals. Even Napoleon is a puppet of the Knitter Drowsed. Even Time lends but a
shadowy and specious grandeur to the human scene.

Yet Time, as everybody knows, is all important in Hardy's
concept of things, as it is also in Mann's. It is antiquity that
deepens the narrow stage of Hardy's stories. Roman legions are
buried beneath the ground on which walks the Mayor of Caster-
bridge; the Middle Ages live in the walls of Jude's Christminster;
shadows of ancient Egypt accompany the Melstock Choir; and an
even more distant past surrounds Tess while she milks her cows
or works in the fields. The epic drama of *The Dynasts* itself,
enacted not in the world of historical events—these are but il-
lustrative projections of the real one—but in the Overworld of
Spirits, is fundamentally a debate on this very subject of Time,
between the Spirit of the Years and the Spirit of the Pities. The
young Spirit of the Pities addresses the Spirit of the Years,
"eldest-born of the Unconscious Cause," as a pupil might an
implacable schoolmaster, pleading with him to "don" the "poor
mould" of Humanity, to "put on and suffer for the nonce" its
"feverish fleshings" that his soul might be "won to sympathy";
and the Spirit of the Years, like an elderly schoolmaster in genial mood, consents to "humour" the youngster, knowing, however,
that his "unpassioned essence could not change" did he "incarn
in moulds of all mankind." Here, then, is the argument for what
had been dramatically objectified in the novels, in Tess, in Jude,
in the lives of nearly all Hardy's heroes and heroines: the difference between perception of events and the events themselves,
for which neither emotional nor intellectual understanding, nor
an external sympathetic apprehension, are relevant. The Spirit
of the Pities, according to the Preface, is the only one of the
"phantasmal Intelligences" that "approximates to 'the Universal
Sympathy of human nature—the spectator idealized' "; and from
this definition emerges the tragic significance that man's keenest
consciousness of his experience, whether as one who lives through
it or who looks on, can hold no inkling of its reality. The pity of
it, as distinguished from the tragedy, is that although the Spirit of
the Pities is wrong, it cannot help itself: "I feel, Sire," it replies
to the Year's rebuke,

> as I must! This tale of Will
> And Life's impulsion by Incognizance
> I cannot take.

The Spirit of the Pities "cannot take" what the Spirit of the Years knows to be true; and it is the Spirit of the Years who alone among all the others is endowed with absolutely certain knowledge. Time only, that is, Time not as history but as the unconscious, cumulative progress itself of events, the appearances or shadows of which history records, as real as every moment present to consciousness and loading it with an accumulated and profound richness, Time only, it appears, is capable of truthful vision, but what its Spirit recognizes is that even it itself is an instrument of the Unknown. To the problem of the Realities, implicit in all of Hardy's works, the answer in *The Dynasts* is most clearly given: that unrecorded, uncommented events contain a truth more sure than any human consciousness of it. Such is the essence of his hopeless message: that which is true cannot be understood, can scarcely be perceived by the living. He himself, the artist-observer, is on the heights, looking on in a never unified vision; he feels with the Pities and sees with the Years, for he is both the Spirit who understands and the creature who doesn't, a dual being sadly convinced of his own limitations, knowing that, in spite of the loftiness of his position, he is capable only of gathering impressions and making conjectures.

And for this reason, although acutely aware of Time, Hardy has no clear concept of Eternity. In his view, Time realized is a remembrance of things quite dead, quite gone; and only unsentient matter, Egdon Heath, the Cliff without a Name, very epitomes of an unconscious that has no link with consciousness, are Sphinx-like symbols of the eternal. For man, therefore, as he sees him, all experience is shockingly one. However deep in years the history of his people, whatever his ancestors might have suffered, whatever the antiquity of the scene of his living, his little life is separate and unique, with neither repetition nor celebration in it; there is no feeling for him of unity with the past; he is crushed by the ever fresh novelty of his sufferings—a passive creature, pitiful rather than tragic, and great only through the shadow he casts. Thomas Mann's work, on the other hand, conveys remarkably the sense of eternity. In his concept, the present and a future without end are united to a past of untraceable beginnings; and this, in a union that calls for no outside Spirit to perceive it, but is known, felt, "celebrated" by men themselves. It is, if one likes, a "psychological" unity, whereby to the otherwise "poor and valueless single character" is added "a mythical value." In this extension beyond itself, in this identification with a legendary past, experience is given dignity; this

is understood by man, and his understanding makes his life
no mere, separate, and meaningless occurrence, but a "celebration." For when Mann writes that man's "dignity and security
lie all unconsciously in the fact that with him something timeless
has once more emerged into the light and become present"
he uses the word "unconsciously" not with reference to an individual's knowledge and awareness of where he stands, but to
his evaluation of this knowedge. Mann, that is, is not blind to his
role as celebrant in the eternally human ritual, but he may not
realize how much his security depends upon this role nor how
dignified he is in it. The man of antiquity, "before he did anything," so Mann reminds us, citing Ortega y Gasset, always took
a step backward "like the bullfighter," into the past of legends,
and thus "disguised and protected" rushed upon his present
problems. And in this noble, and not at all unconscious borrowing of tradition, Mann sees a truly human gesture and one most
hopeful for humanity. That "man sets store by recognition,"
that "he likes to find the old in the new" gives his life a deep,
calm, necessary assuredness. "From that recognition he draws a
sense of the familiar in life, whereas if it painted itself entirely
new, singular in time and space, without any possibility of resting
upon the known, it could only bewilder and alarm"—as indeed
it does bewilder and alarm in the work of Hardy, where the sense
of recurrence serves but to emphasize the meaningless and unknown. That is why there is with Mann a sense of immediacy
about the past, with Hardy only a feeling of remoteness, even
with reference to the present; why Mann's characters are at
home in the world even when they are cast in the role of guests,
as Hans Castorp in the Sanitarium at Davos, or of foreigners, as
Jacob in the land of Laban or Joseph in Egypt, whereas Hardy's
in their own, familiar, ancetral Wessex are all strangers in life.
Time as chronology, which notes the progress of events as they
occur and pass in ordered sequence, is annihilated in their repetitions. And these repetitions are not mere accidents; they are
foreseen and *unconsciously willed.* Nor is the latter phrase a
facile paradox, for the unconscious of Mann's conception is not
Hardy's inscrutable and senseless Thing that differs from consciousness so completely as to have nothing in common with it;
it is a force for which volition is not only possible but all important, by which indeed consciousness itself is motivated. This view
of the annihilation of chronology in a meaningful apprehension of
time is developed and deepened in Mann's novels. It proceeds
from an individual's unconscious remembering of all things in his

own past, as Tony Buddenbrook's harking back, even in old age, to the youthful, unfulfilled, and only love of her life; to his recreating them under new circumstances, as Hans Castorp, in his passion for Clavdia Chauchat living through again his boyhood infatuation for Pribislav Hippe; to his repeating in his personal life experiences not of his own but of a communal past, as in the case of Joseph who relieves the history of his race, perhaps that of mankind. In this process, as the individual's significance is heightened, his consciousness of his role is proportionately increased. Castorp is better aware of what he is living through than Tony, and Joseph infinitely more than Castorp, so much so that an individual's greatness is seen as in part measurable by the degree of his consciousness. The greater the man the better he recognizes that events in his life are both repetitions and prophecies.

The remarkable foreshadowings in the lives of Mann's heroes are naturally, therefore, of a more cheerful mystery than the dark premonitions of Hardy's. For Hardy prophecies can be of evil only; the crowing of a cock, the prick of a rose thorn, can bode no good. They seem to occur as confirmations of an underlying anxiety, as proofs for the view that men are united to the earth and to each other only in a fearful, unuttered expectancy of doom, that only meaningless destruction is repeated in each man's experience, that his life and all his endeavor end in absolute death. The history of humanity presents to Hardy the spectacle of complete loss and waste. But Mann sees in it an extraordinary tenaciousness, a remarkable lastingness and conservation. His work is luminous with the deeply optimistic conviction that the "metaphysical consciousness" of an individual genius, such as Goethe, for instance, "of being at all times and absolutely certain of the favour of destiny" is true also of the human race. For the history of the human race, as he sees it, is the history of man's spiritual growth: the story primarily of man's triumph and not of his various failures, wherein individual experience, including that of suffering, is but one term in a dialectical opposition, the ultimate synthesis of which is not annihilation but a progressively intelligent consciousness. The individual is immeasurably important through his place in a community that extends beyond the bounds of his country and his epoch to the earliest unrecorded beginnings of man. His role is not only that of activity within a limited number of years; in what he does, what he thinks, and what he is, he embodies all similar doing, thinking, and being in the past, and contains the undeveloped future. So Hans Castorp, alone in the snow, on the mountain, reflects in uninhibited, deep musings:

> We dream anonymously and communally, if each after his
> fashion. The great soul of which we are a part may dream
> through us, in our manner of dreaming, its own secret dreams,
> of its youth, its hope, its joy and peace—and its blood-
> sacrifice.

Even in dreams, even in death, a man contributes to the conscious and the living. There is no such irrevocable separation between dreaming and waking, between dying and living as there is with Hardy. For Hardy, death is simply the ceasing of an individual existence, and the vast span of history is the recorded sad accumulation of these cuttings-off For Mann, death is seen as linked to life in an indivisible process of birth, decay, and rebirth— and this by way of no mystical or solipsistic philosophy but through open-minded respect for the concrete realities of empiricism. With the death of Hardy's creatures, with Jude, with the Mayor, even with Tess, another individual puppet passes, a puppet endowed, of course, with eternal and eternally lovable qualities, which is what makes us sorry for his passing; but with Mann when a man dies, an epoch or a way of thought dies with him. The theme of rebirth, which could have had no interest for Hardy, preoccupies Thomas Mann and is most clearly developed in the Joseph books. In *Buddenbrooks*, in *Death in Venice*, in *The Magic Mountain*, there are preparations and adumbrations of it: first, a survival of qualities in one being as if in compensation for the loss of those that perish with another, as when in little Hanno's death the love of music dies but that for poetry lives on in his young friend Kai; then, the closely knit relationship, within one man, of life, love, and death, so magnificently worked out in the story of Aschenbach; next, the rebirth to a death more concrete than the vaporous sterility of a living one, as with Hans Castorp. Finally, the recasting of a man in a mould of greater nobility, as with Joseph's descent into the pit. That the pattern of the ideal may develop in ever expanding repetitions, individual incarnations of it must be destroyed; to lend meaningful dignity to Jacob's loss of Joseph, Abraham and Isaac must have died; before the Resurrection can become plausible in the history of human aspirations, Joseph must be cast into the pit and rescued from it. Suffering, that is, need not be wasteful; and since reincarnation implies death, death is not only necessary but beneficent.

But Thomas Mann must not be accused of having fallen into the mistakes of those very artists whom he calls artists of the "plastic fancy," whose "disproportionate, fevered, and dogmatic presumption of spirit" he thinks "to all eternity" in conflict with the "truth, power, calm, and humility of nature." Schiller and Dostoyevsky he puts in the category of these presumptuous thinkers; and he would not, and indeed must not, be classed with them, but with the "sentimental" artists, with Goethe and Tolstoy, whose imagination is "intuitive . . . the inborn sympathy of the child of nature with the organic." This, despite, or perhaps because of, his realization that it may be very difficult to steer between the entrancing, sterile wastes of spirit and the life-giving sources of nature. How easily, for instance, does Hans Castorp confuse the deathland of snow with the life-giving sea, so terrifyingly similar in their effect on the human being! Hans Castorp's heroic effort to break away from the "horizontal" leads only to another disaster. On his skis in the snow, lost without sight of human habitation, and willingly so lost, he is the mind's play in its perilous metaphysical adventures, breaking with lethargy only to hazard itself in the void. The giving way to the spirit's urge for solitude, for snowy mountains, the wandering about in dizzy and unpeopled heights is "quite as mad and bad" as the body's Walpurgis-night craving for the intimate and physical; both are senseless: that is, without the truly human sense of union with the organic, both passively given over to death. But although the tale of Castorp is one of disaster, there is in it the possibility of regeneration, because "out of death, and the rebellion of the flesh" there came to him as he "took stock" of himself, "a dream of love." This great story of man's failure closes on a question:

> Out of this universal feast of death, out of this extremity of
> fever, kindling the rain-washed evening sky to a fiery glow,
> may it be that Love one day shall mount?

But the question is answered in the Joseph books; *The Magic Mountain* is, as it were, the Pit out of which the story of man's hope emerges. It does not matter that the life of Joseph took place chronologically at an earlier date than Castorp's; these heroes represent something more than a strictly historical past.

For Mann is not a realist in the Zolaesque definition of realism as accurate photography and scientific experimentation. Neither, of course, is Hardy. Both are symbolists. Yet they differ in their use of symbols: Mann's is the way of the fable, Hardy's of the emblem; Hardy's is a search for epitomes, Mann's is an extended probing of individual, concrete instances; Mann's creatures are entities in which all others are comprised, Hardy's are starting points for extended comparisons. And although in the timeless sweep characteristic of his vision, Mann's people—Castorp, Joseph, even, in a more limited sense, Thomas Buddenbrook —represent not men but mankind in its spiritual experimentation, whereas Hardy's—Tess, Jude, even Napoleon—in that atomization without links suitable to "impressionism," are but shortlived creatures within the measurable span of their single existences, Mann's respect for the concrete is greater than Hardy's. The "lifeless land" with its "empty, rolling spaces" in which Castorp gets lost might be the very land of Hardy's Immortal unknown Shadows.

The difference is once again the fundamental one between the dualism implicit in all Hardy's perceptions, and the integration characteristic of Mann's. And here perhaps some speculation as to the nature of these two men might not be out of place. Mann has spoken of his short stories, in the preface to the volume in which they are collected, as "an autobiography in the guise of fable," and elsewhere has expressed admiration for the autobiographic quality of Tolstoy's work. That being so, it is allowable to read his own as symbolic self-revelation; but Hardy would have considered such an interpretation of his productions as nothing short of impertinent. Can it be doubted, indeed, that Thomas Mann is constantly writing about himself, whereas Hardy always tried to conceal himself in his writing? And the problem as to how much this difference makes for their relative excellence as artists is not unimportant for aesthetics. Does not Hardy's perpetual denial of himself, his wish to be dispersed and disseminated in the realities which he observes, his wanting almost to forget that impressions imply an observer, does this not speak of a man at war with himself; while, on the other hand, does not Mann's constant, frank reshaping of his own experience suggest one who, accepting himself, works with and through the contradictions of his being? And is this not the reason also for that character of *division* in Hardy's work which, in spite of careful patterning, always leaves one conscious of the author's own tacit, extraneous commentary on what he himself is saying, and never impresses with the wholeness of undivided inspiration; whereas Mann's orchestral design, infinitely more complex than Hardy's architectural one, gives an effect of perfect unity—certain, calm, and undogmatic, so that in T. S. Eliot's memorable definition of the terms, Hardy might be called a "reflective" but Mann an "intellectual" artist. Certainly Mann's characters develop and are transformed by experience in a process that is of growth, and Hardy's are static, battered down by something outside themselves in a process not of growth but of disintegration—which seems to stand for the progressive clarification of a philosophy on the one hand, and, on the other, for an abdication of thought in favor of continuous exercise in artistic composition—in its result, as beautiful and as much the "very marrow of death" as the "six-sided crystalline symmetry" of Castorp's snowflakes. In every way Mann's work seems to be of one who sees from within and is at home in his experiences, whereas Hardy's is that of a man who looks on from outside and is a stranger even to the most intimate revelations of his soul.

Hardy could not trust his own reason to explain himself, nor any man's reason to explain the universe; and so his way is that of negation, denial, and obscurantism. The mystery of Egdon Heath broods over all his productions. But Mann is nothing if not a lover of thought and reason; the silent, incommunicable symbol of mystery in his work, the Sphinx, represents for him, in Harry Slochower's phrase, "a wild, dead, and false eternity." The deep, unconscious bond of "the child of nature with the organic," the source of his admiration and optimism, is the very reason for Hardy's melancholy. For the essence of Hardy's view is one of unresolved conflicts—the individual at war with society, society with nature, and the good, wherever it might be, always vanquished—in a kind of fundamental unity of belligerent antagonisms. What Mann holds, on the other hand, to quote again Slochower's illuminating essay, * is:

> that man is the high-meeting point between the waking and dreaming state, between Eros and Logos, Chaos and Cosmos, magic and casuality between nature and spirit "on their yearning way towards each other"

and that

> the human way . . . is that which resolves opposites, not by destruction, but by assimilation.

This is no superficial optimism, no Rousseauistic assertion of human goodness, no laughing prophecy of Utopia that shuts its eyes to the disasters of the present; it is a statement of hopefulness in man's potentialities, in his ability to make much even of

---

* *Thomas Mann's Joseph Story.*

tragedy and to understand things as they really are. It is, in the
face of the terrible legacy to which it has fallen heir, the answer
of the twentieth century to the dubious questionings of the
nineteenth.

[1939]

PART IV

Thematic

DEATH AND THOMAS MANN

Lydia Baer

The concept of death is one of the outstanding themes of Thomas Mann's work. It appears conspicuously in almost all his narrative creation, from its beginnings to the present day; it is a habit of mind and a mode of thought that is more than simply a preference; it is inherent in the structure of his being. Its shadow dwells implicitly within many a work that bears no outward visible sign of the dread or welcome presence; it looms large over all his most significant work. His is a temperament attuned to a minor key, and in that key he composes: from an early attempt, characteristically called *Death*, a little sketch charged with mystic premonitions, sadness and fate, to the great symphony of death, *The Magic Mountain*, which concludes the direct line of death with a great metaphysical and concrete reckoning.

More than twenty years ago, when the first storms of criticism had launched themselves against Thomas Mann for his youthful preoccupation with problems of decadence and decay, so closely allied to and interwoven with the concept of death, Ernst Bertram constituted himself Thomas Mann's spokesman. He saw the inherent tendency of this writer to succumb to the fascination of dubious phenomena which have ever attracted the poet and writer in all literary history; but he saw also the eminent artistry of this particular writer and he defended his right to create according to the truth that was in him. He adds Goethe's opinion that a writer's own world must be accepted as he has made it.

It is not easy, or even feasible, to adhere too closely to any one canon of methodology in dealing with such a writer as Thomas Mann. One might well say that death was a problem in his writings. But it does not stand out thus clearly and in isolated fashion; it is interwoven and interrelated with the more obvious problem of decadence, of disease and the decay of the flesh; it is directly related to the conflict between art and life, between the individual and society, which were long irreconcilable to Thomas Mann, despite all his attempts to harmonize them. The danger of categories and labels is overwhelmingly revealed by an intensive study of his lifework in its totality. There is a romantic readiness in him to unravel his own psychic and mental processes —a willingness which by the very excellence of its reasoning has at times almost the effect of obscuring the issue. It is well to remember Walzel's sensible admonition not to accept a writer's own interpretation of himself without careful investigation.

Nevertheless, in examining critically and concretely the nature of the concept death, its function and its manner of presentation by Thomas Mann, his essayistic and explanatory bent must be taken into account. He applies to his own mental and creative habits the same painstaking analysis to which he subjects his characters; he strives to clarify and expound the inner laws which have made him and his work what it is; he gives a careful and exacting account of the functions and the processes that he believes he observes in himself. No romanticist has made a more penetrating survey of his inner inventory or handled the "romantic irony" in a cleverer and more interesting way. Like Goethe, he has an autobiographical tendency; he considers it an obligation to contemporary life and to posterity to enter the confessional and tell unreservedly what has actuated and animated him. Amid the upheavals and disastrous passions of the war, he found mere aesthetic contemplation to be more impossible than ever; in the *Reflections of a Non-Political Man,* with its Nietzschean title, he became his own advocate and critic and that of the lost cause of the German monarchy. The depth of his self-contemplation revealed and enhanced the intensity of his preoccupation with the idea of death, this "Sympathie mit dem Tode," this "Faszination durch dem Tod" and "Todesvagabondage" so profoundly rooted in him that it makes of him a real "Dionysier des Todes."

Can emphasis on the concept of death ever contribute to a dynamic view of being? Is death all negative, does devotion to it preclude all growth or change, is it unqualifiedly a static concept? Thomas Mann recognizes the inconsistency of calling himself a German writer if that name is synonymous with idealist. He knows that he is a good European in the sense that Schopenhauer was one. He asks and answers his own question by new assertions as to what is and is not German. With characteristic ironic discernment he makes his point by referring to Heinrich von Kleist, whose name figures so prominently in the late war as an inspiration to patriotic thinking.

What more natural than this alignment with a poet whose

whole life has a personal experience of growth toward the death concept, for whom the three phases of consecration to death, of ripeness for death, and of victory in death were a supreme reality? Kleist could never adjust himself to life, and life on the other hand, never met him even halfway; so his whole life was a ripening for death and his death only the fulfillment of his own ethical ideal: a death of love and of sacrifice which should be only the beginning of a richer existence. Here the line is sharply divided between Heinrich von Kleist and Thomas Mann. Though they both meet on the common ground of life content and aesthetic content, they part on the method of solution of the problem. Kleist threw away his life with a grand gesture; Thomas Mann sought to live his as normally as possible and thus to heal the breach. His dualistic nature held him in continuous tension between the polar forces of life and death; though the rhythm of both is almost always apparent, the emphasis seemed for a long time to be on the side of death. Death triumphed externally over Kleist, but the "Prinz von Homburg" makes us wonder whether in reality the victory was not his. Since *The Magic Mountain* Thomas Mann has been proclaiming the gospel of life with increasing vigor and earnestness.

Thomas Mann is not concerned with immortality, with Christian eschatology, with palingenesis in the manner of the great and inspired writers from Herder to Goethe. He is a child of the nineteenth century, the century of science, psychology and naturalism. Heir of romanticism though he calls himself, his experiences of death are in a large measure aesthetic ones through the medium of Nietzsche, Schopenhauer and Wagner: a trio which is a unity to him, deep and indissoluble. His soul is attuned to moralism—popularly known as pessimism—through the experience of Schopenhauer; but its ethical atmosphere, this very Christian air of cross, death ,tomb, is in Wagner. And it is Nietzsche, he says, who has converted this primary tendency of his into his work as a psychologist of decay. But it is Nietzsche from whom he has absorbed one supreme formula which he would place above all others, and that is the idea of life.

The work of Thomas Mann is indeed filled with the rhythm of life and death. Up to *The Magic Mountain* death is a negative concept, and the emphasis is in its favor, but increasingly life assumes the ascendancy and positive values are stressed in *The Magic Mountain*.

Looking back of the aesthetic experiences, it is inevitable to ask what were the more primary experiences that turned Thomas

Mann's thinking in the way in which it has gone and which helped to create the dualism in him. This dualism expresses itself in the conceptual antitheses with which his intellect is constantly battling, it is in the artist-burgher problem, it is in the conflict between life and death. It does not seem to lead too far afield to assume that a child which has had the shrinking reactions toward school, toward life, toward its fellow-beings—the similarities with Hanno Buddenbrook are striking—has had "Urerlebnisse" that account for one phase of the dualism. Such an observing, meditative child with a strange psychic structure must have watched the process of disintegration that went on in his own family with that keen inner eye that transformed his "Bildungserlebnisse" and made his weltanschauung a dualistic one. Death was in all probability one phase of his primary experiences. It is not surprising to hear Thomas Mann's confirmation that he loved Heine and the fairy tale, Homer and the sweet languor of life at the ocean, that he was always passionately devoted to music. His first poems have all the sad resignation of Heine and Storm.

In Thomas Mann's endowment there is another factor, a North-German coldness, aloofness, matter-of-factness that may have assisted in drawing him to the side of naturalism in a century of natural science. All his "Bildungserlebnisse," Turgenev, Goncharov, Tolstoy, the Scandinavians, the Goncourts, served to feed the dualism: death and life, romanticism and naturalism. With such a background of natural tendency and intellectual absorption it is not surprising that Thomas Mann took over from romanticism the concern with death. His "Sympathie mit dem Tode" as a natural heritage may have come from his mother, as has often been assumed, or it may be a part of the decadence of an old family into artistry, as he himself has ironically said. But it is primary, and the moving story of his two sisters, both of whom ended their own lives, sheds another light on this tendency.

It is a truism to repeat that Thomas Mann is not the only "German" poet whose concern with death is deep and fundamental. Heine, Lenau, Conrad Ferdinand Meyer, Storm knew of "Todessehnsucht," as had the romanticists. There is a chapter on death in Friedrich Schlegel's *Lucinde*, filled with this yearning. Novalis has come to mean more and more to Thomas Mann with increasing years. Novalis loved death because it was the gateway that released and guided the captive human spirit into a realm where mere earthly, hampered personality was merged

in greater and perfect being. His magic idealism protected him
from phenomena; he was, as Friedrich Schlegel wrote him in
March, 1799, perhaps the first of his age to have "Kunstsinn für
den Tod."

Thomas Mann too has "Kunstsinn für den Tod," but he is
unable to assuage his yearning and his longing with the comforts
of romantic philosophy. He walks in the path of new romanticism,
in theme and essential philosophy that of Schnitzler, Hofmannsthal, Ernst Hardt—all of them deeply moved in an aesthetic way
by this death from which there is no escape—all of them imbued
with a mysticism of death, nineteenth-century mysticism. In them
all lies a supreme and transcendent expression of longing that
knows no bounds. Thomas Mann has nothing of Schnitzler's exaggerated, Freudian, Viennese emphasis on sexual eroticism.
The darkly brooding fate of Hugo von Hofmannsthal is not so
tangible in Thomas Mann's writings. Death as a passion and an
aesthetic cult, as it appears for instance in Ernst Hardt's *Priester
des Todes*, has a parallel only in that early sketch, *Death,* which
Thomas Mann did not incorporate in his collected works.

In discussing the central theme of death, it is impossible to
divorce from the concept the outward mantle in which the main
idea is clothed. If the preoccupation with death is a romantic
mode of thought, so is the form in which death is presented. Almost all of Thomas Mann's writing is gently, subtly—sometimes
more patently and obviously—ironic. It is something in the manner of Heine, for whom he has such great admiration, but with
Heine's overedged sharpness and bitterness removed. Thomas
Mann seldom uses pathos; he has only intellect. For him irony is
the pathos of the middle, the mean. It is a suitable style, the
romantic weapon by which the poet of that generation kept himself above his subject and looked down upon it. Irony is intellectualism to the highest degree, it is the pathos of distance. Irony
becomes almost distortion and caricature when it is infused into
the concept of death as in *Tristan* and *The Magic Mountain*. Indeed, of the latter he says that death has become a comic figure,
in the same breath that discusses its "ethical pathos."

The landscape that Thomas Mann chooses pre-eminently is
the landscape of death. For the sea, its rhythm, its musical trans-
cendence, is "present in almost all his books in some way or
other," and for him it is not really a landscape, it is the experience of nothingness, of eternity and of death; it is a metaphysical
dream. When he places Whitman in the category of the poets who
love death, he says that his love of the ocean would have be-

trayed him, if he had not himself betrayed his dangerous affection by the confession that the waves of the sea of eternity whisper to him "Death, death." Love for the sea, he repeats, is nothing more nor less than love for death.

To this tremendous ocean landscape, so natural a choice for a North German, who has grown up and experienced the ocean, is added an acquired experience in *The Magic Mountain*, the elemental and overwhelming impression of eternal ice and snow. This, too, is a suitable and similar setting for the song of death that Thomas Mann sings in every key.

The new humanism of Thomas Mann, "Der Mensch soll um der Güte und Liebe willen dem Tode keine Herrschaft einräumen über seine Gedanken," is the note that we hear from him again and again since *The Magic Mountain*. It is his very real will to believe, rather than a logical development of his hero's character. It is a manifestation of his growing friendliness to life, which is a legitimate part of his nature just as much as his previously emphasized "Sympathie mit dem Tode." A quarter century of husbandhood and fatherhood induce him to affirm marriage and procreation; to recognize the sterility and unfruitfulness of death-bringing beauty in *Death in Venice* or of Thomas Buddenbrook's denial of the value of continuity. But his Hans Castorp, while he is a "delicate child of life," is nevertheless definitely a child of life and not of death, as were Gustave Aschenbach and Thomas Buddenbrook. Mann knew at twenty-four all about these metaphysical flights of exhaustion into the individualism of death; but knowledge was only a part of his being, and he lived otherwise than he wrote.

Since the *Reflections of a Non-Political Man*, a volume of self-searching and self-clarification, Mann has turned increasingly to the essay for utterances on timely subjects. In the three volumes that have appeared since that time, the theme of death occurs over and over again in discussion, but the protagonist life sits firmly in the saddle and all the emphasis is on the concept of life. On his fiftieth birthday, Thomas Mann expressed as his deepest wish that posterity might say of his work that it was friendly to life, though it knew death. And he adds that there are two ways of affirming life: one which is simple and robust and knows nothing of death, and another which takes cognizance of death. And he thinks that only the latter way, that of artists, of poets and writers, has full spiritual value.

[1932]

THE DIALECTICAL HUMANISM OF THOMAS MANN

A. F. B. Clark

> But nature is not spirit; in fact this antithesis is, I should say, the greatest of all antitheses.

> Effortless nature—that is crude. Effortless spirit is without root or substance. A lofty encounter of nature and spirit as they mutually yearn towards each other, that is man.

> THOMAS MANN (in *Goethe and Tolstoy*).

The situation in which Thomas Mann finds himself to-day is almost unbelievably symbolical of his whole career, temperament, and achievement. The man who was proclaimed in his youth the poet of decadence and who confessed his own "sympathy with disease and death," has in the evening of his life become an activist and is prophesying on public platforms "the coming triumph o democracy"; the author of the *Reflections of a Non-Political Man,* for whom his embattled Fatherland appeared as the champion of a personal, spiritual culture against the hostile, socialized civilization of the *Entente,* is now attributing the enslavement of his people to their fatal indifference to political questions; the one-time creator of the Buddenbrooks, the family which declined in proportion as it became intellectualized and ceased "to think with its blood" (in Hitlerian phrase), is now disengaging from the Biblical block of marble a Joseph who represents a synthesis of spirit and nature. But to anyone who knows his Thomas Mann all this implies no violent conversion. Pope's "Sporus" was described as being "himself one vile antithesis." If we substitute "endless" for "vile," the phrase sums up Thomas Mann perfectly. He is, perhaps, the most "dialectical" in temperament of all imaginative writers—and, as such, perfectly representative of the nation that produced Hegel. This applies to his art as well as to his thought. Were there ever novels so naturalistic in their methods of description, characterization, and dialogue, yet lit with such an underglow of symbolism and poetic suggestion? Was an author ever so emotionally absorbed in his characters, yet so ironically detached from them? Was subject-matter ever so morbid and repulsive, yet treatment and atmosphere so instinctively refined and humane? Was intellectual weightiness ever relieved by such all-pervading humour and wit? Did novels ever so combine timeliness with timelessness?

The importance of Thomas Mann has dawned but slowly on the non-Germanic world. Not till 1916 was any work of his translated into English, when *Royal Highness* appeared in London; then in 1923 a nation of dog-fanciers was made acquainted with his minor work, *A Man and His Dog.* Only in 1924—almost a quarter of a century after its publication in Germany—did *Buddenbrooks* appear in the first of Mrs. Lowe-Porter's superb series of translations. Even yet, not all of Mann's miscellaneous writings are available to English readers, and one cannot avoid the feeling that it is the distinguished German *émigré* and anti-Nazi propagandist who looms in the public eye rather than the author of *The Magic Mountain* and the Joseph novels. Most competent critics are now agreed, however, that in Thomas Mann we have the greatest literary artist of our time; certainly since the deaths of Hardy and Conrad, France and Proust, it would be difficult to set up any rival to him in the Western world, merely as a master of language and of the art of fiction. This aspect of him I have no desire to neglect, but I am even more concerned to call attention to his ideology, for this is both a stumbling-block to his foreign readers, less accustomed than Germans to associate metaphysics with fiction, and yet an integral part of the texture of the fiction itself, not—as in the case of most intellectual novelists—a mere superimposed commentary. Moreover, I believe that the evolution of Mann's thought is most interesting and significant to study in connection with a movement that created quite a stir in America some years ago and which should not be assumed to have lost all its impetus yet—the New Humanism. It will be recalled that the New Humanists were leading a crusade against "naturalism," the worship of nature or instinct, in the name of "the higher will," "the inner check," "the intuition above the reason," and other slogans. Now what is this but the tension between "nature" and "spirit" that animates all Thomas Mann's life and work? But whereas the Humanists were fanatical propagandists and one-sided advocates (most of them were probably by nature—if the Hibernianism may be permitted—anti-naturalists), Thomas Mann is an example, if ever there was one, of "the civil war within the soul" with the contestants almost equally balanced. His works are one long debate between Mann the humanist and Mann the naturalist. It follows from this that Mann's exploration of the terms themselves is much more thorough than that of the American Humanists. Yet the conclusion to which he seems to be slowly coming after a life devoted to the most conscientious and patient weighing of contraries, may not be very different from theirs and will serve as a powerful confirmation of it. Thomas Mann may turn out to be, not only the greatest literary artist, but the greatest humanist of our time.

II

How did Thomas Mann's interest in the "nature-spirit" antithesis arise? * He has himself supplied us with abundant material for answering this question, not only in the autobiographical passages in his novels, but in his numerous critical articles. His very parents represented the two terms of the antithesis— his father, the normal conservative, Philistine merchant was "nature"; his exotic mother with her love of music and her Bohemian ways was "spirit." The austere, simple city of his boyhood, Lübeck, was "nature;" the city of his adoption, the "arty" Munich of the nineties, was "spirit." He found himself, as he grew up, torn between two worlds, the world of "nature," which he equated with the *bourgeoisie,* the simple, unsophisticated middle-class, and the world of "spirit," which he equated with the artistic or Bohemian set; or, to quote the famous passage from *Tonio Kröger:* "The mixture was no doubt extraordinary and bore with it extraordinary dangers. The issue of it—a *bourgeois* who strayed into art, a Bohemian who feels nostalgic yearning for respectability, an artist with a bad conscience. For surely it is my *bourgeois* conscience that makes me see in the artist life, in all irregularity and all genius, something profoundly suspect, profoundly disreputable; that fills me with this lovelorn *faiblesse* for the simple and good, the comfortably normal, the average unendowed human being." There we have, in its ironic pointedness, the early form of the Mannian "nature-spirit" equation; and, if it seems to us extravagant and perverse to confine "nature" to the stolid *bourgeois* and "spirit" to the intellectual smart set, let us note first that it is all to the credit of Mann's severe self-discipline that in his first desperate desire not to fall forwards in the direction in which he inclined, he should lean too far backwards

---

* Of course, it has been deeply embedded in German thought ever since Schiller's Uber naïve und sentimentalische Dichtung.

and exaggerate the dangers of intellect and art; and then let us consider the period in which he began to write.

This was the age known to English aesthetic history as the "naughty nineties" or the "mauve decade"—an age of baroque decadence and irresponsible individualism. We have only to recall the names of Oscar Wilde and Gabriele d'Annunzio with their perversities and highly perfumed exoticism. More significant still, it was the period when Maurice Barrès and André Gide were pursuing the *culte du moi* and when the former was about to turn in revulsion from this form of "spirit" to the "nature" of the *culte de la terre et des morts*. All over Europe adventurous young minds had leaned so far over the abyss that in terror they were drawing back before vertigo dragged them down. It may be that the curious mixture of decadence and ardent nationalism in Barrès and d'Annunzio corresponds in some way to the tension between spirit and nature in Mann. At all events, it must be emphasized that it is on that now vanished background that the early Mann must be projected, if we are to understand him.

The purely intellectual factors in Mann's early development are both cosmopolitan and native. To the former belong the great Russians and Scandinavians and the French realists (particularly Flaubert, whose very voice seems to speak out of Mann's ironic definition of the writer as "a man to whom writing comes hard"). His art as a naturalistic miniaturist he no doubt learned from the latter, and also something of his ironic portraiture of the *bourgeois;* but there is behind this irony in Mann a profound human sympathy and a lyric quality utterly lacking in Flaubert. It is rather the influence of Dostoyevsky that appears in the very earliest short stories of the pre-*Buddenbrooks* period; in form they are terse, pointed little *contes* like Maupassant's, but in content and spirit they are tales of "the injured and insulted" in the unequal contest between sensitive spirit and brutal nature or life. However, cosmopolitan as Mann's culture was already at this early period, it was even more profoundly national, and his first great work was to reveal the truly German writer who might have learned some foreign tricks of art but whose content and inner form were of native inspiration. Above all, the imprint of the three great Germans whom he had chosen as his special masters was on every page of this work—the imprint of Schopenhauer, Wagner, and Nietzsche.

The essence of Schopenhauer's pessimistic philosophy was an almost Buddhistic sense of the futility of the strivings of the human will; only two avenues of escape were open to man from

the misery resulting therefrom; one was to objectify these strivings in works of art (best of all in music which seemed to embody
mysteriously the movement of the Will itself); the other was to
let the Will still itself in Nirvana or death. This idea is the key
to Mann's equating of the art-instinct with the "sympathy for
disease and death," of which he makes so much in later works;
but in *Buddenbrooks* the stress is almost wholly on the latter.
Mann found Schopenhauer the very food his spirit craved. He
tells us himself: "I have in me much that is Buddhist, much heavy
and sluggish yearning for the form or non-form of consummation,
which is called Nirvana or nothingness." (This Buddhistic tendency is another link between Mann and some, at least, of the
New Humanists.) Mann absorbed his Schopenhauer both directly at the source (his discovery of *The World as Will and Representation* was an event in his life) and through Wagner whose
indebtedness to Schopenhauer is well known, and reveals itself
particularly in *Tristan and Isolde*, with its "night," "yearning
for death," and "love-death" motifs. But a comparative study of
the death-theme in literature reveals its wide European extension; it appears in Poe, Novalis, Baudelaire, Leopardi, among
others. It is one of the *leit motifs of* Romanticism, and merely
attains its latest and most richly orchestrated form in Thomas
Mann.

Wagner served, not only as a transmitter of Schopenhauerian pessimism, but as a main objective in himself. In that eloquent
tribute, *The Sufferings and Greatness of Richard Wagner* (1933),
Mann has told us all what the great musician meant to him in his
youth. Mann has always been a passionate lover of music, and
music plays a greater role in his works than, perhaps, in those of
any other novelist. No doubt Wagner particularly attracted him
because he felt in Wagner the same dichotomy that he perceived
in himself. Nietzsche had already pointed out in a famous passage of *Beyond Good and Evil* that Wagner's music sums up the
German soul in its completeness, both its tendency to romantic
disintegration and its stolid Philistine vitalism; but it was no
doubt "the sympathy with disease and death" of *Parsifal* and
Tristan and Isolde that fascinated the youthful Mann rather than
the sturdy healthiness of *The Mastersingers* or the heroic strength
of the *Siegfried music*. For this reason he comes to equate music,
too, with the ideas of disease and death; when Hans Castorp in
The Magic Mountain sees the skeleton of his own hand in the
X-ray laboratory and "for the first time in his life understood
that he would die . . . at the thought there came over his face the

expression it usually wore when he listened to music: a little
dull, sleepy and pious, his mouth half open, his head inclined
toward the shoulder."

The pessimism of Thomas Mann, the "sympathy with death,"
which comes from Schopenhauer and Wagner, must not be confused with the theme of "decadence," so prominent in his early
work and culminating in *Buddenbrooks*. Schopenhauer's pessimism is an expression of the universal destiny of man, now and in
all ages; whereas decadence, by definition, implies a state of
health from which one can decline. Here we come to the third
great German master of Mann, Nietzsche. Mann's relation to
Nietzsche is not as simple as his relation to Schopenhauer and
Wagner. The non-Germanic world thinks of Nietzsche generally
as the prophet of the Superman, the advance-agent of "the blond
beast." This affirmative, aggressive side of Nietzsche affects
Mann, the ironic artist, almost not at all. It is the other side of
the shield that interests him—Nietzsche, the analyst of *bourgeois*
decadence, the forerunner of Spengler. To Nietzsche, the root of
bourgeois decay lies not in a falling-off in virtue, but in a relaxing
of the vital forces. It is from Nietzsche that Mann gets the positive
conception of "life" or "nature" and the negative conception of
"spirit" or "mind" which runs through all his earlier work. It is
from him, too, that the tragic aspect of his works gets its peculiar
colouring; in Mann tragedy consists not in the yielding to sin,
but in connivance with an ebbing vitality.

III

These are the necessary prolegomena to a study of Thomas
Mann. Let us now examine his principal pieces of fiction, both
as works of art and as carriers of his dialectical humanism.

The short stories referred to above were the overtures to
Buddenbrooks (1901), perhaps the most extraordinary example
of literary precocity on record. That a young man of twenty-five
should produce a novel so steeped in the odour of mortality is not
the astonishing thing; what takes our breath away is the maturity
of the literary art and, above all, the power of seeing his characters both from the inside and the outside, of portraying them
both sympathetically and ironically—a feat that seems beyond the
reach of even the most brilliant youth. Take the figure of Tony
Buddenbrook, surely one of the summits of modern character-
drawing. What reader can ever forget that conscientious and
courageous, yet somewhat naive and fatuous girl, whose very
power of rising serene from the blows of fate comes largely from

her lack of "spirit" or "mind"? "She was not consumed by the inexpressible. No sorrow weighed her down, or strove to speak but could not. And thus it was that her past left no mark upon her. She knew that she had led a troubled life—she knew it, that is, but at bottom she never believed it herself." Only Thomas Mann could, with one sentence like that, dash his heroine's hopes of becoming a modern Antigone, a tragic victim of family piety— and at the same time alienate forever the sentimental reader.

Buddenbrooks is both the first real naturalistic novel in German (as Mann claims) and the first German novel of that peculiarly national type known as the evolutionary novel or *Bildungs-roman,* to make a universal appeal outside Germany. It is indeed a rather special variety of the latter type, an inverted *Bildungs-roman,* a story of evolution not upward but downward, an epic of degeneration. At first sight it seems quite similar to many a French or English novel of the realistic school. It is a family chronicle representing four generations of the Buddenbrooks, patrician-merchants of Lübeck, from the beginning to the close of the nineteenth century. The material and social background is inventoried with Zolaesque attention to detail. So far it closely resembles a work like Galsworthy's *The Forsyte Saga.* But look closer and you soon discover that Mann is aiming at something much more subtle than a period-novel. *Buddenbrooks,* in its essence, is the story of a family-destiny working itself out, an evil destiny, the destiny of decadence. And note further that it is not primarily a physical or even a moral decadence; there is no bad heredity in the family, as in Ibsen's *Ghosts,* nor has any Buddenbrook committed even the most venial of crimes; it can only be described as a vitalistic decadence. By a sort of unconscious cultural development, characteristic of the nineteenth century, each successive head of the Buddenbrook family is a more intellectualized, sophisticated, complicated being than his predecessor; he trusts less to instinct, to intuition, to "nature," to tradition, in the conduct of his life and his business, and thereby loses more and more his grip on reality, to which man is guided (this is Thomas Mann's thesis), not by that by-product of nature, the intellect, but by nature herself. The more self-conscious and critical he becomes, the less wisely does he act:

> The native hue of resolution
> Is sicklied o'er with the pale cast of thought

As a work of art and as an embodiment in fiction of the Nietzschean theory of *bourgeois* decadence, *Buddenbrooks* is cer-

tainly deserving of the highest praise. In the building up of
Mann's "dialectical humanism," on the other hand, the novel represents only a tentative first stage. The "nature-spirit" antithesis
forms the framework of the novel; but the actual representatives
of both "nature" and "spirit" are of a kind from which no convincing philosophical arguments could be drawn. One might
almost conclude from a consideration of his characters that at the
date of its composition Mann had really no very high opinion of
either "nature" or "spirit." For "spirit"—represented primarily
by Christian Buddenbrook and Hanno—appears either as wholly
futile or passively sensitive (at all events without creative power), while "nature" is represented only by vulgar "go-getters"
like the Hagenströms or by the bravely resilient but most unsuc-
cessful and muddle-headed Tony; as for Thomas Buddenbrook,
who tries to reconcile "nature" and "spirit," his shipwreck is
complete. The pessimism of *Buddenbrooks* is too all-pervading
to leave any opening for humanistic hopes.

Tristan (1903), the first of what are called the *Künstler-nov-
ellen* (studies of artist-types), is a brisk, dramatic *conte* in the
French rather than the German manner, worthy of the pen of
Maupassant. It is the most pungent (almost cruel) expression
of the Art-Nature antithesis that Mann ever achieved. The closing scene in which Herr Spinell, the aesthete—who has been making Platonic "night-and-death" love in the "Tristan" manner to
the consumptive wife of Herr Klöterjahn (the latter the type of
coarse, common place humanity), but who is merely unnerved,
not heart-broken, like her husband, by the news of her impending death—is completely routed by his unexpected encounter
with Life itself in the guise of the healthy, bouncing baby of the
dying woman, is one of the neatest "curtains" in the history of
the short story and a masterpiece of bitter humor and devastating
irony. As a contribution to humanism, however, the story is no
advance over *Buddenbrooks*. Who can take the fatuous Spinell,
who is staying in the sanitarium not because he is consumptive
but because it is decorated in the Empire style ("Now there are
times when I simply can't live without Empire"), and whose
novel is printed in such a way that "each letter looked like a
Gothic cathedral," as a serious representative of "spirit"? He
recalls too vividly the Gilbertian magnet which yearned for "a
silver churn" not to suggest a deliberate satire on the "mauve
decade" from which the world was just emerging. And what
champion of "nature" will welcome the unprepossessing Herr
Klöterjahn as its representative? If *Buddenbrooks* reveals Mann

in a mood of unrelieved pessimism, *Tristan* seems to have been written in an access of savage cynicism.

The clouds lift with *Tonio Kröger* (1903) to reveal the true humanism (in every sense of the word) of Thomas Mann. No wonder that this charming *Novelle* has remained the most universally beloved of all the author's works. If *Tristan* suggests an exercise in the French manner, *Tonio Kröger* is thoroughly German in its confessional warmth, its patient balancing of opposites, and the lyric beauty of its style. It is, of course, the most frankly autobiographical of all Mann's works; he has dowered Tonio Kröger with his own intellect and heart, with his own excruciating dilemma. The opening chapters describe Tonio's boyhood in Lübeck with his perfectly normal friend Hans Hansen and the girl he (Tonio) loves, Ingeborg Holm, who, being a child of nature, cannot understand Tonio, the child of art (though he can understand her). The middle section deals with his life in Bohemian circles in Munich, and consists, not of narrative, but of a long discussion of the problems of the artist. Later Tonio, now a mature man and celebrated writer, revisits his northern home, and at a Danish seaside-resort sees two people who are for him the reincarnation of the two friends of his boyhood, unspoiled by art. IIe is moved by the love he feels for them to write a letter to his Bohemian friend in Munich.

Not only de we meet for the first time worthy embodiments of "spirit" and "nature" in the successful and brilliant writer, Tonio Kröger, and in the idealized figures of ordinary humanity, Hans Hansen and Ingeborg Holm, but in the above passage we have clearly formulated Mann's first step towards a synthesis of the two elements in Tonio's "longing after the bliss of the commonplace." But the characteristic "touch of contempt" is enough to prevent him from ever achieving a union of "spirit" with "nature."

That curious and ambiguous work, *Fiorenza* (1906), Thomas Mann's only attempt at the dramatic form, gives several unexpected twists to the author's thought and art. The historic setting and the long semi-dramatic, semi-philosophic speeches are a far-off adumbration of what was to be attempted on a much grander scale in the Joseph novels nearly a generation later. The treatment of the Nature-Spirit complex is peculiar in the extreme, and seems to betray some fault in logic. Nature appears to be represented—and this is a reversion to the more than "a touch of contempt" with which she was regarded in the pre-*Tonio Kröger* writings— by the frivolous hangers-on of Lorenzo's court.

Spirit, on the other hand, appears in what seems at first new and striking guises, as Lorenzo, the spirit that seeks to embody the beauty of life as it is, and as Savonarola, the spirit that is hostile to the beauty of life, the spirit "in sympathy with death," the spirit of asceticism. The new thing is that, in both these aspects, "spirit" is for the first time represented, not as merely passive and analytic, but as dynamic and activist. The weakness of the presentation seems to consist in the fact that Mann makes both of these manifestations of "spirit" mere seekers after personal power, whereby their opposition to each other loses all the profound, dramatic symbolism it might have had. The explanation of the apparent ambiguity of the author's purpose in this work probably is that he was here attempting an exercise in that side of Nietzscheism which, as we pointed out above, was least congenial to him—the doctrine of the Superman and of the Will to Power. But in the development of Mann's ideas *Fiorenza* nevertheless marks an important *étape;* "spirit" assumes a more active guise; and perhaps one might venture the suggestion that Lorenzo and Savonarola are preliminary sketches for Settembrini and Naphta respectively in *The Magic Mountain.*

With his second full-length novel, *Royal Highness* (1909), Mann at last attained, in a sense, a synthesis of "nature" and "spirit," but, in my judgment, a somewhat precarious synthesis, as the later works seem to show. No work of Mann has been more variously judged, both as art and as philosophy. On one of its characteristics everyone may agree—it stands out like a sunlit clearing in the dark forest of its author's work. Here at least Mann has followed the slogan of his own Hans Castorp, and has "let death have no sovereignty over his thoughts." It has two other interesting features; it is the most neatly constructed of its author's longer works; and it is, previously to *The Magic Mountain,* the one that conforms best to the ideal of the *Bildungsroman.* It is the story of how Prince Klaus Heinrich, ruler of a small German principality, strives to get into the proper human relationship with his people, and how he finally—by the aid of Imma Spoelmann, the *Dollarprinzessin* from America—succeeds in doing so and in serving his people as well as "representing" them. It is—viewed from the most superficial angle—a delightfully picturesque and humorous record of life in a small German court of the pre-war period (and, as such, of historic value now). But, though Thomas Mann may seem in this novel to have taken a holiday from his more gloomy musings, he has not, after all, departed as much as may appear from his central theme—the ten-

sion between "spirit" and "nature." For he sees the Monarch—
exalted above his people, living in a rarefied atmosphere, yet in
a sense having it as his very function to "represent" his people,
to express their natures and aspirations on a higher plane—he
sees the Monarch as occupying a position curiously like that of
the Artist and suffering like him estrangement from common humanity. This analogy between Artist and Monarch is well
brought out in the scene of the interview between the Prince and
the poet Axel Martini, an exquisite example of Mann's humour
and irony at their best. The latter has just received a prize (a
silver goblet awarded by the Prince) for his poem "The Joy of
Living," and it is incumbent on the Prince to receive him and
congratulate him on his success. The Prince is inwardly a little
dismayed, and at the same time a little exhilarated, at the
thought of meeting a man capable of writing on such a dangerous, nay almost shocking, subject as the joy of living; he expects
to find a Bohemian whose life is all "wine, women, and song";
but he is surprised and somewhat disappointed to learn from the
poet that, though he has written a poem, "The Joy of Living," he
knows as little as the Prince himself about the subject from personal experience. He too is "spirit," not "nature." For his health
is so precarious that, if he indulged in any of the joys of living,
he would have no energy left to write about them. He has to preserve all his strength for his poetic activities.

How does the synthesis of "nature" and "spirit" come about?
By the Prince's falling in love with Imma Spoelmann and marrying her, as soon as he has shown himself capable of throwing off
his monarchical stiffness and of taking a practical interest in the
affairs of his people as well as of "representing" them. The fairy-
tale-like close, with the people in raptures over the brilliant wedding, is full of charm. But I cannot help feeling that there is
something rather "external" about this synthesis—and I understand that Thomas Mann shares this feeling, though not all his
admirers do. No doubt Love is capable of transforming a man;
but what is there in common between this sentimental conversion
and the slow, groping, intellectual *Bildung* that is the characteristic process in the novels of Mann's post-war period?

At all events, we hear no more about the synthesis in Mann's
next important work, which, on the contrary, embodies the most
tragic collision of "nature" and "spirit" he ever depicted. *Death
in Venice* (1912) is, along with *Buddenbrooks,* undoubtedly the
most universally known work of Thomas Mann. It lacks the profound human warmth and the humour of his other stories; but it

is perhaps the most consummate work of pure art—somewhat in
the foreign manner of a Flaubert or an Oscar Wilde—that he has
ever produced. It has a sculptural perfection of form, a *galbe*,
and a fusion of story, characters, and atmosphere into a perfect
unity of impression that go to make one of the most overpowering
things I know in literature. Its style, too, in its lofty intellectual
precision and purity, is as different from the flowing prose of
Tonio Kröger as from the dramatic style of *Tristan*. It is fascinating to see how by these qualities of aristocratic dignity and serenity of style Thomas Mann manages to mitigate the repulsiveness
of his subject-matter. For, in its essence, it is a nightmare of horror; and I know of only one other short story in modern literature
(Henry James's *The Turn of the Screw*) where horror is transformed so wonderfully into beauty. From the first line to the last
we are bathed in an atmosphere of mysterious foreboding, sultry
oppression, decadence, disease, and vice, as we watch the gradual
collapse of the aging, distinguished author, Gustave Aschenbach,
who, thinking to pursue his dream of pure, intellectual beauty,
finds himself in fact pursuing through the cholera-infested lanes
of the crumbling city of the lagoon the beautiful Polish boy for
whom he has conceived a mad passion.

IV

An interval of twelve years—and what years!—separates
Death in Venice from *The Magic Mountain* (1924). The war
years were devoted to what started as a polemical book on the
war and ended as a thorough thrashing-out of Mann's own intellectual presuppositions on such subjects as "nature," "spirit,"
"culture," "democracy," "freedom," etc. The pregnant book embodying this "coming to terms with himself," *Reflections of
a Non-Political Man* (1918), has never, to my knowledge, been
translated into English. That is regrettable, for passages like that
on the *Zivilisationsliterat* (here condemned by Mann as the type
of the Westernizing demagogue of political "reason" and "freedom"), for example, throw light on the guises in which "spirit"
appears in the great novel and on characterizations like Settembrini and Naphta. The great critical essay, *Goethe and Tolstoy*
(1923), is, however, available in English, and throws much light
on the intellectual preparation for *The Magic Mountain*.

This astounding work has left many a well-intentioned
reader breathless. It is the ass's bridge among its author's books.
Never before has a novel been loaded with such an intellectual
cargo. It is not to be recommended to people who cannot enjoy

a novel until they are quite sure they understand all it means. But those who want (like the hero) to probe the meaning of Life, from the meanest of the bodily functions through the questionings of the intellect up to the sensual and emotional mysteries of love, to see in a novel *for the first time* the three aspects of Life (physical, mental, and emotional) driving abreast without one pulling ahead to the detriment of the other, will find here one of the richest pieces of imaginative writing of our time (backed up by the solidest intellectual culture ever possessed by any novelist), a great scientifico-philosophical poem in prose, which (if he had produced nothing else) would alone stamp its author as the greatest living master of literature.

The Magic Mountain, which was started by Mann before the war as a small-scale satirical sketch of life in a sanitarium and gradually became enlarged to take in the reflections provoked by his war-experience, is thus the result of twelve years' gestation. It tells how a young man, Hans Castorp, comes to visit his cousin, Joachim Ziemssen, who is undergoing treatment for tuberculosis in Hofrat Behrens' sanitarium on the summit of the Magic Mountain. Partly because Behrens discovers in Hans, too, a slight tubercular tendency, but mainly because the young man with his inborn love of the morbid (the familiar "sympathy with death") is fascinated by the atmosphere and life of the place, he spends not a few days, as he planned, but seven years on the mountain, where he learns all there is to know about corruption and death, physical and moral, and from which he is recalled only by the thunderclap of the Great War, in whose noise and smoke he vanishes at the end from our view.

This brief outline suggests the profound symbolism of the work, the equating of life in a sanitarium with the feverish heightening of consciousness that spirit (or art) signifies. The mountain-top represents the rarefied atmosphere in which the "intellectual" has his being, far above the "lowlands" of ordinary life. The keen air, the over-abundant food, the comfortable routine, the enforced idleness, on the one hand—and, on the other, the hospital atmosphere, the omnipresence of death and decay— in short, the *danse macabre* in a hotel *de luxe*—combine to stimulate the senses and the nerves of all the inmates. It is life at fever-pitch, "life's fitful fever" raised to the nth power. Mann's peculiar gift (which Henry James alone shares with him) for treating the morbid and the "questionable" (a favourite word with him) in a tone of aristocratic refinement and ironic humour reaches its greatest heights here. As for the great gallery of characters—remarkable syntheses, each one, of the individual and the symbol—here indeed is God's plenty, sufficient to set most contemporary novelists up for the term of their natural book-writing life. Particularly to be noted for their humanistic significance are, on the one hand, the two opposed intellectuals, the *frères ennemis* of "spirit," Settembrini, the Italian rationalistic liberal and Naphta, the Jesuitic nihilist, who undertake from opposite angles the philosophical education of Hans Castorp and who in their lengthy arguments traverse almost the whole intellectual field of our time, spatio-temporal metaphysics, rationalism versus mysticism, democracy versus autocracy, socialism versus capitalism, militarism versus pacificism, romanticism versus classicism; and on the other, Mynheer Peeperkorn, perhaps Mann's grandest imaginative creation, the old Dutchman who, by sheer "personality" and in spite of incoherency of utterance, draws the attention of everybody away from the eloquence and wit of the two "intellectuals" the moment he enters a room and whose only philosophy is "to do homage to Life."

Perhaps the most unique impression that one takes away from this extraordinary work is its singular blend of the scientific and the emotional. We see the human being as an animal organism and simultaneously as a suffering, experiencing spirit. For example, Hans Castorp reinforces the intellectual training he gets in listening to the disputes between Settembrini and Naphta by his own researches in vast tomes on anatomy, physiology, and pathology, as he lies on his balcony under the starry, wintry sky, with a thermometer in his mouth, doing his daily "rest-cure." The knowledge he there acquires of this mysterious body of ours becomes so inextricably mingled with all his thoughts and feelings that when, during the Carnival celebration, and in a state which, it is true, clouds his faculties for discrimination a little, he makes love to Clavdia Chauchat in a declaration such as no mortal woman can ever have heard before or since, he caps the climax by imploring her to give him an X-ray photograph of her skeleton to put in his breast-pocket next his heart (the modern form of the *Liebestod*)!

A great controversy has raged in Germany as to whether *The Magic Mountain* is a real *Bildungsroman* or not. Obviously, if *Bildung* must terminate in a transformation of character or of *Weltanschauung*, the answer is negative. When the Great War calls Hans Castorp down to the "lowlands" again, he is pretty much the romantic with "a sympathy for death" who came up seven years before. I think the proper way to regard *The Magic*

Mountain is as a novelistic counterpart to the theoretical *Reflections of a Non-Political Man,* a canvassing of all the pros and cons, a marshalling of forces preliminary to a new advance from the plateau gained in *Royal Highness* to higher ground. Seen from this point of view, what a superb *Bildungsroman* it is! How incomparably more profound than in any previous work the study of the terms "nature" and "spirit"! With what sharpness all the issues of "humanism" and "naturalism" are focused on the screen! And with what artistic mastery is plastic form given to these abstractions in such symbolic personages as Settembrini and Peeperkorn! Particularly noteworthy is the new appreciation shown for the more "activist" forms of both "spirit" and "nature." Settembrini, the propagandist for Reason, Democracy, and Progress, is made a really attractive figure, although some kindly mockery is spent on "the hand-organ man" and Hans Castorp accuses him of thinking his "free-thinking line." Naphta, on the other hand, the negating spirit, though he has been thought by some to represent the secret depths of Mann's own temperament, is a much less sympathetic figure. As for Peeperkorn, "nature," who has had to be content heretofore with often attractive but usually very retiring representatives (like the admirable Ziemssen in this same novel), finds at last an eloquent, if sometimes inarticulate, spokesman. Although the almost Gallic *malice* that is the Mannian Puck cannot resist making him appear sometimes a little ridiculous (the author sees now that even "nature" can be romanticized), no reader is left in doubt that he is intended to be an imposing figure. How magnificent is his paean to "feeling"! "Feeling, you understand, is the masculine force that rouses life. Life slumbers. It needs to be roused, to be awakened to a drunken marriage with divine feeling. For feeling, young man, is godlike. Man is godlike, in that he feels. He is the feeling of God. God created him in order to feel through him. Man is nothing but the organ through which God consummates his marriage with roused and intoxicated life. If man fails in feeling, it is blasphemy; it is the surrender of his masculinity, a cosmic catastrophe, an irreconcilable horror."

V

And so to Mann's "work in progress," the Joseph legend (1933-). Its already enormous size and the fact that it is nevertheless incomplete at the present moment render impossible a treatment of it here proportionate to that accorded to Mann's other works. Though each successive volume has a narrative unity of its own, yet "the story of Joseph" will not be complete till the last installment appears; and as for the philosophical significance of the work (which concerns us most) it becomes increasingly evident that the full secret of that, too, will not be disclosed before the termination of the work. Any attempt at a final judgment on the artisic or philosophic value of the great enterprise would, therefore, be premature. Yet the work is sufficiently advanced to permit a provisional estimate.

At first sight the new work seems to be an entirely fresh departure for its author, having no relation to his previous naturalistic and pessimistic fiction. Yet we have not gone far before we recognize that it is but the last stage in an evolution towards symbolism that had been going on quite steadily. *The Magic Mountain* had really marked a great advance in this direction, but its strong realistic and contemporary aspect had partly concealed the fact. Yet, if the reader will recall the obsession of Mann with "time" and its phenomena in *The Magic Mountain,* he will perceive the link that joins that work with its successor. Above all, there are very significant passages in the earlier work on the "circularity of time," the phenomenon of "recurrence" (viz., Hans Castorp's borrowing of a pencil from Pribislav Hippe and later from Clavdia Chauchat), that point straight towards the Joseph story. For what else does the study of "the psychology of the myth" (by which phrase Mann has defined his purpose in the Joseph story) involve than the realization on a man's part (in this case, on Joseph's part) of the significance of those experiences of his that seem to be a "recurrence" of previous experiences of his own or of his ancestors and which, therefore, have a "symbolic" value for him and perhaps for all humanity?

Much discussion of the Joseph story lays great stress on its applicability to contemporary history, to its almost allegorical and even propagandist significance. This sort of thing may be overdone: I think Thomas Mann is too great an artist to be an allegorist, though he is undoubtedly a symbolist. Yet these two facts, first, that the very theme of the work is "recurrence" and secondly, that Mann began writing it when the Nazi doctrine (as also, of course, the other European revolutionary doctrines) of "a new world," "the new Fascist era," etc., were already rife, may indeed justify us in seeing in the novel an attempt to react against the idea that the world ever makes literally a fresh start, to claim that, on the contrary, the way to a better future is pointed by a reference to the past. That "recurrence" does not, however, mean literal repetition, but that the history of man is to be thought of as a spiral ascent, partly circular, partly upward, is, of course, an equally stressed idea in the work.

But another link between *The Magic Mountain* and *Joseph* is to be found in the more liberal attitude towards "spirit" that was shown in the previous work. The negating aspect of "spirit" was, as we have seen, embodied in a brilliant but unsympathetic character (Naphta), whereas the affirmative and forward-looking aspect of it (which Mann had previously associated rather contemptuously with the *Zivilisationsliterat*) took the charmingly humane even if slightly pedantic form of Settembrini. As for the "hero," he resembled his prototypes in Mann by inclining towards the dark gods, towards "a sympathy with death"; yet he differed from them in making at least a serious intellectual effort to escape towards the light. Now what strikes every reader of Mann's previous works who opens Joseph is that here at last we have a hero who is decidedly "spirit," yet is not sick, physically or morally. On the other hand, it must be stressed that, though he is not "sick," Joseph shares with his artist-predecessors a sneaking interest in the "questionable." When we first meet him, he is engaged in highly doubtful flirtation with the moon-goddess and other materialistic divinities who represented a stage of theology that Jacob, Isaac, and Abraham had long outlived. Nor does he share his father's utter horror of the land of Egypt, "the monkey land." His "spirit" is not the dry, clear Latin "reason" of a Settembrini; Joseph is a dreamer and like a modern Freudian, he believes that the "unconscious" may be used as a guide to a higher, not a lower life. Moreover, he is not averse to playing with moral fire, which brings him within an ace of succumbing to Potiphar's wife (who may symbolize the forces of death and reaction). Finally, he is by nature an egotist, proud of his intellectual superiority and convinced "that everybody loved him more than they loved themselves," which results in his flaunting his coat of many colours (symbolizing this superiority) before his brethren and being thrown into the well.

But from each discomfiture Joseph rises, not only triumphant, or rather not triumphant at all in a vulgar sense, but a wiser man; and wiser, because he recognizes in his experiences "recurrences" of similar events in his ancestors' lives. From his incarceration in the well (symbolizing the descent into death, whence the resurrection—in body or in spirit), which he recognizes as a new form of Jacob's bondage to Laban, he learns that his pride of intellect was wrong, so in his later life in Egypt he becomes humble and helpful, makes his "spirit" or "culture" serviceable to others; and it is to be assumed that the continuation of the novel after his second going-down into the pit at the close of *Joseph in Egypt* will (it is to be called *Joseph the Provider*) show him establishing a sort of collectivist economy in Egypt. So the cycle taken as a whole will be a great *Bildungsroman,* showing a development of "spirit" from aristocratic individualism to cooperation with common humanity ("nature").

Common humanity or "the masses" (and therefore, we must suppose, "nature") seems to be represented by Joseph's brothers, whose portrayal is one of the artistic triumphs of the novel. Now, whereas "nature" had previously been represented as sometimes attractive, sometimes not, but always as having a certain self-sufficiency, as holding the secret of successful living, and having no yearning towards "spirit" as "spirit" yearned towards her, that no longer holds true here; the brothers are pictured as a crude, brutal, but also somewhat helpless crowd, who underneath their exasperation with Joseph (largely justified by his outrageous vanity and tactlessness) have a sneaking respect and even love for him (the opposition appears particularly in the remarkable portrayal of Reuben). And Joseph, on his side, yearns for the love and appreciation of his brothers. Here, then, at last, we have the reciprocal yearning of "nature" and "spirit" towards each other. Moreover, Joseph is himself both "nature" and "spirit." He is the synthesis of all that is attractive in both Tonio Kröger and Hans Hansen; he has the intellectual brilliance of the one, and the natural human charm of the other; all he needs to do is to mature and to learn how to make the one part of him serve the other and both serve humanity.

Casting a retrospective glance, then, over the long road Mann has come since *Buddenbrooks,* we see that it has been gradually converging towards, and has at last run into, the main highway of the New Humanists. Beginning with a faith in "nature" as the true guide to sound human living and a distrust of "spirit" as a disruptive and negative force, he has almost (though not quite) reversed his position, and now inclines to see in "nature" blind and destructive instinct which requires the shaping guidance of "spirit" if it is not to land itself and the world in ruin. And what makes the identity of Mann's latest philosophy with that of the Humanists still more unmistakable is the fact that "spirit" is obviously not mere "reason" but rather that "higher intuition" or "imagination" which sees, as by divination, in dreams, or in the "unconscious" the recurrent pattern in life's manifoldness, the One in the Many.

[1938]

THOMAS MANN IN EXILE

Lion Feuchtwanger

The curious and solicitous keep asking: How can you German writers work in exile? Is your art not jeopardized by the hundredfold distress of being a stranger, by a strange environment and a strange language?

Instead of a long reply a simple reference to Thomas Mann suffices. There is no need of a long philological analysis; a single glance at Thomas Mann's writings and publications of the last ten years will reveal that exile weakens only the weak, while it benefits him who already demonstrated his worth in his home land.

Fundamentally, Thomas Mann has been a finished writer ever since his first, very early work, a writer whose countenance is unmistakable. Like Minerva from Jupiter's head, the young Thomas Mann sprang completely matured into German literature. And yet this perennially even artist seems perennially different; he furnishes a valid example of how the true writer, in adapting himself to his material, impresses on this material the earmark of his individuality.

The colors which the young Thomas Mann applied to *Buddenbrooks* in his native land are fundamentally identical with those the mature Mann used abroad for *Joseph*. It is the same wary, slightly ironical, tender and balanced tone with which the events are put before us. Still, a change has taken place in the language. The linguistic resources of *Buddenbrooks* would, with all their richness, have been inadequate for transfiguring the simple and yet so pregnant Bible story into the tale which radiates into every nook of human curiosity and knowledge. Just as the Egyptian Joseph differs from the Joseph in the home land while still preserving his identity, just as he added tremendously to his knowledge without changing himself, so Thomas Mann's intrinsic linguistic structure has remained the same during his work on *Joseph*, even though his diction has become still more ramified and still more delicately accented in his exile. Philologists may indicate some day just how much vastly richer the vocabulary of *Joseph* is than that of *Buddenbrooks*, how much the contact with the foreign language affected the language of the author. But the cadence, the ultimate instrinsic means with which the literally formidable material has been mastered, have remained the same.

It is tempting to consider how Consul Buddenbrook and Hans Castorp have been transformed into Jacob's favorite son and into Joseph the Provider. Everywhere behind the features of the three figures can be discerned the countenance of their creator, his inner and external qualities, his fortune and his friendly weaknesses—of which he is proud to a certain degree. Only a man forced to test his calibre in exile, to measure himself continually against new faces and events, only a man forced by the grace of destiny to be incessantly mirrored by the vast looking-glass of exile, can let his intimate and outer qualities flow so freely and directly into an imagined figure.

Two qualities have helped Thomas Mann to master his exile so readily: his delight and his steadfastness in change.

Admiring (and sometimes carping) comments have been made about the kinship of Thomas Mann's diction with the style of the old Goethe. Certain external similarities catch, of course, everybody's eye. The amazing thing, however, is that the style of the young Thomas Mann is much nearer and probably also intrinsically more related to the aged Goethe's style than that of the older Mann. The extraordinary maturity of *Buddenbrooks* is striking; one can hardly believe that this wise mellow work is really the work of a twenty-five-year-old. In *Joseph*, on the other hand, and especially in the last Joseph volume, it is the power and the freshness with which the huge abundance of the work is bound together that is striking, its youthful archness, the delight in colors and the immediacy with which Thomas Mann caught the beautiful lustre of this world.

There is no question about it: his stay abroad has agreed with this author. In the decade of his exile, in his seventh decade, Thomas Mann has grown younger.

[1945]

THOMAS MANN AND RUSSIA

André von Gronicka

I

Mann's Attitude Toward Russia and Its Literature

Thomas Mann's discovery of Russian literature was a highly personal event, not the result of a general intense interest in the subject which might have surrounded the young man and guided his attention in that particular direction. It was in the summer of 1898 during his visit with his brother Heinrich in Rome that in the solitude of his study he turned with fervor to Turgenev, Goncharov, Tolstoy, Dostoyevsky, Gogol, and Merezhkovsky. He sought and found in the works of these Russian authors assistance and inspiration in his quest for a personal style, in his arduous labors on his first novel of truly epic proportions, *Buddenbrooks*. Thomas Mann's numerous expressions of admiration and love for Russian literature are truly rhapsodic. His introduction to this "holy," this "beloved sphere" he places alongside his momentous acquaintance with the philosophy of Nietzsche, thus including Russia among his basic cultural experiences. Nietzsche and Russia, they both, each in a different way, brought the "son of the Ninetenth Century," of the "bourgeois epoch," into contact with a new era, "protected him from torpidity and spiritual death, built for him bridges into the future." Both were for Mann "matters of existential significance," "experiences of a religious nature—religious in a new, vital, and forward-looking sense." In Nietzsche young Mann recognized the champion of a new humanity which was to achieve a loftier religion, realize the age-old dream of the "third kingdom" where spirit would attain corporeality and matter its spiritualization. This very quest for the new religion, for the "third kingdom," he found again in the Russian soul. Gogol and Tolstoy had waged this tremendous battle only to sink back in the end into an "ascetic radicalism" which held that "to live in God meant living outside one's body." "But the struggle," Thomas Mann concludes, "continues in the Russia of Gogol as well as in the Germany of Nietzsche, and to recognize it, to partake of it by dint of knowledge and of love, that is what I have meant when speaking of a 'matter of existential significance'."

Such a personal interpretation of, and relation to, Russian literature could hardly have arisen from superficial browsing. It is the product of a serious, sincere effort to grasp the deeper message of Russian literature, though it is to be stressed that in this effort Mann received much help and guidance from the admired critic and "world psychologist," Dmitri Merezhkovsky, whose masterful study of Tolstoy and Dostoyevsky had made, avowedly, such a deep impression on the twenty-year-old youth and whose monograph on Gogol young Mann "hardly laid aside at all." The profound influence of these studies on Mann we shall find reflected in some of his most important works.

Russia was to young Mann the land of his longing, yet his hopes of visiting Russia came to nought. A lecture tour on which he was to appear in Moscow, St. Petersburg and Riga had been tentatively arranged but was disrupted by the outbreak of the First World War. When Thomas Mann was about twenty-five, the news reached him that Tolstoy was expected to speak at the peace congress at Christiania. He took stock of his finances and was well-nigh decided to make the trip in the hope of meeting the worshiped "master." But Tolstoy fell ill, and thus remained for Mann a "mythical figure." Years later Merezhkovsky intended to visit the now famous Thomas Mann. Though nothing came of the visit at the time—we do not know for what reason—Mann did meet Merezhkovsky nearly ten years later on a visit to Paris, in 1926. This trip brought many other contacts with Russians who had sought and found refuge in the French metropolis. Two of these meetings, Mann describes in some detail: the tea at Leo Shestov's, the gifted author of the study on Nietzsche and Dostoyevsky, and the brief visit to the utter poverty and squalor of Ivan Shmelov's "three-room-with-kitchen" lodgings in the Rue Chevert. At Shestov's the visitor found himself surrounded by a "genuinely Russian atmosphere" which he defines as *"large, childlike, and of a grand good nature, relatively speaking not without a slight touch of wildness."* Especially the host impressed him as "extraordinarily Russian: bearded and broad, enthusiastic, cordial, amiable, 'mähnschlich.' " One of the first of Shestov's friends to be introduced to Mann was Ivan Bunin, the famous author of *The Gentleman from San Francisco,* a work which Mann places at the side of some of Tolstoy's most powerful, plastic creations, such as *Polikushka* or the *Death of Ivan Il'ich.* With

Bunin, this White-Russian émigré and "bourgeois counterrevolutionary," our author immediately felt "sympathy, solidarity—a sort of 'Eventualkameradschaft.'" For as Mann adds prophetically, "I need have no doubt that under certain circumstances his fate might well become my own, even though at present [1926] we in Germany have not yet arrived at the point where a writer of the approximate make-up of a Bunin need shake the dust of his native soil from off his feet and eat the bread of the West."

Ivan Shmelov made a disturbing impression on Mann. The appearance of this "Russian writèr and martyr," in whose "furrowed, emaciated face" all the horrors of Revolution had left their gruesome imprint, stirred up feelings of pity mixed with those of shame, yes, even of personal guilt. For Mann remembered only too well the passage in Shestov's historical novel, *The Sun of the Dead*, in which the writer poured out his scorn on the Western peoples, who like green students sat by and watched with detached curiosity the progress of the "interesting experiment," while in Russia millions were being slaughtered or—like Shmelov—were being maimed in body and soul by the insufferable impact of bestial brutality and unspeakable privations. Mann knew this novel of Shmelov well indeed, for he had read its German translation in manuscript and had urged its publication in *Die Neue Rundschau*, having found in it not only a stirring historical document but a creation of true literary talent as well.

Shmelov's novel was by no means the only Russian work which Thomas Mann helped introduce to the German public. One of his most extensive efforts in this direction was a *Russian Anthology* on which he collaborated with Alexander Eliasberg for the *Süddeutsche Monatshefte*. In his introduction to the volume Mann states explicitly that several of the selections were included on his personal recommendation or at least with his express approval. Thus he insisted on the inclusion of Chekhov's *The Boys* instead of many better-known short stories of this writer because he saw in it a particularly "happy example of Russian humor springing from sheer unsapped vitality" and "a deeply exhilarating sprightliness." He pointed to the episode of Soldier Avdeev in L. N. Tolstoy's *Khadshi-Murat*, since it had impressed him as a matchless example of "the powerful directness (*Selbstverständlichkeit*) of style" so characteristic of the Russian master, and he approved heartily the selection of Sologub's *The White Birch*, which he loved for its "soulful sorrow, helpless longing, morbid sweetness, and tender hopefulness."

This introduction to the anthology is worthy of further analysis, for it sheds some interesting light on Mann's appreciation of Russian literature. Essentially the essay may be defined as an able variation on themes furnished by Merezhkovsky in his monograph on Gogol: Russian literature as the grand arena for the struggle of spirit and matter, the incessant quest for a lofty synthesis of these two opposing forces, the spiritualization of matter, the materialization of the spirit; Gogol as the harbinger of a new epoch of Russian literature in which Pushkin's "sensuously rediant, naive, serene poetic sphere" was to be replaced by the spirit of "criticism," by religious questing and by the Gogolian comicality which does not, as did Pushkin's humor, well up from blissful serenity, but which springs from the desire "to make a laughing-stock of the devil," that is, from metaphysical contemplations. It is this "Russian humor with its truthfulness and warmth, with its fantastic quality and its deep, heart-winning drollery," which Mann considers the "most lovable, the most delighting in all the world"; he places it above the English and the Jean-Paulesque German humor, not to speak of the French, which he calls *sec*. He marvels at the easy accord in Russian literature of a most intense sensuous enjoyment of nature, of a happy, healthy sense of life with a profound insight into the world of sickness and the torments of Golgotha.

But not only the spirit and quality of Russian literature in general is thus broadly defined in this essay; some interesting characterizations and evaluations of individual authors and specific works are also given. Pushkin is called the Goethe of the East, Dostoyevsky the East's Dante, Tolstoy its Michelangelo, comparisons which rest on well observed, significant traits that link these pairs of creative giants. Alexei N. Tolstoy, the "expressionistic Gogol," is likened to his illustrious forebear particularly in his "melancholy imagination and in his humanity." Finally Mikhael Kuzmin is aptly characterized as a "modern citizen of Petersburg," a highly cultured type, a European, hardly very Russian any more, with leanings toward Rococo and Gallic style. In sum, this introduction furnishes a telling testimony of Mann's marked interest in, and understanding and fondness of, Russian literature.

Yet the most important essayistic contribution by Thomas Mann on the subject of Russia and its literature is undoubtedly to be found in his study *Goethe and Tolstoy*. To be sure, this essay is more than an introduction of certain Russian literary figures to the German reading public. Like everyone of Mann's important contributions, this also is a document of the author's untiring speculation on the relationship of nature to spirit, and of art, the artist and man in general to these two spheres. Unquestionably, the vivid portrayal and comparison of Goethe, Tolstoy, Schiller, and Dostoyesky aims, above all, to set forth in concrete form, to objectify in symbolic figures Mann's musings on this central theme. Yet at the same time this portrayal and comparison serves admirably to "bring home" to the German reader the relatively unfamiliar figures of the Russian authors. The German reader sees them here in the company of his classical poets, Goethe and Schiller, sharing with them many of their experiences, thoughts, and emotions. Thus the "exotic" Russians tend to lose for him some of their far-off, bizarre qualities and to acquire a much more immediate human interest.

Of the two pairs of figures, those of Goethe and Tolstoy occupy the foreground; Schiller and Dostoyevsky, by comparison, are treated rather "more timidly." In contrast to the "God-like" Goethe and Tolstoy, Schiller and Dostoyevsky represent for Thomas Mann the types of the hero and the saint; they both are *Leistungsethiker*. Both are of lowly birth, both suffer poverty, poor health, an early death—all this in keeping with their appointed role upon the stage of life. And yet, doomed as they are to a humble social station and ill health, they bear upon their brow the mark of the nobility of spirit (*den Adel von Geistesgnaden*). They are shown to be the born representatives of what Mann calls the "critico-moral" attitude in life and art, which frowns upon the gray mediocrity of everyday existence and reaches for all that is extreme, intense, lofty, pure, and noble, even at the price of losing touch with mother earth and soaring off into the world of sentimental, emotionalized, rhetorical idealism (Schiller) or into the realm of shadowy, grotesque, apocalyptic visions (Dostoyevsky).

As against this attitude and form of being, Thomas Mann sees Goethe and Tolstoy marked by "the calm, the modesty, the truth and strength of nature" and as representing, basically at least, the "aesthetic-plastic principle," which enabled them to create works of truly epic quality and scope, surcharged with life's vitality and vigour. But for all the important traits which Thomas Mann shows that these two "aristocrats of nature," these "favorites of the gods" possess in common, he does not fail to stress their characteristic differences. In the main, these differences can be reduced to a basic group: Goethe, the humanist, classicist, and scion of an old German Patrician family; Tolstoy, the "peasant-aristocrat and son of a young race," the "arch-Russian of enormous ethnic genuineness and colossal Eastwardness (*Östlichkeit*)," or, to express it with Mann, metaphorically: Goethe—the Olympian; Tolstoy—a sort of Russian pagan god.

From this basic set of contrasts Mann develops all others in the life and work of the two men, bringing out in unforgettably vivid scenes Tolstoy's exuberance, his wild, colossal energy, naive expansiveness, unrestrained surrender to instantaneous moods, an elemental urge for self-expression and self-assertion. Tolstoy's tendency toward a freedom bordering on libertinage and anarchy Mann illustrates impressively by a rather detailed presentation of Tolstoy's pedagogical views and a comparison of these with Goethe's. Tolstoy's philosophy of education is seen to center in the demand of absolute freedom for the students. "Let us release all students from behind their benches," he quotes Tolstoy as saying. In these revealing words, in Tolstoy's whole theory of education, Mann sees "the revolt of his [Tolstoy's] basic Russian nature against Peter the Great," the Slavophile, anti-western, anti-humanistic attitude of the prophet of Yasnaya Polyana. "The greatness of Tolstoy," Mann concludes, "is of a proto-heathen, wild kind, antedating all civilization. It lacks the humanistic element, *das Menschliche*." It derives exclusively from Tolstoy's intimate contact with nature. In his life as well as in his work "the sensuous element asserts itself far stronger, more direct, more carnal than in the life and work of Goethe."

To be sure, in Goethe, too, Mann sees a genius deeply rooted in the sensuous sphere, grasping life vigorously with all his senses. At the bottom of his personality he detects that same elemental force, that darkness, that nihilistic neutrality, that mephistophelian mischievous love of confounding and confusing, that diabolic love of negation, so typical of Tolstoy. Yet at the same time he points to Goethe's matchless power to rise above the dark, chaotic, and amoral realm of nature into the lucid, harmonious sphere of ethics and reason. Secure in the possession of a rich humanistic heritage, Goethe, in his struggle toward the light, does not disavow or destroy his sensuous self by a radical asceticism as did Tolstoy, but succeeds, according to Mann, in striking a happy balance between instinct and intellect, vitality and refinement, nature and culture.

This essay of Thomas Mann again impressively demonstrates the author's wide and penetrating reading in Russian literature. It indicates acquaintance even with such relatively minor works of Tolstoy as the novella *Lucern,* with Tolstoy's confessions, with his diaries and letters, with Tolstoy-biographies (Birukov), with Turgenev's, Garshin's and Aksakov's pronouncements on the Russian master. Yet by far the most significant aid and inspiration Thomas Mann has derived here from Dmitri Merezhkovsky's Tolstoy-Dostoyevsky biography, and, especially, from Maxim Gorky's *Recollections of Tolstoy.* We have already quoted Mann's high praise of Merezhkovsky's work. Gorky's little book he considered "the best work" ever written by that author.

Only a critical edition of Mann's essay could trace all the subtle references to, paraphrases of, and quotations from these works. It must suffice here to point to some leading themes which the two Russian biographies suggested to Thomas Mann or at least helped crystallize in his mind, and to some of the most vivid biographical material which was furnished him, particularly by Gorky.

Above all it is the interpretation of Tolstoy as an Antaean personality drawing his powers from contact with mother earth which Mann shares with, if not actually derives from, Merezhkovsky. Together with Gorky, Mann underscores Tolstoy's Slavophilism and shares with him the unorthodox interpretation of Tolstoy as "a sort of Russian pagan god seated upon a maple-throne under a golden linden-tree, a god who, though perhaps not very majestic, is shrewder than other gods." They both stress Tolstoy's diabolic nihilism, his mischievous whimsicality, his delight in confusing and confounding his fellow men and playing rough tricks on them in the manner of the Russian folk-heroes (e.g., Vaska Buslaev). Both discover under Tolstoy's democratic exterior an aristocratic dignity, yes, even a haughtiness which, suddenly breaking forth, could send the back-slapping comrades packing, with "frozen noses, wincing and squeaking." Having made this point, Gorky as well as Mann proceed to call Tolstoy the most human of men, *ein menschheitlicher Mensch, chelovek chelovechestva,* a man with an uncanny ability to win the confidence, admiration, and love of the most diverse people.

Some ten years later (1935), Thomas Mann returns to the figure of Tolstoy in his essay *The Sufferings and Greatness of Richard Wagner,* this time to compare the Russian epic writer with Germany's greatest operatic composer. He finds striking similarity in their lives, both of which have been thought to contain a "break," a radical turn-about in spiritual orientation, while as a matter of fact both traversed a path of the most logical, consequent development. Just as the old Tolstoy was "pre-existent" in the Pierre Besuchov of *War and Peace* or in Levin of *Anna*

Karenina, just so Wagner's Christian-romantic, emotional world of the *Parzival* was present already in his *Tannhäuser.* Both men are characterized for Thomas Mann by the same "social ethos" whch seeks to purge humanity of love of luxury, lust for money and lack of affection and sympathy for fellowmen. Giants both, capable of sustained creative effort and determined not to spare their audience any details, but to elaborate upon them, to drive them home by means of the leitmotiv, that distinctive stylistic device common to both artists.

II

Mann and the Russian Revolution

Thomas Mann's sustained interest in Russia, traced here in some detail, is not confined to the literary sphere but extends to the socio-political as well. Here his earliest pronouncements carry a somewhat critical note. In the "Gedanken über den Krieg," for example, he calls Czarist Russia the "most depraved police-state" and in his essay on Frederick the Great he speaks of Russia's "elemental, irresponsible expansionist tendencies . . . its blunt and limitless willingness to enter wars in its instinctive knowledge of its invincibility." These statements, however, carry little weight in the face of Mann's repeated confessions of profound admiration for Russia, especially in his *Reflections of a Non-Political Man.* Here Russia is eulogized as the home of true, human democracy and Christian brotherhood, of a "democracy of the heart." Germany he considers in every respect far more akin to Russia than to its Western neighbors, France or England. Germany's war of 1914 against Russia is for the Thomas Mann of the *Reflections* a fratricidal folly, "a false, erroneous, damnable war" and Russia's alliance with France a "mesalliance of the human soul with politics." He is elated at the news of peace on the Eastern front for now he sees hope again for the realization of his fervent dream of a united Russia and Germany "marching hand in hand into the future." The Russian Revolution, at the time of its volcanic eruption, perturbed Thomas Mann. To be sure, he had early recognized in Russia a fertile ground of "communism" in the sense of a democratic, Christian, fraternal communality, but the brutal, chaotic, the political form in which communism actually came to Russia could not help but repel Thomas Mann, the anti-political, conservative German bourgeois of the *Reflections.* He saw in the movement nothing but a "frenzied scuffle (*desperate Katzbalgerei*) between the democrat-

ic-bourgeois French spirit and anarchical Tolstoyism." This was
an off-hand judgment in the heat of his polemic against Western,
Gallic *"Zivilisation"* and its representative, the *"Zivilisationsliterat,"* (i.e., Heinrich Mann). Yet several years later, in the
essay *Goethe and Tolstoy* his attitude toward the Russian revolution, though changed, is hardly less critical. No longer is there a
grappling between the "democratic-bourgeois French spirit" and
"Tolstoyan anarchism." Tolstoy has won, Tolstoy, the arch-
Slavophile and reactionary, the enemy of Peter the Great. No
matter what Marxian, Western trapping the Russian Revolution
might be flaunting, Mann is now convinced that in Czar Nicholas
there was murdered the spirit of Peter the Great, that his fall
"opened the way for the Russian nation, not toward Europe, but
homeward, back into Asia." He recognizes now in the Russian
upheaval the "end of the Western-liberal, the European epoch
of Russia." In fact, he sees in it a dire signature of an "anti-
liberal reaction," an early symptom of Europe's turning its back
upon the "Mediterranean-classical-humanistic tradition," its "disgusted turning away from democracy and parliamentarism toward dictatorship and terrorism." This point of view Mann once
more expresses most emphatically through the mouth of Naphta in
The Magic Mountain and underlines Bolshevism's total disregard
for the freedom and dignity of the individual who is swallowed
up in the anonymity of the mass, is sacrificed on the altar of an
ideology.

While Mann thus disapproves of Bolshevist Russia, he feels
a growing gratitude and admiration for the great Russian literary
figures, who furnish him with that inspiring example of strength
and steadfast courage in face of spiritual trials and physical ad-
versities, of which he, the citizen of a Republican Germany, upon
whose shoulders devolve ever heavier responsibilities and duties,
is more than ever in need. "Let us draw strength," he exclaims,
"in contemplation of the mighty mien of Tolstoy at his work!"

Only slowly, with the inexorably unfolding events and with
a steady growth in social consciousness, does Mann's view of
Bolshevism undergo a change. This change is one of the clearest
indices of the author's ability to participate in new ideas arising
in a swiftly-moving world without cutting loose from cherished,
basic traditions, from his *humanistic* heritage. For this change is
not an abrupt turn-about; it is a subtle relocation of accents.
While he had previously stressed the totalitarian, anti-liberal,
anti-idealistic, anti-humanistic aspect of Communism, he now
pays tribute to its social achievements and even nods approval to

collective and planned economy which promises to erase or at
least relieve poverty and suffering. Seeing clearly the dangers of
excessive liberalism and of an irresponsible individualism in the
Western democracies, he points with praise to the salutary emphasis on collective effort, on economic justice, on social consciousness and social responsibility in the Russia of today. No wonder
that a shrewd observer, the Soviet-Russian writer Ilya Ehrenburg
has recently triumphantly exclaimed: "Thomas Mann has expressed his admiration for the integrity and justice of our cause."
Yet Ehrenburg is only partially justified in his triumph. Unless
Russia has in the meanwhile reinstated the rights of the individual
Mann will withhold his full approval and admiration. For although
Mann is duly impressed with the need of socialization, he will
not, it is safe to assume, cast aside lightly his humanistic heritage,
will insist in the future—as he has in the past—on the sacred
rights of the individual as over against the state, on the proper
respect for the dignity and sanctity of human personality.

III

Russian Elements in Mann's Imaginative Work

Thomas Mann's intense and sustained preoccupation with
Russia, its literature, its social and political life, is reflected in
every one of his major creative efforts up to and including *The
Magic Mountain,* with the lone exception of *Royal Highness.*
Since a complete survey of Russian elements in Mann's imaginative work would far exceed the limits of this essay, it was decided
to focus the analysis upon *The Magic Mountain,* not only for its
world-wide fame, but also because this masterpiece presents the
most inclusive and characteristic record of Mann's views on Russia and of his indebtedness to Russian literature as a source of
inspiration and material.

The Magic Mountain is replete with references to Russia; its
pages, particularly the first part up to Madame Chauchat's temporary departure, are literally crowded with Russians. As Settembrini remarks, in his best satirical vein: "Asia [Settembrini
identifies Russia with Asia] swallows us up—wherever one turns,
a Tartar physiognomy . . . Genghis Khan . . . wolves of the
steppes, snow, vodka, the knout, Schlüsselburg, Holy Russia."

The unassuming little traveling salesman from St. Petersburg, Anton Karlovich Ferge, with his first-hand experience of
the Russian steppes is quite as typical a representative of this
"Slavic sphere" as are the "bearded, elegant Russians" down in

the village, "looking so barbarically rich." The Russian students, "with their shocks of hair and black blouses closed to the throat, showing not a vestige of linen"; the "lively, little old Russian lady" chattering in her "soft, spineless tongue"; Madame Chauchat's husband, that Russian official in far-off Daghestan, the slovenly Russian couple, ill-mannered and addicted to erotic excesses; pretty Marusja with her ruby ring, her orange perfume and irrespressible fits of laughter, they all are not only human beings in their own right, with their personal traits and idiosyncracies, but they serve at the same time as characteristic details of Mann's vast canvas of Russia, a picture so colorful, realistic, and vivid as is not easily found again in German *belles-lettres*.

Moreover, even the exotic Javanese, the "great personality," Mynheer Peeperkorn, has certain connections with the Russian sphere. To be sure, the main model for this character was Gerhart Hauptmann; yet at the same time and in a similar manner Tolstoy, too, served this function. A biographical note may introduce and buttress our argument. It is well known that Thomas Mann while working on *The Magic Mountain* was at the same time writing the essay *Goethe and Tolstoy*. In his work on this essay he used, as we remember, for one of his main sources of information and inspiration Maxim Gorky's *Recollections of Tolstoy*, a work which he considered Gorky's best. This biography contains extremely vivid descriptions of Tolstoy. Thus Gorky draws an unforgettable picture of the Count in the park of his estate. Yasnaya Polyana. We see Tolstoy, with head thrown back, intently watching a hawk circling high above, hesitating to strike. "And Leo Nikolaevich Tolstoy strains upward, shades his eyes with his palm, utters broken exclamations, in tense suspense, the bird might dive—now, now—upon its prey." Does not this scene recall a very similar one in *The Magic Mountain*, though, to be sure, one raised from the realism of Gorky's biographical study into the realm of stylized art? Do we remember Peeperkorn, standing there, head thrown back, shading his eyes with his hat, extolling in broken, stammered words the eagle circling majestically high in the blue? And Peeperkorn, just like Tolstoy, fervently wishes to see the king of birds dart upon its victim. On another occasion Gorky shows us the Russian author surrounded by a motley gathering; there sits Prince Nikolai Nikolaevich, an uneducated painter Ilya, a social-democrat from Yalta, a nameless musician, the writer Bulgakov; they all sit silently around Tolstoy, looking at him with the same enamored eyes. And Tolstoy expounds to them the abstruse philosophy of Laotse. "But it seems to me," Gorky continues, "as if he were an unusual *man-orchestra* who has the gift of playing at one and the same time on various instruments." And of Peeperkorn seated amidst the motley crowd of his admirers, Thomas Mann says: "He proceeded to command silence round about him as an *orchestra conductor* who . . . collects his orchestra to begin a number." "What did he utter? Something highly incomprehensible. . . . Yet everyone hung on his lips and succumbed to feelings which for self-abnegation and intensity far exceeded the accustomed gamut of these people." The parallelism is too striking to need much elucidation. With Thomas Mann as with Gorky a heterogeneous group of people bestow their enamored admiration not upon the content of the speech, but on the "great personality" of the speaker, on a personality which Gorky compares to a "man-orchestra" and Mann to an "orchestra conductor." Surely such a far-reaching identity of motives could not be the result of mere chance, especially in view of the fact that Mann had thoroughly studied Gorky's essay!

But once we have been made aware of the interconnection between Peeperkorn and Count Tolstoy by these external parallels, we soon come to recognize that even the very core of Peeperkorn's philosophy of life is akin, if not actually based on, a confession of the aging Tolstoy recorded by Gorky in his study. This confession bears witness to a deep despair which had gripped the aging Tolstoy, this great creative genius and virile personality, in the face of the inexorable approach and senility. "Nature," he laments, "torments man cruelly and mockingly beyond endurance: She takes from him his strength and leaves him with the wish to live. . . . Only man is called upon to endure the full torture of this shame and horror." What is expressed in these agonized words is not the fear of death, rather it is shame and terror of being no longer equal to the demands of life. Throughout the last days of the sick and aging Peeperkorn this panic terror at the threatening inability to meet, master and make the most of life runs as a steady leitmotiv. To prove oneself adequate in the face of the demands of life Peeperkorn considers a divine commandment. "If man fails in feeling, it is blasphemy; it is surrender of His masculinity, a cosmic catastrophe, an irreconcilable horror," he expounds to Castorp in their last great dialogue. The naked fear of growing old, which Tolstoy confesses in a crassly realistic manner, finds here a metaphysical basis, is philosophically embellished and enhanced. Nevertheless, the core of Tolstoy's and Peeperkorn's experience remains the same:

terror and shame roused by the sense of failing vitality, of approaching senility.

In pointing out a certain dependence of Peeperkorn on Tolstoy, we do not wish to imply mechanical borrowing by Mann from Gorky. The effectively enhanced form in which Tolstoy's confession reappears with Mann should be sufficient proof of Mann's creative independence. Nevertheless, it is evident that even in his portrayal of this Dutch Mynheer, Mann's interest in Russia, its people and its literature has furnished him some effective details. Some salient traits of Gorky's Tolstoy live on in Mynheer Peeperkorn.

The most comprehensive and subtle embodiment of the Russian spirit, however, is Clavdia Chauchat, Hans Castorp's paramour. Castorp meets Clavdia shortly after his arrival at the Magic Mountain; actually he had met her as a schoolboy of thirteen in the person of Pribislav Hippe. For Hippe and Chauchat melt for Castorp into a single personality, into the symbol of the Slavic spirit, of "Northerly exoticism," which "appeals to him as nothing else in the whole world. This predilection of Castorp's is a piece of autobiography. Thomas Mann once confessed virtually in the words of Castorp, that the exoticism of the Northeast is for him of the deepest, the most fascinating kind. "The brown exoticism with its blubber lips and swaying earrings is as nothing," in his opinion, "compared with the ice-green slit-eyes and the cheekbones of the steppes." Thus in Castorp's fascination for the Slavic East we are afforded perhaps the deepest insight into Mann's sympathy and predilection for the Russian sphere, which appear to be rooted in the author's subconscious.

It does not seem that Hippe and Chauchat, as individuals, have exact prototypes in Mann's life. Though Mann has probably obtained many characteristic details by keen observation of Russian types, it was the artist's creative imagination that fused them into the complex personality Hippe-Chauchat, objectifying a whole philosophy of life, a way of being. Chauchat's cat-like walk, her lithe, supple, bewitching movements, as well as her little vices of door-slamming, self-exhibitionistic posturing, biting of fingernails, her bad orthography, her incurable unpunctuality, they all objectify important elements of the Russian character as seen by Mann.

Attempting to analyze Madame Chauchat's character, it proves impossible to decide which qualities to trace to Clavdia's lax, languorous feminity, which to her sickness, which to her Slavic provenience, and this for the very good reason that the author

himself has made such a separation impossible by intertwining
these elements, by identifying far-reachingly the Slavic sphere
with languor, lassitude, and laxness, with conscious overemphasis
of the physical, with the predisposition to sickness, with the
"sympathy with death." Chauchat's languid movements, her "posture that left so much to be desired" when viewed superfically
may be taken as the results of her sickness, yet fundamentally
they are organic concomitants of her Slavic disposition. Settembrini and Ziemssen are also tubercular, yet show no trace of Chauchat's lethargy and moral as well as physical laxness. On the
contrary, they oppose them to the last. Moreover, Mann links
Castorp's fateful fascination by the Slavic sphere, i.e., Hippe-
Chauchat, explicitly to the old scars and fresh moist spots in his
lungs, to his "experiments in the organic realm," to his interest
in sickness and to his "sympathy for death." Perhaps the most
striking instance of the interconnection of Hippe-Chauchat with
death we find in the chapter "Snow," where the color of the
surrender-provoking, death-dealing snow is exactly that of the
fateful "slit-eyes" of Castorp's two Slavic friends, Clavdia and
Hippe.

Chauchat may not, of course, be considered an all-embracing
symbol for Mann's Russia. Thus Marusja, for instance, is an important complementary figure, in which Man symbolizes the gay,
naive side of Russia. With Marusja, bursting with merriment and
vigor, sickness is a lamentable, physical affliction, not, as with
Chauchat, the symptom of a deeply problematic psyche. We can
well imagine Marusja, minus the tubercular sores, a mother of
healthy children, a faithful, helpful wife down in the *Flachland*.
Mann knows that such Marusjas, untainted by sickness, such simple, vigorous children of *Matushka Rossiya*, have made that country one of the most fecund nations of the world, able to bear
hardships which would have crushed most other peoples.

Madame Chauchat is a typical member of pre-revolutionary
Russia's "intelligentsia." Dostoyevsky atmosphere surrounds her.
She is Russian in Dostoyevsky's definition of one of that nation's
most characteristic traits. "To become truly Russian," he proclaims in his famous address on Pushkin, "is to become the brother of all peoples, to become *pan-human* (*vsechelovekom*)." It
is of this basic Russian quality that Chauchat in her *Mähnschlichkeit* [!] partakes. There is in Clavdia's *Mähnschlichkeit* that
all-embracing sympathy, understanding, and tolerance for the
human spirit in all its individual and regional manifestations
which transcends the narrowly national. At the same time Chau-

chat's tolerance has for its characteristic reverse an insistence on absolute freedom for her own person from all demands and restraints of etiquette and convention, freedom to live *herself* in the most absolute sense of the word, to follow every impulse, whim, and fancy. Zeimssen, with the hostile instinct of a Prussian soldier utterly devoted to the stern military code of honor, discipline, and duty sees in this *Mähnschlichkeit* but a "blind for all sorts of slovenliness and laxness." As a matter of fact, Chauchat's disregard of the social code does not confine itself to minor infractions such as the slamming of doors and habitual unpunctuality. She does not hesitate to shake the very foundations of Western society. Though married, she prefers to lead a "dubious existence" at the side of a man to whom she is bound by ties of admiration and love, not by those of convention. She is disdainful of the bourgeois concepts of love and marriage with their ulterior social purpose of family and children. Her passion is like a force of nature, untethered by moral or social considerations, unpredictable, wild, ruthless. It is this passion that is reflected in her eyes which have an uncanny way of "melting into the very hue of mystery and darkness," of looking at Hans Castorp "with an inconsiderate boldness and fierce severity," which lifts him from the safe confines of his bourgeois existence and rouses in him a "reckless joy he had felt but once when, experimentally, he had cast off the burden of bourgeois decorum and had enjoyed the abysmal advantages of disgrace."

Hans Castorp is no less aware of dangers lurking in Chauchat's *Mähnschlichkeit* than is Ziemssen. Of *Mähnschlichkeit* "in the sense of unlimited *guazzambuglio* of self-indulgence, I have my own suspicions," he confesses to Clavdia, "but in the sense of freedom, goodness, *esprit (Genialität)* . . . it is great." Here the ingenious Hans Castorp goes beyond his upright, military cousin, he recognizes in Chauchat's *Mähnschlichkeit,* alongside its dangerous tendencies, the very breath of humanity and kindness, yes of genius, that bold and fearless individualism, that freedom and breadth of vision, inseparable from all truly creative existence.

It is important to realize that this spirit of freedom, of unconventionality, alive in Clavdia's Russian soul, her pronounced independence and individualism, have nothing in common with *Western* individualism. That was born in the Renaissance, characterized the ages of enlightenment and classicism, and survives, though hard pressed, in contemporary Western humanistic culture, defended and extolled by such valiant and eloquent champions as Settembrini, this implacable enemy of Chauchat, whose antagonism to the East and all it stands for is so deep as to be instinctive, beyond all debate—which is saying a great deal with reference to this man of enlightened reason and lucid argument. Clavdia's "individualism" is rooted in a pre-social, pre-moral self-hood, in substratas of human history untouched by humanism or by concepts of bourgeois morality. It is akin to the nomad's craving for freedom of movement. It is a mystical individualism which presses on to God and to self-salvation by *seeking*, not by *avoiding* evil, totally unconcerned with the social consequences of its acts.

This Slavic "individualism," this asocial or even anti-social attitude, has a startling way of vanishing before the impact of a compelling affect such as love, of changing as by magic into the most fervent self-denial, into readiness, yes, even eagerness for self-sacrifice. Thus in her love and admiration for Peeperkorn, Chauchat sheds all selfishness and simply and naturally shows herself ready to accept hardship and humiliation for the sake of the beloved. To be sure, Clavdia attributes this unselfishness to her femininity. "One would not be a woman if one were not willing to bear humiliation for the sake of a man like that," she explains to Castorp. The attentive reader is, however, left in no doubt by the author that this willingness to bear humiliation, born as it is of Clavdia's love for Peeperkorn is part and parcel of her *Slavic* nature, a nature completely dominated and conditioned, not by reason and logic, but by *affects*, by emotions.

Clavdia is by no means ignorant of this characteristic organization of her Slavic personality; and far from seeking to change or deny it, elevates it to a life's philosophy which she contraposes to Hans Castorp's, the German's, the Westerner's make-up and manner of life. In one of the most thought-provoking passages of the entire work, Mann has Madame Chauchat accuse Hans Castorp of selfishness and egocentricity on the ground that his is a personality and way of life totally devoid of *passion*. "I am extraordinarily relieved," she remarks with irony, "to hear that you are not a passionate man. But how should you be? You would have to become estranged from your kin and kind. Passionate—that means living for the sake of life. But it is well known, that you all live for the sake of experience. Passion, that is self-forgetfulness. But what you all want is self-enrichment. . . . You don't realize what revolting egoism it is, and that one day it will make you an enemy of the human race!"

This prophetic denunciation is aimed beyond the little per-

son of Hans Castorp, at all like him, at Germany and beyond
that nation at all representatives of Western humanistic culture.
For in this significant passage, with its stratas of implication,
Thomas Mann places his finger squarely on the central weakness, not of the German character alone, but of the make-up of
humanism in all the Western lands. It is the inherent individualistic egocentricity; the aristocratic exclusiveness and selfishness
of humanism which Mann exposes here, significantly, through
the medium of the Slav's differently conditioned and oriented
psyche. To be sure, Mann is not the first to discover this fateful
shortcoming in humanism. Goethe, for instance, in the wisdom
of his old age had become very conscious of it, sought to correct
it in the *Wanderjahre* no less than in his *Faust*, when, all too
abruptly perhaps, he has Faust, that highest incarnation of man
bent on self-perfection and self-enrichment, find salvation in
social activity. Yet it is Mann's contribution to have shown in the
Slavic spirit a possible antidote to the West's malady of solipsism
and to have called for the fusion of the East's "passionate" anti-
egocentricity with the West's conscious glorification and cultivation of the great personality, its dignity and inviolability.

Settembrini, this *homo humanus*, voluble champion of Western civilization, this more genial *Zivilisationsliterat* of the *Reflections*, would have Hans Castorp clearly decide between East and
West, between what he calls the "Asiatic and the European principles." For him, these two "principles," Asiatic force, tyranny,
superstition, sloth, immorality, inertia and darkest reaction on
the one hand, European justice, freedom, knowledge, progress
on the other, are in perpetual conflict for possession of the world.
He sees the time rapidly approaching when Castorp and his native land, Germany, this country midway between East and West,
will have to decide on which side to take up its position. Hans
Castorp, however, faced with this decision, "sat, his chin in his
hand. . . . In his eyes there was a certain obstinacy. He was silent." He refused to turn his back on the East for which he—like
his creator Mann—had such a deep, inborn predilection. To be
sure, he knew Russia's shortcomings, but he also appreciated its
virtues, its greatness of soul, its deep humanity. its latent
strength. His sympathetic understanding embraced both the Eastern and Western spheres, "again he was the lonely boatsman on
the Holstein lake, looking with dazzled eyes from the glassy day-
light of the Western shore to the mist and moonbeams that
wrapped the Eastern heavens." No, Castorp was not one to make
a clear-cut decision between East and West. He kept silent, pon-

dering on fusion and synthesis, as was in his nature and that of
his creator, Thomas Mann. Since then Mann has broken Castorp's
silence, has called in speeches and essays for the introduction of
Russia's social consciousness, its spirit of communality, its "democracy of the heart," into the humanistic tradition of the West,
thus creating what he has called an "Aristo-Democracy," a society of free, creative, unregimented personalities, imbued with
a keen sense of social responsibility and spirit of co-operation.
To be sure, Mann's hope that Germany would lead humanity to
this lofty goal was rudely shattered when his native land chose
to crush its humanistic heritage and to spurn the democratic spirit. All the more fervent is his belief in America's ability to succeed in the most difficult and noble undertaking of creating a
society at once free and socially conscious (*verantwortungsvolle
Freiheit*).

IV

Conclusion

Concluding with a summary of our findings, it seems important to stress that Mann has arrived at his view of Russia
chiefly through the medium of Russian literature. His is, in the
main, the Russia of Dostoyevsky, Tolstoy, Gogol, Turgenev, Goncharov, and some other masters of Russian letters. In turn, this
Russia as represented in the characters and works of the great
Russian writers is often viewed through the eyes of Dmitri
Merezhkovsky, whose role as guide and mentor of Mann in his
explorations of the Russian spirit could hardly be overstressed.
Nevertheless Mann's uncanny gift of "observation and intuition"
must not be underestimated. In a brief defense of his novel *Royal
Highness,* Mann has aptly defined this great gift. In twenty minutes' observation of a Wittelsbach prince holding a reception or
Wilhelm II laying a cornerstone, this gift, so Thomas Mann points
out, enables him "to gain more intense, essential, noteworthy impressions of royalty and the representative form of life than some
court-marshall would acquire in twenty years of loyal service
in the royal household." Surely this gift is operative in the case
of Mann's startling grasp of Russian character as well. Even the
briefest contact with Russians must have conveyed to this keen
observer more of the essential Russian nature and orientation
than a protracted stay in Russia itself would have furnished a
less gifted person. Moreover, there can be no doubt that Mann
is endowed with an inborn predisposition and sympathy for Russia, its people and its literature, which has given him access to

deeper recesses of the Slavic soul than dispassionate observation alone would ever have opened up to him.

What then have we found to be Russia's special fascination for Mann, what the essential features of the Russian spirit as viewed by him? Above all, Russia to him is a vast land of profound soulfulness, "*das weite seelenvolle Land*," in which he finds a spirit of true communality, of true democracy, a "democracy of the heart." It is the country where live "the most human of humans," full of unsapped vitality, close to nature and fellow-men, scarcely touched, to be sure, by the cultural traditions of Western humanism, but gifted with intuitive knowledge of the human soul, with a profound social consciousness and inborn tact. Even in the bitter social critique, in the satire and irony of Russian literature Mann finds reflected this deep humanity of the Russian, for in his view, the Russian's satire and irony do not spring from mephistophelian nihilism and cold cynicism, are not the product of hate and intolerance, but are engendered by a profound sympathy and love for fellow-men, by the fervent desire to succor, to set free, to educate and elevate. In the great Russian authors Mann admires the bold explorers into metaphysical and social problems, who bravely strike out beyond the stifling, stagnant confines of narrow bourgeois morality and convention, who press on toward the solution of basic human problems, utterly fearless of censure and condemnation. "Is not the Russian literature," he exclaims ecstatically, "is it not the most human of all—holy in its humanity?" It is this all-comprehensive, "fierce," and tender humanity, this holiness alive in the Russian soul that holds perhaps the deepest fascination for Thomas Mann, the member of an old and highly formalized civilization with its dangerous tendencies toward "dehumanization," smugness and conceit. We recall that it was this passionate force of Russia's deeply human, loftily striving, soul-searching, ever questing spirit that helped "protect [Thomas Mann] from torpidity and spiritual death and build for him bridges into the future."

[1945]

THOMAS MANN IN AMERICA

Agnes E. Meyer

It is interesting to remember that Thomas Mann's mother fixation and his Dantesque belief in numerology once led him to prophesy that his death would probably take place in this, his seventieth year. Instead a transmutation so momentous as to be akin to death and rebirth took place in his life. For Mann during these fateful twelve months renounced his German citizenship and became an American.

As his enthusiasm over the American scene had been genuine from the outset and had deepened with time and more varied contacts, this final step in spite of its many implications, merely legalized an inner conviction that he now had more in common with a country striving toward world-wide democracy than with the unfortunate land of his birth.

What have been the effects of this formative process upon Thomas Mann as a human being and as an artist? At the end of *The Magic Mountain,* we find the author at least intellectually if not emotionally rejecting his romantic preoccupation with self, and in the anti-Nazi essays of the following period, we find a conviction of duty to mankind that was powerful though more philosophical, moral and humane than social or political in its nature and origin. But the successive volumes, specifically the last two, which were written after the American influence had begun, reveal ever more clearly how Hans Castorp's snow-bound vision of an ideal humanity is fulfilled in Joseph's complex personality with its wise concessions to social necessity, its renunciation of romantic isolation, and its rejection of a culture centered upon death and the past, in favor of democratic disciplines, practices and sympathies, and a democratic orientation toward the future.

As far as the purely artistic quality of Mann's post-European work is concerned, let those who insist that the early European works are superior, read only one chapter, the one in which Lotte and Riemer explore their relationship to Goethe. For sheer intensity and beauty of style, depth of psychological insight, interplay of reality and imagination, irony and wit, and for the exact portrayal of human strength and frailty, these few pages exceed anything that this celebrated author has ever written.

In other words, his growth has been uninterrupted by exile and as far as its direction can be defined, it seems to have been nourished by our peculiar soil. On the other hand, since Thomas Mann's evolution as an artist, ever since he left his native city of Lübeck as a youth of seventeen, had been independent of subsequent environmental influences, it can also be argued that his more recent novels would have been written exactly as they now exist if he had gone to live in Timbuctoo instead of the United States.

And yet I am inclined to feel that his ideological content was enhanced by our republican mores because his democratic transcendentalism is strongly reminiscent of Emerson, whom Thomas Mann has probably never read. The spiritual relationship of the two men is not surprising when we remember that Emerson set himself the same task that confronted Thomas Mann, of allowing his German idealism to expand under the warm sun of our democratic American climate. Not only had Emerson's literary predecessors in New England been deeply influenced by their education in German but he, himself, went from Coleridge and Carlyle to their chief inspiration, Goethe and German philosophic idealism, the identical springboard from which Thomas Mann had to take off when he began to think his way into the democratic atmosphere. Both men are concerned with the importance of the inner life, and express an unswerving faith in the omnipotence of spiritual and moral laws in the affairs of men whether they are triumphant, or whether they suffer, as they do today, the most humiliating defeat. They are both convinced that human beings have been set down upon this earth to accomplish high and sacred ends, and that every man is worthy of honor precisely because he is not wholly a biological phenomenon. Both emphasize the humane element of democracy and see in it what Plato saw in the Republic, the government most friendly to the education of the highest type of individual. Both insist, moreover, that self-reliance can work a revolution in all the offices and relations of men; never should the advantages of a collective life release the individual from his personal responsibilities, from independent thought, from ethical resolve and tenacious adherence to his own conclusion, since without these individual contributions, collective strength is but a myth.

In both the American and the German authors there resides

an earnestness that amounts to piety. Both not only feel democracy
as having religious overtones, but see it as actually synonymous
with art, poetry, philosophy, yes with history itself, because all
of them result from a synthesis of related opposites, from the
polarity of the individual and society, intuition and reason, freedom and necessity, from the action and reaction of matter and
mind, nature and soul. For both of them "the value and beauty
of the human being lies precisely in the fact that he belongs to
two kingdoms, that of nature and that of spirit. No romantic conflict or tragic dualism is inherent in that fact," Thomas Mann
now declares, "but rather a fruitful and engaging combination
of determination and free choice."

But there is this important difference between the two men,
aside from the fact that Emerson is the greater essayist and Mann
the greater artist. Emerson has remained a prophet, revered but
far too little heeded by later generations, because he preached
his summons to a life of the spirit in opposition to a rising
materialism, without making it as clear to others as it was to himself that "romantic egotism must be resisted," that "a man must
ride alternately on the horses of his private and public nature—
plant one foot on the back of one and the other foot on the back
of the other." Thomas Mann's bitter ordeal during the First World
War and his enforced reorientation through formative realities
caused him to become constantly more pragmatic. Thus he parts
company with Emerson on such questions as the inviolability
of property, for Germany's poverty and despair after her defeat
taught him that democratic cooperation is an illusion unless society has an economic basis that makes freedom possible for the
vast majority of the population. In those humiliating years when
leniency on the part of the victors might have changed the history of the world, he realized that life is a marriage of ends and
means, that philosophy may be the guide of life but that it also
springs from the conditions of life and the nature of the social
structure.

John Dewey has called Emerson the philosopher of democracy. Thomas Mann, whose critical essays and whose art, particularly in the Joseph novels, link the transcendental individualism
of the New England sage with the human pragmatism of John
Dewey, may rightly be called the poet of democracy—not, to be
sure, of democracy as we practice it today, but as it must strive
to become, an integral democracy which seeks with mind and
heart to live up to its highest aspirations. Only through such a
renewal of the timeless potentialities of democracy, says Mann,

will the mechanical dynamism of the authoritarian states be confronted with the organic vitality of a truly democratic people. Only by such a rediscovery of ourselves can we gain the fruits of victory that he holds out to us, "a democracy of states in which freedom and equality have reached a new creative balance."

To these bold assertions Emerson would give an unqualified blessing just as Thomas Mann, in *The Coming Victory of Democracy*, agrees to the clarion call for self-reliance and world leadership, which was hurled at us by Emerson as if with divine prescience: "We are not minors and invalids in a protected corner, not cowards fleeing before a revolution, but guides, redeemers and benefactors obeying the Almighty effort and advancing on Chaos and the Dark."

[1945]

THE ARTIST AS BOURGEOIS

Charles Neider

I

Thomas Mann's position in the artistic tradition is clear. It is not surprising to find him preoccupied with himself as the isolated artist. Because of his burgher forbears and his own naturally conservative temperament Mann tends to regard the artistic impulse in himself as something suspect, verging on the criminal. His preoccupation has been quite frank in a literary sense, being the inspiration of his entire output, both fictional and didactic. It has led him to a personal variation of the artist myth, a consideration of himself (and the artist in general) as the middleman between burgher and bohemian, nature and spirit, tradition and revolt. It has also led him to attempt to bring the artist back into the fold of good society after his nineteenth-century escapades, to bridge the chasm between the artist's nineteenth-century isolation and his expected respectability in the coming world state. In the sense that he is a middleman he is a bourgeois; but he is also a bourgeois in relation to his family life and to other aspects of his outward existence. Because of his professed role of mediator and his patrician bearing Mann has been found unpalatable in certain company and has been compared unfavorably (particularly by Europeans) with his brother Heinrich. A contrast of the brothers is illuminating. Heinrich, in his mercurial temperament, carries forward the tradition of the nineteenth-century artist as inspired and admirably bohemian. Intellectually, however, he is an eighteenth-century product. On the other hand Thomas is eighteenth century in behavior (much like Goethe) and nineteenth century intellectually with his love of myth, Schopenhauer, Nietzsche and Wagner.

We shall distinguish three periods of Mann's development. The first period (which I arbitrarily call the pre-war or pre-*Magic Mountain* period) was more temperamental and literary than practical. In his second period (the *Magic Mountain* period, including the *Reflections of a Non-Political Man*, which preceded the novel) Mann made his metaphysical peace with his burgher-

artist role. In his third period (the *Joseph* period) he carried out
the political implications of the role. Thus his work and life constitute the development of the isolated artist-type into the artist as
one of and provider for the people.

I said that Mann's position in the artistic tradition is clear;
but it is clear only if one regards it as part of a tradition as
old as Western society itself. The position of the artist in Western
society has ever been a delicate one, particularly since, with
the advent of philosophy and the self-consciousness which it
entails, Plato rejected the poet from his ideal state. It took a poet-
philosopher to do that, a man full of the ambivalence and sensuous indulgence of the poet and the fears and moral strivings of the
philosopher. But surely Plato, even during his most conservative
phase, must have realized that by the same token he ought to
have excluded himself. Anthropological studies seem to indicate that among primitives the artist's position is secure because of a general cultural solidarity based on the primitive's
difficulty in distinguishing between the individual and the class.
Any such innocence which might have existed in Greece was
disrupted by the rise of philosophy, which made the artist's comparative isolation inevitable, since self-consciousness, whether in
individuals or states, inspires moral judgments. Plato's complaint
was, of course, based on the artist's irregularity, his tendency to
disorder and the illicit as well as on his aversion to the established order of things. He intimated that the poet's main function
was something suspiciously close to titillation. His complaint has
been echoed many times. This mistrust of the artist stems, apparently, from the notion of the "divine afflatus," the belief that
the artist receives his inspiration from the muses or from some
other oracular source while in a state of madness, a notion whose
modern counterpart finds expression in the conviction that the
artist's creations must well up from the unconscious to have
real beauty and significance. The role of the Greek oracles, particularly those of Delphi, Dodona and Apollo Didymaeus, in the
establishment of the tradition is clear. The tradition itself is voluminous.

Such an aspect of the artist's position is not without its com-
pensatory side. The artist has found it convenient to accept
and enlarge the "divine afflatus" myth in order to attain a license
denied to lesser mortals, and to exploit his so-called naiveté and
madness, often however, ending by believing the myth himself.
He has cultivated his personality to the point of eccentricity, not
because he has inherently desired to do so but because eccentri-

city has been more or less required of him by tradition. The individualism of the Western world has forced the artist, that neurotic and extremist whose business it is to deal with the subjective and the individual, to assume the mantle of the pariah. There have, of course, been variations in the tradition, one of the most evident being found in a contrast of the eighteenth and nineteenth centuries: the eighteenth emphasized reason and the typical, and the nineteenth emphasized the emotions and the individual. The individualism of Western society reached its peak in the latter century, and this extreme was prepared by the comparative absence of individualism in the eighteenth. Nor must one forget the technological side of the new science and its part in determining the position of the artist in the nineteenth and twentieth centuries. The artist of the last century revolted doubly: against the money-grubbing imperialism of the Industrial Revolution as well as against the stylized passion of the Age of Reason. The artist was obviously an unwanted man. There was little or no place for him in the midst of a furiously expanding technology at a time when states had little use for his humanitarian and liberal impulses, little use for the fine arts and perhaps even less for literature, a less tangible form of art (when the tangible was exceptionally important) than architecture, sculpture and painting.

Such forces created that era of proud artistic revolt whose figures often ended in tragedy: Kleist, Schiller, Novalis, Keats, Byron, Shelley, Pushkin, Lermontov. . . . Many of the deaths were violent: Kleist shot himself; Pushkin and Lermontov were killed in duels; Byron died in the Greek wars; Shelley was drowned in a storm. . . . Irregularity, isolation, vanity, tragedy: these were the norms. One thinks of Schopenhauer, with his terror of assassination, his poodle, his diary with the unprintable references to sex and marriage; Nietzsche, with his severe neurotic strain ending in madness; Wagner, with his antisocial traits amounting at times to the frankly criminal, with his mysticism, violent myths, perfumes and satins; Hebbel, having to give up his faithful Elise to marry a beautiful and wealthy actress on the ground that otherwise his talents would have perished in the "miserable struggle for existence"; Baudelaire, Mallarmé, Rimbaud, Flaubert, George, Wilde; Dostoyevsky, gambler, epileptic, economic freebooter, with his experience before the firing squad and as a convict for four years at Omsk; Pushkin, under house arrest for suspected revolutionary activity; Lermontov, arrested, court-martialled and expelled from the Guards because of his poem "On the Death of the Poet" (about Pushkin) addressed to the tsar; Tolstoy with his monstrous wrestling with the angel in his effort to atone for the sexual excesses of his youth; Gogol, with his melancholy, his destruction of many of his manuscripts; Turgenev, with his self-imposed exile; Van Gogh, with his self-mutilation, his sun worship, his madness.

The nineteenth century saw, as we have said, an extreme form of the artist's traditional isolation. But there have also been times when the artist's fare was considerably more palatable, times when prosperous states, glorying in their power, tolerated the artist, sometimes even regarding his attacks upon themselves as not altogether uncomplimentary *divertissements.* Such states were evident during the Mediterranean Renaissance. Others, balancing on the tightrope of tyranny, were supersensitive to criticism, such as Russia in the last century, with her countless emasculation of works of art through a rigid censorship and terrorization of artists with the threat of penal servitude. Much, naturally, depends on tradition and on the personalities of rulers and artists in determining the amount and quality of the artist's freedom. Thus Elizabethan England, in all the burst of toleration following the destruction of the Spanish Armada, still knew how to censor both the spoken and the printed word. Enlightened despots like Lorenzo de' Medici stimulated art; others, ignorant or barbaric or even moronic, stifled it. As for the influence of the personalities of artists, it is obvious that figures such as Leonardo, Goethe and Tolstoy inevitably gain greater freedom for lesser men as well as for themselves. One recalls the dramatic moment when the tsar proclaimed Tolstoy "untouchable," beyond the power of Russian terrorism. The fact that Tolstoy's disciples were still persecuted does not detract from the weight of his subsequent attacks on the hulking body of Russian feudalism.

From the preceding it would seem that the artist has increasingly been assuming the role of social leper. Have there been counterinfluences? There have—and again with science as the cause. The role of science during the eighteenth and nineteenth centuries was dual. While through the medium of expanding technology it tended to unify the physical world, to make its parts interrelated and interdependent, and in this sense began the achievement of that spiritual synthesis which religion had failed to accomplish on a universal scale, at the same time it was destructive in its effect on those myths of religion, philosophy and mores which largely sustained the balance of western civilization. The geographical synthesis which science was accomplishing was soon found to be insufficiently sustaining spiritually when viewed in terms of the deleterious effect of science in imperialism, war and the technological revolution. A new ethic was required, which meant that out of the ashes of the old ethic and out of the atomistic array which was science's humanistic contribution in the last three centuries—out of these a new humanism had to be created. That meant imaginative synthesis, legend, myth, tradition: for the achievement of which the artist is indispensable. This counterinfluence underlines the "respectable" part which the artist will play in the world state, the collective, democratic state of the future. A preview of his new role can be seen in the Soviet Union, where the artist, who is the aristocrat in terms of living standards, was conscientiously kept out of the front lines during the recent conflict.

II

One of Mann's earliest published stories, *Little Herr Friedemann,* is a study of the artist as crippled and outcast, the artist's spiritual deformity, his irregularity, being symbolically expressed by a hunchback. The psychology of the protagonist is Mann's; and while it is undoubtedly melodramatized it is at the same time genuine in tone and direction. All of the familiar notes of Mann's preoccupation with the artist are struck in this early piece: the artist's incapacity for athletics because of his introversion and frailty, the use of music (with Wagner the favorite) to heighten the elements of yearning and isolation, the artist as pariah. Friedemann hopes for a sexual union with Frau von Rinnlingen, who represents the normal and extrovertive (and cruel); when she rejects him the blow is too much for his injured ego and he drowns himself in the river beside her garden. Even in a small tale like *Disillusionment* there is a hint of Mann's ever-present theme: here it is in the artistic perversity of being forever dissatisfied with the actual—a spiritual jadedness very *fin de siècle.* (The story was written in 1896.) Another early story, *The Dillettante,* is largely autobiographical, expressing the feelings of doubt and anxiety of the young man gambling on a career in literature. It contains, in addition, a number of interesting overtones, among them the earliest expression of the mother-artist, father-burgher motif. Part of the story suggests the *Buddenbrooks* material which was soon to appear, while part of it hints at *Tonio Kröger* and the motif of yearning for the blue-eyed, blond and extrovertive (the healthy burgher type in

Mann's allegorical vocabulary, based on romantic tradition and particularly on Nietzsche). Mann's decision that happiness (and therefore external success) for him is *de rigueur*, is also seen here at this early date (1897): "I could not permit myself to be unhappy, could not stand the sight of myself in such a role. I should have to hide in the dark like a bat or an owl and gaze with envy at the children of light." But perhaps the most illuminating element in the piece is an implied one. If one equates "dilettante" with "bourgeois artist," the artist as middleman, as official compromiser, one finds the hidden autobiographical core of the story. "Dilettante" here stands as a symbol of the bourgeois artist's tortured striving for direction between the poles of burgher and bohemian. Soon, in *Tonio Kröger*, after the strengthening exercise of *Buddenbrooks*, Mann will firmly rationalize his middle position.

In his early period Mann took sadistic pleasure in projecting what he considered to be the artist's spiritual deformities on to his characters in the form of physical ones. *Tobias Mindernickel*, for example, is a portrait of a love-starved, psychopathically sadistic outcast whose cruelty is matched only by the cruelty of Mann's prose. *Little Lizzy* is a story of adultery in which the cruelty of Amra toward her unhealthily stout husband, Jacoby, is reminiscent of Gerda von Rinnlingen's cruelty to Friedemann. *Little Lizzy* is particularly interesting because of its early pronouncement on artists. Speaking of Alfred Lautner, the young musician who is Amra's lover, Mann says that "He belonged to the present-day race of small artists who do not demand the utmost of themselves, whose first requirement is to be jolly and happy, who employ their pleasing little talents to heighten their personal charms. It pleases them to play in society the role of the naive genius. Consciously childlike, entirely unmoral and unscrupulous, merry and self-satisfied as they are, and healthy enough to enjoy even their disorders, they are agreeable even in their vanity, so long as that has not been wounded. But woe to these wretched little poseurs when serious misfortune befalls them, with which there is no coquetting, and when they can no longer be pleasant in their own eyes." Mann has learned to speak in the voice of the artist as well as the bourgeois. He will not tolerate any trifling with art on the part of the healthy ones (he describes Lautner as blond, with a sunny smile in his eyes), just as they will not tolerate his trifling in their affairs. Whereas Mann considers happiness *de rigueur*, he heartily resents it in those whose primary aim is to be happy—i.e. in those untainted by conscience and *weltschmerz*. Thus his middle role gradually reveals itself even in these very early pieces, written before *Buddenbrooks*. In *Buddenbrooks*, while paying his literary debt to realism and to his nineteenth-century masters, Tolstoy, Flaubert and the Scandinavians, Mann considerably clarifies his notions concerning art and the artist, examining the problem of burgher versus bohemian in his comparison of Thomas and Christian Buddenbrook, portraying the former as a stalwart but decaying burgher and Christian as the dilettante bohemian suffering from neuresthenia and hypochondria. The theme of art as related to disease is here developed with exceptional vigor. The decay of the burgher family through increasing refinement results in disease and art. The figure of little Hanno, last of the *Buddenbrooks*, is the most intriguing in the book for at least two reasons: first, because he stands closest in an autobiographical relation to the author and second, because he is the inspiration for the most beautiful and characteristic passages in the novel. Besides, Hanno foreshadows with precarious frailty the coming Tonio Kröger. *Buddenbrooks*, in this connection, is in several ways a preparatory exercise for *Tonio Kröger*. Among other considerations, the success of the novel, artistically and externally, encouraged Mann to speak of himelf openly henceforth in terms of the artist and to take a more positive position as middleman.

In *Tonio Kröger* Mann brings to a *forte* his previously faint articulation regarding himself as artist. That he was expressing the notions and yearnings of his time, particularly among artistic circles, was evidenced by the warm reception which the tale received on its appearance in 1903. In Mann's own words (1936), this tale and the group of stories of which it is the spiritual center "all bear the impress of much melancholy and ironical reflection on the subject of art and the artist: his isolation and equivocal position in the world of reality considered socially and metaphysically and as a result of his double bond with nature and spirit." The story is delightful because of its lyric bloom and its intellectual core, the latter found in Tonio's conversations with his friend, Lisabeta Ivanovna. Here one comes upon Mann's disgust with bohemian apparel, his reiteration of the decadent idea that simple feelings are banal and that "only the irritations and icy ecstasies of the artist's corrupted nervous system are artistic," his suspicion of the artist-type, his desire for the "normal," his insistence that "The kingdom of art increases and that of health and innocence declines on this earth," his contempt for the dilettante and so on. Despite its evidence of a strangely prolonged adolescence in the author, the tale portrays perfectly the psychology of the sensitive young outcast who seeks acceptance and regularity. It is a blood brother to Joyce's *Portrait*, except that whereas Stephen is proudly scornful of the regular, Tonio regards the regular with irony not unmixed with yearning and compassion. *Tristan, The Hungry, The Infant Prodigy* and *Gladius Dei* all center around *Tonio Kröger* in time and spirit and continue Mann's probing into the psychology of the artist. They precede his work on *Royal Highness* and the stories which more or less accompanied his second novel, among them *At the Prophet's* and *Felix Krull*. Around this time, also, Mann composed his only play, *Fiorenza;* and it too, as almost everything he touched in those days, was concerned with the motif of isolation and the artist. *At the Prophet's* is a satire on the bohemian artist and is similar in tone to *Tristan*, which satirizes the aesthete. In *Felix Krull* the theme of artist as criminal, which was hinted at in *The Infant Prodigy*, is fully developed. Not until the First World War was Mann's conception of the artist as isolated seriously shaken. Until that time all of his major figures—Hanno, Tonio, Klaus Heinrich, Felix Krull, Aschenbach—lived in isolated spheres removed from action and direct social responsibility.

III

Mann's *Magic Mountain* period stems from his experience in the First World War. The war found him embroiled in bitter controversies with his brother Heinrich, who, as spokesman for a European and democratic enlightenment, opposed Mann's nationalistic and sometimes Prussianistic views, views which expressed in political terms his heaviness of character and his temperamental conservatism, Seen from today's perspective, Mann's behavior during the war seems strongly reactionary. It seemed no less so to many of his opponents during the conflagration. In his efforts to defend his position while at the same time searching his mind and conscience, Mann gathered material which in 1918 appeared as the *Reflections of a Non-Political Man*. He has been attacked for this book on many grounds and on many occasions, some quite recent. He has, however, repudiated it; and it is worth noting that he has never had it translated into English along with his other didactic works. Mann himself has indicated that without the experience of the *Reflections* he could not have written *The Magic Mountain*. The *Reflections* cleared the political and metaphysical ground for the novel. It cleared the emotional ground as well. As though in atonement for his

political isolation during the war, Mann makes Hans Castorp, his
alter ego in the novel, leave the sanitorium, where he has been
secluded for seven years, in order to take up arms and thus merge
his identity with that of a larger identity of international importance. Castorp is not, of course, presented as an artist; he is, however, an artist on two grounds: because he is Mann's *alter ego*
and because of his keen acceptance and synthesis of experience.
But Castorp is not, like Heinrich Mann, a man of action or of
political responsibility. He is still, like the author, a man feeling
his way along the misty road to politics. *The Magic Mountain* is
simply the education of Hans Castorp, but it gives us no indication as to how Castorp applies that education except for the
detail of his breaking the spell of Davos and going off to the
wars. Thus Mann's second period, while theoretically mature,
is still characterized by practical, political immaturity. In the
artistic sphere Mann had not been standing still. He had
arrived from the exploited naturalism of *Buddenbrooks* to the
highly polished, involved and musical symbolism of *The Magic
Mountain*. Nor had he turned his back altogether on naturalism:
he had rather given it a sense of play, a sense of wonder and no
little irony. The complex intellectual demands of the second
period had called forth a comparably complex and unbehavior-
istic artistic technique. Let us examine the latter for a moment.

Broadly speaking, it may be said that there are three types
of symbol in modern literature. The first, exemplified by the
cross, ram, sun, flag, etcetera, is the oldest, simplest and most
thoroughly social, although it is obviously enhanced with personal
overtones by each individual. The second is autobiographical,
having its origin and meaning in an experience which may be
flatly objective but more commonly is so subtle that it is barely
articulable. Whereas the first is immediately evident, the second
warrants an example or two. For instance, the description of a
cloud as Mary-colored might be founded on a Mary-experience,
Mary being a person's maid, who is incomplete in his mind
without her characteristic color, the flamingo-pink of her smock;
while the description of a person as Mary-lovely might be founded
perhaps, on a Mary-experience in which Mary, a religious person
of fine spirituality, wears a delicately wrought gold cross. The
third type of symbol is a fusion of these two. To illustrate: I walk
into a strange room and see a crucifix on the wall—a symbol of
the spiritual life, Christianity, Christ, the Crucifixion. I may
also be reminded of Mary with the golden cross, and of all the
moods and incidents her image evokes. The crucifix is therefore

a double symbol, both social and autobiographical. It may become even more complex. Suppose that for me a crucifix stands
for religious persecution or that it brings to mind a particularly
pleasant (or obnoxious) sexual experience characterized by the
chance pattern of a cross on a scarred wall. Now suppose that
my host walks in and we discuss the crucifix as a work of art or
the place of religion in the twentieth century or the virtues of
Catholicism. If a fine novelist were to describe the situation and
play off my words against my thoughts, or one of my mental
images against another, the result would be interesting irony,
especially if the novelist were to make sly, ironic comments. But
if the novelist were Thomas Mann, then social and individual,
objective and subjective would be harmonized, contrasted, fused
or accentuated in a startling contrapuntal symbolism. For with
Thomas Mann this third type of symbol becomes a remarkable
synthesis of the other two. It has been most perfectly exploited
in *The Magic Mountain.*

Synthesis—and yet not, for synthesis implies a new whole
with indistinguishable parts, whereas with Mann the re-creation
emphasizes with great clarity the forms of the old yet offers
something new. Irony and music; contrast, harmony, social versus
individual, plain versus clandestine—counterpoint is the word.
The autobiographical merges with or dominates the social, the
social merges with or dominates the autobiographical; social because the symbol signifies an idea, or an experience broader than
the personal, and autobiographical because the symbol signifies
an intensely personal experience. Whose experience? Castorp's,
Settembrini's, Peeperkorn's, Naphta's. But what if the symbol
is made to carry the weight of Mann's own biography? Then the
ironic play becomes really interesting! Irony is duality, in the
crude sense antithesis, but in the hands of a humanizing master
it is form and content playing with themselves in a multitude
of ever-shifting lights whch combine and separate like the me-
lodic lines of a Bach fugue. In his hands it is humane, intelligent
and in a sublime sense creative, for it presents at once a realistic
image of life and an examination and criticism of it. And in
counterpoint it achieves dynamic transparency in addition to
the transparency afforded by each partially self-conscious and
self-critical symbol, for each of which there is a more or
less hidden and ironical explanation by author, symbol or opposing symbol. It is like an X-rayed living body, in which the
flesh, though warm, is lucid, and in which the deeper structure
is made apparent while in motion. It is this transparency, this

intelligibility, which secures Mann's work against the attack of
being decadent, esoteric and antisocial. While in the profoundest sense Mann's main intention may be to write autobiography,
his burgher-artistic conscience prompts him to give first consideration to story, second to idea and only last to autobiography. It
is in this respect that his work is thoroughly social.

And now let us present the number seven as an illustration
of the foregoing. The reader may justifiably ask: Why seven?—
the book teems with interesting symbols, many of them intellectually more profound and far-reaching, such as the figures of
Naphta and Peeperkorn, or, more important still, Hans Castorp,
and many of them possess the double virtue of abstraction and
concreteness, such as the pencil Castorp borrowed from Hippe
and later from Chauchat; while seven is an abstraction in all
simplicity and is incapable of conjuring up an image in the
sense that Settembrini's checked trousers, Clavdia's Kirghiz eyes
or Peeperkorn's sea-captain's hands can conjure them. An even
stronger objection may be: Since it is the contention that Mann's
symbolism is the synthesis of objective and subjective or social
and individual symbols, and since individual symbolism is necessarily autobiographical, it must follow—if so abstract and social
a symbol as the number seven can in this case be called representative of the third type—that seven is autobiographical—that
is, intensely personal—with Mann. Where is the proof? Who
can say with certainty regarding the work of any author, much
less the work of so profoundly imaginative and social-minded
an artist as Mann, that this item is autobiographical or not?—
unless one has it from the author himself. A good objection; however, there are clues. Mann believes in his "destiny," made clear
to him by the regular occurrence of important and auspicious
events in his life. He believes in this "destiny," this inner rhythm,
this physiological time-organ controlling and directing his physical and spiritual growth and decay, to the extent that he pre-
dicted the year of his death—1945, at the age of seventy. And
was it a strange coincidence or even stranger inner design which
caused Mann to reject precisely seven sections of the manuscript
of *Der Zauberberg*, the unpublished sections deposited at Yale?
It is not altogether fantastic to assume that numbers in general
and seven in particular are personal with Mann. Be that as it
may, the answer to the objection lies in the genius Mann has
evinced for taking the cold symbols of his objective plan and experiencing them so thoroughly as to recreate them in his own
image, so that thus transformed they serve as "autobiography in

the guise of fable" as well as fable itself. But the chief reasons
for the selection of the symbol seven are that it is, first, the leading leitmotiv and, second, the key symbol of the novel.

Number symbolism is almost as ancient as language itself and
probably dates back to the earliest verbal communication of primitive man. Three major sources of number symbolism are the
primitive, the astrological and the Pythagorean. In the first are
included such concepts as twenty meaning a man—ten fingers and
ten toes; from the second, the Babylonian system of astrology,
are derived numbers referring to planets, stellar revolutions and
constellations; the third, the Pythagorean number theory, fixed
the relationship of numbers to one another. Certain basic numbers have possessed parallel meanings in all cultures. One, for
instance, is an indication of unity, two of division and antithesis, three of totality. Three is also a holy number and consequently it signifies the spiritual (the Holy Trinity, the three disciples
present at the Transfiguration); while four symbolizes the material and natural (the four winds, the four corners of the earth).
Seven, a combination of the two, stands for finality, wisdom and
godliness—particularly in astrological sources—and is a favorite
number of the Bible and of Christianity (seven deadly sins, seven
cardinal virtues, seven sacraments, seven gifts of the Holy
Ghost). It has also been widely used in other contexts: Seven
against Thebes, Seven Wise Men of Greece, Seven Wonders of
the World, Snow-White and the Seven Dwarfs, the Seven Sleepers of Ephesus. Its symbolism is multiform. Among other things
it has stood for sin, and for servitude and perseverance (Jacob's
seven years' labor under Laban). But most important is its
magical significance. It is in connection with the latter that
Thomas Mann chose it as the basic symbol in his symphonic
novel, *The Magic Mountain.* Symphonic and symbolic, these are
words which aptly describe the book: symphonic through need—
the author's organic need to shape it so; and symbolic through
intention—to create a "transparency for ideas to shine through."
The sojourners on the mountain are the modernized seven sleepers
of the legend, asleep to reality (the flatland) until the thunderbolt
of the First World War awakes them and sends them scurrying
earthwards. Castorp, Chauchat, Behrens, Naphta, Settembrini,
Peeperkorn and Ziemssen—they are seven, and their names
either contain seven letters each or suggest seven: Castorp, Clavdia, Behrens, Mynheer and Joachim; Napht(h)a, from the corrosive substance of which the communistic Jewish Jesuit is the
human counterpart; and Settembrini, from September, the an-

ciently seventh month. (Giuseppe Settembrini, Ludovico's revolutionary grandfather, is modeled on Luigi Settembrini (1813-77) an Italian patriot and man of letters.) Everywhere the number seven is in evidence—there are seven chapters; Hans stays on the mountain for seven years; at the end of seven weeks he finds he is ill and asserts his freedom from the flatland; after seven months he wins Clavdia; Joachim goes down to the flatland after seven times seventy days; the thermometer is held under the tongue for seven minutes; there are seven tables in the dining hall, at each of which Hans spends a year; Joachim's room is number twenty-eight (seven times four); Clavdia's room is number seven; Hans's room is number thirty-four (three and four make seven); Hans arrives in the seventh month, in 1907, seven years before the outbreak of the war; he is portrayed as a seven-year-old at his grandfather's; supper was served at seven; seven go to the waterfall; Vingt et Un is played (three times seven); Edhin Krokowski's name contains twice seven letters: a host of names contains seven: Berghof, Kurhaus, Mancini, Marusia, Hermine, etc. And thus, through one symbol, the author achieves a leading leitmotiv for his musical structure and a key to the symbolism of his novel.

The salient features of Mann's symbolism, then, are musical, social and ironic. In symphonic style, Mann introduces the number seven immediately, in the foreword (or overture). "Not all in a minute, then, will the narrator be finished with the story of our Hans. The seven days of a week will not suffice, no, nor seven months either. Best not too soon make too plain how much mortal time must pass over his head while he sits spun round in his spell. Heaven forbid it should be seven years!" And then begins the music of the great prose symphony, and when Hans and his fellow-sufferers are most absorbed in their little world, and we with them, the seven is slyly introduced and the effect is like a faint, gentle jeering at their absorption in themselves. We are made aware that all is not what it appears to be, and we are imbued with a sense of fantasy which brightens and makes not only more significant but also more pleasing the book's realism. At last the symbol, only hinted at before, is given clarity. It becomes self-conscious and turns upon itself in farewell irony. "Seven years Hans Castorp remained amongst those up here. Partisans of the decimal system might prefer a round number, though seven is a good handy figure in its way, picturesque, with a savour of the mythical; one might even say that it is more filling to the

spirit than a dull academic half-dozen." And thus the finale as
we prepare to take leave forever of Hans Castorp.

IV

Mann's third period fills the political gap of the second, for
Joseph is portrayed not only in reference to his education but also
to its political and intellectual implications. The Joseph novel itself falls into three sections, corresponding to Mann's three periods: the period prior to the first pit, in which Joseph is the
vain dreamer who sets himself off from his brothers and resembles Tonio; the Potiphar period, in which Joseph's Egyptian (cosmopolitan) education takes place and in which he resembles
Hans Castorp; and the Pharaoh period, in which Joseph, now a
political man, acts as the provider for the people. It is the early
part of Mann's Joseph period which contains *Mario and the
Magician,* the symbolic and prophetic story of Italian fascism.
Later *The Beloved Returns* appears. The Moses story falls into
the latter part of the period. In it we have the artist as inspirer,
provider and molder all in one. Mann several times refers to
Moses as a sculptor chiseling and blasting and carving his people.
This conception brings to mind the lines from Heine's *Confessions*
concerning Moses: "I failed to perceive that Moses, notwithstanding his enmity to art, was nevertheless himself a great artist, and
possessed the true artistic spirit. Only, this artistic spirit with
him, as with his Egyptian countrymen, was applied to the colossal
and the imperishable. But not, like the Egyptians, did he con-
struct works of art from bricks and granite, but he built human
pyramids and carved human obelisks."

It is Mann's final period which contains the rise of Hitler,
Mann's exile and his subsequent polemical activities against the
Nazis by means of pamphlets and BBC broadcasts to the German
underground. This period is climaxed by the publication of
Joseph the Provider, the last volume of the Joseph tetralogy,
and by Mann's publicy declared pro-Roosevelt stand in the election of 1944, the latter taken to the extent of lectures urging people to vote for the President.

There is a notion, rather fashionable in certain "realistic"
circles, that Mann has decayed since *Buddenbrooks,* with the
implication that *The Magic Mountain* is a German metaphysical
hulk rather than a novel and that the Joseph books are altogether incomprehensible and out of the world. A representative
member of these circles found *Joseph the Provider* difficult,
heavy and hardly profound, although he admitted that as simply

a novelist, whatever that may mean, Mann is supreme. He added that while *The Magic Mountain* is Mann's greatest novel, his most interesting one is *Buddenbrooks*. In these circles symbolism, thought and musical construction seemingly possess no value. They would have Mann repeat himself in the manner of lesser novelists, always remaining faithful to the *Buddenbrooks* formula; and they would exclude all un-novelistic elements, comforting themselves with what would remain, a primitive compote indeed, consisting only of tale and character. Their attitude clearly evidences their low opinion of the novel form; and, of course, their own undeveloped taste.

The long tetralogy which was begun in pre-Hitler Germany, continued for five years in Switzerland and finished in California, under skies which the author has compared to those of Egypt, is rich in time, art, spiritual overtones, wisdom, story, pathos and in the unique texture which can somehow make suspenseful that which is already so well known to everyone. One recalls the magnificent prelude to the first book, a prelude with a life of its own and which is a sonorous organ prologue offering orientation and perspective in a style that is a beautiful and complex weaving of themes and ideas. And one remembers the first book itself —largely an introduction to the series, so that its prelude is really a prologue to a prelude—and the poignant story of Jacob, ending with the winning of Rachel and with Rachel's tragic and untimely death. One thinks of the tortuous treatment of time, with numerous foreshadowings and flashbacks, a technique suitable when the story is well known to the reader in advance. Gradually the pattern and its meaning emerge. In the Joseph books the myth has been thoroughly humanized and therefore serves as a sword against reaction and against reaction's exploitation of the myth for its own savage ends. Myths, having their origin in prehistory, are folk legends containing much communal wisdom. Their authorship is communal as well and, while they may look naive on the surface, they are often fierce and cruel, in accordance with the mores of the times which gave them life. And yet they are strangely attractive and exciting to our modern ear because, like the individual's dreams, they are full of the explosive wisdom of the unconscious. They are thus—because of their savagery and emotional appeal—obvious tools of reaction. The myth can be used by the forces of progress just as readily as by those of reaction, since it is a composite of tradition and the present— and even of the future—and therefore stands on the middle ground between two conflicting worlds, the world of ignorance, division, the past, on one hand, and the world of enlightenment, unity, the future, on the other. Mann has made it serve progressive ends in the Joseph novels by humanizing it with psychology and humor. Since he believes that the future holds in store an era of collectivism and communal strength, he has aptly chosen and explored an art form symbolizing the collective—the myth. He was attracted to the Joseph myth because of personal and artistic reasons; because of his interest in the myth as tradition and tradition as recurrence; because of his conception of the myth as the eternally and essentially human and because of his conviction that the concept of humanity must be reëxamined and reaffirmed at a time when reaffirmation is urgent, when a new unity and faith, deriving from a consciousness of strength in the typical, the communal rather than in the peculiarly individual, are necessary to usher in the democratic world out of the ashes of the reactionary one. Therefore he chose the Joseph myth as a symbol of unity emerging out of strife, and humanized and "civilized" it into a myth of peace, of communal and spiritual progress out of something which might, in less humanistic hands, have been exploited for its primitive, violent and divisive aspects.

In Mann's case there is a peculiarly tight relationship between the man and the artist, and therefore to study the evolution of the artist in his works is, among other things, to study Mann's development as a political man, his development from a non-political and shoulder-shrugging citizen to the famous and vociferous resister of reaction. In Joseph, Mann recapitulates all his artist themes, in Joseph can be traced all his other figures as well as Mann's biography, in Joseph can be seen the various stages from the isolated to the ultimate stage of completion, of sharing the world's sufferings and joys while contributing to the world. Joseph is all the others. In his role as Hans Castorp, for example, he leaves the flatland of Canaan to enter the catholic Davos of Egypt. And here he strangely becomes a Goethe-figure, reminding one of Goethe ruling at Weimar and the portrayal of Goethe in *The Beloved Returns*. But of course Joseph rules from below as well as from above, in contradistinction to Goethe, who ruled only from above. Joseph arrived almost together with Hitler and they matured at about the same rate. While Mann was writing about Joseph's exile into Egypt, he himself was forced into exile from Germany. He was the prophet as well as the tool of events. With his Joseph he became the artist who took his place in society without equivocation, aligning himself with progress and truth against reaction and lies, speaking out, accepting exile rather than the honors of the New Order, and finding new inspiration on American soil. In short, he became the thoroughly good citizen, the bourgeois.

It has been said that Mann regards himself as primarily a bourgeois and this is not difficult to believe, in spite of his enormous interest in himself as artist, for he has never been the conventional artist in the sense of being bohemian. Mann has never worked at great cost to his burgher existence: he has taken care to marry, to raise children, and to lead a good life, segregating his artistic labors to the morning hours. Thus he has always come to art as an amateur; and while his love is unique, nevertheless he keeps art at a distance. One result is that his work has not been as prolific as it might have been, hardly as prolific as his brother's. Another and more interesting result is that he has preserved toward his art a remarkable freshness, art being for him a holiday, an excursion, no matter how burdensome at times. This explains his articulateness about his labors: it is as if he is explaining to other burghers his fantastic morning adventures, like some Marco Polo come home out of strange lands with spices and tales.

In a work whose theme and symphonic amplification is the myth, it is not too surprising to discover that a leitmotiv—and perhaps the chief leitmotiv—is a myth itself, particularly when the author is Mann, noted for his musical construction. I refer again to the number seven, now to its mythical significance. It is used subtly but extensively in the Joseph work. In *The Magic Mountain* it was the key to a novel of symbolism and magic and therefore its use was along symbolic and magical lines. But in the Joseph its mythical and Biblical aspects are exploited. Thus Mann has achieved a musical continuity between his two maturest works through the choice of a number as leitmotiv for both, whose traditional reference has been dual: magic and godliness. After employing the number in his novel of modern magic what could be more natural than to employ it again in a novel of ancient magic, particularly since the original text of the new novel required its use to an important extent? But the use of the number in the Joseph is by no means as sophisticated as it is in *The Magic Mountain*. In the latter it is highly cultivated, a hothouse product, clandestine and sly, ironic and highly musical; but in the Joseph it is naive and straightforward. And it is unmusical except in relation to external form; it is not musical from within, it does not pulsate at the core of things, it is modest and fairly self-evident. It represents acceptance and elaboration, no more; there is no synthetic transmutation of value and significance. In other words, its simple, mythical element is stressed rather than its symbolic.

The internal evidence is indicative:

In *Joseph and his Brothers,* Jacob flings himself down seven times before Esau on his return from his sojourn with Laban; Simeon and Levi tell Jacob that Dinah is seven-and-seventy times avenged after they destroy Shechem; Jacob, like Falstaff, describes a defeat and humiliation as a victory when he tells people about being attacked by robbers and his slaying seven times seven of them and about the robber captain's sword being shattered into seven times seventy pieces; Jacob serves Laban twice seven years for Rachel; Laban, in justifying his substitution of Leah for Rachel on Jacob's wedding night, says Leah is unspotted and worthy to mount the seven stairs into the arms of the god; Laban pursues Jacob for seven days.

In *Young Joseph,* Joseph learns of the seven planets and bearers of the command; of how the planets move around the dam of the zodiac in seven circles; of the seven-tiered tower; of seven being the moon's number, its quarters being seven days each; of how the woman of the city of Uruk converted the man of the forest, Engidu, to civilization by seven days and seven nights of love; of the seven evil winds. Joseph relates a dream to Benjamin and tells of the seven halls of Zebul, the seven hosts of angels there, and the seven fiery altars; in the same dream the Lord puts a heavy ring with seven times seven stones on Joseph's head; Jacob and his sons make offering, in Shechem, of leavened bread to God seven weeks after the spring full moon; Joseph's brothers sing that Cain shall be avenged seven-fold and Lamech seven-and-seventy fold.

In *Joseph in Egypt,* the Ishmaelite who bought Joseph questions him to see how bright he is: he asks Joseph how many times seven goes into seventy-seven; the caravan guide says several times that he might have waited for Joseph for seven jubilee years; Joseph arrives in Egypt in the twenty-eighth year (four times seven) of Pharaoh's reign; Joseph is gift number seven of the Ishmaelite to Mont-kaw, Potiphar's steward; Mont-kaw says farewell to the Ishmaelite with "Come again—in six or seven years' time!"; Joseph serves Potiphar seven years before Mut-em-enet, Potiphar's wife, develops her passion for him and begins his downfall; Potiphar's dining room is lit by sunlight coming through seven doors of the western outer hall; Potiphar gives an entertainment for seventy guests; Joseph abstains from consummation with Mut-em-enet because of seven reasons; Joseph is seventeen when he comes to Egypt and twenty-seven when he is thrown into the second pit.

In *Joseph the Provider*, there is the seven-branched river near Joseph's prison; it takes seventy days to prepare Pharaoh's coffin; there are seven fat and seven lean kine and seven fat and seven lean ears of corn in the young Pharaoh's dream; Pharaoh is seventeen; Pharaoh's mother says that according to the chronicles there were seven previous times of famine in Egypt; the Egyptians believe that the soul must pass through seven times seven regions of terror; an old Pharaoh went out to slay the kings of Asia and took seven of them alive; there are the cities of the seven mouths; Benjamin marries seven years after Joseph's disappearance; there are the seven kine of Osiris; the brothers stay with Joseph seven days before going home to tell Jacob he is alive; young Pharaoh builds a new palace with seven courts; the brothers had returned from Dothan to Jacob seven days after the latter had received the sign of Joseph's death; the tribe of Israel leaves for Egypt seventy strong; Jacob lives in Egypt for seventeen years; Jacob's body is bathed in saltpeter for seventy days in process of embalming; the Israelites obtain seventy days' leave to take Jacob's body to his Hebrew home.

And the external evidence is conclusive: just as *The Magic Mountain* contained seven chapters, so Book I of the Joseph series contains a prelude and seven chapters; Book II, seven chapters; Book III, consisting of two volumes, contains five chapters in the first and two in the second; and Book IV, rounding the cycle, contains a prelude and seven chapters.

In reading the Joseph books one is struck by the work's enormous allusiveness, which sounds and resounds in one's inner ear like musical overtones of great volume. One wonders about the relation between Mann's personal life as an artist with that of Joseph the artist-type and the Joseph legend in general; about the book's relation to our time and its relation to Mann's other books in symbolism, style, and outlook; about Mann's development—from a genealogical novel like *Buddenbrooks,* with its entertaining though static symbolism, to the completely bourgeois and musically ironic *Magic Mountain,* and finally to the mythical Joseph books; about the relation of the Joseph work to Faust and of Mann to Goethe; about the relation of the myth in Mann to the myth in other modern authors; about Mann's interest in himself as artist; and about many other things constantly impinging upon and then fading from consciousness. Allusive-

ness and musicality—those are two words certainly characteristic of *Joseph's* author, for there is a constant ringing in one's
ears, and bells seem to sound when one comes in contact with
Mann's style.

It is always a little presumptuous and unfounded for a critic
to assume autobiographical content and symbolism in an author's
work, even when he is encouraged to do so by the author's own
confessions, for authors are notoriously apt to read into their
work, once it is out of their hands, things private, secretly delightful, and confessional in spite of the fact that the cold observer,
like the child in the fable, sees the emperor naked and nothing
else. But in the case of the Joseph books and in other of Mann's
writings, certain analogies between life and fable are sufficiently
evident to justify giving them considerable thought. The case
of Joseph's two pits is a good example. Twice Joseph is thrown
into the pit, once by his brothers and again by Potiphar; the
first time because of Joseph's exceeding self-love, even arrogance,
the self-love of the dreamer who has begun to make an ivory-
tower cult of himself; the second time because of his renunciation of this same self-love, which appears to him now in the form
of sexual manhood, love of his maleness, the fleshly. And here
irony becomes plain, for the cause of Joseph's double downfall
is identical, each time being the same self-love but with this
distinction—that Joseph's first fall results from its acceptance
and the second from its rejection. Thus the second fall is the
more noble and mature; as a matter of fact it is blameless, even
virtuous, for it is the renunciation of the flesh—of consummation
with the lovely Mut-em-enet—in favor of the spiritual, in favor
of physical purity, and loyalty to Potiphar, Joseph's friend and
benefactor.

So much for Joseph's two pits; but what about Mann's?
Mann's first was his Prussianism during the First World War,
when he wrote the *Reflections of a Non-Political Man*, as though
a man interested in the welfare of humanity can ever stand
blameless on the sidelines and call himself non-political. The
second pit is his exile from his native land and the consequent
loss of his German-speaking audience. Note the following striking parallel: the cause of Mann's two falls in each case is the
same as it was with Joseph: first because he accepts and then
because he rejects—and, as in the case of Joseph, it is precisely
self-love. Of course it is a more complicated, more sophisticated,
less obvious self-love but nevertheless it is that same self-love
of the dreamer, the artist; and in both Joseph and Mann it is

expressed on two planes: in personal egotism and in heightened
spirituality—the latter, with Joseph, a belief in God and in his
being God's favorite; with Mann, his belief in himself as an
artist with a mission, an artist loyal to the humanizing ideal of literature and to literature's covenant with the humane. But what
is the nature of Mann's double fall? It is this: in the first instance
he deserted his loyalty to things of the spirit. In short, by joining
the ranks of the German militarists he forsook his loyalty to the
word, to his art, and to his destiny as an artist—in practical terms,
to his continuing influence as a writer and his continuing ability
to win an enlightened, civilized and worthy audience. And, like
Joseph, he was punished with smarting in the pit, with smarting,
like Joseph's, of an inner nature, a smarting of guilt and revaluation. Now for the second instance: in this he was cast into the
pit of exile and thus deprived of his German-speaking audience
(something not to be underestimated as an enervating, depressing
force), suffering because he renounced that which was largely
responsible for his first fall, now expressed in the form of German fascism. Why did he, like Joseph, turn to renunciation?
Because, like Joseph, he now refused to compromise his artist-
purity, his conscience, having firmly established it in the smarting and revaluation of the first fall. Joseph's self-love is Mann's
self-love, just as Joseph is Mann, for both are artists and both
are egotistic. Joseph is more primitive and therefore more naive,
but the impulse is the same, except that Joseph's feelings of
artist guilt—feelings which largely derive from an excess of self-
love—are not so strong as Mann's, since Joseph falls back on the
assurance that his role is destined by God and therefore will, in
the long run, be one of honor. Mann, however, though not an
ordinary believer in God, finds relief from his feelings of guilt
in a device not very dissimilar to Joseph's; in fact his device, too,
is precisely destiny, his personal destiny of playing an honorable
role among men.

Thus we see that there is indeed a broad yet intense parallel
between Joseph's two pits on the one hand and Mann's on the
other. But at this point a disturbing question arises. Did Mann
choose the Joseph legend because of this and similar parallels between the fable and life? If so, then he must have known of his
coming exile. Is one therefore to assume the existence and validity of the occult? Is the artist truly, as it has so often been
written, a prophet and seer? Does he sense the nature of coming events? Fortunately, it is not necessary to answer such
questions to present a sound case. It is undoubtedly true that

Mann chose the legend because he felt some inner affinity with it. He himself has said so. Aside from being definitely explicit about his choice, he has given the following insight into his productive mechanism, which is certainly relevant here: "A work must have long roots in my life, secret connections must lead from it to earliest childhood dreams, if I am to consider myself entitled to it, if I am to believe in the legitimacy of what I am doing." But aside from this affinity his choice had political overtones, and it is here that we find the answer to the disturbing question. At the time that Mann was thinking of his new work, events in Germany had already come to such a pass that only the blind (and there were many such) could not sense their direction, only the blind were without some dark suspicions concerning the nature of future events. Nationalism, militarism and despotism were already rife, and a wave of anti-semitism was engulfing and shaming the country. Indeed, so far had fascism progressed that even Mann, still quite a non-political man, chose the Old Testament as the subject for his new book—not by accident, but strictly by design. He writes: "Well, the selection of the Old Testament subject was certainly not mere accident; most certainly there were hidden, defiantly polemic connections between it and certain tendencies of our time which I always found repulsive from the bottom of my soul: the growing vulgar anti-semitism which is an essential part of the fascist mob-myth, and which commits the brutish denial of the fact that Judaism and Hellenism are the two principal pillars upon which our Occidental civilization rests. To write a novel of the Jewish spirit was timely just because it seemed untimely." In brief, Mann had already chosen the course of renunciation and defiance of the New Order, though not overtly as yet. Therefore the second pit needed only the further development and strengthening of the New Order for it to achieve existence. It was already foreshadowed, for it was plain that the Hitlerites would punish those who resisted them. Therefore the particular form of the pit—in this instance exile—was to some extent accidental, but the coming of the pit itself was never in doubt.

Have we stated the case completely? Not quite. Some of the facts chafe under isolation; they belong partly to another context, to another pattern, another parallelism. In short, certain key words possess value in a second pattern, from the point of view of which the first can be seen in a new and equally striking light. The self-love which twice endangered Joseph's life is, as has been stated, the self-love of the artist. But what about the

pits? They too are the pits of the artist, for only an artist could
have gotten himself into them for such causes as we know about.
Relegation to these pits is not caused by the irregularity of the
criminal or the social or political revolutionary; it is caused by
the irregularity, in the first instance, of the insufferably vain
dreamer and in the second of the insufferably loyal purist. And
renunciation? It is the ambivalent renunciation of the artist-
type, which shuns that for which it hungers and which craves
precisely and perversely for that from which it keeps aloof—it
is the renunciation whose aftermath is suffering. And the maturation following the suffering in the first pit? It is the maturation
not of whole wisdom but again of ambivalence, of trying to play
with fire while avoiding it, in other words, the maturation of the
middle man. The story of Joseph is, among other things, the
parable of the artist as a success among men, and for this reason,
if for no other, it must have appealed strongly to Mann, who as
an artist has always proclaimed a strong bond with tradition
and the regular and who considers happiness and success necessary in this life. Mann is almost the prototype of the regular-
irregular artist, the man who refuses to wear a velvet jacket and
long hair in sign of his trade but yet flirts lovingly with death
and the illicit in his artistic explorations. Almost but not quite
the prototype—for there is always Goethe, Goethe as model and
master. Success, however, is not the whole story, nor does Joseph
achieve it without danger and struggle—all of which fits in nicely
with Mann's experience as an artist. Joseph is the outcast dreamer, full of vanity, physically rather fragile, a decadent from his
brothers' burgher and regular point of view, a silly mental man
and not a shepherd, not a man who labors in the field or with
the flocks. And what of Mann? Mann as a young man is the
shady member of a solid burgher family; he is irregular, decadent
and unhealthy in their opinion; he has a bad conscience, he
suffers from feelings of guilt; he doesn't work as regular people
do—on the contrary he dreams, scribbles and dabbles in disturbing things. And so Mann as a young writer writes of the artist
who is desperately alone and who dreams of union with the gay,
blithe and blue-eyed, the unfrowning regular folk. For Mann
is never completely the artist in the old Bohemian sense of complete revolt. He is the new type of artist as middle man, the mediator between tradition and revolt as well as between flesh and
spirit.

Joseph, then, is cast out because he is unbearable, a misfit
in a land of tents and shepherds. But he is not the only unbear-

able one, for to him his brothers too are unbearable; to fulfill his talents he must escape their way of life, he must go down to a country where his gifts will be prized instead of despised and where he can attain a sizable piece of urban wealth, not the wealth of flocks and fields, for he is ambivalent, he is not the man to despise the material simply because he loves the spiritual. Therefore he must go to a country with an advanced culture, a decadent country which will prize his "decadence" and shower him with wealth and honor because of it. And so he goes (or arranges to have himself sold into, which is the same thing from the viewpoint of fate) to Egypt, knowing that a prophet is not without honor except in his own country. There he rises to greatness and becomes the provider, not only for his own people, who once cast him out, but for all others as well.

And again we note the cogent parallel, this time of ambivalence and success. Mann gains great honors in the foreign land of literature, where his decadent dreams bring a good price, and in the end he showers wealth and honor not on his people alone but on all people; in the end he is the provider, the artist as father and teacher; the artist, in more or less figurative terms, as savior of the people.

V

Burgher, artist, tradition, revolt, nature, spirit—these are social terms and we have accepted them conveniently from Mann thus far because they have historical insight and validity. But we are aware that Mann's work is a web of highly personal symbolism too—perhaps so personal that Mann himself is not altogether aware of it. What, let us ask, are the above broad terms disguising in Mann's psychic history? What clues can they afford to a subterranean symbolism general in his work and as yet unsuspected by us?

In *Tonio Kröger* the father-mother dialectic is more directly presented than elsewhere in Mann. As usual, the father is the good citizen, the mother the somewhat suspect hot-blooded creature. The latter comes from somewhere "far down on the map" and is named Consuelo (Mann's own mother came from Brazil). The mother is equated with license, passion, the south; the father with conscience and order; the mother with the new, the father with the traditional. All that Mann has written about the artist's intermediary position is now seen by means of the symbolism of his fiction to be disguises of a basically sexual motif: the ambivalence between masculine and feminine traits in the artist; or, more expressly stated, the artist's ambivalence between his father and mother. That the sexual motif is indeed basic is indicated by the richness of the unconscious symbolism (soon to be discussed) which pervades the works.

The father symbolizes conscience; this is indicated by the sentence "It might have been his father in him, that tall, thoughtful, fastidiously dressed man with the wild flower in his buttonhole, that made him suffer so down there in the south. . . ." It is in the south that Tonio's heart becomes "dead and loveless," and that he descends "into the depths of lust and searing sin," suffering "unspeakably" thereby. Tonio is seriously ambivalent. "So for all result he was flung to and fro forever between two crass extremes, between icy intellect [father] and scorching sense, [mother] and what with his pangs of conscience led an exhausting life, rare, extraordinary, excessive, which at bottom he, Tonio Kröger, despised." Art is the product of this ambivalence, this disease, this neurosis, and it is directly proportional in excellence to the severity of the neurosis, according to the tale. Thus Mann writes: "But as his health suffered from these excesses, so his artistry was sharpened, it grew fastidious, precious, *raffiné*, morbidly sensitive in questions of tact and taste, rasped by the banal." Art is compulsive. "He worked, not like a man who works that he may live; but as one who is bent on doing nothing but work. . . ." The artist, like the Oedipus neurotic, is of doubtful sex. "Is an artist a male, anyhow? Ask the females! It seems to me we artists are all of us something like those unsexed papal singers. . . ." Tonio desires to be normal, to be like Hans Hansen and Ingeborg Holm; that is, he desires to be like his father. But he is torn by the illicit, which is the feminine in him, and is not in the least surprised to be taken for a criminal on his visit to his native town. His visit is in a sense a journey of rebirth, a journey into the womb of the past, with all its touching nostalgia, and it ends with rhapsodies on the sea, that classic symbol, in mythology and psychoanalysis, of regeneration.

In *Death in Venice*, Aschenbach, the man of iron will, the descendant of strict and disciplined forebears, is the victim of energies which he has been repressing for years. These overthrow him on two counts—moral and physical. They seduce him to the illicit level of homosexuality and, having witnessed his progressive degeneration, slay him with the plague. The conflict in Aschenbach is between the forces of the conscious and the unconscious minds. Fatigued by his sapping work, and worn-out by a lifetime of repression, Aschenbach unconsciously seeks a new life, a rebirth. That is why he heads instinctively towards the sea, the symbol of woman, the womb and parturition. He travels south because the south for him symbolizes the sensuous, the feminine and disorder—in brief the illicit—traits he has inherited from his mother, the daughter of a Bohemian musical conductor. * The unconscious, the primitive, makes powerful demands of him. It stirs up primitive images—of jungles and tigers. Aschenbach's yearning for rebirth is indicated even by his repugnant attempts to beautify himself at the Venetian barber's.

Rebirth entails death. That is why Aschenbach must die. It is also why the symbols of death pursue him— the North Cemetery, the stone-mason's yard, the snub-nosed man in the portico, with his fangs showing, the old sailor with the goatee, the horrible old man in the rakish panama. Aschenbach's "yearning for new and distant scenes," his "craving for freedom, release, forgetfulness," are cravings for death so that he may be reborn. As always in Mann, there is the equation between father and discipline and order, and mother and the sensuous, illicit and beautiful. The sea plays a great role in the novella. Its importance for Aschenbach is made clear by Mann: "His love of the ocean had profound sources: the hard-worked artist's longing for rest, his yearning to seek refuge from the thronging manifold shapes of his fancy in the bosom of the simple and vast; and another yearning, opposed to his art and perhaps for that very reason a lure, for the unorganized, the immeasurable, the eternal—in short, for nothingness." This is also a true description of Mann's own interest in the sea.

With these facts in mind one can easily discern a classic pattern of behavior—the pattern of the Oedipus type of neurotic, torn between his desire for both parents and by his incestuous leanings toward his mother. Aschenbach (or Mann), the Oedipus, represses the feminine in him because it is illicit; it is illicit because it involves incest; but in the last analysis his powerful defenses crumble before a sudden if late attack by his primitive unconscious. The homosexual component, emphasized by the figure of Tadzio, is classic in the Oedipus neurosis. All the elements are clear: the ambivalence between the parents and their symbolic equivalents, the fear of incest and consequent punishment, the yearning to return to the womb and to achieve rebirth, the homosexual overtones, result of a too-strong identification with the father. "Thought that can merge wholly into feeling,

---

* The coupling of music and the illicit. as well as music and the sea, is prominent in Mann's work.

feeling that can merge wholly into thought—these are the artist's highest joy." This sentence from the tale is but a disguised statement of the neurotic's search for stability and mental health between the opposing poles of the conscious mind (thought) and the unconscious one (feeling).

At first glance it would seem that *The Magic Mountain* contradicts this thesis of the rebirth quest, but the symbols need only to be stripped of their superficial disguise for all their regularity to become transparent. The novel is a tale of Castorp's rebirth on the mountain, in the shadow of death, after he has died in terms of the flatland. Now the earth, like the sea, is a great female symbol—witness the traditional expression Mother Earth. A mountain is an excrescence not unlike the female breast, so that the fertility and feminine motifs are strengthened. As always the feminine motif is powerully linked to the notions of disorder, disease, the illicit and erotic for Mann—all elements prominent in the life of Davos. The masculine motif is disguised by two father images, the grandfather—stern and orderly, a citizen of good conscience—and Consul Tienappel, the guardian and also a solid burgher type. One of the most interesting disguises is the mountain itself, which stands for the depths of the womb. This use of the opposite for purposes of secret symbolism is profoundly apparent in the study of dream censorship and—and now we speak of communal dreams—in the censorship of folklore and mythology. The gods on Mount Olympus are personifications of forces in the depths of man's unconscious.

Hans Castorp psychologicaly descends into a pit although actually he ascends a great mountain as he approaches the Berghof: he experiences giddiness and nausea as if he were seasick, and this is apt, inasmuch as he is figuratively immersing himself in the sea, the sea here disguised as space and time. That the sea is not overlooked even literally is suggested by Castorp's carrying a copy of *Ocean Steamships* and from his remark to his cousin about the eternal snow on the mountain (water in any form is a rebirth symbol). As a matter of fact, the sea motif is extremely prominent, although it is likely to be overlooked in the massive novel, with its shifting focus highlighting the themes of death and time. Hans is a ship engineer, he comes from Hamburg, "a seaboard city," he loves water as he does music, the climactic sequence of the novel, in which he experiences the process of rebirth, is called "Snow," another is called "By the Ocean of Time," there is an important scene at the waterfall, and Hans, in his great dream, while almost freezing to death, conjures up fertility symbols—the rainbow, showers, and especially the sea. This descent into the depths has other aspects as well: Hans descends into the pits of psychoanalysis (depth psychology), the erotic, music, death, the occult. It is such hidden symbolic elements which lend the novel its mythical charm.

And the Joseph saga—the entire story is an effort to return to the womb of the past. Here the theme of rebirth is explicit—in Joseph's pits and arisings therefrom. Mann's sexual symbolism grows increasingly explicit with his profound assimilation of the Freudian explorations.

We have found, therefore, even in this far from inclusive sketch, that Mann's great theme, hidden beneath the surface of his works and probably hidden from himself to a large extent—the theme which is compulsive for him and which wears countless masks—is nothing less traditional and grandiose than that of the Oedipus quest in modern dress. One thinks instantly of the Sophoclean Oedipus and of Hamlet—and of course of Freud. Nor is that all—for doesn't one also bring to mind the entire gallery of great modern novelists—Proust, Joyce, Lawrence, Kafka, to make only a beginning? Are they not all on an Oedipus quest, with their obsession with anti-paternal revolt, maternal love, ambivalence, frustration, sex? Proust strives to descend into the womb of present time, Joyce into the womb of language-myth, Lawrence into the womb of past time (primitivism) and sensualism, Kafka into the womb of slyly hidden personal and pyschoanalytical symbolism. The neurotic hero is the modern hero and he is the artist in disguise. The modern great novel is truly the portrait of the great artist as an Oedipus neurotic.

[1946]

THOMAS MANN AND THE RELIGIOUS REVIVAL

Philip Blair Rice

Some of the meteorologists who record shifts in the winds of doctrine are labelling the second quarter of our century a period of religious revival; others put it down as a time of "failure of nerve." It has been at any rate a period of great heat about religion; we could ask for more light. I am presuming to speak for that considerable faction, not yet very vocal on the subject, who are distressed by the terms in which the issue is being stated in public controversy. This has tended to resolve itself into a dog fight between the neo-orthodox (supported by those who would be neo-orthodox if the faith were not lacking) and the upholders of scientific method against a resurgence of superstition.

The spokesmen for neo-orthodoxy are often shrewd and cultivated gentlemen, and I for one can read them in moderate doses with profit. They have a keen eye for the flabbiness of religious liberals and the crudities of naively science-minded naturalists, though they tend to center their attacks against versions of naturalism which are no longer flourishing. But their net effect is that of a kind of philosophic sniping. They are very clever at picking off the foolish and unwary outposts of the naturalistic movement, but are unable to carry an assault in strength against the fortified philosophies of contemporary science and humanism. The ordnance is rusty. The neo-Catholics seek to retain the metaphysics and theology of St. Thomas while rejecting the science and logic of science which were very much of a piece with them. Protestant neo-orthodoxy, going back to Augustine and Tertullian via Kierkegaard and existential philosophy, has some very sensitive psychology of the moral experience to offer, and beyond that little but paradoxes. These are the philosophers and theologians of neo-orthodoxy. Of their allies among literary men, who are on the whole a more ingratiating if no less vulnerable crowd, I shall speak later.

The most active opponents of neo-orthodoxy can claim with considerable justification that such desperate remedies constitute a kind of failure of nerve, or battle fatigue of the philosophic fox-holes. Yet it will not do to treat the neurotic as bedevilled, and to set one witch-hunt against another. Too ofen, abandoning their own professed clinical attitude, its critics eye the neo-religious movement as a manifestation of something like Original Sin, the heritage from the devil consisting in this case of willful resistance to the revelations of scientific method. If our age has undergone a collective failure of nerve, it would be the way of understanding to ask: Why are we so nervous? The answer may not be found wholly in such obvious social causes as the wars and the economic upheavals. It may be that contemporary naturalism or humanism itself is not yet sufficiently imaginative, that its battle slogan of "scientific method" is too shrill and monotonous, that like monotheism on certain interpretations it does not offer a sufficiently fine and diversified pattern to fit the predicaments of living.

I am speaking of scientific method as a slogan, or a panacea. If we take it simply as a logic, the logic of empiricism as that is now understood, it has not been shown to be inadequate. The efforts of anti-naturalists to combat it or supplement it with apriorism or intuitionism or authoritarianism have been singularly ineffectual. The logic of hypothesis, deductive prediction and experiential verification has been too fruitful, not only in the physical sciences but also in the sciences of man and even in the value studies (though here its steps are still hesitant) for us to say, Thus far shall it go and no farther. It appears as the sole reliable method for warranting assertions. This would be clearer in the "humanities" themselves were it not for that perversion of scientific method known as pedantry. Yet granting all this, and insisting upon it, we can still find some truth in the statement: *Non in dialectica complacuit Deo salvum facere populum suum.* Even though empirical method is the sole valid way of warranting assertions, this is not our whole business. We have to act and feel, to work and fight, to create and enjoy, even perhaps to, worship, as well as to know. All these activities are related, but to point to their mutual dependence is not to identify them. So it is that the adoption of "scientific mehod" as a slogan tends to frighten practitioners of the arts and professors of the humanities, as well as other worthy people who can find some guidance in the religious tradition itself. Sometimes the slogan scares them into the bailiwick of anti-empirical and supernatural doctrines which in the past have been able to live with, and even at times to foster, the arts and humane conduct.

It is not, of course, true that recent naturalists have failed entirely to attempt sympathetic reinterpretation of the religious tradition, as the writings of Santayana, Cassirer, and lately Mrs. Langer, testify. But the most militant naturalists, those who have led the assault on the current theologies, have been the American instrumentalists, the logical positivists and the Cambridge analysts. These have all been concerned primarily with the furthering of science, and it is not to be wondered at that they should consider the religious tradition, especially in its neo-orthodox representatives, as mainly an obstacle to enlightenment. Even Dewey and his school, who among the devotees of scientific method are the most inclusive and humane in their interests, have given very little detailed attention to the religious tradition. Dewey himself has written, in *Art as Experience,* a profound and fruitful book on aesthetics, but has attempted nothing comparable to it on philosophy of religion. Here is, for example, his definition of the religious attitude from *A Common Faith*: "Any activity pursued in behalf of an ideal end against obstacles and in spite of threats of personal loss because of conviction of its general and enduring value is religious in quality." So far as it goes, this is admirable, and most of the official religionists of any age could well take it to heart. Yet this heroic ethico-social attitude, divorced from the traditional context of religious practice and wedded to scientifically established ideals, seems to be *all* that Dewey can salvage from the tangled wreckage of religious systems. Myths, legend and other religious symbols as modes of awareness are dismissed as pre-scientific. This is where a naturalist who is more centrally preoccupied with the arts and humanities is likely to part company with him.

Some prima facie significance can be derived from the fact that imaginative writers from Homer through Aeschylus to Yeats, Mann, Eliot and Auden have continued to ransack the religious tradition for instruments of vision. Where the main current of religious orthodoxy has not seemed viable to them, they have often, as did Baudelaire, Rimbaud and Yeats, found nourishment in heretical occultist sources, or, like Blake, George and Lawrence, they have constructed kindred heretical mythologies of their own. As sometimes with Rilke, their gods and angels are mere patent objectifications of their personal anxieties and compulsions. It is always difficult in the case of a poet to disentangle the belief from the literary strategy. But none of these men was a simple aesthete or entertainer using religious symbols for afflatus and decoration, and some conceived themselves to be prophets. That so many of them were forced to seek their salvation in fantastic and heretical byways may suggest inadequacies in the religious, humanist and scientific orthodoxies. Yet whatever choice prospects it can afford, the tradition of high heresy—that which was nourished by Gnosticism, neo-Platonism, Cabbalism and Rosicrucianism—is itself a kind of ivory tower of the spirit, a very special refuge available only to those who are not offended by posture and mystification. Compared with it, the main Judaeo-Christian structure may seem spacious, liberating and full of mansions. Many diverse hands have worked on it, largely in public view and under the control of functional specifications. So it may be on the whole a sign of relative health, or of yearning toward health, rather than of irredeemable neurosis, that the leaders of the contemporary religious revival in literature, such as Eliot, Auden and Mann, are seeking refreshment in the main current of Hebraic-Christian experience rather than, as did so many of their immediate predecessors, in the magic elixirs of high heresy. I am not suggesting that each of these men would pass the tests of some one of the rival orders that claim to be the present repositories of orthodoxy, and there is no indication that Mann in particular would make the effort. Yet his heresies, if such they are, consist in an imaginative reworking of the recognized elements of orthodoxy—though not without incidental benefits from arcane sources—rather than a partial revolt on behalf of doctrines equally tainted with superstition but less fraught with human experience.

The conversions of Eliot and Auden were too rapid and too whole-hearted to make their progress altogether intelligible to others who are still, what they began as, children of the Enlightenment; and their own elucidations have not helped. But Mann's interest in religion is less of a break with his past, and not at all aggressive. We know that Eliot is for the Church, and that Auden is against naturalism. Thomas Mann's present attitude both toward ecclesiastical institutions and toward philosophcial naturalism as that term is understood in America remains, so far as I can learn, unstated. Though the Joseph story is a philosophical novel, it is not a treatise in theology or metaphysics. It is a book not about God, but about what the religious liberals used to call "the idea of God in human experience." Not only its tone of sweet irony in handling the more grandiose pretenions of theodicy seems to place it on the humanistic side, but also such passages as the following, though they are not unequivocal:

> Yes, Abram had known how to communicate his exaltation of spirit. He was named Abiram; that is to say: "my father is exalted," or also, probably just as correctly, "father of the ex-

alted." For in a way Abraham was God's father. He had
perceived Him and thought Him into being The mighty properties which he ascribed to Him were probably God's original
possession. Abraham was not their creator. But he not so,
after all, in a certain sense, when he recognized them,
preached them, and by thinking made them real? The mighty
properties of God were indeed something objective, existing outside of Abraham; but they were also in him and of him.

The ambiguity lies in our freedom to interpret the "objectivity"
of God's properties as we will, whether with the naive realism
of the supernaturalist or naturalistically after the fashion of the
modern critical realist. Because Mann is writing not about God
but about Abraham's experience of God, it suffices to relate that
the patriarch felt these properties as coming from outside him.
Since the supernaturalist would not be likely to define Abraham's
role with respect to the divine properties as "by thinking to make
them real," and since Mann at once proceeds to have God answer
Abraham's questionings of divine justice by enveloping Himself
in "benevolent silence," the weight of the passage if any is not
on the side of theodicy. But most probably Mann's ambiguity is
intentional. His book contains nothing that would offend a humanist or imaginative naturalist, and at the same time nothing
that could be denied by an honest supernaturalist. This does not
mean that it is milk-and-water, or that it straddles, but rather
that it affords a good starting point for a testing and reworking of
the religious tradition. It makes a minimum of assumptions.

II

In order to get a foothold on religious tradition, Mann has
had to go behind, not only institutional religion, but even Christianity itself, to its two ultimate sources or precursors, the experience of the patriarchs and the pagan mystery cults of the
Near East.

Going back so far, Mann is able to find the God-idea to be
an unqualifiedly progressive one. Not only did El Shaddei substitute the ram for the sacrifice of the first-born son but He did
not yet need an establishment to protect His word from the
vagaries of the uninstructed and dole it out to the spiritually
inept:

> Why did Jacob live like an Ishmaelite or a Bedouin, in tents
> outside the town, in the open country, not even in sight of
> the citadel of Kirjath Arba; beside the well, the caves, the
> oaks and the terebinths, in a camp which might be struck at
> any time—as though he might not stop and take root with

the others, as though from hour to hour he must be awaiting the word which should make him take down huts
and stalls, load poles, blankets and skins on the pack camels
and be off? Joseph knew why, of course. Thus it must be,
because one served a God whose nature was not repose and
abiding comfort, but a God of designs for the future, in
whose will inscrutable, great, far-reaching things were in
process of becoming, who, with His brooding will and His
world-planning, was Himself only in process of becoming, and
thus was a God of unrest, a God of cares, who must be
sought for, for whom one must at all times keep oneself free,
mobile and in readiness.

This recalls Matthew Arnold's idea that Western civilization
derives its moral energy from Hebraic sources, but it goes back of
the explicit reflections of the ethical prophets to the legendary
fathers' austere awareness of a not-self, or ideal other, who would
not let them rest content with things as they were. For the patriarchs, the progressivism of the God-idea was not rootless; it
was pious, or backward-looking, as well as forward-looking.
These nomads were men who "did not precisely know who they
were." They became conscious of their identity by role-taking,
by re-enacting old patterns—the brothers' strife over the blessing, the blessing-bearer's exile, the wooing of the distant bride.
Yet this was not a slavish Egyptian imitation of stereotypes, but
a creative use of forms, a pouring of new wine into old bottles.

Joseph inherited this God-awareness from his fathers. Even
in the sober version of Genesis, Joseph stands out from these
dun, tortured men like his coat of many colors from the attire
of the shepherds. He is less provincial, more labile, better in-
structed, endowed with the heathen as well as the Hebraic virtues. As Mann represents him, he fuses Arnold's "Hellenic
culture"—or its approximation in the lore of the Babylonians, the
Canaanites and the Egyptians—with the moral earnestness of
the Jew. Being free from Jacob's puritanism, the young Joseph
is fascinated by Tammuz and Osiris, the gods who die and are
reborn. His sin, or missing-the-mark, is in consequence one
against which the Greeks felt it more necessary to warn than
did the Hebrews—the presumption of a man's fancying himself
a god. In the sphere of human relationships, this hybris takes
the form of insensibility to the feelings of others, and in particular
of imagining that others love him more than they love themselves. Joseph lands in the pit.

But if Joseph's lability makes him more susceptible to transgression, it also renders him more capable of learning. The "twice-born" Joseph whom the Israelites carry into Egypt, and who serves Potiphar so discreetly, can no longer imagine himself to be a god, though he is still confident that he is the instrument of divine purposes. The counterpoint of *Joseph in Egypt* is elaborate. Joseph is resurrected, yet he is all the time Osiris Joseph, a dead man in the land of the dead. He bears the creative principle in a sterile culture, among a people who are not ancestors but descendants. The coughing little folk who build the king's tomb under the lash of his overseers are dead, and so are the nobles who appear before them in the immobility of a mortuary statue. The Enlightenment of Potiphar, who shares the new liberal cult of Atum-Re, is the thin idealism of a eunuch. Even the quickening of Potiphar's wife before the charms of maturing Joseph is not a rebirth of the person in love but the tumescence of an erotic dream.

Joseph himself must die again. The first sojourn in the pit did not rid him entirely of hybris or want of foresight. His "pedagogical" designs on Potiphar's wife spring from his arrogant confidence that he can teach the unteachable, that he is a "virtuoso of virtue" who can push matters to the uttermost in order to carry off a greater triumph.

III

In *Joseph the Provider* the atmosphere changes. Egypt is no longer a dream landscape, the underworld, but is itself undergoing a renascence. It is a splendid imaginative stroke of Mann's to identify the Pharaoh whom Joseph served with Ikhnaton, the universalist reformer who tried to stir Egypt from its dynasties-old sleep, and some of whose hymns to the loving sun-god Aton have, according to Breasted, found their way into our own Book of Psalms. Mann represents the young Pharaoh as something of a Hellenist, who collects Cretan lyres and Cretan tales, and who in his directions to his artists for a portrait of his sister anticipates the *stil dolce e nuovo*:

> Make her sweet and easy, make her according to the truth, which is the light, and in which Pharaoh lives, for he has set it in his inmost heart! Let one hand be putting to her mouth a piece of fruit, a pomegranate, and her other hand be hanging down easily—not with the palm turned stiffly to the body but the rounded palm turned backwards, thus will the god have it that is in my heart and whom I know as no other knows him because I come of him.

This last volume has many of the earmarks of an *Ode to Joy* rather than the tragic resolution of Mann's earlier novels; and Joseph's personal fortunes, as some reviewers have pointed out, bear the interest, or lack of it, of a success story. Yet it would be an oversimplification to take this as the full import of the tale. For Jacob's blessing goes not to Joseph but to the tormented Judah. How does Mann make artistically plausible this interpretation of Genesis?

Our expectations for Joseph have been raised high. For the first time, Mann brings together into something approaching a synthesis the antitheses which have beset him throughout his life as a writer. Joseph is, what none of the Buddenbrooks succeeded in being, both a business man and an artist. He combines Aschenbach's discipline with Tadzio's natural grace. He is at the same time a Child of Nature and a Child of Spirit. Unlike Hans Castorp, he achieves a unification and magnification of the several good qualities which Hans descried, in however life-tarnished form, in Mynheer Peeperkorn, Settembrini and Naphta—he even possesses some of Clavdia Chauchat's feminine perceptiveness and Asiatic inscrutability. All this sounds like a monstrous achievement, but it does not exhaust Joseph's multiplicity-in-unity. Though Joseph knows that he is not a god, or even a perfect man, the oppressed of Egypt identify him with Adon. We are even at times tempted blasphemously to see in Joseph—the bringer of the new time, the reborn harbinger of God's Kingdom—intimations of the risen Christ.

Yet Joseph does not receive the blessing. On his death bed, Jacob, clear-sighted if incoherent, bestows the gift of the spirit on the conscientious but unexceptional Judah. He has previously told Joseph that the blessing is not for him:

> "God has given and has taken you," murmured Jacob, "and he has given you back, but yet not quite, for He has kept you too. . . . He has elevated and rejected you both in one, I say it in your ear, beloved child, and you are wise enough to hear it. He has raised you above your brothers just as in your dream—and I have, my darling, ever held your dreams in my heart. But He has raised you in a worldly way, not in the sense of salvation and the inheritance of the blessing. . . . Through you salvation is not to reach the peoples and the leadership is denied you."

It is evident, then, that there is an element of tragedy in the conclusion of the Joseph story. One of Jacob's two reasons for denying Joseph the blessing is clear. As a matter of historical fact, the religious and political achievements of Ikhnaton's reign were soon swallowed up by the reactionary House of Amun, and the God-idea and the moral energy of the Hebrews were transmitted to us by the undistinguished eleven.

Jacob's second reason, that God has raised Joseph in a worldly way, offers difficulties. It is true that Mann has told us earlier in the story that the young Joseph was more calculating than Jacob, that he had a sharper eye for the main chance. But Jacob also is a rich man and can likewise be a rogue on occasion. Any slight difference of degree in these respects might seem to be counterbalanced by the many admirable qualities in which Joseph excels Jacob. Even Joseph's accommodation to the gods of Egypt is made to seem not a betrayal of the God of his fathers but a universalistic extension of His conquests. As we see Joseph after his second rebirth he is not a worldling who pursues his own interests at the expense of others. He is a man thoroughly dedicated to his task. Arrogance has been purged from him; his forgiveness of his brothers is so complete that he does not regard it as forgiveness.

It is true that Joseph's most spectacular accomplishments are political and economic. But we know that Mann is no longer an unpolitical man, that he does not consider redemption of the world a task beneath the dignity of spirit. And Joseph's political eminence is not a mere vulgar personal success, a grab of power for power's sake. Mann has cleverly interpreted the exploits of Joseph as recounted by Genesis so that they do not appear as a feat of monopoly and extortion but as a triumph of economic democracy, within the possibilities of the second millennium B. C. Joseph the nourisher squeezes the rich for the sake of the poor, and does so because that is his mission.

It seems likely that Mann's fascination with the character of Joseph, abetted by the Biblical suggestions of Joseph's many-sidedness, has led Mann to endow him with so many perfections that he bursts the bonds of the traditional story. So that the necessity, imposed by Mann's reading of Genesis, of denying him the blessing, comes as something of an anticlimax. By this line of thought, we are led to suspect that Mann's own propulsions have driven him toward an ideal fusion of the Jew, the Greek and the modern in Joseph, but his literal reading of the story requires him to make the award to pure Hebraism—which was, after all, the blessing that Jacob had to give.

We may also be tempted to metaphysical speculations of the type evoked by the interpretation of legend in Greek tragedy, leading us to see the tragic element in the Joseph story as a universal one. It is not precisely the universal tragedy of near-perfection, that it cannot maintain itself. Knowing Mann's ironic temper and his romantic German idealism, we might interpret his conclusion as a kindred yet subtler type of universal tragedy— the tragedy of embodiment, that anything which is realized is tainted with compromise and relative to local conditions. This is perhaps something that can be salvaged from the myth of the Fall and the generally repellent doctrine of Original Sin. The nearest to perfection falls short of universal validity; it must wither and die, and the advance start over again from a cruder but less defined matrix: from Judah rather than from Joseph. In other words, Spirit, though generated out of Nature and dedicated to reclaiming it, must always surpass and elude its achieved embodiments in Nature.

Such fancies may not be without texts in the Joseph story. But we should not be too disturbed at discovering in this fourth part of the novel elements which cannot be fitted into a tight artistic structure like that of *The Magic Mountain, Death in Venice* or *Joseph in Egypt,* or into a neatly paraphrasable pattern of thought. Mann has never been coy about challenging comparison with the greatest, and he may have dared here, as did other writers in the masterpieces of their old age, *Oedipus at Colonus, The Bacchae, The Tempest* and *Faust Part II,* to set down insights which do not yield wholly to the form-giving impulse. Instead of answers, he states problems for those who come after to solve if they can. Such, instead of the supplying of finalities, is for him in any case the vitalizing function of the God-idea.

IV

It would seem that Mann has made the religious tradition, or an early segment of it, available to us as a kind of serious ethical and cosmological poetry, if nothing more. To call it poetry is to discredit it only for those who think poetry is of no consequence. But a distinction is needed here. Santayana has said: "Poetry is called religion when it intervenes in life, and religion, when it merely supervenes upon life, is seen to be nothing but poetry."

This is an attitude that will appear to the neo-orthodox to fall short and to the devotee of scientific method to go too far.

The neo-orthodox in his spiritual fox-hole is lost unless religion gives him certainty about cosmic riddles; the science-minded naturalist will ask how poetry can give us even probabilities on more modest issues. Both alike will question the claim that poetry can seriously intervene in life.

It will be necessary to discuss the question somewhat technically if briefly. Involved are, first, the nature of poetic and religious symbols, and second, the manner in which they operate. I shall suggest that poetic symbols and religious symbols are similar in their nature, both belonging to what may be called—to use a term of Mrs. Langer's, though not precisely her conception —"presentational symbols"; and they differ in their mode of functioning.

Religious symbols, such as myths, legends, and the acts and stage properties of ritual, are like aesthetic symbols in that they do not merely indicate objects and instigate operations, as do the symbols of science, but depict or enact or evoke what they signify; and at least part of what they signify consists of certain value qualities, which convey the immediacy and particularity of the object as experienced. The two types of symbols agree further in that they, or some of them, may organize a considerable area of experience by their systematic ambiguity or multiple reference, whereas the symbols of science are chosen for their univocal signification. Thus the crimson carpet in the *Agamemnon* organizes the play by bringing into focus at least three elements: the blood-soaked atmosphere of the play in general, and more specifically the bloody deeds of Agamemnon and Clytemnestra; Agamemnon's hybris—Oriental despots walk into their palaces on crimson carpets, which in Greece are spread only for the statues of gods entering their temples; and the blood feud whose struggle with civic justice is the main theme of the trilogy. In the Joseph story a like role is played by such symbols as the bridal veil, the Nile, the dying god, the strife of brothers over the blessing.

In their aesthetic functioning, such symbols are intransitive; they organize only the little world of the poem or the novel, and they organize it for perceptual or contemplative enjoyment. Their meanings may be derived from the great world of practical and cognitive experience, and are potentially extensible into it; but in so far as we adopt the aesthetic attitude—and perhaps we can never do so completely—such reference to the great world is excluded, suspended.

Symbols functioning aesthetically are not assertions; they do not give us transitive knowledge. Poetry of course contains sentences in the indicative mood: we are told that Macbeth killed Duncan. But this is a pseudo-assertion, or an assertion about the imaginary world of the play, not about the great world in space-time.

Such considerations are behind the denial of empiricists that art when it is functioning aesthetically gives us knowledge in the full sense. They may grant that it gives us "knowledge by acquaintance" of value qualities, as *Macbeth* can show us what it feels like to commit a murder. But value qualities are predicates, or propositional functions, and not propositions. In the aesthetic experience the subject of which they are predicated is the aesthetic object itself; the symbols function reflexively, within a microcosm. Even when we say that *Macbeth* shows us what it feels like to commit a murder, we are overstating the case. Responded to aesthetically, the play merely shows us what an imaginary character was imagined to feel like upon committing an imaginary murder. When we generalize from this we are not necessarily saying something false, but we are going beyond the evidence supplied by the aesthetic experience itself, and we must verify the statement by scrutinizing the reactions of real murderers, or at least by inference from our own experiences of transgression.

So far, all this is in accord not only with empiricist logic but with everyday observation. Any one who has fed on imaginative literature in adolescence must undergo a series of shocks in order to learn that his fund of vicarious experience derived from literature cannot be carried over directly to life without much painstaking and painful "verification."

Presentational symbols when functioning aesthetically, then, do not give us warranted knowledge; but such symbols when functioning in other ways may contribute to both knowledge and practice. Rather than to establish moral and cosmological truth forthwith, the transitive use of aesthetic experience is to help us discriminate immediate qualities, to stamp in attitudes, and to supply us with "hypotheses" which subsequent experience can confirm or disconfirm. When we exploit aesthetic symbols for these purposes, we may be doing something legitimate, but we are no longer using them aesthetically.

The religious attitude would seem to fall within this nonaesthetic, or not wholly aesthetic, use of presentational symbols. It is poetry "intervening in life," in the ways in which it can profitably do so. The posture of devotion or worship involves the assumption—if not always the explicit assertion—that the pattern of the act is transferable beyond the immediate experience, that it refers to a stable relation between man and the cosmos, or can organize his life beneficently on week-days. The religious attitude presupposes that the value qualities evoked by the symbols attach to such-and-such an object in the real world, or will be fostered by an act of such-and-such a kind. When this assumption is made explicit, it challenges verification, and thus easily comes into conflict with science or empirical method. When in such conflicts theology lays claims to some supra-empirical avenue to truth, it always gets licked. So that religion for us today must not be pre-scientific, or post-scientific, but co-scientific. It fills in the verifiable hypothesis with the particular detail, the context of consummatory qualities, that science leaves out, and it may rehearse us for their realization in action.

In a religious novel like the Joseph story, the presentational symbols are functioning for the most part aesthetically. It shows how the old myths and rites might have operated in the lives of certain legendary personae. The co-scientific character of Mann's own method is attested by the elaborate but unobtrusive use he has made of archaeology, anthropology, Freudian analysis and Biblical criticism: on this point another essay could be written. In the ways in which tradition, together with their own free adaptations of it to experience, enabled the patriarchs to "learn who they were," we are given a kind of paradigm of the operation of the religious consciousness. Since Mann is writing obliquely about our own time, and all time, as well as the second millennium B. C., he gives us hints as to how those hypotheses can organize our own chaotic world. But the testing and the verification are for us to carry out.

As to the larger claims of theodicy, I can find nothing in the Joseph story which will help the neo-orthodox to resolve the problem of evil in the age of Dachau, Lidice and Buchenwald. Instead of meeting a voice from the whirlwind, we are carried through irony to "benevolent silence." The tone of such chapters as "Prelude in the Upper Circles" we could derive from Kafka, if we did not remember that Mann's own *Royal Highness* was written before *The Castle*. As in Kierkegaard, we find paradoxes, and there is some anxiety. But the anxiety here is an instrument of human growth, not an ultimate surrender of man's natural powers; and the paradoxes do not lead to a *credo quia absurdum*: they are stages in the unending search for a perspective of perspectives rather than toward a cancelling of all perspectives in a supra-rational ecstasy.

On the other hand, Mann does not, like the naturalist of the unimaginative variety, impose a final barrier to speculation. The cosmological adventures of religion may not give us an unequivocal answer, but they keep alive the sense of mystery. Without this, science itself becomes cocksure.

[1945]

THE IDEA OF UNIVERSAL CULTURE

Harry Slochower

Thomas Mann's distinguished position in contemporary letters derives from a liberal manipulation of the catholic values in world culture. Perhaps more than any other writer today Mann would at once preserve the link with our ancestral heritage and meet the demands of the hour. The key-terms for this dual aspect in Mann's work are "association" and "identification." In his case, again, war and fascism made for variations in range and degree.

Mann's pre-war identification was mainly with the Germanic *Kultur* tradition of a musical esthetic and an idealistic dialectic, which was suspicious of Mediterranean civilization geared to practical concerns. It is a period of *Tonio Kröger, Buddenbrooks, Death in Venice*, culminating in the essay on Frederick the Great and Mann's war against the political internationalism of his brother Heinrich. It is dominated by Schopenhauerian esthetics and voluntarism, Wagnerian Nirvana mythology, Nietzschean metaphysics of disease and Freudian probings into chthonian regions. The First World War closes Mann's aristocratic *Kultur* association. *The Magic Mountain* and the critical essays of the twenties embody Mann's painful leave-taking of German idealism and bring him closer to the social-pragmatic values in the Latin and European tradition. The arrival of Hitlerism completes this development. It frees Mann toward World Citizenship, which he discovers in the Hebraic-Christian heritage. These international values are embodied in the Joseph cycle. The whole marks the transition from an esthetic attitude to the ethical act. Yet—and this is the unique feature of his *Weltanschauung*—Thomas Mann does not discard his past. His present outlook is deeply permeated by his former allegiances.

In Thomas Mann's pre-war work the nineteenth-century battle between commercial and spiritual values is fought out to an esthetic conclusion: the characters retreat to the realm of artistic and philosophic freedom. Thomas and Hanno Buddenbrook elude the financial schemings of the Hagenströms by embracing

Schopenhauer's static pantheism and Wagner's musical dialectics. Spinell and Frau Klöterjahn resist the prosaic robustness of old and young Klöterjahn by losing themselves in the love-yearning of the *Tristan* score. Aschenbach is liberated from a close-fisted Prussianism by Tadzio's exotic beauty which he enjoys "purely" from a distance. Young Castorp is saved from the technics of engineering by a hermetically sealed Olympian mountain. There he "grows," feeding on cerebral talk and formless Walpurgisnachts, rendering piety to disease and romantic music. If Tonio Kröger still yearns for the simple, the blond and blue-eyed, if Spinell and Thomas Buddenbrook maintain some contact with the material world of the Klöterjahns and Hagenströms, Gustave Aschenbach and Hans Castorp break almost completely with the "real" world. Here Mann pictures the ultimate stage of alienation which began with the Germanic *Kultur* dualism between matter and spirit, existence and value.

But is there an "escape"? Do not empirical compulsions themselves condition ascents to enchanted castles, and do they not continue to operate and affect the "escapist"? Do those who flee become immune to happenings in the spatial-temporal concretum? That was the persuasion of nineteenth-century romanticism. But this persuasion was weakened in the next hundred years, in which the reality of technics and industry intruded upon the "ideal." Modern writers sense that there is no escape. They send their heroes "away," but do so with a bad conscience.

Such reservations already appear in Mann's early work. Tonio Kröger envies the simple and uncomplicated. His final esthetic consolation is mixed with nostalgia and regret. Detlev Spinell is pathetically helpless before the robust physicality of Klöterjahn. Thomas Buddenbrook turns to Schopenhauer, but the latter stills his agony for only a brief moment. He dies, having lost his past and without hope in the future. *Death in Venice* is Mann's last stand at the Hindenburg line of estheticism. Even here the "truth" flashes before Aschenbach when, at the end, he observes Tadzio's beautiful face being pressed down into the sand. With Castorp's descent from the Magic Mountain, Mann returns to the realistic battlefield. Yet Castorp fights for the very powers he distrusted seven years earlier. He abandons the esthetic realm, but he remains between two worlds as he sings Schubert in the service of the German war-machine. Castorp's retreat does not save him from politics. *The Magic Mountain* showed that there was no escape. The issues between Settembrini and Naphta could not be settled by the word but only by the act. In *The Magic Mountain*, however, the act is as ambiguous as the word.

In 1929 Mann published *An Experienve in the Occult* and *Mario and the Magician.* Here art is no longer pure magic; it has become *black* magic. If, in the occult experiments, artistic sleight-of-hand is confined to relatively harmless pranks, the story of Mario, acted in the land of black fascism, holds more terrifying possibilities. The magician Cipolla, though ugly and deformed, succeeds in forcing his audience to do his bidding, to dance against its will, even to show physical affection for the misformed juggler. Here art is no longer "distant": Cipolla mixes freely with the audience. But the contact is used to impose a more direct exploitation. The older art erred negatively through objective withdrawal. It was merely out of date. This art "interacts" to produce inhuman practices. Cipolla employs his "comradely" approach to establish the notion of the leader-follower principle. The capacity for self-surrender, Cipolla tells his audience, is but the reverse side of that other power to will and to command. In the leader the will is obedience, the obedience will. If, in *The Magic Mountain,* artistic disinterestedness is manipulated toward a war dictatorship, in *Mario and the Magician* art is used directly in the interests of a somber fascism.

The idea of a universal poem is perhaps as old as human consciousness itself. We find it in our legends of Moses and Jesus, of Prometheus and Parsifal, of Faust and Siegfried. In Goethe, Marx and Nietzsche, the concept of universal culture becomes a programmatic demand. Yet even as Goethe's Faust enunciates his vision of a free people he remains a Utopian leader separated from his following by heroic exclusiveness. Nietzsche's Zarathustra is a lone, almost lost voice in the wilderness, torn by discords over his own solitude. Karl Marx formulates the social conditions for the development of the "universal man." He sees that human freedom requires social freedom as a prerequisite. A sociologist rather than a poet, Marx does not face the problem of poetic creation of situation and character. But even as a critic he is constrained to place the emphasis on repudiating the old mores. He has less to say about the *vita nuova.*

Our own century brought the trend toward collectivism to a climax. It established the warped coördination of fascism and the idea of international socialism born in the Russian Revolution. Paradoxically, the fascist cataclysm has accelerated and encouraged the forging of human solidarity. It has been our war-torn era which has once again brought forward the idea of universal culture.

The theme of collectivism runs through all of Mann's work. In his earlier writing it takes the form of a metaphysical or musical universalism. Thomas Buddenbrook finds solace for the loss of his personal heritage in the Schopenhauerian thought that he is at one with the cosmos and Hanno is enveloped by an all-embracing Wagnerian Nirvana. Aschenbach's self dissolves in the contemplation of the Platonic, and Hans Castorp loses himself in the magic timelessness of the cosmopolitan Berghof. When Castorp leaves the Berghof, he exchanges, to be sure, a metaphysical collectivism for a concrete sociality, but this new affiliation turns out to be a tragic error on another plane. It marks an advance over his circular abstractions, for it "quickens" him toward action. But this action is on a destructive plane. The Joseph story would translate Castorp's identification, at odds with the interests of the individual, into a collectivism where the self is neither subsumed nor destroyed. The Joseph cycle represents Mann's hope of "supra-personal, supra-partisan, supra-racial standards and values." This orientation is foreshadowed in Hans Castorp's snow-dream on the Magic Mountain.

Castorp's vision follows his rejection of the two dialectical pedagogues, each of whom represents a confused form of collectivism—Settembrini defending a capitalistic world republic and Naphta an ambiguous Jesuitical communism. To resolve their "morally chaotic All," the author takes Castorp away from the civilizatory concordances of the Berghof to dream amid the "inhumanity" of nature's stillness. Castorp's dream is "anonymous and communal," merging the observer with the object observed. His vision is something he had "always" known. "Always and that always went far, far, unthinkably far back." He beholds a pastoral scene by a Mediterranean seashore, peopled by children of the sun and the sea, joyous and winning, friendly and courteous to one another. It is an agrarian setting in which people live in complete social harmony. They play seriously and they work gladly. "Art" and "life" appear happily joined. But this pleasurable "wish" of the dreamer is disturbed by the critical censor, who half-awakens Hans Castorp by the picture of the social blood sacrifice. Behind the Utopian sociality a realistic struggle goes on among groups and classes. But before he is fully awake Casstorp formulates that synthesis which Mann's characters had vainly sought for, the union of thought and action. The dream is forgotten by Castorp as he returns to the Berghof, but it remains stored away in his subconscious, where he has "always" known it. For Mann, dreams are *promises,* not merely recollections of things past.

The First World War and fascism helped bridge the distance

between the hesitant note of *The Magic Mountain*, and the Joseph story. The thunderbolt which dynamited Mann's *Kultur* concept showed that estheticism was propagandistic in its consequences ("Music is politically suspect"). There followed Mann's spirited concern with the "demands of the day," his participation in the struggle against the Nazi menace, culminating in the Joseph story. Yet Mann found his universal theme as he was about to be alienated from his native grounds. This circumstance is, as we shall see, not without import for this work as well.

The story of Joseph is the legend of man's eternal sources and the recurrent cycles of his existence. The author leaves the historical distractedness of the bourgeois world to pierce deeply into the human. In terms of the Freudian metaphor the work may be called a monument to the immortal wish of man's unconscious, to his legendary Titanism which has been obscured by temporal shadows. The myth would render homage to man's ancestral and traditional roots. It is a work of piety and loyalty to essential forms in an age of unrest and bewildering change. In paying tribute to the power and inspiration of the past, the story becomes a repudiation of those authorities in the present that demand coördinated fealty. The story is a Freudian charting of man's infantile stage, revealed as encompassing the landmarks of humanity's permanent way.

However, Mann's story is not a mere retelling of the primitive legend. It is not pure regression and literal recurrence. His myth is garbed in all the complex forms of modern insights. As Castorp invaded the wild primitiveness with "civilized" instruments, so Mann approaches the early history of man with the aid of modern anthropology and psychology. It is an attitude toward man's beginnings on the part of a modern. The hypotheses and implications are *ours*. While the ending is given to us and the forms remain externally the same, the content and process vary. Time is real and history does not repeat itself exactly. As against the simple authoritarianism of the fascist myth and the permanent absolute of the Thomist view, here man's will and imagination are factors in his fate. The reversion to the past is no search for a lost paradise. The pattern binds us but varies when it is enacted in the particuar. It is an "I" and a single individual "through whom the typical and the traditional are being fulfilled." This "I" is "from God and is of the spirit, which is free." The dreams of our myths must be interpreted, not to avoid the "purposes of God," but "to anticipate and provide against it by proper foresight." In Mann's work, the myth is still *to be ful-*

filled, and that depends on our work in the present and future.

Mann has chosen a story which stands on the border line between the revealed and the historical. It is a period when the separation has already taken place between the hero-demon and the sky-god. And his characters both know and don't know. Their problems are not those of primitive tribes. Mann treats of exceptional, differentiated individuals. They are separated from their ancient prototypes by what has come between, by the Socratic question, by the quest of Don Quixote and the dilemmas of Hamlet and Faust. They have eaten from the tree of knowledge, and they know their tears.

Thomas Mann's Joseph story is rich and iridescent in suggestiveness, and no amount of critical labor can hope to exhaust it. The interpreter of its conceptual import faces the task of making clear Mann's amazing synchronization of multiple perspectives. Events appear simultaneously as *happening* according to physical causation, logical sequence, human motivation, purposeful direction, and withal as molded by individual *doing*—a kind of translation of Aristotle's four "causes" into a world where free will obtains.

Mann's choice of Hebrew characters strikes centrally into the ambivalent nature of his work. Mann is concerned with people whom history has fated to be restless wanderers. The Fathers and Sons in Mann's story are given over to endless quests, from Abraham the moon-wanderer to Jacob and Joseph, forced to leave their fathers' homes. They are Odyssean characters, uprooted and homeless, representations of mankind's eternal unrest. They are a nomadic group, forming a bridge between East and West. To Mann the choice of Hebrew characters does not exemplify the fortune of a single people. For he is well aware that the Ahasueran nature of Jewish history has been conditioned by specific historical exigencies. Similar factors operating in the post-war era have produced an analogous situation for all peoples. In fact, Mann stresses the *interracial* character of his group, which stamps it as a prototype of mankind itself. Their Hebrew affiliation simply makes for a greater accentuation of what is a dominant motif in the story of man as a whole and particularly of modern man. In Mann's work the element of disquietude is bound up with his category of *Geist* or Spirit. In its broadest meaning, Spirit makes for doubt, criticism, questioning. It is the warring emissary which "stirs up emotions of disquiet and exceptional wretchedness in the breast of one single man among the blithely agreeing and accepting host, drives him far out of the gates of the past and the known into the uncertain and adventurous." It moves among "coulisses and abysses" (*"Küstenkulissen und Brunnenschlund"*) and is forever bargaining with Mephisto yet never selling the soul to him. Spirit is Mann's equivalent for Goethe's Faustianism, the determination not to tarry in the moment; for Nietzsche's transvaluation of values and continuous "self-surpassing." Mann's other favorite term for it is "irony." It is the attitude which seeks knowledge of the "other side" and of the total situation. And since such knowledge cannot be gained "locally," man must be ever migrating. From this desire for the other arises humaneness, sympathy with the alien. This constitutes the *international* ingredient of the Ahasueran man.

The legend tells that the Hebrew God was Spirit and that he "blessed" Abraham. Abraham is blessed in the sense that he *has* the blessing of the spiritual, for he would serve none but the Highest. This makes for his blessing, a blessing which is transmitted to Jacob, Joseph and Judah, the fathers of coming generations.

But pure spirit is dangerous to man. Mann's early characters, Spinell, Hanno, Aschenbach and Naphta, suffered from incest of the spirit, attempting to create out of their own substance, out of art and logic. They shunned the material sphere and tended toward self-regression, auto-eroticism and homosexualism. They reflected the truncated artist- and thinker-type whose images are the reflex of his own desires. Castorp is saved from this circular route by the realm of matter, in the shape of the war. But he receives it as uncritically as he shunned it, and his problem is dissolved rather than resolved. And where pure reason or rhetoric leads is shown in the self-contradictory act of Leo Naphta.

In the Joseph story, too, the characters are exposed to this peril. Jacob faces the wrath of Esau, whom he tricked by his rhetoric. He flees from Laban, whom he likewise deceived, and loses Rachel, the wife of his choice. When he ventures further, gives the coat of many colors to Joseph instead of to Reuben, the first born, thereby continuing to show preference for the spiritual over the legal, he loses the beloved son of Rachel as well.

Joseph has the blessing long before the father bestows the ketonet on him. Young Joseph is beautiful and learned, combines the imaginative with the speculative. He is a superior character. His deviation has not the freakish nature of Mann's former "marked" men, of little Herr Friedemann, Tobias Mindernickel. He does not suffer from the diseased loneliness of Hanno Budden-

brook and the ambiguous apartness of Gustave Aschenbach.
There beauty is seen as the price paid for exclusion from normal
living and communal participation, and art as possible only in
opposition to the world. Here excellence is to be nourished by the
world. Here the characters are not made sensitive by disease.
Mann has chosen healthy people, chosen a legend which ends
with Joseph the artist providing for his community as he in turn
is nourished by it.

The Beloved Returns and The Transposed Heads, which followed Joseph in Egypt, seemed at first glance to have no connection with Mann's Joseph myth. The first was characterized
as a tribute to Goethe, and the Hindu legend as a "finger exercise" in the rest period made necessary by the exacting labors on
the Joseph story.

Now the conception and execution of these novels fall into the
time when Mann continued to work and deliberate on Joseph's
final stage. This circumstance recalls the fact that Goethe interspersed his work on Faust with other projects, all of which
reveal in some way Goethe's preoccupation with the "main business" of Faust. Sounded for similar clues, Mann's novels also appear as ruminations on his "main business," as convergences from
distant peripheries toward the center of the Joseph story.

The story of Joseph, following his descent into the Pharaoh's
prison, is to take an ascending curve. But where was Mann to
find the source for such inspirational direction? He himself was
an exile, and all signs of this time (1938-40) pointed to the
continued triumph of fascism. With the historical present holding the spirit imprisoned, what was the artist to draw on for
Joseph's elevation from the prison-pit?

The Goethe novel we interpret as a backward look to history
for a prototype and approximation of the Joseph personality.
The subject of Goethe offered Mann a historical analogy to himself and to his theme. More than any other historical figure
Goethe has been Mann's own prototype. Moreover, Goethe himself once planned a drama dealing with Joseph. And just as Mann
has tended to identify himself with the great German, so in The
Beloved Returns Goethe is likened to Joseph, endowed with
"blessings of heaven above, blessings of the deep that lieth under." While "waiting" for Joseph's visions to take form Mann
invokes the past for a nineteenth-century foreshadowing. Goethe,
by whom Mann himself has been nourished, is resurrected to
serve as the "nourisher" of Joseph's future. Mann's regression
in The Beloved Returns is an invocation to the Mothers of History to give up the son.

Mann shows Goethe at the period of his fullest maturity. He is sixty-seven (approximately Mann's own age at the time the novel was written), at work on the second part of *Faust* and ready to close the circle by reintegrating his beginnings in the higher phase. To his followers he is a kind of God-Father, androgynous and complete ("womb and seed"), combining opposites in an all-embracing irony. He is pictured as embodying a divine disinterestedness, "at once absolute love and absolute nihilism and indifference." Goethe appears here as an absolute, but his public perfection as artist has been gained at the cost of deep private tragedy.

Goethe has attained absolute stature by disallowing himself living participation in events and people. Beneath his Olympian serenity, Mann discloses the searing pain of the human being who has sacrificed his body to art and spirit. Goethe did love, but he never allowed himself to "live out" his love, to marry and have a family. He flirted and kissed, but no children come from kisses. "The making of children," Goethe muses, "is no affair of poetry's." Consummation he achieved only in his art. Here again Mann treats sex-fulfillment as an obstruction to the creative stress. Renunciation of the physical increases the tension and thereby spurs man on to *symbolic* fulfillment through artistic and spiritual refraction. This, Mann shows, was the case with Goethe. His fusion of nature and art, of physics and ideality, of "kisses" and "children" was largely in the symbolic sphere. He was averse to wedlock in order to enjoy the perpetual honeymoon of poetic ecstasy. He refused to "settle down," in order to allow his spirit to be eternally transformed. The result is a majestic portrait, admired and worshipped by the many who are pilgrims to his seat at Weimar. But these see only the mask of the spirit, not the terrible aloneness of the man. Goethe did marry, but Christiane Vulpius never ventured to address the great man with the familiar "thou." He did have a son, but August is shown as a weak echo of his father, an imitator who coarsens, sensualizes and stratifies his qualities. Goethe had a large following, but the Riemers and the Meyers are servants who fawn and bow. In short, Goethe's life failed of the interaction which his work effected. His progeny is more in the character of Thomas Buddenbrook who denies his son, of the faded Peeperkorn, of the eunuch Potiphar, than of Joseph, destined to become a father of a family and father to the people of Egypt.

Lotte—the Lotte whom Goethe wooed as a youth—is the representation of the nature element which Goethe renounced.

Where he chose "kisses" and the parody of life through art, Lotte chose to give up the lover Goethe for the husband Kestner, to live in orderly bourgeois wedlock and become a mother of many children. Her simple nature preferred the stability of organized, sober living to the might-have-been which Goethe's adventurous genius held out to her.

However, this is no simple repetition of the Tonio Kröger theme, in which the artist is deprived of the blond and blue-eyed ones. Mann's work has taken him through the magic values of enchantment which enriched the personalities of Gustave Aschenbach and Hans Castorp. If art suffers from deprivation of nature, the latter in becoming conscious, feels the lack of art. If Goethe has missed a wife and marriage, Lotte has missed the honeymoon with the lover. And so, after forty-four years since the days of Werther, she undertakes a pilgrimage to Weimar in a somewhat childlike attempt to recapture the poetic past. In a final mythical setting, in a talk carried on amid the shadows of Goethe's rolling carriage, they reveal to each other their reciprocal incompleteness. Goethe speaks of the hidden agony behind his dignity, of his body-sacrifice that the light might burn: "I am the drunken butterfly that falls to the flame—figure of the eternal sacrifice, body transmuted into soul, and life to spirit." As in *Royal Highness*, renunciation remains the poet's pact with the Muse and life the forbidden garden. The final words, "Peace to your old age," are Lotte's, whispered to him who can now look forward only to the last Antaean compensation, to death, the ultimate transformation of nature into the flame. But the words may as well have been addressed to Lotte, who has also come to feel the need of "the other." The dream-nature of this scene suggests an identification of the two characters with these spoken words applying to either and to both.

The Beloved Returns thus questions the possibility of complete fusion between the spiritual and the physical. Goethe was the genius who, like his Faust, left no offspring. Lotte was nature who produced many children that remained unknown. It is the story of unfulfillment seen from the distinct perspectives of art and nature. It presents the either-or between the genius and the simple people, between the aristocratic individual and the folk, between honeymoon and wedlock. However, now when they are at the end of the holy season of renewal and rejuvenescence, they may hope that in the final "flight into the flame," the sublimation of their individual existence may yet mean their union in the "All-in-One."

In *The Beloved Returns* Mann goes to specific history for aid in establishing the Joseph coördinates. *The Transposed Heads* regresses to the prehistoric. It is an even purer myth than that of Joseph, for it stands outside historical time altogether. Mann's Hindu legend is an approach to the Joseph problem from absolute beginnings unencrusted by historical contingencies. It takes place in the land which gave birth to the mother-tongue from which our Indo-European speech developed. It is the land which, according to legendary tradition, was the site of Paradise. Mann is in quest of the first enactment of the human drama, repeated in more involved forms in later ages. Here perhaps may be found the original formula in simple, naked outline, before it became obscured by moralistic canons and guilt associations brought by Western religions and civilizations. In this early pattern there is as yet a minimum of "false" consciousness and no fear of punishment in an after-life. For these people know of only one world, the world of Sansara or Appearance. The realm to which the departed go they call Nirvana or Nothing.

As a "plain" summary of human relations, *The Transposed Heads* encompasses the entire gamut of man's way, beginning with his state in paradise, the innocent plane of unity and peace, through his awakening to consciousness, passion and knowledge which split the original oneness and bring divisiveness and war, to the final reintegration by "flight into the flame." In this necessary process, man is fated ever to strive for unification, ever succeeding to a limited extent and always feeling the insufficiency of both satedness and want. What distinguishes this story of Mann's is that, for the first time, the tragic surd is treated from the vantage point of high comedy, viewed as part of nature's way and accepted with cheerful sympathy ("*heiteres Mitleid*").

In this tale Mann transposes the problem of "head" and "body," of genius and organization, of art and business, into an elementary plot involving a woman's desire for simultaneous enjoyment of a lover and a husband. Sita is married to Schridamann with the wise head but unimpressive body. Her marriage only awakens her to the knowledge of lust, and in the arms of her husband Sita longs for the lover, for Schridamann's friend Nanda, the youth with the coarser head and the manlier body. When the heads of the two friends are transposed, Sita is happy —she now possesses the lover's body as well as the husband's head. In the Hindu legend this rearrangement makes for their common happiness. Thomas Mann's account diverges from this happy ending. There is bliss at first, but even this "at first" is questionable, and the author suggests that what transpires later makes itself felt from the very beginning. The acquired lover-body becomes the husband-body, and the distant husband-body takes on the qualities of the longed-for lover. Having what she had desired, Sita now desires what she has not.

Together Schridamann and Nanda combine the wisdom and practicality which Joseph's personality embodies. In the opening paradisiacal setting they are united in friendship, each finding it inconceivable to live without the other. Their first stage is an innocent male union. They "intrigue each other," by virtue of being perfect complements to each other. This peaceful state is upset by the appearance of the beautiful girl. Sita is the "Snake" emerging from the waters, bringing to them the fruit from the tree of knowledge and sin, the Eros element arousing them from the quietude of their existence to a Maya-longing which becomes a longing for absolute beauty and happiness that can be stilled only by death. Through her the two become divided, differentiated, awakened to the particularity of their sex-beings. She is the "Fall," making for individuation and estrangement. But this is only her lower phase of "customary" sensuousness. (This aspect is also suggested by Mann's play on her name: "*Sitte*," "*sittsam*," "*sitzen*.") She is also the liberator from appearance, leading out "beyond the darkness of confusion to knowledge and truth." She is the Earth Spirit in the dual role of awakening matter to consciousness (the Nanda-evolution) and conversely of materializing the spiritual (the Schridamann development). She is the "furrow" through which the two men find their common road, the "All-Mother" and "All-Nourisher" of both the simple and the complex, who find the meaning of life and death through her. In the attempt to bind to herself the wisdom of Schridamann and the immediacy of Nanda, in her desire for both husband and lover, Sita reënacts Jacob's dual wooing of Leah and Rachel, Mut's effort to hold Joseph while wedded to Potiphar and Lotte's craving for both her good Kestner and the romantic friend. (Mann subtly "modernizes" Sita's error in putting the heads back. Her error is the truth of her subconscious will.) Sita is, finally, a foreshadowing of Joseph's attempt to wed his prophetic gifts to the practical business of politics and government. Mut and Lotte failed. Even Jacob soon lost his beloved Rachel. To be sure, the world's goal is "union between spirit and beauty, a bliss no longer divided but whole and consummate." But the story of Sita, Mann tells us, is an "illustration of the failures and false starts attending the effort to reach the goal." The dream visions, when translated into the actual, become grounded and limited. Hence, "makeshifts, renunciations and resignations are the common lot." Mann's story of the "original" failure is a preview of the later Joseph when the enthusiasm of his lyrical beginnings is stabilized and regulated.

Still, the isolation and difference which Mann's characters suffer constitute a value. For,

> difference makes for comparisons, comparisons give rise to uneasiness, uneasiness to wonderment, wonderment tends to admiration; and finally admiration turns to a yearning for mutual exchange and unity.

Ultimately this spells tragedy. Yet by *knowing* that all peace, harmony and silence are illusions, that man has the power to arouse desire but not to sate it, he can raise himself above the tragic, can even smile at his fate in cheerful sympathy. In *The Beloved Returns* Goethe muses on the high value of the light touch:

> The depths must laugh! Profundity must smile. . . . All seriousness springs from death and its reverence for it. But dread of death is despair of the idea—is the stream of life run dry.

Never before has Mann treated a tragic subject with the same equanimity and aloofness. There is a sort of debunking of the tragic through common-sense humor when Nanda calls Schridamann's longing for death after he sees Sita simple "lovesickness," and when the Goddess treats the whole episode in a rough, matter-of-fact manner as something entirely normal. At the end this light touch is carried out by the three characters in the nontragic way in which they decide to die together. What makes all this possible is that the head has now assumed undisputed leadership as the all-important factor in establishing human identity. In the end, "the head decides the value of the body."

The tale has a concrete issue as well. It is the son, the common fruit of the three parents. He is called Samadhi, which Mann translates as "Sammlung." The German term has the double meaning of "collection" and "concentration." Samadhi is nearsighted, and we are led to imagine that this handicap will restrain him from looking as far a field as his parents did. It may also lead him to concentrate on those goals which lie within man's limited periphery.

Thomas Mann's Joseph story points to tragedy on two levels, the human and the divine. In the development of Joseph we find

the law of human life, which, "of course, one only gets somewhere near." It moves from dreams to their interpretation and
formalization, from spiritual wooing to the gathering of worldly
goods, from universal sympathy to limiting nationalism—in short,
from spirit to biology. It is "ambition directed downwards," in a
craving to be like the rest, and away from spiritual exclusiveness. The evolution of man is from God's image toward the ani-
malistically fruitful, a declension to the folk-god and biologic
self-enjoyment. The other way, the way of Jacob, seeks the adventurous, the otherworldly and the universal. It never allows
itself to be localized and to "enjoy life." It knows evil and sin
because it preserves maximum conscience. This is man, a being
"notoriously unstable and embarrassing."

The theme of insufficiency in Mann is known to us from his
earlier works. In his Tonio Kröger period, Mann wrote of the
artist as "detached and disinherited." The crassness of his society
was seen as "prejudicial" to his moral well-being, giving but a
hollow silence to his questioning of the meaning and purpose of
man's existence. Yet these characters loved the life which they
shunned, even as their creator was a highly honored member of
his community. The Joseph story promised to resolve the dualism.
But even as Mann worked toward this end he suffered personal
exile.

The Joseph story shows that Mann "remembers" the dilemma on which his earlier work focused. He has retained the con-
vnction that is it the ineluctible fate of man "in no condition and
under no crcumstances ever to be entirely at ease upon this
earth: no form of life is wholly suitable nor wholly satisfactory
to him." In the Prelude the author breaks the frame of the
legend to confess: "To me too has not unrest been ordained,
have not I too been endowed with a heart which knoweth no
repose?" He once spoke of further plans he had even as he was
still working on Joseph, and added: *"Ich komme nie zur Ruh'!"*

"To become conscious," Mann writes, "means to acquire conscience." And conscience gives knowledge of man's natural limitations. Thomas Mann accepts the Christian doctrine of original
sin in the sense that it expresses the deep feeling of man's in-
firmities. This insufficiency is a painful mystery. Yet because
man is "notoriously unstable and embarrassing," he is for that
very reason in need of mercy and grace—that is, he is also the
source of the good. For Thomas Mann, original sin is polarized
toward "spiritual conscience." If we deny the former there is no
need of the latter. And without conscience there is no humanity,

no thought or criticism. Spiritual restlessness urges man to strive for change, promising alleviation. Through it man's animal nature "judges itself in a being which belongs at the same time to itself and to a higher order of things." Man thereby acquires knowledge of good and evil. Thus the mystery of the spirit may be a "very honorable one for man," widening his horizon toward the strange, the foreign and the unknown. It makes for man's collective interest, his interest in humanity. The art in Thomas Mann's Joseph story has this charitable humanity. Nowhere is his characterization more tolerant. Nowhere is he more patient in explaining the natural roots of human weaknesses. Throughout, man appears as *das kranke Tier,* suffering from the burden and strain of his midway position between the animal and the divine. The way of Jacob and the way of Joseph unite to form this ambivalent story of man. It is neither wholly a divine comedy nor a human tragedy but oscillates between the two poles.

There was a time when Mann's ambivalent approach made for an ambiguous neutrality. And while the author of *The Magic Mountain* protested against the charge that his ironic reservation might be interpreted as "liberal anemia," he continued to remain silent about the Third Reich. The mounting barbarism in the land of the Nazis forced Mann out of his cultural retreat. To the Rector at Bonn who informed Mann that his name had been struck off the roll of honorary doctors, he wrote: "I could not have lived or worked, I should have suffocated, had I not been able now and again to cleanse my heart, to give from time to time free vent to my abysmal disgust at what was happening at home—the contemptible words and still more contemptible deeds." Mann has abandoned the position of that liberalism which would allow freedom to the enemies of freedom. The weakness of the old humanism issued from "its leaning toward indulgent scepticism. . . . This weakness, under certain circumstances, can be fatal." And Mann calls for a "militant humanism, a humanism which would affirm its virility and which would be convinced that the principles of liberty, of tolerance and of free thought, must not be exploited by the fanaticism of its enemies."

In the classical myths of Odysseus and Prometheus, of Theseus and Beowulf, of Siegfried and Faust, the hero experiences rebirth in the pit of humiliation and learns humility. The work of Heinrich Mann and Anna Seghers, of John Steinbeck and Mikhail Sholokoff, of André Malraux and Thomas Mann also acknowledges the power of circumstances, those from above and those from below. And they look back to history and the myth for the prototypes of human fate. But they reach back not out of love for the dark night, as is the case with anti-intellectualism, but because, with Freud and Marx, they seek the categories which on a higher level chart a liberating future. If, for Spengler, Ezra Pound, Proust and Joyce, history and the myth are the abandoned dreams of man to be passed in review as historic ruins, they are for these men the promises of continuity and recurrence. Their work reclaims our faith in the rationality of man's natural history. It is a kind of moral-esthetic counterpoint to the physical disorder of our day. Their art is the contemporary secular equivalent of man's divinity. In this sense it has Catholic character—with a difference: for their universality functions as contingent particularity and receives form by individual critical consciousness. These writers know that we cannot avoid the "purposes of God," but they also know, as Mann's Joseph adds, that we can anticipate them by foresight. In this sense the idea of the universal man is not opposed to reason. The archetypal forms remain the same, but the process, meaning and direction depend on the impact of the individual will and of the imagination on the force of circumstances. In short, man can *define* the process of his microcosmic history. To that extent he can mold his fate.

[1945]

PART V

General

THOMAS MANN

Félix Bertaux

Thomas Mann is not an imaginative writer. His books grow out of events, and the source of his material is his own experience. Looked at as a whole, his writings are a continuous novel of the development of the author and his times. Nevertheless his standard of selection has this distinctive feature, that he invariably takes life at a point where it seems about to degenerate, to struggle against destruction, to seek a discipline. The plot of every one of his novels concerns an organism whose vitality is threatened; one can never be sure whether the crisis will end ineluctably in death or whether it is not instead the critical point in a rebirth. In *Buddenbrooks* he has chosen as his subject a family which represents the Hanseatic bourgeoisie taken at the point where it is threatened by the various forces of decadence of the nineteenth century—social changes, moral revolutions, rise of the musical and artistic spirit. In *Tristan*, the equilibrium of a bourgeois family is again threatened through the illness of the heroine, through Wagnerian romanticism and the attractions of love and death. In *Royal Highness* the reigning family of a small principality is threatened with extinction unless an American woman supplies new blood and new money. *Death in Venice* depicts the problem of the intellectual who, believing that he has organized his existence on a rational basis, finds that carefully organized existence breaking up under the onslaught of demons and abandons himself to dissolving passions. *Tonio Kröger* is an anti-romantic story of the poet who stumbles into the labyrinthine passions of an artistic community and is overcome by a nostalgia for the lost paradise of his bourgeois youth. Even the wartime essays—*Frederick the Great and the Grand Coalition* and *Reflections of a Non-Political Man*—are the work of an uneasy German who, watching his nation in a crisis, is seeking first a sign of vitality in the crisis itself by considering that crisis as an explosion of German demonism; second, through the example of Frederick II, a discipline capable of channeling that demonism effectively. The big postwar novel, *The Magic Mountain,* is again the story of an organism passing through a crisis. It concerns the inhabitants of a sanatorium in Davos, come from every corner of the world; and the illness against which they are fighting is the illness of Europe struggling to regain her strength.

Whereas Heinrich Mann set out to seek the sources of power in contemporary society, one might almost say that Thomas Mann set out to seek the sources of weakness. But curiously enough, although they differed in the objects of their search, each found what he was seeking in the same place. Where Heinrich Mann sees a *Befreiung*, a liberation of vital dynamism, Thomas Mann sees the appearance of the forces of breakup and decline. Heinrich is considered a revolutionary, Thomas a conservative. But these are untrustworthy formulas. Thomas Mann is a revolutionary also; he does not preach violent revolution, but he lives in a state of instinctive revolt, a state in which the obscure forces of the soul are so freed that he feels it necessary to seek a *Bindung*, a restraint, to hold them in check. For a long while the great difference between the two brothers was that Heinrich felt that restraint would be found in reason, and hence demanded a dictatorship of reason; whereas Thomas Mann, like Luther, saw in reason a disturbing force, and felt that instinct offers not only a source of disorder but a source of restraint as well. Finally they met on common ground: the conception that *Geist* and *Musik*, the spirit of lucidity and the spirit of musicality, should not be considered as separate, but should be united in a higher form of reason and perform a work of both construction and destruction.

Heinrich Mann's novels give the impression of social pessimism; Thomas Mann's of national optimism. As a matter of fact in both cases the two are united, and both writers finally embrace an optimism of pessimism. In Heinrich Mann it is the optimism of a sturdy nature which does not hesitate to cut open a wound; in Thomas Mann it is the optimism of a sensitive personality fearful of interfering, and leaning rather upon man's faculties of adaptation—man's ability to overcome evil by skirting it.

It is easy to be misled by Thomas Mann's apparent facility. His smile is agreeable, but it illuminates features twisted by effort, and represents a continual struggle. He has taken health and normality as his ideals, but he has done so precisely because neither health nor normality is natural to him. He is a troubled artist who feels an original sin deep within him, senses the threat of destructive forces which he must prepare to oppose; and for this reason he has tried to evade the vast and the dreary, and constantly to rebuild a tissue of sensibility which forever tends to tear itself to shreds.

Less direct than his brother, he has attainted his own particular heights of optimism only with difficulty, by circuitous paths, by dint of insinuation, by counter-balancing. The virtue of his art is in the fact that he has been able to dissimulate the effort and leave only an impression of sensual enjoyment. His artistic talent seems compounded of facility and compliance; as a matter of fact it is the result of much labor. Those who have compared him to René Bazin have been deceived by appearances. Those who have called him a German Barrès have been misled by a certain similarity of preoccupations between the two writers. The faith, the scepticism, the egoism, the patriotism of Barrès are made of a different stuff from the faith and scepticism and egoism and patriotism of Thomas Mann. It was not the German writer's task, as it was the Frenchman's, to develop a novel of national energy; on the contrary, in Thomas Mann's case, Germany's national energy seemed already to have reached its peak, and the observer's task was rather to show its deficiencies. Thomas Mann has a greater frankness than Barrès, together with more irony and greater emancipation of spirit.

Heinrich Mann sets up a conflict between the individual taken as a whole and a unified society desirous of change. Thomas Mann places the conflict between the artist ego, tending to escape from the forms imposed upon it, and the social ego, tending to hold the artist ego within the formal limits of tradition. His distrust of his art is by his own admission the distrust which the universal bourgeois feels for the implications of boldness, license and indecency contained in all art. But it has other bases as well. It is a Protestant distrust both of Catholicism, which canalizes sensuality, and of Luther, who transposes sensuality into popular sentimentality. To bend the Protestant conscience, the Protestant morality, to the ends of enjoyment is to play with fire. Conscience and morality make him distrust the very play of the senses—as if there were something essentially reprehensible in sensual enjoyment, even when it takes a non-religious or an aesthetic form. Thomas Mann is of course too clever not to make this censure a matter of degree. He does not conceive the artistic temperament as always following the same model, and he has varied his characters accordingly: Christian Buddenbrook, the mere mimic; Gerda, his sister-in-law, the dilettante; Johann, one of her sons, a consumptive; Tonio Kröger, a hybrid whose two sets of desires destine him to compromise; Spinell, the ecstatic;

Aschenbach, the cold demoniacal type, whose demon ultimately melts his icy crust; Felix Krull, the virtuoso of simulation. In his ironical condemnation of Krull, Thomas Mann also condemns the essential sham in all art.

Thomas Mann feels that the artistic urge calls forth a whole gamut of poisons. But though like Mithridates he fears them, like Mithridates also he makes no effort to flee them. He introduces them into his system, and thanks to his eclecticism finds a certain charm in the very threat of danger which their introduction carries with it. His intellect and his sensibilities are so active that we cannot tell whether it is tragedy or pleasure for him to half open the door upon events, to live at once a whole life and a measured one, to feel madness seep into his mind and soul without ever losing his reason, and, like the quinquagenarian in *Disorder and Early Sorrow,* to live in sympathy with both the spirit of life and the spirit of death.

Underneath the masterfully arranged exterior broods a somber passion. This passion has no definite object; it is rather the attraction of the abyss. Music stirs it or accompanies it; it is always allied to music; it is music. Now an air from *Carmen* played on the sanatorium phonograph, now the song of the Tilleul in the *Battle of Verdun,* now the mad aria of a wandering singer in Venice, now a movement from *Tristan* ally themselves with the soul in tumult, raise moving problems of the moral universe. A big book and fine book could be made by collecting the writings in which Thomas Mann describes musical emotion. Music for him is like the cathedral organ for Gretchen: it brings to the surface deep hidden thoughts which would otherwise never reach the point of expression; it permits forebodings to take form in consciousness. The whole forms a symphonic tragedy in which the music is a perpetual prelude to death. But it is a death in the Holbein manner, a dance of death, which draws into its wild movement beings who are living at their greatest intensity, caught at a moment when life surpasses itself, and which tends toward its own destruction—the condition which precedes metamorphosis.

Strangely, but in accordance with a profound logic, the theme of love and the theme of death are indissolubly allied. To love is to wish to die; this theme recurs in successive novels. Johann Buddenbrook, the heroine of his *Tristan,* Aschenbach, Hans Castorp are all condemned to die. They are awaiting destruction, and music turns the period of waiting into ecstasy. They see and feel while rapt in a wild dream like that of Aschenbach

when the plague breaks out in Venice, in the midst of the swarm-
ing activity of nature—a constant, intoxicating process by which
bodies are returned to their elements and new bodies formed
from the elements again. It is the theme of death looked upon
as the annunciation of divine resurrection—a theme within the
traditions of both paganism and Germanism, and at the same
time in the tradition of Christianity, which gave subtlety to the
Oriental idea of redemption.

It is likewise in the Wagnerian tradition. Music for Thomas
Mann means above all the music of Bayreuth. Wagner represents
one pole of his existence. The artist ego which he distrusts is the
ego which tends to yield to the spell of Wagnerian music. And
it is this ego which is dearest to him, this ego which he was com-
bating most strongly when in *Death in Venice* he said: "As poets
we can be neither wise nor worthy, we are fated to go astray
and be destroyed. Mastery of style is a snare and a delusion. Education through art is a risky undertaking which should be forbidden. For of what use in education is a thing which by its very
nature tends irresistibly toward the abyss?"

The other pole of Thomas Mann's existence is the bourgeois
tradition, a fact which is true less because he is conservative in
mind than because he is conservative by instinct. He does not
merely, like Thomas Buddenbrook, feel the desire to be correct:
he feels an organic necessity to unite himself with the mass of
that which exists, to partake of its stability. In the life of good
bourgeois society there is poetry also, a poetry diametrically opposed to the romanticism of passion. This poetry has a rhythm
dictated by events listed in the bourgeois calendar or consecrated
by a rational tradition. Ritual festivals, picnics, baptisms, birth-
days, weddings, funerals, fill the forty years of *Buddenbrooks*
with a majestic sweeping rhythm. As in Proust, but with none
of Proust's Bergsonism, Time is the principal hero.

The other important hero is the bourgeois family. Thomas
Mann has dealt chiefly with the old bourgeoisie. Families like the
Grünlichs and the Permaneders are considered mésalliances and
remain in the background. The Hanseatic families represent a
patrician class pure in its dignity, equally removed from the business bourgeoisie, which lacks the sense of honor and the class
consciousness of the Buddenbrooks, and from the Philistines,
who attempt to deny their pettiness by masking it beneath a confusion of stars and blossoms.

The entry of this old German bourgeoisie into German literature is a new phenomenon. Even Goethe in *Hermann and Doro-*

thea did not achieve it, for he took an attitude of condescension toward his characters, and, though he hid his smile, the gravity which he gave them left them without true pride and greatness. Tony Buddenbrook, on the contrary, is a woman obviously proud of her bourgeois condition. As in any aristocracy of race, she takes pride in the feeling that in her is embodied a whole greater than herself. That whole is both family and function in society, the honor of the one dependent upon the honor of the other. Everything is a part of it: the firm with its grain vessels, its offices, its employees, its credit with the banks, as well as ancestors and the elder members of the family, brothers, husbands, cousins and the family's reputation in the city. The desires, the renunciations, the whole existence of the heroine depend upon the concept of an indivisible heritage. Tony comes unsoiled through mésalliances, divorces, disappointments; no matter what happens she still represents all the beings and things included in that rich plural—the Buddenbrooks. From the family she acquires a sort of impersonal dignity so great that her virtues and vices no longer seem to her to be her own, but those of her family itself.

Thomas Mann, like the naturalists, depended for his material upon experience of reality. But he differs from the naturalists in that he does not approach the problems of his time systematically or from without. His was a single problem: it was born in him, he lived it within himself, he watched it take every possible form—individual, family, social, national. A single spiritual destiny, seen from different viewpoints, was at stake, threatened by what was called the decadence of the times. Did Thomas Mann ever entirely believe in that decadence? Probably not, no more than he believed absolutely in the virtue of the tradition which he said he embraced. When he set out to depict a bourgeoisie at once so proud and so seriously undermined, a caustic touch crept into the work. He never entirely lost the "*schweres Blut*," a drop of which mixes well with humor. But there is champagne sparkling in his veins also, and a malicious twinkle in his eye. He brought to German literature the bantering note which it had previously lacked. Banter is his mode of criticism. He does not engage in open satire of the customs and institutions of the German nation. His is an art of understatement, rather than of hyperbole. Where his brother employs sharps, he uses flats. He marks the point at which the German novel began to free itself of the excess of emotionalism with which it was overloaded. The tremendous desires and the tremendous hungers of the individual

are often scaled down in Thomas Mann's work to the dimensions
of the gluttonous pastor who was served a Lenten meal by an
irritated housewife, or to little Thilda, the poor relation who took
pleasure in mocking idealism by exhibiting before the assembled
family the fruits of her questionable activities. Thomas Buddenbrook, deranged by Schopenhauer, dies of an abscessed tooth; his
son, wasted away by musical ecstasy, in finally carried off by a
commonplace attack of typhoid fever. Thomas Mann pretends
to show such an excessive reverence for authority that his mocking detachment becomes obvious, as when Miss Spoelman jostles
the guardsman in front of the royal castle at the sacred moment
when the guard is to be changed. Delicately, in his own fashion,
he has attacked the remaining evidences of feudalism in the
social and political structure.

   Although he early discovered in art a natural ferment dangerous to morality, Thomas Mann was quick to see in it the germ
of a new grandeur. The bourgeois class which he was depicting
no longer included all the basic conceptions of contemporary
society, and this may have accounted for its decline. It had grown
greater only just so long as a will to growth was allied with its
desire to conserve. Initiative, the taste for innovation, and a sense
if not of revolution at least of necessary evolution, had all been
part of the true bourgeois tradition. But that tradition was now
threatened by the introduction of artistic elements. Every thrust
of the artistic is a revolutionary thrust. The question was whether
the disrupting influence of the artistic was not itself a demand
for change, was not preparing the way for a transposition of the
bourgeoisie to a higher plane. Thomas Mann, as his career has
progressed, has tended more and more to answer this question
in the affirmative.

   Just as in his own life Thomas Mann tends toward conformity, so in his literary style he seems to make an effort to
avoid originality. He is a stylist, but his style is not a creation
bearing new promise, nor is it likely to undergo any sudden evo-
luton. It represents rather the highest mastery in the utilization
of already existing means of expression—all means of expression.
He combines the resources of Latin logical composition with a
German capacity for musical composition. The plot of *Death in
Venice* is developed on a musical theme of death, just as Mar-
guerite's tragedy is developed around a theme of fidelity. After
a Wagnerian overture, the theme which has been stated reappears, flows out, swells to a tragic finale. In others of his novels
part of the charm even of secondary characters lies in the fact

that their interior life progresses like a melody whose rhythm
is marked by the recurrence of a favorite phrase: Hans Castorp is a "little bourgeois still wet behind the ears"; Tony's "I'm
no longer a stupid goose"; Christian's "My nerves are too short
on the left side." This is a curious psychology, but it fits to perfection characters who never analyze themselves, who live their
lives like a song, who take up the refrain again in every reincarnation.

Indeed Thomas Mann's is a complex art. He respects tradition, but conceives of it as being in process of evolution, capable
of assimilating heterogeneous elements from outside itself. In it
are joined culture and nature, conservation and revolution, the
individual and the social, music and reason. In Thomas Mann's
thinking the influence of Nietzsche counterbalances that of Wagner, and on a plane above either is the inspiration of Goethe.
The conception of art as suspect has been replaced by the conception of a great art which does not parody nature or attempt to
modify nature's law, but which seeks out nature at living founts
and imposes upon it restraints which are at once esthetic and
moral. In this conception the spirit of music is no longer a purely
German attribute, nor the spirit of lucidity a purely Latin one.
With *Rede und Antwort* (*A Full Account*) and *The Magic Mountain,* that encyclopedia of the present, Thomas Mann achieved a
truly European outlook. While he does not attempt to show how
a Europe on the way to dissolution should be rebuilt, he maintains within himself that condition of passionate questioning
which was common to the German élite even throughout the
period of the Hohenzollern empire.

Bemühungen and *Die Forderung des Tages* are essays for
the times. Although he avoids the role of *praeceptor Germaniae,*
Thomas Mann is nevertheless, like his brother, one of the great
who draw inspiration from reason. In Germany, which, unlike
France in the eighteenth century, had no encyclopedists to clarify the opinions of the people; in which Lessing's voice was
drowned by the clamor of romanticism; in which even Goethe
did not wield the influence that was his due, Thomas Mann has
come increasingly to feel that he partakes of Goethe's tradition.
His growing prestige has allowed him to address to a German
public, deluded by the obscurantism of the National Socialists,
that *Appeal to Reason* of which all nations as well as Germany
stand in need. The strength and nobility of the views which he
expresses in that document make it far more than an appeal to
ideologues. He has stated the commanding ideas to which we

must turn if we hope to find an effective solution of the present universal spiritual crisis.

Fascism, which Thomas Mann satirizes so neatly in *Mario and the Magician;* dictatorships which hold things together temporarily—these are solutions which are powerless to create the new order which the world demands. During the twenty centuries of the Christian era the bourgeoisie, whose bankruptcy is everywhere proclaimed, has steadily manifested a creative energy whose products subsist today in what we call Western civilization. There is no question but that that creative energy has now become wholly conservative, that that civilization demands fresh inspiration and new forms. But no new civilization can be created unless we maintain the concept of order, enriching it with new elements from the present. Thomas Mann is on the side of those who are working for this metamorphosis of the old traditions. He is the last bourgeois of the past, and at the same time the first prescriber of a future which shall also have its order, though the name by which that order shall be called is as yet unspoken.

[1935]

THE PROMISE AND BLESSING

Philo M. Buck, Jr.

There is more than a slight analogy between the self-imposed exile of Thomas Mann from his native Germany, now sacrificing in high places to strange gods, and the flight of the ancient forefather of his hero Joesph from the heathen Ur of the Chaldees. For early Abraham had learned that "one must serve the Highest alone," and the gods of Ur were powers lesser and sinister, and ministers of death. So he became an exile, a man apart, the founder of a new tradition. Likewise his descendants, Jacob and his son Joseph, in their lonely adversity found comfort in the fulfillment of a divine plan: "Not in vain shall have been thy torment." For it led to the discovery of something that is ultimate, 'the nature of man,' and in this there is bound up also another blessing: by discovering the nature of man Abraham discovered also peace. Thomas Mann is devoted to the same quest. Peace, how can it be sought in a world given up to vain strivings and worship of the brute, strange abortions of the imagination, without pity or reason, grotesque monsters and symbols of dark power? Abraham left the ease of the fruitful plains to save his integrity and keep alive his faith, and moved, a questing spirit, upon the uplands and arid hills of a new world, that in their stillness he might hear the voice of his newly found God. The analogy is not only a personal one for Thomas Mann the exile from Nazi Germany. It is the paradox of every sensitive soul of today, who in the contemporary din can hear only the alarmed and menacing cries of the beast; where in this clamor of unhuman tongues can he find the solitude in which man can discover reason and the will of God and peace?

It is interesting to observe how an old epic narrative can serve a contemporary purpose and give meaning and direction to life, To the Greeks, Homer was more than an old story of a people's mythical and divine beginnings; his poem was a textbook in contemporary conduct and laid the foundation of classical civilization and art. Virgil in the life story of the devoted Aeneas saw the pattern of the Roman Augustus and the constitution of Rome. Thomas Mann, as he turns to a much earlier episode in the history of humanity in the prose epic of the Hebrew conscience and its beginning, finds it full of significance for the bewildered and anxious contemporary mind.

There is yet more in the analogy of Abraham and Thomas Mann. It was this arch-ancestor's great discovery that the charm and the sweetness in the lands of Ur and Egypt were the allure of death and annihilation. It was to discover life that he resisted its sensuous appeal. Such, too, was to be the experience of his descendants Jacob and Joseph. And as one reads from the beginning the long series of novels and essays of Thomas Mann, with their themes from the beginning of our century to these days of tragedy, they tell the story of this our western civilization rounding to its period of death. There was a time, when he wrote *The Magic Mountain* and *Death in Venice,* that it seemed he was writing the obituary of Europe, the gradual sickening of will and reason, when men play with shadows in a world of shadows, and succumb to the fatal sweetness and charm of the mortal malady in the empire of the tomb. Later, when the crisis was even more alarming and the clamor of Cerberus beyond endurance, he wrote the hope of a rebirth. For his hero he sought in the well of time for the man that made the great discovery of God and man and the consciousness of human destiny. An age that has lost God and in consequence belittled man needs the discovery.

In this Europe and America that may be on the point of setting up the tradition of the state or the church as the Absolute, his return to the individual human conscience is not unlike Luther's defiance of Pope and Oecumenical Council and proclamation of the virtue and necessity of non-conformity. In more ways than one Thomas Mann is in the orthodox Protestant tradition. Life has a meaning, human destiny is a pattern woven by the combined efforts of man and God. Man must be admitted to "the secrets that lie behind man and things." These are not written in constitutions of states or revealed to deliberative councils, nor can they be expressed in the dogmas of any church. They are discovered only by such as Abraham and his successors, who while they live in the world are yet apart. "Yea, often it hath seemed to me as though the world is full of such loud rumors to the end that it may better hide the hidden beneath them and out-talk the secrets that lie behind men and things."

But before one can hear the call to come out and be separate, one must have known in one's own life the fatal sweetness that is the foretaste of death. So before there could be the Thomas Mann of the *Joseph and his Brothers* there was the younger Mann, a generation ago, of *Buddenbrooks,* then afterwards of *Death in*

Venice, of *Tonio Kröger*, and last, but greatest, of the *Zauber-berg, The Magic Mountain*. Great as are these books, and especially the last, they are all like Part I of Goethe's *Faust*, the preparation, the necessary training, the vision of Vanity Fair, that later the pilgrim of life might be led to the region of the final vision and reality.

Buddenbrooks belongs to the pre-war generation; and its theme is not unlike that of the family novel, where the laws of heredity and environment work the regeneration, but far more often the disintegration, of a family. It reminds one not a little of Zola, if one removes the Zolaesque obsession with the unfortunate flotsam and jetsam of contemporary civilization. Much more is it like the chronicle of the Forsyte family by Galsworthy. And yet in it there is something more, a distrust of some of the most admired motives of life, and especially of art and music; but not precisely as the Philistine distrusts culture, as one of the unpractical ornaments of life that distract from the business of making a living and founding a family fortune. Thomas Mann in his own family had seen an honest, well-to-do manufacturing family lose itself in a later generation in the impractical pursuit of art and culture. He has a deeper motive for distrust.

In this novel he tells the story of the slow paralysis of the will to live and create by the creeping nihilism of prettiness. And there rises naturally in the mind of the reader, as in the then yet immature imagination of the author, the active doubt: are art and music, are these obsessions with what is called Beauty, wholesome? Are they not rather a sign of decay and even of approaching death? Here almost in his youth the author, in the decade before the war, posed a question to which he will recur as one of the dominant motives of all his later thinking. It later became the central theme in the two interesting short novels, *Tonio Kröger* and *Death in Venice*. The answer in these had so stout a conviction, that it was almost possible to say of the author that he was obsessed with the beauty of disease and death.

But all of these, the *Buddenbrooks*, the two little novels, are minor items in the development of Thomas Mann's genius. They point the way to his major enterprise, the epic of the Europe before the war, *The Magic Mountain*. I expect in a generation or two, when the books of the first third of the twentieth century are balanced and audited, that this novel will be among the very near first, in the final assessment of the creative imagination of our time. Yet the novel differs from every other great novel of the nineteenth century. For its closest analogy we shall have to go back to the beginnings and call up the spirit of Cervantes and his *Don Quixote*. For though both abound in realistic description and background that all can confirm, both are founded upon a fantasy. Each in its way is a vision and each an allegory. Perhaps, and this is no vain conjecture, this very quality is the hall mark of their greatness.

But nowhere is the contrast between the spacious, humane days of the Renaissance and ours more manifest than in the attitude of Cervantes, which while it could laugh could also chide and hope for human betterment through discipline and insight. The case of the Don was not hopeless. His excesses were due to wrong-headedness and folly, natural but eradicable human frailties. And at his side there was always the pedestrian Sancho, who, though he could not aspire, at least recognized the difference between windmills and terror-mongering giants. The world was at heart sound and wholesome, as sound and wholesome as the highways and sun and clear air of Spain. The world was much more nearly right than the Don in his folly deemed; its ailment was rather of the head than of the heart; only he was the last man in the world qualified for the adventure of setting it right.

But the comedy of the Zauberberg is bitter and unqualified. Its background is not a real world at all, but a place of unrealities, spectra of people, and phantasms for ideas, and no motives strong enough more than to utter their impotence. It is a place as empty as the imagination that creates it, and, except for its gloss on the condition of the world, as purposeless. The characters are driven not by folly but by mortal illness, and though they move and talk as men and women, they are shadows of humanity, humanity in dissolution, yet able to simulate thought and action; they are the puppets of their malady. Don Quixote was rescued from his folly and his eyes opened by a jolt from his horse. It required the shock of a world war to scatter these shadows of the Magic Mountain.

To make another comparison, *The Magic Mountain* may also be compared with Goethe's *Faust*. And this comparison is doubly appropriate, for Mann is more than an admirer of the aristocrat of the German tradition of excellence. *The Magic Mountain* is Goethe's *Faust* in reverse. For as the theme of the great dramatic poem is the gradual regeneration of man through the wise use of experience, the theme of the novel is the allegory of human disintegration through the simulacrum of experience, until will becomes atrophied and reality is lost in a Walpurgis Night of kaleidoscopic illusion. In the former, time and causation are real, because both are directed and measured by an active will; here all sense of time disappears and human endeavor is directed only to its annihilation. The one is occupied with life and how it may be lived more abundantly, in spite of the cynical temptation of Mephistopheles whose reward is death; the other slowly submits to the luxury of death. So far has the spirit of optimism at the beginning of the nineteenth century been transmuted into its opposite in the narrow compass of a hundred years. Such is the sentence one of its keenest critics passes upon the Europe of the days before the Great War.

For the Magic Mountain is Europe. In the story it is a cure in Switzerland and its patients the miscellaneous victims of tuberculosis from everywhere in Europe; and as we get acquainted with them an amazingly cultured and proper selection from all the proper walks of life. It is a microcosm of Europe. Curiously, and yet for a good reason, only the workers and the peasants are not represented. The hero, Hans Castorp, freshly graduated from an engineering school and ready to begin his career as a marine engineer, has a few days of leisure and runs up to the mountain to visit his cousin Joachim, an officer of artillery, who has contracted the disease and is impatiently submitting to an enforced furlough. The story begins as casually and innocently as any realistic or naturalistic novel; and it is not until one has been captivated by its alluring subtlety that one begins to realize that behind all this easy charm there is a deadly serious purpose; and that one is being read a moral and alarming lesson.

For Hans Castorp is by no means only the well-meaning but more-or-less-purposeless young German engineer. He is Everyman, the Everyman of pre-war Europe. Cultured and efficiently trained, loving art and music, cosmopolitan in his background, and at the same time a competent technological expert, he has in him all of the potential motives of the age that could talk of music and pictures and operate modern machinery. There is only one thing lacking. His actions are nearly all of them purely automatic. He is sensitive, none too intelligent, but beautifully curious about everything, including the latest researches in science. He is Everyman. *"Du bist nicht irgend ein Mensch, mit einem Namen . . . du bist ein Vertreter."* You are not a person with a name— you are a type.

The Magic Mountain itself is not a place on any map of Switzerland, or anywhere else. It is Europe. It is a place of disease and imminent death, as Europe is a hospital whose vocation is disease and death. The motives of all the patients are vain, in-

fertile, the ceaseless talk of Vanity Fair, maya, the world of illusion, that expends its time in vapid exploitation of all motives,
none of which are carried into action, endless talk on endless
subjects, but no accomplishment except death, that silently and
without notice lurks behind all the idle philanderings and purposeless chatter. For compensation there are the aimless gaiety,
parties, dances, masquerades, even lectures on science that the intellects of the inmates might not be neglected, and music and art,
above all music and art. These are not pursued as professions or
as creative activities, but only as distractions, to keep people
from thinking on life and death, to make them forget time and
themselves. The Magic Mountain is a pseudo-world, a world designed as an escape from the world, a place of refuge for those
who would play only with abstractions and substitutes.

For Thomas Mann is convinced that art and music, when
they serve only as distractions from life, a cultured form of idleness and a relief only to the emotions when these have no con-
sort with reality, are the way of death, and not of life. This is the
main theme of *Death in Venice*, the story of the gradual disintegration of what once may have been a very real artist. More than
once he returns to the same theme in this novel. Hans Castorp
easily finds his place in such a world of shadows.

All are preoccupied with the prince of shadows, Death. For
there is no other preoccupation that is more sensuously thrilling. A sound body with a sound imagination is only occasionally
alert to the sensuous call of life. Its concern is with matters beyond itself, the world in which it plays its part is far more interesting and absorbing than the telegraphic record of peripheral
nerves. To the ill, cut off from most of the activities of life, little is
left except the luxury of an abandonment to sense. Here on the
Magic Mountain, as the young hero at once discovers, all creative activity has ceased, and the campaign with death has become each inmate's personal adventure, symbolized by the fever
chart each displays as the chief *objet d'art* over his bed. Hans
Castorp too begins early to keep the curve of his fever, and
study the X-ray photos of his lungs, with its light and dark areas
like the surface of the moon.

Even when he falls in love—for there is also the shadow of
love in this world of shadows—the photograph that he begs from
Clavdia is not one a living lover would carry, but the X-ray picture of her thorax, that he may immortalize her illness. And on
the evening of a masquerade there is a conclusion of a liturgy
in lovemaking without parallel.

In this region where life pauses and awaits annihilation there is also the annihilation of Time. Now there are two ways of rising above time, a positive and a negative, and of escaping its bondage. For time, to those who would throw off its chains, is the routine of the commonplace, the table of conventional necessities that binds man to the wheel and destroys freedom. The Buddhist seeks its annihilation by rising above the desire for individual existence, by slowly throttling all selfish motive, and thus discovering by the discipline of yoga that the world of self is the world also of illusion. Time is only the last illusion and most persistent. He thus attains the great victory whose end is the bliss of nirvana. We have seen how this philosophy that denies the reality of the world of sense has colored and given substance to the poetry of the Indian Tagore. There is a caricature of this philosophy in the effort of Proust to gain immortality for the moment by fusing in recaptured memory the sentient past. For these moments are timeless in that they are unselfish, freed from the bondage of the present and immediate individual desire. Proust literally was searching by the discipline of a new yoga for a sort of psychological nirvana, and its compensating joy.

But the patients of the Berghof had neither the opportunity nor the motive for any such discipline. The oriental mystic is convinced that behind the illusion of time lies the only significant reality, the eternal, and he would live free of all illusion. For the comrades of the cure there is only one reality, the negative one of Death. It too, like eternity, is timeless, and in the cult of the dance of Death all are joined, the serious and the gay, the intellectual and the purely sensuous. In their world of fleeting illusions there is also a victory over Time. But time is not swallowed up in Eternity, it is annihilated in Death. It is an illuminating sojourn, this. So a visit begun as a careless gesture becomes a pilgrim's progress toward timelessness and Death. The fact that Mann here in his symbolism is using a well-known psychological reaction of most tubercular victims towards time only adds to its force.

It is an interesting group of characters that Hans Castorp is introduced to on this mountain of illusions, characters who are wraiths of ideas and not real personalities, for they have been denied the power of action. Rather they seem fixed attitudes; *idées fixes*, that have all the convincingness of live and mobile ideas, except that of carrying themselves into action. As we pass them in review are they not a generous handful of the ghosts that haunted the voluble corridors of the pre-war decade? For as they are impotent for creative action they cultivate the gardens of speech and persuasion—all except one.

He is Joachim the soldier, grimly taciturn and impatient, impatient to go below to the world of action and his profession of war. He is the only character with a positive motive, who counted the days and refused to be compensated by any world of shadows. Does Thomas Mann, seeing the preparations that the pre-war nations of Europe, and especially Germany, were making for war, find the only positive signs of life in the motives of the soldier? He at least had the virtue of his profession, and the world of illusion about him was a continuous and irrelevant bondage. The generous and chivalric soldier—but he too, though he saw through it all, had the disease. For war is no longer the profession of the chivalric and generous; so he dies before his cousin Hans Castorp's sojourn is complete.

There is the charming and lovable Settembrini—the name is allegorical—the symbol of the decay of enlightened liberalism with its appeal to the best in human nature. He is cynical but not bitter. He is rhetorical as liberalism has always been, from Voltaire to John Bright to Woodrow Wilson. But this is liberalism now in its disintegration, more voluble than ever, and more humane and more lovable, but loosed now from all power of action. He can cite the victories of the past, and the hopes for human regeneration, and deal bitterly with all that oppose, and especially with the most dangerous foe of all liberalism, the Jesuit Jew advocate of the totalitarian state and force, Naphta.

Herr Naphta, by the very combination of opposites in his blood and training, is a force, but only a stage villain engaged in a masquerade of danger. His real power will not be given him until the war has driven Europe out of the mountain of illusion and closed its gates. A great deal of very recent history is locked up in this personage, who yet is as much a ghost as his opponent in these verbal duels. The intensity and moral conviction of the Jew, the training and discipline and will to obedience of the Jesuit, the conviction that institutions are greater than the individual, and above all the moral creed that the end will justify every, even the most bloody, means; it isn't hard to classify Herr Naphta. Of all its patients he seems the most out of place in this Eden of the lifeless. But what motive in those carefree years before the war seemed potent for evil? It was the age of perfect tolerance, when tolerance meant perfect indifference.

There is Clavdia Chauchat, whose unconventional photograph Hans Castorp carries and to whom he makes feverish love.

If Naphta and Settembrini bring Castorp under cascades of ideas enough to bewilder and confound, Clavdia is an unpredictable geyser of sensations and emotions. She is as spontaneous and unpredictable in her comings and goings. She is the breaker-up of smug order, she never fails to slam doors as she enters or leaves the otherwise peaceful and orderly dining room. But she is no less disorderly in her views. Clavdia is an interesting person, the new eternal feminine. But again how unlike Goethe's *ewig weiblich,* who brings order and peace and direction into the miscellaneous life of Faust. Instead she is the angel of a chaos of impotent ideas and impotent passion.

In all this Hans Castorp becomes a genius in absorbing experience that leads nowhere. Nor does he even learn whether his illness is real or imaginary, so well does he fall into the life of diseased futility. He offers himself to these pseudo-adventures with the full knowledge that their only effect will be on that all important fever line. In this "epic of disease" he even learns to find disease interesting; perhaps it reveals more of the spiritual nature of man than health. Perhaps, even, it is a part of the order of nature and is *eine Form der Leidenlichkeit;* one of the forms the life of passion ordains. Perhaps characters are even ennobled by it, and in its exquisiteness it is to be preferred to gross health. Perhaps love itself is a disease, in its richest ecstacy available only to those that have the mark of the malady. *"C'est de mon ancien amour por toi; que ces marques me restent qui Behrens a trouvées dans mon corps, et qui indiquent que jadis aussi j'étais malade."* Faust makes the grand adventure to discover Helena that he may be made whole, but Hans Castorp. . . .

The Great War was the thunderbolt that broke up the adventure in diseased futility. As we last see Hans Castorp—millions of Hans Castorps—"feet heavy with mould, the bayonet swinging in his hand," "farewell, honest Hans Castorp, farewell . . . . Out of this universal feast of death, out of this extremity of fever, kindling the rain-washed evening sky to a fiery glow, may it be that Love one day shall mount?" War was one way out of the mount of illusions; it was a reality bitter and malignant and only temporary. Can there be a better hope for the civilization of Europe? And that answer Thomas Mann is now engaged in unfolding in his story of *Joseph and his Brothers.*

Though the title turns the spotlight only on Joseph, the story is the epic of four generations, the Biblical prose epic of Abraham, Isaac, Jacob and Joseph, the founders of the tradition of a chosen people, and the reason and manner of their choice. But Thomas Mann is of too catholic a nature to suggest that it is of the nature of the Hebrew tradition that he is speaking; much rather it is of the tradition of humanity. Abraham and his descendants are the allegory of humanity in general in the process of an evolution from savagery, and the end of the process is only remotely suggested, "the fulfilment of God." For each in his way had the vision, the vision of the place of Man in a divine plan, and the ardent need of co-operation with God that the will of God may be made to prevail. Each had the ambition, "that was no base ambition: to live in the light of the silent conviction that God had unique designs regarding him. Ambition is not the right word for it; for it was ambition for God, and that deserves a higher name."

Vision—the word has long had a sinister meaning, as one thinks of the ecstasies of medieval ascetics and now knows some of the psychological motives that have given them birth. There often is more of the psychopathic than spiritual in the orgiastic excesses of a vagabond imagination. But there is vision of a quite different varitey, without which one shudders at what level human life would be left stranded. Even science and the scientific mind are not without a debt to those who had visions regarding the meaning of things and their relationship. The commonplace pedestrian mind is content with things as they have been presented, not looking behind and around for pattern or significance beyond the bare needs of everyday life. But a moment of thought and quickly the inquiring mind feels the queerness of the universe, large or small, in which it tries to discover a meaning. The scientist G. B. S. Haldane is reported to have said of it, "The universe is not only queerer than we suppose, but queerer than we can suppose." It is only vision that can discover a clue to the manner of its queerness, and how to read its meaning.

Vision accepts life not at its face value. And from this point of view there is no essential difference between the vision of the scientist, that of the poet, and that of Abraham and every mystic who challenges the accepted values. The only check is the practical one after the event, of whether it can be made to work; by their fruits do we know them, the visions of scientist, poet, and mystic. So Sir Isaac Newton, from the simple facts known from the beginnings of time, came upon the law of moving bodies. His imagination leaped the gap from experience to a formula that transcends experience and measures the stars. So Einstein corrected Newton, supplying something that in his day was beyond the earlier philosopher's scope. So has come every great discovery in science through the freed and heightened consciousness, the imagination or vision, that insisted on seeing beyond the face value of things, into the invisble.

It is this same "imaginative enfranchisement accompanied by a greater degree than ever before of comprehension" that is the gift of great poetry. Homer, before the beginnings of human history, read the story of a world of gods and men and made it intelligible to human reason. Intelligibility of the world in which we live, the postulate that man's reason can comprehend and thus at least partly control the world in which it works—without this postulate all life becomes the victim of a benevolent or mischievous caprice. Once open the door to caprice, and science is impossible. It was the poet's vision that made science possible. More than once in the history of human progress the poet has pointed the way that science has followed.

Exactly of the same worth was the vision of the meaning of life that came to forefather Abraham. It came with the convincingness of a motive that polarized personality and freed it for action. It made him suddenly feel the abyss that separated him from his neighbors, who continued to accept the currency of the age and life at face value. Abraham escaped from the Magic Mountain of illusion and death. From this day forth he became the ancestor of all who demand reality of life and a personal, vital motive for living. Abraham was different.

As Goethe's *Faust* was an epic of humanity, so will this sequence of novels, when it is complete, be an epic. But there is a difference, not only in its philosophy, but also in the background of its science. Goethe's *Faust* carried an optimistic faith in human nature, in that morning of science, that could remove mountains. The compact with Mephistopheles was unfair to the spirit of evil, who himself is perplexed by his impotence. He confesses himself baffled, the spirit that "ever wills the bad, but works the good." Faust was never in danger of damnation. In our day, on the contrary, we are troubled by the dubious fate of man, and damnation has again a very real, though no longer a theological, significance. And a wager with the spirit of evil today is no jesting matter. As if we slipped a coin into some cosmic slot machine, the law of averages seems against us. The saga of Joseph is more serious than the drama of Faust.

It casts also a much wider net. Time—Goethe remarked once that at his death Faust was a hundred years old. But the story of these four generations is unfathomable in the well of time. They are four generations; they are also four epochs in the evolution and discipline of humanity. They are the discoveries that man has made as the tradition of humanity took form and grew and became a mighty power. Abraham, Isaac, Jacob, Joseph are here each in his own person, and each in his own age; but again their times are first obscure and distant, then clearer and close to ours. It was always also a personal discovery, in spite of the tradition; and the blessing each possessed involved only the power each gained to act; the vision had to be repeated and passed with its blessing to the coming epoch. Above all, each must act in the faith and light the vision conferred.

A long tradition and a growing one of man's conflict with his chief enemy. The enemy was always Death, stagnation, disbelief in the living essence of humanity and its divine coadjutor. To Abraham, back in the primitive days of human nature, the enemy was symbolized by the story of Nimrod, savagery. Isaac, of a later epoch, found his enemy in Ishmael, the code of the restless nomad. Jacob, of a day not far removed from the modern, had two enemies, one of temperament and one of a code for life. He had his twin brother rival, Esau, the spirit of romantic excess and uncertain temper and lack of discipline, passionate and unpredictable. The other foe was his relative Laban, a man of commerce, given up to the pursuit of wealth and industry for its own sake. Jacob must learn to deal righteously and yet firmly with both, and live apart. Joseph, the contemporary, finds the effete and dead culture and refinement of Egypt, with its art and beauty and sensuousness and obscenity, the most insidious and difficult foe of them all. Joseph must live in Egypt, the land of the cult of Death, and yet find life and not falter in pursuit of the blessing.

And the vision is the discovery of man, and in that discovery also the discovery of God. A double discovery. There is an upper, and can become wholly absorbed in the nether world, of matter. Man shares of the natures of both, but forgets the upper, and can become wholly absorbed in the nether world, the abode of matter and death. The upper world, the nether world, and the story of the evolution of history is by Mann symbolized by the cults of the dying god in the regions about Palestine from whose sensuous appeal the earlier patriarchs must hold themselves aloof. It was symbolized in Egypt by the aesthetic cults of animals and birds, the creatures of the appetites, and by the feasts and art dedicated to the dead. Each had its cults of fertility and its obsession with sex, but fertility is only matter perpetuating itself, and sex an aesthetic obsession with sensual appetite. Thus each serves only the lower life. They are not life dedicated to an end beyond itself, but life obsessed with its own processes in the prospect of death, like the obsession of the patients on the Magic Mountain with their own fever charts. There was beauty, but in these paganisms that the four generations lived to conquer, it too is dedicated to itself and death. There is exquisite taste, but it is meaningless. These are symbolized in the *Joseph in Egypt* by the attractive figure of Potiphar, lovable but impotent, whose highest ambition was realized when he was allowed to call himself the unique friend of Pharaoh. He was a eunuch.

Abraham, the founder of the new tradition, learned one more truth, and a perilous one, that one may fall away from God, and the soul may again lose itself in matter.

> For here was the important fact: through Abram and his bond something was come into the world that had never been there before and which the peoples did not know—the accursed possibility that the bond might be broken, that one might fall away from God.

And the plot of the novel is the successive temptations that came to Jacob and again to Joseph, to let go, to permit one success to take the place of perpetual non-conformity with the cults and practices about them, and to forget "the silent conviction that God had unique designs regarding him."

In return for this silent conviction and conformity to the unique designs, each of the generations had the blessing and the promise. The blessing was a source of power, and the promise for the future. As they had given the spirit in man the victory over matter, and the soul was brought into conformity with its higher origins, the old uncertainty and meaninglessness of life was now replaced by a quiet dignity and confidence, serenity, and above all the power to act. Each is now to bring life into the world and to drive out evil and death, and thus to "fructify many souls." As the story progresses, how true this is of the beautiful Joseph. Potiphar, even the impotent, is given through him a feeling of self-confidence. He "strengthens my heart in my own regard." Such is the blessing: "For let a man once have the idea that God has special plans for him, which he must further by his aid, and he will pluck up his heart and strain his understanding to get the better of all things and be their master." So Joseph rightly exclaims, when he resisted temptation: "How

could I commit such folly and sin against God?" Though far
from perfect, Jacob and his son Joseph avoided folly, with its
penalty of "shame, guilt and mocking laughter," and remained
masters.

Each of the four generations had the "promise." This was to
be the fulfillment of God."

> There would come a day, the latest and last, which alone
> would bring about the fulfillment of God. This day was end
> and beginning, destruction and new birth. . . . The realization
> of God's great and boundless kingship was reserved for that
> first and last day, for the day of destruction and resurrection;
> when out of the bonds wherein it still lay, His absolute splen-
> dour would rise up before the eyes of all.

It is with this central theme that Thomas Mann tells the
story of Jacob and Joseph, clothing the simple lines of the prose
epic in Genesis with contemporary spiritual meaning: the story
of how Jacob and then Joseph, his favorite son, finally attained
the "blessing." There is first the story of Jacob's theft of the birthright from his temperamental twin Esau, and the consequent
long sojourn in a strange land, with his kinsman Laban. Then
how his power and sense of a unique destiny are awakened by
his love for Rachel, and his return to the land of "promise." Next
we have the two great incidents in the life of his favorite son
Joseph—this youth who had more than human beauty and more
than human intelligence. It is a story of how Joseph first came
into the region of Death when he exalted himself above his
brothers, and was in return by them put into a pit and then sold
into slavery. Schooled by this shock Joseph advances himself in
the household of Potiphar in Egypt until he catches the attention
and the mad infatuation of Mut, his Egyptian master's beautiful
priestess wife. And finally how he escaped the last and most
formidable temptation. There was a "parallel between his sin
against Potiphar's wife and his earlier sin against his brothers.
Once more he had gone too far, in his craving to make people
'sit up'; once more the waking of his charm, which it was his
good right to employ, for his own enjoyment and for the honor
and profit of his God, had been allowed to get beyond control,
to degenerate into actual danger." So again Joseph was punished.
But the Creator in punishing Joseph made "misfortune a fruitful soil whence renewed good fortune should spring." And this
will be the theme in the next novel of the sequence.

There is much more in this interesting sequence of novels
on the meaning of man and his destiny. The author has thrown
a wide net of scholarship over the latest research in anthropology,

comparative religion, and' myth. And all has been used, as by
Goethe in the scenes of the Walpurgis Night in the *Faust*, alle-
gorically to represent contemporary states of mind and folkways.
But all this, just now, is beside the mark. What has Thomas
Mann to say of the right faith that shall furnish a motive for
life today and lead us away from the sensuous poison and impotent ideas of the Magic Mountain? It may even be given us to
doubt the final place of *Joseph and His Brothers* in literature, for
it is weighted with its message until the axles of the novel groan
under the burden; and the symbolism obscures the features of
life like the mask of learning the instructor is forced to wear
when he lectures. But again be this as it may, it too is now
beside the mark. What has Thomas Mann to say of a motive for
life in this changing and sceptical age?

First he has much to say about this our age of supposed
unique change. It is not unique. He dives into the "well of
time" and discovers that the tradition of humanity has been
much the same since man became man. The rolling sphere—now
man is God, now God becomes man. A period of enthusiasm
and a glimpse of vision, and then disillusionment and sensuous
cynicism and the exaltation of the animal. Man has always come
back after a period of romantic excess to earth and reality, as
to a cheerless house on a cold night with no fire on the hearth
to gladden his return. In exchange for impotent cynicism and
make-believe with illusions, our author offers the long tradition
of the man with the blessing and the promise, a perilous tradition
for it is the gift of a vision that will not allow a man to falter or
use half measures in his devotion.

It is this tradition and faith that has made humanity and
given progress, for it alone preserves against stagnation and
death. It writes the history of humanity in the lives of those
unique and chosen individuals who had the faith. This faith is
not a creed, nor the philosophy of a school or community. On the
contrary it is an insight possessed alone by the unique individual,
a faith in himself and his destiny, which somehow is tied up
with that of the spiritual power that is working for intelligence
and order, a faith that "there would come a day, the latest and
the last, which alone would bring about the fulfillment of God."
Here is the creed of a professed individualist, in this day when
the repudiation of individualism has perhaps gone farther than at
any time since the Roman Empire.

This belief in the perfectibility of the individual and in the
supreme worth of vision is the thing that I called at the begin-

ning the protestantism of Thomas Mann. "Forefather" Abraham came out from, actively protested against the mass creeds and mass traditions of the people about him. He could act only as the message came from his own heart, for in its austere purity and in its assertion of life, he recognized the voice of powers greater than his own, spiritual powers that were at work to round the sum of human destiny. With these powers he felt himself called to co-operate to the end that justice and the will of God might be made to prevail. This insight and mission gave him the power and serenity that imposed itself upon others and made of him a leader.

[1942]

A NOTE ON THOMAS MANN

Arthur Eloesser

Thomas Mann's literary ancestry goes back to the decadent school; he derives from Nietzsche and Wagner. The course that he followed from *Buddenbrooks* to *The Magic Mountain* was the record of a highly personal experience, yet at the same time of a more than personal progress from isolation to communion with humanity. The best products of German fiction have always been novels of education or cultural development, and this is the type of novel that Thomas Mann has revived. Culture stands for time fruitfully employed in the building up of personality, for growth consisting partly in elimination, for loss which is also gain; and it would hardly be possisble to imagine a great novel which might not bear as a second title that of "Lost Illusions," or which does not reveal to us, if only from a distance, what Goethe called an "educational province." In Thomas Mann there was a conflict between the artist and the bourgeois, between that intelligence and the world. As he reaches a higher stage of life and maturity, the artist desires to become a sage, and his art becomes a gamble with the deepest things, in which life itself is staked in order that it may be won again. The decadent movement was a second stage of Romanticism and, like it, drew its inspiration from sympathy with what was dead from the moods induced by a period of decline. The turning point in European conditions became that of Thomas Mann's destiny as well, his emergence from the selfish attitude of an aesthete, which had come to seem antisocial, to a positive attitude of service to his people and the State. "Through poetry," to quote a fine saying of Novalis, "there arises a sense of solidarity both in feeling and in action"; it is the master minds that help us to live. The course that Thomas Mann's development was following was not recognized soon enough, and it was not till he reached the height of his power that it was seen mounting steadily upwards, like a predestined road, on which every work marked an irrevocable stage.

Reprinted from *Modern German Literature* by Arthur Eloesser, by permission of Alfred A. Knopf, Inc. Copyright 1933 by Alfred A. Knopf, Inc.

Thomas Mann was born at Lübeck on June 6, 1875, four years after his brother Heinrich. The Buddenbrook family is based upon that of a wholesale tailor with a large family who, in the first half of the eighteenth century, moved his business from Nuremberg to the old Hanse town of Wismar, in northern Germany. This ancestor was not an invention, but did really trace his origin back to the city of Albrecht Dürer, Peter Vischer and Hans Sachs, which stands for the flower of bourgeois civilization in Germany. Mann's father was a great merchant and a senator, deputy burgomaster of the old free Imperial city and Hanse town of Lübeck. His mother, Julia Bruhn da Silva, who lived to see both her sons famous, was the daughter of a German who had been a planter in Brazil and married a creole lady of mixed Portuguese and Indian blood. In his book of essays entitled *Rede und Antwort* (*A Full Account*), he relates how he was filled with enthusiasm for the Homeric heroes by reading an old schoolbook of his mother's and, in the character of the victorious Achilles, dragged his little sister three times round the walls of Troy. The Homeric type of art, which he recognized in Tolstoy among the moderns, remained his standard for judging all epic art. Mann has left a record of the world in which he spent his childhood and youth in *Buddenbrooks,* in which the family dies out in the person of little Hanno, by the fortuitous intervention of an attack of typhus. We can picture young Thomas Mann as a blend of persevering resistance to poor health and an irritability that he mastered through reticent self-control, being readily susceptible to nervous shocks, but strong enough to control outbreaks of nerves; as a young man he was old for his age, but he was one of those stoical natures which know how to wait, even when there is no special object in view, and appreciate the lapse of time as a thing beneficial in itself. Thomas Mann did not do well at school, but he read a great deal, especially such things as he thought to be useful for requirements that he felt, but was as yet unable to define. It was a novel of the ubiquitous Hermann Bahr, *The Good School,* that gave him his first ideas of the modern world, and initiated him into its artistic refinements, though without turning him into a literary prodigy. His contributions to a monthly paper brought out by him and his school friends still echoed the sobs of Heine, while an early attempt at lyric poetry shows a certain geographical affinity with Theodor Storm, who had lived on the other side of Kiel Bay. But though he soon abandoned lyric poetry, its qualities had become firmly implanted in the innermost cells of his work and served to sustain the flowing rhythm of his prose and modulate its periods.

After his father's death and the breakup of the proud old firm, which left the family with only a modest fortune, the Manns moved to Munich. Thomas, who was no rebel, accepted a post that was found for him as an unsalaried employee in an insurance office. His first story, *Fallen*, which has little to distinguish it from numbers of other impressionistic studies of the nineties, attracted the attention of M. G. Conrad's *Die Gesellschaft*, but more particularly that of another employee in an insurance office, Richard Dehmel, who had already won himself the nickname of "literary superintendent" by his unselfish and eager zest in the discovery of new talent. Thomas abandoned his desk, which he had surreptitiously misused for purposes of literary work, and, following a chance suggestion of the discriminating old Wilhelm Hertz, tried to complete his academic education at the University of Munich. He next followed his brother Heinrich to Rome, for each of them had a small income, and both of them were full of doubts on the score of their ability and vocation. Italy became Heinrich Mann's own special domain, the scene of his great trilogy of novels, *The Goddesses*, and of a number of short stories, for which he required a more typically Southern race, with more clearly defined outward forms and a readier gift for the dramatic aspects of life. Thomas Mann remained a Nordic type, a son of the sea, for which he had an inborn love, as he also had for sleep, both of them standing to him for a sort of Nirvana of the formless, whose infinitude brought a sense of relief from the limitations of time and space. "All this *bellezza*," says his Tonio Kröger in later days, "gets on my nerves. Nor can I endure all these appallingly animated people, with their black eyes like those of beasts. These Romance peoples have no conscience in their eyes." Thomas had no turn for landscape; his inner Nirvana maintained itself through music; nor had he much affinity with the plastic arts. His landscape was mankind; he was fond of calling himself a moralist, which, in the old French sense revived by Nietzsche, signifies an investigator, one who feels compelled to examine thoroughly into evil and temptation.

His beginnings were tentative and on a small scale; no peal of bells ushered him into the world of literature. When he published his first little tales under the title of *Little Herr Friedemann*, they could be classed as products of the decadent school, distinguished from their many neighbors only by their more carefully polished style. They are for the most part sketches and studies of humble people who have had a poor time in life and seek to find compensation in some kind of eccentricity. Within their narrow limits they displayed exactitude of apprehension and finish and neatness of contour, combined with a graphic zest pushed to the verge of caricature. It is only by looking back from his later works that we can see how much of the real Thomas Mann there was in these sketches, with his favorite theme of the clash between human intelligence and the world. This volume of short stories had not yet been published when Thomas Mann returned to Munich from Italy, which was to him indeed a *Purgatorio*, but certain isolated contributions had obtained him a position as collaborator and sub-editor on the staff of *Simplicissimus*. His bourgeois bringing-up prevented him from feeling at home in this madhouse of the wits, nor did Thomas care to join a noisy, jovial band and indulge in festive drinking-parties. His shy reserve emboldened him to seek little friendly intercourse except with Kurt Martens of Leipzig, who was not much older than himself; Martens' talented *Roman aus der Décadence* had won him standing as an important spokesman of this movement, and in his later works of fiction—for instance, in his interesting book of short stories, *Katastrophen*—he turned his psychological experiments to use in the analysis of vampirism and Satanism as well. The great bond between them was that Martens belonged by his origin to similar surroundings, being the son of an old patrician family who had drifted into writing; but he had had a wider experience of life, having associated with the literary opposition circles which were keeping the bourgeois in a state of agitation in Berlin, Munich, and Leipzig and pouring ridicule upon the existing political system, based upon the authority of the monarchy, the *Landrat* (chief district administrator), the lieutenants of the reserve, the inexhaustible varieties of councillor—*Kommerzienrat, Konsistorialrat,* or *Kanzleirat* (commercial, ecclesiastical, or chancery councillors)—and all who were loyalists to the marrow. Those were the days of incessant harrying, when the penal laws were still trying to purge art and literature of unsound opinions by clauses dealing with immorality, blasphemy, and, worst of all, *lèse-majesté*. Never had talent been more hostile to the social order and the State than during the period of Wilhelm II, which soon proceeded to try to drill the universities as well, the only people whose rebellious spirit it failed to coerce into standing to attention being the "indecent painters (*Schmutzmalers*)," from Liebermann to Thomas Theodor Heine, and the "harmful" writers, from Hauptmann to Wedekind. But Thomas

Mann refused to let himself be drawn on to the war-path on which his brother had already started out with a novel of Berlin society containing some social criticism. In the home of his ancestors at Lübeck, Thomas had imbibed patriarchal traditions which applied to intercourse with workmen among others; after which he chose Munich as rather a chance sojourning-place, and Italy as a refuge in need or a place of escape, where he had soon to find his true self.

His *Buddenbrooks* was started in Rome and finished in Munich, but the writer was not really present in either of them when he turned his attention inwards, and there, in the course of his profound researches into himself, discovered his forefathers. Thomas Mann had written his first short stories in Italy, *"pour se faire la main,"* as the French say, and master the necessary flexibility of technique. But an epic type of art demands copiousness, mass, and weightiness, all of which can arise only out of an objectivization of the personality. The creative genius must first become a world in itself, in which only discoveries, and not inventions, remain to be made. Thomas Mann read Tolstoy's great novels, as well as those of the Goncourts and the Scandivanians, and as soon as he had clearly thought out the form of epic art, he found it no more than an empty vessel waiting to be filled. His attitude towards life was pessimistic and continued to be so, in spite of his porings over Nietzsche, whom Mann had always regarded as the Romantic exponent of the sacredness of pain and intellectual suffering. The decadent movement might be a festal thing, conjuring up all vanished beauty once more and garlanding itself for a Dionysiac orgy of decay, as was happening in Vienna. Decadence might use the methods of analysis, and having converted literature into a sort of biology—a process which fills the good Hans Castorp in *The Magic Mountain* with wild enthusiasm—study the rampant wantonness of cell-formation up till it ends in atrophy or decomposition. Thomas Mann was himself his own subject-matter. His forefathers lay dead with him, and the old simple relation to life had been broken. But in process of analyzing his own blood he found, on going back to the past, that of his ancestors as well, and imparted life to them by his unconscious attachment to them. Though this novel came into being during one of the most uneasy periods of his life, it turned out to be one of the most pleasing of German works, in spite of the fact that it treats of the decay of a family. The German middle classes rediscovered in it that past which Freytag's *Die Ahnen* had failed to bring back to them.

It had not been the author's intentions to write either a his-

torical or a social novel. What interested him was the human soul,
which has always been the fertilizing element in the German
novel, from *Wilhelm Meister* to *Der grüne Heinrich* and *Eman-
uel Quint*. It was only half-consciously that he included in it a
sociological and political element. He did not worry much about
such things, and it is evident enough that he held at arm's length
those with whom he had no affinity, the plebeian and new middle
classes that were encroaching upon the aristocratic race of the
Buddenbrooks. Books have a destiny of their own, and they sometimes take it into their own hands; thus, when this novel was at
the very beginning of its career, it was plainly apparent that,
quite against the will of the author, which he was as yet unable
to impose upon it, this story of his ego was spinning itself out into
the story of a family extending over four generations. Yet, as it
grew up, it all formed an organic whole, and we should not like
to be without any part of the story of the Buddenbrooks, from
the period of gradual transition from the rococo and rationalists
periods to the early "Philistine" decades of the nineteenth century, which had turned once more to religion, and again from
these to the modern age, to which the old family could no longer
adapt itself and in which the last head of it turns to Schopenhauer for consolation amid the atmosphere of an age of decline.
The great merit of the book is that the progress of time is never
represented in the abstract, but that, as the process of seething
disintegration goes on, the resultant precipitate, whether in the
shape of senile exhaustion, pessimism, music, or art, finds expression in the various characters, including, on the one hand,
Christian Buddenbrook, who is already an utter degenerate and,
living on terms of brotherly familiarity with the idea of death,
represents the posturing folly that is a preliminary to the artistic
stage; and, on the other hand, the splendid and imperishable
Tony Buddenbrook, who performs the womanly office of tending the family health with a superb narrowness of outlook. It may
have been Thomas Mann's intention to analyze the decline of a
family, as it were, by biochemical methods, but the public understood it otherwise and was quite content with its deductions. By
a misunderstanding that had far-reaching consequences, the part
which he had meant to be played by love was exaggerated beyond what he had originally ventured to attempt, and love gave
rise to humour, which in itself unconsciously implied a farewell
to the decadent movement.

Buddenbrooks provided a table to which all could sit down,
and one spread, too, with a truly Homeric banquet, so that it had

won the affection of the public even before the critics had quite made up their minds what to think of it. Some of them actually detected the beneficial effects of "regional art" upon this composition, of which Thomas Mann could justly say in later days that it had Europeanized German prose fiction. By his book of short stories entitled *Tristan,* Mann won the good graces of the younger generation, who not long ago had still been positivist, Socialist, and revolutionary, after which, again, an uneasy sense of the difficulty they felt in explaining their standpoint, and the heady excitement to which they had worked themselves up as a result of their feuds, impelled them to seek transient compromises between such opposites as Nietzsche and Dostoyevsky, Stefan George and Strindberg. In one of these short stories, *Tonio Kröger,* Nietzsche's "dithyrambically conservative" conception of life, to quote Thomas Mann's emphatic words, became developed into a sort of irony of love, an enamoured assertion of vital force and beauty, which he rather sentimentally finds realized in the world of middle-class life and the beatitude of the commonplace. Tonio is a vagabond haunted by a nostalgia for a comfortable nursery, an artist with a bad conscience, standing sadly aloof behind the glass door from ordinary, simple pleasures, and though his thought may dwell with Nietzsche, his longings are with Theodor Storm. The magic of this writer is unseemly in its effects. The process of expressing ideas in words exhausts him and renders him mortally weary of representing human affairs without participating in human experience. The tales brought together by Thomas Mann in this volume are not true *Novellen* in the old strict interpretation of the term, according to which the writer is bound to observe the apparently impartial detachment of the chronicler; they may be generally described as promenades about a central point, consisting in a certain view of life and fixed point in life. Whether the author steps out cheerfully or his footsteps drag, it is always as though he were taking the air after sitting for years over some exacting work. When human intelligence and life mock at one another—a process in which both come off equally well—they give rise to tragicomedies, comedies, and very merry tales such as, for instance, the story *Tristan,* which gives its name to the book and has as its subject a writer who carries on a literary flirtation with an excellent middle-class woman and finds literature a burden in spite of his daemonic talent. "If anyone had watched Herr Spinell at work, he would certainly not have had the impression that words came crowding to him. For one whose bourgeois profession was that of writing, he was painfully slow at getting under way, and anyone observing him must have arrived at the conclusion that a writer is a man who finds more difficulty in writing than other people do."

Thomas Mann's mode of work leaves no room for any adventures save those of the intellect, but it always observed the laws of historical inevitability, never shirking problems or failing to allow for chance occurrences, however smoothly it may seem to have grown up in the subdued atmosphere of an apparently contemplative existence. Not the least of the problems of which he treats is that of the strained relations between the bourgeois and artistic worlds; this situation has its personal aspect, but under this is a more general problem, a deeper distress —the dread, that is, of losing touch with life. In the long run life convinces us of its existence only through its relationships, and when Goethe says that duty is capable of great things, but love of infinitely greater ones, these narrow limitations already open up the full range of life's possibilities. What is a writer? One whose life is symbolic. Thomas Mann somewhere expresses the firm conviction that he has only to write about himself to loose the tongues of his age and of life in general. And so, even in the novel *Royal Highness*, which was received with some surprise, he did not deliberately choose his subject with a view to displaying his virtuosity, but quite as much with a view to telling the story of his own life, in doing which he hoped at the same time to ennoble the German novel as a form of art. At the close of this comedy in narrative, which might equally well have been entitled "All for Money" or "All for Love," all the bells peal, all the bands strike up, and all the court ladies drop their curtsies, while Klaus Heinrich, heir to the crown of a little country, but also to enormous debts, leads the "dollar princess" Imma Spoelmann to the altar. Little Imma is scared by the people's enthusiasm and gratitude, for all, neither she nor her little prince knows anything about life. "What, nothing at all, little Imma? What is it, then, that has given you confidence in me and led me to make such practical studies for the common weal? Can he who knows love know absolutely nothing about life? Henceforth this shall be our affair: both nobility and love—a strenuous happiness." The book is the production of a happy young husband, balancing his new responsibilities against his new wealth. Up to that time Thomas Mann had written about loneliness, the discrepancy between life and art, and the necessity for coming down to earth from this indeterminate state and once again taking root in it. In this work two types of loneliness, those of noble birth and of wealth, are brought together to create yet another cell in the building up of the social structure. Even a princely existence, lifted above social ties and the fraternal community of souls, is a formal, unreal, artistic type of existence, on a plane above that of real life. It is love that proclaims the will for fruitfulness, which starts with self-abnegation. Thomas Mann has also invented a little state with touches of penetrating comic genius, not as a realistic picture of manners, but as a fantastic tale, a graceful symbol, which has, however, no romantic significance, but rather implies a rationalistic and even democratic summons to serve humanity and increase its share of happiness or comfort. It was this reasonableness that was to cast its spell over the public, the charming contrivance of an honest mind which had done more than merely devise a higher and more austere mode of existence for itself. This display of virtuosity was like a garland offered up to the gods in a serious spirit on the part of one who desired to appease them by treating his good fortune as a responsibility.

The novella *Death in Venice* arose out of a similar situation, as though, after laying his garland before the gods, he had next dedicated to them a marble column, erect and strictly proportioned, though all the marble used for this work of art has arteries and nerves and seems even to breathe. The famous writer Gustave Aschenbach, the descendant of a family of army officers and officials, has a sense of the responsibilities laid upon him by his distinguished descent and the general confidence that he enjoys, and, after a period of effete decadence and moral nihilism, proceeds to serve the common cause and the State in as austere and self-abnegating a spirit as his forefathers had done, though by different means. At the age of fifty he feels discontented, wearied out, and conscious of the emptiness of life. He is forced to travel, whereupon important encounters and significant signs combine to attract him to Venice and the Lido. Against a background of wine-coloured sea, Homer's sea, once sailed by the ships of the Greeks, stands a foreign boy of another race, whose very language he is unable to understand—one of Nature's own works of art, full of that mute harmony in which Greek statues justify us in believing. The artist sees the incarnate reality of what he has himself created out of words, and recognizes in the divine form of this body the order and precision which his own ideas have expressed in a form having the hardness and coldness of marble. The catastrophe that comes upon the artist is brought by strange ways into relation with the cholera, which

is "death in Venice." It is Eros-Thanatos, the god of love and
death, leading his orgies in the ardent, sultry world above, who
seduces the artist from duty and order and looks on, indifferent
to life and death, as he sinks into the abyss of daemonic passion.
Thomas Mann's intention was to depict a devastating passion
such as undermines even the most stable fabric of life. By making Aschenbach succumb to the attraction of one of the same sex
as himself, he once more succeeded in representing the loneliness of a great artist in mute and tragic isolation. The problem
of homosexualism, which had probably survived in his mind as a
memory of his childhood, led him in later days to take an interest
in Platen and enabled him to throw an illuminating and understanding light upon that poet's tragic commerce with the beauty
which brings death in its train; but he does not seem to have
been attracted by Stefan George. It should be understood that
these masterly short stories, which are among the noblest examples of German prose, were the work of a happy young husband
at the height of his virility. Yet even, as it were, in broad day-
light a ghost had risen from the abyss and forced him to look
into its depths. What is experience, and of what is it capable?
High noon, when the sun at its height puts men to sleep, brings
them bad dreams. This audacious composition, trusting to the
purity of form that ennobles, is a pious spell, an atoning sacrifice,
in whose flames all that is superhuman and inhuman is consumed.

The war found Thomas Mann but ill prepared. It took him
by surprise, as it did the whole German literary world, which
contained no Barrès or Kipling of whom it might be said that
he had had a part in the intellectual mobilization for it. During
the four years of the war, which caused a gap in his literary
production, Thomas Mann drew up a sort of statement of accounts in *Reflections of a Non-Political Man,* in which he threw
down a challenge to his brother Heinrich in an aggressive and
what he himself calls a "cantankerous" spirit, arraigning him as
a typical *"Zivilisationsliterat,"* the champion of Western, democratic ideas copied from French models. In the course of this
fraternal strife in the Mann family, which subsequently ended
in an honourable reconciliation and which corresponded to the
similar one that took place in the German family as a whole,
German literature was reproached by the politically-minded
for having always remained passive in politics, thus showing its
lack of morality and defective sense of responsibility; while it
won praise from the opposite quarter, from the non-political
party, for having always refrained from taking part in politics,

caring for nothing but asserting its leadership in what was of universal human interest. After Romanticism had tried the brilliant experiment of setting up a universal communion of the mind, side by side with the classical work of education and the humanist realm of Kant, Goethe, and Schiller, and after the Young Germany movement had provided poetry with a fresh stimulus in the shape of the democratic idea, German literature only fell to pieces all the more thoroughly. Decentralization was at once its charm and its weakness. Thomas Mann took no further part in the naturalistic revolt, fostered by historical materialism and Socialism. The somewhat older generation of Hauptmann, Dehmel, and Wedekind had the honour of being persecuted or having its works prohibited, but this ceased as the two spheres of authority and intellect became separated by an ever widening gulf. The relation between intellect and the empire based on force came in the end to be one of irony and mocking skepticism, as though the latter were a thing merely mechanical and material, not to say bombastically theatrical, which had no real existence and could not, in any case, exist for long, for the very reason that it was anti-German. Germany was reaching out towards Europe, and Europe towards Germany, or that Germany, at least, which was preoccupied almost to excess with the question of what lines were to be followed by its spiritual growth and its impulse towards realizing the form latent within it. "Among us Germans," says the art critic Juluis Meier-Graefe, "art was not a class distinction, an enervating form of dilettantism, or a luxury, but the one and only reality, the ultimate altar, the final bond holding humanity together. For the first time we believed ourselves to be discovering it, and stood, stirred to our depths—not before beauty alone, for we scarcely saw it: what carried us away was the human appeal, the heroism that struck no attitudes."

Thomas Mann, a son of the decadent movement, who believed his artistic ancestors to have been Nietzsche and Wagner, belonged to a still older past in which both Goethe and Novalis had had a part and which gave this native of northern Germany a kinship with Fritz Reuter, Storm, and Fontane as well. No catchwords roused him to passion—neither that of the politicalization of intellect, of modern democracy, nor of literary activism. He remained indifferent to all formulas and abstractions, living upon his own resources alone, and his talent was so consistently plastic in character that it found an adversary—though a complement as well—in his brother Heinrich, whose temperament was militantly and passionately political and loved to tear the veil from reality by satire. Thomas' *Reflections of a Non-Political Man*, filled with disquiet by the national anxieties and fears arising out of the experiences of the war, are an inquisitorial self-examination; in this internal war with himself, which consequently resembled a war between brothers, Thomas Mann rallied his conservative tendencies in his desire to find a firm foothold, though as a matter of fact the result was to make him bid a last farewell to many things. This scrupulously conscientious process of clearing up his ideas enabled him, first and foremost, to endure the war, which had paralyzed his creative work. This "non-politician" came out of the catastrophe a democrat and a republican, who, while profoundly in touch with Germany's inner life, had also incorporated the speculations of Novalis in his ideal scheme for educating the community. "The State," he said in one of his speeches, "has lapsed into our hands since the abdication of those powers which were destroying the spirit of the body politic and alienating the inner consciousness of Germany. The form assumed by a democracy is immaterial; its content is a profession of faith in humanity, a vow taken by every people in its own tongue. Liberty means responsibility and is a great school of duty. What use is the writer unless he is in a supreme degree responsible, and how should his talent be employed, if not expressing itself, in the form of character, in the building up of the community?"

In the course of this development or, rather, gradual unfolding, of his faculties, Thomas Mann travelled from *Buddenbrooks* to *The Magic Mountain*, and both of these novels surprised their author by outgrowing his original intention and developing from what he had intended to be an analysis into a great sythnesis of epic breadth and fullness. A passing visit that he had made before the war to a sanatorium had inspired him with a desire to write a little satiric drama. It had been his intention to describe solely from the comic point of view the patients' existence high in the upper air, remote from reality— typified by the Flachland, or plain—together with the amorous association of eroticism and ill-health, and the hypnotic obsession of the idea of death. His idea had been to take a very inexperienced, innocent, and unprejudiced young man and bring him into contact with the combination of intellectual and sensuous seductions provided by this dance of death. This young man, Hans Castorp, who bears unconsciously within him a varied heritage drawn from the past of his native Hanse town, is provided with a partner in his discussions, Settembrini the rationalist, a belated

Voltairian who professes the democratic ideas of the West with
unalloyed faith. Settembrini in turn led to the conception of an
opponent, in the shape of a converted Jew, a fanatical Jesuit, a
clever champion of all forms of absolute and anti-individualist
authority, from the Inquisition and the Counter-Reformation
down to Lenin's Communist dictatorship. All that was still required was a representative of the unformulated, instinctive,
ardently sensuous side of life, and this is the role of the imposing
Mynheer Peeperkorn, the wealthy Dutchman whose function in
the novel is to bring back Madame Chauchat to the Zauberberg,
after Hans Castorp has waited for her for seven years. Madame
Chauchat is the Russian of dubious origin who appears in every
fashionable sanatorium, the Venus of the enchanted mount, standing for the uncanny power of sickness to produce profligacy, the
temptation that caresses the nerves and enters into the very
marrow, the narcotic spell of the East, lulling the will to sleep.
All this typifies the unhealthy state of Europe before the crisis,
though the symbolism should not be labored as an end in itself.
These people talk a great deal, for they have nothing to do but to
be ill; but they are all real, and if the humblest of them becomes
of equal significance, this is due to the mind working in them all,
that of a great realist. Mann has aimed high in every respcet,
without turning dizzy on the heights, and he raises us with him
to lofty altitudes from which we have a wide outlook. All great
novels are symbolic self-portraits revealing the laws of human
development. Hans Castorp has reached the way of reason
through the romantic view of life—the way of "genius." Man
must grasp and master opposites; freedom of mind is nobler than
death, and piety of heart is nobler than life. This does not sound
very original as the upshot of such an imposing display of cleverness, and rather indicates a compromise. But how can life hold
its own save as a compromise? It seemed original enough on the
Zauberberg, where the higher the curves of the fever-chart, the
the greater the patient's prestige, for he could say: "I am worse
than you are." The good European, the healthy European, is he
who has a will. The novel was intended as a farewell to Roman-
will outlive many farewells yet. Coming when it did, the book
represented a victory, and hence an education, and so it was
understood by Europe. It begins in a twilight mood with a dance
of death, and ends in a morning atmosphere with a summons to
new life, and its reveille has a sober but clear and heartening
ring.

[1933]

THOMAS MANN'S ARTISTIC MISSION

Hanns Fischer

"North and West and South a shambles
Thrones are crashing, empires tremble
Eastward go! Breathe freely there
The pure and patriarchal air."

Goethe: *West-Eastern Divan*

On the sixth of June, Thomas Mann will be seventy years
old. When my generation was still in its childhood his first book
appeared and made him famous overnight. It was a novel by a
writer under thirty but already fully matured in his point of view
and his way of seeing, and master of his medium to a remarkable degree. We were given the colorful reflection of human life
in the setting of a Hanseatic town, as outlined against the horizon
of reality in the years preceding the First World War; the glory
and decline of a German middle-class world, mirrored in a middle-
class temperament formed of love and irony, detachment and resignation, in a poetic blend of incomparable individuality. Such
were the Buddenbrooks, born out of the sultry twilight of Wagnerian music and begotten with the clear, courageous pessimism
of Schopenhauerian philosophy; a family whose firm, close-knit
order slackens more with each generation, until it dissolves entirely with its last, most spiritual, most tender offshoot. A middle-
class *Götterdämmerung,* but composed at a lower pitch, without
the Wagnerian bombast of kettledrums and fanfare of brasses,
and therefore deeper, purer in effect. Forty years later we have
the completion of a huge Biblical novel which is beyond compare in scale and scope. But now, as the sons are gathered around
Jacob's death-bed, the solemnity of the old man's blessing, the
concentrated vitality of this life which is not an end but a beginning, radiates a mystical aura penetrating the darkness of thousands of years, its shimmer ascending out of the "well of the
past" toward us, sending into the future of mankind rays of love,
irony, and wisdom—but now love is dominant, announcing this
time no twilight of the gods but rather the dawn.

Between the poles of this esthetic and human evolution lie time and space. We leave the narrowness of patrician Lübeck behind; our way goes past the court of a petty German prince, past Venetian and Florentine palaces, over the Magic Mountain heights of Davos, where the worlds of Settembrini and Naphta, individual autonomy and the new religiosity of mass-deification, engage in mortal combat onward into the clear sun of Hindu fable, where the tragic conflict between Spirit and Beauty—a theme that recurs like a vivid clue throughout the life-work of Thomas Mann, beginning with *Buddenbrooks, Tonio Kröger, Death in Venice*—is serenely resolved in a gay and masterful paraphrase of the Goethian pariah-legend (*The Transposed Heads*); and down at last into the patriarchal expanse of the ancient Egyptian landscape, where Joseph is restored to his father, who had believed him dead only to find him risen to high honors in life. Jehosiph, son of the true bride, whose eyes were the eyes of Rachel with their veiled glance and melting darkness, and in whose person beauty and spirit were fused to a unique perfection, only to be forever parted: for it is not Joseph who inherits the paternal blessing, but the dull and carnal Judah, who is to carry the God-idea through the sequence of generations.

The scene changes with the revolution of time. Not too distant from our own today, close to our still vivid yesterday, there looms up the figure and reality of Goethe, the work and the world of the poet in his sixties, seen once more with love and reverence, with knowledge, irony, and a drop of bitterness not entirely explained, perhaps, by Dr. Riemer's "strained oxen-eyes" and Adele Schopenhauer's spinsterly-clever chatter. And when this world has sunk below the horizon, there is disclosed to our startled and charmed vision the ocean of the deepest past, with its sun-warmed bays enclosing present and future. From the "well" of unfathomable depth there rises up before us a panorama of human-kind with a wealth of individuals and their actions, sufferings, thoughts: an inexhaustible, unforgettable procession.

There is Abram, the wanderer of the desert and seeker of God; and Jacob, endowed with the false blessing from the abyss and the true blessing from above; Jacob, whose tireless courtship of Laban's child is so basely cheated. But his revenge for the shameful wrong done to him by his uncle and father-in-law, whom the "rigors of husbandry" have hardened into a gloomy devil of a man, is as thorough as it is witty. It is the same Jacob who, a life-span after these events, knows so well, in the solemn frailty of old age, how to uphold his dignity before Pharaoh. And there is Leah, unloved but fruitful, with her slightly red-rimmed, squinting eyes; the brothers, from the towering Reuben, "the rushing torrent," to Dan, "the adder" whose cunning and shrewdness lead to his becoming a judge; not to forget Dinah, the little minx, for the sake of whose virginity so much evil comes to pass. There is the old Ishmaelite, for whom Jehosiph invents such a variety of charming good-night speeches. We see Mizraim, finally, the Lower Realm with its ominously fixed rituals of fertilization and death for both gods and men; yet there is room here for the simple humanity and the simple death of Mont-kaw, the house-steward; for the intrigues of a stumpy-armed dwarf; and for the superior wisdom of Potiphar the "War-Lord," a man of impressive appearance but unfortunately so disqualified for sporting with his ravishing spouse Mut-em-enet, "the moon-nun with her pleasing voice," that grave complications ensue. Who can fathom the bottom of that well, its depth of time and thought, leading us down—or, better still, up—to the Prelude in the Upper Circles, which like the *Book of Job* and the Prologue to *Faust* also treats of the relationship between God and man, the Fall, and the imperfection of Creation—which springs from the idea of Creation itself—in a manner that is thoughtful and witty, graceful and gay. Who can encompass the wealth of characters, events, scenes, and insights of this immense work, the fruit of twenty years' labor, from *Joseph and his Brethren* to *Joseph the Provider,* without conjuring them all together, rounding out the picture without precedent, so full of life and color, and all accomplished with such consummate artistry.

At about the same time I read *Joseph the Provider* I recently read, quite by chance, two other Biblical novels which have attracted some attention, less on their own account probably than because of the author's background. How stale and featureless do the figures of *The Nazarene* and *The Apostle* appear beside the personalities of the Joseph novel; what inexpressible boredom emanates from that style: so lifeless, and weighed down by priestly solemnities that would have pleased Stefan George, who dismissed *Buddenbrooks* as "decadent." What a sad waste of lavish stage-props, what with high-priests, leprous beggars, nards and spices, the dawn-lit battlements of Fort Antonia—all for the sake of presenting us with a few bloodless phantoms whose Homunculus-spark is extinguished as soon as we have turned the page.

The development of Thomas Mann through time and space is extraordinary in that it has meant a steady growth of poetic

substance. That long years of practice of his craft develop in the
writer a mastery of his own, concentrated, individual style is
well known; on the other hand, the power of his creative imagination usually declines with age. His later work generally reveals
a loss of warmth and immediacy; it develops, instead, the spa-
ciousness and clarity of an autumn day. Witness Goethe's purest
gems of literary form, his *Helena* poem and his *Pandora*, written
in his sixties and based more on reflection than on experience. In
the realm of literary creation it is a rare event to find the work
of riper years pulsating with a living warmth of invention, content, feeling.

Thomas Mann is one of the few exceptions. His vision, cool
and clear from the first, grows richer with warmth and life in
each new book. In *Tonio Kröger* we feel the poet's heart-beat
for the first time. Sheer formal excellence drives it into the
background once more in *Death in Venice* and *Fiorenza*. But
later, in *The Magic Mountain*, there are scenes such as the death
of Joachim, the chapter "Snow," and Hans Castorp's love-
speeches in his halting French; scenes that open up worlds unknown to the writer's youth: the experience of nature, the secret
of love and death. His intellectual awareness and his emotional
power are now interwoven into a new synthesis. Here, suddenly,
is more than the brittle order of a middle-class world and its
masterfully drawn protagonists; more than the brilliantly formulated ideas which carry and bury them. Here, at one stroke,
as if a heavy fog were suddenly dispersed, the heroic landscape
is disclosed to full view, 'the day open to judgment," as C. F.
Meyer puts it; we sense the primeval power that leads us to the
summit and dashes us into the abyss: Disorder and early, ancient, eternal sorrow. "Inmost warmth, warmth of the soul,
center-point," is the way young Goethe once defined the basic
poetic emotion; and here we have it all, profoundly moving,
great, convincing. It is such scenes that have stamped Mann as
he has remained ever since: a poet, simply, "the strange son of
chaos." Only a poet could have done what he did, recreating
with visionary calm, amidst the raging hell of the Third Reich,
the work of another's old age, in that fabulous monologue which
fills more than a hundred pages of *The Beloved Returns*, magnificently fusing together Goethe and James Joyce. And only the
stored warmth of ripeness could have peopled the infinite horizon
of the Biblical landscape with its unforgettable figures: Joseph
the lamb, who falls into the pit, and wins worldly power; Tamar,
the woman whose fixed stare seeks the future and whose unholy

womb bears the seed of salvation. This life-work, the inner unfolding of which indescribably moves and inspires us, whether
we are contemporaries of the writer or younger, is deeply rooted
in the form and spirit of music. Even at a superficial glance we
see that one of Mann's most characteristic devices, the repetition
of a typical phrase, forcibly reminds us of the musical figure of
imitation. As, for example, when Sesemi Weichbrod, the board-
ing-school director in *Buddenbrooks* apostrophizes the pupils,
generation after generation, with her stereotyped blessing: "Be
happy, you good cheeild." Or in *Royal Highness*, where it is
stated repeatedly, with admiration, that someone "had let the
wind blow around his nose." There is Hans Castorp's reiterated
opinion that Settembrini's well-formulated remarks are "worth
hearing"; it served him well as a kind of asbestos armor against
the straw-fire of the literary liberal. And, finally, there is
Joseph's fantastic and presumptuous declaration that he was, one
might say, of virgin birth, which is echoed with reluctant respect
by Potiphar himself.

The changes of external or internal situation in which such
phrases are recapitulated provide a perfect analogy to the en-
harmonic change of key by which a musical figure is modulated.
It is not by accident, therefore, that the good news of Joseph's
rebirth in Egypt is announced by means of song, pouring from
the sweet lips of little Serah, Jacob's grand-daughter, in seraphic
jubilation.

Thomas Mann's highly individual, unmistakable diction, is
rooted in the love of ornamentation, figurative expression, in
the joy of characterization and verbal luxuriance: in a word, in
the element of form, its closest parallel in the harmonic mobility
of musical structure. Economy of expression is not his concern:
his way is that of the musical theme which gains in content and
significance only through repetition, displacement, consistent
development. It is not the sound and fragrance of his prose that
invite the comparison with music, but its harmonic interplay, its
wealth of color, rather than the lyrical quality itself.

But this similarity brings to light still other deep-rooted
affinities. The atmosphere of Thomas Mann's early stories is
saturated with music. The experience of Hanno Buddenbrook, of
Tonio Kröger, are unthinkable without the undercurrent of the
Tristan chromatics by which they are accompanied. The shadow
of Richard Wagner hovered for many years over the creations of
this last literary master produced by the German middle-class—
darkening, illuminating, inspiring his work.

Not until relatively late in life did he free himself from that domination, sealing his detachment with that marvellous essay written, if I am not mistaken, just before the outbreak of the Third Reich, which after all represented the political embodiment of the Wagnerian feeling complex with its Vertigo, Will, and Valhalla. This essay, composed with an intellectual incorruptibility and sobriety made possible only through great insight, counts for more in the struggle against that demonic element, in my opinion, than the passionate diatribes and accusations of Nietzsche, who was too close to it himself, and whose temperament was too saturated with *studium et ira* for objectivity.

The fact that he has outgrown Wagner and come home into the freedom of purer forms establishes a special, intimate link between Thomas Mann and the younger generation. For most of my generation are just old enough to have passed through this struggle ourselves, though we were able to resolve it more speedily. When I was twenty and just back from the war, I remember my mother taking me to a performance of the *St. Matthew Passion.* I declared then that one could not listen to such things anymore; *Parsifal* was our world. My mother, whose instinctive taste for the enduring in art was proof against confusion, smiled. Two years afterward it was all over and when we said goodbye to *Tristan*, conducted by Furtwängler, shortly before we left the country, it was quite easy to leave before the third act without the slightest sense of guilt. By the same token, we are not likely to miss too acutely our author's own novella, *The Blood of the Walsungs*, which he himself suppressed although, despite the ungratifying content, it happens to be exceedingly well-made.

Perhaps another experience may help to show Mann's deep affinity to music. It must have been in 1918, during the Munich Music Festival, that I happened to hear for the first time a performance of Palestrina by Pfitzner and was more powerfully stirred by it than I have ever been since by any work of art. Shortly afterward the profundity of Thomas Mann's understanding of music was revealed to me when I read his excellent essay on the same impressive work in *Reflections of a Non-Political Man,* where the great non-musician points out the overwhelming beauty of the passage, "There lies my Rome," following the vast night passages of the mass.

Since that time, Thomas Mann has represented to us the literary artist animated by the spirit of music. And when, confronted by his latest giant production, to the stature of which

our posterity will do homage, we see the past he has conjured
rising from the bottomless gulf of time and opening up before
us into a vividly present experience; when, behind the spoken
word, we surmise the unspoken, the inexpressible; when "beginning and end fuse into one" and "all that is passing is but a
parable," then we know what remains to us now that our homeland has fallen away: The vision and the word of the great
German artist.

Almost the very moment at which he crosses the threshold
of the Biblical age has been destined to mark a turning point
in the world's history. The demonic spectacle of the European
Walpurgisnacht which has devastated his world, our world, has
been engulfed by the hell whence it came. Twilight of the gods,
twilight of the idols, for the last time on this part of the road,
this season of the century. And if, in this night of nights, much
has been lost that was dear to him, such as the Holstentor in
Lübeck and the Frankfort Römer, the residence in Würzburg,
and perhaps even a certain garden-house in Weimar, then may he
find cheer, on this day when his work has come to its sublime
completion, in "The glow of morning over the mountain-range
of humanity," and may he be comforted by the sure knowledge
that his work will endure:

"A poet's words, I think you know,
Up to the gates of heaven go
And gently knocking, make their plea
For love and immortality."

[1945]

WHAT WE HOPE FROM
THOMAS MANN

Albert Guérard

There are uncrowned sovereigns of the spirit. Voltaire was such a king, and after him Goethe, Victor Hugo, Tolstoy. "The monarchy of wit" is the most substantial of all; few scholars could tell offhand who was the rector, bishop or provost of Paris *under* Villon; and by the side of Tolstoy, the tsars who strutted in his lifetime are shadows. Yet this eminence is elusive; it is the miraculous component of antagonistic forces. The King of Humane Letters is not the rebel or the pioneer. He is not permitted to voyage through strange seas of thought alone. But neither can he be King Log, inert in contented conformity. He must win the respect of artists and the acclaim of the untutored. Above the strife, he is a vital part of the strife; timeless, he is a living force in the events of the day. No rootless cosmopolitan is eligible, yet the chosen ruler must spurn and transcend the petty "sacred egoism" of his tribe. He must be of this earth, wise in his generation, a shrewd, capable, sociable man; yet he must live also on a different plane: he is fated to be, half-consciously, a legend, a symbol, a myth.

Such is the greatness that the times have thrust upon Thomas Mann: it cannot crush his own inherent greatness. Zola, Wells, Bernard Shaw, deliberately worked for mastership—not unworthily, yet the artists in them suffered from the strain. Anatole France submitted to his elevation, with a rueful deprecatory smile; and posterity smiled in return, with a touch of irony and pity. Not so with Thomas Mann. His position is secure, because he neither sought it nor shunned it. He accepted the burden, as Eisenhower did, with earnestness and with simplicity.

Such a burden is never light: even a sense of humor brings little relief. At the present hour, it demands superhuman strength. For what we expect of Thomas Mann is an achievement more complex, more far-reaching than Eisenhower's. It is for Mann (not single-handed of course, but as the responsible, the indispensable leader) to win the decisive battle, now that Eisenhower has cleared the way. This war will not be over until catharsis has come to the German soul.

The task is not to destroy, but to purify, and Thomas Mann can direct us. Not because he is a "clever" writer and a "best-seller." If these vulgar advantages are not wholly irrelevant, it is only because they enhance his opportunity. Fame is an amplifier: it enables a man to speak gently and be heard. Thomas Mann—and, I believe, Thomas Mann alone—is fully qualified to bring, not appeasement, but atonement. For he came to us, and was accepted by us, grown to his full stature, such as Germany had made him. He has gone through the shadow of death with his people. He could not serve the world so well today if he had not written *Reflections of a Non-Political Man* twenty years before *The Coming Victory of Democracy*. He can save Germany from despair; he can save us from complacency.

I need hardly say that I do not believe Thomas Mann should go into politics, least of all into German politics—the Lamartine of a Second Republic. At the proper moment, he has not shirked the rough-and-tumble of civic life. Today, he belongs to the world, and he belongs to us. He can serve Germany best by serving the world. And to fulfill his appointed task, he needs serenity.

Thomas Mann is Europe. No work could be more deeply rooted in its native soil than *Buddenbrooks*, but European literature is one. Mann received his impulse to novel writing from the doubly alien Goncourts. He composed his Lübeck epic (which horrified Lübeck) in Rome and Munich. To me, brought up in France, his Lübeck was not stranger than Mauriac's Bordeaux; to Edmond Jaloux, it evoked his native Marseilles. The commercial background reminded me at times of *Soll und Haben*, at times of *Dombey and Son*, at times of *The Forsyte Saga*. If its subdued irony is consciously akin to Theodor Fontane's it bears a likeness also to the quiet humor of William Dean Howells. Every writer is unique: themes, moods, techniques, ignore political and linguistic boundaries. Art for Art's Sake, Decadence, which Mann used with contrapuntal effects in his decline and fall of merchant princes, were European motives in the decade that preceded *Buddenbrooks*. Mann alone could have written *Death in Venice*, and he wrote it alone. Yet it reveals a temporal affinity with his elders, d'Annunzio, Barrès and Gide—not to mention Oscar Wilde.

Already before the first World War, Mann was, not a political novelist, but a social critic, perhaps without knowing it. The chronicle of *Buddenbrooks* implied a satire, not of a family and of a city, but of the bourgeois order. Its secure wealth creates opportunities for culture which it cannot satisfy. In the bourgeois scheme of things, culture, an ornament and therefore a parasite, becomes a disease; it preys upon the system which has made it possible. The bourgeois who ceases to be pure Philistine is doomed. But the writer whose art is severed from the *mores* of his people is spineless, defenseless. Gustave von Aschenbach welcomes physical annihilation, because he feels annihilation within. The center of his life has become a tragic futility, an ardent quest without hope and without purpose.

To Thomas Mann himself, by all accounts, *Royal Highness* is but a fairy tale. Prince meets Princess, and they live happy ever after. I read it about the same time as Heinrich Mann's *Der Untertan,* and I saw in both the same satirical intent. It is almost impossible for a dynastic ruler to be a full-grown man. His education is unreality. Wherever he turns, he sees the same admiring conventional smile. Bluster as he might, Wilhelm II of the withered arm was another Klaus Heinrich with the crippled hand; the gaudy empire with its antiquarian trappings, like the duodecimo principality in the novel, would have fallen into shabby-gentility and decay, if it had not been saved by commerce and industry. Aristocracies (of blood as well as of mind) cut off from the common earth must wilt and rot.

When the First World War broke out, Thomas Mann reluctantly but deliberately left the Ivory Tower. He fought—in 630 closely packed pages—against the forces which were assailing Germany: Western Liberalism, "Civilization." But his guiding thought was not "My country, right or wrong!"—the blasphemous fallacy which impelled Niemoeller to offer to kill in Hitler's name and for Hitler's glory. What he was attempting to vindicate was a conception of the world. Germany, in his eyes, was but the champion of the cause. He himself admitted later that the faith he was then defending—"the acceptance of a determinism," "the soil and the dead"—had been admirably expressed by a Frenchman, Maurice Barrès; while among the *Zivilisationsliteraten* upon whom his scorn was poured, stood his own brother Heinrich.

The battle he was fighting then was over a hundred and fifty years old. It was the conscious rebellion of Romantic primitivism against conventional Society, that Society which had reached its perfection with the Enlightenment. There again, alleged national psychology would be an unsafe guide. The masters of "obscurantism" were Vico and Rousseau as well as Hamann and Herder.

This rebellion was not sheer nihilism. At its origin, we find the idea to which Mann has ever remained true: that of human dignity. For all its cosmopolitanism and equalitarian ideology, the Enlightenment acknowledged, emphasized or even created distinctions which were humiliating to the majority of men. It had assumed a Franco-British pattern; Mediterranean Europe was branded as decadent, Nordic Europe as uncouth and "Gothic." It was sophisticated, the possession of an exquisite elite. The rebellion was at the same time national and democratic. It asserted that German ways were not necessarily inferior to French ways; that the rules of French tragedy, the etiquette of Versailles, the wit of Parisian salons, were not infallible badges of excellence. Not the Germans alone, but the common folk everywhere, the unsophisticated, the naive, were purer in spirit than the learned.

There was more to the Romantic rebellion than an inferiority complex. Beyond the victory of the bourgeois Enlightenment, the Romanticists could descry only a world that was colorless and mean. Adam Smith pointed to the Promised Land where the Profit Motive would hold undivided sway. To the unwary, the Enlightenment seemed to ignore the power of the irrational, for good and evil. The Encyclopedists appeared to live on a smooth, well-lit plane, which was but a small, obvious, uninteresting section of reality. This impression was not fully justified. Voltaire was conscious of the "dark forces," which he called "L'Infâme," and Diderot felt strongly the power of imagination and passion. The deeper difference is that the Enlightenment was disciplined effort, and Romanticism surrender. There is an idyllic, a quietistic brand of surrender: "Relax; fret not; in Nature and in Nature's God you will recover innocence and bliss." There is a tragic, a daimonic kind: "Let yourselves be carried by the profound, chthonic forces, and you will feel through your whole being the glory of their power, even though the end be destruction." Two ways—poles asunder—of not resisting evil.

To complicate matters, the great battle of the eighteenth century, which is still raging, was and remains three-cornered. Romanticism in its purity is not conservative, but radical. It is not satisfied with "the wisdom of prejudice." It assails civilization as an elaborate, oppressive superstructure, whether it be founded upon tradition or upon reason. It was Conservatism, forced out of its ancient citadel, Tradition, that sought refuge in Romantic darkness. In some essential aspects, Romanticism was an appeal to the people, and represented "the wave of the future," but it became a highly successful camouflage for superstitions and privileges: "Enemies of reason, unite!" Mann has very

aptly defined that trend: "There is within Romanticism a historical school which may be described as reactionary. One finds in it
that pious passion for the night, that Joseph-Görres complex of
Earth, Folk, Nature, the Past and Death—a world of thought
and feeling whose magic is well-nigh irresistible. . . ." It is the
world of Wagner, of Thomas Mann—and of Hitler.

The kinship cannot be denied. It has not been renounced: in
his fine essay *Kultur und Sozialismus*, Mann explicitly, courageously refuses to abjure his *Reflections*. In *The German Record*,
William Ebenstein dwells heavily on that point. No doubt it
would be ludicrous to equate Mann with Hitler: both redeemed
or both damned. Fellow travelers come to the parting of the
ways. I have worked all my life for Franco-German reconciliation; but there was a moment when I turned against Otto Abetz.
I have labored for peace: yet I had to fight those who advocated
defendnig justice "by all means short of war and that would not
lead to war." We must be ready, at any moment, to denounce the
lunatic fringe. Above all, we must be on our guard against the
men who "muscle in," who seek to turn to their own sordid gain
all sacred things—religion, patriotism, art and love.

But it is well to remember the common background. Yes, the
German people, in their bewilderment, took flight into the primitive, the subconscious, the dark forces of the blood and the earth.
They surrendered to an ideology which had no power to with-
stand the monstrous madness of Hitler. But that ideology was
Thomas Mann's. He had denounced as shallow and Philistine
the Western cult of the intellect. And, among the cultured, he
was not alone. Even an all-too-conscious artist, a cosmopolitan,
like Stefan Zweig, who seemed destined to be a *Zivilisationsliterat*, had followed the same trend and extolled the daimonic.
Let those who have never been false to the Enlightenment, never
sneered at "logic" and "clarity," cast the first stone.

What made Hitler's Germany formidable was the conjunction
of Romantic madness and Prussian efficiency—the army, the
state. Here again Thomas Mann was with the many. He did not
realize the fundamental evil of these magnificent creations when
they became idols instead of tools. The army and the state had
killed conscience; but they had no spiritual power of their own.
They were but instruments after all, and they could not resist,
when they were picked up by a demented primitive. The army
and the state in their perfection were incarnated in Frederick
the Great; and Thomas Mann had praised that sharp, intellectual,

"Enlightened" cynic, the least Wagnerian of men. No less illogi-
cally, Heinrich Mann, the *Zivilisationsliterat,* worshipped Napoleon.

We must consider Thomas Mann therefore as the exponent,
not as the accuser, of the German spirit. He followed the same
road as millions of other Germans. Confessedly, it was a perilous
path. Those who attempted it tumbled easily into Hitlerism. But
Hitlerism was the abyss, not the goal. The sanity of genius kept
Thomas Mann steady; many, who were not criminal at heart,
fell. Climbing back to sanity will be hard.

It must be hard. I have no thought of sparing the Germans'
feelings. Any conversion at the point of the sword, even if it be
perfectly sincere, is a wrench, and is apt to leave a dangerous
wound. I wish another way of salvation had been possible. Harshness is now the only cure, as Thomas Mann told the German
people on the day of unconditional surrender.

But we did not ask of Thomas Mann when he cast in his lot
with us, we cannot ask of the German people, that they should
abjure their entire past and adopt *in toto* our way of life. We
cannot be so criminally smug as to offer ourselves to our enemies
as patterns of perfection. We cannot hold up to them as an ideal
our own frailties and blemishes. We cannot tell them that a
realistic policy based on force is monstrous when it is called the
Axis and virtuous when it is called the Big Three. We cannot
tell them: "Be humble; work hard; when you have served your
sentence, you may graduate into party politics and the profit motive." We cannot offer to them as a spiritual guide the religion
of the average "Liberal," threading his bemused way in the
middle of the road. We cannot help them out of the pit and lead
them into a morass.

The Germans must transcend their follies—and so must we.
The way to world harmony is not assimilation, standardization,
Gleichschaltung: that is a Totalitarian nightmare. It is the method
which the French have at last adopted for their colonies: *converging evolution.* We do not want to Americanize Germany, and we
do not want America to be Germanized. Our hope is that the
best in Germany and America will ultimately meet and merge.

Such has been Thomas Mann's achievement. He has not
altered his course. What he has gone through, what he has left
behind, remains an integral part of his being. He is the Thomas
Mann of *Buddenbrooks* and *The Magic Mountain,* and the Thomas
Mann of *Reflections.* He has skirted the abyss and emerged
into safety, not merely with us, but ahead of us. *The Coming*

Victory of Democracy might easily have turned into a Fourth
of July address. He has made it a challenge. He has restored
dynamism to our faith. He has made us realize that human dignity cannot be attained simply through magic formulae such as
liberty, equality, the will of the people. It must be deserved. The
eternal verities are not static, as of 1776. They call for constant
purification and constant action. Democracy is unceasing peaceful revolution. The immediate goal Thomas Mann assigns to us is
social democracy, or, to borrow a French phrase, "economic humanism." Before the world reaches that stage, the Germans will
have much to unlearn. But so shall we. The coming victory of
democracy is above all a victory over our own sloth, selfishness
and confusion.

Perhaps we had too easy a time on this rich continent, without dangerous neighbors. We were apt to forget the "dark forces"
under a thin veil of comfort and reasonableness. Those forces
are there. They cannot be denied, but they can be tamed. Perhaps the most profound and the most helpful of Mann's essays
is *Freud's Position in the History of Modern Thought.* To many,
it was Freud who revealed the unconscious and the subconscious.
He gave romantic intuition the confirmation of experimental science. His mission, however, was not to capitulate, but to heal.
He explored, but he cleansed the abyss. He brought light into
the recesses. Freud was the exact reverse of an "obscurantist."
The light he used was that of the intellect. Feeble it may seem,
but it is persistent, and it conquers. Freud proclaimed as his
ideal "the primacy of reason." Thomas Mann's last great public
effort before he left Germany was *Appeal to Reason.* So Romantic confusion is transcended, and the Enlightenment triumphs at
last. But it is an Enlightenment that conquers, absorbs, organizes,
not one that simply denies.

[1945]

THE RESPONSIBILITY
OF THE SPIRIT

Erich Kahler

The purpose of this essay is not to celebrate Thomas Mann as the great artist—others will do this sufficiently—but rather as the consummate representative of the man concerned with matters of the spirit. What is a man who is concerned with matters of the spirit? The western European languages have no word for it—they know only "intellectual," a term which is by no means identical with that of the man of the spirit and which should not be confused with it. Only the German language makes this important distinction. An intellectual is anyone who concerns himself with the arts and sciences and perhaps also with their practical application; it is a concept embracing many occupations and professions, a specific level of life. But few artists and scholars are really men of spirit, and in order to be one, one need not necessarily be an artist or a scholar. We call a man of spirit him, and him only, for whom supra-personal problems and decisions are a personal concern, one who no longer distinguishes between the personal and the supra-personal, since in his innermost passionate efforts he has completely identified himself with these questions. The man of spirit is he to whom understanding the world and shaping it is close to the heart—in short, a man who feels a personal responsibility for the condition of the world and humanity.

It is of this attitude that I am thinking when I call Thomas Mann the perfect representative of the man of spirit. This attitude prevails in all his work and lends his art its specific character and its profundity. But also in his critical and theoretical essays this attitude found a specific and separate expression; they are most intimately connected with his purely artistic creations, more than with most contemporary writers. These essays are often preliminary steps to his narrative works; they often prepare or interpret them. Their sequence begins with that extremely problematical book which has the significant title, *Reflections of a Non-Political Man.* The challenge of the title im-

plied its negation, for the author ceased to be "non-political" at
the moment he uttered the challenge. Since then it has become
impossible to express anything of weight without involving the
sphere of the "political"; for at that time began the great crisis
which was to engulf everything.

Reflections of a Non-Political Man is doubtlessly a disputable
book; it is so not only today, but was from the beginning. For
it is a book full of questions. It mirrors the perhaps somewhat
belated process of detachment from the well-protected realm in
which it was possible for the poet and the thinker, and especially
the German poet and thinker, to follow his calling, transcending
the business of the day, in complete remoteness from that business. In this book Germany appeared as a bastion against the rest
of the world, particularly against western Europe. But the issues
of this battle surpassed by far the battle itself. Germany represented "Kultur" against "civilization," organic cultivation of
profound inner values against the quicksand of material well-
being; Germany represented that which was living and genuine
in opposition to the merely superficially esthetic, oratorical and
literary; she stood for the eternal spirit against ephemeral existence, against mere economic activity and its restlessness. Germany stood for the eternal and for that which was in the making,
and which began to dawn beyond the obsolescent world of material progress. Germany stood for the loneliness of the artist, the
thinker, the statesman and for his obligation toward himself; she
opposed their being drawn into superficial obligations of a public and collective nature. This was the meaning of the term "non-
political" in contrast to the political; it was the opposition of an
aristocratic to the democratic principle.

That which is given here in outline was, however, no longer
a firmly held conviction. The *Reflections* book is in a state of
continuous fluctuation. Here atavisms are in conflict with premonitions, the aspects are shifting constantly, and the positions
taken—in spite of their being passionatley defended—are without
exception undermined by conscious or unconscious questions.
The whole book is a battlefield, a desperate struggle for assured
self-reliance, for objective judgment in the midst of the growing
turmoil. But all efforts were in vain; the artist was irrevocably
drawn into the sphere of the political, whatever he touched turned
into a political question and his fundamental problem of old,
the problem of his position toward the world and in the world
(the problem of *Tonio Kröger* and of *Death in Venice*), became
a burning question of the day. Thus a direction was indicated:

for especially in so far as he had been in bitter earnest with everything which Germany as a defensive bastion meant for him, and in so far as this was identical with his innermost concerns, the contact with the political arena resulted in assigning him his place and in showing him where he had to look for truth, humanity, the central interest of the spirit and of the future. His eyes were opened to the reality of the situation, and what followed was, step for step, a development toward a social, democratic republic.

Although in the *Reflections of a Non-Political Man* there are many things which are no longer tenable, and some which were never fully tenable, it remains a memorable and praiseworthy book. I know few books in the literature of the world in which the spiritual drama, the struggle for a transformation and a decision which is at the same time intimately personal and supra-personal, reveals itself in such touching sincerity with all its errors, its probing and searching, with its passionate reflection and its reflective passion. I hardly know a book from which one can learn better what it is to be a man of spirit. All political convictions to which Thomas Mann gave expression later would be of lesser weight if they had not been obtained in the struggle fought out in this book.

But the significance of this oscillating and ambivalent, this stormy and inconclusive book is still not exhausted. It represents a kind of dividing line between two epochs and because it poses extreme questions it throws light upon the exceptionally precarious, even tragic position of the man of spirit in our time.

The growing peril threatening the man of spirit has been deeply felt through the whole nineteenth century, from Goethe and Stendhal to Flaubert, Burckhardt and Nietzsche; but it became of immediate concern only after the First World War, when the man of spirit was confronted directly and inescapably with political and social reality, when he was forced to take a stand.

Only now the deep conflicts to which he was exposed have become clearly visible. For a century the world of the masses had been surging forward with ever-increasing impetus. This new world necessarily brought with it a leveling and standardization of life, the predominance of the average man, of mediocrity, of routine, an increasing noise of publicity, of teeming actuality; and the lonely voice which does not resort to shouting—for the most essential and the most subtle things do not lend themselves to shouting—was hopelessly drowned out. The world of the masses brought with it the emptiness and ugliness of materialized

and mechanized life. It meant the atomization of human knowledge, the accumulation of facts and the diminution of meaning.
The man of spirit, however, knows from experience that genuinely receptive and creative activity requires an atmosphere of
leisure, of reflection, and slow maturation; he knows that truth
is a very delicate thing and does not permit itself to be over-
simplified mechanically, that even in its simplicity it is never
clumsy, but embraces a multiple and often paradoxical complexity. He knows also that individual truth does not thrive without
an individual conduct of life. To all this the drift toward collectivism is opposed. He is forced to recognize the damage
resulting from the oversimplification of issues in the political battles, the harm done by hasty production of art and by scientific
specialization; he is forced to acknowledge that the slogans of
political, social and commercial advertising produce an atmosphere of falsehood which oppresses and numbs the consciousness
of the people and prevents a clear understanding of the actual
situation. The rulers are no longer men who can talk to men, but
slogans broadcast by mechanical means and the emotions stirred
up by them, against which the individual is helpless. These were
some of the reasons which drove many of the best minds of the
nineteenth century, in protest, into an attitude of conservativism.
This conservativism overemphasized individuality; it pushed the
artist to romanticism, esthticism, epatism, hero worship, resignation and the ivory tower of *l'art pour l'art;* it pushed the philosopher into solipsism, East Indian quietism, or nihilistic revolt. The
Reflections of a Non-Political Man are an echo of this protest,
which, after the First World War, made many intellectuals ad-
herents of a movement which led them into a falsehood even
worse, into a tyranny of slogans which was even more vulgar than
that against which they had protested, and which finally resulted
in a complete betrayal of themselves.

On the other hand there is no excuse for the man of spirit
to shun the new realities. He is of necessity a revolutionary; he
must desire the new and espouse its cause, not for the sake of its
novelty but because it is the future; this future he must perceive
earlier than others; it is his task to bring it about. His place is
at the furthermost outposts of knowledge; he must grasp that
which can hardly be grasped, for everything is completely true
only in the moment of its creation. There was the new reality,
and he was called upon to master it. There was the order to
create a democratic world; it was irrevocably pronounced with
the industrialization, mechanization and rationalization of life,

from the moment the masses appeared. This order was given from the moment when the capitalist system, which had turned hybrid, usurped power and brought with it unspeakable misery. It is certainly least of all the mission of the spirit to defend the world dominance of money. Hardly any other system was as pernicious for the basic human values as that of capitalism.

In the nineteenth century the protest of the spirit was directed particularly against the world of the bourgeoisie and of capitalism. The dangerous phenomena which had aroused the disgust of artist and thinkers had appeared in the guise of purely formal political democracy, and what was actually hidden behind this veil was the oligarchy of the powers of money. Those who felt a revulsion against this world could either withdraw into the fading era of aristocratic and heroic values, as was the choice made by Goethe, Stendhal and the romanticists, or they could anticipate the future of social justice which was to reestablish the human values together with human rights, as was the choice of the socialists, of Tolstoy, Ruskin and Carlyle. But at their time the historical process was still proceeding slowly, and a reflective and inconsistent attitude was still possible. It was the same Flaubert for whom the bourgeoisie was nauseous, progress a plague, "politics" a *saleté*, who nevertheless in his epic work accomplished the breakthrough into a new reality, and who with embittered love described in its nakedness this loathed world of the bourgeoisie. The same Dostoyevsky who was an enemy of socialism opened a vista of the human misery which called for it; it was he who created the concept of universal man, a concept which is capable of realization only in a socialist order. In the nineteenth century these radical contradictions are common to all minds of any significance. They are most obvious in Nietzsche's insights and prophecies and their unreconciled ambivalence.

During the great crisis, however, which began with the First World War, the middle class began to defend itself against the growing threat of socialism with the same individualistic arguments which had been used against itself in the nineteenth century. In the violent struggle which now ensued, these arguments became dogmatic and hypocritical slogans. People who had long forgotten what it means to be an individual, a fully developed human personality, used the slogan of individual liberty in order to protect the system of unrestrained private enterprise which had long ago been organized in trusts. The annihilation, the repression, the manipulation of democracy, the mysticism of nationality, of tradition, of religion, of blood, of hero worship—all this was now mobilized in support of the capitalistic system. In this witches' dance the man of spirit was forced to take a direct stand.

The alliance with the individualism of the middle class was extremely questionable and subject to suspicion. It meant a front against the future, against the new technical and social realities, against the human rights of the weak and of the awakening and still ignorant and helpless nationalities, and in actuality this alliance led to the most despicable brutality and wild chaos. On the other hand the consequences of collectivism had further developed: the levelling and banalization of life, the drugging of consciousness through mass slogans and mass concepts in literature, radio and films. The sense for the values of human personality, the greatest values of man, threatened to disappear. The complexity of reality, its overcrowding with facts, increased in the same degree as the general power of the intellect became weakened.

These factors brought another old conflict of the man of spirit to its most acute stage. The further the artist and thinker advances in his work, the more successful he is in his search for truth and the more profoundly he probes, just so much wider becomes the gap between him and the capability of the masses for assimilating his work. The more deeply he enters into the hidden primeval layers of reality, the further he loses touch with the immediate present. And yet it is the present which needs ever more urgently to be mastered and elucidated by the spirit. And when the fruits of this effort at elucidation finally reach the broad public, after having passed through several intermediate filters, then they not only have become half-truths, but have usually arrived too late, for the political and social development has meanwhile taken another course, a shorter and easier one, into which it was directed by passions, economic interests and mental laziness. What position should the man of spirit then take? If he sacrifices the truth for the sake of immediate influence he ceases to be himself. If he sacrifices influence for the sake of truth then his efforts, which were destined to serve man, appear slightly ridiculous and quixotic. He must carry responsibility for what occurs, for that is in the essence of his being; he is even called upon to give an account; he has often been blamed for his inability to prevent the horrible things which have taken place and are taking place again and again. But his position is not in any way official and the more deeply he feels his responsibility the smaller is his influence. Then, too, there is no easily recognizable mark of identification by which he can be distinguished from his half-brothers whose influence is far greater than his.

The man of spirit seems therefore faced with a dilemma incapable of solution: he has to choose between human rights and human values which are really inseparable, and he has to choose between truth and influence, which are useless if separated.

In reality he has no choice, for him the only problem which exists is how to reconcile concretely truth with influence, human rights with human values, or rather in what order of things this reconciliation is possible. This is identical with the problem of democracy.

We cannot go back, we can only go forward; for the historical processes are non-reversible. We cannot preserve, we can only conquer. Democracy is on the march. We cannot get rid of it any longer, nor can we restrain its development without perpetuating and multiplying a hundredfold the present destruction and anarchy. The leveling of standards through mass production and mass consumption, the dizzying growth of intellectual and physical communication and, resulting from it, the mutual dependence of peoples, nations and continents—all this leads in the purely technical field to an increasing participation of everybody in everything. It was the capitalistic system which brought about these conditions and it is irrevocably bound to them—but only to a certain degree. The goal of capitalism must be to enable the greatest number to participate in the consumption and therefore also in the production of goods, but this is only in so far as the economic process is directed to the advantage of the producers and not of the consumers. Avoiding the technical terms of economics, this means: to the advantage of money and not to the advantage of the people. The people have to be taken into consideration only in so far as they are customers. They have to be well treated and kept in a state of sufficient well-being, because only then are they able to purchase, and welfare itself must become a purchasable object. These are the limits set to the welfare of the masses. We are accustomed to these well-known facts: the goods must be attractive rather than of good quality, they may be of good quality only to the extent that they do not last too long and therefore do not prevent the need for new goods. On the other hand, new inventions and discoveries may be made accessible to the general public only in so far as they do not devaluate the existing goods and their instruments of

production. The goods must not be too select, because then they
are too expensive for mass consumption and are not profitable,
but they must not be too abundant either, because then they
depress the market and again are not profitable.

The democracy of our day does not conceal its origin in the
capitalistic system. The democratic way of life is based on the
principle of supply and demand. The competing party machines
and candidates offer the voting public their "platforms," and the
methods of political propaganda (not only of the National-So-
cialists) are exactly parallel to those of advertising. The voters
select their candidates according to offers and accomplishments
related to their own private interests and needs. They have
neither the opportunities nor the abilities for active participation in the fundamental political decisions. Their influence does
not go beyond the act of voting and the time of election, their
insight into the actual situations and into the significance of the
current problems does not transcend the horizon of their news-
papers and their radio commentators, and these, in turn, with
few exceptions, present the issues only in a manner which fur-
thers the practical interests of their customers, the parties, the
economic groups, the buyers of advertisements and the social
group which is their audience. Everywhere public life does not
center around the people as a whole or the individual, but around
customers. The attempt to change this incomplete and false
democracy into a full and genuine one means nothing other than
to transform the service for the customer into a service for the
nation and the human individual.

From the economic point of view the customer is identical
with the nation, and in spite of the fact that even here his genuine
interests are not served, by the degree of personal and physical satisfaction he obtains from the goods he has purchased everybody can determine whether he has fulfilled his needs and desires
for an adequate price. He has been trained to yearn for ever
novel things; now he desires and obtains them. Thus even in
the social and political sphere begins the discrepancy between
personal satisfaction and common good, between the merely
immediate and the lasting benefit. When the citizen votes for
a party because it promises him a lowering of taxes and the
abolition of irksome controls, he is not aware of the fact that he
may have to pay for these immediate advantages with his ruin
in a coming crisis or with the life of his children. He is offered
a tangible advantage—he is unable to calculate its fatal consequences. He is satisfied as a customer and deceived as a citizen

without knowing it. This knowledge is the central issue; we have reached the decisive point.

The widest gap between the demands of the customer and the welfare of the human being exists in the cultural sphere. Nowhere better than here is there an opportunity to study the harmful effects of the system of supply and demand. The people as customers desire an education which is useful for quick advancement in practical life; they desire and obtain a kind of literature, film and radio program which provide them in their rare leisure with entertainment, excitement and food for their romantic dream wishes. Even the serious-minded who want to inform themselves, after their day of work naturally desire that which is easy, which offers the least resistance, the superficially new which at bottom is the old. In the numbing rush of satisfactions of this kind, which, hardly enjoyed, are already forgotten, and leave behind only a confused and overcrowded world of impressions, how could they conceive the idea that this flood of distractions is cheating them of their truth, of their sense of truth, of the highest values of their life? How should it dawn upon them that with the destruction of the basic value of truth all other human values are destroyed, that, without their being aware of it, together with human values, human rights are carried away; how should they realize that the horrors of modern battlefields, of bomb cellars, of torture and gas chambers have their beginnings in this growing inner emptiness of man?

Of all this they are unaware, and this is true also for the merchants in culture who serve their customers, the teachers, the publishers, the film producers, the professional writers and journalists. They do not believe it possible, and even if they were conscious of it, under the present system they probably could hardly conduct themselves otherwise than they do now. For they are only the extreme exponents—exponents in the basic meaning of the word, "displayers"—of an attitude which is characteristic for the whole traditional system of democracy: adjusting oneself to the wishes of the customers; that is to say letting oneself be guided by the people as "public," by the most quickly passing and most superficial whims of the masses, accepting the accidental present conditions as immutable and incorrigible and thus blocking the way for future developments. The technical foundations of our life are in constant change, they have been gradually altered in such a decisive manner that the human conditions of our life are no longer true—but the human beings

are being prevented from changing, man is prevented from preserving his existence through its transformation.

The comment of the "conservatives" to this will be: There
you have it. The people are not mature enough for self-determin-
ation; they will never be mature enough for it; they need a
guiding hand, a monarch, a leader. But taking this attitude means
closing the book of history. The only way out is the radically
opposite conclusion: the masses must be made more and more
mature for determining their own life more and more fully, they
must be put into a position to understand the factors governing
their life, they must learn to walk on their own feet instead of
being pushed. They must learn not only to elect officials but to
understand their own basic problems and to make the decisions
themselves. They must grasp clearly what today they perceive
only vaguely and passively. How can this be brought about? We
are caught in a vicious circle. In order to put the masses into a
position where they can determine their own life, a new public
order is necessary; and the establishment of this new order calls
for a new way of thinking, a fundamentally new orientation. But
how can man reach this new orientation, how can he hold out
in a social order which punishes the adoption of this new way of
thinking with starvation? It is easy enough to preach that each
one of us individually should begin with himself. This is all very
well but it does not get us very far. There are too many isolated
individual persons and as individuals they are much too weak
against the masses of all shades of conviction, these masses which
are the pillars of the existing society. The individual is too weak
against the firmly established positions and is forced to submit to
the rules of the game if he wants to live. It is not only the isolated individual who must adopt this new way of thinking; it
must be adopted by whole groups, for they alone can carry out
the reconstruction of society. This task calls for active support.
From whom can it come, if not from that kind of man for whom
supra-personal problems and supra-personal decisions are a matter of personal concern, and who feels a personal responsibility
for the state of the world and of man? Who can offer this
assistance if not the man whom we have called the man of spirit?

In order to do this, the man of spirit will have to take upon
himself a much greater burden than he has carried until now.
He should not give up any of his labor at the inner front, at the
most advanced outposts of the expressible and thinkable, and at
the same time he will have to make possible the impossible. and
keep in touch with the outer front of the day-by-day battle in the

field of society. The dangerous rift between the vanguard of human consciousness and the life of the masses, which arose during the last century and which left the spirit without influence and political development without guide, this distance can only be reduced if the man of spirit is willing to put his own existence at stake and to form a bridge between theoretical truth and practical reality. He will have to interpret his own findings, he will have to translate himself into a language understandable to the public masses. If he never loses sight of the fact that, however remote the object of his research may appear, still it is concerned with human problems and destined for human beings, if he can demonstrate to his fellow men the delicate connection between his most subtle research and their life, then perhaps he may persuade them to make an effort to meet him half way, to listen to his insight and to his advice. The man of the spirit will even have to become aggressive, he will have to organize himself with his equals, if he wishes his voice to be heard, he will have to become more and more "political-minded."

This is the way which Thomas Mann has shown to us in the course he himself has followed.

[1945]

IN THE SERVICE OF LIFE

Rudolf Kayser

It is not going too far to ascribe symbolic greatness to the work and personality of Thomas Mann, a greatness which lies not so much in his individual books as in the totality of his spiritual existence. Since Nietzsche no creative German has sensed his historic hour as acutely as Thomas Mann. For him, the present is a time of great vindication: vindication of a humanist creed, of a European tradition and of a creative activity which is free because entirely determined by the personality of the artist. All the dark powers of nihilism have raged against this conservatism—and such it is in the noblest sense of the word—for decades. They have not been altogether silenced as yet, but the time of their wildest excesses appears to be over. We may look back upon their presumptuous ambitions with liberating irony. And irony also means to Thomas Mann "the pathos of the middle . . . its morals, its ethos." Irony is for the artist the unlimited freedom to create dreams and figures out of his own heart. It is the art of an enduring spiritual transformation of the world, often playful and gay, often filled with warning and pathos, but, in Thomas Mann's technique, always informed by a sense of responsibility toward human fate.

In Thomas Mann's stories, this ethical irony illumines the totality of life in its most secret corners. As *leitmotif* it proceeds from the *Biedermeier*-mildness of *Buddenbrooks* to the metaphysical depths of the Joseph novel. In between we see an abundance of characters and adventures, not isolated from the time and place out of which they emerge, but sprung from the living reality. And this is why Mann's epic work represents a history of European man in his last epoch, an epoch of unrest and crisis, of longing and desperation.

Tonio Kröger already experiences the general conflict of his age, that is to say the conflict between spirit and life, or between art and reality. He is deeply shaken at the thought of the solitary mission of the artist but he is also proud of his "burgher love for everything human, alive and common." This love is Thomas

Mann's source of strength. It is not a passion for the social, as
in Balzac or Zola, but rather a devotion to the miracle of individual existence in things small as well as great. This miracle
reveals itself even in the most trivial events and makes us ask
the question as to the meaning and achievement of life itself.
The answer is not a system of philosophy. It lies in the colors,
sounds and backgrounds of human fate and can be given only
in the language of the poet.

From Thomas Mann's earliest stories through *Buddenbrooks*
to *The Magic Mountain* we can recognize an entire epoch contained in his characters. All of them lead a double life: first their
own real one, and then a second one, symbolic of the decay of
the age. We can trace this decay in all stages of life. The threat
of chaos wanders through the souls of men. The crisis of the age
emerges ever more clearly and becomes the basic theme of *The
Magic Mountain*: "A book of spiritual abnegation of much that
had been beloved before and of many a dangerous sympathy,
spell or temptation to which the European soul was and is inclined. . . . Its service is service to life, its will is health, its goal
the future."

"Serving life," then, is the real content of Mann's humanism. As a poet he sees life concretely, sees the pulsating, bloom-
ing world of reality. But the more cracks this reality shows and
the more miserable the men who live in it grow, the stronger
becomes the need for values which outlast all crises. For Thomas
Mann the road to Biblical mythology signifies escape from life
as little as it did for Goethe when he turned toward the "pure
East." Mythos is the philosophy not only of pre-historical, but
also of unhistorical man. It is in him that life actually proves its
legitimacy. And "foundng life" is always the issue if a nobler
future is to follow upon the decline.

Such then is the essential meaning of the Joseph novels,
which represent the most magnificent synthesis of old and new
elements of existence. Faith and reason, "Eros" and politics, spirit and deed. will and dream—they all meet in this, the richest
epic work of our time. Here is a world inhabited by many peoples, types and characters, filled with such a wealth of fantasy
and wisdom and goodness as we have rarely seen in a work of
epic art. The old "burgher love" of man rises up to God. "God's
and man's sanctification" are one and the same, being mutually
interdependent. On the road to this goal we re-experience the old
Biblical legends in a new, purely human light. The sharp outlines of the Biblical characters are filled with new, personal ex-

periences. The misery and the glory of his own personality first
strike Benjamin when he has a foreboding that the powerful
Lord of Egypt is his own, lost brother. "And there is a cry forth-
coming in this world which, however, is not yet a cry and
with which in our breast we cannot return home to father to
live as formerly, while the cry is about to break out into the
world and to fill the world, for all of which it is tremendous
enough."

Though the Joseph stories may represent the epic climax of
Thomas Mann's career as an artist, they are by no means an
ending point. Life and its experiences are too colorful, too manifold today. *The Beloved Returns,* that calm and mature tale of
the life of the aging Goethe, was completed in the midst of work
on *Joseph.* And at the same time, Thomas Mann stepped upon
the political scene after many hesitations. His struggle against the
nihilistic powers was aimed not only at the destruction of a hated
system but also at the redemption of Germany for the higher
task of her "return to Europe."

This Europe is more than a geographic term, more even than
a cultural unity. Goethe's and Nietzsche's concept of the "good
European" is being newly re-interpreted in every period. Today,
in an age darkened by utter lack of faith, it means the ideal of
religious communion with all those enduring spiritual powers
which alone are capable of saving us from the agonizing destruction of the present. Thomas Mann's work and existence are a
summons to a new faith in the old Christian-humanistic forces
which have created the idea of Europe. And this faith, too, is
like a cry in our breast which is about to break out and to fill a
desperate world.

[1945]

THOMAS MANN AND THE GERMAN TRADITION

F. J. H. Letters

British students of contemporary German could have felt little if any surprise when the Nobel prize for literature was awarded to Thomas Mann. Not only must it have been clear to them that with Gerhart Hauptmann he held the highest place among his country's living authors; they would know, too, that as German writers are in a much more favourable position, both geographically and linguistically, for due consideration of their claims by the Scandinavian committee which awards this prize than their English competitors have ever been, it was only a question of time before Thomas Mann should win the recognition that ought so much earlier have been Thomas Hardy's.

On the other hand, those whose knowledge of modern German tendencies derived from the stream of English translations in the twenties might have been pardoned if they had confused the writer with the Labour agitator of the same name. This curious post-war phenomenon—the translation of German novels and essays in quantities that left renderings from the French far behind, had not, it must be peremptorily affirmed, introduced the English reader to work of the best quality. The enormous sales of Remarque's *All Quiet on the Western Front* and Feuchtwanger's *Jew Suss* are notorious instances of the type of book that engaged the curiosity of the public and the energies of translators. In these times when *Ulysses* may any day become a university textbook, we can hardly apply to the realism of Remarque and Feuchtwanger the obsolescent epithet "daring." That realism, however, was then novel enough in an English garb to whet and satisfy an appetite not sufficiently catered to elsewhere. The frankness of the type of author favoured by translators was always of a kind understood by the people. It had the advantage of being democratically clear. This was not usually the case with contemporary English realists, whose stylistic peculiarities at least made them caviare to the general. Compare the relative obscurity of D. H. Lawrence with the popularity even in England of Lion Feuchtwanger. *Jew Suss* and *All Quiet,* in fact, like most German books then advertised throughout the Empire, were admirably adapted for that large class of persons who can only be persuaded to read at all by every resource of modern publicity. As these will always form the majority of the public, it is hardly surprising that such productions were in greater demand than far more important German works.

Thomas Mann, of course, though a novelist and thinker of a very different calibre, had already been partially translated into our tongue. But there is no doubt that until recently his name was almost unknown to English readers, and probably even now much of his work remains untranslated. Certainly in our language there are few or no critical studies of this remarkable writer. A few scrappy notices and articles might no doubt be collected from magazines and volumes of essays. But we have nothing like Eloesser's *Thomas Mann's Leben und Werke* or Martin Havenstein's more purely critical and very profound essay *Thomas Mann: Der Dichter und Schriftsteller.*

It was inevitable, however, that the international recognition resulting from his winning the Nobel Prize should gain him more attention in the Empire and in America. As, besides, he was still in his early fifties, it was unlikely that the "finis" he subscribed to the enormous *Zauberberg* would also come to symbolise the conclusion of his work as a novelist.

Nor has it. He has since produced *The Beloved Returns* and the massive Joseph legend series of old Testament novels. But as these have received sufficient attention from English and American reviewers, I intend to limit this essay to a study of Mann's development up to the appearance of *The Magic Mountain.*

German literature is characterised by certain marks found in no other, and those marks are not wanting even in Mann's most original work. Alone of modern, and with the apparent rather than real exception of Italy among ancient nations, Germany's self-expression burst out simultaneously in many branches of intellectual achievement. Normally the process of such development in a given country is in the sequence of poetry, narrative prose, philosophy, and scholarship, though special historical causes may, of course, introduce variations. This is the order of the purely literary evolution; sculpture, painting, architecture, music and science do not, it is true, emerge in regular processional form, and very rarely have all attained a high stage of development in any one nation. Perhaps ancient Greece alone excelled in each of them, and even Greece could hardly have advanced very far in the complexities of which music has proved capable, while her astonishing greatness in philosophy, paradoxical as it may seem, is one of the causes of her relative barrenness in science. She penetrated far into the depths of mathematics. But Greek mathematics remained a pure science, untainted by the vulgarity of application to utilitarian ends. Here is one of the few points at which antiquity and the middle ages touch, and where Plato and Aquinas are in accord. Both eras developed an elaborate philosophy while remaining comparatively indifferent to science.

In Germany, on the other hand, we witness the singular phenomenon of a simultaneous awakening of poetry, philosophy, literary criticism, scholarship historical and verbal, science, and music. Not only is this a complex situation in itself, but each of these activities reacts upon the rest, and the same writer often takes several of them as his province. Winckelmann, critic and scholar, exerts a profound influence over the broader and more creative genius of Goethe. The poet who gave the Faust legend its final and most marvellous form, wrote purely scientific treatises (of varying value, indeed) on botany and optics. In *Faust* itself, particularly, though not exclusivey, in the second part, where the firm outline of the drama grows at once looser and more intricate, Goethe involves contemporary metaphysics and scientific theory in the huge and cloudy symbols of classic and Germanic mythology. Whether he has not injured his stupendous work by making it at times obscurer than much ultra-modern verse is another matter. What is worth observing is that the foil to the restless genius of Faust, the Wagner who attaches himself so constantly to the master's steps, is hardly, except in name, the Wagner of Marlowe's *Dr. Faustus*. Even in Marlowe, it is true, he is the placid pedant. But in Goethe he sums up all the pedantries of modern Germany, so mercilessly satirized in Heine's prose—a pedantry that at any rate presupposed the astonishing development of verbal scholarship and philosophy that made her the most erudite country in the world.

This jostling of intellectual interests, the quarrels and alliances of their various exponents, continued with the nation's history. They have not ceased today. German philosophy, not subtly, but directly, exerted great influence over German music. When we come to Wagner, we find that to understand his operas we must know something of Schopenhauer and Nietzsche. Moreover, apart from the relation of the contending philosophies of these two to its mood, we have to consider how the form of Wagnerian opera is due to Wagner's own very systematic philosophy of music.

Prose was the last instrument of self-expression to gain formal perfection in Germany. She had some great, and many fine poets when Lessing was her one stylist in prose; and even Lessing did not reveal all the possibilities of German prose. It was still characterised or deformed by interminable periods constructed on much the same principle as that which Marcel Proust has used, *mutatis mutandis,* to produce his strange, labyrinthine French. Clearness and comparative lightness of touch were won for it by the genius of Heine, chiefly no doubt through his thorough education in classic French. But it was not until towards the end of the last century that it had developed all its resources, and it was only in the present generation that prose became the chief vehicle of expression for German genius. Gerhart Hauptmann and Thomas Mann completed what Nietzsche virtually began. Yet the inter-action of the various intellectual forces characteristic of the German writers of more than a century ago still continues in the genius of Thomas Mann. He is a philosophic novelist in a sense impossible to predicate of any Englishman, even of Thomas Hardy himself. Hardy exhibits a pessimistic scepticism that owes nothing to any speculative system. Discussion of Meredith's philosophy of the comic spirit is hardly more than discussion of Meredith himself, since he likewise has no apparent affiliation with any purely formal thinker, English or foreign. Besides, neither Hardy nor Meredith is much concerned with the major issues of metaphysics. Their systems, if they can be said to have any, are looseknit and fragmentary, conformable with the English tradition in the realm of pure thought.

Mann is typically German in that he betrays everywhere not only the influence of pure metaphysics, but of metaphysics as treated by his countrymen. We have not made the first step towards understanding him unless, as in Wagner's case, we have some grasp of the conflicting viewpoints of Nietzsche and Schopenhauer. A writer of this stamp has obviously far more claim to be termed a philosophic novelist, at any rate in the technical sense, than the English authors just mentioned, neither of whom presupposes the reader to be familiar with English or even German metaphysicians. Speculation and literature in Germany, in short, act upon one another far more vigorously and directly than in any other country. That philosophy, nay, metaphysics, has won its way into the most popular form of literary expression without subduing (usefully to borrow metaphors from Shakespeare and Goethe) life's native hues to the pale cast of thought, or its green to the grey of theory, is the special achievement of his country in the person of Thomas Mann.

There can be no doubt, on the one hand, of the vividness and reality of practically all his characters. Without this creative power, Mann's style and thought would in themselves make him a distinguished writer. His essays, *Frederick the Great and the Grand Coalition* and *Reflections of a Non-Political Man,* are a sufficient proof, if any other proof than his novels were necessary. But, of course, style and thought alone could never make a great novelist. On the other hand, his philosophic qualities are not of the kind usually required even by supreme masters of fiction. Practical psychology with him stands in closer relations with formal metaphysics than is the case with any English author. In reading him we can never forget that he has been more profoundly influenced by thinkers than by fellow-craftsmen. More persistently than to any writer of his class, whether English, French, or even German, does the problem of life present itself to him. This phenomenon darkens or illumines his every work, from *Buddenbrooks* to *The Magic Mountain.* But his greatness in this field is rather that of Hamlet than of Shakespeare. His perpetual brooding over the meaning and tendency of human existence does not result in a new philosophy of his own. Shakespeare is never didactic, but we can easily trace certain broad but distinct convictions, at least in the realm of morals, underlying the whole cycle of his plays. But neither Hamlet nor Mann finds clear answers to his questioning. Hamlet is not co-extensive with Shakespeare, but Hans Castorp is surely none other than Mann himself.

Hamlet and Mann are, in consequence, supreme ironists. They state contending theories with perfect fairness and profound understanding, and juxtapose the actual facts of life with the competing theories. But they stop short at juxtaposition, leaving adjustment to robuster faiths than theirs. In consequence, they lack the interest of characters who plead with power the cause of their beliefs. But they are interesting in another way. Our attention is not drawn so much to the validity, as to the cause of their mentality. They do not attract us by any promise to solve the final secret of the universe, but by provoking us to attempt to solve the secret of their own nature. The personal interest thus finally over-balancing the abstract, they become of more im-

portance to the lover of pure literature than to the student of formal philosophy.

For what may be termed the tone of his ideas, Mann, as already mentioned, is most indebted to Nietzsche and Schopenhauer, thinkers whose pre-eminence both in literature and in
philosophy witnesses to the interaction so special to Germany
of these two modes of intellectual expression. From this aspect,
his peculiar importance consists in his introduction into the modern novel of a new conception of tragedy.

Whatever be its informing spirit, it has generally been felt
that the spirit that broods over the evolution of the ancient
drama is that of fatality. According to this view, what befalls the
heroes of the Attic stage is inevitable. Its crises result from the
clash of the human will with forces that govern the world from
afar, and that are variously conceived as a transcendent necessity at the back of all things, against which we strive in vain, or
as an Olympus that over-rules us. Thus the real cause of tragedy
is of a remote character, and works far away from the world of
man.

There is no need to show that this interpretation of Greek
tragedy is incomplete; sufficient to observe that its very superficiality testifies to its obviousness. Add to this the fact that classical irony, which depends for its effectiveness on the spectator's
"fore-knowledge absolute" of the catastrophe, tends to deepen
his sense of its inevitability, and we are in a position to understand the fatalistic overtones of the Athenian dramatists. They
are common to Aeschylus, Sophocles, and Euripides, however
variously subdued or heightened by each. Sometimes it is the will
of the gods on Olympus that is represented as bringing to nought
the designs of men. At other times, and especially in the most
philosophic part of the drama, that is, in the lyrics of the chorus,
whose aloofness as spectators from the fierce interests that engage the actors proper, permits of profounder and more abstract
thought, the mysterious and impersonal *ananke,* or necessity, is
substituted for the will of divine beings.

This necessity rules not only the earth, but the heaven-
mountain Olympus itself. The gods cannot save their mortal fa-
vourites from doom. Nay, beyond what may literally be termed
the "earthly Paradise" of Olympus, from beyond the very stars,
it moves all things on their inevitable course. For the Greeks
this sense of inevitableness, sustained by dramatic irony, must
have largely contributed to the power of Attic tragedy. No poetry
is more philosophical, for none provokes deeper speculation on

the ultimate meaning of human destiny. Yet it is apparently a merely external frustration of the aims and instincts giving life significance that inspires those intimations of mortality heard most piercingly in the choral lament of Sophocles: "The happiest destiny is never to have been born and the next best by far, is to return, as swiftly as may be, to the bourn whence we came."

From this impression of human impotence as directly connected with powers outside and above man, an irresistible fate working independently of his will, or a pantheon that over-rode it, we pass to the next really great group of tragedians in history. These are the Elizabethans. For the heroes who trod Rome's short-lived stage, and who survive for us solely in the plays attributed to Seneca, introduce no modification of their Athenian originals. But the Elizabethans, and particularly the sovereign Shakespeare, present us with a different scene. The principle that baffles the yearnings of humanity is indicated more distinctly as extending from heaven to earth, from the gods to man, from the divine to the human will. Tragedy results from the action or inaction of the human will in given circumstances, the doing of a wrong, the neglect of a duty. Macbeth stands as an illustration of the one, as Hamlet of the other case. The antinomy of fate and free-will is, of course, reflected both in Shakespeare and in the classical dramatists. Determinism in its most rigid and metaphysical form does not find universal expression in the Greek tragedians. The very ascription of tragedy to the will of the gods admits the existence of free-will somewhere, and that admission is found frequently enough in the choruses, not only in their passionate, but in their most meditative utterances, though alternating wit hthe conception of an impersonal destiny controlling all things human and divine, and only riveting more glittering shackles on the ankles of the gods than on feet that tread the dust. Yet the freedom of human, as distinct from divine will, is also amply recognized. In truth, the inconsistency of Greek tragedy is not peculiar to it. It is anticipated in the naiver epics of Homer.

None the less, there is no doubt it is to the interaction of the twin motives of humanity and of fatality that Greek drama owes most of its poignant beauty. Shakespeare, on the other hand, stresses our freedom no less powerfully, even when he limits the field of its exercise. "The fated sky allows us verge enough" sums up, if any single sentence can sum up the most many-hearted of poets, the underlying idea of Shakespeare's philosophy.

The cause, it will be seen, has now taken on a transcendent-immanent character; immanent, because man himself is responsible for his own tragedy, transcendent, because this view presupposes as well the objective existence of duty. In short, Fatality has been replaced by Morality as the dominant factor that makes tragic occurrences interesting, and not merely terrible.

In both these views, though in different degrees, the milieu in which the characters find themselves is of vast importance. In Greek drama we are almost tempted at times to regard the very landscape as part of the machinery of relentless fate. It is the objective situation against which the Grecian hero dashes himself to death. Who can think of Oedipus apart from the Thebes that proved his doom, and the doom of his race? For it is not merely the flawed character of Oedipus that leads to his blindness and ultimate disappearance from the face of the earth. It is impossible to say that the sorrowful king and seer incurred his mysterious doom by any sufficient moral transgression of his own. Sin, of course, lies at the back of all the woes of the Greek drama. But here as usually, it is, to speak theologically, not the "actual" but the "original" type that is in question. It is the offence of his line that is to be expiated by the ruin of Oedipus, and the subsequent sacrifice of his noble daughter, Antigone. Yet it is to the necessary rather than the moral character of this expiation that our attention is drawn in reading the masterpieces even of so religious a poet as Sophocles. And that necessity becomes visible, so to speak, as Thebes. Had Oedipus not wandered thither, fleeing into the invisible danger he fancied lay behind him in Corinth, he would never have become the portent we know. But, of course, it was ineluctable Fate that drove him on his way.

In Shakespeare, principally on account of the significance he ascribes to the will, external circumstances are not so tyrannically absolute. But they are of great importance. Hamlet, no doubt, would carry his questioning into any state of life into which he might have been born. Still, he would have escaped the great tragedy of his career had a few events never occurred. Had his father not died through the poison whose effects are so graphically described, had his mother not married the murderer, he would not have been able to summarise his fate in the poignant cry:

> The time is out of joint; O cursed spite
> That ever I was born to set it right.

What is true of Hamlet is even more so of all the other Shakespearean heroes, none of whom are initially so soul-sick as he, so tragic apart from the objective situation. With Hamlet, indeed, we are approaching, although we have not yet reached, the type of character, and the conception of tragedy with which Thomas Mann has familiarized his generation.

In this third and latest conception, the transcendent-immanent bond has parted at the transcendental end, and now constrains the human will by fouling or entangling it. In other words, the tragic principle has become purely immanent. Tragedy, it is conceived, may be the result of neither of the two causes hitherto adduced. It may merely result from a form of mental or physical illness or abnormality. To express the position succinctly, the centre of interest has shifted from Morality to Vitality.

However incomplete and one-sided this view may be, there is no denying its originality, and the extraordinary skill and power that mark its exposition in the prose of Thomas Mann. Like most writers of eminence today, he has written much, though he is rather a bulky than a prolific author. *Buddenbrooks, Royal Highness,* and *The Magic Mountain* are Cyclopean novels each running into about a thousand closely printed pages, but each remarkably free from that *Langweiligkeit* or tediousness which is apt to beset even good German work constructed on so merciless a scale. In all of them, as well as in his smaller works, the author is forever preoccupied with his novel dramatic theory.

As all Edgar Allen Poe's heroes are mad, all Mann's are sick. Their deficient vitality sets them apart from the world of action —always in spirit, and sometimes in body. In reading Mann, the sense of tragedy arises in us through our carefully fed conviction that all these characters are doomed to sink in the stream of life. The *Tendenz zum Abgrund,* tendency to the abyss, which pulls them down, body and soul, to the grave, works without speed and without rest, whether the will of the sufferer resists or surrenders. All that the will can do is to lengthen the process without affecting the issue, and sometimes, as in the case of the tubercular soldier, Joachim Ziemssen, the very energy of resistance hastens the enemy's victory. For the wrestling is not with flesh and blood, but with principalities and powers of darkness. The foe is not one who faces the combatant outside with equal arms, for he has already crept into the citadel in the body of the victim before his presence is known, and he captures the town of Mansoul not by siege but by sortie. Whether in the form of a malady garrisoned in the nervous system, or a bacillic army

marshalling in the blood-stream, he lies screened equally from
the resistance of the spirit and of the body, by occupying an area
beyond the regions to which either can reach; not sufficiently objective for physical, nor subjective enough for mental opposition
to engage, the radiation of his cancerous conquest slowly forces
body and soul to collapse together.

[1945]

THE IDEA, THE WORD AND THE DEED

H. T. Lowe-Porter

"Es war der Hang zur Gedankenverbindung, welcher Jaakobs Innenleben in dem Grad beherrschte, dass er geradezu seine Form ausmachte und sein Denken fast schlechthin aufging in solchen Associationen."

Even as Jacob's garments were fringed and full-fashioned, so also were his mind and thoughts. In his musings, one thing always led to another, he dwelt above all upon the connections between ideas, as did his son Joseph, in fact (though with a difference, for he was a man of action) as did our good Hans Castorp, in his unassuming way (who was a man of no action at all); as also does the creator of these. He too, in all his "tales" is bent on this one thing: to link up and combine, to adumbrate a picture of a whole. Here lies the province of all those who, like Jacob, are "played upon by chords and correspondences"; who move in a world of chiaroscuro, of yes-and-then-again-no and one thing endlessly melting into another; of deeply entangled fringes of feeling and thought, of shifting associations and combinations, no shadowless brilliance of atomic exactitude. Such power of evoking the racial unconscious will always be found combining what is hard to combine and yet what *has need to be combined*. It is possible that here lies the explanation of Thomas Mann's popular success, in the face of this scholar-artist's bulk and weight of erudition, in the face of a style so conditioned, as style should be, by its content, that it can by no means be read while running. Probably we are in great present need of his services. When not alone the average today but the very sagest stand staggered at their inability to combine the mutually annihilating elements of our civilization into any imaginable pattern; now it is we have need of such an artist, weaving the garment of his time for us to see it by. For first our morbid state takes comfort, as like from like, in this art, it addresses itself soothingly to our ills. But after that we are led on, we take lessons in the art of combining, we seek sanity in the persistent effort to relate all things to the whole. Not the artist, of course, nor we, nor any coming age, will ever succeed. The task must ever be done anew; yet precisely today we have a grievous need to be at work on it.

It may make an odd impression, when one whose concern has so explicitly been with this writer's words, dwells so particularly upon his thoughts. But the antithesis, of course, is a false one. For to the artist, word and thought are like body and mind and cannot be divorced. Indeed, no one so well as the translator can measure the affront dealt to this artist by our time, in that his work must be known so largely in other tongues than his. Finally, in these few lines it is scarcely upon the Word as Thought that the writer of them would lay stress. Rather she would be at pains to condemn another divorce, equally unfortunate, which takes place in our common thinking when we make an antithesis between words and actions. For now, today, in our present anguishes, surely we may, in appraising the work of Thomas Mann, speak of the Word not alone as Thought but even more cogently and inevitably as Deed.

[1945]

IN SEARCH OF THE BOURGEOIS

Georg Lukacs

What are we to understand by "In search of the bourgeois?" Is he not to be found everywhere, and is not our present-day civilization in all its aspects, not only in the economic field but also in poetry and music, the product of the middle class? And is this question not superfluous particularly with regard to Thomas Mann? Has he not always stressed his allegiance to the world of the middle class more strongly than is usual today?

This problem is even more complicated by the total absence of utopian traits in Thomas Mann's art, although they are not entirely missing in his thinking. This we say in order to characterize his work, not for the purpose of ranking it according to value. Thomas Mann is, with exceptional faithfulness, devoted to reality. In the details of his stories and novels, as well as in their plots and problems, he may not cling mechanically to the surface of everyday life, his artistic procedures may have nothing in common with naturalism—and yet at bottom the essence of his work never transcends reality. In his books Thomas Mann portrays the German middle class; he supplements this by describing the genesis of the class and by unfolding its problems, whose dialectical development in turn naturally extends beyond the circle of the class; but he never offers a utopian perspective into the future, superimposing it upon the present. Not a few important works of realism show utopian traits; one need only think of Goethe's *Meister* novels. However close the affinity between the two may normally be, in this respect Thomas Mann is at the opposite pole from Goethe.

These observations only serve to emphasize the fact that for Thomas Mann the world of the middle class is both a form of life and an artistic principle. The general public is justified in considering Thomas Mann to be the representatve present-day German writer. Such a representative function can assume different forms within the same nation. There are representative writers who are ringing prophets of the future, and there are others whose genius and whose calling it is to be "mirrors of the world."

Schiller's forward urge is of the same symbolic value as Goethe's serene attachment to the present. But even if we assign to Thomas Mann a place in the neighborhood of the type represented by Goethe, Balzac or Tolstoy, even if his work is for us a "mirror of the world," even then we have not distinguished him sharply enough from others. We mentioned the utopian traits of the *Meister* novels, motifs which we find also in Balzac, Keller or Tolstoy but not in Thomas Mann. He is representative in a unique fashion presenting a complete picture of the middle class with all its problems but he describes this world at the present specific stage of its development. (We should not overlook, however, the fact that this portrayal of the German middle class embraces only the pre-fascist era; the fascist or anti-fascist German has not yet become a subject of his work.) This is why so many Germans find in Thomas Mann's writings a much more profound and exact, intimate and sympathetic portrait of themselves than in the books of other novelists. Here, where the problems are given artistic expression, questions are merely asked, never or only indirectly answered; here many relationships, associations and correspondences are revealed but at once cancelled out with irony. This is why Thomas Mann's influence extends so much farther than that of his contemporaries. In his narrative method he expects a great deal of artistic sensitivity on the part of his readers, and the finely spun web of his questions and reservations is intellectually exacting: still his plots and characters are simple and natural and easily understandable. And since his writings reflect a particular moral condition, they will be of lasting influence: each of them contains a record of the German middle class at a specific stage of its development; whoever is conscious of his individual and national past will always have to return to these works.

This special representative function is strengthened by the slow organic development of Thomas Mann. Here again he is in harmony with the gradual processes of reality. But the time in which he is living is more than tempestuous; and was so particularly during the second half of his career. This stormy tempo inevitably had its effect on his writing. Nevertheless contemporary events were not able to alter the essentially epic character of his work, which is based on a leisurely and contemplative way of experiencing life; not only in that the works which reflect these violent happenings preserve their calm epic-ironical character; their writing also consumed a great deal of time. These books give artistic expression to problems which have already reached ideological maturity; they describe the step forward which historical development has taken or is about to take, and the conflicts preceding this step in the psychological and moral realms. The historical crises themselves, however, never become the subjects of these works; Thomas Mann makes visible only the reflections of them in the everyday world. The slowness of these procedures sets Thomas Mann clearly apart from any kind of naturalism. The ideological substance of Thomas Mann's works never corresponds to the accidental fashions of thinking of the German bourgeoisie. Just the opposite is true. The further he advances in maturity, the more outspoken he is in his opposition to the reactionary currents which dominate the German middle class. But the manner of his opposition and the intellectual weapons of his resistance are the culmination of that stage of moral development of which the bourgeoisie was capable at that moment, and even in his opposition to it Thomas Mann the artist never detaches himself completely from the middle class. The depth and breadth of his influence rest upon this attachment to his social origin; he is the symbol of that which is best in the German middle class.

All we have said so far applies, however, only to the concrete artistic qualities of Thomas Mann's work. Its easy, almost casual perfection is the result of a prolonged and tormenting struggle with the manifold problems of the world of the middle class, particularly with its moral problems, and the contours of this art are an organic outgrowth of that world. Thomas Mann the artist is the diametric opposite of the philosopher Schelling, about whom Hegel said that he "obtained his philosophical education before the eyes of the public." Thomas Mann's work represents the full synthesis of completed stages in the historical sequence. Nevertheless his philosophical development of necessity takes place before the eyes of the public.

We consider it misleading to use the theoretical utterances of an important writer as the basis for the interpretation of his art. His bold efforts to master the conflicts of his time in philosophical form result at best in the honest formulation of antinomies, where often the conflicting attitudes are simply juxtaposed without any attempt at reconciling them; sometimes these theoretical efforts even lead to false or reactionary conclusions. The abstract, theoretical treatment of the problems transforms them into a state of rigidity, while, when treated artistically, they acquire the maximum of fluidity obtainable within the limits of the given historical possibilities. But works of art of this kind in

their most outstanding examples represent more than a mere
rounding out of fragmentary conceptions in artistic form. Here
reality itself, which the author has mirrored with such passionate
devotion, has made the necessary corrections upon the errors
contained in his ideology. There is no more convincing refutation
of Balzac's utopian legitimism than in his story *The Cabinet of
Antiquities,* or of Tolstoy's Christian-plebeian utopia of a frater-
nization with the peasants than in his *Resurrection.*

Thomas Mann is an extreme example of that type of author
whose greatness it is to be a "mirror of the world." This does not
imply that he is a philosophical dilettante or that he may be lacking in logical consistency. The exact opposite is the case. He is
in full possession of the most highly developed philosophical traditions of the German middle class of his time; few among his
contemporaries have, like him, mastered in their ultimate consequences the leading reactionary thinkers of this period, Schopenhauer and Nietzsche; few have so thoroughly experienced the
intimate relation which exists between these philosophical systems and methods and the fundamental problems of the middle
class of the time. Not many can be found among his contemporaries who have so completely fused their painfully acquired
philosophical convictions with their artistic work as has Thomas
Mann.

This is why the erroneous elements in his theoretical writings, those tendencies which are hostile to progress, in his narrative work are so easily confuted by the artistic autonomy of his
characters, his plots and his situations. A small example may
serve as an illustration. *Buddenbrooks* was written at a time
when Thomas Mann and an essential section of the German
middle class intelligentsia considered Schopenhauer to be the
leading philosopher of a typically German Weltanschauung. In
Thomas Mann's opinion, to which he clung long after the completion of this novel, the intellectual development of Germany
led from Goethe to Schopenhauer and then to Wagner and
Nietzsche; Nietzsche was to be the foundation of a genuinely
German philosophical culture of the present and future. It is
therefore not surprising that Schopenhauer influenced *Buddenbrooks* and that his attitude toward life here found artistic
expression. But how is this influence presented in the novel itself? Thomas Buddenbrook is a broken man. He has failed in
his efforts to give his business a fresh impulse; he has lost all
hope that his son, who will succeed him and continue his life's
work, will be able to accomplish that which was denied to him.
The intellectual and emotional bond with his wife is becoming

ever more problematical. In this situation he happens to read
The World as Will and Idea. In what way does this book affect
him?—"He was filled with a great surpassing satisfaction. It
soothed him to see how a master mind could lay hold on this
strong, cruel, mocking thing called life and enforce it and condemn it. His was the gratification of the sufferer who has always
had a bad conscience about his sufferings and concealed them
from the gaze of a harsh, unsympathetic world, until suddenly,
from the hand of an authority, he receives, as it were, justification
and licence for his suffering—justification before the world, this
best of all possible worlds which the master-mind scornfully
demonstrates to be the worst of all possible ones! . . . He felt that
his whole being had unaccountably expanded, and at the same
time there clung about his senses a profound intoxication, a
strange, sweet, vague allurement which somehow resembled the
feelings of early love and longing."—Even the most convinced
opponent of Schopenhauer could not find a better way of presenting him as a leader of decadence.

[1945]

THE CONVERSION OF THOMAS MANN

Lavinia Mazzucchetti

In almost all churches converts are held in special favor. The congregation of believers in a federated Europe may therefore also be permitted to have a special predilection for a great convert to the cause of supra-nationalism and of political co-operation among all countries, and to extend to Thomas Mann devoted and cordial homage upon his seventieth birthday.

We do not wish to commit the indiscretion of claiming Thomas Mann for the federalist movement simply because he finally descended from the clouds and established contact with the concrete political situation of our days; rather, by tracing back the slow and steady development of his thinking during the last twenty-five years, we shall appreciate doubly the comforting value of his solidarity with this cause, a support which came to us from such an opposed camp.

In 1918 Thomas Mann published the *Reflections of a Non-Political Man*, the carefully weighed and weighty document of his Teutonic convictions which were then conservative, opposed to democracy and parliamentarism and to the Western, Latin world. The polemics of this book which originally was directed mainly against his brother Heinrich became in Germany the center of heated discussions of a more far-reaching nature, which were symptomatic of the crisis through which Europe was passing at that crucial moment. I recall that I published in those years (in the old, fervently democratic *Secolo* of Pio Schinetti) a long article, full of juvenile boldness, on the fascinating duel between the two men who symbolized the two Germanies facing one another in the search for a new balance. I observed that for us, incurable (or at least so I believed) democrats and people of the West, it was of much more fundamental importance to understand and combat the dangerous weapons of Thomas Mann than to listen to the obvious truths of his brother. In this dialogue with himself, in a book of more than 600 pages, Thomas Mann furnished a model of true polemics, because here he gave a comprehensive and faithful exposition of the ideas of his opponent.

The book aroused in me respect, but also reassurance, because at the end its author came to the bitter conclusion that Germany, too, would finally be "corrupted" by cosmopolitism, internationalism and the imitation of the evil French example.

Nevertheless, the dialectical superiority of the great "reactionary" was so evident and so fascinating that I feared his cause might be victorious, and I was filled with gloomy forebodings. I asked myself the question: Would the momentary success of Heinrich, the European democrat, really matter much, if the *homo germanicus* were in his essence incurable beyond remedy, as the conservative Thomas describes him? Unfortunately the rapid course of events refuted the fears of the "non-political" prophet and confirmed mine, the humble observer. To this article by me, the unknown writer, the always urbane and generous master replied in an amiable note in which he said that for the country of Mazzini it was only too natural and in agreement with its historical traditions to be "anti-Thomas Mann." It was my good fortune that this letter brought about a meeting with Thomas Mann which later developed into a most valuable friendship. I therefore followed with increasing interest and sympathy the inner development of Thomas Mann, which finally led him to state his views in a sincere public confession of his own errors and to declare himself an adherent of the new faith which he had acquired in the light of reality. He himself had occasion at a later date to define the *Reflections* as a stage in his auto-analysis which was indispensable to the slow dialectical development of his mind; this book was, so to speak, a symptom of the latent crisis which was to be accelerated by the events.

The sickly German democracy was an artificial creation born out of the uncertainties of defeat and officially sanctioned by the false democrats of Versailles. At the time when this flimsy structure was about to go down in a resounding collapse, Thomas Mann discerned on the horizon the approaching shadow of the apocalyptic Anti-Spirit, and felt himself obliged to revise all his convictions. These were the years of his so-called minor writings and of his essays, in which he appears to scatter himself in discussions with too many partners (*Rede und Antwort, Bemühungen, Pariser Rechenschaft*), years in which he answered the reproaches of vanity and lack of concentration with the significant title of his next book of essays: *The Demands of the Day.*

This, in short, is Thomas Mann's great conversion: he became aware that in the totality of the human problem the social and political aspects occupy an essential place. From this newly gained insight into the inseparability of the spirit and of political activity in the highest sense of the word, derive all the later stages of his development, all his courageous conclusions. The year 1923 is the year of his first great message to the new world, his solemn declaration of allegiance to the new Germany, *Oration for the German Republic*. Even before the dark scourges of barbarism had descended on his country, Thomas Mann felt impelled to "unseal his lips." Later, when thinking back on the long road he had travelled, he said: "I am grateful to my good genius for not having concealed my faith in democracy. Where would I find myself today if, because of my conservativism, I had remained faithful to Germanism? Germany, in spite of all her intelligence and all her music, was not able to save herself from the plunge into the idolatry of brutality and into a barbarism which threatens the very foundations of Western civilization."

Thus the great artist who had begun as an individual became the voice of society and of political conscience. In the meantime the super-Germanic artist, the retiring and timid man who hid himself discreetly in the secluded tower of his strenuous work and of his inherited middle class habits, the man who for fifty years had instinctively recoiled from speaking any language other than the mother tongue of his Nordic Hanseatic blood, he who even outside the borders of his country preserved his full identity like a drop of oil in the sea of other ethnic masses—he now felt with ever increasing urgency the necessity of looking beyond his borders, of becoming acquainted with different mentalities, of examining remote social and political experiences, in short, of becoming a true citizen of the world.

His intimate familiarity with father Goethe, particularly with the "old Goethe," during the past few decades, which has been his constant companion (I need only to mention his various essays on Goethe and his bold conjuring up of *The Beloved Returns*) undoubtedly had its share in transforming him into a cosmopolitan mind, without the superficialities sometimes accompanying this change. I remember the Sunday gatherings in his house in Munich, over which he presided like a father, without austerity, but with a special kind of auto-ironical shyness, still a young man in comparison to his grown-up sons who were already his colleagues in literature, and much too subtle for the simplicity of the younger children. I sometimes noticed that he directed many questions to us birds of passage in his busy home, thus creating the impression that we did not rob him of his precious time but on the contrary that we provided him with material for his nest. I dared to tell him once, jokingly, that his house resembled a modern Weimar "Frauenplan" where everybody came to render homage to a poet and where the visitors instead were subjected to unexpected examinations on rather prosaic European events. When we think back to his *Lehrjahre* of political self-education, it is a source of satisfaction to find that he never had even the slightest illusions about fascism in its early stage and that he later always kept a lively interest in the fate of Italian resistance.

The international recognition he received through the Nobel prize in literature in 1929 only confirmed and strengthened his position as a fighter. This honor spurred him to seek even more frequent contacts with foreign countries. In the period preceding Hitler's rise to power, Mann had already made open profession of his philosophical and cultural convictions. When the famous and unforeseen "assumption of power" came, Thomas Mann was by chance outside Germany as an ambassador of German culture, lecturing on Richard Wagner. Not without pain, but without hesitation, he chose the route of voluntary exile. The new regime, lacking in intellectual values, at first showed a curious tolerance toward him, an embarrassed passivity, which strangely enough lasted until 1936; it was as if it appeared too hard, even to Hitlerites, to renounce before the whole world this "pure blood," with its millions of readers. After a short stay in southern France, Thomas Mann enjoyed the hospitality of Switzerland; he received the honorary citizenship of valiant Czechoslovakia, and finally, shortly before the outbreak of the War, he accepted the invitation of America, where he is now living.

In the memory of all good Europeans his anxious appeals during these years of the gathering storm are still alive. These were the years which, through the mental lethargy of the Anglo-Saxon nations, were made perhaps even more tragic than were the following years of lightning and storm.

Thomas Mann's denunciations of the anti-Semitic crimes, his prophecies of inevitable disaster, his castigations of the crimes committed in Spain, his implorings and warnings against the approaching war, have made of him since 1933 more than a German in opposition to the Nazi regime; he has become the voice of the great army of the spirit which took its place on the side of the allied military power. After having fought in vain with the ardor of a David struggling against Goliath or of a St. George wrestling with the dragon for the cause of the good, he took part in the war with the only weapon given him, that of admonition and criticism and the tenacious hope in an ultimate repentance and moral reawakening of his unfortunate mother country. To those familiar with the restraint and reserve of his style, the discreet chastity of his mode of expression, some of his gloomy messages, which faithful B.B.C. sometimes brought us at night, were extremely depressing and disconcerting. They did not reawaken the Germans but we cannot and will not believe that they were seeds sown in vain. The greatest living German has detached himself from his countrymen and allied himself with all free and righteous minds in the world; by this gesture he has broken a gap in the wall of Teutonic unanimity and opened a breach for a breath of hope in the future. Fortunately it was a German who raised the most vehement protest against "Hitler's most impudent lie, namely the criminal perversion of the European idea, the brazen distortion of his pillaging and plundering into an attempt at European unification." It was a German who first solemnly prophesied that Germany would become European, in opposition to Hitler's dream of a Germanized Europe.

Thomas Mann, who after a long pilgrimage came to a supranational conception of the basic ethical and political problems, is today one of the strongest allies of all those who work for a new, concrete and effective universal brotherhood.

He once said that to formulate the human problem in political terms and to approach it this way means for everybody, but especially for the poet, saving his own soul. On the other hand, Harvard University conferred upon him an honorary doctor's degree because "he, together with a small number of his countrymen, has safeguarded the dignity of German civilization." We, as humble and distant co-workers on the edifice which other indefatigable minds are trying to erect, wish to assure him of our great gratitude and sincere devotion. He has not only saved his soul and saved German civilization; he has kindled in the darkest night a flame of faith that all souls of sincerity and good will can be saved. He has been one of the few Germans who promoted life in these last years, while the others promoted death.

Seventy years are brief for a perfect Goethean! Many more years of European wisdom can receive light from his will for good. We do not ask him for a new *Faust*, but we do ask him to continue fighting for us and with us for a more livable future!

[1945]

THE OTHER GERMAN DISASTER

Gabriela Mistral

Hitler has lost for Germany a great portion of its moral being, several cities, Austria, Einstein and Thomas Mann. This last alienation is of no less importance than the others. Any enlightened and honest man of letters knew that Mann was the first writer of the continent.

The great Führer, full of arrogant contempt for superior German culture, afforded himself the supreme delight of eliminating the two first citizens of the Fatherland. They were two bulky acorns lodged in his riding boots; he felt them at each step on his march through Prussia, Brandenburg and Saxony.

I remember the morning when my illustrious friend Curtius sent his colleague, Flasche, to take me to the University of Bonn. There, at the entrance on the bulletin board of university announcements, displayed for greater mockery, hung a copy of the decree expelling Thomas Mann from the University as Doctor Honoris Causa.

To cast out this man from his homeland, stripped of all civil rights, to make of him a wanderer without a country, was to offer him as a citizen to all other nations of the world, nations containing disciples, imitators and friends: an entire family— the great horde of humanity.

No one on earth has the right to slice off from a nation, whose primary excellence springs from its culture, the essence and the epitome of that culture, any more than one has the authority to eliminate the mathematical concept of the unit *million*. In the Capital of Specialism, in Berlin, the expulsion decree demanded the signature of a figure at least equivalent to Mann in magnitude. No such person exists. Neither Goethe nor Nietzsche, if they could rise from their tombs, would have the power to sign a repudiation so fatal despite its imbecility, an edict pernicious to the whole nation.

Totalitarianisms, from the Central American to the German, take for granted in such a case that the silence of a despoiled nation, the stark silence, is equivalent to approval. Among the real and certain guilts of the German people is found the mute authorization of that monstrous travesty. The minority parties could not or would not protest: the conservatives maintained silence because the incident concerned not a traditionalist but a modern; the communists because it referred to a "superb bourgeois." Thus there remained only one voice within all Germany that did not adulate the owners of the hour, the lords of circumstance—Thomas Mann.

Mann emigrated and, as he is a man of decency who has been integrated by acute consequence, he wished to express to the utmost his gratitude; he did not remain a refugee but adopted with his soul as well as with official seals the country that gave him shelter.

I have asked other, lesser, men who have done the same their reasons for not returning to Germany, since return is so sweet when called a vindication. Their answer is as decisive as a hatchet blow: "We were offended not only by Hitlerians in shirts. Civil Germany, professional Germany, and even Christian Germany abandoned us to the furies. No one aided us in our peril and we do not want to live among the former partisans of Hitler."

An extraordinary secession—that of Germany on the one hand and of Einstein and Mann on the other. The severance of those two great colossi from their native land can be compared to geologic displacements, or to the rending of those mountains that in the world of myths are hurled to far regions of the planet, or to the sundering of those glaciers that are flung across the ocean in ambulating cathedrals fleeing in a great silence.

Germany of today has no one who can fill the immense void left by Mann and Einstein. There are many men of secondary importance in German science and literature. But, to the woe of fools, it is impossible in a forest to substitute for the cedar of Lebanon pine trees that have been hoisted one upon another. . . . You may mount five trees in this abnormal fashion but you will never make a cedar. Neither can you bind together several rugs from anywhere and hope to replace with them the great tapestry of Persia that has been torn from the hall of an ancestral manor.

There will be some German readers who will say to all this, "And why so much ado over a mere teller of tales?" Tellers of tales, yes—a relater of physical milieus, of epochs, of social classes, of heroes, patriarchs, of the bourgeois, of the wanderers of the earth. This is equivalent to being a deep-sea diver who penetrates the inmost recesses of man and who puts into our hands and reveals to us, their owners, the most secret parts of ourselves that we never saw before save through those intruders, those scarifiers, those distillers called Dostoyevsky, Balzac, Mann.

In order to write life into his characters, this "mere entertainer" had to smelt down and accumulate vast reserves. He had to mature completely, from forehead to feet, at the precise moment of the century when the concern of the world centered on the palm of the hand; he had to achieve through his own wits and through art an aggregate of faculties that only two or three individuals on a continent are ever able to attain. He labored to bring the fruits of his work to the point of crucial ripeness, to the level of "integral expression," until he was as much a lord of language as of breathing and of walking. He came to be worth several universities put together, without bearing the burden of their dross, carrying within himself the living word. He has bequeathed to the world a broad chronicle of the things of the soul, and in him, as in Shakespeare, none of these seems to be lacking. Mann, the gainer and the rememberer, who had rooted himself in the German and in the European way of life, now, at the age of seventy, is able to adopt a new and opposed civilization without losing any portion of his integrity.

A man with such a combination of gifts and virtues deserved to be cared for, sheltered, venerated, in the land where he attained his genius. Thus does England with people of less stature than Mann: her Masefield and even her Shaw. Mussolini himself did this with Marconi. Classic Germany knew it, and knew it well, but the Germany of boots and revolvers—how could it conceive of this?

What rendered Mann unpardonable, a man to be rejected to such a degree by the Germanies—the Hitlerian (the middle and military class), the popular and the aristocratic Germany? The scandal that a fashioner of novels, upon the advent of the totalitarian debauch, should unthinkingly bring forth from his breast a civil man, a classic liberal in the style of the Athenians . . . or of the English.

They believed him to be a simple weaver of plots; at the most they thought they had the sumptuous luxury of a consummate man of letters, but what they had was the luxury of a universal and eternal man.

Let us consider what has happened. The totalitarianisms are

a kind of general dispensary of drugs—drugs to strengthen the weak, to inebriate the imaginative, to overcome the temperate, to redouble the delirium of the mad; drugs that deaden hunger, that make one forget the Decalogue, that volatilize written and lived history: that submerge the entire memory. To this dispensary—dear God!—almost all came and took the potion from vials that were alike, and of unique stamp: the Basque-Germanic-Aztec swastika. . . .

Upon returning from the distribution of these drugs it was not strange that they should forget Einstein and Mann. Everything tumbled headlong in a matter of moments: cathedrals fell, Kant, Goethe, Schiller, Dürer crashed to the earth. The drugged nation first stunned the world; then it anguished us—there were many of us who loved Germany; finally it shocked us into indignation.

Oh, the marvel of men that did not sip the draught even when they saw "respectable" and "honorable" men drink: marshals, prelates and educators. Einstein and Mann, without need of approaching the tribal pharmacopoeia, breathed in the air its stench, and came to detest it with the same holy hate that sane families of drug addicts feel. To speak, to argue, to try to convince, all this they did there within Germany; but madness was the mistress of the streets, not to mention seats of learning, pulpits, offices, factories.

My Austrian doctor tells me in Rio of something like an interplanetary infection. . . . Thanks be to God that the entire world did not enter into this dementia; but Germany was the Orpheus of the world and in addition the muse of philosophers.

The ultimate adventure of Thomas Mann, the same one that he tells us happened in the grotto of the Goddess Kali, replete with blood and skulls, did not overwhelm him with that dizziness suffered by the native Nazitoides; it was as if there had been a thin current of pure air for him from the beginning to the end of the great debauch.

This man of imagination whose trade is fantasy, frequenter of myths, submerged in the delirium of peoples, becomes a phenomenon; the simple saneness of the German master overwhelms the reader as much as the cycle of the histories of Jacob and Joseph.

On choosing the soil for the last walks of an old man, Thomas Mann must have thought of liberty as an incalculable blessing worth more than a continent, more than the planet itself. His eyes were fixed on the United States. He chose a country that would be *forever* free, without alternations of servitude and independence; a country bred and bound to a liberty as certain as the quadrilateral of its sides. It was natural that this free spirit should choose those people who conquered the enemies of freedom and won for themselves its constant blessing.

[1945]

THE PROBLEM OF ANTI-INTELLECTUALISM

Friedrich Carl Sell

I

Anti-intellectualism in modern Germany is a strong movement that tries to eliminate the preponderance maintained by the intellect in various fields of civilization, in particular in letters, the arts, and philosophy, Although officially sanctioned it is not only a weapon in the political fight against the conservative attitude of mind but a serious problem with a long past and many implications. It has attracted the attention of many distinguished thinkers, among them that of the most prominent German author in America, Thomas Mann. In a way it is the key to his philosophy, which we must understand if we wish to appreciate what he has written, at least in his later year.

It would lead too far afield to analze the political and psychological sources from which anti-intellectualism dervies its strength. They are rather accidental and certainly not as important as the intellectual sources, which deserve a special examination. In this respect our phenomenon is associated with a more general trend in history. The evolution of European civilization may be regarded as a continuous alteration of rationalism and irrationalism in various *nuances*. Rationalism comprehends and guides life preferably by reason; it appreciates reality. The classical Greek civilization, the Renaissance, the Enlightenment, and the technical age are its outstanding representations. Irrationalism believes in religious feeling, in the creative genius, in visions, in music, in instinct, in intuition, in unconscious vitality. Early Christianity, medieval mysticism, Gothic art, the ecstasies of the Counter-Reformation and the Baroque, and Romanticism mark its phases.

The Nineteenth Century was under the spell of rationalism as exhibited by the capitalist bourgeoisie and its well-being. In Germany a reaction began when the despairing cry of Friedrich Nietzsche became audible, protesting against the shallow platitudes of bourgeoisie and liberalism, the superficiality of religious beliefs and conventional morality, or in brief, against the predominance of reason in its most unattractive form. Nietzsche found what this modern civilization lacked: an influx of the Dionysian element which once had formed the true Greek culture before it became static, reasonable, and Apollonian. "Dionysian" means consenting to life, though it inflicts the greatest hardships; it means a will for life, a desire for, including even a joy in, destruction. Its discovery determined Nietzsche's philosophy, culminating finally in the "will to power."

Ridiculed first, later dreaded as a revolutionary, Nietzsche ultimately was praised by a constantly growing public. His fearless opposition, his monumental outlook, the respect for greatness and singularity fascinated progressive minds. Even outstanding liberals, like Max Weber, the sociologist, and Ernst Troeltsch, the philosopher of religion and history, were deeply influenced by him. In Germany, Nietzsche's doctrine impressed and directed the intellectual movement which was called by the very unsatisfactory name of Neo-Romanticism. We should better say: Neo-Irrationalism. Its outstanding author was Stefan George, a poet of truly creative power. He regarded himself as the prophet of a future age, shaped on the lines of Nietzsche's superman. Convinced of his vocation, he formed a sort of sacral union with a few unconditionally devoted followers and friends amidst the prosaic surroundings of modern civilization.

To this circle, which partly resided at Schwabing, the center of the Munich bohème, three men were attached who became fatal to the development of anti-intellectualism: Karl Wolfskehl, Alfred Schuler and Ludwig Klages. At the beginning in close co-operation, later in hostile jealousy, these three concentrated upon a theory which they believed would solve the problem of modern civilization and decadence. Karl Wolfskehl came across the forgotten ideas of Johann Jakob Bachofen (1815-1887). This quiet patrician of Basle had discovered gynaecocracy as the original and formative principle of human society. In prehistoric times the mother, not the father, was the ruler and the representative of the family. Motherhood as a supreme social value stands in full harmony with nature, reflecting the unity of the universe and the pains of mortality: physical health, beauty, instinct, the connection with the maternal earth, but not the intellect. It was patriarchism that used the intellect in order to abolish the rule of motherhood and to gain control of the forces of nature which so far had dominated life.

Schuler and Klages eagerly seized these ideas, with which Wolfskehl had made them familiar. According to Bachofen's

belief in the influence of cosmic powers, they experienced cosmic
ecstasies, whispering about a coming *Blutleuchte,* the great catastrophe which was at hand. These supersensitive and self-
centered intellectuals cherished the hope that the human soul
would reassume its original powerful simplicity and that the
hateful present order of things would be overthrown. They found
themselves disappointed when nothing happened, and when Stefan George refused to take public action as redeemer of the
world. This brought about a break between him and Klages as
well as Schuler, a break that became irrevocable through the
singular and majestic maliciousness of George.

Henceforth Klages buried himself in graphology and psychology for two decades until he finally produced a work that was
the outcome of those early impulses and the standard proclamation of modern anti-intellectualism: *Der Geist als Widersacher
der Seele* (1929-32), intellect as the enemy of the soul. Body,
soul, and intellect are the elements of human nature; but only
body and soul are real poles of life. Into their union the intellect
intrudes like a wedge, trying to disrupt the harmony by depriv-
ing the body of psychical and the soul of physical influences. In
fact, the intellect kills every kind of life it can get hold of.

Klages described the fatal career of the intellect from Socrates, the founder of its supremacy, down to Americanism, whatever that may be to his mind. Under the influence of the intellect,
vitality degenerated into mere activity, and imagination into
rationalism. Klages' animosity against everything he believes to
be intellectual is unlimited; and he resents the logical principles
of thinking as well as the causalities of science and the moral
regulations of Christianity. Still, it is amazing to note what he advocates in the place of the ominous predominance of the intellect,
viz., a sultry swamp of unbridled instincts and passions, thinly
concealed, if concealed at all, behind some pathetic Dionysian
formulas.

II

It does not appear likely that Thomas Mann had any connection with this strange phenomenon. He never belonged to the
peculiar circle of Schwabing, having met Schuler only once and
Wolfskehl occasionally. His personality is as contrary as possible
to that of mystical priests and prophets of a new creed. He was,
however, a keen observer of what was going on in literary life,
and the problem, raised by Nietzsche and complicated by Klages,
affected him especially because it is the very problem of his art:
the controversy and the antagonism of life and *Geist.*

Thomas Mann's career began when the period of European decadence had reached its final phase. His first and most brilliant narrative, *Buddenbrooks*, "der vielleicht erste und einzige naturalistische Roman," presents a picture of decadence resulting from biological exhaustion, pathological degeneration, and refinement of aesthetic sensitiveness. The situation is without hope: it is a picture "der leidenden Seelenlage des Abendlandes" at the end of the Nineteenth Century. Refinement is separation from actual life; and this was his own problem, extensively related in his self-confession, *Tonio Kröger*. Here what he calls *Geist*, the gift of sensitive understanding and creative observation, is confronted with natural, innocent, instinctive life. The artist is excluded from the life his soul yearns for. This topic of exclusion is varied again and again in Thomas Mann's works, in *The Dilettante, Tristan, Little Herr Friedmann*. It turns in a more positive direction in *Royal Highness*, the story of the lonely prince amidst his subjects in the typical German *Kleinstaat* and his love for the equally lonely daughter of the American millionaire. But this highly amusing and technically excellent work was not convincing. Thomas Mann himself regarded it rather as a play, "ein Kunstspiel, nicht Leben," a momentary forced eruption, an attempt to find a solution, to break the ring of isolation by developing a sense of social responsibility. The following novel, *Death in Venice*, however, shows the terrible danger the refined and high-spirited intellectualist and artist runs if he is suddenly exposed to an attack by life, by abnormal passion, which affects him infinitely more than it would an average man, and which completely wrecks him.

Spiritual refinement must be paid for by the exclusion from life, this is the conviction of Thomas Mann in this period. A secret and profound sympathy with death compensates those cultivated individuals for the loneliness they must suffer.

The results of the first fifteen or sixteen years of Thomas Mann's literary effort show the influence of the three great powers who determined his intellectual attitude: Schopenhauer, Wagner and Nietzsche.

Schopenhauer's grand pessimism, his doctrine of the individual's return into nothingness as the most desirable thing in life, was the favorite philosophy of European decadence in the second half of the nineteenth century. In *Buddenbrooks* Thomas Mann expressed his admiration for the superior brains which mastered and condemned the strong and brutal and cruel life by mercilessly revealing its futility. Yet he already indicated a

coming change in the sinister doctrine, in that Thomas Buddenbrook, reconciled to his individual end, believes that his existence
will be perpetuated in other, more vital individualities.

Richard Wagner's art has fascinated Thomas Mann during
his whole life, "die Passion für Wagners zaubervolles Werk
begleitet mein Leben," and he was deeply impressed by the
moral pessimism, the mood of decay of the magnificent music,
the romantic glorification of the dark and the night, and the
sympathy with death. Nevertheless, his objective critical vein
was not silenced by devotion, and we owe to him the best and
most broadminded analysis of Wagner's place in history. The
romanticism of Wagner, however was a danger, a kind of alluring seduction which he more and more resisted, aligning himself
with the opposition of Nietzsche against Wagner, despite an everlasting, though hidden, passionate love.

Nietzsche's influence on Thomas Mann's intellectual life was
the most important one. In the first place he adopted Nietzsche's
criticism of the artist's character in the period of decay: it is
the critique of Hanno Buddenbrook, of Tonio Kröger, of Gustave
von Aschenbach. Nietzsche taught self-denial of spirit and intellect in favor of life, "an enthusiastic, erotically intoxicated
submission to power." Yet Thomas Mann did not adopt Nietzsche's doctrine without reserve. First, he is in open sympathy
with spirit and intellect, although they are doomed to failure.
Secondly, there is a very interesting difference between Nietzsche's conception of life and Thomas Mann's. Nietzsche set an
imaginative Dionysian and heroic life against the intellect of
decadence, whereas Thomas Mann, more realistic, saw from the
beginning that this conception of life was a fiction. Brutal life,
which overrules the decadent, subtle intellectual he is so fond
of, is not heroic; it is cruel, banal, trivial. It is the disillusioned
truth, which in fact makes Thomas Mann's pessimism more toler-
able than Nietzsche's illfounded enthusiasm, for it produces his
outstanding artistic quality: a merciless, and by its very accuracy
and its irony, a delightful naturalism. The chief instrument of the
naturalism was irony. Irony was implied in the self-denial of the
intellect, and so this self-denial was not absolutely serious, not
complete. "Irony tries secretly to win people for the intellect
(*Geist*), although without hope."

III

A delicate melancholy with a humorous touch, this is the attitude of Thomas Mann during his first phase of subjective in-

dividualism, made attractive by his dignified self-discipline. Yet intellect or mind or spirit—whatever translation for *Geist* one chooses is undoubtedly separate from life; and he too stands on the side of romantic death.

It was the war that brought forth a crisis. Mann had thought to speak for himself, to deal with personal problems. The war taught him that everybody is connected with society, even unconsciously. "Man glaubt nur sich zu geben, nur von sich zu reden, und siehe, aus tiefer Gebundenheit und unbewusster Gemeinschaft gab man Überpersönliches." The crisis became evident in his *Reflections of a Non-Political Man*. This peculiar and voluminous book, published in 1918, was directed against his own brother Heinrich Mann, whom he branded as the type of a *Zivilisationsliterat,* representing the Western spirit, Western rational criticism, Western belief in democracy and progress. He confronted this Western spirit, which propagated the victory of Western democracies over German reaction, with what he thought to be the real German spirit, with Schopenhauer's noble pessimism, Nietzsche's irrationalism, conservative romanticism, with everything which was dear to hm. Nevertheless he seemed to be extremely unhappy, for the fronts of this controversy were, in fact, confused. He believed he was fighting for the true spirit against superficiality of life and cruelty of cold reason. But was this really true? Could he deny that he himself had liked the idea of freedom, and was not the Western, in particular the French, mind in its classical clarity equally spiritual with the German?

The final solution he found in this dilemma was his abandonment of the original antithesis of intellect, or *Geist,* and life. During the following years he learned that the victory of democracy by no means produced the general standardization of the mind that he had dreaded so much. None of the dangers he had foreseen actually occurred; and now he parted with his individual isolation, feeling a new social responsibility and turning away from the sweet, alluring romanticism of Wagner and the ecstasies of Nietzsche towards the deliberate service of life itself. His essay *Von deutscher Republik* (1922) and *Rede über Nietzsche* (1924) mark this new turn. It is interesting to observe how general the terms of his praise of Nietzsche become now, in view of his former, very definite statements. The "fair beast" and the Dionysian ecstasy apparently disgusted him and he confines his praise to phrases like "a friend of life, a prophet of higher humanity, a leader into the future"—that is, away

from romanticism. He describes the evolution of that time as
follows: "No metamorphosis of the mind is more familiar to us
than that which begins with the sympathy with death and ends
with a resolution for life."

What, then, is the part intellect and spirit play in his new
conception of life? It is at this time that Goethe gains importance
with him. In the great essay *Goethe and Tolstoy* he describes these
two individualities as natural and naive geniuses in contrast to
Schiller and Dostoyevsky, who are sentimental and represent
the *Geist*. *Geist* still means morbidity and romanticism. Yet, after
all, it is the outstanding indication of what is really human. *Geist*
is what distinguishes man from all other organic life, and the
question is "whether man is not the more human the more dis-
severed he is from nature." Here Thomas Mann takes up an idea
which Herder had discussed when trying to define what humanity really means.

The poetical expression of this change is *The Magic Mountain*. This book is the final overcoming of the sympathy with
death, the turn toward life; and it is not without irony (typical
of Thomas Mann) that a confession of will for life contains more
about death than all the preceding books of pessimism. His new
insight is revealed by Hans Castorp's adventure in the snowstorm: "Der Mensch soll um der Güte and Liebe willen dem
Tode keine Herrschaft einräumen über seine Gedanken." *The
Magic Mountain* was intended to be, the author says, "a book
of good will and of resolution, a book of farewell to many beloved
things, many a dangerous sympathy, a book . . . of educational
self-discipline. Its service is service of life, its will is health, its
aim is the future. . . ." This was the author's intention; whether
he succeeded in making it completely clear in his extraordinary
book is perhaps another question.

The problem of *Geist* versus life is completely dropped as far
as the original antithesis of art and life goes. Yet it reappears in
another form. The impartial satire describes three attitudes toward life, three extremes: those of the rational intellectualist,
the rational anti-intellectualist, and the unconscious instinctive
irrationalist. As the protagonist of rationalism, of progressive life,
of spirit against the body we have the Italian *litterateur* Settembrini; the antagonist of reason, of liberalism, of intellect and humanity, and the propagator of discipline, obedience, primitive
devotion is the intellectualist Naphta—Jesuit, Jew, and bolshevist.
Natural, instinctive, vital life is represented by the majestic and
foolish figure of Mynheer Peeperkorn, who never finishes any

of his mysterious sentences. It is said that he is to a certain extent a portrait of Gerhart Hauptmann. The hero of the novel does not identify himself with any of those principles, for the idea of life and humanity he finally reaches is "die Idee der Mitte." This is not a clear solution, and in that it resembles life, which seldom solves definitely any problem. Thomas Mann worried in particular about Naphta, the fighter against rational humanism. For it was now that he came into touch with the doctrine which threatened to undermine the position he had recently gained.

In the essay *Freud's Position in the History of Modern Thought* Mann surveys the intellectual tendencies of the Nineteenth and the Twentieth Centuries. These stand opposed to rationalism, intellectualism, and classicism, emphasizing instead the shadow side of nature and the soul as the actual life-conditioning and life-giving element. It is the cry: back into the night, to the sacred primitive, to the romantic, prehistoric mother womb. The powerlessness of mind and reason and their shallow optimism is contrasted with the dynamics of passion, the irrational the unconscious. This historical line begins with Romanticism and continues to Klages and Spengler, the prophet of the decline of the West. There is no doubt about Thomas Mann's attitude toward this theory. As early as 1924 he wrote against the "iron scholar" Spengler in most bitter terms, calling him a defeatist of humanity and his treatment of mind and reason a snobbery.

He is, however, fully aware of the feebleness of the reason and the intellect, their oft proven incapacity to condition life. In his opinion, this should give rise to the desire to pity and protect the weak, not to treat them as though there were danger that they might become too strong, as Klages and his followers do. He admits that the new science and knowledge of the subconscious depth, the exploration of the unconscious driving power of the instinct means progress. It is not so much the idea he criticizes as the fact that those intellectual anti-intellectualists do not worry about the abuse of the new doctrine for the purpose of destroying humanity. "There is today no false and hypocritical conversation, no hatred and fear of the future, no cant or stupidity, no spirit of brutal reaction . . . which has not felt itself strengthened by the sympathy with the irrational displayed by modern research . . . has not tried to establish contact with it . . . to make political capital out of it, to translate it into terms of social anti-revolution and thus make a crude reaction appear in the disguise of revolution." To the mind of such people social amelioration, sympathy with humane aims, with the world's yearning after spiritual unity is simply shallow internationalism and pacifistic sophistry. "Against all that, there stands in the revolutionary freshness of youth the dynamic principle, mindless nature, the folk-soul, hatred, war." War is the final issue of this tendency.

The essay on Freud is not the only place in which Mann has discussed this question. His appeal *Achtung Europa!* contains even more precise formulations of the lack of responsibility shown by the modern theorists of anti-intellectualism, who disregard the fact that intellect and morality share a common fate in that contempt of mind and reason is followed inevitably by a decay of morals. By the time this essay was written Thomas Mann was already involved in the fight against National Socialism. The essay on Freud was published in 1929 at a time when he was able to speak with greater objectivity than at present.

Disclosing its dangers does not solve the problem of modern irrationalism. The example of Freud gives proof how it should be handled. Freud's psychoanalysis acknowledges the actual superiority of the impulse over the mind. "The voice of the intellect is low," says Freud, "but it does not rest until it gets a hearing. In the end, after countless repulses, it gets one." Freud believes the civilization of the present day to be unstable and insecure, similar to the state in which a neurotic patient, without a will to recovery, comes to terms with his symptoms. Progress can be made by increasing consciousness. Mann was deeply impressed by the problem Freud put before him. The question of the relation of instinct and reason, of increasing consciousness, becomes more and more important in his eyes. It is indeed the central problem of his greatest piece of prose fiction, the still unfinished Joseph novel.

This extraordinary work of already 1,555 pages is not always easy reading on account of the epic slowness of the narrative and a certain abundance of detail. It uncovers perhaps too much Thomas Mann's method of working, that careful elaboration of what he once called his *Kunstgespinst,* the original plan of which underwent fundamental changes. Nevertheless it is a wonderful Oriental carpet that he spreads before us, with admirable and impressive details. We seem to smell the desert and the Bedouin camp, to see the stony hills of Palestine and the magnificent splendor of ancient Egypt. The author succeeds in making the past live as the present. Nevertheless, it is not just another historical novel. Not facts and events of the past but the *myth* of the past is the subject of Mann's story, a myth presented in an unusually careful and sometimes ironical fashion. Nevertheless, this modern style does not spoil the illusion in the least degree, and this is one of the major charms of this book.

The nature of this myth is explained in the strange introduction, "Prelude," which has discouraged many a reader from further reading. "Prelude" means the return into the mysterious, sinister, and terrible depth of the past, a past so far away that the limits between centuries and ages have become dim, and myth and reality confused. It is the myth of soul, matter, and *Geist*, whose relations form the novel of the adventures of the human soul. Soul and matter were original principles, possessing life, but neither knowledge nor consciousness. God sent *Geist* in order to explain to the soul that only its mixture with matter had formed the world and created death. If the soul would leave matter, the world of forms would disappear together with death; and this process will be due to the interference of *Geist*. Yet this original idea of liberating the soul was gradually changed under the influence of world and life. *Geist* feels itself to be the deadly principle. This was the conceptoin of the biblical story of the fall of man. It is also the modern theory of Klages.

Whether we accept or reject this idea depends on our individual decision. So far Thomas Mann is perfectly tolerant with regard to such views. But this decision should be made according to the individual's gift and character, otherwise it would be *Verderbnis*, perversion. This remark obviously aims at those intellectualists who oppose intellectualism.

The mythical conflict of *Geist* and life is the leading idea of the entire Joseph novel. Young Joseph, handsome, intelligent, pleasant, is much shrewder than his unconscious and instinctive brothers. His arrogance makes them feel inferior and arouses annoyance and resentment. He represents the superior intellect segregated from the sphere of simple and primitive instincts and impulses. His downfall and humiliation chasten him; in captivity his mind learns to adapt itself to the surrounding world and to develop a moral firmness which is based on sentiment as well as reason. What saves him in the moment of temptation is the feeling of obligation, not to his master, but to his moral self, that issue of tradition, of soul and reason. This is as far as the story has gone. The final volume, *Joseph the Provider*, containing the reconciliation of Joseph and his brothers according to the biblical story, must present a reconciliation between the purified mind and the penitent instincts, a harmonization of principles hitherto opposed to each other.

Is there, however, any substantial reason to assume that such a thing ever has happened or was believed to have happened? Here we must turn again to the preface. Myth and mysteries deal very freely with a succession of events and may exchange past and future. They tell things as occurrences in bygone ages which are expected to happen in a coming time. "It is possible that the verdict that soul and *Geist* have been a unit means that sometime they may become one. This seems to us the more conceivable since the *Geist* represents the principle of the future . . . whereas the piety of the soul is devoted to the holy past." Thus the story of Joseph does not state a fact, but expresses a hope. It is not the one-sided expectation that *Geist* will absolutely predominate as nature without spirit. It is perhaps the secret hope of God that both will be combined, permeating and hallowing each other. This would produce "ein Menschentum, das gesegnet wäre mit Segen oben vom Himmel herab und mit Segen von der Tiefe, die unten liegt." This passage offers the clue to the novel and summarizes Mann's philosophy at the same time.

The clue to the novel! We can not help wondering why Thomas Mann, the realist of the modern age, selected this far-fetched subject, why he became fascinated when he was asked to write a few pages of preface to a series of lithographs on Joseph. A myth condenses a human problem and eliminates any accidental elements, and this must have attracted him. Moreover, he may have wished to test his strength in a field completely new to him, as an act of rejuvenescence. But above all, it appealed to him when he sought a way to express his anxiety and his hope in his own style as a narrator. A *myth* with the privilege of taking the past as the future *offered the opportunity to describe in narrative form what can be only a dim, though ardent, hope.* In doing this the novel summarizes what Mann had struggled for and what he had held up against the doubts of his own mind and the hostilities of the outside world: the idea of humanity.

[1940]

THE FATE OF AN ARTIST

B. Suchkov

It seems ironical that Thomas Mann's seventieth birthday should coincide with a momentous event in current history—the capitulation of Germany. A German by birth and language, the author of *Buddenbrooks, Joseph* and *The Beloved Returns* observed his birthday in far-off America, witnessing with horror the downfall of his nation and seeing history stand trial over his fatherland.

Musing over his eventful career, so firmly impressed upon the world, he remembers the quiet streets of Lübeck, the noisy Bohemian life of Munich, and leafs through the pages of *Reflections of a Non-Political Man*—written in those dark days of World War I and conceived during the period of social instability of the Weimar Republic; and he recalls the streets of Berlin and the bonfires which destroyed his writings. Has he striven enough to prevent these fires from rekindling? What has been the nature of his creative development? "There are no accidents," Voltaire said. "Everything in life is either experience or punishment or laurels or resourcefulness." What were the fruits of Thomas Mann's long and creative years as a pillar of German culture? Were they Maidanek, Oswieczim? What did he foresee when he wrote of the downfall of German patricianism or presented the stoicism of his heroes—the "little people," the Piepsams, Minder-nickels, Friedemanns? Did he visualize—out of the Germans' *Gemütlichkeit*, the respect for "order" and "discipline"—the birth of a soulless robot, the Hitlerite soldier the world came to know? Did he, in his studies of Nietzsche and Schopenhauer, anticipate that their theories of will and force would lay the foundation for fascism—the ideology of killing? Did he anticipate that the passive resignation of his heroes to their historically predestined fate, their willingness to die, were factors in the German frame of mind which the ecclesiastical wisdom of his writings could not penetrate? Yes, he hated prussianism; he passionately and fiercely denounced "Pan-German Reaction"; with all the forces at his disposal he—as a gifted pamphleteer—

wrote against the heinous philosophy of Spengler and other such theorists. He raised his voice in anger against fascism and, most German of Germany's writers, he turned against her, condemning Hitlerism. And so, in his later years, he possesses only that which he has lived through—that and disillusionment, experiences for his future work (for his talent is ever productive) and regret for the past, because his creative career has been, perhaps, full of errors.

Thomas Mann is a writer of extraordinary intellectual range. None among his contemporaries is able to handle difficult philosophical problems as easily and competently. Few western writers have as deep a feeling for the pace of history. He possesses the rare gift of penetrating to the depths of the human psyche, where nothing is small or insignificant to him. He identifies a social process with every psychological development. His *Magic Mountain*, an almost Socratic work based on the intellectual arguments of its three heroes—Castorp, Settembrini and Naphta—is primarily a sociological novel which deals with the burning problem of life in Europe between two world wars—the question of the genesis of fascism. The Joseph novel, notwithstanding its Biblical coloring, represents the author's reflections on the future of humanity. And *The Beloved Returns*, ably and artistically written in the maner of Goethe, has nothing in common with the notorious biographical novel that occupied so important a place in the literature of pre-war Europe. In this work, dedicated to the problem of the fate of Germany and her struggles between the forces of reaction and progress, Thomas Mann excels at handling sociological factors. The brilliance of his psychology is only the inner lining, the special quality of his realism.

Thomas Mann entered the field of literature as a social artist. His first novel, *Buddenbrooks*, which brought him acclaim throughout Europe, is an almost scientific analysis of the reasons for the collapse of the patriarchal middle class system under the newly created conditions of imperialism. That, in short, is the basic subject of the novel. Yet, as a masterfully executed social study, it is of far-reaching importance. In working on *Buddenbrooks* Thomas Mann arrived at an unexpected conclusion: he discovered that with the extinction of the Buddenbrooks and their traditions the whole social structure and concept of government disappeared; the very system which had produced people like the Buddenbrooks and their traditions collapsed.

In those days at the beginning of the century Thomas Mann still tackled problems of the kind which were dealt with by

Rolland in his famous books, *Farewell to the Past* and *Death of a World*.

The passion and sorrow of *Buddenbrooks* are witnesses of Mann's attachment to a dying world. History gave him the opportunity to choose between the newly formed social forces which tried to rebuild the world and those which were intent on maintaining the status quo. Thomas Mann, unlike Rolland, decided to take the conservative path. This decision became the turning point of his creative career. While Mann's brother, Heinrich, tried all his life to escape the yoke of the ruling class, Mann voluntarily accepted it. His art regressed from the forthright and progressive to self-centered seclusion, assuming the characteristics of aristocracy: refinement and superfluous philosophy. Thus began a trying and extended period in the life of the writer, a period of conflict within himself, conflict against the forces of the good, the decent, the unspoiled.

Thomas Mann solved this conflict (which was caused by something common to all Europe—the increased activity of the masses and their influence on the social way of life) in typically German fashion—i.e., he transferred the practical problems of life to the realm of metaphysics. This reaction was typical, not new. The history of "German ideology" is full of such compromises. Fichte and Schelling, Hegel and Richard Wagner willingly served the German bourgeoise, sacraficing their half-hearted "freethinking." In the course of time the reservoir of "freethinking" among German ideologists ran dry and the aggressiveness of the German bourgeoisie increased. Once having become the slave of the cynical and uncouth bourgeoisie, the "ideology" of the new era took great pains to justify and defend prussianism and plutocracy, and in the end served as the basis for the humanity-hating ravings of Houston Chamberlain, O. Spengler and, finally, Rosenberg. The reactionary element of German ideology engulfed Thomas Mann too. The concepts of historic evolution and social development which he had evolved had been formulated under the combined influences of Schopenhauer and Nietzsche. And, although the healthy foundation of his art, untouched by decadence, saved him from the extremes of nationalism, he stained his spotless biography as an artist by writing such books as *Frederick the Great and the Grand Coalition* and *Reflections of a Non-Political Man.* These were not merely innocent excursions into history and international politics; during the period preceding the First World War and during the war itself they were available to the German nationalists.

How easily the capital truths of so-called humanism are sometimes forgotten! However, Thomas Mann was soon to remember
them, although under changed historic circumstances.

The great adventure of Kaiser Wilhelm came to an end—
the intoxication of general chauvinism gave way to a grievous
hangover. New social movements which had had nothing in
common with nationalist reaction sprang up in central Germany
as well as in the Ruhr, Saxony and Bavaria. It was then that
reactionaries of all descriptions, filled with the lust for revenge,
embarked the country upon a wave of white terror, bent on
wiping out all opposition within Germany. The "Black Reichs-
wehr," Von Epp's brigade, composed of youths who had been
bandits, did not lack the financial support of the magnates of
capital, the Krupps, Thyssens, et cetera. Blood flowed freely.

Thomas Mann realized that his abstract position covered
many issues with which he did not agree. He made an important
step to the left, not toward nationalism but toward liberalism.
And although, as before, he sided with the governing ideology,
he took a stand against the obviously detestable deeds committed
by the governing clique. In his *Magic Mountain* he pointed to the
beginnings of fascism. Leo Naphta—Jesuit, Catholic, fascist and
forerunner of totalitarianism—evokes Mann's wrath and condemnation. In the character of Settembrini, Mann satirizes the barrenness of "democratism," the leftist phraseology of various and
sundry upholders of "humanitarianism." And although the writer
had nothing to say in opposition to the social reaction except an
appeal to humaneness, nevertheless he did not withdraw from
his ideas but strove toward the solution of common problems,
toward humanity as a whole. Mann was by now fully aware of
the danger which fascist-inclined Germany constituted, yet he had
difficulty in freeing himself from the meshes of "German ideology." The studies of the new social structure to which Mann
devoted himself after the First World War are half-hearted and
inconsequential. As before he regards history as a struggle between reaction and progress; and as before he considers the focal
point of social development the socially isolated human being,
beside whom the never-ending stream of life flows unceasingly
and hostilely. True, Mann no longer considers society a tragic
balance of the powers of good and evil—and into his outlook
there enters a new note, the belief in the final triumph of humaneness, in the ability of man to fight off the powers of evil.

If humaneness is developed in the human being, muses
Thomas Mann, he will, after having gone through a great many

difficult experiences, reach a god-like status and will establish righteousness on earth. It is easily noticed that his concept of history carries the stamp of the decadent theory of "eternal restitution," of the "cycle of history," softened by the absence of cynical skepticism. It is also obvious that Thomas Mann had undertaken only the first steps in his fight against fascism. That is why the staid hero of *The Magic Mountain* is the simple, mediocre, ordinary, righteous, moderate bourgeois typical almost to the point of banality. Although he is educated to be a thinking human being, a being capable of distinguishing between good and evil, Hans Castorp, in his transformation, does not produce an active, aggressive personality capable of fighting fascism. That is also the reason why the style of the novel is so tedious and abstract and why it falls so far short of being a real and great work of art. *The Magic Mountain* is a novel written by a great artist, but by one who has spent his intellect and talent unproductively.

The efforts of Thomas Mann are reminiscent of those of inventors of perpetual motion machines: brainracking contraptions brilliantly conceived, but without motion. Mann's trouble was that, while moving toward a more progressive viewpoint, he remained a metaphysician in his art. However, his next great work, the *Joseph*, was nevertheless an anti-fascist novel.

As long ago as his Weimar days Thomas Mann had determined that fascism aimed at the destruction of culture and the establishment of barbarism. Writing, as he did, against fascism, he attempted to point out that a fascist victory was unthinkable. For the struggle against fascism was one of the skirmishes of the eternal fight between the forces of reaction and progress, in which humaneness emerges victorious. To amplify his thesis Mann turned to the history of Joseph the Excellent, retaining in the details of his plot all of the Biblical myth.

In the first book of Genesis, in the section on the fate of mankind, there is a curious thing: the story consists of a series of repetitions. The incidents in the life of Abraham are repeated, in greater detail and under different circumstances, in the life of Isaac; the latter's life, in turn, is repeated, to a lesser extent, in Jacob's; and incidents similar to those in the latter's love-life are experienced by Joseph. Thomas Mann utilizes this theme of repetition in his novel in order to analyze the history of mankind as a recurrence of events, a process of changing sameness, as it were, during which society slowly but steadily is humanized in its lengthy struggle against the historically evil forces.

The hero of the novel is Joseph the Excellent—an ideal hero, personifying humanity, whose fate is the fate of humanity. The mishaps in his life fail to injure the nobility of his personality. Humaneness, embodied in Joseph, emerges victoriously throughout his experiences. Thus contemporary humanity will triumph over fascism, for humaneness is eternal and evil mortal. This main thesis of his novel is strengthened by Thomas Mann by means of original argumentation: to the effect that humanity had always believed that its soul was eternal. Verification of this fact is found in the myth of the rebirth of gods—Dionysus, Christ, Adonis, Osiris. The involved Semitic, Egyptian, Assyro-Babylonian, antique mythologies are utilized by Mann to stress a simple point: the human being as such is great, and the ravages of fascism will not halt his progress. The novel champions humanity and is directed against the gloom of fascism. This belief in humanity and in its creative genius and strength turned Thomas Mann into a champion of anti-fascism.

The history of the pre-war European mind attests to the fact that only those who believed in the creative power of humanity did not succumb to the influence of fascism. The indifferent cynics and the decrepit sceptics, one of whom made the infamous statement that "it is better to be a live German than a dead Frenchman"—all these Judases outdid each other in submissiveness to the prussian boot. Those defeatists, those corrupted souls, kept whispering to humanity: "Give in, be afraid, don't trust yourself!" Those sorry bootlickers of fascism! And then there were the writers who had experienced fear for their lives or had preferred to recede into the narrow sphere of intellectualism—a crystal world, as it were—in order to avoid contact with the burning issues of the contemporary world. They did not offer their helping hands to humanity, bleeding to death. They silently waited to see who would win, scanning the map for a haven where fascism might not reach them. Thomas Mann, however, was among those others who eyed the impending danger fearlessly and called for resistance. Alas, his ideas had been widely accessible, although he had directed his writings toward humanity. Thomas Mann finally understood, as the dark smoke of the crematoriums rose to the sky, that fascism could not be countered with essays on the beliefs of primitive nations but had to be fought with the simple and forthright language of the bayonet.

In his articles published from 1941 to 1944 he gave due credit to the feats of the Soviet warrior, who annihilated the fascist beasts, and called on the freedom-loving nations to be pitiless toward Nazis and Nazism. History taught Thomas Mann simplicity.

The fate of Thomas Mann is a dramatic lesson. Truly great art is nourished by the juices of a progressive ideology and responds to the demands of the people. All too long did Thomas Mann search for the truth in a place where its light did not shine. He paid a great price for his blindness.

Fate equipped him with a great artistic genius. He earned the world's acclaim. History offers him the opportunity to free himself of erroneous illusions and false hopes. The living forces of his talent, his belief in mankind and his love of the truth, currently enjoy powerful support. The rest is up to art and conscience.

[1945]

ON POETIC FICTION

Joseph Wittlin

The old man who for several years now has been delivering my daily bread to my house in Riverdale, in the outskirts of New York, was born in Sicily. He has charm. His Italian is pure, untinged with any dialect, and he knows it. He takes a modest satisfaction in correcting my mistakes in his native tongue. On occasion he has proverbs and maxims handy, some of which recall the times when Greek gods were still trodding the Sicilian soil.

Many years of his life have been spent baking bread or delivering it, and yet he seems to be aware that man lives not by bread alone. One indication of this awareness appears to be his interest in my work. One day he asked me whether I had read *The Divine Comedy*. When I told him that I had, he inquired further: "What do you think—was Dante ever really in hell?"

With this astonishing query he touched on the essential problem of all poetic fiction, no matter whether it meets the reader's eye in *terza rima*, in hexameters, or in prose. What did the old baker mean by stressing the word "really" in his question? Presumably, the spell to which he succumbed in reading the *Inferno* was too strong for him to believe that any man could possibly describe the appearance, the structure, the institutions and inhabitants of hell in such precise detail without having passed through it on his own feet and having seen all of its horrors with his own eyes.

As late as a few years ago, certainly until the outbreak of the war, I should have found it less difficult than today to give my Sicilian a satisfactory answer. I might have ventured to tell him in those days that no living person had yet set foot in hell—that only the souls of men were going to hell, not the feet of men. This subject might have so intrigued our baker as to oblige me to add an explanation: that hell is an ancient fiction of mystical visionaries and mystical moralists among almost all the peoples of antiquity—a fiction which was later taken over by the escha-

Written in honor of Thomas Mann's seventieth birthday.

tological religious systems of the Middle Ages, and which celebrated its poetic triumph in *The Divine Comedy*. Probably, in
those days, I should have mentioned also that medieval art and
literature always represented hell as something worse than earth
—a place in which those who have sinned on earth suffer eternal
punishment because the heavenly judgment has not deemed them
worthy even of purgatory. As for Dante, I might have said that
he created his own hell on the basis of some antique and medieval
visions, that he populated it as he saw fit and described it so
plastically as to give us the illusion that he really had been there.

So this is a game, fixed up between him and us—for we often
give the poets a measure of credit for telling us fictitious, generally fantastic incidents as if they had really taken place. Perhaps
I might finally have pointed out to our Sicilian that there are
such things as hallucinations and mental borderline states between dream and wakefulness—and in so doing, of course, I
should have fully respected his Catholic faith.

Now, however, after six years of this war, I should be compelled to revise my ideas of what hell really is and where it is.
Of Dante's hell we know that it was located far underground—
to be exact, beneath a mountain. But today at times all his
terrors seem mere idylls—even though like idylls full of nightmares—in comparison with all the things that have occurred on
the ground, especially on that of my native country. Dante's
visit to his *Inferno* was an exceptional case, due to the special
patronage of Virgil; and besides, it was not extended and was
followed by other inspection trips, to purgatory and to heaven.
For today's hell on earth no patronage is required. By now this
hell has permanently devoured several millions of people who
were anything but gifted poets, and only a very few have managed to escape from it. I myself know a man who recently was
in hell and gave a very talented description of all that he saw
there in his book, *The Story of a Secret State*. His name is Jan
Karski. He was an officer in the Polish Army and from 1939 to
to 1942 served as a courier in the Polish underground. Rather
than by a poet of antiquity, he was guided through one of the
many sub-divisions of hell in Poland—through one of the extermination camps—by a bribed member of the Estonian militia
who was on guard duty at the camp. With the guard's aid and
in the disguise of an Estonian militiaman Karski witnessed the
extermination of several thousands of Polish Jews. He was a
witness in the very sense in which the Greek word *martyros*
means witness. With his own eyes he saw a few armed men cram

many thousands of defenseless, naked, starved, half-crazed human beings into freight cars. . . . Thousands of men, women and children suffocated there; they died like flies. Neither devils nor demons nor fallen angels were encountered in that hell by the witness to these "Dantean" scenes. The work of the devils there was done by mere uniformed men. They inflicted torments on those naked and defenseless people without any wrath; calmly and cold-bloodedly, like expert technicians, they tortured these people before death and forced them in groups of a hundred and twenty apiece into railroad cars able to hold fifty at most. Then they poured quicklime over the railroad cars. Those defenseless people were unquestionably damned, like the characters in Dante's hell. But it was not God who had damned them; it was not He who had sentenced them to suffer their protracted agonies, but a man—one whose doctrine was then spread by more than four Evangelists and twelve Apostles. Karski's book is not a figment of his imagination, nor that of another's. It is, in fact, the classic counterpart to a work of poetic fiction. Nor is it the report of an indifferent traveler touring hell under a safe conduct, for on its pages we find descriptions of tortures suffered by Karski's own body and by his own soul. All the horrors described there were *really* experienced by the author, in the sense in which the Sicilian used the word "really."

Books of this type are very numerous today, although their authors are not always as gifted as Karski. These books belong to the literary category of reporting. In the past few years this category has developed to a certain degree of perfection—for one thing because the respective authors came to be thoroughly trained specialists with new observational methods at their disposal, but also because our time abounds in improbable and yet real occurrences straining the very limits of human imagination. Among the different types of reporters two in particular stand out: the professional and the accidental ones. Those of the first type look for and pursue dramatic situations in the outside world; deliberately they expose themselves to dangers so as to describe them afterwards. They always push into the thick of things, squeeze into tanks and submarines, go out on missions with the bomber crews. Many a daredevil of this sort pays with his own life for his ardent desire to grasp life at its most torrid. But the present also favors the accidental reporters. They often are people transformed against their will into not only witnesses but also heroes of the dramatic events which they describe once they have had the good luck to get out of the danger zone.

There are, however, such books as *My Prisons* by Silvio Pellico, and Dostoyevsky's *The House of the Dead*—owing their existence to the fact that both the dramatist Pellico and Dostoyevsky were sentenced to death in similar circumstances and after commutation of their sentences languished for long years, one in jail, the other in the *katorga*—and these books scarcely will be classified as reporting. In *The House of the Dead* especially, it is hard to tell how much of this book is "fiction" and how much is "truth." Both of these works originated in a time when poetic fiction was still rigidly contrasted with truth—that is to say, with authenticity. In Dostoyevsky's case we clearly see the author follow the innate proclivities of a poet—that is, the proclivities of a writer who makes the action of a book conform to his will by deforming the so-called reality. Dostoyevsky's poetic proclivities impelled him to seek authenticity in the souls of those who were with him in the *katorga*, rather than to photograph the *katorga*. Nor did he waive that one of the poet's privileges which I might call "transfiguration."

Today the development of reporting, charged with the exact photographic reproduction of authenticity, would seem to pose a serious threat to the poetic novel and the novella. It also would seem as though the continued existence of these literary categories required a certain combination of the old elements of poetic fiction with the newer elements of reporting. And in fact, some praiseworthy steps already have been taken in this direction: *Journey to the End of the Night*, the *roman picaresque* by L. F. Céline, or a few of A. Malraux's works, might be cited as instances of such a happy marriage of convenience. But on the other hand the belletristic work of Thomas Mann might serve to show how the novel in our time has victoriously defended its independence. The reporter has no ambition to transfigure in his books the people he meets on his travels; nor has he the least wish to form and express their mental processes. He is satisfied with an expression that is subjectively or objectively characteristic and mostly achieved in compliance with recognized formulas. The novelist, on the other hand, must visualize his characters "for the first time," so to speak—as if no one had ever seen these people before—even if they are popular, historical figures. This is what I mean by "transfiguration."

A man writing a novel or a novella has not merely the right but the duty to suggest the most improbable and irrational traits in his characters. He has the right to stage the most fantastic spectacles with the aid of these people. Thus, for example, in

Thomas Mann's novel, *Joseph the Provider,* we find an Egyptian jailkeeper, Mai-Sachme, whose soul and character were endowed by the poet with traits so beautiful and noble as probably no prisoner in the history of the world has yet observed in "reality."

There is even more to this. In reading works of poetic imagination we often feel pleasure even if their sole subject is the ugly and the repulsive. If my memory is correct, it was Schiller who called this "the delight in awful things." What we demand of the reporter, on the contrary, is that he satisfy our curiosity. So we must not deprecate the enjoyment offered us by the art of a poet. Often this enjoyment is our only indication as to whether we are reading a work of art. Such works as *The Divine Comedy, The Human Comedy,* the novels of Dostoyevsky, or *The Magic Mountain* afford us great intellectual, moral and aesthetic pleasure, although so much occurs in them that is repugnant. It would be hard to say that Jan Karski's excellent book is "beautiful." It is only a shattering document of a time when hell moved from the nether world to the surface of the earth. But Dante's hell is beautiful, and from it we already get a presentiment of heaven. For none but the poet is able to lend a metaphysical aspect to the menace and ugliness of human existence, thereby linking our earth with those spheres toward which every man is aiming, consciously or unconsciously, with or without the help of religion.

In reflecting on the form in which I ought to honor Thomas Mann, I became convinced that I should do best by honoring in his person the two types of poetic prose in which he is a master: the novel and the novella. The more so, since his work is part of an epoch which allegedly sees the frontiers between the imaginative story and the eye-witness report begin to fade.

Thomas Mann, in our time, faithfully keeps that good tradition of the European story-tellers' art which began with Bandello, Boccaccio, Cervantes and Madame de Lafayette. He is one of the few contemporary writers who in their works simultaneously express, as Dante once did, what the Catholic liturgy calls *"visibilia et invisibilia."* By the very style of his narrative he is able to transport the reader, tortured by the "reality" of our life, into the world of his equally real, albeit fictitious harmony. And the art of transporting people from one world into another is a privilege of great artists alone—of those who *really* were within other people's souls. And there, too, are found a hell, a purgatory, and a heaven.

[1945]

NOTES ON CONTRIBUTORS

Conrad Potter Aiken (1889-), American poet, critic and short story writer.

W. H. Auden (1907-), English poet now living in the U. S.

Julius Bab (1880-), German author now living in the U. S.

Lydia Baer, assistant professor of German at Swarthmore College.

Joseph Warren Beach (1880-), American critic, professor of English at the University of Minnesota.

Berthold Biermann (1903-), former member of the press department of the German Foreign Office. Fled Germany in 1933.

Lienhard Bergel (1905-), member of the German Department, Queens College, New York.

Félix Bertaux, French critic.

Tor Bonnier (1883-), president of the firm of Albert Bonnier, Sweden's leading publishing house.

Menno ter Braak (1902-1940), Dutch essayist and historian, regarded as the intellectual leader of the anti-fascist movement in the Netherlands.

G. A. Borgese (1882-), Italian novelist, scholar, critic now living in the U. S. Married to Elisabeth Mann, youngest daughter of Thomas Mann.

Philo M. Buck, Jr. (1877-), American critic, professor of comparative literature at the University of Wisconsin.

Kenneth Burke (1897-), American critic and translator.

A. F. B. Clark, professor of French in the University of British Columbia.

Arthur Eloesser, German critic.

Lion Feuchtwanger (1884-), German novelist now living in the U. S.

Hanns Fischer (1894-   ), German attorney, musician and writer.

Hedwig Fischer, widow of the late German publisher, S. Fischer, who published Thomas Mann's earliest works.

Bruno Frank (1887-1945), German novelist and playwright.

André Paul Guillaume Gide (1869-   ), French novelist and essayist, Nobel Prize winner for literature, 1947.

André von Gronicka (1912-   ), assistant professor of Russian and German at Columbia University.

Albert Léon Guérard (1880-   ), author, and professor of general literature, Stanford University.

Martin Gumpert (1897-   ), German physician and writer now living in the U. S.

Henry C. Hatfield (1912-   ), member of the German Department, Columbia University.

Chares Jackson, American novelist.

Erich Kahler (1885-   ), Czech essayist and author now living in the U. S.

Fritz Kaufmann, associate professor of philosophy at the University of Buffalo.

Rudolf Kayser, German author, former editor of *Die Neue Rundschau,* now member of the German Department, Hunter College, New York

Hermann Kesten (1900-   ), German novelist and playwright, now living in the U. S.

F. J. H. Letters, Australian critic, member of the faculty of New England University College, Armidale, New South Wales.

Harry Levin (1912-   ), American critic, associate professor of English at Harvard University.

Ludwig Lewisohn (1882-   ) American novelist, critic and translator.

Robert Morss Lovett (1870-   ), Amercian author, educator and editor.

Georg Lukacs, Hungarian-born critic living in the U. S. S. R.

Helen T. Lowe-Porter, authorized English translator of Thomas Mann's work.

Erika Mann (1905-), author, lecturer, correspondent, eldest child of Thomas Mann.

Heinrich Mann (1871-), German novelist, playwright and essayist now living in the U. S. Elder brother of Thomas Mann.

Klaus Mann (1906-), novelist, essayist, playwright, second child of Thomas Mann.

Monika Mann (1910-), fourth child of Thomas Mann.

Lavinia Mazzucchetti, Italian publisher of Thomas Mann's works.

James H. Meisel (1900-), German author and playwright now living in the U. S., secretary and assistant to Thomas Mann, 1939-40.

Agnes E. Meyer, American journalist, author, lecturer, social-worker.

Gabriela Mistral (1889-), Chilean poet and educator, Nobel Prize winner for literature, 1945.

Helen Muchnic (1903-), member of the faculty of Smith College.

Lewis Mumford (1895-), American Biographer, essayist, critic.

Charles Neider (1915-), American writer, editor, critic.

Alfred Neumann (1895-), German novelist now living in the U. S.

Reinhold Niebuhr (1892-), American author and clergyman, professor of applied Christianity, Union Theological Seminary.

J. B. Priestley (1894-), English novelist, playwright, essayist.

Philip Blair Rice (1904-), American critic, professor of philosophy, Kenyon College.

Friedrich Carl Sell, member of the Department of German Language and Literature, Mount Holyoke College.

Harry Slochower, American critic, member of the German Department, Brooklyn College.

B. Suchkov, Soviet critic.

Dorothy Thompson (1894-), American journalist, lecturer.

Vernon Venable (1907-), associate professor of philosophy, Vassar College.

Bruno Walter (1876-), German symphony and opera conductor now living in the U. S.

Hermann Joseph Weigand (1892-), Professor of German, Yale University.

Joseph Wittlin (1896-), Polish novelist, poet and essayist now living in the U. S.

Stefan Zweig (1881-1942), Austrian playwright, essayist, biographer, short-story and novella writer.